BOLLINGEN SERIES XCVI

FRANZ BABINGER

Mehmed the Conqueror
AND HIS TIME

Translated from the German by
RALPH MANHEIM

Edited, with a preface, by
WILLIAM C. HICKMAN

BOLLINGEN SERIES XCVI
PRINCETON UNIVERSITY PRESS

Copyright © 1978 by Princeton University Press

Published by Princeton University Press, Princeton, New Jersey

All Rights Reserved

THIS IS THE NINETY-SIXTH IN A SERIES OF WORKS
SPONSORED BY BOLLINGEN FOUNDATION

Translated from *Mehmed der Eroberer und seine Zeit:
Weltenstürmer einer Zeitenwende*, by Franz Babinger, Munich:
F. Bruckmann KG., 1953; second edition, 1959;
with further revisions by the author and editors

*Library of Congress Cataloguing in Publication Data will be
found on the last printed page of this book.*

Princeton University Press books are printed on acid-free paper,
and meet the guidelines for permanence and durability of the
Committee on Production Guidelines for Book Longevity of the
Council on Library Resources

ISBN 0-691-09900-6
ISBN 0-691-01078-1 (pbk.)

Second printing, for the paperback edition, 1992

3   5   7   9   10   8   6   4   2

PRINTED IN THE UNITED STATES OF AMERICA

TABLE OF CONTENTS

LIST OF ILLUSTRATIONS

Plates

Text Figures

Maps

EDITOR'S PREFACE

Franz Babinger's *Mehmed der Eroberer und seine Zeit* (Munich: F. Bruckmann) was enthusiastically received in the year of its publication, 1953, the 500th anniversary of the conquest of Constantinople by the Turks. For the first time, the life and times of Sultan Mehmed II, conqueror of Constantinople, was subjected to rigorous investigation by an Orientalist well equipped to deal with the wide range of source materials available, but not always easily accessible, for such a study. A French edition appeared the following year: *Mahomet II le Conquérant et son temps* (Paris: Payot), translated by H. E. del Medico, and with an introduction by Paul Lemerle. An Italian translation followed soon after: *Maometto il Conquistatore e il suo tempo* (Turin: G. Einaudi, 1957), translated by Evelina Polacco. The German edition was republished in 1959, and a second, revised Italian edition appeared in 1967. Most recently the book was published in the Serbo-Croatian translation of Tomislav Bekić, *Mehmed Osvajač i njegovo doba* (Novi Sad, 1968). Other translations had been mentioned in print, by reviewers and by the author himself, but did not materialize.[1] While successive editions of the book were greeted with continuing enthusiasm, some reviewers withheld specific criticism pending appearance of the volume of notes promised from the outset by the author, for the book had been published without either footnotes or bibliography. Babinger, however, did not live to fulfill his promise. He died in Albania on June 23, 1967, at the age of seventy-six, only three days after completing the preface to the revised Italian edition.[2]

Long before that, however, steps had been taken which would lead to the publication of a further revised edition of the book, this time in English. The project was undertaken by the Bollingen Foundation in the United States; the draft of an English translation was completed by Ralph

[1] A Polish translation is in preparation at the time of writing.

[2] A brief account of the life of the author with an appreciation of his work is given by Louis Robert in the *Comptes rendus des séances* (*Académie des inscriptions et belles-lettres*), 1967, 487–493. See also the note of H. J. Kissling, *Südost-Forschungen* 26 (1967), 375–379. A volume of studies was presented to Babinger on the occasion of his sixtieth birthday as *Serta Monacensia*, ed. H. J. Kissling and A. Schmaus (Leiden, 1952). Nearly complete lists of reviews of the several European editions of the work may be found in the bibliography of Babinger's publications (see n. 3 below).

Manheim in 1965. Meanwhile, however, the inability of the author to complete the complementary volume with notes and sources resulted in the first of a long series of delays, and with Babinger's death the project came to a halt. Finally, in 1972 the present editor was asked to see the work through to completion, now under the direction of Princeton University Press, which in 1967 had assumed responsibility for the publication of the Bollingen Series.

Interested in a wide range of problems from the history of the Ottomans, and especially of their conquest and rule over the Balkan countries, Babinger made one of his first major scholarly contributions with the publication of "Schejch Bedr ed-din, der Sohn des Richters von Simaw," *Der Islam* 11 (1921), 1–106. (This study of a controversial figure from early fifteenth-century Ottoman history was subsequently complemented by the publication of the Turkish "life" of the scholar-sheikh: *Die Vita [Menāqibnāme] des Schejchs Bedr-ed-din Mahmud*. Part 1 [Leipzig, 1943]. The second part was destroyed during the Second World War and was never published.) Babinger's fascination with the accounts of travelers to Turkey and the Levant led, in 1923, to his edition of the diary of Hans Dernschwam: *Hans Dernschwams Tagebuch einer Reise nach Konstantinopel und Kleinasien (1553–1555)* (Munich). Two years later he published the text of the chronicle of the fifteenth-century Ottoman historian Uruc: *Die frühosmanischen Jahrbücher des Urudsch* (Hanover). His interest in the accounts of the Turkish annalists came to an early culmination in the landmark publication of *Die Geschichtsschreiber der Osmanen und ihre Werke* (Leipzig, 1927), a bio-bibliographical survey and catalogue of more than three hundred Ottoman authors. *GOW* (as it is known to readers in footnote abbreviation) has remained an important reference work down to the present.[3]

For the next twenty years Babinger dealt with an equally wide variety of topics, but it was not until 1948 that there appeared the first of a series of articles connected by a common theme: the life of the seventh Ottoman sultan, Mehmed II. While the comprehensive biographical study *Mehmed der Eroberer*, in 1953, summarized and expanded the results of several of Babinger's previously published research papers, his interest in the Conqueror did not cease. Articles pertinent to the biography continued to appear, to the extent that this preoccupation with the dominant figure of

[3] A comprehensive bibliography of Babinger's writings from 1910 to 1961 was published in the first of two volumes of papers collected and reprinted as *Aufsätze und Abhandlungen zur Geschichte Südosteuropas und der Levante*, ed. H. J. Kissling and A. Schmaus (Munich, 1962 and 1966; as *Südosteuropa. Schriften der Südosteuropa-Gesellschaft* III and VIII).

fifteenth-century Turkish history must be counted one of the most intense of Babinger's many interests.[4]

In his preface to the French edition Babinger noted that the first full-length study of Mehmed was the *Histoire du regne de Mahomet II* of Guillet de Saint-Georges, and that in the two hundred and fifty years since that author's death no other writer had attempted a comparable *étude d'ensemble*. While research in Ottoman history has advanced considerably since 1953, the emphasis has been on the publication and analysis of archival material, an area in which Babinger himself made notable contributions.[5] Even so, and despite the wealth of such official documents, scholars in Ottoman history have continued reluctant to publish broadly conceived, synthetic studies. And Babinger's book remains the only full-length account of the rule of a single sultan which, based on Eastern and Western sources alike, at the same time surveys institutional organization and cultural activity.[6]

A few words remain to be said about the English edition. When the present writer came to the project, Ralph Manheim's draft translation (made from the second German edition supplemented and corrected by the second Italian edition, together with additional unpublished notes of the author) had already seen a great deal of editorial work. Significant changes had been made, especially in the organization of material, all of which had been approved by the author before his death. (As a result of the rearrangement of numerous passages throughout the book, it may prove difficult to move back and forth easily between the English and the older editions. This convenience has been sacrificed, however, for the

[4] Details of Babinger's studies on Mehmed are to be found in the above-mentioned bibliography. For works after 1962, see especially J. D. Pearson (ed.), *Index Islamicus, Second Supplement 1961–1965* (Cambridge, 1967) and *Third Supplement 1966–1970* (London, 1972). Cf. H. G. Majer, "Osmanistische Nachtrage zum Index Islamicus (1906–1965)," *Südost-Forschungen* 27 (1968), 242–291.

[5] An appraisal of Babinger's contributions in the field of diplomatics and paleographic studies is given by Jan Reychman and Ananiasz Zajaczkowski, *Handbook of Ottoman Turkish Diplomatics*, trans. A. S. Ehrenkreutz and ed. T. Halasi-Kun (= *Columbia University Publications in Near and Middle East Studies, Series A* VII; The Hague, 1968). See especially 73–75.

[6] As Babinger noted in the final chapter of this biography, Turkish interest in Mehmed continues to grow. A list of publications in that country alone in 1953 is compiled by S. N. Özerdim and M. Mercanlïgil: *Belleten* 17 (1953), 413–428. For periodical studies published in the West the best guide is J. D. Pearson, *Index Islamicus 1906–55* (Cambridge, 1958), and the five-year supplements (see above, n. 4).

sake of clarity.) During the ensuing editorial work the content of the book has remained essentially unchanged, with only minor exceptions: observations now outdated by the mere fact of recent publications have been deleted, as have highly opinionated comments of the author, at two or three places only, on matters of no scholarly significance.[7] The editor wishes only to make clear that he does not share the personal views frequently expressed by the author in various books of this work, especially the last.

The careful reader will detect, here and there, an internal inconsistency in Babinger's narrative, apparently the result of his reliance on sometimes unreconciled evidence. These inconsistencies have been allowed to stand, rather than erase what may be significant disagreement in the sources.

The principal task of the editor has been the addition of footnotes, primarily bibliographic in nature. It was the mutual understanding of publisher and editor that a completely revised and annotated edition of *Mehmed* was no longer possible after Babinger's death, however much that had been the original aim of the Bollingen Foundation in undertaking to publish the English edition.[8]

The notes, it need hardly be emphasized, would not be those which Babinger himself had promised to write. No attempt has been made to provide references to the sources, primary and secondary, at every point of the way, much less to include the exhaustive bibliography of works, from the fifteenth century to the twentieth, which the author customarily added to the notes to his own scholarly studies. It was felt rather that the notes should serve primarily as a guide to further reading. They would have an *ad hoc* character. Where recent research has brought forward new facts or suggested different interpretations of the old, these are brought to

[7] A single German word from the original edition has consistently proved awkward in translation: *Renegat*. The English "renegade" has a strongly pejorative connotation. More important, Babinger used the term often as a blanket description of high-ranking Ottoman military men of non-Turkish origin. That group, however, included both voluntary converts to the Ottoman cause—where the word "renegade" would be fully appropriate—and involuntary subjects, particularly men who were conscripted into the Ottoman system through the mechanism of the *devşirme*. I have retained the term "renegade" when it seemed entirely applicable, otherwise using a circumlocution such as "forced or voluntary converts."

[8] Throughout the later years of his life Babinger expressed the hope that the English edition would become the definitive version of his work. The author took an interest in the culture of the English-speaking world and had published a handful of articles in the language. It may be remarked here parenthetically that Babinger's personal library has found a home or rather homes in the United States, the Turkish-language books having been purchased by the University of Washington (Seattle), those in European languages by the University of California (Los Angeles).

the reader's attention. The editor has refrained throughout from taking sides. At the same time documentation of some of the major sources—both those available to the author and those published since his death—seemed appropriate. Further, the editor has tried, throughout, to direct the reader to more detailed discussions, in English whenever possible, which themselves provide appropriate bibliographic references. (Many of the printed books—not to mention manuscripts—to which Babinger had recourse are unavailable even in a large American university research library. It would be presumptuous and misleading to refer to them, except indirectly through references in other works.) Among the non-English works, Babinger's books and articles have been given precedence. Attention is equally drawn to scholarly works published in Turkey. The volume and quality of such publications since 1953 makes hazardous now the task of any who would deal seriously with Mehmed II without a knowledge of Turkish. Notably, the work of Halil Inalcïk must be taken into account by any student wishing to grasp the realities of early Ottoman history, and his research, in Turkish and English, is amply cited in the notes.

A final observation may be in order here regarding the book as it was left by the author. Despite its appearance, the text consists of rather disparate parts: on the one hand, those which represent the fruit of Babinger's own extensive research in the sources and, on the other, those in which his original contribution to "received tradition" remained limited. In the former case the notes point to the documented publications of the author, which require little further comment. In the latter case Babinger sometimes followed his predecessors closely, making little or no addition to their statements. An effort has been made to indicate some of the places where this dependence amounts to little more than paraphrasing. Others could be pointed out, but the editor has not assumed the task of following and marking every footstep of the author. In particular the reader will find only very limited reference to the three standard histories of the Ottoman Empire which Babinger obviously knew well and used: those of J. von Hammer-Purgstall, W. Zinkeisen, and N. Iorga. Their narratives roughly parallel that of Babinger's work and the interested reader can make the comparison for himself. Nor has reference been made to three Turkish works: Ismail Hakkï Uzunçarşïlï, *Osmanlï Tarihi* I and II, 2nd ed. (Ankara, 1961 and 1964; as *TTK*: XIII. seri, no. 16ªl, 16ᵇl); Selahattin Tansel, *Fatih Sultan Mehmed'in siyasi ve askeri faaliyeti* (Ankara, 1953; as *TTK*: XI. seri, no. 4); Ismail Hikmet Ertaylan, *Fatih ve futuhati*, 2 vols. (Ankara, 1966). Critical comparison of these works and the studies cited in the notes with Babinger's book must remain the task of a future biographer of the sultan. It is hoped that *Mehmed the*

Conqueror will serve as a challenge and a stimulus to those who would attempt such a study. As the author of the book so clearly demonstrates, Mehmed II ranks as a major figure in the history of world civilizations and deserves continued interest.

As has been said, a great deal of work on the text was done by others. At a time when the fate of the project was uncertain, Professor Hans J. Kissling, who succeeded to Babinger's Chair of History and Civilization of the Near East and Turcology at the University of Munich, first undertook to keep it alive. In that he received the assistance of Dr. Hans Georg Majer of the same university. At an earlier stage, Wolfgang Sauerlander, of the Bollingen Series editorial organization, worked for several years to shape the book as it now appears, frequently in consultation with Professor Babinger, and the final text contains numerous contributions from his hand. Furthermore, Ralph Manheim, the translator, went beyond his primary responsibility as translator by consulting with the author in regard to many details of the text. Finally, William McGuire, now of Princeton University Press, who had supervised the project from its inception at the Bollingen Foundation in 1961, has personally provided an invaluable link between the present editor and the earlier stages of work on the text. It need hardly be added, however, that while many revisions were made or suggested by all of these, the final responsibility for the text, insofar as it differs from the manuscript approved by Franz Babinger, rests with the undersigned.

In order to illustrate the present edition, we have departed somewhat from the selection of pictures and maps used in the previous editions. While some of the subjects have been retained, most are new; altogether, there are forty-seven subjects on plates and as textual figures, and eight maps, especially drawn, in place of four. The aim was to provide illustrations more closely related to the text, more informative, and of better graphic quality. The list of illustrations indicates, besides the sources of the photographs, persons and institutions that have been helpful. In particular we wish to thank the Honorable Kemal Çiğ, Director of the Topkapï Palace Museum, for his kind interest; Nuri Temizsoylu, of the faculty of the Academy of Fine Arts, Istanbul, for specially photographing the Sinan portrait of the Conqueror, in the Topkapï; and Fanny Davis and Talat S. Halman, respectively, for their much valued advice. The maps, which have been replanned, were executed by Adrienne Morgan. The display of a *tuğra* (signature) of Mehmed II or another personage at the head of each Book is a decorative innovation of the present edition.

Berkeley, November 1973 / March 1977   WILLIAM C. HICKMAN

NOTE ON SPELLING AND
TRANSLITERATION

THE PROBLEM of transliteration of Oriental terms is an awkward one. Where a term has been generally accepted in English we use a standard spelling: *vizier* and *serai*. Otherwise we follow modern Turkish orthography, rather than any one of the more complex systems of transliteration in scholarly use, thus: *devşirme* and *hisar*. Difficulty is encountered with proper names especially when they belong to both Turks and Arabs or Persians. The Turks now write Celaleddin (or Celalettin) where scholarly transliteration of this (Arabic) name would be Jalāl al-Dīn, or any of a number of variants. We use the Turkish spelling of the name except where to do so would erroneously identify its bearer too closely with the Turkish-speaking world. In the latter case we adopt a slightly modified scholarly transliteration. So we write Cem Sultan, speaking of Mehmed's son and would-be successor, but Mullah Jami, referring to the Iranian poet. (Some discrepancy will also be noted between the spellings of, for example, Yakub and *azap*, but here we simply follow current Turkish convention.)

In the matter of place names, we have made a departure from the original text. For the most part, the modern names of cities are used. In a book devoted to the life of a Turkish sultan, it seems unnecessary to persist, for example, in writing Adrianople when the Turkish name of the city is Edirne, a form closer to that used by the Ottomans in the fifteenth century than the anglicized form of Hadrianopolis. Following the same practice, we have chosen, for example, Sibiu and Shkodër, rather than the German Hermannstadt or Italian Scutari. Two groups of exceptions are the names of prominent cities or regions which have well-established modern English forms: Athens, Belgrade, Macedonia, Trebizond (in its imperial significance; post-conquest, Trabzon), and so on, and those modern names which present too jarring an anachronism: we use, for example, Braşov instead of Oraşul Stalin. Furthermore, place names have been spelled according to present usage in the country of their location or have been transcribed according to a standard modern system. (The same applies to other proper names as well.) Our guide here has been *The Times Atlas of the World* (Mid-Century Edition), ed. John

Bartholomew (London, 1956). An extremely useful work for the historical identification of place names is *The Columbia Lippincott Gazetteer of the World*, ed. Leon E. Seltzer, 1952 edition with 1961 Supplement (New York, 1970). An attempt has been made to verify all locations, but several, especially of military fortifications, could not be positively identified. The appearance of Donald E. Pitcher's *An Historical Geography of the Ottoman Empire* (Leiden, 1972) facilitates the task of following Babinger's narrative, with its numerous maps and region-by-region historical summaries.

Because of the choices of spelling mentioned above, readers may encounter some difficulties in pronunciation, but these should not be insurmountable. The following equivalents may be found useful.

For Turkish:
 c: as *j* in *jury*
 ç: as *ch* in *church*
 g: always hard, as in *gain*
 ğ: silent, but lengthens a preceding vowel
 ï: as *i* in *cousin*
 ö: as *o* in *word*
 s: as in *sound*
 ş: as *sh* in *shun*
 ü: as *ü* in German
 z: as in *zone*
So *çavuş* is pronounced "cha-vush"; *doğancï* is "doe-awn-ji."

For Serbo-Croatian:
 c: as *ts* in *waits*
 č: as *ch* in *church*
 ć: *ch*
 j: as *y* in *your*
 s: as in *sound*
 š: as *sh* in *shun*
 z: as in *zone*
 ž: as *s* in *pleasure*
So Jajce is pronounced "Yay-tse"; Vukčić is "Vuk-chich"; Priština is "Prish-tee-na."

For Hungarian:
 c: as *ts* in *waits*
 j: as *y* in *your*

s: as *sh* in *shun*
sz: as *s* in *sound*
zs: as *s* in *pleasure*
´:   indicates vowel length
So Székesfehérvár is pronounced "Se-kesh-fe-hair-var."

For Romanian:
j: as *s* in *pleasure*
ş: as *sh* in *shun*
ţ: as *ts* in *waits*
So Braşov is pronounced "Bra-shov."

For Albanian:
ë: an indeterminate, reduced vowel
j: as *y* in *your*

ABBREVIATIONS

A&A   *Aufsätze und Abhandlungen zur Geschichte Südosteuropas und der Levante* (see above, n. 3).

BZ   *Byzantinische Zeitschrift* (Munich).

DOP   *Dumbarton Oaks Papers* (Washington, D.C.).

EI   *The Encyclopaedia of Islam*, 4 vols., ed. T. W. Arnold, et al. (Leiden, 1913–34).

EI²   *The Encyclopaedia of Islam, New Edition*, ed. H. A. R. Gibb, et al. (Leiden, 1960–).

GZMBH   *Glasnik Zemaljskog Muzeja u Bosni i Hercegovini* (Sarajevo).

IA   *Islam Ansiklopedisi* (Istanbul, 1940–); Turkish edition of *EI* with many articles newly written or substantially revised.

IED   *Istanbul Enstitüsü Dergisi* (Istanbul).

TTK   *Türk Tarih Kurumu* (Ankara).

MEHMED THE CONQUEROR
AND HIS TIME

Book One

THE OTTOMAN EMPIRE AT MURAD'S ACCESSION.
BIRTH OF A PRINCE.
BALKAN CAMPAIGNS—HUNGARIAN COUNTEROFFENSIVE.
THE CRUSADE OF VARNA.
A CHILD SULTAN.
THE CAMPAIGN IN GREECE.
MURAD'S LAST YEARS.

MURAD II had just turned eighteen when, in early July 1421, at Bursa, he mounted the throne of the Ottoman kingdom, restored by his talented father, Mehmed I.[1] It seemed at this juncture, as though the Republic of Venice would soon take possession of the crumbling Greek and Frankish states in southeastern Europe, while Hungary was striving to extend its sovereignty, if not its actual rule, over present-day Romania and the Slavic territories as far as the gates of Constantinople. However, the military and diplomatic skills of the republic were put to a severe test by the need to bring to a halt the advance of Ottoman power, which was pushing relentlessly westward from the interior of the Balkan peninsula.

The front was hundreds of miles long, extending from Zadar (Zara) in Dalmatia to the Aegean Sea, and almost every vital point was threatened by discord and rebellion which the Venetians, despite their still uncontested sea power, were unable to put down. Venetian power in the Levant was further impaired by the fateful policy of the great doge Francesco Foscari (1423–1457), who, not content with the hostility of Genoa and Hungary, the traditional rivals of Venice, antagonized the Milan of the Visconti, so orienting Venetian policy, to its detriment, toward the

---

[1] Because of discrepancies among the sources, it is difficult to fix precise dates for numerous events in Ottoman history, among them birthdays of the early sultans. A useful modern reference work is A. D. Alderson, *The Structure of the Ottoman Dynasty* (Oxford, 1956). Cf. Gültekin Oransay, *Osmanlı devletinde kim kimdi? I. Osmanoğulları* (Ankara, 1969), based on the standard late Ottoman reference work of Mehmed Süreyya, *Sicill-i Osmani*.

Italian mainland.[2] The shrewd Genoese merchants and bankers in their trading posts in Rumelia and Anatolia, on the shores of the Black Sea and in Constantinople, were trying, through far-reaching concessions to Byzantium and the Ottomans, to safeguard their old possessions. But it was clear that their brilliant role in the economic life of the Orient was drawing to an end. The island dynasties of the Aegean, for the most part of Genoese origin, outdid one another in intrigues, political maneuvers, and family feuds. Still, they seemed to be in no imminent danger as long as the Ottomans lacked an effective fleet with which to seize one island after another. By then the remnants of the Byzantine Empire amounted to little more than Constantinople, the ancient capital, and its narrow hinterland, exposed on all sides to the Ottoman threat [pl. XIII]. Its territory had been reduced to the peninsula extending from the Bosporus to Silivri (Selymbria) on the Marmara and Terkos, Misivri (Mesembria), and Anchialus (now Pomorie [Pomoriye]; Turkish Ahyolu) on the Black Sea. It included also the sacred Mount Athos, the city of Thessaloniki (Salonica), a pair of islands in the Aegean Sea, Imroz (Imbros) and Lemnos, and the so-called Despotate of Mistra (Misithra) [pl. IV b]; and Thessaloniki was soon to be lost forever. How long the shadow sovereignty of the Palaeologi would endure depended entirely on the will of the Ottomans.[3]

The statesmen of the Western world were very slow to realize that the schism of the Church, internecine strife, private feuds, and political rival-

[2] A useful survey of Venetian history and culture is D. S. Chambers, *The Imperial Age of Venice: 1380–1580* (London, 1970). More exhaustive is Frederic C. Lane, *Venice. A Maritime Republic* (Baltimore, 1973), with emphasis on economic history and extensive bibliographies.

[3] Halil Inalcïk, *The Ottoman Empire, The Classical Age, 1300–1600*, trans. N. Itzkowitz and C. Imber (London and New York, 1973), must now be considered the best general treatment of early Ottoman history. For the background of Ottoman relations with the West, see D. M. Vaughan, *Europe and the Turk. A Pattern of Alliances 1350–1700* (Liverpool, 1954; a new edition has been announced). A pioneering work of great value still is Paul Wittek, *The Rise of the Ottoman Empire* (Royal Asiatic Society Monographs XXIII, London, 1938; reprinted 1965). And see the same author's "De la défaite d'Ankara à la prise de Constantinople (Un demi-siècle d'histoire ottomane)," *Revue des études islamiques* 12 (1938), 1–34. For succinct narratives, see also the chapters by Inalcïk in the *Cambridge History of Islam* I (Cambridge, 1970) and those by Franz Taeschner in the *(New) Cambridge Medieval History* IV, part 1 (Cambridge, 1966). One of several standard accounts, George Ostrogorsky, *History of the Byzantine State*, trans. Joan Hussey (New Brunswick, 1969), treats the Palaeologi period in his final chapter. A more detailed full-length study is Donald M. Nicol, *The Last Centuries of Byzantium* (New York, 1972). Donald E. Pitcher, *An Historical Geography of the Ottoman Empire* (Leiden, 1972), provides the most up-to-date atlas, with newly drawn maps.

ries impaired the military power of the West to a suicidal degree, thus enabling the Ottoman state, which had been almost hopelessly defeated by Tamerlane at the battle of Ankara (Angora) in 1402, to recover its earlier position and prestige.

Well informed about developments not only in the neighboring countries but also in the more remote lands of Christendom (thanks particularly to the reports sent from far and near by his Western advisers and, in all probability, by spies), the young sultan Murad saw himself faced with vast and tempting tasks which only a ruler with his power could hope to confront. He was an able statesman, with a clear understanding of the political situation of the times, but by no means a man who found satisfaction in war. Not only his compatriots, coreligionaries, and court annalists but the Byzantine historians as well spoke of him as a loyal, forthright, and trustworthy man.[4] His chief concern—determined, no doubt, by his basic character—was to consolidate the internal order of the state, still threatened here and there by religious and social unrest, and to repair the damage and heal the wounds caused by the turmoil following the disaster of 1402. His deeply religious nature, which tended toward mysticism, encouraged his decidedly charitable leanings and a patriarchal solicitude for his people. In simple garb, bearing no indication of his identity, he mingled with his subjects. At the ceremony of mourning for his mother he was dressed so unassumingly that one Western eyewitness, as he has related, was unable to recognize Murad until the sultan was pointed out. He was famed for his affability, tolerance, and maturity of judgment. His architectural ideas were admirable, seldom excelled even in the most brilliant periods of Ottoman history. Particularly Bursa (Brussa) [pl. I b], the former capital, and Edirne (Adrianople) [pl. I a], the capital of the newly consolidated state, benefited by his public spirit and love of splendor. Everywhere construction was under way: streets, mosques, hospitals, inns, bridges, and monasteries for dervishes. And the nobles of the realm sought his favor by vying with him in this activity.[5]

[4] The three major Byzantine chroniclers for the period are Chalcocondylas, Ducas, and Phrantzes. For translations of select passages from the first two see below, book 2, nn. 13 and 2. For Phrantzes, book 2, n. 12. Their works are not otherwise available in convenient modern translations. For brief biographical notes and references to the texts see Ostrogorsky, *History of the Byzantine State*, 467–469. Cf. Steven Runciman, *The Fall of Constantinople 1453* (London, 1965), 192–194. — Now available is Harry J. Magoulias's annotated translation of *The Historia Turco-Byzantina* of Ducas (Doukas): *Decline and Fall of Byzantium to the Ottoman Turks* (Detroit, 1975).

[5] No book has been devoted to the life and sultanate of Mehmed's father and predecessor, Murad II. The article "Murad II" (H. Inalcïk) in *IA* VIII, 598–615 (in Turkish) provides a thorough survey of the major events and problems con-

Murad took a particular interest in his army. It was he who from about 1438 on organized the selective conscription of Christian boys in the territories of the state as replacements in the Janissary corps and to serve in the imperial palaces. In Murad's own lifetime this levy of boys (*devşirme*) opened up the highest positions in the state to Christians thus impressed into service. For nearly a century and a half these converts set their stamp on the conduct of Ottoman military and civil affairs. As for the Janissaries themselves [pl. XXII a], the so-called new troops (*yeni çeri*), while the origins of this infantry corps date back to the early years of Ottoman history—the period when the confederation of *ghazis* and *akhis* put their imprint on Ottoman society—it was to Murad that they owed the severe training, martial discipline, and tight organization which made them so redoubtable as defenders of the state and, when needed, as leaders in offensive operations. In a detailed and colorful account of the Ottoman military establishment, Chalcocondylas, the contemporary Byzantine chronicler, greatly praised the organization, efficiency, and discipline of the army and conveyed a good idea of the adversary whom the states of Christendom would have to face in case of war.[6]

Apart from the authority of the sultan and the institution of the *devşirme*, it was the feudal system, perfected under Murad II, which

nected with his reign, based on primary sources. For the architectural monuments of Murad's reign, see Godfrey Goodwin, *A History of Ottoman Architecture* (Baltimore, 1971), chap. 3. Cf. E. H. Ayverdi, *Osmanli mi'marisinde Çelebi ve II. Sultan Murad devri, 806–855 (1403–1451)* (Istanbul, 1972).

[6] For the Ottoman levy of non-Moslem children, see "Devshirme" (V. L. Ménage), *Encyclopaedia of Islam* (2nd ed.), II, 210–213, where reference is given to the document (from 1438) referred to indirectly by Babinger. Cf. Claude Cahen, "Note sur l'esclavage musulman et la devshirme ottoman, à propos de travaux récents," *Journal of the Economic and Social History of the Orient* 13 (1970), 211–218. The monograph study of B. Papoulia, *Ursprung und Wesen der "Knabenlese" im Osmanischen Reich* (Munich, 1963; as *Südosteuropäische Arbeiten*, 4a), is examined by Ménage, "Some Notes on the Devshirme," *Bulletin of the School of Oriental and African Studies* (London) 29 (1966), 64–78, and by S. Vryonis in *Balkan Studies* 5 (1964), 145–153. The latter's own studies include "Isidore Glabas and the Turkish Devshirme," *Speculum* 31 (1956), 433–443; and "Seljuk Gulams and Ottoman Devshirmes," *Der Islam* 41 (1965), 224–252.

For the Janissary corps, see Hamilton A. R. Gibb and Harold Bowen, *Islamic Society and the West* I, part 1 (London, 1950), 39ff. The loose organization of *ghazi* (*gazi*) warriors for the faith is described by Irene Melikoff, "Ghazi," *EI²* II, 1043–45. The urban brotherhoods of Anatolia are treated by F. Taeschner, "Akhi," *EI²* I, 321–323. An account of *akhi* circles and their hospitable activities is provided by the 14th-century traveler Ibn Battuta, *The Travels of Ibn Battuta* A.D. *1325–1354* II, trans. H. A. R. Gibb (Hakluyt Society, 2nd series, CXVII; Cambridge, 1962). See especially 418ff.

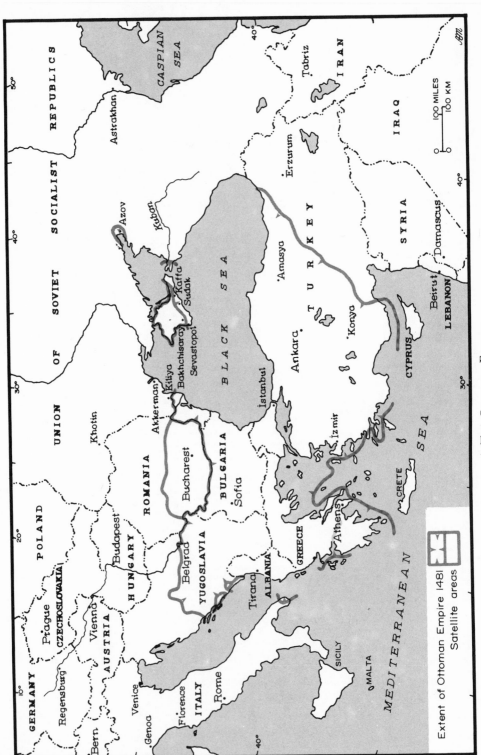

Extent of Ottoman Empire 1481
Satellite areas

1. The Ottoman Empire

provided the basic "energy of this empire and consequently the success of its efforts," encouraging the tried warriors who were its beneficiaries to hold themselves in constant readiness for new conquests. For many years, newly conquered territories had been divided into fiefs, the larger termed *ziamet* and the smaller *timar*, whose holders obligated themselves to take part, mounted, in military operations and to supply a number of soldiers or sailors proportional to the income from their estates. It is relatively certain that the Ottomans had taken over this system of military vassalage from the Byzantines, but its history will become fully known only when the early Ottoman land registers become available, making possible a study of the feudal estates of Rumelia. It is safe to assume, however, that from the end of the fourteenth century on, large estates were distributed among trusted march wardens (the *uç beys* of the frontier regions) and became hereditary in their families. Feudal families established themselves on the Danube, in the southern part of present-day Serbia, in Macedonia, and in Thessaly. Centuries later we still find them in possession of enormous estates.[7]

The most important positions of the realm were accessible to any servant of the sultan, and not infrequently, especially in the course of the fifteenth century, former slaves rose to the highest ranks. With few exceptions, this is the story of the keepers of the imperial seal, the grand viziers. As late as the sixteenth century, reports of German and Venetian ambassadors reported with amazement that the wealth, administration, strength—in short, the entire ruling apparatus—of the Ottoman Empire depended on and were entrusted to men who were born in the Christian faith but had been enslaved and raised as Moslems. Even in the reign of Murad II, the nature of Ottoman political organization was determined by this institution, and it alone saved the empire in a number of crucial situations. "Forgetful of their early childhood, parents, and home," those carried away as boys to the palace (*saray*) knew no fatherland other than this, "no lord and father other than the sultan, no will but his, no hope but in his favor." They knew "no life except in strict discipline and unconditional obedi-

---

[7] For an introduction to the study of Ottoman feudal practice, see Halil Inalcïk, "Ottoman Methods of Conquest," *Studia Islamica* 2 (1954), 103–129. The same scholar has published one of the oldest existing Ottoman registers giving details of land holding in Albania in 1432: *Hicri 835 tarihli suret-i defter-i sancak-i Arvanid* (Ankara, 1954; as *TTK*: XIV. seri, no. 1). For further discussion of the subject, see below, pp. 445f. The quotation at the beginning of the paragraph is from Leopold von Ranke, *Die Osmanen und die spanische Monarchie im 16. und 17. Jahrhundert* (Leipzig, 1877). Cf. the English translation of W. Kelly, *The Ottoman and the Spanish Empires in the Sixteenth and Seventeenth Centuries* (Philadelphia, 1845; reprinted New York, 1969), 13–14.

ence, no occupation but war in his service, no aim for themselves but pillage in life and in death the paradise to which warfare for Islam offers the key."[8]

It was Murad I, assassinated on June 15, 1389, after the victorious battle of Kosovo, who had first opened up high careers to foreigners. By the time of Murad II, his great-grandson, only a very few leading positions in the state were given to sons of native, old Anatolian families, chief among them the Çandarlï, in whose family the highest government office, that of grand vizier, had for a time been hereditary. All other positions in the administration, and still more so in the army, were shared by former Christians from Serbia, Albania, and Greece. Hatred and envy of the intruders seem to have made their appearance in native circles at an early date, and even under Murad II we find signs of serious dissatisfaction. Nevertheless, non-Turks continued, up to the seventeenth century, to obtain many of the leading positions.

Fortunately for the young sultan, the internal strife that had dangerously shaken the empire during the terrible civil wars of the interregnum (1402–1413), and still under his father, Mehmed I, had come to an end at the time of his accession. Not long before, in the summer and autumn of 1416, the former army judge Sheikh Bedreddin, a profound scholar and friend of the common people, had fomented a serious uprising in Anatolia and Rumelia, his goal the elimination of the old institutions, including perhaps even the Ottoman throne; this rebellion, however, had been nipped in the bud, its instigator taken prisoner and hanged in the marketplace at Serrai (Serres; Turkish Serez) on December 18, 1416.[9] A few weeks later a certain Seyyid Ali al-ula, a missionary of the Hurufiyya, a heterodox sect which had spread from Persia to Anatolia and which was closely allied with currents that later became institutionalized in the Bektaşi order, was executed because of his intrigues in the empire and perhaps also because of the influence he had acquired over the troops.[10]

[8] The quotation is from von Ranke, *The Ottoman and Spanish Empires* (Kelly trans.), 12.

[9] For details of the life of Sheikh Bedreddin and comments on the insurrection, see "Badr al-Dīn b. ḲĀḌĪ SAMAWNĀ" (Hans J. Kissling), *EI*² I, 869. By the term "army judge" (*Heeresrichter*) Babinger referred to *ḳadi-i asker* (more commonly *ḳadi asker*, or simply *ḳazasker*), the title given to the holder of the highest judgeship in the Ottoman state. On the division of the office into Anatolian and Rumelian supreme judgeships see below, p. 400. For the institution of religious scholars (*ülema*) more generally, see Gibb and Bowen I, part 2 (London, 1957), 81–138.

[10] For this sect of Persian origin see the article "Ḥurūfiyya" (A. Bausani), *EI*² III, 600–601. On the penetration of their ideas into Bektaşi circles John K. Birge, *The Bektashi Order of Dervishes* (London, 1937), 58–62. Hurufi doctrine in its poetic

Few records of such heretic and subversive activities, so odious to the Orthodox clergy, have come down to us, and these quite by accident; for the reign of Murad II they are almost totally lacking. The dervish orders seem, under Murad, to have been content with a quiet period of growth. As the petty Anatolian principalities, which were particularly accessible to the influence of the dervishes, had with few exceptions been shattered and absorbed into the Ottoman state, the dervishes exerted little influence outside of eastern Anatolia. Only the principality of Karaman, by far the most important of these Turkmen states in Asia Minor, managed, thanks to the clever statesmanship of its prince Ibrahim Bey (1423–1464), to survive the collapse of the Anatolian Seljuk state. Ibrahim's whole life was spent in intermittent war with the Ottomans. But he was married to a sister of Murad and on more than one occasion this alliance may have saved him from ruin.

The Grand Karaman (*Gran Caraman*), as he is called in distinction to the Grand Turk (*Gran Turco*) in the fifteenth-century Italian sources, remained by far the greatest rival of the Ottomans, for soon after his accession he had been astute enough to enter into diplomatic contact with the countries of the West, offering his services for a concerted attack against the hated enemy, a kind of pincers movement from the East and West at once. His project had aroused keen interest. We shall have ample occasion to speak of it.

As to the internal order of the empire, it was menaced not so much by social unrest as by the plots of real and alleged claimants to the throne. In every case Murad responded swiftly, ruthlessly eliminating rebellious brothers and provincial governors and thus safeguarding the empire against the disintegration to which the Arab caliphates had fallen victim. In fact, throughout his reign Murad displayed unflagging energy and astuteness in dealing with the outward pressures on both parts of the empire. There was permanent danger of a clash on three fronts, where the interests of the expanding Ottoman state were in conflict with those of neighboring states: the Danube frontier, Dalmatia-Albania, and the Greco-Frankish world.

The first decade of Murad's reign, marked by the dramatic but unsuccessful siege of Constantinople (June 10 to September 6, 1422), by the elimination of his rivals, and finally by the capture of Thessaloniki (March 29,

---

context is treated by Kathleen R. F. Burrill, *The Quatrains of Nesimi, Fourteenth-Century Turkic Hurufi* (Columbia University, Publications in Near and Middle Eastern Studies, Series A, 14; The Hague, 1972). See also further below, p. 34.

9

1430), left such shrewd observers of the situation in southwestern Europe as Ducas in no doubt about the future. The chronicler saw the fall of Thessaloniki, principal center of the Venetian Republic's trade in the Levant, as a harbinger of the event that would take place less than a quarter of a century later: the fall of Constantinople and the final collapse of the Byzantine Empire.

The compromise which Murad granted Venice in the Peace of Gallipoli (September 4, 1430), allowing all subjects and merchants of the Venetian Republic to travel and trade freely throughout his territories, could not compensate for the loss of Thessaloniki, though it should have been clear from the outset that the Venetian acquisition of that city in 1423 was bound to provoke Turkish countermeasures. In addition, Venice had to agree to pay an annual tribute to the sultan. This treaty provided only a seeming guarantee of the Venetian possessions in the Morea, hastily acquired in the preceding generation. The agreement by which the sultan promised to leave the Signoria in peace by land and sea, on all its islands and in all its castles—in short, wherever the banner of San Marco waved—had temporarily dispelled the Venetians' fear of losing Negropont (Euboea). But the Turkish invasion of Epirus immediately after the capture of Thessaloniki—this campaign, said to have been led by Sinan Bey, one of the sultan's generals, ended in a treaty (1431) providing for the surrender of Ioannina (Yannina) and vicinity to the Ottomans—and the ensuing raids on Albania, further to the north, could not fail to open the eyes of the Venetians to the sultan's long-range plans.

If the chroniclers are reliable, the year following the conquest of Thessaloniki was one of peace and tranquillity. In accordance with the Ottoman rulers' custom of issuing new coins every ten years, silver and copper coins were minted in Edirne, Serrai, and Novo Brdo (Novar) in 1431 (= 834 H.).[11] Murad spent the summer in the northwestern quarter of his capital in a modest summer house, the ruins of which are still extant, on the mountain slope known as Çöke where he escaped the oppressive heat of the city. For the remainder of the year he seems not to have been greatly troubled by the affairs of the world. Ali Bey, his treasurer, went to Dubrovnik with a communication from the sultan; the previous autumn this city had for the first time sent ambassadors to the Porte in an attempt to secure recognition of its possessions in the hinterland (September 1430); the ambassadors had been well received in Philippopolis (now Plovdiv; Turkish Filibe) and had gone on to Edirne, where they

[11] Description of the silver akçe (asper) minted at this time in Amasya, Ayasoluk, and Bursa, as well as the three cities mentioned by Babinger, is given by Nuri Pere, *Osmanlilarda Madeni Paralar* (Istanbul, 1968), 84 and plate 5.

obtained a commercial charter, written in Serbian (December 6, 1430).[12]

The next year (1432) was also to be a quiet one. Murad apparently spent the whole of it in his capital city of Edirne; the sultan's palace, which appears to have been built in 1417 by Mehmed I, lay not far from the later Selimiye Mosque (1568–1574) on Poplar Square (*Kavak meydani*) in the center of the city. There at dawn on Laetare Sunday, March 30, 1432, his third son, Mehmed Çelebi, was born. Murad can scarcely have suspected at the time that this child would twice accede to the throne and become one of the most powerful figures of the declining Middle Ages. The identity of the child's mother is still shrouded in darkness. Nowhere is her old family name recorded. Named in no inscription that has thus far come to light, she is mentioned only in the deed of a pious foundation, fragments of which have been preserved, but there simply as Hatun bint Abdullah, "the distinguished lady, daughter of Abdullah." Her own name is not given, while the name given to her father, Abdullah —as converts were always called—attests clearly her non-Moslem origin.[13] At the time the document was written she was living in Bursa, presumably where she died. There she was apparently known as "the lady" (Hatun), while her tomb is popularly known as the Hatuniya *türbe*. Later she was called Huma Hatun after *hüma*, the bird of paradise of Persian legend. (Xerxes' mother had also borne that name.) According to a tradition that has not yet been substantiated, she was an Italian woman named Stella (Estella). Since in those days this name was customary only among Jews and is merely a translation of the Persian name Esther—i.e. *stella*, "star"—one might be tempted to conclude that

[12] For the medieval history of Dubrovnik and the background of its relations with the Ottomans, see N. H. Biegman, *The Turco-Ragusan Relationship* (The Hague, 1967); Francis W. Carter, *Dubrovnik (Ragusa), A Classic City State* (New York, 1972); and Bariša Krekić, *Dubrovnik in the 14th and 15th Centuries* (Norman, Okla., 1972). Note the last author's remarks on the use of the names Ragusa and Dubrovnik (p. 3). Cf. the article "Ragusa" (F. Babinger), *EI* III, 1098–1100. For the charter of 1430 see Ciro Truhelka, "Tursko-slovjenski spomenici dubrovačke arhive," *GZMBH* 23 (1911), 5–6 (document 2). Summary Turkish translation is given in *Istanbul Enstitüsü Dergisi* I (1955), 42–43.

[13] Babinger himself earlier discussed in greater detail the problems of Mehmed's birth date and the identity of his mother in separate articles: "Mehmeds II., des Eroberers Geburtstag," *Oriens* 2 (1949), 1–5; and "Mehmeds II., des Eroberers Mutter," *Münchener Beiträge zur Slavenkunde* (= *Festgabe für Paul Diels*; Munich, 1953), 3–12. The articles are reprinted in Franz Babinger, *A&A* I, 167–171 and 158–166, respectively. On the use of the name Abdullah by converts to Islam, see the excursus to the article of V. L. Ménage, "Seven Ottoman Documents from the Reign of Mehemmed II," in *Documents from Islamic Chanceries*, ed. S. M. Stern and R. Walzer (Oxford, 1965), 112–118.

Mehmed's mother was a Jewess. It is curious to note that according to the Old Testament, the Jewess Esther was the second wife of Ahasuerus, that is, Xerxes, king of the Persians.

It seems quite certain in any case that the prince's mother was a "slave." This much is reported by Ducas and other contemporary sources, but unfortunately we know nothing more. Why the origin of this wife of the sultan, who bore him the heir to the throne, is so cloaked in mystery can only be surmised. According to a legend taken up by Ottoman historians of the sixteenth century, Huma Hatun was a French princess. There is no more truth in this story than in the fairy tale to the effect that the mother of Bayezid II was a daughter of the king of France. All we can know for certain is that Mehmed's mother was neither a Frankish nor an Oriental princess, and that if she was indeed a "slave" she cannot have had a Turkish father, for there were no slaves of Turkish origin. Furthermore, custom required that slaves conceal their ancestry. Our ignorance of his mother's identity excludes any serious discussion of his maternal heredity. This is unfortunate, because it seems certain that his essential traits of character came to him from his mother's side: they differed radically from those of his father or his grandfather Mehmed I, as attested both by Ottoman and Byzantine sources. Yet, though we know nothing of Mehmed II's maternal ancestry, there can be no doubt that strains of Turkish, Slavic, Byzantine, Frankish, Persian, and probably Arab blood made for a strange and colorful heredity, whose genetic components it will never be possible to determine.

It may be assumed that the first years of Mehmed Çelebi's life were spent in the harem of the Edirne palace, in accordance with Oriental custom.[14] Hundi Hatun, usually called Daye Hatun, a Turkish woman, is mentioned as his wet-nurse; in her later years she came to be extremely wealthy and built several mosques; she survived her young charge by several years and died in Istanbul on February 14, 1486, taking the secret of Prince Mehmed's maternal ancestry with her to the grave.

In the summer of 1434, probably accompanied by his mother and wet-nurse, Mehmed was sent to Amasya (Amaseia) [pl. V a] in eastern Anatolia, where his father, Murad, had been born in the spring of 1404. Mehmed's half brother Ahmed Çelebi, who had also been born in Amasya (in 1420), became governor of the city at the time of the young

[14] Princes of the Ottoman house, at least until the mid-16th century, were granted the title *çelebi* following the given name. (The title *sultan çelebi* was also used for the princes.) Thus Prince Mehmed was known as Mehmed Çelebi. He should not be confused, however, with his grandfather, who, as Sultan Mehmed I, was known as Çelebi Mehmed or Çelebi Sultan Mehmed. For the term *çelebi*, of uncertain origin, see "Čelebi" (W. Barthold and B. Spuler), *EI²* II, 19.

prince's arrival. Murad's second son, Alaeddin Ali Çelebi, found himself in Mehmed's retinue. It was customary in those days (and occasionally in later periods) for the sultans—as a safeguard against popular uprisings and troop mutinies—to have their sons and possible heirs educated in the interior of Asia Minor. Frequently one of them would act as local governor under the supervision of reliable dignitaries. It was Mehmed II who first put an end (and for many centuries) to this peaceful method of obviating palace rivalries by his promulgation of the so-called fratricide law.[15]

Since the days of Bayezid I, known as Yĭldĭrĭm (Thunderbolt), Amasya had been the favored residence of these princes. And indeed few cities of the Ottoman Empire can have been better suited to the purpose. In 1838, Helmuth von Moltke described the "ancient city of Amasya" as the strangest and most beautiful place he had ever seen.[16] Its numerous mosques, minarets, and dwellings are crowded into a bowl formed by the confluence of two large mountain streams. On December 27, 1939, the romantic city was partly destroyed by a great earthquake. But even today one can see sumptuous gardens and mulberry orchards, watered by the mountain streams and enclosed by the high mountain walls in which centuries ago the tombs of kings were hewn. At the upper left, on a lofty crag, stands an ancient, strangely shaped castle, which was first built in the most remote antiquity but in the Middle Ages still served as the citadel of such Turkmen overlords as the Eretnas and the poet-prince Kadi Burhaneddin (d. 1398). The memory of these rulers is still preserved in a number of impressive public buildings—mosques, poorhouses, schools, and mortuary chapels (türbe)—that have escaped the frequent earthquakes. The serai of the Ottoman governors, who established their residence there after Bayezid had occupied the city, has long been in ruins. The palace lies on the left bank of the Green River (Yeşil Irmak) below the citadel. The once splendid buildings set into two magnificent gardens—the men's quarters (selamlĭk), the women's quarters (harem), the servants' quarters, the two baths, and the kitchens—are all also in ruins.

It was here that the little Mehmed Çelebi took up residence when Prince Ahmed Çelebi assumed the governorship in his native city.

In those days, and for many years to come, the character of Amasya

---

[15] See below, book 2, n. 3.

[16] See von Moltke's letter of March 10, 1838, in his *Briefe über Zustände und Begebenheiten in der Türkei* (Berlin, 1893), 212-226. A Turkish translation of the letters, by H. Örs, appeared as *Türkiyedeki durum ve olaylar üzerine mektuplar* (Ankara, 1960). For other accounts of the city and a brief historical sketch, see "Amasya" (F. Taeschner), *EI²* I, 431-432.

was dominated by a group of wealthy and influential native families, while the life of the palace itself was influenced also by the religious scholars and particularly the Persian dervishes who, with the city as their base, wandered through the countryside preaching. The Ottoman princes who lived in this city and served as the highest officials over *Rumiye-i sughra* (Little Rum, or Asia Minor) maintained social contact with the upper class and intermarriages were not infrequent. Among the most influential families at the time was that of Şadgeldi Ahmed Pasha, whose daughter Şehzade Hatun had married Bayezid's son Mehmed (later Sultan Mehmed I), father of Murad II. Among the pasha's descendants we find several of the chief advisers of the young Ottoman princes.

In 1437, Prince Ahmed Çelebi died suddenly in Amasya. The cause of his death has never been fully established. According to one version, he was buried in Amasya in the so-called Türbe of the Princes; according to another, in Bursa with his ancestors. The governorship was transferred to the five-year-old Mehmed Çelebi, while his brother Alaeddin Ali was sent in the same capacity to Manisa (the ancient Magnesia ad Sipylum), northeast of Izmir. Murad appointed as the new governor's adviser his former freedman Hïzïr Pasha, and as teacher Hïzïr Çelebi, a son of the distinguished religious scholar Ilyas Fakih. Burak Bey, a descendant of Şadi Bey, became his military commander (*serasker*). Murad himself had been governor of Amasya for a considerable period and one of his wives, Yeni Hatun, was a granddaughter of the powerful Şadgeldi Ahmed Pasha, while both her sisters had successively been married to the influential Yörgüç Pasha, who is said to have been granted the right to mint coins in his own name. Thus the sultan, through his kinship with the city nobility, was thoroughly informed of local conditions and was certainly guided by this knowledge in choosing counselors for his inexperienced son. There is good reason to suppose that it was they and not the boy Mehmed who made all important decisions.

In June 1439 significant changes were made in the personnel of the government at Edirne. Ishak Pasha, the first vizier, a convert probably of Greek origin, who for many years had stood in high favor with the sultan, was suddenly deposed. He was replaced by Çandarlïoğlu Halil Pasha, scion of an illustrious Turkish family which for generations had supplied the empire with high dignitaries.[17] Ishak Pasha became second

---

[17] For this family, important in the 14th- and 15th-century history of the Ottomans, see "Djandarli" (V. L. Ménage), *EI*² II, 444–445. (In Turkish the word *oğul* ["son"] may be suffixed to a name, as in many other languages, to produce a new proper name. The addition of the possessive suffix results in the loss of the medial vowel, as here: Çandarlïoğlu.)

vizier, while the post of third vizier went to Zaganos Pasha, another Greek renegade. As non-Turks, both these statesmen were looked upon with disfavor and suspicion by the old Turkish nobility. It is safe to assume that the reorganization had been brought about by pressure from the nobles. The conflicts that arose from the admission of non-Turkish converts (voluntary or forced) to the highest posts in the government, above all in the army, were a threat to the stability of the state and a source of lasting concern to the sultans. Particularly under Murad II, who at this time (ca. 1438) had vigorously promoted the *devşirme*, the rivalry between the two groups became acute. It was to play an important and often crucial role in the destinies of the state throughout the thirty years of Murad's reign.

In the late spring of 1439, either immediately before or after the change in government, the circumcision of the two princes, Alaeddin Ali and Mehmed, was celebrated in Edirne, both princes having been summoned from their posts in Anatolia. Traditionally this event was an occasion for prolonged festivities, to which in later years foreign rulers of both East and West came to be invited. Entertainments of all sorts were provided for the populace, while scholars, poets, magistrates, each in his own way, did their best to embellish the magnificent festivities at court. On this occasion, however, the expenditure was still relatively moderate, a far cry from the lavish ostentation of subsequent reigns. The patriarchal simplicity with which Murad celebrated the circumcision of his two sons is perhaps best indicated by a detail recorded in the Turkish chronicles, that on this occasion Sheikh Seyyid Natta of Baghdad, who under Bayezid I had come to Anatolia from Mesopotamia and established a profitable family benefice in a monastery at Bursa, introduced leather tablecloths into the sultan's dining halls, a refinement hitherto unknown among the Ottomans. This apparently accounted for the sheikh's surname (Nattā', from *nat'*, "leather tablecloth"), which to all intents and purposes replaced his real name, Husayn.

The marriage of one of Murad's daughters with Ismail Bey, son of Murad's brother-in-law Isfendiyaroğlu Ibrahim Bey, who led an obscure existence as princeling of Kastamonu (Kastamuni, in northwestern Asia Minor), was celebrated on the same occasion. Mehmed II, as we shall see, was not to deal very kindly with his brother-in-law.

The celebrations had scarcely ended when the sultan decided to reverse his Anatolian governorships and send Alaeddin Ali to Amasya and Mehmed to Manisa [pl. II]. The reasons for this measure are not clear, but the move seems at least partly attributable to the influence of the sultan's political advisers, a conclusion to which the tragic end of Prince

Ali seems to lend weight. Yet gravely as the change was soon to affect the destinies of the empire, it was overshadowed at the time by the military enterprise in which Murad began to involve himself soon after the end of the family festivities in Edirne.

The Serbian despot George Branković had hoped in vain to purchase the sultan's favor by the marriage of his daughter Mara—who seems to have been about sixteen at the time—to Murad on September 4, 1435. But, as it became increasingly clear in the following years, no sacrifice on his part could change the sultan's policy toward George's tottering throne. A pretext for the campaign against Serbia was provided by the death of Emperor Sigismund, who, aged almost seventy, died at Znojmo (Znaim) on December 9, 1437, on his return journey from Bohemia to Hungary. The sultan had concluded occasional truces with the emperor. To negotiate one of them he had sent a legation of five nobles to Basel, where the council was in session at the time (November 1433). Here the emperor received his guests in great state in the cathedral; the ambassadors presented him with twelve golden goblets full of gold coins and silken garments embroidered in gold and set with jewels; having received sumptuous gifts in return, they were dismissed with assurances of peace. But when on New Year's Day, 1438, Sigismund's son-in-law Albert of Austria, with his wife beside him, was crowned king of Hungary at Székesfehérvár (Stuhlweissenburg; the ancient Alba Regia), Murad, reportedly goaded by his entourage, took advantage of the change of rulers to make a surprise attack on Hungary and Serbia.

Probably as a diversion, a party of raiders (akĭncĭs) was sent against Transylvania, commanded by Ali Bey, son of Evrenos and scion of an old feudal family. The Serbian despot and Vlad II, Dracul, prince of Walachia, were called upon as vassals of the sultan to participate in the campaign and each appeared with troops. In the autumn of 1438 the Ottoman army burst into Transylvania by way of the Iron Gate, vainly besieged the walled city of Şibiu (Hermannstadt; Nagyszeben) for a whole week, devastated Sighişoara (Schässburg) and Mediaş, and burned the suburbs of Braşov (Kronstadt; now Oraşul Stalin). We are told that the country was laid waste for as much as forty-five days on end. More than 70,000 people are said to have been carried away into slavery, among them "Brother George" of Mühlenbach, who, on his return home after more than twenty years in Turkish captivity, wrote a record of his experiences. Frequently published both in Latin and in German, this work is one of our most important sources of information about the Ottoman Empire at this time—its manners, customs, religion, sects, etc., which Brother

George, having had ample occasion for observation, described with an accuracy and understanding rare in his time.[18]

While the Turkish bands were devastating Transylvania, other expeditions broke into Serbia, where they pillaged castles and monasteries.

But all this was a mere prelude to the main offensive that was undertaken in the following year. Murad in person led his army before the walls of Smederevo (Semendria), capital of the despotate, whose vast fortifications had only recently (1430) been completed. Branković's eldest son and his brother-in-law Thomas Cantacuzenus defended the city heroically but waited in vain for help from the West, which had other preoccupations at the time.

In the cathedral of Florence a council of Roman and Greek priests was in session, attended by John VIII Palaeologus, emperor of Byzantium. After interminable deliberations it finally (July 5, 1439) brought forth the decree of union between the Greek and Roman churches, the implementation of which was unfortunately rendered impossible by the confusion and tribulations of the ensuing years. King Albert was at odds with the Hungarian nobility, who were doing their utmost to curtail his authority; he finally agreed, however, to show his good will by sending the despot a small body of soldiers.[19]

After a siege of three months, Smederevo [pl. IV a] fell on August 18, 1439, putting the Ottomans in possession of nearly all of Serbia. Only the region of Novo Brdo in the south, with its invaluable silver mines (worked for the most part by Saxon miners, while the ruling class, the mine owners, goldsmiths, and mint masters consisted of Ragusans), escaped Turkish occupation for a time. The chronicler Critoboulos records with enthusiasm that gold and silver sprang from the Serbian soil as from natural springs; wherever one dug, one ran into rich deposits, more productive even than the famous mines of India. Though these natural resources as well as the region of Zeta remained in the possession of the despot, it was clear to all observers that in the long run the Ottomans would take over. Ishak Bey, Evrenos's other son, who had previously been in charge of Skoplje (Üsküp) on the Vardar, became the first commander over the new territories.[20]

---

[18] On Brother George and the manuscript and printed editions of his work, see J. A. B. Palmer, "Fr. Georgius de Hungaria, O. P., and the *Tractatus de Moribus Condicionibus et Nequicia Turcorum*," *Bulletin of the John Rylands Library* 34 (1951), 44–68.

[19] For a detailed treatment of the background to and aftermath of the council see Joseph Gill, *The Council of Florence* (Cambridge, 1959).

[20] For Critoboulos see below, book 2, n. 23; for Novo Brdo and its mines, see

The roads to Bosnia were now open to the Turks. Their raiders advanced almost unopposed from Sarajevo (Vrh Bosna; Turkish Bosna Saray), which with its environs had been occupied for some time past, to the outskirts of Jajce, the Bosnian capital, pillaging the countryside. Hungary itself was protected against Ottoman incursions only by the barrier of Belgrade.

The military success of 1439 encouraged Murad to carry on with his Serbian plans. At the end of October 1439, King Albert died suddenly of dysentery on his way to Vienna. The ensuing quarrels over his succession put Hungary in a state of turmoil and even the papal legate, Cardinal Giuliano Cesarini, was unable to impose a solution. The sultan was quick to take advantage of the situation. His next aim was Belgrade, the powerful bastion which had been annexed by Hungary on the basis of an exchange. Beginning in April 1440, Turkish forces laid siege by land and water to this important fortress which, situated at the confluence of the Sava and the Danube, was well protected both by nature and by manmade fortifications. At the same time Turkish expeditions raided Transylvania and Hungary as far as the Tisza River, devastating the countryside. From the land side the besiegers, led jointly by the sultan himself and his trusty general Ali Bey, son of Evrenos, threw up a wall around Belgrade from which they hurled stones into the city, while the besieged replied with cannon fire and mines. More than a hundred warships plied the Danube. The besiegers were finally thwarted by the bravery and ingenuity of the defenders, and in September, Murad was forced to withdraw. For the present this fortress guarding the frontiers of Christendom was saved, having brilliantly fulfilled its mission.

Yet the heroism of the Belgrade garrison could not delay the fate of the despot George Branković. The Hungarian succession had not been settled in accordance with his purposes and desires. The fifteen-year-old King Ladislas III of Poland, a representative of the Lithuanian Jagellon dynasty, had emerged victorious from the elections; the despot's own youngest son had been defeated. George's son-in-law, the powerful and immensely wealthy Count Ulrich of Cilli (ca. 1406–1456), husband of the despot's younger daughter Catherine (since April 20, 1434) and hence brother-in-law to the sultan's wife Mara, withdrew the support on which the old man had been counting. Young Ladislas seized the despot's palace at Buda and numerous other possessions, which he distributed among his henchmen. In despair, the aged Serbian prince left the estates of Count

pp. 126f. The older standard history of Serbia is Constantin Jireček, *Geschichte der Serben*, 2 vols. (Gotha, 1918).

Ulrich of Cilli and set off southward, accompanied only by his wife Irene and a few hundred horsemen. Like Venice on an earlier occasion, Dubrovnik (Ital. Ragusa) now gave him a friendly reception, but its friendliness was short-lived. The news from his remaining Serbian territories in the interior became more and more desperate. Novo Brdo, "Mother of Cities," surrendered (June 27, 1441) with its inexhaustible mines, to the Rumelian governor, the eunuch Şihabeddin Pasha, a convert. But even more crushing was the report of the cruel fate that overtook two of his sons. Gregor, who had fallen into Turkish hands at the fall of Smederevo, and his younger brother Stjepan, who had been taken into custody in Edirne, were accused of secretly corresponding with their father. At the command of their own brother-in-law, Murad, they were thrown into chains on Easter Sunday (April 16, 1441). On May 8 they were blinded at Tokat in central Anatolia, site of the ancient state prison (Bedevi Çardak), where for many years prisoners regarded as politically dangerous were confined. The intercession of their sister Mara, who was not without influence on her husband though she had clung to her Christian faith, had come too late to avert their bitter fate. In the end there was nothing for the despot to do but return to Hungary, submit to the young king, and join him in planning vengeance against those who had seized his possessions. But to his dying day George Branković never forgot this humiliation.

The proud, freedom-loving Ragusans were soon to feel the consequences of the Ottoman occupation of Serbia. The entire region from the Kvarner (Quarnero) to Durrës (Durazzo; Turkish Draç) had been under Venetian sovereignty from 1205 to 1358, but was ceded to Hungary by the Peace of Zara (February 18, 1358). Soon afterward (May 27), in a treaty with Louis the Great of Hungary, Dubrovnik had acknowledged its allegiance to the Hungarian crown. But the king of Hungary had no permanent representative in Dubrovnik, which actually became an independent oligarchy on the style of the Italian city-states, managed through the unusual ability of its senate to preserve its independence. The first half of the fifteenth century was the period of its greatest prosperity, to which numerous churches and palaces still bear witness. The disorders in the neighboring territories and the Ottoman conquests in the western Balkans gradually cut down Dubrovnik's overland trade, but thanks to its ships, its local industry, and above all to its political resourcefulness, the city long preserved its old importance as a mart for the products of the western Balkans and the textiles of Italy. It also remained a hotbed of diplomatic intrigue and continued to figure prominently in the political plans of Venice. The commercial settlements of the Ragusans, not only in Bosnia, Herzegovina, Serbia, and Albania but also in Sofia, Turnovo (Trnovo), Provadiya (Pravadi), Philippopolis, Edirne, and Constantinople itself, compelled the city fathers to take increasing account of the sultan's political whims and to pay increasing tribute to the Porte.

In September 1440, a treasurer of Murad had appeared in Dubrovnik to demand, in his master's name, the institution of an annual tribute. The senate's rejection of this demand resulted in the immediate imprisonment of all Ragusan merchants not only on Turkish soil but also in Serbia and in the Bosnian territory of Stjepan Vukčić (Stephen Kosača, Duke of St. Sava), vassal and compliant tool of the sultan. Alarmed for their rich depots in the Balkans, the Ragusans yielded forthwith. Only by a solemn undertaking to dispatch a thousand ducats' worth of silver plate each year to the sultan's treasury were they enabled to preserve their freedom to trade in the territories of the Ottoman emperor and his vassals; and even so they were hardly secure against further extortion.[21]

The westward thrust of the Turks had rudely awakened the rulers of the countries most immediately affected, particularly Hungary. The Ottomans had sent raiding parties as far as Slovenia and the Tisza River, where they spread terror among the population. Young King Ladislas entrusted two distinguished generals with the defense of his menaced frontiers: Nicholas Ujláky and John Hunyadi, voivode of Transylvania, whose brilliant feats of arms in the years that followed were to inspire all Christendom with hope that the Turks would ultimately be repelled. A petty Transylvanian nobleman of Romanian descent, Hunyadi had already earned glory in battle against the Turks and the Hussites and was thoroughly experienced in the art of war.

From his headquarters in Belgrade, John Hunyadi began to make raids on the Turkish countryside in 1441, inflicting a considerable defeat on Ishak Bey, commander of Smederevo, to whom this discomfiture must have been a bitter blow, particularly as his influence on the sultan's military plans was far from negligible. This same defeat led Şihabeddin Pasha, governor of Rumelia, to build the fortress of Žrnov (Avala) on a height (1700 feet) nine miles south of Belgrade, where its ruins still dominate the landscape. The aged Mesid Bey, the sultan's chief equerry, who had invaded Transylvania and was preparing to besiege Şibiu, was put to flight and killed along with his son. The battlefield was strewn with Turkish corpses and soon the news of Hunyadi's brilliant victory spread far and wide. A wagon so heavily laden with booty and battle spoils that ten horses could barely draw it was sent to George Branković,

[21] For more details and references to the sources for the *ahd-name* of 1442 see Biegman, *The Turco-Ragusan Relationship*, 26. Cf. Carter, *Dubrovnik*, 200.

Hungary's ally. It was topped with the impaled heads of Mesid Bey and his son and carried an elderly Turk who was compelled to deliver a speech presenting the trophy to the despot. Şihabeddin swore grim revenge and appeared at the head of a mighty army, boasting that his adversaries would run hundreds of miles at the mere sight of his turban. However, he incurred a defeat far more disastrous than that of Mesid Bey which he had hoped to avenge. The Ottomans lost thousands in dead, including members of illustrious noble families; numerous prisoners and some 200 banners were taken. The spoils, which Hunyadi distributed among his troops as a reward for their bravery, were reported to have been enormous.

Tidings of this victory reached the court of the Hungarian king in Buda shortly after the arrival of a legation from Murad, who demanded the surrender of Belgrade or at least an annual tribute in pledge of a projected alliance. Whether this was the real purpose of the sultan's mission, or whether it had merely been sent to obtain more reliable information about the state of affairs in Hungary than his spies could provide, remains an open question. It seems more than doubtful that Murad harbored any illusions concerning the prospects for his mission at a time when in the West the fortunes of war had turned against him. Confident in their military superiority, the Hungarians dismissed the Ottoman envoys out of hand. On the basis of their report, it became clear to the sultan that sooner or later the defensive warfare of the Hungarians would develop into a large-scale offensive.

In Hungary political dissension had been lessened appreciably by the unexpected death of the queen dowager, Elizabeth (December 24, 1442). Fired with enthusiasm by the success of Hungarian arms, the splintered forces of the nation began to unite. Everyone spoke of making war on the infidels and driving them out of Europe. John Hunyadi was honored as the national hero and savior. The captured banners and insignia of the Ottomans were distributed among the churches of the land. Here Christians gathered in prayer and thanksgiving, from which they drew strength for their great undertaking.

Word of Hunyadi's victories had spread far beyond the borders of Hungary. Throughout the Western world enthusiasm for the war against the heathen seemed to be on the rise. The Holy War, a favorite project of Pope Eugenius IV, had first been proposed at the Council of Florence (1431). In moving letters to the rulers of Christendom, the pope described the pitiful situation of their coreligionaries in the Orient. But time and time again the disastrous schism between the Western and Eastern churches, the endless negotiations for the union of the split faith, and the political turmoil of Italy into which the Holy See was drawn had prevented the pope from carrying out his plan for a crusade. Early in 1443, Eugenius issued an encyclical in which, deploring the insufficiency of his own resources, he called upon all the princes of the Church to collect a tenth from all their churches, convents, and benefices for the war against the Turks. By way of setting a good example, he undertook to set apart a fifth of the entire income of the Apostolic treasury for the equipment of an army and a fleet. He concluded a military alliance with the Republic of Dubrovnik; he had previously sent his legate, Cardinal Giuliano Cesarini, to Buda, not only to settle the internal dissensions of the Hungarians but above all to press for a crusade against the Turks. The cardinal was a tragic figure. Thanks to his influence and energy, he was destined to play an important and ultimately disastrous role far beyond the confines of southeastern Europe. His impassioned eloquence had brought internal peace to Hungary and won decisive support for a great campaign against the infidels. But most of the sovereigns of the West greeted the papal summons to holy war with an indifference which almost entirely frustrated his hopes. Notable exceptions were Poland and Walachia, which levied both infantry and cavalry, though allotting funds sufficient to pay them for only six months. Only the common people were more enthusiastic. From all sides penniless crusaders and fortune hunters thronged to Hungary, eager for adventure and hoping to fill their empty pockets.[22]

One important reason for the widespread lukewarmness toward the crusade was a deep-seated hostility to the Byzantine emperors, who, it was generally thought, had most to gain by it. Only in those countries which were themselves threatened was direct support forthcoming. Elsewhere there was always some good reason or pretext for declining to supply troops. Emperor Frederick III (1440–1493), interested only in enlarging and consolidating the power of the house of Hapsburg, was, as usual, unequal to the situation. His pretext for neither participating nor sending troops was the unrest in Bohemia. His real reason was that he had no wish to add to the already increasing power in Hungary of the Polish king Ladislas, lest the latter turn his victorious arms against Austria.

Murad, who had covered the entire Balkan peninsula and perhaps Hungary and even Germany with a network of able spies, was informed of the grandiose projects for a campaign against him and his empire. He

---

[22] For the papacy under Eugene see Joseph Gill, *Eugenius IV* (London, 1961). Cf. Ludwig Pastor, *The History of the Popes* I, trans. F. I. Antrobus (St. Louis, 1902), especially 324ff.

was equally well informed of the designs of his own brother-in-law and adversary, the Karamanoğlı Ibrahim Bey, on the neighboring Ottoman Anatolian provinces. The Ottoman chroniclers and Western writers of the time allude frequently to a pact between Ibrahim and the kings of Hungary, and it is certain that there was such a pact, though few details of it are known to us. It provided, no doubt, for concerted action against the Ottomans, similar to that projected at a later date by the Persian Safavids and Charles V.

Just as a major crusade was being organized in Buda, Ibrahim Bey, the "Grand Qaraman," struck in Asia Minor. Murad in person led the campaign against his brother-in-law, presumably in the spring of 1443. His son Ali Çelebi was summoned from Amasya to join him in all haste, and soon their united forces brought the rebel to his knees. Ali Çelebi, we are told, distinguished himself by his courage and astuteness. His strikingly powerful physique, it is said, called forth great admiration. Ibrahim Bey sued for and obtained peace, thanks no doubt to the intercession of his wife, Murad's sister. The sultan, accompanied by his son, then returned to Bursa, where they parted.

At this point a strange tragedy occurred, the mystery of which will in all likelihood never be cleared up. Kara Hizïr Pasha was sent to Amasya after Ali Çelebi. Creeping into the palace at night, he strangled the prince in his bed. And that was not all. The prince's two sons, aged six months and eighteen months, were also killed and buried, first together in the Turumtay *türbe* in Amasya, later probably in Bursa. Ali Çelebi was replaced as governor of Amasya by Mehmed Pasha, son of Lala Şahin Pasha, the conqueror of Philippopolis (1364).

The news of the sudden death of Ali Çelebi, said to be his favorite son, filled Murad with profound grief and consternation, or so, at least, we are told by our Ottoman and Western sources; all of them, however, are mistaken in their dating of the tragedy.

As a result of the death of his brother the eleven-year-old Mehmed Çelebi in Manisa now became heir to the throne and was recalled at once to his father's palace. Up to this time Mehmed Çelebi does not seem to have been a source of great joy to his father. His impetuous, headstrong spirit and his refusal to obey or to accept the slightest admonition had made it difficult, if not impossible, to give him any education. The sultan had assigned him a number of tutors; their names have come down to us, but the results of their teaching are more than doubtful. One of these was the mullah Iyas Efendi, who along with the future grand vizier Mahmud Pasha had come to Turkey as a Serbian prisoner of war and had later taught in Bursa. Iyas had not seemed the right man for the task. Given to occasional ecstatic absences, he retired in the end to a monastery to follow a mystic vocation. When all efforts had failed to induce young Mehmed to study, and when he had rejected instruction in the articles of faith and Koran reading, his father called on the celebrated mullah Ahmed Gürani (Kurani), from the village of Kuran in the Kurdish region of Şehrisur. After studying jurisprudence and the Koran in Cairo, Gürani had made his way to Anatolia; at the behest of the sultan he accepted a position at the *medrese* founded by Murad I in Bursa. Apparently a man of sufficient energy and prestige to bend the rebellious prince to his will, he was called to Manisa. According to some of the older sources, the sultan handed the mullah, an imposing man with a long dyed beard, a switch and gave him express permission to use it should the boy prove recalcitrant. Switch in hand, the sources continue, the mullah went to the prince. "Your father," he said, "has sent me to instruct you, but also to chastise you in case you should not obey me." When Mehmed laughed at these words Mullah Gürani gave him such a beating that the boy stood in awe of him forever after. In a short time he had learned the Koran. Richly rewarded by Murad for his success, the mullah rose to high government position when his difficult charge had become sultan, although his frankness and brusque manners often brought him into conflict with the young ruler. Another of Mehmed's teachers, Mullah Sinan, later became a vizier. Mullah Hamiduddin, surnamed Efdalzade—like Gürani, a student of the famous theologian Mullah Yegân—seems also to have been one of the young prince's tutors at this time in Manisa. He later achieved considerable fame as a professor in Bursa and Istanbul.[23]

Manisa, where Mehmed Çelebi had lived for four or five years with his mother and teachers, was a picturesque city. Today bare vestiges mark the site of the former serai, from which one can enjoy a sweeping view over the city, rising in terraces up the mountain slopes from a deep ravine, its numerous mosques towering over the green of the trees. But from now on the young prince was to live close to his father in Edirne so as to gain an understanding of government affairs. He arrived at court at a critical moment; no sooner had Murad returned to Europe from Anatolia than news came that the Christian armies had set out from Buda in a southeasterly direction (early July, 1443).

[23] More details on the lives and works of these and other scholars living under Murad II and Mehmed may be found in the oldest of the Ottoman biographical dictionaries, *Al-Şaka'ik al-nu'maniye*, written in the mid-16th century by Taşköprüzade. The book has been translated into German by O. Rescher as *Eš-Šaqa'iq en-No'manijje* (Constantinople, 1927). On Mullah Gürani see also "Gūrānī" (J. R. Walsh), *EI²* II, 1140–41.

The small but impressive host of the crusaders was headed by the youthful king Ladislas; an advance guard of 12,000 horsemen was led by the battle-hardened John Hunyadi, accompanied by the cardinal-legate Giuliano Cesarini and the landless Serbian prince George Branković. Not far from Smederevo, which was still in Turkish hands, the army crossed the Danube and continued southward. Nowhere was there any serious resistance. The army of roughly 25,000 horsemen and archers was joined along the line of march by more than 8,000 Serbs, mounted and on foot. The combined host encountered an Ottoman force first on November 3, 1443, between the castle of Bolvan (near Aleksinac) and the city of Niš. Here Kasĭm Bey, then governor of Rumelia, Ishak Bey, and other standard-bearers were defeated. Without serious difficulty the Christian army, by way of Niš and Pirot, reached the walled city of Sofia, which was quickly stormed and pillaged. The Bulgarians went wild with joy, welcoming the Poles as their brother Slavs. Now there was no obstacle to the main advance into the Thracian plain, and the crusaders seemed perfectly justified in their confidence that they would reach Edirne in another week. The Serbian despot, who knew the country inside and out from his years as a vassal under Sultan Bayezid I and his sons, was able to guide the Christian army through the inhospitable countryside and the snow-covered passes of the Balkan Mountains (the ancient Haemus). The closer the host, followed by an enormous provisions train, came to its goal, the more obstinate became the resistance of the Turks. The ancient Gate of Trajan and the entire military highway leading from Belgrade to Constantinople were blocked with felled trees and the passes were well guarded.

When on December 12, 1443, in bitterly cold weather, the army reached the basin surrounding the locality of Zlatitsa ("Izladi" of the Ottoman chronicles), whence it planned to pursue its course through the beech forests of the Sredna Gora near the town of Panagyurishte, it encountered the stubborn resistance of the massed Ottoman armies. At this point the extreme cold, the impossibility of replenishing their supplies, and the renewed attacks of the Ottomans under Kasĭm Bey, who had meanwhile escaped, obliged the crusaders to turn back. The Ottomans followed in pursuit but were repulsed in a battle fought at Melshtitsa near Sofia on Christmas Eve. On January 2, 1444, near Mount Kunovica between Pirot and Niš, the Ottomans were again defeated by an attack from ambush and many of their leaders, including the sultan's brother-in-law Mahmud Çelebi of the Çandarlĭ family, were taken prisoner. Serious consideration was given the despot's suggestion that the entire army spend the winter in fortified positions in Serbia and resume its eastward advance in the spring. In the end, however, because of the bitter cold and the critical lack of supplies, the plan had to be discarded, and the Christian host started on its homeward march. By late January the crusaders reached Belgrade after a difficult journey across icy fields and mountain passes. In February what was left of the exhausted and decimated army arrived in Buda. Emaciated from hunger and cold, clutching the captured banners of the infidels in their bony hands, the warriors entered the Hungarian capital amid the rejoicings of the population. To speed their march, the troops had cast away and burned all unnecessary baggage; whole wagonloads of captured weapons were buried and all superfluous horses and beasts of burden were killed. Faithful to his oath, the young king made his entry on foot. Before repairing to his castle, he and his generals went to the cathedral to give thanks to Providence.

This was the end of the strange expedition which lasted roughly six months but has become known in Hungarian history as the "Long Campaign."[24]

This bold incursion of a relatively small Christian army into the heart of Ottoman territory made a lasting impression. Throughout southeastern Europe the Christians began to raise their heads. On all sides there were uprisings against the Ottoman overlords and soon the Turkish garrisons were driven from a number of important castles and fortresses. But it should not be supposed that the Balkan peoples joined in common revolt against Ottoman rule. By prompt payment of the *harac*, the tribute always imposed on them, the Christians of the conquered countries purchased the right to live unmolested in their faith and to maintain their customs and many of their institutions. Most of the tribute went to the sultan's treasury. The Jews also paid their share. In addition each Christian was liable to a pasturage tax graduated according to the number of his sheep, goats, and oxen, and a tenth was levied on each harvest. If we may rely on the Burgundian Bertrandon de la Broquière, Murad received in 1432 an annual tribute of 25,000 ducats.[25] Those who paid their taxes fully and punctually enjoyed a life scarcely different from that of pre-Ottoman times. Such, at least, was the case in the fifteenth century. It was only much later that bribery, extortion, blackmail, and usury made their ap-

[24] The Long Campaign is the starting point for Babinger's earlier study of events between 1443 and 1446: "Von Amurath zu Amurath," *Oriens* 3 (1950), 229–265; reprinted in *A&A* I, 128–157.

[25] The account of the Burgundian traveler is contained in *Le Voyage d'Outremer*, ed. Ch. Schefer (Paris, 1892). An English translation appears in Thomas Wright, *Early Travels in Palestine* (London, 1848), 283–382. A detailed discussion of taxation in the Ottoman Empire will be found in the article "Djizya" (H. Inalcïk), *EI²* II, 562–566.

pearance in the Ottoman provinces, that the officials, often spurred by insatiable greed, began to suck the blood of the population, and that all life was poisoned by deception and distrust. But this was in the decadence of the seventeenth and eighteenth centuries; conditions were very different under Murad II, who, as we have noted, was respected even among his adversaries for his sense of justice.

Thus it was not so much the people who rebelled against the new masters as the would-be rulers, who feared for their lands as well as for those privileges and liberties which they still retained. The Byzantine emperor John VIII was to play a lamentable role in the drama that now began to unfold. To be sure, he promised to support the Western princes who had drawn their swords against the Turks, but his promises were pure hypocrisy, a cloak for his weakness. The crusading movement had filled him too with new hope for the survival of his house and his shadow empire. Not without reason has it been maintained that in Byzantium, as in Rome, the dream of expelling the Ottomans from Europe had become a consolation for the misery of the present and the obvious hopelessness of the future.

Emperor John VIII was one of the first to send ambassadors to Buda to congratulate the king on the end of his campaign in the Haemus. As Filippo Buonaccorsi (Callimachus)[26] records, perhaps with a slight irony, in his history of King Ladislas, the Rhomaeans (i.e. the Byzantines) could think of no better way to express their joy over what had already been done and what was to be hoped for in the future than, blending the human and the divine, to announce to all the world that, at the very hour when King Ladislas was winning the brilliant victory that cost Mahmud Çelebi his freedom, a white-clad youth on horseback had appeared at the Macedonian Gate in Constantinople. After prancing about for a while as a sign of rejoicing, the phantom had suddenly vanished. At first the news of this apparition had been greeted with alarm, for no one knew what to make of it. But soon the people had understood that the rider was a messenger of victory, sent to let the Byzantines know that the time had come for them to take a hand. With such old wives' tales the Byzantines sought to divert their minds from the seriousness of their situation. For it was clear to anyone in his right mind that Murad was prevented only by his activities in other parts of his far-flung realm from reviving his old plan, shelved in 1422, for the conquest of what remained of the Byzantine Empire. And when, ten years later (1432),

[26] The reference is to P. Callimachi Geminianesis, *Historia de Rege Vladislao, seu clade Varnensi* (August Vindelicorum, 1519).

the Genoese had launched their bold but unsuccessful attack on Constantinople, the not unreasonable suspicion that they were in league with the sultan made the prospects for Byzantine survival look dim indeed.

Yet at first it seemed as though the inevitable might be delayed. From the Morea the emperor's two brothers, Constantine, despot of Mistra, and Thomas, despot of Patras, fomented an uprising north of the isthmus. The Walachians of Mount Pindus rebelled against the Turks, and by the summer of 1443 bitter hostilities had broken out in central Albania. It is hardly surprising that, when informed of these developments, the Hungarian diet should have decided to carry on the struggle against the enemies of Christendom by every available means. Pope Eugenius IV (by birth a Condolmieri, member of one of the newer aristocratic families of Venice), the Venetian Republic, Duke Philip of Burgundy, and Dubrovnik—all offered to join in fitting out a fleet. The spoils were divided in advance. There is no doubt that Murad, the common enemy, found himself in a perilous situation.

In Asia, Ibrahim Bey of Karaman, his old unreconcilable enemy, was threatening a new attack in the hinterland, obviously in collaboration with the sultan's European foes. The imminence of the Karamanian war as well as the alarming stirrings in Albania, Serbia, and Greece made it seem more than advisable to Murad to conclude a peace as quickly as possible with the Western powers, especially Hungary. The delicate negotiations were handled by the sultan's wife Mara, daughter of George Branković. Under conditions of deep secrecy her envoy, a Greek monk, went to Dubrovnik at the beginning of March 1444, and proceeded in a vessel made available by the senate, up the Adriatic to Split (Spalato), whence he hastened on horseback to Hungary to meet the despot George. But this was not the sultan's first attempt to come to terms with the West. The preceding January, while King Ladislas was on Serbian soil with his army, a messenger had come to him from the sultan to arrange for an Ottoman deputation and discuss the main points of a peace treaty or armistice. According to the projected agreement, Serbia was to be returned to George Branković, and his two blinded sons were to be sent home. Thus George Branković, especially after receiving the Greek envoy, had indeed every reason to argue warmly in favor of the sultan's peace proposals before the Hungarian diet in April 1444, for by now he had high hopes of restoring the fortunes of his house.

The events of the next few months would still be totally unknown to us were it not for some letters that came to light only recently. They were written by Ciriaco de' Pizzicolli (b. 1391) of Ancona, more com-

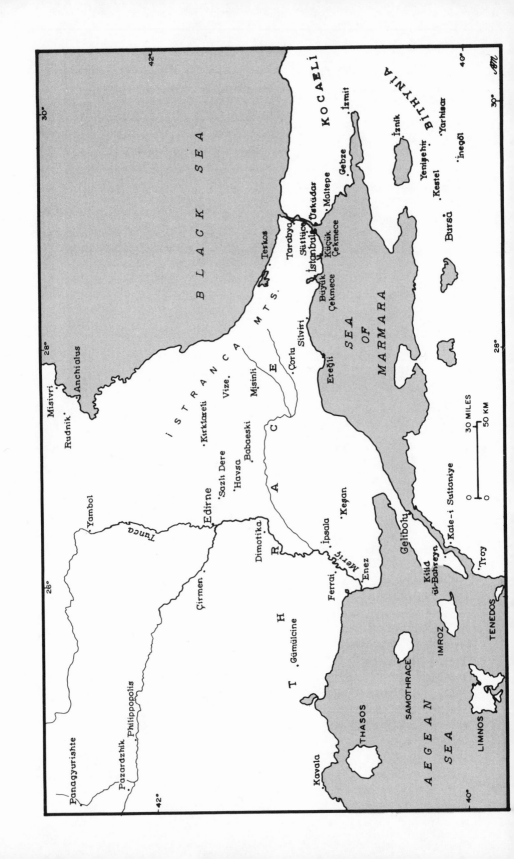

monly known as Cyriacus of Ancona or Anconitanus. More than once in recounting the history of the next decade we shall have occasion to speak of this remarkable figure who made it his business, in the course of innumerable journeys through the countries of southeastern Europe and the Levant, "to awaken dead men from the grave," as he once put it. His archaeological (and political) travels found a worthy patron in Pope Eugenius IV. Ciriaco combed the Greek mainland for antiquities, at the same time establishing ties with the local princes; his travels took him to Constantinople, which he had first visited as a merchant in 1418, and also to Thrace, Thessaly, Macedonia, the Aegean islands, Crete, and Egypt. Wherever he went, he looked for vestiges of the past, kept diaries, and wrote to friends in Italy. Murad, to whom he had succeeded in being presented, provided him with a safe-conduct (*berat*) which enabled him to travel throughout the Ottoman Empire unmolested and immune to customs duties. The last years of his life—he appears to have died about 1455 in Cremona—are still shrouded in mystery. Today it can be taken for certain that Ciriaco de' Pizzicolli also carried out political missions in the Balkans and Asia Minor. But thus far only fragmentary evidence of his activity as a spy has come to light.[27]

Early in 1444, while on a trip through the Morea, Ciriaco was over-joyed to learn of the preparations for war that had been made by the despot and the emperor's two brothers. At the end of February he was at the sultan's court in Edirne with Francesco Draperio, a wealthy Genoese, or rather Galatian, merchant and owner of alum mines in Yeni Foça (near Phocaea, north of Izmir), who had been commissioned by Genoa to carry on certain negotiations with the sultan.[28] On May 22 he and one Raffaele Castiglione accompanied Draperio to an audience with Murad, and the same day, in a Latin letter to his patron Andreolo Giustiniani-

---

[27] For this Italian traveler and his letters, see F. Pall, "Ciriaco d'Ancona e la crociata contro i Turchi," *Bulletin de la Section Historique de l'Academie Roumanie* 20 (1938), 9–68. Further details are also given by Babinger in "Notes on Cyriac of Ancona and Some of His Friends," *Journal of the Warburg and Courtauld Institutes* 25 (1962), 321–323. Cf. also E. W. Bodnar, *Cyriacus of Ancona and Athens* (Brussels, 1960).

[28] The town referred to here as Yeni Foça was founded by the Genoese early in the 15th century. A few miles to the south lies the settlement once known as Eski (Old) Foça, now simply as Foça. Babinger seems to use this shorter designation for both places on occasion (cf. below, p. 44). For a survey of the history of the alum trade, see Charles Singer, *The Earliest Chemical Industry* (London, 1948), especially 89–94 for mining at Foça. Cf. Jacques Heers, *Gênes au XVe siècle* (Paris, 1961), 202 and especially 394ff.

Banca on Chios (Scio; Turkish Sakïz Adasï), Ciriaco painted a vivid picture of the ceremony. As the Italians entered, the sultan sat on an outspread carpet "in regal splendor of a barbaric kind," surrounded by his dignitaries; beside him sat Prince Mehmed Çelebi, the heir apparent. The letter goes on to describe briefly but strikingly the reception first of the sultan's son-in-law Isfendiyaroğlu Ismail Bey of Kastamonu and then of Francesco Draperio, both of whom had brought lavish gifts. From this letter we first learn that the young crown prince was in residence with his father at this time.[29]

But far more important than this description of an audience with Murad, such as the Burgundian knight Bertrandon de la Broquière had written twelve years earlier (1432), is Ciriaco's account of an event which occurred on June 12, 1444, and for which we have no other source. On this day Murad received in solemn audience a delegation of four ambassadors from the West, who had come to deliver a communication signed in Buda on April 25, 1444, by King Ladislas III.

This delegation was headed by a Serb, Stojko Gizdavić, serving as ambassador of the king of Hungary and Poland; he was followed by one "Vitislaus," representing John Hunyadi, and two envoys from the Serbian despot George Branković, one of whom was Atanasije Frašak, metropolitan of Smederevo, the other probably a man by the name of Bogdan, the despot's chancellor. The strange procession was rendered particularly impressive by an escort of sixty horsemen. One is astonished to learn that a Hungarian legation was headed by a Serb who, despite the flowery epithets with which he is graced in the letter, is otherwise unknown, that John Hunyadi, who, as voivode of Transylvania was nothing more than a vassal of the Hungarian king, was represented by a special envoy, and finally that George Branković had appointed two of his highest secular and ecclesiastical dignitaries as his spokesmen.

The sultan granted the envoys several audiences. They were received each time in the same order: first Stojko Gizdavić, then the two envoys of the despot, and finally John Hunyadi's representative. At the final audience, June 12, 1444, Murad dismissed the Western legates with a document granting a ten-year truce, guaranteed with all the usual oaths and speaking expressly of the conditions under which Vlad Dracul, prince of Walachia, was to be freed from Turkish allegiance. In conclusion it provided that Süleyman Bey, as envoy (çavuş) of the Porte, should repair to Buda, there to receive equally solemn confirmation of the agreement—

[29] The text of Ciriaco's letter is given by O. Halecki, *The Crusade of Varna, A Discussion of Controversial Problems* (New York, 1943), appendix 3 (following the work of Pall, cited above, n. 27).

recte et fideliter sine aliquo dolo, faithfully and in all due form, without guile of any kind.[30]

Having thus, supposedly at least, covered himself in the rear, Murad was able to turn his main attention to the threat of his brother-in-law, Ibrahim Bey, in Konya (Iconium). It is safe to assume that Ibrahim had a secret understanding with Hungary at the time. Edirne lived in great fear of coming events. Ciriaco de' Pizzicolli, who left this city for Constantinople soon after the departure of the Western envoys, wrote John Hunyadi from Pera on June 24, 1444. In a characteristic introduction, this communication refers to a previous letter dispatched from Edirne on June 12: "I wrote what was possible from Adrianople, most Christian Prince, in a moderate form, in order to avoid certain destruction at the hands of the Barbarians" (in case his letter should fall into the hands of the Turks). He goes on to speak expressly of a "forced peace" and to tell how the people of Edirne were busy strengthening the city's fortifications. Clearly the sultan and his entourage put little trust in a peace with the Western powers. As we know from other sources as well, particularly from the informative poem of Michel Behaim, the Swabian Meistersinger, at the news that the Hungarian king had embarked on a new southeastern campaign, many of the wealthier inhabitants, especially merchants, not only of Edirne but also of Gelibolu on the Hellespont, fled to Bursa in Asia Minor.[31]

The situation in Anatolia permitted of no delay. In the above-mentioned letter of June 24, Ciriaco had informed the voivode of Transylvania that the sultan intended to leave Mehmed Çelebi and the trusted first vizier Halil Pasha behind in Thrace (i.e. Edirne), and to cross the Dardanelles to Asia with a considerable army.

This makes it clear that before the middle of June, when Ciriaco left Edirne, the sultan had planned his campaign and decided to entrust the government of Rumelia to his twelve-year-old son Mehmed, under the supervision, to be sure, of his vizier Halil Pasha of the house of Çandarlï, who enjoyed his unlimited confidence. Most of the chroniclers, even the Turkish ones, report that Murad abdicated at this time, but this was certainly not the case. Mehmed Çelebi merely became regent of the Rumelian territories. Murad crossed the straits with his troops on July 12, 1444, and remained absent from Europe for almost exactly three months.

---

[30] For Ciriaco's account of Murad's reception of the Western delegation and the text of the truce see Halecki, appendixes 4 and 5.

[31] For Ciriaco's letter to Hunyadi, see Halecki, appendix 6. For the poem of Michel Behaim, see Babinger's "Von Amurath zu Amurath," *Oriens* 3 (1950), 237–238 (= *A&A* I, 135), and the sources given there.

During this time the youthful prince Mehmed reigned under the guidance of Halil Pasha and of his stern tutor Mullah Husrev, who as army judge was the highest juridical authority in both parts of the empire. Thus his power was second only to that of the grand vizier.

The summer months of 1444 witnessed important events, which it is still impossible to elucidate in every detail. Accompanied by a Greek named Vranás, Süleyman Bey, as the ambassador of Murad, repaired to Buda, where he must have arrived before the end of July. Concerning his reception and the result of his mission, opinions are widely divergent.

Until recently it had been generally supposed that at the end of July, or at the latest on August 1, 1444, King Ladislas III in Szeged swore to observe the agreement made in Edirne, but that only a few days later, on August 4, he proclaimed a holy war against the infidels, so nullifying his signature and breaking his oath. However, the Polish historian Oskar Halecki has endorsed the interpretation, previously proposed by some Polish scholars, that Ladislas never signed the peace treaty, that a kind of separate peace was concluded between Murad and George Branković, and that Ladislas firmly refused to be a party to it.[32] It is further inferred that on the basis of these separate agreements the Serbian despot recovered the Serbian cities occupied by the Ottomans, including Smederevo, and the important fortress of Golubac (Turkish, Güvercinlik) [pl. VI], which had been refused him up to the last moment. Under the year 1444, it is true, the Serbian annals report that on August 15 the despot concluded with the "emperor"—i.e. the sultan—a peace by which he recovered Smederevo, Kupinovo, Novo Brdo, and all Serbia, and that he entered Smederevo on August 22. If the Polish assertion were founded, it would prove that the sultan had succeeded in shattering the Serbo-Hungarian alliance, a pact no doubt unique in its kind, thereby ensuring that Serbian troops would not participate in a new campaign of the Western forces. In the "Long Campaign" of the previous year George Branković had supplied at least one-third of the Christian army, and his help had surely very much facilitated the march through the difficult terrain of Turkish-occupied Serbia. Now that Branković was no longer to be feared as an enemy, the sultan, without diminishing his own power, was in a position to restore the despot's lands and return his blinded sons. It is definitely established in any case that before September 20, 1444, the assumed date on which the Western armies set out on their campaign,

---

[32] Babinger refers to the above-cited work, *The Crusade of Varna*. Cf. his own "Von Amurath zu Amurath" and Halil Inalcïk's *Fatih devri üzerinde tetkikler ve vesikalar* I (Ankara, 1954; as *TTK*: XI. seri–III, no. 6).

a far-reaching agreement had been concluded between George Branković and the Porte and that the Porte had fulfilled all its terms.

Weighty arguments can be adduced against the Polish contention that Ladislas committed no breach of oath. It is certain that at the diet convened in Buda on April 15, 1444, in the presence of Cardinal Giuliano Cesarini, the papal legate, Ladislas promised to resume the Turkish war that same summer; this did not deter him, however, from dispatching Stojko Gizdavić to the sultan's court a few days later to inaugurate peace negotiations. At approximately the same time, Ladislas assured Giovanni de Reguardati, the Venetian ambassador to the king of Hungary, of his determination to make a new war on the sultan. On July 24, 1444, he informed the king of Bosnia that he was about to launch a campaign against the infidels. But the very next day, St. James's Day, he left Buda for Szeged to meet Süleyman Bey and Vranás the Greek, and to receive from their hands the peace treaty to which the sultan had sworn, for the purpose of affixing his own signature. We shall probably never know for sure whether the young king, whose duplicity can be explained only in part by the spirit of the times, was master of his own decisions or whether he was merely the plaything of outside forces, especially of Cesarini. That he either disregarded the sultan's offer or, if he accepted it, grossly violated it, is proved beyond a doubt by the agreement signed at Szeged on August 4, 1444, in which the king and the lords of his realm solemnly swore by the salvation of their souls, by the Holy Trinity, the Virgin Mary, and both patron saints of Hungary, Kings Stephen and Ladislas, that before September 1, 1444, they would cross the Danube at Orşova with their troops and do everything in their power to drive the Turks from Europe before the year was out. This remarkable document, signed by the king and all the lords present, was sent forthwith to the Byzantine emperor, to the commander of the papal fleet, and to all those Western princes who were allied with Hungary. But the expulsion of the Turks was more a pious wish than a serious political project. The Western allies had counted without the sultan.

As for the agreement of August 15, 1444, between the Porte and George Branković—which was equivalent to a separate peace—we have little reliable information apart from the sparse indications in the Serbian annals. It is no doubt largely, if not entirely, explained by the despot's fear that if he took part in a crusade, he was in danger of losing for good the lands he had just recovered. Such an attitude would also account for the loyalty with which he observed his pact with the sultan. It may be worth mentioning that from Szeged the Serbian prince returned directly home in the company of the Turkish ambassador. If a separate pact between George Branković and the Porte was actually made in Edirne, this can have occurred no later than the first half of August; the despot must then have dealt with Prince Mehmed Çelebi and his advisers, for at the time Murad was far away in Anatolia.

On June 14, before conclusion of the truce negotiations in Szeged, the crusading fleet, assembled largely by the efforts of Pope Eugenius IV, had left Venice for the Levant. The Venetian galleys were commanded by Alvise Loredano; the fleet as a whole was headed by the Apostolic legate, Cardinal Francesco Condulmer, a close relative of the pope. It put into the Dardanelles too late to prevent the sultan from crossing over to Anatolia. The crusaders planned, however, to block Murad's return to Thrace after his Karaman campaign, or so at least the cardinal wrote in a letter to Szeged, urging the hesitant king to hasten his departure. If advantage is taken of this favorable moment, says the missive, it will be possible to conquer the country with a small force and send the heathen back to the land of their origins; let the king reflect on his promise to the princes of Christendom and consider the efforts they have made to fulfill their own engagements.

It is perfectly true that the prospects of a successful crusade were brighter that summer than ever before, for Thrace had been almost entirely depleted of troops. Apart from the garrisons dispersed throughout Rumelia, Mehmed Çelebi had no more than 7,000 or 8,000 men at his disposal, if we can trust the testimony of the Burgundian Waleran de Wavrin.[33] In Edirne, moreover, strange happenings had been spreading confusion and alarm among large sections of the population.

Both from an Italian and an Ottoman source we learn that in the late summer, probably in September, a religious fanatic from Persia, representing himself as an emissary of the so-called Hurufiyya, won a considerable following among the people.

A Shiite sect, founded toward the end of the fourteenth century by a certain Fadlallah from Asterabad in Persia, the Hurufiyya soon spread through the Ottoman Empire.[34] In time its religious ideas were largely accepted by the Bektaşi order of dervishes, through whom Hurufi doctrines probably gained acceptance among the Janissaries as well. The religious views of the Hurufiyya—literally, "interpreters of letters," so named because they attached a certain significance to each character of the Arabic alphabet and its numerical value—and particularly their con-

[33] See the monograph of Halecki, p. 60 and p. 68, n. 56.

[34] For the founder of the Hurufi order, see "Fadl Allāh Hurūfī" (Abdülbaki Gölpinarli), EI^2 II, 733–735. See also above, n. 10.

nections with other dervish groups in Anatolia and Rumelia have not been sufficiently clarified. This can be attributed partly to their practice of concealing their doctrines and rites and partly to the inadequate study of their books, written in obscure and difficult language.

Since the appearance of Sheikh Bedreddin, Rumelia had been fertile soil for religious agitation. Over and over again, down to the seventeenth century, we hear of religious preachers who gained considerable following by holding out the promise of a reconciliation between Islam and Christianity. Dispersed followers of Sheikh Bedreddin, who seems to have held such ideas of reconciliation, remained active throughout Bulgaria long after his execution at Serrai in 1416. It is not unlikely that there was some connection between them and the crowds who flocked to the Persian missionary in the summer of 1444.

That the Persian should have been able to move freely about the capital spreading ideas repellent to all orthodox believers is easily explained. None other than the precocious Mehmed Çelebi himself took an interest in his teachings and accorded him and several of his followers personal protection. The religious dignitaries of Edirne were scandalized, most of all Fahreddin the Mufti (as the dignitary later designated as sheikh al-Islam was then called), himself a native of Persia. Having resolved to take action against the heretic, who by then had a following of several thousand in the city, the mufti consulted with the grand vizier. The upshot was that Halil Pasha invited the missionary to his house, where he informed him that he, the grand vizier, took a special interest in his views. Fahreddin, who was hidden not far off, overheard the entire conversation. Unsuspectingly, the missionary set forth his opinions and, as he was developing a particularly heretical view, the mufti sprang furiously from his hiding place and tried to seize him. The heretic managed to escape to the sultan's palace, where Fahreddin followed him. Apparently distressed at the turn of events, Mehmed Çelebi abandoned the man, whom he had previously protected, to the mufti Fahreddin. The Persian's doom was sealed. The mufti repaired to the mosque and harangued the faithful who had meanwhile assembled, calling upon them to drag the dangerous heretic to the place of execution and promising a reward in the other world to all those who would help put him to death. The Persian was dragged to the public prayer site, where the infuriated crowd gathered wood. He was probably dead before the flames enveloped him. According to the legend, the flowing beard of the mufti, who in an excess of zeal helped personally to feed the fire, was singed by the flames. The Persian's followers suffered a similar fate.

If it is true, as the Ottoman sources tell us, that the grand vizier had feared to anger the prince by expressing his horror at these heresies, and that the Persian, pursued by the zealot Fahreddin, was able to seek refuge in the crown prince's palace, we can only infer that even as a boy Mehmed showed the liking for Persians and free thinkers that in later years was to arouse the indignation of the Orthodox clergy and the native population. It would also show that relations between the youthful regent and his advisers, appointed by Murad, were already marked by the grave tensions that would soon lead to open conflict.

This was not the only dangerous incident. A few weeks later the Janissaries demanded an increase in pay and mutinied when it was not granted, setting fires at several places in the capital. The flames spread quickly in the summer heat, engulfing the central bazaar, which was full to bursting with precious wares and stuffs, and soon reduced to ashes the quarter of Taht al-kale (Under the Castle). Other bazaars were also destroyed; Hoca Kasĭm, the superintendent of markets, and a number of his clerks lost their lives. A large part of the city, consisting chiefly of wooden houses, was destroyed in a few hours. Many people were killed and the loss in goods, assembled from all parts of the empire, was immeasurable. The fury of the troops was directed chiefly against young Mehmed Çelebi's special adviser, the eunuch Şihabeddin Pasha, who saved his skin only by taking refuge in the palace. The enraged Janissaries gave up the pursuit and assembled on the hill of Buçuk Tepe, whence they issued grim threats that filled the whole population with dread. Finally, the prince consented to a daily pay increase of half an *akçe* (asper), putting an end to this unusual rebellion. In view of the tensions between the Ottoman families and the Christian converts, there is a certain plausibility in the contention that Halil Pasha—if only to give the prince a warning—had a hand in stirring up the Janissaries against the influential Şihabeddin Pasha, who was detested by all the old Turkish families.[35]

There is no doubt that personal relations between Halil Pasha and Mehmed Çelebi were extremely strained and that in the long run the two men could not be expected to collaborate fruitfully in carrying on the affairs of state.

Meanwhile the crusading army advanced slowly, in arduous marches, delayed by bitter battles with the Turkish garrisons of the Bulgarian

---

[35] The events of the summer of 1444 are discussed in greater detail by Babinger and Inalcĭk in the works cited above (n. 32). The increase in pay granted by Mehmed to the Janissaries must have amounted to approximately 10 percent; cf. below, book 2, n. 9. For the Ottoman silver coin, see also the article "Akče" (H. Bowen), *EI²* I, 317-318.

cities and fortresses along their path, toward the Black Sea, hoping to proceed without difficulty down the coast to Constantinople, under the protection of the papal fleet. Thanks to Murad's military talent, the war with the Karamanids had been brought to a victorious end, perhaps more quickly than he himself had expected. Once again Ibrahim Bey saw that longer resistance was futile, and through the mediation of the learned mullah Sarï Yakub, a native of Karaman, he concluded a speedy peace with the sultan, even offering him military assistance.[36]

It was high time. In all likelihood, messengers dispatched by the grand vizier to the camp in Asia Minor had made it clear to the sultan that his youthful son was capable neither of dealing with the situation in the capital nor of resisting the invaders. After Ibrahim Bey's surrender Murad hastened north with his armies. Reaching the Dardanelles in early October, he found the crossing blocked by the Christian fleet. His forces numbered roughly 40,000; the Westerners, their imaginations fired by fear and false rumors, set the figure at no less than 100,000.

In the end the sultan's army was obliged to cross the straits at night above Constantinople, near Anadolu Hisarï on the Bosporus. The sources provide widely divergent versions of this strange crossing, but it seems quite certain that the "infidels" received help from the Christians themselves, who for money provided boats and even military supplies. In a bull issued in October, Pope Eugenius IV saw fit to excommunicate all those found guilty of such offenses.[37] We learn from Chalcocondylas that a violent storm prevented the papal fleet, anchored at the entrance to the Dardanelles, from entering the Sea of Marmara, and this too may be in keeping with the facts. But there is good reason to believe that the Genoese and perhaps also the Venetian sea captains gave the sultan decisive help in his undertaking, all the more willingly because he is said to have offered a gold piece for every soldier landed in Europe. All this happened presumably in the second half of October. Strengthened by remnants of the Thracian army that joined him en route, the sultan hastened to Edirne. The Byzantine emperor, to whom messengers had been sent summoning him to provide troops, managed to sidestep his obligation. He had no desire to antagonize the sultan and still less the Hungarians, whose support would be indispensable should the fortunes of war turn against Murad.

In the capital the sultan saw his son but remained within the walls for only a short time. He proceeded northward by forced marches toward

---

[36] For the peace pact of Ibrahim with the Ottomans see I. H. Uzunçarşili, "Karamanoğullari devri vesikalarïndan Ibrahim Bey'in Karaman imareti vakfiyesi," *Belleten* I (1937), especially 120ff.

[37] See Gill, *Eugenius IV*, 155.

Varna, near which, only a few miles distant from the Christians, he pitched camp on the seventh day. A moonlight night enabled the Christians to observe the Ottoman army from the neighboring heights and estimate its strength by the number of campfires. The situation of the Christians was highly precarious; cut off by the Ottomans from their natural line of retreat, they had behind them only the city of Varna and the Black Sea; the fleet was nowhere to be seen, and by land the only possible escape route was through the inhospitable Dobruja. John Hunyadi decided to give battle in the open field. On the morning of November 10, 1444, he had barely time to draw up his army in battle formation, insofar as the highly unfavorable terrain permitted. To westward, facing the Christians, divided from them only by a slight depression, the Ottomans, now some 80,000 to 100,000 strong, nearly four times more numerous than the Christians, had drawn up their battle lines. For three hours the armies stood motionless, face to face under a serene sky; then suddenly a violent storm arose from the mountains to westward and beat down upon the Christian armies. In a short while the wind had torn all the banners and pennants to tatters—an evil omen—except for the banner of St. George. Despite their advantage in numbers and position, the Ottomans, perhaps uncertain about the enemy's strength, hesitated for a long while to advance. Finally, at about nine o'clock in the morning, the auxiliary cavalry (*akĭncĭs*) and foot soldiers (*azaps*) started a skirmish, followed by a serious attack.[38] The Hungarians resisted with courage and skill. The *akĭncĭs* were defeated. But in the heat of battle the leaders of the Hungarians failed to notice that Karaca Bey, the governor of Anatolia and husband of the sultan's sister Seljuk Hatun, had advanced with his *sipahis* ("feudal cavalry") to attack the right wing of the embattled Christians; this was put to flight, leaving only a few hundred horsemen to guard the *Wagenburg*.[39] King Ladislas and John Hunyadi now launched a powerful offensive which soon cost the Anatolian *sipahis* 3,000 men and their leader Karaca Bey. Meanwhile, the Christian left wing was hard pressed by the Rumelian *sipahis*: only the astute intervention of John Hunyadi, who persuaded the king to reoccupy his old position in the center with his personal troops and to hold it while he

[38] The irregular cavalry and infantry forces are dealt with in the articles "Akĭndji" (A. Decei) and "'Azab" (H. Bowen), *EI²* I, 340 and 807, respectively.

[39] The *Wagenburg*, apparently of Russian origin, was essentially a defensive arrangement of carts or wagons, immovable when in place, on or between which were set up stout shields to protect against an assault of cavalry armed with bows and arrows. For a description of the *Wagenburg* and of its use in battles of the fifteenth century see Charles Oman, *A History of the Art of War in the Middle Ages* (Boston and New York, 1923) II, 363ff.

himself hurried to the aid of the left wing, decided the battle in favor of the crusaders. On the Turkish side only the Janissaries still held firm. The rest of the army broke into a wild rout, fleeing southward to Edirne and on to Gelibolu.

At this point King Ladislas was misled by his warlike spirit and by his Polish knights' jealousy of Hunyadi's prowess into disregarding the agreement he had made with Hunyadi. With only 500 of his best cavalrymen he attempted a rash attack on the sultan's infantry. The first attack was actually successful. Despairing in the possibility of victory, the sultan was about to take flight. The Janissaries—or so, at least, we are told by the Byzantine chronicler Chalcocondylas—were able to keep him in their midst only by fettering his horse. Driven by necessity and awareness of what was at stake, both sides fought desperately. But before Hunyadi could reorganize his troops, scattered by the long battle and the final pursuit, news came of the king's death. He had fallen from his horse and one of the Janissaries, the Moreote Hoca Hizïr, had chopped off his head and brought it to the sultan, who had it impaled and displayed all over the battlefield. Even Hunyadi's courage failed him at the sight, and the troops, who until then had stood fast, were seized with panic. Night fell, leaving both victors and vanquished in uncertainty over the outcome of the battle. Both sides turned away from the battlefield at once. The Ottomans withdrew to their camp in good order, while the Christians fled wildly in all directions. Cardinal Cesarini, who had fought bravely to the last, also sought safety in flight and was never seen again. It is not known where and how he met his death. The stories contained in the sources are widely divergent.

The remnants of the Christian army wandered for days in the direction of the Danube and only a few reached their homes. Scattered far and wide, they spread the news of the pitiful end of this last crusade. Hunyadi himself, with a few faithful followers, reached Walachia and hurried on toward Hungary. On the way, however, Vlad Dracul, who had an old grudge against him, took him prisoner and held him for some time under close guard, but in the end released him and even sent him off with presents.[40]

The day after the battle the Ottomans were still uncertain about the enemy's intentions. For a long time they feared that the Christians had merely hidden and would try to take them by surprise. Murad spent

[40] Vlad had not personally taken part in the battle. For his relations with Hunyadi and the Romanian background to Varna, see Radu Florescu and Raymond T. Mc-Nally, *Dracula* (New York, 1973), 38. For Cardinal Cesarini, Gill, *The Council of Florence*, 328–333.

three days on the spot in indecision. At length the Turks ventured to storm the abandoned *Wagenburg* and had no difficulty in capturing 150 richly loaded wagons. Thereupon Davud Bey, the governor of Rumelia, scoured the countryside as far as the Danube for two days and nights, mercilessly slaughtering every straggler who fell into his hands, and returned to the sultan's camp laden with booty. The losses of the Ottomans were enormous: 30,000 men, it was rumored, approximately one-third of their troops. The best of their captains, including Karaca Bey, were among the dead. Accompanied by one of his intimates, Azab Bey, who later built a mosque in Bursa, Sultan Murad explored the battlefield. "Is it not amazing," the sultan is reported to have said, "that they [the Christian dead] are all young men, not a single graybeard among them?" "If there had been a graybeard among them," Azab Bey replied, "they would not have embarked on so rash an undertaking."

The sultan decreed that those of his generals who had taken flight at the first impact of the Hungarians should be severely punished. The guiltiest were condemned to death; the others were to be led through the camp in women's clothes, exposed to the mockery of the soldiers. Only the vizier's intervention prevented the severe sentence from being carried out.

Murad sent letters announcing his victory to all the rulers of Islam and presented the sultan of Egypt, the Mamluk Çakmak, with twenty-five captive cuirassiers, by way of showing "what men of iron he had defeated."

So ended the battle of Varna, one of the most decisive events not only of Ottoman but of all Western history. A severe blow had been dealt the Christian hope of driving the Ottomans out of Europe. For years to come, a pall of discouragement lay over European Christendom. The defeat of the crusading army was looked upon as divine punishment for the sacrilegious breach of the oath King Ladislas had sworn on the Gospel at Szeged. Especially the states bordering on the Ottoman Empire were paralyzed with fear. At the news of the disaster, John VIII of Byzantium made haste to conciliate the sultan with gifts to restore good-neighborly relations as far as possible. The pope's influence was at a low ebb. It was formerly believed that George Branković, responding to Murad's hopes in him, had blocked the mountain passes against George Castriota, who supposedly tried to come to the crusaders' help with his Albanian troops. But recent research has shown this to be untrue.[41]

It was only in the south of Greece that the hope of defeating the Turks

[41] Most recently on the roles of Castriota and Hunyadi, see F. Pall, "Skanderbeg et Ianco de Hunedoara," *Revue des études sud-est européennes* 6 (1968), 5-21.

still lived. There the indefatigable Constantine Palaeologus had not hesitated to support Hungary and Venice in this war on Murad, with the aim of restoring Greek sovereignty north of the isthmus at the expense of the Turks and the Florentines of Athens, as he had succeeded in doing fourteen years earlier in the Morea.[42]

From Varna, Murad returned directly to Edirne. There his first acts were to bury his fallen brother-in-law Karaca Bey and to appoint the Albanian Ozgur governor of Anatolia in his place. The Janissary Hoca Hïzïr, who had given King Ladislas the death blow at Varna, so deciding the outcome of the battle, was rewarded with rich estates in Rumelia. Murad sent the head of the Hungarian king, preserved in a cask of honey, to the bailiff of Bursa, where the rejoicing inhabitants went out to receive the gruesome gift before the city gates. Having been carefully washed in the Nilufer River, the skull was mounted on a lance and borne in triumph through the old Ottoman capital. All this happened in the last weeks of November.

Immediately afterward, in late November or early in December 1444, Murad, then in the fortieth year of his life, took a step whose motives will in all likelihood never be known: he suddenly resolved to abdicate in favor of his son Mehmed Çelebi, despite the sorry experience of the boy's regency the preceding summer. The protests of his viziers, and especially of Halil Pasha, the grand vizier, were of no avail. Escorted by a few of his most trusted companions, among them the second vizier, Ishak Pasha, and Hamza Bey, the chief cupbearer, he left his capital and crossed over to Asia Minor, where he had reserved for himself the fiefs of Menteşe, Saruhan, and Aydïn. As his place of retirement he chose the idyllic Manisa, where his son, now the sultan, had dwelt as governor only a short while before. Again he chose Halil Pasha, the grand vizier, and Mullah Husrev, army judge, as his son's special advisers. Although the Venetian sources speak of a "sultan of Europe" in reference to Mehmed, there can be no doubt that the prince, not yet thirteen years old, had become the sole ruler of the Ottoman state and that Murad had withdrawn from the duties of government.

It is futile to search for the motives of Murad's sudden abdication. Nevertheless, we may assume that he was not, as most historians have supposed, impelled by world weariness and love of solitude. Murad's rule apparently aroused oppositions, which sprang in part from the antag-

[42] For speculation on opposition to Turkish rule elsewhere in Greece, see Apostolos Vacalopoulos, "A Revolt in Western Macedonia: 1444–1449," *Balkan Studies* 9 (1968), 375–380.

onism between the old Turkish nobility and the *devşirme* or renegade converts. Certainly Murad knew that the young Mehmed Çelebi was incapable of dealing with these difficulties. Had it not been for his utter confidence in the statecraft of Halil Pasha, his trusted grand vizier, he would scarcely have taken so drastic a step.

On his way to Manisa, Murad spent a few days in Bursa. He had always felt a particular attachment for this city. There lay his ancestors in their magnificent tombs; there his brothers, sisters, and sons slept the sleep of death. He too wished to be buried in Bursa, when the time came. From the year 848 H. (April 1444 to April 1445) we possess both copper and silver coins, minted at Bursa, Amasya, and Tire (Aydïn Eli), which clearly bear his name, although we do not know why they were issued at this time. The first silver and copper pieces bearing the name of young Sultan Mehmed were coined in the same year—that is to say, in the first four months of 1445, at the latest—in Edirne, Ayasoluk, Amasya, Bursa, and Serrai. The Friday prayer (*hutbe*) was proclaimed in his name.[43] The privileges of minting coins (*sikke*, It. *zecca*) and of being mentioned in the weekly prayer were two of the principal prerogatives of the Moslem sovereign. In January 1445 solemn missives, the wording of which has in part come down to us, were sent to the Moslem princes in the east and south of the empire, informing them of the young sultan's accession and assuring them of his friendly intentions.

The effect in Christendom of this unexpected change of sovereigns can hardly be gauged from the records or documents that have thus far come to light. For a time, no doubt, the Christian leaders were too discouraged by the crushing defeat of the crusaders at Varna to take cognizance of the new conditions. Until late in 1445 many refused to accept the truth of the disaster and in particular to believe that the young Hungarian king was dead; for many years, indeed, the legend went round that he was still alive, living as a hermit somewhere in Spain.

While probably not the first Western power to recognize the new situation, Venice seems to have had the most realistic view of the matter, for the republic soon took steps to come to suitable terms with Mehmed. Toward the middle of March 1445 the Signoria had to defend itself against the papal accusation that Venetian galleys had enabled Murad to cross over from Asia to Europe. The answer was that Venice had made every conceivable effort to give the Turks battle and to hold them in check

[43] For an exemplar of the silver *akçe* minted by Murad at Serrai and Edirne, see Pere, *Osmanlilarda Madeni Paralar,* 84, #63 (and plate 5); for the first coins of Mehmed, 90, #84, and 91, #90 (and plate 7).

despite the Turkish raids on Negropont, Albania, and other Venetian possessions, raids which were still going on. The crews of the Venetian vessels, it was added, had incurred serious losses. A few weeks later, on April 4, the senate once more justified its past and present conduct with the same arguments, pointing out further that Genoa and other Christian allies had already made peace with the Turks. Thus, the document continues, no one need be surprised if the Signoria also found itself compelled, for reasons of political necessity, to sign a formal peace treaty with the sultan in the very near future. On April 26, the senate resolved to send a message to the Holy See, pointing out that the pope had refused to supply additional funds for the united fleet in the Aegean and reiterating that other Christian states had already concluded peace treaties with the Ottomans, who meanwhile continued their attacks on Negropont, on the other Venetian settlements in Greece, and on Albania, so that Venice was now constrained to proceed in the same manner as the other Western states. The senate voted on the message and approved it by an overwhelming majority (ninety-one for, two against, and only two abstentions). Thus the project of peace negotiations with the Turks was as good as approved.

On May 11, 1445, the Venetian admiral Alvise Loredano was instructed to remain in the straits until peace with the sultan should be concluded.[44] It was hoped that a reasonably honorable treaty might be obtained. In accordance with the advice of Andrea Foscolo, the Venetian *bailo* at the court of Byzantium, it was decided to send a suitable intermediary to the "sultan of Europe," to negotiate an agreement concerning the freedom of Venetian trade in his states and, in the ensuing peace negotiations, to renew the accords arrived at in Gelibolu, on September 4, 1430, between Murad and Silvestro Morosini—if possible, however, without the humiliating tribute clause. The "Turk," it was further decided, should promise to obtain his father's confirmation of the treaty. From this stipulation it may safely be inferred that at least the politically shrewd Venetians still looked upon the abdicated sultan, whom they seem to have regarded as a kind of sultan of Asia, as a figure to be reckoned with.

In compliance with this crucial deliberation of the senate, Andrea Foscolo dispatched Aldovrandino de' Giusti (Zusti), presumably a wealthy and astute merchant residing in Pera, to Edirne as an intermediary. The text of the treaty was agreed on Wednesday, February 23, 1446, and subsequently sent to Venice with a letter dated March 9.

---

[44] For a summary of the instructions from Venice on this date see F. Thiriet, *Régestes des délibérations du Sénat de Venise concernant la Romanie* III (= *Documents et Recherches* IV, ed. Paul Lemerle; Paris, 1961), 124.

The messenger to the doge Francesco Foscari was Mehmed's "slave," Yunus Karaca, the commander of mercenaries (*ulûfeci başï*), who was accompanied by Dimitri, the secretary of the sultan's Greek chancellery and himself undoubtedly a Greek. The treaty was written in Greek; it was the custom of the fifteenth-century sultans to have their missives to the Slavic nations couched in Slavic and those to the peoples of the West in Greek, and to maintain special Greek and Slavic chancelleries for this purpose. The Greek original, preserved in the state archives of Venice, is probably the only document of the first reign of Mehmed II to have come down to us. The text comes very close to the provisions of the treaty concluded with Murad II in 1430.[45]

While Mehmed, assuredly under the influence of his wise and experienced counselors, was preparing to conclude a profitable treaty with the Western powers, his father was enjoying a peaceful and, we are told, pleasant existence in the quiet and seclusion of Manisa. Concerning the happenings there in the first months of 1446, welcome information is provided by letters written from the immediate vicinity by Ciriaco de' Pizzicolli to friends. After wanderings in the Cyclades and Crete, the tireless traveler reached the coast of Asia Minor, where his presence in January 1446 is attested with certainty. On March 13 he was living in Lesbos as the guest of Duke Dorino I Gattilusio; from there he wrote his friend Andreolo Giustiniani on Chios that an Ottoman attack on this island, which his friend feared, was not to be expected. Ciriaco did not carry out his original plan of returning to Constantinople, but went instead, at the end of March, to Manisa. On April 7, 1446, he was back again in Foça near Izmir, the principal center of the Genoese alum trade, in which his friend Francesco Draperio played a leading part. On April 9, Ciriaco went to Manisa in the company of Draperio, who helped him obtain the safe-conduct from Murad mentioned above. The audience with the sultan took place on Easter Sunday (April 17, 1446). Three days later Ciriaco, in a new letter to Giustiniani, described the audience, in which the two Italians were graciously received, not in the throne room or reception hall (*arz odasï*), where it was traditional to receive ambassadors, but in the sultan's private chambers.

[45] The document is treated in Babinger and F. Dölger, "Mehmeds II. frühester Staatsvertrag (1446)," *Orientalia Christiana Periodica* 15 (1949), 225–258. Further, see the articles of A. Bombaci, "Due clausole del trattato in greco fra Maometto II e Venezia, del 1446," *BZ* 43 (1950), 267–271, and "Nuovi firmani greci di Maometto II," ibid. 47 (1954), 298, n. 3. For documentation of the events of this time see again Babinger, "Von Amurath zu Amurath," 255–259 (= *A&A* I, 148–151).

Not quite three weeks later, on May 5, 1446, Murad left his place of retirement and set out for Europe accompanied by 4,000 warriors. This is reported by Ciriaco in a letter to Giustiniani, written from Foça on May 11, in which he remarks that the sultan was going to Edirne in response to an urgent plea from his son, the "Cialaby" (Mehmed Çelebi).[46]

In fact, it was the alarmed Halil Pasha who, no doubt because he lacked confidence in the young sultan's statecraft, though his exact reasons are still unknown to us, recalled Murad to the throne. This, however, seems to have escaped Ciriaco, which is surprising when we consider that he and Draperio spent three days with Murad on his return journey to Thrace, accompanying him past Bergama (Pergamum) as far as Ayazmend, on the coast opposite Lesbos. Here the sultan turned northeast toward Bursa, while the two friends returned to Foça. Later on, says the letter, Ciriaco planned to follow the sultan's itinerary to Europe.

Another Italian who later spent years at the Turkish court as the prisoner of Mehmed II and was thoroughly familiar with the events of the time—namely, Gian-Maria Angiolello of Vicenza (1451-1525), the author of a Turkish history (*Historia turchesca*)[47]—tells us in speaking of the present events that young Mehmed had been planning an offensive against Constantinople and that his viziers apparently did not approve. The Ottoman chroniclers, who relate all these events confusedly and with chronological distortions, describe the sudden appearance of Murad in Edirne in a highly romantic light. These accounts have also influenced Byzantine historians such as Chalcocondylas; his version, however, is that on the day Murad was expected in Edirne, Halil Pasha sent young Mehmed out hunting, so that the father, amid the rejoicing of the Janissaries, made his entrance into the capital and resumed possession of the throne in his son's absence. When Mehmed returned from the hunt that evening, the operation was concluded. In reality, the episode was far less dramatic, for Murad was in no particular hurry to return. He seems to have remained in Bursa for a considerable time.

There is, however, one event which more than any other throws a bright light on the situation in which Murad found himself as a result of his sudden recall to Thrace. On August 1, 1446, the sultan drew up his will in Bursa, in the presence of Mullah Husrev, the army judge. By chance this important Arabic document, ten feet long and eight inches

---

[46] For these letters of Ciriaco, see the article of F. Pall cited in n. 27 above.

[47] The work referred to here as Angiolello's *Historia turchesca* was attributed to Donado da Lezze by Ion Ursu, who published it under that name (Bucharest, 1909). For the author see the article "Angiolello" (F. Babinger), *Dizionario Biografico degli Italiani* III, 275-278.

wide and consisting of sixty-three lines, has come down to us. Along with sixty-eight sacks of paper, filled with important old documents, it was sold in Bulgaria in the spring of 1931; later on, it was discovered in one of the fifty-three sacks that were returned to Turkey. This significant document, in which the three viziers Halil Pasha, Saruca Pasha, and Ishak Pasha are cited as witnesses, contains the following passage: "When I die, you are to bury my body in Bursa three to four *arshin* [approximately eight feet] from the grave of my son Alaeddin, not far from my mosque. Do not build a sumptuous *türbe* over it, as for great rulers. Lay my corpse directly in the earth. Over me let the rain fall as the grace of God; only build four walls around my grave and set a roof over them, so that the Koran readers may sit there. Bury none of my children or relatives beside me. For the construction of my tomb I set aside 5,000 gold florins. In case I should not die in Bursa, transport my body there. It should arrive on a Thursday and be laid in the earth on Friday."[48]

These words, far more than any other record of those years, provide an insight into the inner life of Murad. He demands to be buried beside his favorite son, Alaeddin Ali, who had met his death under such unusual circumstances, and expressly forbids that any other member of his family be buried near him. The naming of the three viziers as witnesses proves with certainty that they were in Bursa at the time, along with Mullah Husrev, the army judge, who committed the last will to writing and is expressly mentioned in this connection. Thus, before Murad crossed the straits with his retinue to resume the throne of his fathers, he felt the need to make a last will and testament. This circumstance in itself seems to show that Murad thought the deposition of his son Mehmed Çelebi might involve considerable difficulty, perhaps even mortal peril.

The testament was formally issued at the beginning of September. Soon thereafter Murad must have appeared on Thracian soil and resumed his throne. On his arrival in Edirne he did not go to the palace but to the house of Saruca Pasha. The unclear and often contradictory accounts of the Ottoman and Byzantine chronicles do not enable us to form a reliable picture of these happenings. It is certain, however, that it was Halil Pasha, the grand vizier, who planned and carried out the coup d'etat, perhaps convinced that only Murad's return to the throne would enable him to recover his former influence, of which Mehmed, in an

---

[48] The original Arabic text of the will (*vasiyetname*) has been published in its entirety by Inalcïk, *Fatih devri*, 209–212, together with a Turkish translation. (See also there the photocopies in plates 3, 4, and 5, and the discussion of the author.) For the mausoleum (*türbe*) see Albert Gabriel, *Une capitale turque, Brousse-Bursa* (Paris, 1958) I, 116–118, and II, plates 66–67.

unpropitious moment, had apparently begun to deprive him. Mehmed never forgave him; his lasting grudge undermined all confidence between the two men and was one day to cost Halil Pasha his life.

Accompanied by several faithful followers, Mehmed withdrew to Manisa, where his father had built a palace which must have been completed just before the return to Edirne. The viziers Halil Pasha, Saruca Pasha, and Ishak Pasha were confirmed in their posts. Only Zaganos Pasha, a convert of "Illyrian origin," was exiled to Anatolian Balîkesir, where he probably possessed landed property.[49]

The common people welcomed Murad's return with enthusiasm, and the Janissaries, whose wholehearted favor and devotion young Mehmed apparently never enjoyed, were jubilant. Murad's affability and bonhomie contrasted sharply with his son's haughty, forbidding manner, which had never appealed to the army. Before the end of September, Murad received as the delegate of Andrea Foscolo, the Venetian *bailo* in Constantinople, another member of the Giusti (Zusti) family of Pera, one Bartolomeo, who solemnly handed him the peace treaty ratified by the Signoria. On October 25 Murad sent Dimitri, maintained as secretary of the Greek chancellery, again to Venice along with his "slave" Yahşi Bey, provided with credentials and bearing the treaty which the returned sultan had now ratified, thereby confirming the policy his son had initiated nine months before.[50]

Thanks to this treaty the western frontiers of the Ottoman state were now relatively secure. No serious pressure was to be expected from Murad's father-in-law George Branković, who had returned to power in Serbia; immediately after the battle of Varna the old pact of friendship had been renewed with John VIII of Byzantium, who was at the end of his strength and plagued by gout; and for the present, at least, the sultan's indignation over his ambiguous conduct during the Hungarian campaign had been appeased by rich presents. No danger threatened from Hungary. Accordingly, the sultan's eyes turned toward Greece and Albania, for it was only from these quarters that he envisaged any serious threat to the security of his European possessions. He made up his mind to attack these countries as soon as possible, before they should be in a position to attack him.

The responsibility for order in the north of Greece rested with the

---

[49] For the exile of Zaganos Pasha at this time see Halil Inalcïk, *Fatih devri*, 104, n. 155.

[50] For the documents in question see George M. Thomas, *Diplomatarium veneto-levantinum sive acta et diplomata res venetas graecas atque levantis (1300–1454)* II (Venice, 1899; reprinted New York, n.d.), 370–372.

sultan's loyal servant and general, the Thessalian march warden (*uç beyi*) Ömer Bey, son of Turahan of the old Ottoman noble family of Pasha Yiğit Bey, who could not fail to note that in the south Constantine, despot of Mistra, had been working circumspectly on his plan to reconstitute a great Byzantine empire. Though the defeat of the Christians at Varna had utterly changed the situation in the north of the Balkan peninsula, Constantine continued his efforts to establish Byzantine sovereignty north of the isthmus.

Constantine had earlier strengthened the fortifications of the Hexamilion (so called because it is six miles wide), the narrowest spot of the isthmus, with a wall strengthened by five bulwarks and a deep trench. Once this work was complete, he and his brother Thomas made war on Nerio (Rainer) II Acciajuoli, duke of Athens and vassal of the sultan. In the spring of 1444 Constantine invaded Boeotia and occupied Thebes and Levadhia (Livadia); here he threatened Athens, compelling Nerio to recognize his suzerainty, pay an annual tribute, and provide him with troops. Then he marched northward to the Pindus, encouraged the Walachians and Albanians of Thessaly to throw off the infidel yoke, and occupied Lamia (Zeitun), Lidhorikion (Lidokhorikion), and other places. These exploits appreciably diminished the sultan's power and had doubtless contributed to the latter's willingness to conclude the ten-year truce of the summer of 1444. Of course, it was only under duress that Duke Nerio II, whose territories amounted to little more than Athens, became the vassal and ally of the despot of Mistra; he cannot have been very happy about it, particularly after Ömer Bey, at the sultan's behest, invaded Boeotia and Attica, laid them waste, and returned northward laden with spoils. Immediately after the battle of Varna, Nerio made haste, through envoys, to obtain the sultan's pardon, and offered forthwith to resume his former fealty to the Porte. Constantine punished Nerio's betrayal of the Greek cause by a campaign against Athens, which he occupied, though he soon withdrew from Attica for fear that Ömer Bey's menacing movements in Thessaly might be directed against himself. Now, after his return to power, Murad demanded the immediate surrender of all the cities and provinces Constantine had occupied; when Constantine refused, war was inevitable.

In a last effort to avert the danger, Constantine sent the father of the historian Chalcocondylas to Murad with peace proposals, in which, however, he insisted on full political independence, sovereignty over the Greek provinces as far as Thermopylai, and the right to maintain his fortifications on the isthmus. Enraged at these demands, Murad had the ambassador thrown into chains and, though winter was not far off, decided on an immediate campaign. In mid-autumn 1446 Murad left his capital for Serrai, where he mustered a large army. Then he marched southward. At Thermopylai he met with no opposition. The Greeks had withdrawn to the bulwarks of the Hexamilion. Unopposed, the sultan entered Thebes, where his vassal Nerio II joined him with his troops.

With a considerable army and a gigantic train of wagons and camels, Murad moved toward the isthmus, halting near Mingias. Greeks and Ottomans were separated by the walls of the isthmus fortifications. By 1446 the Ottomans, no doubt with the help of Western instructors, had so well mastered the use of artillery, that most frightful of Western inventions, that the walls of the Greek cities and castles could not resist them for long.

Murad reached the fortifications on November 10 and spent three days opening breaches by means of cannon fire and mines. It was not until December 10 that the assault began. After a desperate battle, this last bulwark of Greek freedom fell to the Turkish army. In vain Constantine tried to rally his troops. While some of the Ottomans pillaged the Greek camp, others hunted down the fleeing Greeks; the surviving fugitives did not recover from their terror until they had reached the interior of Arcadia and Laconia. The nearby castle of Acrocorinth was useless as a haven, for it had been left unmanned, without food or ammunition. Three hundred Greeks had fled to a mountaintop near Kenchreai (modern Kechrias). Murad forced their surrender but had them slaughtered to the last man. According to Chalcocondylas, he purchased six hundred other prisoners from his Janissaries and sacrificed them to the shades of his father, Mehmed I. The entire Morea was paralyzed with dread. The two despots, hidden in the farthermost corners of Laconia, were planning to leave the peninsula with their followers and chattels and seek safety over the seas. The sultan sent Ömer Bey after them, while he himself turned westward to Achaea.[51]

Corinth was taken and devastated. Sikion (Basilika) and Aiyion (Aigion; Vostitsa), forsaken by their inhabitants, were burned. Then Murad went on to Patras. Except for some 4,000 people, the citizens of this commercial city had found safety in Lepanto (Naupaktos; Turkish Inebahti) and other Venetian strongholds on the Aetolian coast. The remainder, men and women, were enslaved by the Turks. The mountain citadel resisted heroically and the sultan had to abandon the siege.

Despairing of further resistance, the despots of the Peloponnese sent

[51] For further discussion of the question of ritual sacrifice for the dead, see Speros Vryonis, "Evidence on Human Sacrifice among Early Ottoman Turks," *Journal of Asian History* 5 (1971), 140–146.

envoys from their hiding places to sue for peace. But Murad had begun his retreat northward. What remained of the isthmus fortifications was razed. The spoils in slaves (allegedly 60,000), precious stuffs, and silver plate were so enormous that the Janissaries carried only the most valuable articles away, and sold the most beautiful slave girls en route for the absurd sum of 300 aspers each. Ottoman garrisons were posted neither in the cities of the Peloponnese nor in Attica nor Boeotia.

When Murad reached Thebes he was overtaken by the envoys of the two despots, who, by undertaking to levy a head tax as tribute, purchased the dubious privilege of continuing to rule over the Morea as Ottoman vassals. With this—so Chalcocondylas tells us—the formerly free Morea became subservient to the sultan.

Thus at the end of 1446 the Peloponnesian League was shattered. Attica, Thebes, Locris, and the Walachian tribes on the Pindus became once more tributary to the Turks; the gates of the Morea with Corinth, Sikion, and many smaller towns were destroyed; the inhabitants of some sections in the north of the peninsula were exterminated and the rest subjected to the head tax.

Constantine's somewhat impractical outlook was largely influenced by his admiration for Georgius Gemistus Pletho (died ca. 1450), undoubtedly the greatest philosopher of the declining Byzantine empire. The supreme judge at the despot's court in Mistra, Pletho founded and directed an academy modeled on Plato's where he expounded his own philosophy, a variety of mystico-religious Neoplatonism. Inspired by Pletho's political ideas, Constantine, shutting his eyes to the elementary realities of his time, had wished to reform the men and institutions of his country. It was the corruption of the Greek upper classes, which he had hoped to diminish, if not cure, by a mild government and wise administration, that ruined all his efforts and resulted a few years later in the political downfall of his entire nation. As for Constantine himself, fate was to spare him for new trials.

Before the winter was out, the sultan made his entry into Edirne. He seems to have spent the remainder of the year 1447 at rest, for no campaign is mentioned in any of the chronicles. His son Mehmed Çelebi had taken no part in the war against the Greeks, but had remained in Manisa. No information has come down to us concerning his life, activities, or plans during this period. On his instructions or at least with his consent, however, Turkish pirates appear to have harried the Aegean Sea and perhaps even to have attacked the islands from bases on the Anatolian coast, in disregard of the treaty with Venice.

In January 1448 a son was born to Mehmed Çelebi in Thracian Dimotika, by a slave girl named Gülbahar. The boy was given the name of
Bayezid and was later (1481) to mount the Ottoman throne as the second
sultan of this name. There is no doubt that this union was beneath
Mehmed's station: Gülbahar bint Abdullah, whom Turkish legend subsequently transformed into a "daughter of the king of France," was a
Christian slave of Albanian origin.[52] It is equally certain, as we shall see
later on, that Mehmed preserved a particular affection for her as long as
he lived. From the fact that Gülbahar Hatun bore her child in Dimotika,
it may be inferred that Mehmed was back in Europe by the beginning
of 1448 at the latest and perhaps even that he was residing there. Dimotika
was the site of an old Byzantine castle, with a double ring of walls,
preserved by the sultans and sometimes used for the Ottoman state
treasury. More than twenty years later, as we know from Gian-Maria
Angiolello, one of Mehmed's sisters, a notorious sadist, lived there. Thus
the castle seems to have been the occasional dwelling place of members of
the Ottoman family. Later Mehmed Çelebi must have returned to Manisa,
if it is true (as Angiolello reports, though in his version Bursa is substi-
tuted for Manisa) that in the course of that same summer his father
called him to Edirne, ordering him to bring with him copper, tin, and
cannon founders for the new Albanian campaign that had already been
decided upon.[53]

John Hunyadi, since 1446 regent of Hungary for the minor Ladislas
Posthumus, had not forgotten the disgrace he had incurred at Varna;
plans of revenge were his constant preoccupation. He looked everywhere
for allies. The Serbian despot Branković, whose granddaughter Elizabeth,
only daughter of Count Ulrich of Cilli, was betrothed at the time to
Hunyadi's son Ladislas, withheld his support, declaring that the Christian army was far too weak to combat Murad's forces with any hope of
success. His real reason, of course, is to be sought in his understandable
fear of once again losing the sultan's favor, to which he attached far more
importance than to the friendship of Hungary and its allies. Chalcocondylas goes so far as to say that George Branković informed his son-in-law
Murad of Hunyadi's warlike plans. Venice, glad to have finally achieved
a profitable agreement with the sultan, permitting it to carry on its Levan-

---

[52] On the birthdate of the heir apparent and future sultan see Hans J. Kissling,
"Die Anonyme Altosmanische Chronik über Sultan Bayezid II," *Grazer und
Münchner Balkanologische Studien* (= *Beiträge zur Kenntnis Südosteuropas und
des Nahen Orients* 2; Munich, 1967), 134.
[53] *Historia turchesca*, 15.

tine trade undisturbed, showed equal reserve. King Alfonso V of Aragon, ruler of Naples and Sicily, was also disinclined to embark on a dubious adventure. In vain John Hunyadi turned to Pope Nicholas V, who had succeeded Eugenius IV in February 1447. Unlike his predecessor, who, although he never attained his ambitious aims, had devoted all his energies to restoration of the papal power, Nicholas was more interested in the arts and sciences than in war. He was a Christian humanist, mild and peace-loving, with no mind for adventurous undertakings, even against the infidels and enemies of Christianity. Twice Hunyadi had sent an ambassador to win the Curia to his cause. He obtained nothing but vague promises of aid against the Turks, a universal indulgence for all who offered to take part in a crusade, and for himself the title of prince, which at the time meant less to him than ever. Not without bitterness Hunyadi gave Nicholas V to understand that if he were to show himself worthy of this honor, what he most needed was the requested help against the Turks.

Even then the pope offered no more than vague assurances. The Holy See seems to have favored a postponement of the campaign until the following year. Hunyadi would not hear of it. His preparations were already too far advanced, and in his opinion the danger of an Ottoman offensive was too pressing to admit of further delay. On September 8, 1448, in a letter to Pope Nicholas from Kovin, across the Danube from Belgrade, he set forth his reasons for believing quick action to be imperative.[54] The eternal enemy of the Christians, he wrote, was approaching his frontiers by land and sea with large forces, and had already attempted to invade his territories at several points. He must therefore take up arms at once, if he were not to be crushed by this mighty army. In a later letter from Serbia, Hunyadi again informed the pope of the need for an immediate offensive, but again in vain. Even if the pope had been willing and able to help Hunyadi, it was already far too late. The regent was compelled to advance precipitately into the interior of Serbia. The core of his army consisted of Hungarians, supported by German and Bohemian auxiliaries. Dan, the newly appointed voivode of Walachia, had contributed some 8,000 men. Estimates of the total strength vary from 31,000 to 47,000 (7,000 horsemen and somewhere between 24,000 and 40,000 foot soldiers). As in the campaign at Varna, the army was followed by an enormous *Wagenburg* of more than a thousand vehicles bearing arms and provisions. Serbia was treated as enemy country. All the cities and villages along the line of march were seized, pillaged, and devastated.

[54] For the letter see J. W. Zinkeisen, *Geschichte des osmanischen Reiches in Europa* I (Hamburg, 1840), 717–718.

At length the menacing proximity of the enemy obliged Hunyadi to make forced marches, which in twenty days took him to the memorable plain of Kosovo, the Field of Blackbirds; here an October 17, 1448, he set up a fortified camp within view of the Ottomans.

During the summer Murad had personally led a surprise attack on eastern Albania. We are without reliable information concerning the size of the expedition or the details of the campaign. At the end of July 1448, in any event, the strongly fortified city of Svetigrad (Kocacïk), whose imposing ruins in the valley of the White Drin, across from Trebenište, still fill the traveler with amazement, was captured by the sultan from its brave Albanian defenders under Peter Perlatai.[55] But the critical lack of provisions in this inhospitable region forced Murad to abandon any project he may have formed for an advance into the interior and to return almost precipitately to Edirne. Only a small garrison was left behind in the captured fortress. Thus the eastern border of Albania had been pacified, but this could not blind the sultan to the increasing threat to his western provinces taking shape in the Albanian mountains, where for the last five years a bold and powerful adversary had been arming for a decisive blow against the hated Ottomans he knew so well. This was George Castriota, known as Skanderbeg. The story of this man, whom Pope Calixtus III once called the "athlete of Christendom" and who for almost a quarter of a century offered brave and successful resistance to Turkish forces far superior in numbers and equipment, reads like a novel.[56]

The assertion, however, that he grew up with Mehmed Çelebi, the future sultan, is pure fiction. Born about 1405, he was carried off or sent by his father, lord of the Matja district in Upper Albania, to Edirne as a hostage. At the time he exchanged his Christian faith for Islam, whether voluntarily or under constraint does not concern us here. His father died in 1431, and when the son escaped to his beloved Albania immediately after the "Long Campaign" (1443), he was almost forty years of age, while his alleged playmate was barely eleven. Back in Albania he resumed the religion of his forefathers, and established himself at the end of November 1443 in the mountain fortress of Krujë (Kroya; Akçe Hisar), where he proclaimed a holy war against the Turkish oppressors. On all sides he won the support of his compatriots, allying himself with

[55] For Kocacik and its defenders cf. Babinger, "Mehmeds II. Heirat mit Sitt-Chatun (1449)," *Der Islam* 29 (1949), 220; reprinted in *A&A* I, 227.

[56] The standard modern biography in English of the Albanian national hero is Fan S. Noli, *George Castrioti Scanderbeg 1405–1468* (New York, 1947). Now see "Iskender Beg" (H. Inalcïk), *EI²* IV, 138–140.

53

the Montenegrins and with Albanian nobleman George Arianit, whose daughter Andronike he married. Before the end of the winter, he had enlisted some 12,000 men and wrested from the Ottomans all the land from the Vijosë River (Aoos) to the Gulf of Arta (Amvrakia). Ties were soon established with King Ladislas of Hungary, and in the summer of 1444, in Venetian Alessio (Lesh; now Lezhë, Upper Albania), a solid military alliance was concluded among all the Albanian and Serbian chieftains along the Adriatic coast from southern Epirus to the Bosnian border. Elected "captain of Albania" by his allies, Skanderbeg opened an offensive war against the Ottomans, seizing the mountain province of Debar (Dibra) and made his headquarters there. Around him formed a league of Albanian noble families, some in possession of large estates and retinues, others impoverished, but all fired with martial spirit, having grown up amid warfare and tribal feuds.

Before the walls of Alessio, Venice concluded a peace treaty with Castriota on October 4, 1448, whereupon the Albanian leader decided to join Hunyadi's army with his troops. Relying on this support, the regent led his forces on to the plain of Kosovo, not far from the mountains of the Albanian frontier.

The news of the Hungarian advance had reached the sultan, who issued a general call to arms and quickly levied all available troops in Asia and Europe. From Edirne, where the sultan ordinarily assembled his troops, Murad himself hastened to Bulgaria to head off the enemy forces before they could cross the mountains. On this occasion Sofia was the principal assembly point of the Turkish forces, or so at least the Ottoman sources report. According to the Turkish reports, 50,000 to 60,000 armed men were there passed in review by the sultan. The Western chroniclers, exaggerating as usual, set the figure at 150,000 men. At Nikopol (Nicopolis; Turkish Niğebolu), where the Walachian prince Vlad Dracul, or at least some of his troops, tried to cross the Danube into Bulgaria, a sharp skirmish had taken place shortly before, in which the Ottoman march wardens had retained the upper hand. The Walachians had been almost entirely wiped out by the Ottoman cavalry.

At the news that the enemy was approaching from the north, Murad left Sofia for the plain of Kosovo; if the Ottoman sources are correct, the sultan arrived on Friday, October 4, 1448 (4 Şa'ban, 852 H., which corresponds actually to October 3, 1448). The battlefield was the same as that on which Sultan Murad I and Prince Lazarus of Serbia had met their death on St. Vitus's Day, 1389, and the Ottomans had gained a decisive victory over the Serbs and Hungarians. John Hunyadi had forgotten the ominous warning.

Mehmed Çelebi accompanied the sultan on this occasion; this was to be his baptism of fire. But while his father remained behind a wall with the Janissaries and the artillery, Mehmed was on the right wing with the Anatolian troops. The Rumelian forces took up their position on the left wing. Both wings were protected by light cavalry, as was the camp itself. Auxiliary troops, the so-called *azaps*, maneuvered before the main lines. Thus overwhelmingly outnumbered, John Hunyadi had to extend his army, divided into thirty-eight regiments, to make his front line as long as possible. He himself with some battalions, presumably Hungarian and Transylvanian, held the center. Voivode Dan occupied the right wing with his Walachians, while the remaining troops held the left.

On October 17 there were violent skirmishes between outposts and on the next day Murad opened the attack with his left wing. The Christians, wearing dark blue armor, according to the Ottoman chroniclers, were equipped with superior firearms and inflicted serious losses on the Turks. Both the Anatolian and Rumelian wings of the army were swept aside. Only the numerical superiority of his forces saved the day for Murad. That night an artillery duel took place. On October 19 the sultan brought in fresh Anatolian troops; when they too were unable to make headway, he attacked Hunyadi in the rear. In great difficulties, the Walachians sent a deputation to Murad and through the grand vizier stated the conditions under which they would change sides. When at length they went over to the Turks, Hunyadi could only recognize defeat. He ordered the Germans and Bohemians who manned his culverins to occupy a position opposite Murad and his Janissaries. He himself, sacrificing those of his troops who had remained in the *Wagenburg*, fled with the rest of his army. On the following day, when the Turks attacked the wagons and artillery, which the Germans and Bohemians defended heroically, the regent had fled northward. Fighting his way through hostile Serbia, he had almost reached the Danube and safety when he fell into the hands of George Branković. It was only toward the end of the year, after he had concluded an extremely unfavorable treaty—which, to be sure, was declared null and void by the pope—that he was allowed to resume his journey to Szeged. His army had lost 17,000 men, including the flower of the Hungarian nobility. Turkish losses seem to have been double this number. The military fame of John Hunyadi is darkened by the defeats of Varna and Kosovo. The latter battle might well have been won if he had waited for the promised help from Albania and made his plans in conjunction with Skanderbeg.

The Walachians derived no benefit from their betrayal of Hunyadi's cause. In the hope of eluding the sultan's vengeance—for it was clear that they would be its first victims if the Christians were defeated—they had offered Murad their services. Murad opened his ranks to them and received their arms in token of submission. But taught by bitter experience, the sultan interpreted this desertion as a ruse on the part of Hunyadi. Ordering the commander of the Anatolian troops to surround them, he had them butchered to the last man. First, however, he had mockingly ordered their weapons returned to them, because, as he said, he did not wish Ottomans to murder defenseless men. This, at least, is Chalcocondylas's version of an incident which the other sources, first and foremost the Ottoman chronicler Aşikpaşazade, who had personally taken part in the battle, pass over in silence.

The enormous Turkish losses seem to have prevented the sultan from following up his victory and pursuing his fugitive enemies. Those of Hunyadi's troops who were able to escape to the north were attacked on the way by the despot's bands and many of them robbed and slaughtered.

Mehmed Çelebi, who had left the battlefield unharmed, hurried to Edirne in advance of his father, who returned in triumph somewhat later. Shortly after the battle, on October 31, 1448, the Byzantine emperor, John, died unexpectedly. He left no children; consequently, the eldest of his surviving brothers, Constantine, despot of Mistra, was the natural heir to the throne. When his brother Demetrius, lord of nearby Silivri, tried to enter the ancient capital by force of arms, the sultan, as several times in the past, was asked to arbitrate this dispute over the Byzantine succession. Before the end of December, Constantine's party, represented by the historian Phrantzes, submitted the delicate question to the sultan. Phrantzes was so successful in arguing the case of his royal patron and friend that on January 6, 1449, Constantine, in the castle of Mistra, received the pearl diadem from the hands of a deputation from Constantinople. The coronation ceremony was performed, and the last Byzantine emperor, carried to the Golden Horn in a Catalan ship, made his entrance into Constantinople amid the rejoicing of the population. He came to terms with his two brothers in Greece and a treaty of partition was signed amid solemn oaths. Yet despite this pact, the two brothers soon became embroiled in a lamentable dispute, which was settled by the arbitration of Constantine and the intervention of Ömer Bey, the Thessalian march warden, who profited by the occasion to raze what was left of the isthmus fortifications.

Such was the situation of the Byzantine Empire when Murad decided to put his own house in order. It was time, he held, to replace the union of his son Mehmed Çelebi with a woman of inferior station by a suitable marriage which might also serve political purposes. The heir apparent was now seventeen, the age at which it was customary to attend to such matters in the house of Osman. The sultan's choice fell on the wealthy and beautiful daughters of Süleyman Bey of the Turkmen family of Dulkadïr (Dhu'l-Kadr), ruler of Malatya and Elbistan, in the center of eastern Asia Minor. One of his sisters had married Murad's father, Mehmed I, while another was married to the aged Mamluk sultan Çakmak in Cairo. Later Ayşe Hatun, Süleyman's granddaughter, would marry the future Bayezid II and become the mother of Selim I, known as the Grim. Süleyman Bey, who is described as a man of unshapely corpulence and pathological sensuality but also as a skillful horseman and the owner of magnificent stables, possessed a considerable army of brave, devoted Turkmen and was fabulously wealthy, two circumstances which in themselves sufficed to incline Murad toward the union of his son and heir with this respected noble family which centuries later, though dispossessed of its lands, was still revered as a family of royal blood. The Byzantine chronicler Ducas was convinced, not without reason, that one of the sultan's chief motives in seeking this marriage was to obtain an ally against the arrogant Karamanids and Jihan Shah, the chief of the Turkmen Black Sheep tribe (Kara Koyunlu).

It must have been in the winter of 1448–1449 that Murad summoned Halil Pasha, his trusted grand vizier, and informed him of the marriage plans—an episode vividly described in the early Ottoman sources. The sultan declared that he wished the prince to marry and this time as he, Murad, saw fit. Halil Pasha approved wholeheartedly of his master's plan, whereupon they decided to choose one of Süleyman's daughters. The wife of Hïzïr Pasha, governor of Amasya, was sent to Elbistan to select the bride in accordance with ancient custom. Her choice fell on Sitt Hatun [pl. III a], the most beautiful of the daughters; the intermediary kissed her eyes and put the engagement ring on her finger. Later the same matron, this time accompanied by Saruca Pasha, the sultan's favored adviser in family matters, returned to the court of Elbistan to bring the chosen bride home to Rumelia. The most distinguished nobles of the land escorted the young girl across the mountains to the former Ottoman capital of Bursa, where the judges, the *ülema*, and the skeikhs of the religious orders came to meet her in solemn procession, and then onward across the Dardanelles. At the news that the cortege was approaching, Murad sent out the grandees of the realm from Edirne to meet his future daughter-in-law, who continued on to the sultan's residence with her imposing retinue.

The wedding took place soon after and was celebrated with great pomp for three months. Popular festivities of all sorts and poetry contests contributed to the rejoicings. The bridegroom, who had not been consulted on the choice of his bride, returned with her to Manisa immediately after the celebration. The marriage seems to have been childless and not very happy. Apparently, the whole arrangement was not to Mehmed's liking. Long after he had removed his court to Istanbul, Sitt Hatun remained behind in Edirne, where she lived, lonely and forsaken, until the end of April 1467. It seems likely that her niece Ayşe, in devotion to her memory, completed the mosque which bears her name and beside which she rests under the open sky in a grave now completely uncared for. The two cracked tombstones have been removed from the shrubbery and taken to the city museum. The mosque is today used as a hay barn.[57]

Weary of the affairs of the world, Murad, who during the whole of 1449 undertook no new military venture, spent his days far from the city's bustle, on the island in the Tunca, on the northwestern edge of Edirne, in the company of scholars, poets, and sheikhs. In Manisa, Mehmed Çelebi continued to send out his filibusters to harass the Venetian possessions in the Aegean; not only were such islands as Tinos and Mikonos raided but also the mainland. "For the last three years without interruption," runs a report of March 1449 from Negropont to the Venetian senate, the Turks have been inflicting heavy damage on this island, carrying away men and beasts. The pirates claimed to be acting with the approval of "the sultan's son," who lived in "Turkey," that is, in Anatolia, and was at war with Venice. So much, at least, can be gathered from the deliberations of the Venetian senate. If these and similar reports are taken at face value, they mean that Mehmed Çelebi had set up·a government of his own in Manisa and had become a law unto himself both by land and by sea.[58]

This view is corroborated by the remarkable copper coin which the prince had struck in 852 H. (1448/49), at Ayasoluk, fifty miles south of Manisa. It leaves no room for doubt that he arrogated to himself the right of coinage. The obverse shows a coiled upright monster, which some

---

[57] For more details on Mehmed's marriage, see Babinger's "Mehmeds II. Heirat," 217–235; reprinted in *A&A* I, 225–239. Cf. the remarks of Halil Inalcĭk (in his review article, "Mehmed the Conqueror [1432–1481] and His Time," *Speculum* 35 [1960], 411), who places the wedding in the winter of 1450–1451. A succinct account of the history of the Turkmen family from which Mehmed's bride came is given in "Dhu'l-Ḳadr" (J. H. Mordtmann and V. L. Ménage), *EI²* II, 239–240. For illustrations and descriptions of the mosque with its inscription date 887 H. (1483/84), see Ayverdi, *Fatih devri mimarisi*, 250–252.

[58] For more details see Babinger's "Von Amurath zu Amurath," 264–265 (= *A&A* I, 156). For discussions in the senate on March 17, 1449, see F. Thiriet, *Régestes des délibérations du sénat* III, 149; and its index, for the Ottomans otherwise.

interpret as a dragon, others as a snake. Actually, it would seem to be a royal dragon or basilisk, whose symbolic meaning in this connection is unclear. Possibly the figure reflects a Western influence exerted through Italian mint masters, a hypothesis made plausible by the proximity of Genoese settlements, which were presumably in contact with the court of Manisa, and especially by the obvious awkwardness and unusual disposition of the Arabic legend on the coin. The representation of animals is very uncommon in Moslem coins of that period; indeed, this coin may be unique of its kind. It would be easier to solve the problem of this coin if we were able to date another, roughly contemporaneous coin struck in the name of Mehmed Çelebi at Amasya and also at Tire, showing a striding lion with head turned forward. A number of considerations make it seem likely that this piece is not younger than the dragon coin but perhaps several years older.[59]

In August or September of 1449, Mehmed Çelebi lost his mother, who seems to have spent the last years of her life in her son's palace. She was buried in Bursa in the so-called Hatuniye Türbe, in a garden some 100 yards removed from her husband's funeral vault. A three-line inscription in Arabic, revealing neither her name nor the date of her death, runs as follows:

> Praise be to God! This illustrious tomb was erected in the days of our lord, the mighty sultan, the exalted Hakan, the sultan and sultan's son, Murad, son of Mehmed, son of Bayezid Khan—may God keep his kingdom!—at the behest of his son, the balm of his eyes, homonym of the Prophet—God bless him and greet him!—the noble lord, the sultan Mehmed Çelebi-Sultan—may God fasten the strap of his authority to the pegs of eternity and reinforce the supports of his power until the predestined day!—for his deceased mother, queen among women—may the earth of her grave be fragrant! The completion [of the edifice] fell in the month of Rejeb, the unique, in the year 853 [= mid-September, 1449].[60]

The relative length of the optative formulas of aggrandizement would in itself show that the tomb was commissioned by the son and not the

[59] For these coins see Babinger's "Mehmeds II. Heirat," 231–234 (= A&A I, 236–238). Further, see also Babinger's "Von Amurath zu Amurath," 263 (= A&A I, 154–155). Pere, *Osmanlilarda madeni paralar* 91 (#91 and #93) and plate 7, gives exemplars of both coins.

[60] For the *türbe* see Gabriel, *Une capitale turque* I, 128, and II, plates 54 and 63. The text of the inscription is found in R. Mantran, "Les inscriptions arabes de Brousse," *Bulletin d'Études Orientales de l'Institut Français de Damas* 14 (1952–54), 110.

husband of Huma Hatun. While the name of Murad is accompanied only by the brief conventional formula "May God keep his kingdom," the formula for Mehmed Çelebi Sultan is far longer and more high-flown—so much so that one would take Mehmed for a sultan in his own right. Mehmed's mother carried the secret of her origin with her to the grave.

In the following year, 1450, father and son seem to have come closer together. Mehmed Çelebi probably transferred his residence from Manisa to Edirne on several occasions; at least, this is fairly certain for the spring of 1450. Another campaign against Albania, where things were going badly for the Turks, had been planned for this time, and the prince was expected to participate by the side of the sultan. From the confused reports assembled by Marino Barlezio in his famous work on Skanderbeg, in which exaggerations and inventions make it almost impossible to distinguish the actual facts, we may infer that certain Turkish generals, one called Ali, the other Mustafa, had suffered dangerous setbacks on Albanian soil, so that the sultan was compelled to intervene in person. In April 1450 father and son seem to have left Edirne with a large army; on May 14 they appeared before Krujë.[61] This time the Turkish advance was directed against this key fortress, near which, on Mount "Tumenist" (Thumana?), Skanderbeg had fortified himself with his 8,000 faithful followers, including many Slavs, Italians, Frenchmen, and Germans. A siege of the mountain fortress of Krujë, defended by only 1,500 or 2,000 men, brought no results. Murad had powerful mortars cast, two of which, according to reliable sources, were capable of hurling 400-pound stone balls against the walls. The Venetians of Durrës provided Skanderbeg with help, the value of which was diminished, however, by the fact that their compatriots in Shkodër (Scutari) sent provisions to the sultan's camp at the same time. Murad tried in vain to bribe Count Vrana (Vranaconte), the defender of Krujë, to surrender the fortress. Then he offered Skanderbeg himself peace terms, demanding only an undertaking on Skanderbeg's part to pay a considerable annual tribute. But again the sultan had no luck. To spare his soldiers the hardship of a winter campaign, he was finally obliged to abandon the five months' siege on October 26 and withdrew to the east. The whole Christian world, so deeply shocked by Hunyadi's defeat at Kosovo, was full of rejoicing. Emissaries

[61] For Barlezio see Babinger's introduction to the reprinted edition (= *Beiträge zur Kenntnis Südosteuropas und des Nahen Orients* 3; Munich, 1967, vii–xv) of Georges T. Petrovitch, *Scanderbeg (Georges Castriota), essai de bibliographie raisonnée* (Paris, 1881).

bearing congratulations, food, and grain arrived from Rome and Burgundy, Hungary and Naples. Pope Nicholas V, King Ladislas of Hungary, the duke of Burgundy, and King Alfonso of Naples sent Skanderbeg large sums of money, and with the help of Western workmen the fortifications of Krujë were repaired. But it was evident to all that Murad would never accept such an ignominious defeat. In Skanderbeg, Christendom had a new hero, who assumed the role of John Hunyadi and played it brilliantly for another eighteen years.

It was probably at this time (1450/51) that Mehmed had a second son, Mustafa Çelebi, who was to be his favorite. Of the mother we know only that she was alive in 1474 when her son died; this rules out Sitt Hatun. It may have been Bayezid's mother, Gülbahar, or another wife, Gülşah Hatun, of whom we know only that she was buried in her own *türbe* near Bursa.[62]

In the following winter the sultan again retired to the island in the Tunca where, it seems, he had previously built a number of country houses and baths. There he rested from the disappointments of the previous year and from the burdens and cares of an agitated reign, and began to build a large palace. But he had spent hardly a month on the island when, a great drinker, he was stricken with apoplexy in the midst of a drinking bout. According to some sources he died on the spot; according to others it was not until four days later, though he never regained consciousness, that he gave up the ghost, on the morning of Wednesday, February 3, 1451, New Year's Day of the Moslem year 855. He had lived only forty-seven years; his glorious and just reign had lasted for three decades. Mehmed Çelebi was not in the capital but in Manisa when his father died. This was the true beginning of his reign.

We have already noted that not only the Ottoman but also the Byzantine chroniclers accord the highest praise to the justice and mildness, honesty and forthrightness of Murad II, to mention only the principal traits of his character. Occasionally this emphasis on the bright side of the sultan's nature has been explained as an effort to paint as dark a picture as possible of his successor, destroyer of the remnant of the Byzantine Empire. But when we examine these historians' words more closely, we see that they were meant in all sincerity. "Sultan Murad," observes Chalcocondylas, for example, "was a man who loved law and justice and had fortune on his side. He waged war only in self-defense.

[62] See Babinger, "Mehmeds II. Heirat," 229–230 (= *A&A* I, 234–235).

He attacked no one unjustly. But when he was attacked by others he took up arms. If no one provoked him, he took no pleasure in campaigns, but the reason for this is not to be sought in laziness. For when it was necessary to defend his empire, he did not fear to set out even in winter, nor did he measure the dangers and difficulties attending his undertakings." Ducas, probably the most reliable of the Byzantine annalists, said to be a man enamored of the truth, gives special emphasis, in his judgment of Murad II, to the loyalty with which the sultan observed his treaties with the Christian powers, and stigmatizes the failure of the Christians always to exhibit the same virtue, as exemplified by their breach of the peace of Szeged. "Murad kept his given word," writes Ducas, "and not only to those of his own people and faith, for he never violated the treaties he had concluded with the Christians; when the Christians transgressed against the treaties and broke their given word, this did not escape the eye of God, which sees the truth. His just punishment befell them. But His wrath was not long-lived, for the barbarian did not follow up his victories. He did not desire the total destruction of any people. And when the defeated sent envoys to sue for peace, he gave them a friendly reception, granted their plea, laid down the sword, and went the ways of peace. For this reason also the Father of Peace granted him to die in peace and not by the violence of the sword."

As European visitors reported over and over again, Murad enjoyed great popularity with his people.[63] Although he exerted no particular influence on the political organization of the Ottoman Empire, but contented himself with keeping the country as his father had left it, his reign, thanks to these same conservative tendencies, preserved an aspect of stability and security. Throughout the empire numerous public buildings for pious and benevolent purposes bear witness to his paternal concern for the welfare of his people. The army, whose quarters, food, training, and discipline he did much to improve, was devoted to him throughout his reign. A contemporary Ottoman chronicle relates that after the raising of the siege of Krujë (1450), one of his advisers suggested a winter campaign. "If I attack," he is reported to have replied, "many men will be killed. I would not give one of my soldiers for fifty such fortresses." Though this remark is hardly comparable to Otto von Bismarck's words about the "sound bones of a single Pomeranian musketeer," such solicitude

[63] Another European traveler whose comments about Murad have been preserved is the Spaniard Pero Tafur, who was received by the sultan at Edirne in 1438. The account of his travels to the Holy Land and Turkey and of his audience with Murad is given in his *Travels and Adventures 1435–1439*, translated and edited by Malcolm Letts (London, 1926).

on the part of a fifteenth-century sultan, endowed with absolute power over the life and death of his subjects, may be said to carry still greater significance. And quite apart from his charity and generosity, hereditary virtues of the Ottoman sultans, there is no doubt that he was distinguished by a particular piety. Several mosques, hospitals, schools, refectories for the poor, and caravansaries still bear witness to these qualities in him. His father, Mehmed I, had already set aside a certain sum of money to be distributed among the poor in distant Mecca; for the same purpose Murad earmarked the income from a number of villages near Ankara, to which he added each year 1,000 gold pieces for the descendants (*seyyid*) resident there of the Prophet Mohammed. He esteemed and trusted the orders of dervishes which already existed in his empire, especially the dancing dervishes (Mevlevi). Thus the native chroniclers do not connect his death with drunkenness, but attribute it to an ecstatic dervish whom he was said to have met shortly before his end, as he was crossing on foot the bridge from the Tunca island to Edirne, in the company of his intimates Saruca Pasha and Ishak Pasha. The dervish was said to have addressed him and informed him of his imminent end. At this Murad was seized with terror, which increased when he learned that the dervish was a pupil of Sheikh Buhari, who thirty years before had predicted his victory over Düzme Mustafa, a pretender to the throne. Looking upon the prophecy as an expression of kismet, inexorable fate, he fell mortally sick and died in the prime of life.

Book Two

MEHMED'S FINAL RETURN TO THE THRONE.
THE FORTRESS ON THE BOSPORUS.
THE FALL OF CONSTANTINOPLE.
CREATION OF AN OTTOMAN IMPERIAL CAPITAL.
REPERCUSSIONS IN THE WEST.
OTTOMAN EXPANSION INTO THE AEGEAN.
THE SIEGE OF BELGRADE.

THE NEWS of the death of his father in Edirne was brought to the young Mehmed, not yet nineteen, in a sealed envelope by special messenger from Halil Pasha to Manisa. As usual, the sultan's death was kept secret from the population. The danger was greater than ever that the people, particularly the Janissaries, with whom Mehmed Çelebi was not popular, might be tempted to protest against his accession before he should arrive in Thrace. Chalcocondylas speaks in this connection of a conspiracy of the "newcomers" (*neilydes*, νεήλυδες) to take possession of the city. They met, he reports, in a place outside of Edirne to launch their attack, but Halil Pasha thwarted their plan by massing troops in the capital. Though we do not know exactly what was meant by "newcomers" (Janissaries?), we can infer from the Byzantine chronicle that the people were in a dangerous state of ferment.[1]

The young sultan is reported to have mounted his Arab stallion with the words "Let those who love me follow me," and to have hurried northward from Manisa. The sources diverge in their accounts of the next few days. Ottoman chroniclers mention no difficulties in connection with Mehmed's enthronement, though they do inform us that Mehmed hid in the palace for three days on his arrival in Edirne. According to Ducas, he spent two days in Gelibolu on the Dardanelles, until all was

---

[1] "Newcomers" (νεήλυδες) is Chalcocondylas's regular term for Janissaries. See Gyula Moravcsik, *Byzantinoturcica* II (Berlin, 1958), 110.

in readiness for his reception at the capital.[2] As he made his way under escort from Gelibolu to Edirne, the people came flocking from all sides to see and welcome the new ruler. From Edirne the viziers, governors, nobles, the sheikhs, and doctors of the law rode out to meet him; when the procession was a mile from the city they dismounted and walked before the sultan on foot. After they had gone half a mile, they stopped and raised cries of lamentation over his father's death. The new sultan also dismounted and held out his hand for his retinue to kiss. Then all remounted and proceeded to the serai. Nearly all the Ottoman chronicles agree that Mehmed did not mount the throne until the sixteenth day of Muharrem, 855 H., or Thursday, February 18, 1451, and that Murad's death had been kept secret from the population for all of thirteen days. We can only assume that some sort of conflict must have occurred in Edirne, but its exact nature remains obscure.

There is an atmosphere of drama in Ducas's account of the young sultan's accession to the throne. The viziers and nobles were gathered around him. Closest to him stood the former chief of eunuchs, Şihabeddin Pasha; at some distance followed Ishak Pasha and Murad's grand vizier, Halil Pasha. Halil certainly had the most reason to fear his new master's anger, for it was he who had obliged Mehmed to relinquish the throne and retire to the solitude of Anatolia. "Why," asked the sultan "do my viziers stand aloof?" And turning to Şihabeddin Pasha, he said, "Call them, and tell Halil to take his accustomed place. But as for Ishak, let him as governor of Anatolia accompany my father's corpse to Bursa." A born ruler, Mehmed knew how to bide his time. He permitted Halil Pasha to kiss his hand and confirmed him, along with the other pillars of his father's throne, in his old position.

Ishak Pasha set out for Asia Minor with the mortal remains of his former master. Great pomp was displayed and large sums of money were distributed among the poor along the way. A second coffin was sent to Bursa at the same time. Ducas tells us that while Mehmed's stepmother, daughter of the *bey* of the Isfendiyaroğlu dynasty, was in the throne room imparting to the new sultan her grief at the loss of her husband, Mehmed dispatched Ali Bey, the son of Evrenos, to the women's quarters to drown Küçük (Little) Ahmed Çelebi, Murad's youngest "porphyrogenite" son, in his bath. This was the inauguration of the fratricide law, which from then on was to be applied over a period of centuries, at every change of

[2] Ducas's account is now available in the translation of J. R. Melville Jones, *The Siege of Constantinople 1453: Seven Contemporary Accounts* (Amsterdam, 1972), 56ff.

sultan. It was Mehmed who later had it enacted as actual law in the following terms: "Whichever of my sons inherits the sultan's throne, it behooves him to kill his brothers in the interest of the world order. Most of the jurists have approved this procedure. Let action be taken accordingly."[3]

It is repeatedly stated in the sources that the little prince was then eight months old, which seems surprising when we consider that his parents had been married for twenty-six years. The child's mother was treated more mercifully. Ishak Pasha, the new governor of Anatolia, was obliged to take her as his wife. A better lot fell to Murad's other nobly born wife, Mara, daughter of George Branković. She was sent back to Serbia with rich presents and an imposing retinue, though it is not known whether Mehmed's conduct was dictated by fear of the despot's vengeance or by the deputation from Smederevo, bearing condolences and the request that the late sultan's widow be permitted to return home. In any event, Mara was a shrewd diplomat and was able to incline Mehmed to her wishes as long as she lived. She seems even to have received ample funds for her support from the sultan's treasury. The good relations between Mara and her stepson may be inferred from the mere fact that after her father's death she returned to Turkey, where she remained until her eventful life came to an end in her widow's residence at Ježevo (Eziova; now Daphni), southeast of Thessaloniki, on September 14, 1487.[4]

Mehmed took advantage of Mara's return to her father to renew the treaty of peace and friendship between Serbia and the Ottomans. In general it was Mehmed's well-considered policy to maintain friendly relations for the present with his neighbors, as well as with certain more distant countries whose hostility he had inherited from his father. Immediately after he mounted the throne, envoys came from all sides. In particular, those Aegean islands and border countries which were already tributary hastened to send the young sovereign their homage and appropriate presents. There were emissaries from Walachia, from the lords of Chios and Lesbos, from the Genoese of Galata, and from the grand master Giovanni de Lastic of Rhodes. On September 10 the sultan without hesitation renewed the peace with Venice; two weeks later (September 25) the monks of Mount Athos had no difficulty in obtaining confirmation of their liberties. Envoys from Dubrovnik brought the news that the small free state had added another 500 florins to its tribute (re-

[3] For a brief account of the "law of fratricide" with reference to the Turkish texts, see Alderson, *The Structure of the Ottoman Dynasty*, 25–29.

[4] On Mara's resting place, see below, book 3, n. 9.

cently increased to 1,000 florins) in the hope of keeping the sultan in a good humor. On September 20 a truce for three years, negotiated in April by Hungarian envoys, was concluded with John Hunyadi, who was in difficulties due to the intrigues of the imperial nobility and, even more, to the hostile attitude of Emperor Frederick III. In concluding this treaty, Mehmed must have thought that as long as Hungary kept quiet, he had nothing to fear from the other Western states. As so often in the course of Ottoman history in the fifteenth century, a Turkish adventurer—in this case one Davud, allegedly a son of the blind "sultan" Murad Bey— was busily at work in Hungary and Poland, attempting in vain to exploit for his own ends his conversion to Christianity and his claims to the throne. Above all he attempted to persuade Casimir IV of Poland to launch a campaign against the Turks.[5]

In the West, Mehmed had acquired the reputation of an incompetent boy who could never be expected to carry on the successful military career traced for him by his father. His willingness to enter into agreements with kings and princes far and near seemed to confirm the Christian world in its hope that the Ottoman Empire, at least in Europe, would be reduced to ruins by the weakness of its youthful ruler. This confidence increased the general indifference toward the hitherto dreaded Turkish peril, dangerously paralyzing the forces of the already divided Christian world. None of the Christian powers felt the need to undertake any measures whatsoever against the Ottomans and their sultan, for nearly all were busy with internal problems and conflicts with their neighbors.

Only Francesco Filelfo (1398–1481) of Tolentino, a humanist with grandiose political ambitions, thought the times were ripe again for him to meddle. He had spent seven years (1420–1427) at the court of Byzantium and had become, as it were, half a Greek by his marriage to a daughter of his mentor, John Chrysoloras. He boasted of having been employed during that time on delegations to Sultan Murad, King Ladislas II of Poland, and Emperor Sigismund, and once offered his services to the Sforzas as ambassador to the Grand Turk, claiming to be eminently suited (*ottimissimo*) to this post. On March 20, 1451, he had written his famous letter to King Charles VII of France, violently attacking the young sultan Mehmed. The letter must have been written immediately after the news of Murad's death reached Italy and its ostensible purpose was to win over the king of France to personal participation in a war against the Turks. It is more than questionable whether the writer hoped

---

[5] Babinger gives more detail regarding Davud in his "Dâvûd-Çelebi, ein osmanischer Thronwerber des 15. Jhdts," *Südost-Forschungen* 16 (1957), 297–311; reprinted in *A&A* I, 329–339.

to make the slightest impression, let alone achieve his aim. The obsequious phraseology leads us to suppose that Francesco Filelfo had personal designs. His letter, in any case, is of interest only as an expression of the mood of the times and in particular of the prevailing prejudices and misapprehensions in regard to the sultan's strength. In view of the disastrous division of Italy and the refusal of the other Western countries to act, it was up to France, says Filelfo, to take the lead in a crusade against the Turks. A man of his eloquence had little difficulty in making a plausible case for the necessity and feasibility of such a campaign. The Ottomans, he declared, were in no position to put more than 60,000 men into the field. A further argument was the incompetence of the present ruler, a weak and simpleminded boy, who had never borne arms, lacked knowledge and experience, and led a dissipated life amid wine and women. Never had the time and circumstances been more favorable for a decisive blow against the Turks; of all Western countries France was in the best position to initiate a campaign. The adroit Filelfo went on to draw up a plan of attack, which in his opinion was sure to succeed because Ottoman resistance was out of the question. The army would advance without hindrance to Constantinople, there join forces with the Byzantine emperor, and so drive the Turks from Europe for good. Nay, more—it would cross over to Asia and break the power of the Saracens forever. "Forward then, King Charles," the letter concludes. "Take Christ himself as your guide and champion and, as your piety and benevolence command, turn all your thoughts to this so necessary, so honorable, so glorious war. You have only a rude, uneducated people to combat, a band of robbers, a mob of venal, corrupt slaves who, despite all the scorn and contempt we feel for them, have nevertheless, like vile, crafty animals, darkened the light of Christendom, by our fault alone."[6]

This preposterous plan and in general the political fantasies of this vain and ambitious scholar could scarcely have been addressed to anyone less suitable than King Charles of France, who at this of all times was certainly in no position to leave his strife-torn country and lead the princes of the West in a campaign against the infidel. Pope Nicholas V, without whose support and approval such a project could not possibly be undertaken, made it contingent on the implementation of the union of the two churches, which the emperor Constantine was even less zealous in promoting than his predecessor had been. This was hardly the moment to raise the question of a common struggle of the Latins and Greeks against

[6] See Robert Schwoebel, *The Shadow of the Crescent: The Renaissance Image of the Turk* (New York, 1969), 150–152, for more on Filelfo and references to the sources.

the Ottomans. Powerful groups in Constantinople were hostile to the idea of union with Rome, not only because of the danger it represented for Greek Orthodoxy but also because they looked upon the reward which the union party hoped from the West—namely, Western help against the Turks—as the greatest of perils to the independence of the Greek world. The Greeks had not forgotten that once, in the course of a crusade supposedly directed againsts the infidels, Byzantium had fallen prey to the Latins (1204-1261). In the opinion of these influential circles, a union with the Roman church would merely substitute Latin for Ottoman domination. In other words, a liberation of Constantinople by the West was regarded as tantamount to a new Latinization of the Byzantine Empire.

This was indeed the intention of the Aragonese Alfonso of Naples, who reunited Naples and Sicily under a single scepter for the first time since the Sicilian Vespers (1282), and in his Oriental policy as well proved a worthy successor of Charles of Anjou. Like all the princes of southern Italy before him, he looked upon the imperial throne of Byzantium as his highest political goal. In 1451, when Filelfo was trying to win the king of France over to his plan for a crusade, Alfonso revived his Oriental projects on a scale more grandiose than ever before. Wishing to become the spearhead in a campaign against the Turks, he concluded an alliance with Demetrius, who had succeeded his brother Constantine as despot of Mistra. His aim, however, was not to free European Greece from the Turks, but rather to acquire all the Greek territories, including Constantinople, for himself. The scope of his plans was revealed by his acceptance that same year of overlordship offered him by the Albanians. Only his deep involvement in Italian politics, the lack of a fleet, and the uncertainty of the situation in his own kingdom deterred him from carrying out his plans in southeastern Europe. But the existence of such plans suffices to account for the rejection by the antiunion party in Constantinople of help from the West.

While the Western world as a whole had no serious intention of taking advantage, with unity, resolution, and dispatch, of the change of rulers in Edirne to drive the archenemy of Christianity from Europe, such conscientious Byzantine observers as the historian Phrantzes were well aware of the dangers to Byzantium and to the Christian West that were bound to follow directly from the death of Murad II. Murad's successor, Phrantzes pointed out, was a young man who since childhood had hated everything connected with Christianity and had repeatedly declared that once he mounted the throne he meant to destroy the Eastern Empire and all Christendom, root and branch. If it should occur to this daring young man to attack Constantinople at once, then what?

In the beginning at least, Emperor Constantine XI does not seem to have reckoned with such a possibility. He too made haste to send ambassadors to Edirne, bringing the new sultan condolences for his father's death and congratulations on his accession to the throne, and expressly requesting renewal of the existing treaties. Thereupon, Ducas tells us, Mehmed swore by Allah and the Prophet, by the Koran, the angels and archangels, to observe the existing peace and gave his sacred promise that as long as life was granted him he would never lay hands on the capital or any of the emperor's other possessions, that quite on the contrary, he was determined to maintain the same friendly relations as his father with the emperor of Byzantium and his predecessor. As though in token of his honorable intentions, he granted the emperor an annual allowance of 300,000 aspers from the revenues of the cities on the River Struma (Strimon) for the upkeep of Orhan, an Ottoman prince then living at the court of Byzantium, said to be a grandson of the Emir Süleyman (son of Bayezid I) and thus second cousin to Mehmed. The circumstances surrounding the life of this prince are by no means clear and there would be no need to mention him if he were not, as we shall soon see, to play a fateful role in the course of the ensuing years.[7]

Mehmed had now every reason to look upon the situation in Europe as safe for the present and to fear no danger to his state from the West. He was free to devote himself more energetically to Anatolia, where, immediately after his accession to the throne, Ibrahim Bey, ruler of Karaman, had once again raised his head. But this time Ibrahim planned no less than to wrest the whole of western Asia Minor from the Ottomans and, with the help of real or alleged scions of disestablished ruling houses of Anatolia, to restore at least a part of the old petty states (*beyliks*). In order to carry out his plan he sent to Menteşe, Aydīn, and Germiyan three young men who were or claimed to be descendants of the former rulers, and ordered troops to occupy a number of fortresses and small towns, while he himself invaded and laid waste the nearby Ottoman territories. Mehmed commissioned Ishak Pasha, the governor of Anatolia, to put down the disorders, after dismissing his general Ozguroğlu Isa Bey, who, previously entrusted with this task, had infuriated his master by his inactivity. Subsequently, after a brief stay in Bursa, where he had visited his father's tomb and otherwise looked after affairs, Mehmed himself appeared on the scene. The mere presence of the sultan was enough to make the ruler of Karaman reconsider. The towns he had

[7] The identity of Orhan remains in doubt. See Alderson, table 24, n. 16.

occupied on Ottoman soil were speedily evacuated, and Ishak Pasha advanced without resistance to Akşehir and Beyşehir. Ibrahim Bey, who had fled to the mountains, sent letters pleading for forgiveness and peace. Finally, envoys who reached Mehmed in Akşehir repeated his message and offered the sultan the hand of one of Ibrahim's daughters. The sultan granted his forgiveness, whereupon Ibrahim undertook to pay perpetual homage and acknowledged that his territories had been a gift from his brother-in-law, Sultan Murad. Ishak Pasha, who as governor of Anatolia had previously resided in Ankara, was now ordered to remove to Kütahya, which from then on remained the residence of the governor of the Asian provinces. Meanwhile he had driven Ilyas Bey, who for many years was tributary ruler of Menteşe and who had rashly taken sides with Ibrahim, from his fief and restored order everywhere.[8]

Sultan Mehmed then returned from the interior of Anatolia to Bursa, where he was greeted by an unexpected event. The Janissaries, apparently being kept in reserve there, came storming out to meet the sultan, demanding a gift of money, a *donativum*, of their commander, who, however, had already been informed of their demands by Şihabeddin Pasha and the aged and battle-tried Turahan Bey. When they renewed their remonstrances, Mehmed swallowed his rage and ordered ten sacks of aspers distributed among the mutineers. This was the first time an Ottoman sovereign was compelled to make the Janissaries a gift on the occasion of his accession to the throne. The custom perpetuated itself: subsequent rulers made the same gift, except that with the steady devaluation of the coinage the amounts became larger all the time. A few days later Mehmed sent for the Janissary agha, or general, of the "new troops," a man named Kazancı (or Kurtcu) Doğan, gave him a violent tongue-lashing, boxed his ears (or, according to other sources, whipped him), and dismissed him from his office, which was conferred upon Mustafa Bey. In addition, the sultan called to account the several *yaya başı*, captains of the foot militia, and had them punished, not only for the indiscipline of the Janissaries but also for their negligent handling of the muster rolls. Mehmed took the opportunity to reorganize the Janissaries, then numbering about 5,000 or 6,000 men, in such a way as to discourage further disorder. Adding to their numbers 7,000 falconers (*doğancı*) and dog keepers (*segban* or *seğmen*), who had previously been under the chief master of the hunt, he kept for himself 500 of the former and 100 of the latter.

[8] A survey account of the several Anatolian principalities in one volume is Ismail H. Uzunçarşılı, *Anadolu Beylikleri ve Akkoyunlu, Karakoyunlu Devletleri* (Ankara, 1969; as *TTK*: VIII. seri, no. 2ª). For the Karaman dynasty, see also especially "Karamanlılar" (M. C. Ş. Tekindağ), *IA* VI, 316–330.

During Mehmed's passage through Anatolia an incident occurred that was to have far graver consequences than the quickly subdued unrest of the Janissaries. Messengers from the Byzantine emperor had appeared in the sultan's camp, complaining on Constantine's behalf that the allowance for Prince Orhan had not yet been paid. They went so far as to threaten that if the allowance were not doubled from then on, the prince would be permitted to put forward his claim to the Turkish throne. Halil Pasha, the grand vizier, who was not as a rule hostile to the Greeks, let fly at the imperial delegation, declaring that the late sultan Murad, a kindly man noted for his sense of justice, had done his utmost to meet the Byzantines halfway, but that they could not expect such consideration from the present ruler, a bold and violent youth who would not hesitate to attack Constantinople. No sooner is the ink dry on the treaty between the two sovereigns, the grand vizier went on, than envoys come over to Asia to frighten the Ottomans with the "usual bugbear" (*mormolykia*). Ducas, who quotes the speech almost word for word, seems to have captured Halil Pasha's manner perfectly and his record of the speech gives an impression of authenticity.

Informed by the grand vizier of the Byzantines' presumptuous demands, Mehmed dissimulated his feelings. He dismissed the envoys with friendly words and the assurance that he would soon attend to the matter in Edirne and communicate with them. The curtain had risen on the last act of the Byzantine tragedy.

When Mehmed reached the straits with his retinue, he learned that they were blocked by Christian ships. A crossing to Gelibolu proved impossible. It was decided to pass through the Kocaeli region on the Sea of Marmara, and to cross the Bosporus near the castle of Akçe Hisar (or Güzel) the "white" (or "beautiful") castle, now called Anadolu Hisari, built by Bayezid I in 1395 [pl. VIII a]. It was here that Murad II and his troops had crossed the straits with Genoese help before the battle of Varna. On this occasion Sultan Mehmed is said to have conceived the plan of erecting, on the European shore opposite the White Castle, a fortress under whose protection troops could be put across to Thrace.

Shortly after his arrival in Edirne (still in 1451), Mehmed confiscated the revenues of the cities on the Struma that had been set aside for Orhan's upkeep and ordered the Greek inhabitants of these same cities expelled. By way of filling the state treasury he had most likely somewhat earlier ordered silver coins, dated 855 (February 3, 1451, to January 22, 1452), to be struck in various mints of the empire—namely, Edirne, Ayasoluk, Amasya, Bursa, Serrai, and finally in the silver-mining city of Novo Brdo; probably the intrinsic value of the coins was again secretly reduced. The Janissaries' pay, which had recently been increased by half an asper a day, and the semiannual renewal of their uniforms, in which silk and velvet were not lacking, may well have necessitated this particular devaluation of the coinage. Distrust of these frequent new currency issues always led the population to hoard the old coins, although the trade value of the old aspers was reduced—twelve old to ten new, despite the diminished silver content. Later on, to be sure, such exchange transactions became rare, for special officials were appointed to ferret out and punish all those who kept the better coinage instead of letting the state treasury realize the profit.[9]

The upkeep of the Janissaries, who, apart from their pay and clothing, had to be supplied with bows and arrows at the sultan's expense, amounted to a considerable sum, roughly 28,000 ducats, and this of course was only a fraction of the total expenditure for the army. But in fact war was almost always a source of profit to the Ottoman treasury, as a contemporary chronicler tells us, for many soldiers on campaign provided their own barley or flour, the regions traversed were obliged to feed the army, and every military governor (*sancak beyi*; lit., "lord of the standard") who arrived at the imperial camp brought costly gifts.

Thus far we possess no specialized investigations of Mehmed's monetary policy. But there is no doubt that in his reign the coinage fell short of its twofold function as standard of value and as legal tender. More than the lack of precious metals, insufficient revenue and the alarming greed of the sovereign seem, even in the first brief reign but particularly after his final accession to power, to have brought about a steady deterioration of the coinage. Under Murad II the traditional preference for good gold and silver money had made for a well-regulated currency and kept the coinage of copper within reasonable limits, but in the new reign the state treasury must have derived considerable profit from currency devaluation. The relation between the copper coin (*mangir*) and the silver asper (*akçe*) fluctuated incessantly. Although Mehmed had new coins, exclusively silver and copper, struck every ten years, and the law required that old coins be turned in for these, the silver changers (*gümüş sarraflari*) he had appointed always found plentiful spoils when they searched natives or foreigners for old coins. The scandalous extortions and frauds of

[9] For the minting of silver coins in 885 H., see Pere, *Osmanlilarda madeni paralar* 90 (#85) and plate 7. Some idea of the value of the *akçe* (asper) may be gained from the fact that at this time the approximate daily wage of an ordinary Janissary was six *akçe*. (See the paper of Halil Inalcîk, "The Policy of Mehmed II toward the Greek Population of Istanbul and the Byzantine Buildings of the City," *DOP* 23–24 [1969–70], 236.)

these detested officials did not outlast the reign of Mehmed, for though his son and successor, Bayezid II, devalued the currency on his accession to the throne, he refrained, allegedly under pressure from the Janissaries, from repeating the performance during the remainder of his reign.

From the very first Mehmed's reign must have brought an appreciable increase in state expenditure; the new ruler was quick to abandon the simple patriarchal customs of his forebears, especially of his frugal father, and to display a magnificence all his own. Shortly before his death Murad had started to build a new palace on the Tunca island on ground which, so it was said, had formerly served the Byzantine emperors as a hunting park. In the summer of 1451 Mehmed gave orders to extend the construction in accordance with his desires; there is no doubt that foreign architects, presumably Italians and Ragusans, were employed. The new establishment consisted of a number of buildings, the most impressive of which were the so-called reception hall (*arz odasi*), the Kum Kasrï, where guests were lodged, and the castle of Cihan-numa, a part of which is still standing. In addition to the women's quarters, some ten fortresslike edifices were built for the court. The serai had no less than thirteen large gates, which gives us an idea of its dimensions. The settlement included mosques, ultimately thirteen in number, thirteen halls (*koğuş*) on ground level, and no less than twenty baths. But the whole establishment does not date from Mehmed II; additions were made by later sultans, especially Mehmed IV (1648–1687) and Mustafa III (1757–1773), who was born there. The Cihan-numa, which consisted of ten rooms, three council rooms and courtiers' quarters, was the sultan's actual residence; a library was installed and, in the sixteenth century, rooms for the Prophet's cloak (*hïrka-i şerif*), the sacred banner, and other precious objects. The Kum Kasrï, some sixty-five feet to the east of this palace, was the residence of the princes. Here Prince Cem was born, and one of the tower rooms long bore his name. Helmuth von Moltke, who visited the place in the summer of 1837, when the buildings were relatively intact, gives us a vivid account of their magnificence: "In the center arises a massive stone edifice surmounted by a strangely shaped tower; its walls are still for the most part covered with marble and jasper; the ceilings, however, have collapsed, and nearly all the beautiful porcelain tiles with gilded arabesques which decorated the walls have been torn down. The building is so solidly and massively constructed that it seems likely to stand for centuries; but it is not very large, and one is reminded of the serai in Constantinople, where amid so many kiosks one looks in vain for a main building. The serai of Edirne, however, does not have the same prisonlike look; the sultans who inhabited it had not yet become invisible to the Moslem population.

In the harem building, the framework walls have caved in and the lead roofs and domes seem to hover in midair. Today this part of the serai is inhabited solely by a stag, who gives visitors a very unfriendly reception."[10]

Next to nothing remains of all this pomp and splendor. The palaces were destroyed on January 17, 1878, by Turkish soldiers retreating from the Russians. Only the great elms and age-old plane trees still bestow their shade, and sheep and cattle graze on the rich "meadows of the Comneni"—a sad reminder of earthly transience. And the city to the south of the island, Edirne, with its domes and minarets, its crumbling walls and towers amid a welter of flat red roofs between which gleam light green bushes and black cypresses, is today a mere shadow of its former greatness and power.

In his throne room on the island Mehmed received foreign emissaries; in the palace of Cihan-numa he took council with his advisers and associated with scholars, poets, and theologians. It was there that he forged his bold plans which always disclosed, side by side with youthful impetuosity and daring, a sharp and penetrating judgment uncommon for his age and which soon made it clear that he was far superior to most of his predecessors and contemporaries in military talent and in political insight and skill. It was here no doubt that shortly after his accession he surrounded himself with a number of Occidentals, especially Italians. His favorite topic of conversation was the heroes of antiquity whom he had decided to emulate, but he also liked to question his guests about conditions in the Christian world. For those years, unfortunately, the name of only one member of the sultan's entourage is attested—his father's personal physician, Maestro Iacopo of Gaeta, who was Mehmed's constant companion to the day of his death and who, as we shall see, more than once exerted an important influence on his master's decisions. Ciriaco de' Pizzicolli may have been one of Mehmed's advisers, but of this we cannot be certain. Edirne was an important market for Western wares, and a number of Italian merchants resided there. Mehmed may well have sought their company, and there is no reason to suppose that he did not.

The Thracian winter was approaching when Mehmed issued an order throughout the Ottoman Empire enlisting a thousand masons and a corresponding number of lime slakers and workmen. Furthermore, he or-

---

[10] Von Moltke's description is from his *Briefe* (see above, book 1, n. 16), 150–151 (letter #28, May 12, 1837). See also the article "Edirne" (M. T. Gökbilgin), *EI²* II, 683–686. A Turkish work on the Edirne serai is Süheyl Ünver, *Edirne'de Fatih'in Cihannuma Kasri* (Istanbul, 1953).

dered that the necessary materials be held in readiness, for in the early spring he planned to build a fortress on the European shore of the Bosporus. The alarming news soon reached Constantinople. Even on the Greek islands the population was stricken with panic. "This is the end of the city!" they cried, according to Ducas. "These are the omens of the end of our race." "These are the days of the Antichrist!" They were not mistaken in their fears.

Emperor Constantine sent messengers to the sultan in Edirne to make representations. They were instructed to say that when Mehmed's great-grandfather wished to erect a castle on the Anatolian side of the Bosporus —namely, the Akçe (or Güzel) Hisar—he had petitioned Emperor Manuel II (1391–1425) as a son might petition his father. Needless to speculate how the emissaries were received. For quite some time there had been no further mention of the meeting with Byzantine negotiators to which Mehmed had consented in Anatolia. He wished to have no dealings with any emissaries or with the emperor himself; indeed, he seemed pleased with this convenient pretext for a final breach with Constantinople.

Mehmed left Edirne in the middle of March, set out from Gelibolu with six fully equipped galleys, eighteen galleons, and sixteen supply ships, and, passing the Golden Horn, reached the Bosporus on March 26. He had personally planned the new fortress and chosen the site; it was there that Darius, king of the Persians, had built his bridge. It was not far from the place then called Asomata, at the narrowest point in the straits, where they are only some eight hundred yards wide and the current is particularly swift. This was the easiest point from which to control the Greek capital's Black Sea trade. Under the supervision of Grand Vizier Halil Pasha and of the viziers Saruca, Zaganos, and Şihabeddin, some 5,000 workmen completed the powerful fortress between Saturday, April 15, and Thursday, August 31, 1452.[11] Building materials had been brought in haste from all quarters: lime and slaking ovens, beams from Ereğli (Heraclea) on the Black Sea and Izmit (Nicomedia), stone from Anatolia. Some of the materials were provided by the ruins of old churches and ancient temples on the Bosporus. The Church of St. Michael, which had occupied the site of the fortress, provided stone and columns. The nobles of the empire, who directed the project, lent a helping hand, and each of the viziers erected the tower assigned to him and his purse as quickly as possible. The sultan himself undertook the building of the walls between the towers. A few inhabitants of Constantinople tried to obstruct the building by picking quarrels with the workmen. There were

[11] For these viziers see Babinger (with F. Dölger), "Ein Auslandsbrief des Kaisers Johannes VIII. vom Jahre 1447," *BZ* 45 (1952), 25–28 (= *A&A* II, 167–169).

stabbings and deaths on both sides. Emperor Constantine sent envoys to the sultan, asking him to post sentries for the protection of the Greek peasants harvesting nearby; at the same time he sent gifts, food, and drink. Ducas records the conversations between the two parties in detail, employing direct discourse. At the news of the incidents at the outposts of the fortress, Constantine had the gates of the capital closed, and a number of Turks found in the vicinity were imprisoned but were held only for a few days. The prisoners included several eunuchs from the sultan's palace who, when brought before the emperor, declared: "If you release us before sundown, we shall be grateful to you. But know that if we have not returned by sundown, our release will no longer be of any use to us, for we shall be condemned to death. Therefore take pity on us and set us free at once; otherwise, have our heads cut off, for we would rather meet death at your hands than at those of the destroyer of the world." So, at least, Ducas records the incident. And to Ducas we also owe a report that the emperor addressed a last plea for a peaceful settlement to Mehmed, who, far from apologizing for his actions, replied with what amounted to a declaration of war against Byzantium: the two imperial emissaries were beheaded (June, 1452).[12]

The enormous fortress, the present-day Rumeli Hisari [pl. VIII b], which its builders called *Boğaz kesen* and the Greeks *Laimokopia*, both meaning "cutter of the straits," or "throat cutter," is a strange edifice. It is shaped roughly like a triangle, with the towers of three of the viziers at its corners and the fourth, that of Halil Pasha, at the center of the east wall. The pinnacled walls were several yards thick and fifty feet high; the roofs were covered with thick sheets of lead. As architect a certain Muslihuddin, surely a renegade, is mentioned, but also a Christian monk converted to Islam. It is evident that the ground plan follows the terrain. Certain authors have expressed the opinion that the contours of its walls followed the Arabic writing of the word Mohammed (the name of both the Prophet and the sultan), but this is not to be taken seriously. The castle is set against a steep slope, consisting in places of rocky cliffs. It is 800 feet long and roughly 160 to 320 feet wide. Its highest tower rises more than 200 feet over the sea.[13]

---

[12] The question of the emperor's bids for peace in the waning months before the fall of Constantinople is discussed in another context by M. Carroll, "Notes on the Authorship of the 'Siege' Section of the Chronicon Maius of Pseudo-Phrantzes, Book III," *Byzantion* 41 (1971), 28–36. An extended study, with translations, of Phrantzes' chronicle by the same scholar is apparently in preparation (see Jones, *The Seige of Constantinople*, xi).

[13] Chalcocondylas's account of the siege, beginning with the construction of the fortress of Rumeli Hisari, is now available in the translation of Jones, *The Siege of*

Mehmed garrisoned the fortress with 400 men and appointed Firuz
Bey as captain. He commanded that all ships passing through the straits
in either direction were to be stopped, and permitted to proceed only on
payment of a toll. If any sea captain should defy the order, his ship was
to be sunk by cannon fire from the fortress. By way of implementing this
order, several enormous brass cannon were placed on the tower nearest
the shore. They were able, Ducas tells us, to fire stone projectiles weighing up to 600 pounds. And his statement finds confirmation in the marble
cannon balls weighing 450 pounds that are still to be seen at the foot of
this tower.

On August 28, 1452, the sultan left the fortress and repaired to the
trenches and walls of the Greek capital; these he inspected carefully for
three whole days, according to tradition. Finally, on September 1, he returned to Edirne with his troops and retinue. The Ottoman fleet also
left the Bosporus and on September 6 reached Gelibolu, where Admiral
Baltaoğlu Süleyman Bey, later to be styled *kapudan paşa,* resided.

The threat to sink any vessel that should fail to lower its sails and pay
the appointed toll was carried out in bitter earnest. After the construction
of the fortress had begun, a cannon founder by the name of Urban, presumably a Transylvanian, deserted from Byzantine service and went over
to the Turks, who received him with open arms. The sultan promised
Urban the highest wages, overwhelmed him with gifts of money, and
asked him whether he would be able to make a cannon capable of breach-
ing the walls of Constantinople. Urban replied without a moment's hesitation that he could make a cannon which no wall, either in Byzantium
or "Babylon," could resist, but admitted that he could not determine the
range in advance. Mehmed bade him start work on the cannon; they
would see about the range later on. In three months Urban built an
enormous cannon for the shore side of the new fortress. Toward the end
of 1452 three Venetian merchantmen coming from the Black Sea approached the fortress. None of the captains was willing to accede to the
Turkish demands. Two of the ships got through safely, but not the third,
commanded by Antonio Erizzo and bearing a cargo of grain for Constantinople. On the captain's refusal to lower sails and heave to, his vessel
became the new cannon's first target, providing a good indication of its
range (November 25). The vessel was sunk and captain and crew taken
prisoner. All were brought to Dimotika, where the sultan happened to

---

Constantinople, 42ff. The most extensive treatment of the fortress on the European
shore of the Bosporus is Ekrem Hakkī Ayverdi, *Osmanli Mi 'mārīsinde Fatih Devri
IV* (Istanbul, 1974; Istanbul Enstitüsü No. 69), 626–662. For the Asian fortress,
617–624.

be at the time. He had the sailors beheaded on the spot, and the captain was impaled. The bodies were left unburied in the street, where shortly thereafter Ducas saw them with his own eyes.

Venice and Genoa were paralyzed with fear at the news of the construction of the fortress on the straits, an act generally interpreted as a preparation for war against Constantinople. The flourishing colony of Pera and indeed the whole Levantine trade were menaced. But only in November, when a last desperate call for help reached Genoa, did the Genoese authorities decide to send an armed ship to the Golden Horn; at the same time they appealed for help to the king of France and to Florence, their ally. As long as Genoa and Venice were at loggerheads in Italy, any collaboration between the two great commercial powers was unthinkable. When at length, on January 26, 1453, the Genoese galleys with 700 soldiers on board landed in Constantinople, Emperor Constantine appointed their commander, Giovanni Giustiniani-Longo, general-in-chief of his land forces, with the honorary title of *protostrator* (roughly, marshal), and at the same time made him a gift of the island of Lemnos.

Neither Venice nor Genoa was able to summon up the old fighting spirit that Enrico Dandolo and Simone Vignosi had once shown in the Levant. Only the Byzantine emperor tried in earnest, though vainly, to prepare for the threatening storm. Throughout 1452 as much grain as possible had been brought from the surrounding country to the city, where many country people had also sought refuge. During the winter everything possible was done to put the city's defenses in order; but despite every effort, the necessary money and soldiers, which only foreign powers could have provided, were not forthcoming. The emperor's glittering promises to several Western princes brought no reply other than words of comfort and vague assurances.

In response to the repeated calls for help from Byzantium, Venice did nothing but send out messages of exhortation: to the pope, to Emperor Frederick III, who had been crowned in Rome on March 19, 1452, to Hungary, Aragon, and finally to France. As for Emperor Constantine's negotiations with the Roman Curia, they brought but one result: Pope Nicholas V again brought up the question of church union.

In November 1452 Cardinal Isidor, bishop of St. Sabine, arrived in Constantinople aboard a Venetian galley. The emperor had no alternative but to have the divine services in St. Sophia held in accordance with the union ritual, in the presence of the court, the senate, and the higher clergy (December 12). The decree of Union was sworn to, under the proviso that it should be reexamined once the Turkish menace had subsided. But this merely added to the dissension among the Greeks. Under pressure from the lower clergy, which was hostile to union, and in particular from the most active leader of the antiunion party, the learned Gennadius in the monastery of Pantokrator, the masses raised a violent outcry. Monks swarmed through the streets, shouting invectives against the Latins, and thronged to the monastery, where they asked Gennadius for instructions. Gennadius gave them a written reply in which he deplored the disgrace into which the ancestral faith was falling, and held out a terrifying picture of the divine judgment that such an act of apostasy was bound to call forth. The monks swept through the city, shouting anathemas against the decisions of the synod and those who accepted them. As usual, the masses sided with the fanatical monks. The populace broke into the taverns, uttering fearful curses against the union and its supporters, and drank quantities of wine in honor of the Blessed Virgin, who alone had the power to save the menaced city. The rioting lasted for some time, and even the staunchest supporters of union were intimidated. The solidarity and fortitude of the population, most needed in these critical times, were undermined. *Tantum religio potuit suadere malorum.*

After he had secured the passage across the straits, Mehmed's next step was to make it impossible for the emperor's brothers, Demetrius and Thomas, who shared the rule of the Morea, to come to Constantine's assistance. On October 1, 1452, he ordered his aged general Turahan Bey, with his two sons Ahmed Bey and Ömer Bey, to set out from Thessaly and Macedonia, of which Turahan Bey was march warden (*uç beyi*), and attack the two despots in the Peloponnese. The diversion was eminently successful. Corinth and the isthmus, which had been refortified, were taken by storm. Burning and ravaging, the Turkish hordes poured through Arcadia and the plateau of Tripolis (Tripolitza) to Mount Ithomi, the natural acropolis of the Messenian territory; advancing as far as the Gulf of Koroni (Coron) they took Navarino (Pylos, Neokastron) and beleaguered Siderokastron, but in vain. From here a column led by Ahmed Bey marched to Leondarion (Leondari), but was attacked on the way by Greeks under Matthew Asanes, Demetrius's brother-in-law; Ahmed Bey was taken prisoner and brought before the despot in Mistra. While Turahan Bey and his troops immobilized the Greek forces in the Morea, Mehmed was busily making war preparations in Edirne.

Well pleased with the success of Urban's cannon, the sultan ordered him to build an enormous siege gun in Edirne, twice the size of the first, capable of hurling projectiles weighing more than a thousand pounds. Fifty yoke of oxen could barely move it, and 700 men were required to transport and service it. When it was ready, it was placed outside the just completed Cihan-numa palace, and loaded with great difficulty. The inhabitants of the Turkish capital were warned, lest they be stricken with panic. At dawn next day the cannon was fired, filling the whole city with powder smoke; the thunder was heard for miles around. The projectile traveled a whole mile and sank almost six feet into the earth.

War was constantly in Mehmed's thoughts. Often at night he strolled through the city incognito, accompanied only by two intimates, to inform himself of the state of mind among the population and in the army. When recognized and greeted with the usual "Long live," Mehmed would stab the unwelcome interloper with his own hand. Ducas, who reports this story, declares that Mehmed took as much pleasure in killing men as anyone else in killing fleas. One night, as the same chronicler tells us, he sent some eunuchs to summon Halil Pasha to his presence. The grand vizier, who because of his former conduct had good reason to fear his capricious master's anger, took a bowl of gold with him. Finding the sultan sitting up in bed, fully dressed, he set the gold down at his feet. "What is the meaning of that, *lâla?*" Mehmed asked. "Custom," the vizier replied, "decrees that when a noble is summoned to his master at an unusual hour, he must not appear with empty hands. It is not my goods that I offer you but your own." "I have no need of your gold," said the sultan. "I want but one thing of you—your help in taking possession of Constantinople." The grand vizier, who was looked upon as a secret friend of the Greeks and bore the dubious nickname *gâvur ortağı* ("accomplice of the infidels"), was not a little perturbed by the sultan's demand. He replied that the Lord, who had already subjected the greater part of the Greek territories to the sultan, would also grant him possession of the capital. All the sultan's servants, he added, were vying with each other in sacrificing their wealth and their very blood to this end. The sultan answered, "Behold my bed, in which I have been tossing from side to side all night! I admonish you not to let yourself be softened by gold and silver. We will fight the Greeks bravely and, relying on Allah and his Prophet, take the city." With this he dismissed the thoroughly alarmed grand vizier. He himself spent the remainder of the night and many more nights working feverishly on his plans. He sketched the walls of the city, the battle lines and outposts, the positions of the siege machines, batteries, and mines; he consulted persons familiar with the situation in Constantinople and the state of the fortifications. At this time, and perhaps earlier, Mehmed appears to have immersed himself in illustrated Western works on fortifications and siege engines. If, as is generally supposed, Ciriaco of Ancona was already a member of Mehmed's entourage, he presumably helped him with the sketches.

An unbiased investigation of the part played by "Franks" that is, Westerners, in preparing for and carrying out the capture of Constantinople would be of the greatest interest. Without Mehmed's astounding gift for assimilating the "teachings of his day" (N. Iorga) and utilizing the ideas and skills of the foreigners he had attracted to his court or at least to his person, it seems certain that Constantinople would not have fallen so quickly. (In giving Urban exclusive credit for the Ottoman triumph, Iorga, who regarded the Transylvanian Saxon or Hungarian as a Romanian, was no doubt carried away by national pride, for his assertion in this radical form is scarcely tenable.) As we shall see in the course of our story, the "Latins" made a vital contribution to the swift downfall of Constantinople. In other contexts as well, Mehmed's European advisers, then and later, played a tragic role in the history of the West. Mehmed's interest in his Western advisers was purely practical. The romantic interpretations that attribute it to the sultan's supposed attachment to humanism and the Renaissance have hardly favored the cause of historical truth.[14]

In this connection the only definitely attested fact is that the Jewish physician Iacopo of Gaeta was living at Mehmed's court in 1452. A diploma preserved from the month of Rebi II, 856 H. (April–May 1452) seems to prove that he participated in the building of *Boğaz kesen*. But whether at this time he already exerted an appreciable influence on the young sultan remains uncertain; nor is it known what role he may have played in the palace of Murad II after the retirement of Murad's previous Jewish physician, Ishak Pasha.[15]

In view of the overwhelming military superiority of the Turks—a count undertaken at the emperor Constantine's behest shows that the Greek

[14] Babinger surveys the contacts between the sultan and the Italians in his "Mehmed II., der Eroberer, und Italien," *Byzantion* 21 (1951), 127–170, where references are given to many of the authors and works alluded to in this book. Translations into Turkish and Italian may be found in *Belleten* 17 (1953), 41–82, and in *Rivista Storica Italiana* 53 (1951), 469–505, respectively. The Romanian historian referred to is Nicolai Jorga (Iorga), author of *Geschichte des Osmanischen Reiches*, 5 vols. (Gotha, 1908–13).

[15] For Mehmed's Jewish physician, see most recently Eleazar Birnbaum, "Hekim Ya'kub, Physician to Sultan Mehemmed the Conqueror," *Hebrew Medical Journal* 1 (1961), 250–222, where full references are given to the sources and earlier studies, including Babinger's "Ja'kub-Pascha, ein Leibarzt Mehmed's II," *Rivista degli Studi Orientali* 26 (1951), 82–113, and Bernard Lewis's "The Privilege Granted by Mehmed II to His Physician," *Bulletin of the School of Oriental and African Studies (University of London)* 14 (1952), 551–563.

forces totaled only 4,973 natives and 2,000 foreigners—the role of the sultan's Western advisers does not seem very important. These figures, compiled by the historian Phrantzes, are certainly worthy of credence. They came as such a shock to the emperor that he ordered them kept secret, lest they add to the general despair. There was little chance of supplementing these forces; neither men nor funds were available. At the emperor's order, the silver vessels were removed from the churches and melted down for coin. A last addition to the Byzantine army was provided by the crews of the ships at anchor in the Golden Horn; in the end there were some 6,000 Greeks and 3,000 foreigners, mostly Genoese and Venetians, under arms. The population of the city was much smaller than generally supposed. In 1437, it had amounted to only some 40,000. In 1453, it was estimated by some observers (J. Tedaldi, for example) at 30,000 to 36,000, by others at a maximum of 50,000. Thus, in the year of its downfall the Byzantine capital numbered no more than 45,000 to 50,000 souls, which, even by late medieval standards, seems a strikingly small population for the capital of a former world empire, especially when the not inconsiderable number of refugees from the surrounding towns is taken into account.[16]

On the land side, Constantinople was then protected by a double wall [pl. X b]. Chalcocondylas sets its length at 111 stadia, or some twelve miles. The inner wall was the higher and stronger; the outer one, however, was protected by a broad trench lined with stones. Measures were also taken for defending the sea side. The emperor had few ships of his own, but he confiscated all the vessels that were anchored in the harbor and those that subsequently put in; on April 2, 1453, he closed off the harbor mouth with a heavy iron chain kept afloat by great round blocks of wood, and extending from Galata to the fortifications on the opposite bank. In all, there were twenty-six ships, including five from Genoa, five from Venice, three from Crete, and one each from Ancona, Spain, and France; the rest were Byzantine vessels. On February 26, 1453, seven ships, six from Crete and one from Venice, the latter under Captain Pietro Davanzo, had secretly left the Golden Horn; 700 persons escaped with them. Otherwise, as Phrantzes expressly remarks, only a few families had fled.

Although war had long been declared, the winter passed without mili-

[16] For the population of the city, see A. M. Schneider, "Die Bevölkerung Konstantinopels im XV. Jh.," *Nachrichten der Akademie der Wissenschaften in Göttingen, philos.-hist. Klasse* (1949), 234-244. A Turkish translation appears in *Belleten* 16 (1952), 35-48.

tary events. In the outskirts the fighting with the Ottomans had never entirely ceased. Virtually cut off on the land side, the capital was like a beleaguered fortress. Only by way of the sea were the Greeks able, up to February 1453, to maintain communications with the outside world.

The sultan had returned to Edirne from Dimotika in the middle of January. Dayï Karaca Bey, governor of Rumelia, prepared the terrain for the army's advance, cutting down the vineyards in order to provide a free view into the city. Sections of the advance guard stormed the fortresses of Studius on the Marmara and Tarabya (Therapia) on the Bosporus, which were still in possession of the Greeks. Because the Byzantine garrisons had refused to surrender, the captured were hanged, in order that the inhabitants of Constantinople might see the corpses. Boat after boat brought *azaps, sipahis,* and all sorts of camp followers over from Asia. Under cover of the new coastal fortress, all were able to land unhindered. Finally Ishak Pasha, governor of Anatolia and husband of Murad's widow, also crossed over to Thrace. In answer to the call to arms, Rumelian troops poured over the roads from the west and north. The Serbian contingent, 1,500 superbly mounted men, had already arrived, but was never put to much use. In addition to artisans and merchants of all sorts, an indescribable horde of camp followers eager for booty had gathered for the occasion.

From Gelibolu, according to Phrantzes, a previously unobserved squadron of more than 300 vessels of varying size, incomparably superior to the opposing fleet, arrived under the command of Admiral Baltaoğlu Süleyman Bey, governor of Gelibolu; son of a Bulgarian boyar, he had won the young sultan's favor by his participation in the embassy to Buda in 1444 and his attack on Lesbos in 1449.

It is impossible to give a serious estimate of the Ottoman armed forces. The figures cited by contemporary observers vary widely. Chalcocondylas sets them at 400,000, Ducas at 265,000 (including 15,000 Janissaries), Phrantzes at 258,000, and Niccolò Barbaro at 165,000. But even the last-named figure is probably an exaggeration. The Ottoman Empire at the time was not large enough to muster 165,000 trained men. Any figure above 80,000 must have included the masses of camp followers who never failed to put in an appearance when a war was proclaimed against the infidel. For centuries the conquest of Constantinople had been represented, on the basis of an invented "tradition" (*hadith*), or saying of the Prophet, as the ultimate objective of Islam. Thus innumerable mullahs and dervishes of every conceivable order assembled that spring to fire the courage and fanatical faith of the soldiers, to participate in the meritorious project, and, it goes without saying, to share in the hoped-for spoils. Though the concentration of soldiers was probably no larger than in any other of the campaigns undertaken by the sultans of the time, it called for an enormous baggage train, which must also have included several thousand men.

In their account of the storming of Constantinople, the Ottoman historians never weary of citing the words of the *hadith* which on at least two occasions had fired the Arabs to make war on the Byzantine capital. The Prophet said to his disciples: "Have you heard of a city with land on one side and sea on the two other sides?" They replied: "Yes, O Messenger of God." He spoke: "The last hour [of Judgment] will not dawn before it is taken by 70,000 sons of Isaac. When they reach it, they will not do battle with arms and catapults but with the words 'There is no God but Allah, and Allah is great.' Then the first sea wall will collapse, and the second time the second sea wall, and the third time the wall on the land side will collapse. And, rejoicing, they will enter in." And even more famous than this spurious *hadith*, made to order for Constantinople, is the following equally inauthentic passage from the collection of "traditions": "They will conquer Kostantiniya. Hail to the prince and the army to whom that good fortune will be given."[17] [pl. X a]

The supreme commander of the Ottoman armed forces left Edirne on March 23, 1453, and arrived before Constantinople with his retinue on the morning of Easter Monday, April 2. A short while earlier the siege machines and the heavy artillery had been put in place. It had taken the whole of February and March to cover the two days' journey from Edirne to Constantinople with the giant cannon, hauled by fifty yoke of oxen and held in balance by 200 men. Road builders and engineers went ahead to prepare the road. Two cannon of smaller caliber arrived at the same time and were set up beside it. On the way Dayï Karaca Bey, to whose care the great cannon was entrusted, took advantage of the opportunity to overrun and capture several towns on the Sea of Marmara as well as the Black Sea. Misivri, Anchialus, and Vize (Byzon) fell at this time. Only Silivri and Epibatos (Bivados) put up fierce resistance and had to be passed by.

Mehmed pitched his camp at some distance from the city walls on the

---

[17] For another view of the "traditions" relating to the fall of Constantinople, see Louis Massignon, "Textes prémonitoires et commentaires mystiques relatifs à la prise de Constantinople par les Turcs en 1453 (= 858hég.)," *Oriens* 6 (1953), 10–17; reprinted in his *Opera Minora* II (Beirut, 1963), 442–450.

hill of Maltepe, facing St. Romanus Gate, which was to be the center of action. Some 12,000 Janissaries surrounded his tent. It was here that the great cannon and its two smaller companions were installed.[18]

The Anatolian army occupied the position to the right of the sultan, from Maltepe to the Sea of Marmara. The left wing, extending down to the Golden Horn, was held by the Rumelian army. Half of the forces, kept in reserve, were stationed behind the sultan's headquarters. The renegade Zaganos Pasha, third vizier and for a time the sultan's father-in-law, and Dayï Karaca Bey, with a few thousand men, occupied the heights beyond the Golden Horn behind Galata, and Kasïm Pasha a site on which a part of Pera now stands. In the early morning the army formed its ranks some two and a half miles from Constantinople. On the following day, Friday, April 6, the entire column advanced to within one mile of the beleaguered city. At the end of the Friday prayer, the beginning of the siege was proclaimed. The detachments took their appointed positions.

On the same day Emperor Constantine left his palace to take up his position at the Gate of St. Romanus, toward which the great cannon was pointed. He was to defend his post bravely to the end. At his side stood Giovanni Giustiniani-Longo with 500 Genoese soldiers. Altogether, 3,000 men occupied this dangerous and most menaced position. The rest of the small garrison was distributed along the seemingly endless circuit of the walls. The Greek cannon, of small size as compared to those of the Ottomans, were still too powerful for the walls, which trembled every time a cannon was fired. When the largest of the Greek cannon burst, a great fury arose against the cannoneer. Suspected of having been bribed by the sultan, he was threatened with execution, but was finally released for lack of proof. The so-called Greek fire was directed by a German, reportedly named Johann Grant. With it the Greeks had succeeded in burning an enormous siege machine, lined inside and outside with three layers of oxhide, which had helped to bring down the tower of St. Romanus during the night. In a single night the tower was rebuilt to the amazement of the sultan, who, according to Phrantzes, swore by the Prophet that he had never seen or heard of anything like it. In general it became clear after the first attempts to storm the walls that nothing

18 The Gate of St. Romanus is the Turkish Top Kapï (or Cannon Gate)-not to be confused with the name later given to the Ottoman palace at the opposite end of the city. For the identification of the numerous gates in the capital city, Alexander van Millingen, *Byzantine Constantinople* (London, 1899), is still useful. The most recent scholarly work on the topography of the Byzantine city is R. Janin, *Constantinople Byzantine* (Paris 1964).

could be accomplished by operations on the land side alone and that the Turkish fleet would have to take a hand. But for the moment developments at sea were also unfavorable. Three freight ships from Chios and an imperial vessel that had met up with them on its way from the Morea gave battle to the Ottoman fleet for several hours on April 20, and fought their way through, putting into the harbor of Constantinople during the night. This first defeat must have cost the Turks dearly. They were reported to have lost some 12,000 men and several ships. Sultan Mehmed, who from the shore saw his men giving way, was said to have flown into a towering rage and ridden into the sea in his fury; up to his waist in water, he shouted curses at the sailors and commanded them to regroup and stand fast. Admiral Baltaoğlu was called to account for his failure to rally his men; in his first surge of anger the sultan wished to have him impaled, and only the intercession of the Janissaries saved his life. He was deposed, flogged, and shorn of his possessions, which were distributed among the Janissaries. Hamza Bey was his successor.

Here we cannot take up the minor details of the final battle for Byzantium, which have been dealt with in countless monographs. We shall be able to consider only the most important happenings. In view of the part played by Western soldiers, one is inclined to agree with Iorga that the last defense of Constantinople was characterized more by Romance chivalry than by Greek religious enthusiasm. The supreme commander, or *protostrator*, as already mentioned, was Giovanni Giustiniani-Longo. The Venetian *bailo* Girolamo Minotto and members of such famous families as the Dolfin, Gritti, Loredano, Cornaro, Mocenigo, Trevisano, and Venier had their appointed posts. A considerable number of Genoese were present and gave a good account of themselves: Girolamo and Lionardo di Langasco, Maurizio Cattaneo, Paolo Bocchiardo, to mention only a few. There were Catalans under their captain Pere Julia, and the Spaniard Don Francisco de Toledo, the "new Achilles," allegedly a relative of the emperor Constantine. Prince Orhan was in command of a force defending one of the harbors on the Marmara shore. The commander of all the sea forces in the harbor was Alvise Diedo, captain of the Venetian trading fleet of Tana (Azov) on the Black Sea, whose sons Marco and Vettore also fought with distinction.

Sultan Mehmed seems to have relied far more on his mortars and cannon [pl. XI] than on deeds of romantic heroism. He expected greater results of his catapults, a whole dozen of which had been brought up to the walls by April 11, than from the use of his troops. But progress was slow and hardly in keeping with the sultan's expectations. One dark night (April 17) the Turks tried to take the city by a surprise attack. After a four-hour battle with the scantily distributed defenders, the assailants were obliged to withdraw. Turkish morale was not improved by the April 20 failure of the fleet in the skirmish against the four relief ships off the Marmara coast. However, on April 21 a section of the wall near St. Romanus Gate was demolished. Previously the defenders had filled in the gaps at night with tons of stone and rubble, but now, as the cannon fire became more and more intense, it was no longer possible to repair all the breaches quickly enough.

At this stage the sultan, undoubtedly advised by a Christian, conceived of a stratagem which soon put the defenders in an extremely precarious position. At a council of war held near the present-day Beşiktaş on the Bosporus, the grand vizier Halil Pasha, who appears to have been in league with the Greeks and to have repeatedly communicated information to them in return for rich rewards, tried to persuade Mehmed to make peace with the emperor, suggesting, it was said, that the sultan should demand the right to appoint police officials in Constantinople and exact an annual tribute of 70,000 gold pieces from the emperor. But Zaganos Pasha, the other viziers, and especially the sheikh Ak Şemseddin, foremost among the popular religious leaders who had joined the Ottoman camp with their followers, insisted that the siege be continued, and the council decided against Halil Pasha. In the course of the deliberations, it was observed that an attack on the land side alone was insufficient, while the boom frustrated every attempt to enter the harbor. The sultan's advisers were utterly at a loss until someone, allegedly the sultan himself, hit upon the idea of moving a part of the fleet overland to the harbor. It appears that plans were made that same night and carried out without delay.

The route from the present-day Bay of Dolmabahçe, near the southern end of the Bosporus, across the vine-covered hills to the north of Pera and down to the district now known as Kasïm Pasha, was cleared of underbrush, covered with planking, and in the steepest spots provided with railings. The track, which resembled a launching runway, was greased with sheep and ox tallow. Over this runway the ships were hauled on rollers from the Bosporus to the Golden Horn. First a few smaller vessels were transported as a test, then larger ones, until in the end a total of seventy-two ships had been moved. A part of the crews did the hauling; other sailors remained aboard, manning the sails and rudders, while still others cheered the work along with drums and trumpets. Amid the cheers of the crews and the deafening din of the kettle drums, the ships were launched swiftly, with sails billowing, into the waters of the Golden Horn, to the consternation of the Christians. There was no battle, and all the efforts of the besieged to destroy the intruders by fire were unsuccessful. Previously, while the Ottoman fleet was still outside the harbor boom, Iacopo Cocco, a Venetian sea captain, had attempted one dark night to attack the Turkish ships and destroy them with Greek fire. But as the Venetians were about to set the fire, the sentries raised an outcry and the entire Turkish fleet, allegedly apprised in advance of the plan by the Genoese in Galata, fell upon them. The crew of one sunken vessel, thirty-three men who had escaped by swimming, were captured and taken before the sultan, who had them executed the following morning within sight of the city. Such was the fury of the Greeks at this execution that all the Ottomans in the city prisons were dragged out to the walls and put to death.

On May 5, as the cannonade continued and the walls were on the point of giving way in a number of places, Mehmed had several cannon set up in Galata, whence they fired on all the ships in the harbor without distinction. When a Genoese merchantman riding peacefully at anchor was sunk and the Genoese protested to the sultan, they were dismissed with empty words. As if this were not enough, the sultan gave orders—on May 19, it is thought—to build a bridge across the Golden Horn just above the city walls; it was made with barrels which the Genoese had apparently put at his disposal. Fastened together with iron hooks, the barrels, nearly a thousand of them, served as pontoons, and over these were laid planks on which five men could easily walk abreast. Repeated efforts of the Greeks to set the bridge on fire met with no success.

Within the city shortages were felt more and more keenly and, especially among the troops, morale was dangerously low. Whenever the Ottoman fire slackened a little, whole bands of men left the walls and returned to their homes. Bread was distributed at various points, but the grumbling, stirred up by agitators, did not cease and, as Phrantzes reports, it often degenerated into open vilification of the emperor.

The sultan's army had already occupied the trenches on the land side and his fleet lay in the Golden Horn, directly under the walls of the hard-pressed city. At this point Mehmed resolved once again to send a legation to the emperor, but not, as some have supposed, in order to satisfy the rules governing Holy War (*jihad*, Turkish *cihad*) against the infidel. According to these rules, the prospective adversary should first be called upon to espouse Islam; if he refused, he was free to choose whether to accept Moslem sovereignty and pay tribute or to fight. Nowhere is it reported that Mehmed, in the course of his long reign, ever followed this rule. In the present case, he was probably more interested in

89

sending an experienced observer to investigate the state of the besieged city and its defenders than in offering the Greeks merciful conditions. And indeed, the emir of Sinop, Isfendiyaroğlu Ismail Bey, his brother-in-law, who had made a personal contribution to the preparations for the siege, went to Constantinople, not as the sultan's emissary but as the personal protector and patron of the Byzantines. Accordingly, he advised them to propitiate the sultan's rage and save themselves from slavery by surrendering. Constantine replied that he would give thanks to God if the sultan, like his forebears, should decide in favor of peace. He observed that none of Mehmed's ancestors who had besieged the city had enjoyed long life. Let the sultan exact tribute, but not the city itself, in whose defense all without exception were prepared to die.[19]

On receiving this response, the sultan on May 24 proclaimed that a general offensive by land and sea would begin on the 29th. The commanders were assembled, and the sultan solemnly swore to permit the army to pillage the city, reserving only the walls and buildings for himself.

From May 26 on, countless fires were seen burning in the enormous Turkish camp, especially at St. Romanus Gate, where the sultan had his headquarters. The entire army was drunk with the joy of anticipation. Criers proclaimed that those who were first to scale the walls would be rewarded with fiefs and high posts in the administration, while all who fled would be beheaded. Sheikhs and dervishes roamed through the camp and incited the army to plant the banners of Islam on the ramparts of the infidel capital, invoking the names of the Prophet and his personal companion Abu Ayyub, who had died before the gates during the Arab siege of Constantinople in 672. At night a general illumination was ordered. Torches and lamps were lit on every ship and tent. The shouting and jubilation were so overpowering that the besieged expected "the heavens to open." Meanwhile, according to Ducas, from the dark city rose laments and cries of supplication: "Kyrie eleison! Kyrie eleison! Avert from us, O Lord, thy just threats and deliver us from the hands of our enemy!"

In that terrible night Giovanni Giustiniani-Longo labored without rest to close the breaches in the walls. Near St. Romanus Gate, where the wall had been entirely demolished, he raised a new bulwark with bundles of branches and entrenched himself behind it. He sent a messenger to Lucas Notaras, the grand admiral and commander of the Greek troops, asking him for cannon. Notaras denied that they were needed in this particular

[19] For details of the particular legal obligations of the sultan in the matter of making war, see Majid Khadduri, *War and Peace in the Law of Islam* (Baltimore, 1955), 96ff. Inalcîk takes the opposite point of view regarding Mehmed's proposals of surrender, "The Policy of Mehmed II," *DOP* (23–24), 231–232.

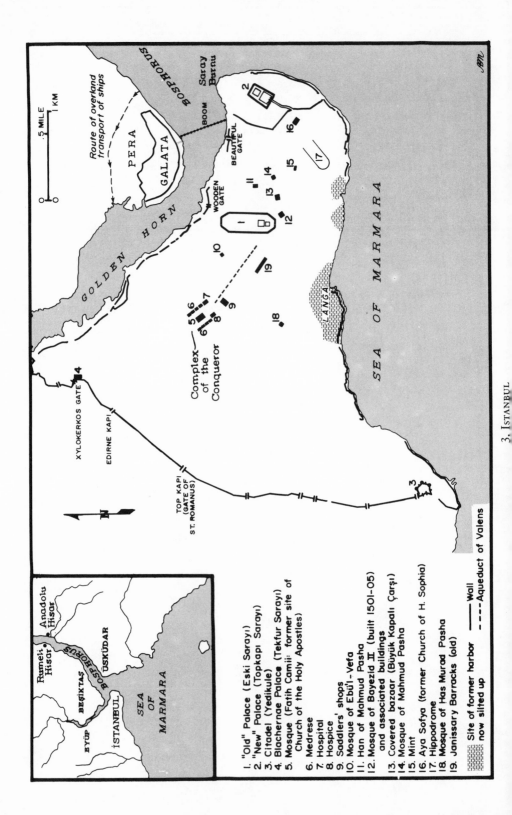

3. ISTANBUL

1. "Old" Palace (Eski Sarayı)
2. "New" Palace (Topkapı Sarayı)
3. Citadel (Yedikule)
4. Blachernae Palace (Tekfur Sarayı)
5. Mosque (Fatih Camii: former site of Church of the Holy Apostles)
6. Medrese
7. Hospital
8. Hospice
9. Saddlers' shops
10. Mosque of Ebü'l-Vefa
11. Han of Mahmud Pasha
12. Mosque of Bayezid II (built 1501–05) and associated buildings
13. Covered bazaar (Büyük Kapalı Çarşı)
14. Mosque of Mahmud Pasha
15. Mint
16. Aya Sofya (former Church of H. Sophia)
17. Hippodrome
18. Mosque of Has Murad Pasha
19. Janissary Barracks (old)

━━━━ Wall
━ ━ ━ Aqueduct of Valens

▨ Site of former harbor now silted up

spot. A bitter dispute ensued. Giustiniani called Notaras a traitor and enemy of his country, and at length the emperor himself had to arbitrate. Giustiniani was a true tower of strength, and for this reason the object of constant envy on the part of his rivals. Reports of his bravery seem even to have reached the sultan, who tried in vain to bribe him. In view of the miserable condition of the walls, however, all the skill and determination of the Genoese commander and his helpers were wasted. The Greek monks, who before the siege had been charged with repairing the city defenses (so we are told by Leonardo Giustiniani of Chios, archbishop of Mytilini),[20] had buried the money put at their disposal instead of spending it on the fortifications, 70,000 gold florins, which were afterward found by the Turks.

In the early morning of May 29, St. Theodosia's Day, the storming of the city began. Three hours before dawn the Turkish armies began to move. At first light Mehmed, in order to tire the Greeks, sent out his poorest troops, who were driven into battle with rawhide whips and iron rods. Whole bands of these Turks climbed the walls and were cut down by the enemy. Their siege machines were smashed and the losses were considerable. At daybreak an enormous din of trumpets, horns, and drums was heard. All available cannon were fired at once. And now the battle began on all sides, by land and sea. The Turks had worked all night bringing their vessels closer to the shore. Eighty biremes occupied a line from the Wooden Gate to the Beautiful Gate. From here on the rest of the ships extended in a double row around the whole city. The besieged knew where the main attack would occur. With some 3,000 men, Giovanni Giustiniani-Longo had advanced to the outer wall near St. Romanus Gate. Grand Duke Lucas Notaras covered the Blachernae quarter, and on the harbor side, from the Wooden Gate (*Odun Kapïsï*; Gate of the Drungarii) to the Beautiful Gate (*Horaia*, Gate of the Neorion; *Bahçe Kapïsï*), stood no more than 500 archers and slingers. The rest of the walls were thinly manned, with only one man to each watchtower and bastion.

The sultan in person drove the assailants on, bearing his iron staff and, as Phrantzes tells us, alternating cajolery and threats. Black powder smoke blanketed the city and obscured the bright May sun. Among the assailants there was a giant, Hasan, from Ulubad in Anatolia. With thirty others he scaled the walls; the defenders resisted with arrows and

[20] The eyewitness account of Leonard is given in translation in Jones, *The Siege of Constantinople*, 11–41.

stones. More than half the Turks fell to the ground and in the end the giant, with his shield over his head, met the same fate.

Inside the walls the defenders fought bravely, while the emperor rode among them, encouraging them by his words and his example. At this juncture a strange thing happened. Severely wounded in the arm or thigh, Giovanni Giustiniani-Longo, the hero of the day in whom all reposed their hope, lost heart and abandoned his post. No remonstrances, not even the emperor's earnest pleas, could restrain him. "My brother," Constantine cried, "fight bravely! Do not forsake us in our distress. The salvation of our city depends on you. Return to your post. Where are you going?" Giustiniani is said to have answered coldly, "Where God himself will lead these Turks." With these words he hastened to the Golden Horn, boarded a ship, and crossed over to Galata to have his wounds dressed.

The Turks were quick enough to note and take advantage of the confusion created by Giustiniani's defection. At the head of a detachment of Janissaries, Zaganos Pasha rushed to the walls near St. Romanus Gate. The defenders fled headlong to the inner gate. Many were crushed and thrown down to the ground. All serious resistance ceased. Finding the gate blocked by an enormous heap of corpses, the main body of the enemy burst into the city through a breach made nearby by the giant cannon. By then, the Turks were already inside the walls at the other end of the city. Kerkoporta Postern, near Xylokerkos Gate, had been well barred because of a prophecy to the effect that the enemy would first enter the city there, but the day before it had been opened for a sortie and left open by mistake. Passing through it, fifty Turks attacked the defenders in the rear and planted their banner on the wall. Now terror spread through the sparse group of defenders around the emperor at rumors that the city had been entered from the harbor. When Emperor Constantine saw the Turkish banner, he flung himself with his faithful followers into the thick of the fray, struck down every enemy within reach, and, even when wounded, carried on the hopeless battle almost single-handed. Convinced that all was lost, his men no longer listened to his commands. When Constantine realized that further resistance was impossible, he hurled himself at the on-surging Ottomans. "Is there no Christian here," he cried, "who will take my head?" Thereupon he fell under the blows of two Turks, one of whom struck him in the face, the other in the back.

So perished the last of the emperors of Byzantium, fighting like a common soldier. The Turks spent some time butchering the defenders until at length, seeing that there was nothing more to be feared from them, they desisted from the terrible massacre and proceeded to pillage the city. The remains of the defending army fled to the harbor and some of the fugitives managed to escape on Christian ships. But when the sentries at the gates saw the surging crowds they closed the gates and threw the keys across the walls, trusting in an old prophecy that the Turks would penetrate to the middle of the city but would then be hurled back by the inhabitants. Already, however, many of the brave defenders had made good their escape. Giovanni Giustiniani-Longo, who received the disastrous news aboard his ship, succeeded in reaching Chios, but died soon thereafter of a broken heart. Cardinal Isidor escaped to Galata disguised as a slave, and Antonio Diedo reached the Aegean Sea with a number of his ships. Betrayed in the course of his flight, Prince Orhan was overtaken and killed.

Meanwhile the crowd had flowed from the harbor side to Hagia Sophia where, in fearful disorder, men, women, children, nuns, and monks sought refuge, again encouraged by the superstitious belief that when the Turks reached the Column of Constantine an angel would come down from heaven, hand a sword to a poor man sitting by the column, and say, "Take this sword and avenge the people of God." Thereupon the Ottomans would immediately turn tail and, pursued by the Greeks, be driven not only from Constantinople but out of all Asia Minor to the borders of Persia, to the Tree Monodendrion. In a short time the whole church—vestibules, galleries, and aisles—was full to bursting. "If at that moment," writes Ducas, "an angel had really descended from heaven and cried out, 'Accept church union and I will drive your enemies from the city,' they would still have refused to profess union and would rather have surrendered to the Turks than to the Roman church."[21]

Breaking down the doors with axes, the Turks entered the church and dragged the fugitives off to slavery. Two by two, the men were tied together with cords, the women with belts, without consideration for age or station. Scenes of indescribable horror ensued. The statues of saints were shorn of their jewels and smashed. The gold and silver church vessels were seized, the altar cloths used for caparisons. Topped with a Janissary's cap, the crucifix was paraded in mockery. The conquerors used the altars as tables; when they themselves had finished eating on them, they turned them over to the horses for feed troughs or used them as beds on which to assault boys and girls. In describing these crimes, Ducas recalls the words of the prophet Amos (3:14): "That in the day that I shall visit the transgressions of Israel upon him I will also visit the

[21] For the legend of the ultimate rout of the Turks, see Apostolos E. Vacalopoulos, *Origins of the Greek Nation: the Byzantine Period, 1204–1461* (Rutgers, 1970), 202–205, and especially the sources in n. 114.

altars of Beth-el: and the horns of the altar shall be cut off, and fall to the ground." Phrantzes also gives a graphic and evidently faithful picture of the horrors enacted in the cathedral. Like wild beasts, inflamed by greed, the Turks fell upon their human prey. The prisoners were seized by their hands, beards, and clothing and dragged away. Churches and private dwellings, palaces and cloisters were searched and looted. Clothes, carpets, precious metals, pearls, jewels—everything that fell into the looters' hands changed its owner. Many Turks selected houses in which they planned to replace the slain or fugitive owner.

The sultan had not entered the city with his troops but remained outside the walls until, toward noon, he learned that Constantinople was wholly in the hands of the victors. At the wide-open St. Romanus Gate, where he had been encamped for almost two months, Mehmed received the news that Emperor Constantine was dead. He gave orders to search the camp for the corpse, and at length a Turk, who was later to be richly rewarded, announced that in the heap of corpses at St. Romanus Gate he had seen a man resembling the emperor. His report was followed up and the emperor was recognized by his purple shoes. The head was cut off and that same day set up on the column of the Augusteum, where it remained till nightfall, bearing witness to the Greeks that they no longer possessed a ruler. Soon thereafter Constantine's head was sent in a precious casket from one Moslem ruler to another, as a succinct announcement that Islam had triumphed over the Byzantine shadow empire. Where the body was buried remained unknown. Centuries later, the Greeks still revered the emperor's supposed tomb in Vefa Square, in a courtyard surrounded by wooden shacks. At nightfall they would light candles in his honor, until the Turks obliterated every trace of the tomb and only a solitary old willow trunk in the corner of the courtyard indicated the site of the emperor's neglected last resting place, a weather-beaten stone.[22]

Accompanied by a few viziers and courtiers, Mehmed II, from now on known as the Conqueror (*Fatih*), entered the city that afternoon on horseback. He went first to Hagia Sophia. On entering, his first glance fell on a Turk who, in a destructive frenzy, was hacking away at the marble floor with an ax. The sultan asked him why he was destroying the floor. "For the faith," the Turk replied. Enraged at such barbarism, Mehmed struck at him with his sword and cried, "Content yourselves with the loot and the prisoners. The buildings belong to me." Thereupon the half-dead ruffian was hauled away by the feet and tossed outside.

[22] See Vacalopoulos, 203, n. 113, for a reference to the sources.

Then the sultan commanded one of those present to go up into the pulpit and proclaim the Moslem creed: *Lâ ilâha illallâh; Muhammad rasûlullâh.* "There is no God but God. Mohammed is God's Prophet." The faithful were summoned to the afternoon prayer. Mehmed himself, we are told, leaped up on the altar and performed his devotions. With this the Byzantine Hagia Sophia ceased to be a Christian church and became a Moslem mosque, henceforth known as Aya Sofya.

Outside the looting continued. The imperial coat of arms with the double eagle was torn from the public buildings and the Turkish flag hoisted everywhere. At the sight of the Crescent waving nearby, the crews of the Turkish ships went ashore. Leaving their weapons on the beach in order to have their hands free for looting, they flocked into the city. A band entering a house for this purpose affixed a pennant to the door, and the sign was respected by other groups of looters. The monasteries and convents received special attention. A horde entered the Church of St. Saviour in Chora (subsequently known among the Turks as Kariye Camii, that is, Kariye Mosque), where the icon of the Mother of God "who points the way" was kept during the siege. The Janissaries hacked it into four pieces, which were distributed by lot.

Late in the afternoon the sultan sent for Lucas Notaras, the grand duke and grand admiral, who had been taken prisoner while trying to make his way to his sick wife and his children, and was being held under guard in his own house. When the sultan chided him, saying that he was to blame for the masses of dead and prisoners because he had refused to surrender, Notaras replied that neither he nor even the emperor had possessed sufficient authority to make the defenders surrender, especially after the emperor had received letters encouraging him to resist. The sultan understood at once that this was an allusion to the grand vizier Halil Pasha, whom he had long suspected of treasonable intrigue. Mehmed bade Notaras be of good heart, gave 1,000 aspers to each member of his family, promised to place him at the head of the city's administration, and graciously sent him back to his palace. He wrote down the names of all the state and court officials mentioned in the course of their interview, sent men to find them in the camp or ships where they were being held prisoner, and purchased the freedom of each one for 1,000 aspers.

The next day, May 30, 1453, the sultan, who reportedly had spent the night at the Franciscan monastery, rode back to the city, this time to the house of Lucas Notaras, who came out to meet him, welcomed him, and led him to his wife's sickbed. "Greetings, Mother," the sultan was quoted as saying. "Do not grieve over what has happened. The Lord's will be done. I can give you more than you have lost. For the present the best thing you can do is to get well." The grand duke presented his two sons and the sultan departed to inspect the city. Deathly silence prevailed in the deserted streets. Inside the houses the looters were still at work. In the course of his rounds, as we are told by Tursun Bey, an Ottoman chronicler who was usually a member of the sultan's immediate retinue, Mehmed mounted the dome of Hagia Sophia. "The ruler of the world," writes Tursun Bey, "contemplated the marvelous works and figures inside the dome and then deigned to mount the outside of the dome. He mounted as the spirit of God [that is, Jesus] mounted to the fourth story of the heavens. From the galleries of the intervening stories, he viewed the sea waves of the floor and then mounted the dome. When he saw that the dependencies and outbuildings of this imposing structure lay in ruins, he reflected that the world is transitory and unstable and would ultimately perish; of the sugar-sweet words which he uttered, deploring [this state of affairs], the following verse reached the ear of this poor man and engraved themselves on the tablet of his heart:

> *The spider serves as gatekeeper in the halls of Khosrau's dome,*
> *The owl plays martial music in the palace of Afrasiyab."*

According to others, the sultan uttered these words while viewing the desolate halls of the Blachernae Palace. It has not yet been discovered to what Persian poet they are attributable, or whether Mehmed himself composed them. In any case, if the Byzantine chroniclers are to be believed, the sultan prepared a great banquet near the imperial palace. Drunk with wine, he ordered the chief of the black eunuchs (*kizlar ağasi*) to go to the grand duke's home and bring back his youngest son, a handsome lad of fourteen. When the order was transmitted to the boy's father, he refused to comply, saying he would rather be beheaded than allow his son to be dishonored. With this reply the eunuch returned to the sultan, who sent the executioner to bring him the duke and his sons. Notaras took leave of his wife and, accompanied by his eldest son and his son-in-law Cantacuzenus, followed the executioner. The sultan ordered all three beheaded. The three heads were brought to the sultan; the bodies remained unburied. Notaras, popularly known as the "pillar of the Rhomaioi," had once declared, "Rather the Turkish turban in the city than the Roman miter." His wish had been fulfilled. The three Byzantine chroniclers Ducas, Chalcocondylas, and Phrantzes, who all relate the incident in detail, abound in mournful reflections and homilies.

Critoboulos gives a different version of the grand duke's tragic end. According to him, Notaras was a victim of the "envy and hatred" of his adversaries, who had slandered him to the sultan. After the enraged sultan had executed Notaras and his two sons, he learned of the slanderers' treachery and malice, dismissed them all from his presence, had some executed and the rest shorn of their positions and privileges. Notaras was believed to be enormously wealthy; this perhaps largely accounted for the total extermination of his family. The same fate befell a number of prominent Westerners who had taken part in the defense of the city, in particular, Girolamo Minotto, *bailo* of Venice, accused of being a "breaker of the peace," his son, and Pere Julia, the Catalan consul, and two of his sons. Forty-seven other Venetian noblemen, who had also been taken prisoner, received permission through Zaganos Pasha to purchase their life and freedom with heavy ransoms. Most of them paid, according to their name and rank, from 1,000 to 2,000 ducats. Seven thousand were asked of Iacopo Contarini, the defender of Studius.

The spoils were enormous: many thousands of prisoners, costly garments, rich fabrics, gold, silver, and above all jewels, which the Janissaries, unaware of their value, bartered for next to nothing. Even the gold, according to Chalcocondylas at least, was often sold for copper. Heaps of the rarest and most magnificent books were thrown in the fire because there was no one to pay the negligible price for which they were offered. The damage incurred by the foreign settlements, notably those of the Italian maritime states of Ancona, Amalfi, Genoa, and Venice, was enormous. The losses of Venice alone were estimated at 200,000 gold pieces. Years later the Turks still referred familiarly to a rich man as one who had taken part in the pillage of Constantinople.

On the third day Mehmed put an end to the looting. The army was ordered back to its camp. The fleet returned to its bases with the greater part of the spoils, under whose weight the ships were close to sinking. Admission to the city was barred under heavy penalties.

Silivri and Epibatos, the two fortresses that had successfully resisted Dayï Karaca Bey, surrendered quietly after the fall of the capital, thus leaving all Thrace in Ottoman hands.

The two Byzantine islands of Lemnos and Imroz, however, managed to evade occupation. At the bad news the Byzantine officials and many Greek inhabitants had fled, but Critoboulos, who was then a judge on Imroz, remained and managed to persuade the sultan to assume sovereignty peacefully and at the same time to bestow the islands on the Gattilusi brothers. Lemnos was given to Dorino I, lord of Mytilini, and

Imroz to Palamede, lord of Enez (Aenos, Inoz). Both had, of course, to pay an annual tribute to the Turks.[23]

The first of the Western powers to receive news of the end of East Rome and the tragic death of the bravest of the Palaeologi was Venice. As the council was meeting on June 29, 1453, letters arrived from the castellan of Methoni (Modon) and the *bailo* of Negropont. Alvise Bevazan, secretary to the Council of Ten, read the frightful news aloud. Such were the general grief and consternation that no one dared to ask for a copy of the reports. From Venice the news went out in all directions. The Signoria dispatched it to Pope Nicholas V on June 30 and it became known in Rome on July 8. According to all reports, the effect on the pope and the cardinals was crushing. Nicholas V sent envoys to the Italian powers to persuade them to cease their internecine quarrels and join forces against the infidel.

Everywhere it was felt that a turning point in history had been reached. The overpowering impression produced by the event showed that Constantinople outweighed whole countries in importance. On the frontier between two continents, where until now the successors of Constantine the Great had ruled over Eastern Christendom, the archenemy of the Christian faith had now established himself. It has rightly been pointed out that this constant menace, which filled all souls with anxiety and paralyzed the Western spirit of enterprise, was bound to exert a disastrous influence on the inner life of the nations and to prevent the peaceful "surmounting" of ecclesiastical and social evils. With good reason the year 1453 has been designated as the dividing line between the Middle Ages and the modern era.[24]

[23] The story of the conquest has been narrated in detail many times, most recently in English by Steven Runciman, *The Fall of Constantinople 1453* (London, 1965), in which is found a bibliography of the major Western sources. To these may now be added Nicolò Barbaro, *Diary of the Siege of Constantinople 1453*, trans. J. R. Jones (New York, 1969). None of the relevant Turkish sources, dealt with summarily by Runciman, has been translated into English. For a German translation of the contemporary Aşıkpaşazade see below, n. 55. The Greek Critoboulos later wrote his account of the years 1451–67 for the sultan: Kritovoulos, *History of Mehmed the Conqueror*, trans. Charles T. Riggs (Princeton, 1954).

[24] Schwoebel, *The Shadow of the Crescent*, 1ff., gives more details regarding the impact in the West of the news of the fall of Constantinople. Five historians deal more broadly with the consequences of that event in lectures given at a symposium in London on the 500th anniversary of the conquest in *The Fall of Constantinople* (School of Oriental and African Studies, 1955). The essays are by S. Runciman, B. Lewis, R. R. Betts, N. Rubenstein, and P. Wittek.

Apart from the pope and Venice, it was principally from Hungary that Byzantium had hoped for help, for at this time Hungary was one of the most powerful states of Christendom and moreover had every reason to feel directly threatened by the Turkish peril. Thus it may be worth our while to recall briefly the part played by Hungary in that decisive period.

In order to prepare adequately for the siege of the Byzantine capital and to carry out his plans undisturbed, Mehmed was forced to safeguard himself against any surprise from the West. This alone can explain why, immediately after his accession to the throne, he sent a friendly message to the bitterest enemy of John Hunyadi, Count Ulrich of Cilli, brother-in-law of his stepmother Mara. Dissension had just broken out between Hunyadi and the partisans of Cilli and this was beginning to undermine Hunyadi's influence. In order to feel fully secure against the Christian nations, the sultan found it necessary above all to establish passable relations with Hungary. For this reason he concluded in September 1451, as we saw, a three-year truce with the Hungarian regent. Two months later, on November 6, 1451, a clause was added to the treaty, forbidding the sultan to build fortifications along the Danube. It seems probable that the Serbian despot George Branković helped to negotiate this agreement, for it was at that time that he was visited by Mehmed's delegation in charge of mediating the peace with the Hungarians. Only after thus safeguarding his rear against the West did the sultan turn against the lord of Karaman in the summer of 1451.

At the beginning of 1452, to distract attention from his military preparations against Byzantium, he circulated the rumor that he was planning an expedition against Hungary. This report terrified not only the Hungarians but the Byzantines as well. Still wary lest the West mount a concerted attack on his empire, with Hungarian participation, the sultan sent emissaries to the various Christian countries with orders to ferret out any plans that might be afoot. When they returned with the news that discord reigned in the Christian camp and that all was calm in Hungary, the construction of Rumeli Hisar was nearing completion, so that for the moment the danger of an attack, at least from the Black Sea, was averted.

It is possible that despite all his vigilance the sultan was unaware of the serious negotiations then in progress between Emperor Constantine XI and John Hunyadi for Hungarian aid to Constantinople. These negotiations were carried on, probably in the first days of September 1452, by a Byzantine legation. At the end of October a Hungarian legation reached Constantinople by sea and promised the requested military aid on condition that their troopships be permitted to enter Misivri, to ensure a concerted and sufficiently powerful attack on the Ottomans from sea and land. The emperor and his council of war haughtily refused the offer, declaring that they intended to defend their fortresses with their own forces. According to Ubertino Pusculo of Brescia, who celebrated the events in verse, the Hungarian intermediaries returned home without having settled anything. The Hungarian request actually may have been prompted by ulterior motives. Indeed, if the chronicler Phrantzes is to be believed, John Hunyadi had demanded sovereignty over Misivri and Silivri, wishing to station there a large contingent of troops with which to come to the help of the capital in case of a siege. There is no reason to doubt Hunyadi's offer of assistance, but he may very well have wished thereby to fulfill Hungary's old dream of permanent access to the Mediterranean. Such a project was more likely to succeed than a large-scale attack on the Ottomans from the West by an army that would have to pass through the entire Balkan peninsula. This was the bitter lesson of the unsuccessful expedition of Varna.[25]

When the situation became increasingly menacing, the emperor abandoned his obstinate opposition to the Hungarian request. In the first weeks of the year 1453 he issued a Golden Bull (*chrysoboullon*), composed by Phrantzes, making over Misivri to John Hunyadi. A special envoy of the emperor hastened across the Danube to convey the document to Hunyadi in person. Too late! Before the siege of Constantinople had begun Dayï Karaca Bey, as we have seen, had already taken possession of the well-fortified Misivri and the other fortresses on the western coast of the Black Sea.

At the same time changes were taking place in Hungary. In December 1452, Ladislas V Posthumus, who had been held captive by Emperor Frederick in Vienna, was released and mounted the throne; John Hunyadi ceased to be regent. Mehmed was at the gates of Constantinople when, in the first days of April, a delegation arrived from Hunyadi informing the sultan of the modified situation and at the same time denouncing the three-year armistice, half of which had run out. The delegation returned the document in question and asked for a receipt.

[25] For the position of Hunyadi at this time, Constantine's secret last-minute acceptance of his offer, and later discussions between Hungary and the rulers of Milan and Florence, see F. Pall, "Byzance à la veille de sa chute et Janco de Hunedoara (Hunyadi)," *Byzantinoslavica* 30 (1969), 119–126. See there note 2 for references to the poem of Pusculo. G. Moravcsik deals briefly with the role of Hungary at the time of the conquest in his *Byzantium and the Magyars* (Amsterdam, 1970), especially 100–102. Cf. idem, "Ungarisch-Byzantinische Beziehungen zur Zeit des Falles von Byzanz," *Acta Antiqua* (Budapest) 2 (1954), 349–360; reprinted in the same author's *Studia Byzantina* (Amsterdam, 1967).

Mehmed was informed that he could do with the king of Hungary as he wished. Ducas relates that one of the Hungarian envoys, observing the incompetence of the artilleryman in charge of the giant cannon, smiled and taught him how to aim and fire it properly. Some of the Hungarian chroniclers deny this story; others, in an odd way, try to minimize its importance. They explain that an aged soothsayer had told Hunyadi after the battle of Kosovo that the ill fortune of the Christians would cease only after Constantinople had been destroyed by the Turks. Hunyadi, according to these writers, had denounced the peace treaty in order to gain a free hand and, trusting in the oracle, to come to the aid of Constantinople after its fall. What task fell to another Hungarian delegation, which was with the sultan during the last week of the siege, and whether it too had been sent by Hunyadi or by the new king, it is difficult to decide on the basis of the available material. It is certain that this delegation threatened war in case the sultan should not come to an agreement with Byzantium. Mehmed and his council of war delayed dismissing the ambassadors. When Byzantium had fallen, the Conqueror left them free to decide as they wished. Now that he was master of Constantinople, the question of peace or war was a matter of indifference to him.

On June 2 the young sultan busied himself with the Genoese in Galata. Lists of inhabitants were drawn up; the houses of those who had fled by sea were entered but not looted. Inventories were made and it was proclaimed that the property of those who failed to return within a period of three months would fall to the state treasury. Mehmed gave orders to raze the walls of Galata, but left those on the sea side standing. During the siege the Genoese had already sent emissaries to the sultan's tent who were empowered to renew the long existing treaties. Mehmed promised them peace and friendship, but insisted that the Genoese must not give help of any kind to the Greeks in Constantinople. The agreements were sworn to on both sides and observed, at least outwardly, by the Genoese. On May 29, 1453, Angelo Lomellino, *podestà* of the Genoese of Galata, had sent the keys of the city to the sultan, and on June 1 the rights and liberties of the inhabitants of Galata were confirmed in a formal treaty, written in Greek, the original text of which has been preserved in London. This firman, drafted and signed by Zaganos Pasha, guaranteed the people of Galata security of life and property; their sons were not to be enrolled in the Janissaries; there was to be no interference with their churches and cult. But they were forbidden to build new churches or to make use of bells and wooden gongs (semantrons). Turkish soldiers and civilians were forbidden to enter the city of Galata.

The resident Genoese were permitted to carry out their commercial affairs undisturbed and tax-free, while merchants from Genoa itself were under obligation to pay the legal duties. The citizens were subjected to the poll tax; further, they were free to choose an elder whose duty it would be to supervise the observance of custom, law, and justice in the conduct of commerce. They were constrained to surrender their weapons, cannon, and ammunition, and to attend to the razing of walls as mentioned above.[26]

After the conquest Mehmed spent twenty-four days in Constantinople or, as it was now called, Istanbul (from the medieval Greek *is tin polin*, "into the city") or Stambul.[27] Not until the night of June 21, 1453, did he return to Edirne, taking with him a long train of booty, including Greek women and young girls. Among the prisoners was the widow of Lucas Notaras, who died and was buried along the way, near the village of Misinli (Messene). It was now that the grand vizier Halil Pasha met his fate. Three days after the conquest he was thrown into a dungeon and on the fortieth day of his imprisonment, on July 10, 1453, having meanwhile been moved to Edirne, he was executed. He was found to have left 120,000 ducats in cash, which was confiscated by the state treasury. His two aides in office, Yakub Pasha and Mehmed Pasha, were also shorn of their possessions, and Halil's friends were forbidden to mourn for him. The sultan had long suspected the grand vizier of taking bribes from the Greeks, as we have already seen in the incident related above which took place between the two men in the palace at Edirne. One day when Mehmed saw a fox tied to the gate, he cried out, "Poor fool, why did you not turn to Halil and buy your freedom?" Frightened at these words, the vizier decided to evade Mehmed's wrath by going on a pilgrimage to Mecca, but shortly after, reassured by a message from the sultan, he postponed his journey. However, Mehmed's secret rancor and distrust did not die down until Halil Pasha, whose family (the Çandarlï) had provided four grand viziers in unbroken succession, had paid with his life for his crimes.[28]

[26] For the document discussed here, see T. C. Skeat, "Two Byzantine Documents," *The British Museum Quarterly* 18 (1953), 71–73, where references are given to discussions of the firman. Mehmed's treaty with the Genoese is given in translation by Jones, *The Siege of Constantinople*, 136–137.

[27] For a recent discussion of the names of the city, and particularly the use of "Istanbul," see Steven Runciman, "Constantinople-Istanbul," *Revue des études sud-est européennes* 7 (1969), 205–208. Cf. "Istanbul," (H. Inalcïk), *EI²* III, 224.

[28] The sources disagree concerning the date of the grand vizier's execution. Inalcïk proposes that it did not take place until late summer. See his review article, "Mehmed the Conqueror (1432–1481) and His Time," *Speculum* 35 (1960), 412.

From Edirne letters of victory went out to the friendly Moslem sovereigns.[29] The envoys of neighboring Christian states and islands who gathered at the Conqueror's court to congratulate him were informed that their annual tribute had been increased. In August 1453, emissaries from the despot George Branković appeared at the court of Edirne, where they gave generous alms to the prisoners and on the despot's instructions ransomed 100 nuns of all ages from slavery; the despot was ordered to send an annual tribute of 12,000 ducats, 10,000 ducats were demanded of the two despots in the Morea, while the Genoese rulers of Chios and Lesbos were to pay respectively 6,000 and 3,000 gold pieces a year. Similarly, 2,000 ducats were exacted from Emperor John IV Comnenus of Trebizond and from other cities of the Black Sea coast. Dubrovnik sent neither delegation nor tribute, although it had incurred the displeasure of the Porte by its hospitable reception of Greek refugees, among them members of the Comnenus, Laskaris, Cantacuzenus, and Palaeologus families, and by welcoming such distinguished Byzantine scholars as Constantine Laskaris, Demetrius Chalcocondylas, Theodoros Spandugino, and Paulos Tarchaniotis, before sending them on to the court of Cosimo de' Medici in Florence. Venice began negotiations at once, whereas the grand master at Rhodes successfully refused to pay tribute.

After the fall of Constantinople, the slave trade must have flourished extraordinarily, especially in Edirne. So many of the inhabitants had been carried off from Constantinople that the ancient capital was seriously depopulated, a situation which Mehmed was determined to correct as quickly as possible. On his departure, he had appointed a certain Karïştïran Süleyman Bey as prefect (*subaşï*) of the city, and left behind a garrison of 1,500 Janissaries. Süleyman Bey was commissioned to clean the city, to repair the damaged walls, to adapt the city administration to Turkish ways, to appoint Turkish officials, and especially to replenish the population by bringing back former inhabitants and by newly settling others. The necessary resettlement measures were quickly taken; in particular, the inhabitants of conquered cities were sent to Istanbul. The transplanted populations of the various towns were assigned each to different quarters which were named after them; some of these names have been preserved to this day. Greeks driven from the Morea were situated not far from the new patriarchate, in the Fener (Phanar) quarter. Numerous Jewish families were brought from Thessaloniki, for it was thought that their commercial ability would do much to restore the

---

[29] For these letters of victory, together with the replies, see Ahmed Ateş, "Fatih Sultan Mehmed tarafından gönderilen mektuplar ve bunlara gelen cevablar," *Tarih Dergisi* (Istanbul) 4 (1952), 11–50.

prosperity of the deserted city. This practice was maintained for many years; at each new conquest new settlements were founded in Istanbul, so that twenty-five years after the conquest the new capital of the Ottoman Empire sheltered some 60,000 to 70,000 souls. The census taken in 1477 by the city judge Muhyiddin lists 14,548 inhabited houses and 3,667 shops.[30]

Perhaps the most important measure inaugurated by Mehmed before the end of 1453 and concluded in the first months of the following year was the election and consecration of a new patriarch according to the traditional ritual and custom. The few archpriests and laymen who had remained in the city soon agreed on the monk Gennadius, formerly the layman George Scholarius, who during the siege had fled from his monastery, been captured by the Turks, and sold as a slave in Edirne. Mehmed had him brought back to Constantinople and at the beginning of the new year, on January 6, 1454—and not, as most historians have written, in the summer of 1453—Gennadius was consecrated by the metropolitan of Heraclea (Marmara Ereğlisi) and installed in his new office. Before the ceremony, the sultan sent for him, received him with special honors, and invited him to share his repast. On his departure, Mehmed presented him with a precious scepter and, in spite of the priest's protestations, escorted him into the courtyard, and ordered that all the Turkish dignitaries present should accompany him to the patriarchate. On a palfrey provided by the sultan, Gennadius rode to the Church of the Holy Apostles, which had been assigned to him as his official residence in place of Hagia Sophia, now transformed into a mosque.

Soon, however, when this site was taken over for the Mosque of the Conqueror, Gennadius transferred the patriarchate to the Church of the Pammakaristos, which was itself later (1573) turned into Fethiye Camii (the Mosque of Victory). Mehmed ordered a document issued to Gennadius to the effect "that no one should vex or disturb him; that unmolested, untaxed, and unoppressed by any adversary, he should, with all the bishops under him, be exempted from all taxation for all time."

By decree the members of the Orthodox church were granted three privileges: first, that their churches not be transformed into mosques; second, that no one interfere with their marriages, funerals, and other church rites; third, that they be free to celebrate Easter with all its rites and that during the three nights of the celebraion the gates of Fener, the Greek quarter, remain open. In conquered Christian cities the sultans

[30] For more complete information from this census see below, p. 354. Further details of the revitalization of the city occupy a major portion of Inalcīk's paper "The Policy of Mehmed II," *DOP* (23-24), 229-249.

had always respected the juridical prerogatives of the bishops and metropolitans, allowing them to retain certain of their revenues and dignities.
But quite aside from this precedent, there is no doubt that in the present
case Mehmed aimed, by preserving the hierarchical structure of the Orthodox church, to perpetuate an institution that could be expected to serve
his designs and to compensate to a degree for the present inadequacy of
the civil administration. And Mehmed's installation of the Orthodox
patriarch served still another purpose: it demonstrated that the supreme
spiritual authority, not only of the Greeks but also of all Oriental Christendom, had fully recognized the new state of affairs. Thus, at the very
inception of Turkish rule over Byzantium, any thought of resistance on
the part of the new subjects and payers of poll tax was rendered unthinkable.

Gennadius held three terms as patriarch, with his last appointment in
1465. Later he retired to the remote monastery of St. John Prodromos,
situated in a picturesque, well-watered ravine on the flank of Mount
Menikion (Boz Dağ), near Serrai. Here, after a life of danger and excitement, he engaged in intensive theological studies. Alone and forsaken,
he died shortly after 1472.[31]

Mehmed's installation of Gennadius as patriarch of the Greek Christians has recently been characterized as incompatible with Islamic law,
on the ground that Constantinople did not surrender voluntarily but was
taken by force (*cebren*). In this view, Mehmed's protection of the Greeks
and their church was one of several instances in which he disregarded
the law. By his tolerance, the argument continues, he hoped to take the
ground from under any possible crusading movement on the part of the
West. It is perfectly possible that in pursuing a policy of indulgence,
Mehmed looked beyond the situation of the moment; it is equally possible
that his purpose was to hasten the repopulation of the deserted city at a
time when Moslems, despite official encouragement, were showing no
great eagerness to settle in the new Istanbul. Quite conceivably the choice
of Gennadius, known for his hostility to Rome, was intended to discourage any thoughts of church union, which would surely have been un-

---

[31] See C. J. G. Turner, "The Career of George-Gennadius Scholarius," *Byzantion*
39 (1969), 420–455, for the life of the first patriarch under Ottoman rule in Constantinople. Cf. also n. 46 below. While no original documents survive, there is
general agreement that Mehmed gave the new patriarch a written declaration
elaborating the rights of the Orthodox community. On the exact nature of the
decree, there is less agreement. See, for example, the discussion in Gibb and Bowen
I, part 2, 216. Steven Runciman treats the broader history of the Orthodox church
in its relation to the Turkish conquerors in *The Great Church in Captivity* (Cambridge, 1968).

welcome to the sultan. There is no doubt that the rights granted the patriarch were very considerable and amounted to the establishment of a Christian state within the state. But it is certain that Mehmed committed no offense against Islamic law.

The concessions which Mehmed had made to the patriarchate did not prevent him from turning one church after another into a mosque. Most of the murals and mosaics in these churches were covered with whitewash. "For obscure reasons" (*per occulta causa*) the sultan gave orders, however, that the mosaic of the Mother of God in the half-dome of the choir apse of Hagia Sophia should be spared. A hundred years later the mosaic was still covered with only a veil, but subsequently it too was painted over. Only in recent years have workmen begun, ever so carefully, to remove the coating from the mosaics; many of them have reappeared in all their radiance and splendor, to the amazement and admiration of all who behold them.[32]

The smaller churches were stripped of their lead roofs, which—as Ducas sorrowfully relates—were used as building material for the sultan's new palace.

Among the few inhabitants of Constantinople to have survived the Turkish seizure of the city were the Jews of the Balat quarter. Not long after the appointment of Gennadius, or perhaps at the same time, Mehmed also selected a chief rabbi to preside over all the Jewish congregations of Turkey. His choice fell on Moshe Capsali, a man of piety and learning, founder of a celebrated family of scholars; Elijah Capsali, who in the sixteenth century wrote a Hebrew history of the Ottoman Empire that is still awaiting publication, may have been descended from him. The sultan, we are told, even made him a member of the imperial council (*divan*), where he was honored by a seat next to the mufti, thus gaining precedence over the Greek patriarch; furthermore, he delegated to Capsali certain political powers over the Jewish congregations of Turkey. It was Moshe Capsali who assigned the taxes to be paid individually or collectively by the Jews, appointed officials to collect them, and transmitted the proceeds to the sultan's treasury. He also possessed penal authority over all members of the Jewish community and the right to confirm the appointment of rabbis. In a word, he was the head and official representative of the Jewish community in the Ottoman Empire.

Under the Conqueror, if the accounts of Jewish contemporaries are to be believed, Turkey was a paradise for the Jews, who were cruelly oppressed in Western Europe. Jewish emigrants from Germany were over-

[32] Further details of the fate of several churches in the capital are given by Runciman, *The Fall of Constantinople*, 152–153 and 199ff.

joyed at the favored position of the Jews in Turkey. They were free to live and trade as they pleased. There was no "golden penny" to pay, no crown taxes amounting to a third of their fortune. They could dispose freely of their property and dress as they saw fit, in silk and satin if they wished. Their enterprise found rich sources of profit, though it is true that they were soon obliged to limit their activities to commerce and moneylending. In 1454 Isaac Sarfati, a Jew born in Germany of French descent, sent a circular letter to the Jews of the Rhineland, Swabia, Styria, Moravia, and Hungary in which he spoke with enthusiasm of the fortunate conditions of the Jews under the Crescent in contrast to their yoke under the Cross, and encouraged his coreligionaries to leave the "great torture chamber" and come to Turkey. The years that followed witnessed a massive emigration of Jews to the Turkish paradise, especially from Germany. Certain countries, Italy in particular, prevented their Jews from leaving.[33]

From the human booty seized in Constantinople, Mehmed seems to have selected persons suited for his court and to have taken them with him to Edirne. Unfortunately, we have no reliable information concerning this measure. In his "Letter on the Fall of Constantinople" (*Epistola de excidio Constantinopolitano*), Angelo Giovanni Zaccaria, *podestà* of Pera, laments that Mehmed had taken his nephew because he "wishes to have a few Latins at his court." It is certain that this was not the only example of its sort, but this record, which has come down to us by pure chance, is the only reference we possess to an individual case. Above all, numerous Greeks were carried off to the Porte, especially those who had filled important administrative posts in Constantinople.[34]

Historians have taken a grossly exaggerated view of the institutions and customs supposedly taken over by the Turks from the Byzantines at the

[33] For Sarfati's letter see below, p. 412. A standard account of the Jews in the Turkish capital is Abraham Galanté, *Histoire des Juifs d'Istanbul*, 2 vols. (Istanbul, 1941–42). See especially, I, 49ff. For the position of Jews in the Ottoman Empire in the 16th century, see Israel M. Goldman, *The Life and Times of Rabbi David Ibn Abi Zimra* (New York, 1970). Mayer A. Halévy, "Les Guerres d'Etienne le Grand et du Uzun-Hasan contre Mahomet II, d'après la 'Chronique de la Turquie' du Candiote Elie Capsale (1523)," *Studia et Acta Orientalia* 1 (1958), 189–198, gives an appraisal of the value of the history referred to by Babinger. More recently on the chronicler Capsali: Charles Berlin, "A Sixteenth-Century Hebrew Chronicle of the Ottoman Empire: The *Seder Eliyahu Zuta* of Elijah Capsali and its Message" in Berlin (ed.), *Studies in Jewish Bibliography, History, and Literature. In Honor of I. Edward Kiev* (New York, 1971).

[34] For reference to the letter of the *podestà*, see Schwoebel, *Shadow of the Crescent* 2, n. 11.

time of the conquest; in most cases there is no justification for this dating. The greater part of these customs and institutions were already traditional with the Turks, having been acquired by the Ottomans of Anatolia in the course of their dealings with the Byzantines in the thirteenth and fourteenth centuries. Another fanciful theory, based on the fact that the geographical expansion of the Ottoman Empire followed very much the same pattern as that of the Byzantine Empire (just as the gradual loss of border regions was similar in both cases), is that by its acquisition of Constantinople, the Ottoman Empire somehow became the political successor of Eastern Rome, inheriting notably its Mediterranean claims and projects. Such a theory throws little light on the policies of the sultans, which resulted almost inevitably from geographical realities and political events.

It seems possible, though not certain, that after the conquest Mehmed took over the crescent *and* star as an emblem of sovereignty from the Byzantines. The half-moon alone on a blood red flag, allegedly conferred on the Janissaries by Emir Orhan, was much older, as is demonstrated by numerous references to it dating from before 1453. But since these flags lack the star, which along with the half-moon is to be found on Sassanid and Byzantine municipal coins, it may be regarded as an innovation of Mehmed. It seems certain that in the interior of Asia tribes of Turkish nomads had been using the half-moon alone as an emblem for some time past, but it is equally certain that crescent and star *together* are attested only for a much later period. There is good reason to believe that old Turkish and Byzantine traditions were combined in the emblem of Ottoman and, much later, present-day Republican Turkish sovereignty. The Arabic epithet *Ebu'l-Feth*, that is, "Father of the Conquest," by which, side by side with *Fatih*, "Conqueror," Mehmed began to be known after the conquest of Constantinople, goes back many years and was applied to Seljuk sultans at the beginning of the thirteenth century.[35]

During the summer of 1453 Mehmed, as his panegyrist Critoboulos wrote, spent thirty-five days in Anatolia, where, as the Ottoman chroniclers remark, he went to the mountains to rest from the strain of the preceding months. He seems, however, to have returned to Edirne before

---

[35] For a recent view of the problem of Byzantine influence on Ottoman tradition and institutions see Speros Vryonis, "The Byzantine Legacy and Ottoman Forms," *DOP* 23–24 (1969–70), 251–308. Detailed references are given to earlier works on the subject. Cf. idem, *The Decline of Medieval Hellenism in Asia Minor and the Process of Islamization from the Eleventh through the Fifteenth Century* (Berkeley, 1971), especially 463ff. For the specific problem of the use of crescent and star in Islamic and other Near Eastern societies see *EI²*, vol. III, 381–385, "Hilāl" (R. Ettinghausen).

the end of August, for according to Ducas, the Serbian delegation mentioned above was received there in that month.

The sultan spent the autumn and winter in his capital, presumably occupied with the construction of his palace on the Tunca island. The fact that work on these extensive buildings continued immediately after the conquest of Constantinople makes it seems unlikely that Mehmed was thinking at this time of moving his capital to that city. But he seems to have changed his plan very quickly, for the so-called Old Serai in Istanbul was begun in the following year.[36]

In early spring of 1454 Mehmed, feeling fully secure in his rear, sent emissaries to the despot George Branković, then almost eighty years of age, bearing a message which, according to Ducas, ran as follows: "The land you rule over does not belong to you but to Lazar's son Stjepan, and consequently to me. I can cede to you the share of Vuk, your father, as well as Sofia. If you refuse, I will fall upon you." But a far more plausible pretext for hostilities was provided by the despot's irregular payment of the annual tribute and his recent alliance with Hungary. Mehmed appears to have demanded certain lands of the despot, including the castle of Golubac on the Danube, the "Taubersburg" of the German chronicles, and the capital city of Smederevo. We are told that Mehmed gave the emissaries twenty-five days in which to obtain the despot's consent to his demands and threatened dire punishment in case of failure. Meanwhile, Branković had fled across the Danube to Hungary; the Serbs detained the Ottoman legation under all manner of pretexts, so gaining time in which to fortify the threatened towns and supply them with provisions. When thirty days had passed with no sign of his emissaries, the sultan left Edirne with his army for Philippopolis, where he met the emissaries on their way back from Serbia. According to Ducas, the despot escaped with his life only through flight to Hungary and the resulting delay in the return of the mission to the sultan.

The Hungarians themselves had meanwhile crossed the Danube and proceeded to pillage the countryside. Mehmed left his retinue and the main body of his army in Sofia and moved west, allegedly at the head of 20,000 *sipahis*. The despot had advised his followers to take refuge behind the walls of the fortresses until help came from the Hungarians. Mehmed divided his army into two columns, one of which approached Ostrovica and the other Smederevo. Ostrovica, situated on a steep rock

---

[36] The conflicting evidence of the chronicles for the chronology of the sultan's travels in Turkey in the months following the conquest is discussed by Inalcik in "The Policy of Mehmed II," *DOP* (23–24), 236–237, where he proposes a slightly different itinerary.

(altitude 2,500 feet) northwest of the mining city of Rudnik, and Smederevo on the Danube were the main strongholds of the Serbian plain, which the Ottoman cavalry were ranging and pillaging almost unhindered. Fifty thousand people were carried off to Istanbul as slaves and settled in the surrounding villages. Smederevo put up fierce resistance, even after the outer wall of the powerful fortress had been forced, while Ostrovica, whose garrison had attempted a vain sortie, was pounded to rubble by the Ottoman cannon. Promised that they would be permitted to withdraw unharmed, the defenders opened the gates of the fortress, but were carried off to slavery by the Turks in disregard of their oaths. The place was renamed Sïrfiye Hisar (Sivrice Hisar). Mehmed ordered the siege of Smederevo to be discontinued and returned by way of Sofia to Edirne with numerous prisoners: he kept the fifth to which he was entitled for his court.[37]

In Serbia, at Kruševac (which the Turks called Alaca Hisar) on the Morava River, Mehmed had left Firuz Bey behind with approximately 32,000 men to resist George Branković and, if necessary, John Hunyadi. The two were not long in attacking. Firuz Bey and his army were defeated; he himself was taken prisoner and brought before the despot in Smederevo (October 2, 1454). Hunyadi ravaged the region of Niš and Pirot, burned Vidin, and after this brilliant cavalry expedition, returned to Belgrade, near which he was met by the despot and his son-in-law Count Ulrich of Cilli. Two Serbian armies were set up, one on the blood-soaked field of Kosovo, the other near Leskovac in the region of Glubočica. Nikola Skobalić, who commanded the second, defeated the Turks advancing from Macedonia at Vranje (September 24, 1454), but in a second battle further south was defeated (November 16), taken prisoner, and impaled alive. The frightful devastation of the country in the course of these battles brought about a mass flight of the starving population. Many went as far as the Adriatic.

Unable to take a personal hand in all these hostilities, Mehmed had entrusted the conduct of the Serbian campaign to his march wardens. On April 18, 1454, he had come to terms with the Venetian Signoria, which two months previously (February 12) had concluded a treaty with Ibrahim Bey, the Grand Karaman, the eternal mutineer and mortal enemy of the Ottomans. On the basis of former treaties between Venice and

---

[37] Elizabeth Zachariadou gives additional details on the events and time of this campaign in "The First Serbian Campaigns of Mehemmed II (1454, 1455)," *Annali* n.s. 14 (1964), 837–840. The identification of Sïrfiye Hisar (Sivri or Sivrice Hisar, according to most authors) with Ostrovica is uncertain. On the fifth part of the booty claimed by the sultan, see Irene Beldiceanu-Steinherr, "En marge d'un acte concernant le pengyek et les aqingi," *Revue des études islamiques* 37 (1969), 21–47.

the Porte, the merchants of both states were accorded freedom of trade in the territories of the other; the duke of Naxos, as tributary of the Venetian Republic, was included in the peace; the taxes of the Venetian possessions in Albania were established at the same amounts as under Murad II; the Venetians were accorded the right to maintain an ambassador (*bailo*) in Istanbul for the protection of their subjects; and finally, they were confirmed in their possession of Negropont. This was a mild treaty, almost taking on the appearance of a diplomatic victory for the Venetians when we consider the sultan's niggardly treatment of their Genoese rivals, many of whose Levantine possessions he soon would ruthlessly destroy; on these occasions Venice regularly seized every opportunity to improve her own position.

The negotiations leading to the new agreement had been conducted by Bartolomeo Marcello, beginning in the latter part of 1453; he had performed the unpleasant task of apologizing to the sultan in the name of the Signoria for the part played by his compatriots in the defense of Constantinople, while saying as little as possible about the murder of Venetian citizens, especially the *bailo* Girolamo Minotto, and the theft of their property. Marcello subsequently became the new Venetian ambassador, the first to the newly conquered Turkish city. He remained at his post until 1456, when he was succeeded by Lorenzo Vitturi.

It is certain that he was accompanied by Niccolò Sagundino (d. March 22, 1464, in Venice), who had been sent from his native Negropont and commissioned by the Signoria to help Marcello in his difficult negotiations. By September 25, 1453, when Marcello sent him back to Venice, Sagundino had gained an accurate insight into the conditions prevailing among the new masters of Constantinople. As a result the pope summoned him to Rome, also arranging for him to submit his report to King Alfonso of Aragon in Naples. The particulars of Sagundino's communications to Rome and Naples are unknown to us, but we do know what he committed to writing, at the behest of the king of Aragon, after delivering an address (*oratio*) on January 25, 1454. His memorandum is extant in several manuscripts and an abstract of it was printed. This *Oratio Nicolai Sagundini edita in Urbe Neapoli ad Serenissimum principem et novissimum regem Alfonsum* is probably the oldest *relazione* concerning the Ottoman Empire; no similar report has come down to us concerning the period before 1496, not even among Marino Sanudo's résumés in his sixty-volume *Diarii*, in which he kept a running account of all transactions of the Signoria.[38]

[38] For the works of Sanudo and especially his *Diarii*, see D. S. Chambers, *The Imperial Age of Venice: 1380–1580*, 197. Cf. F. Babinger, "Marino Sanuto's Tagebücher als Quelle zur Geschichte der Safawijja," in *A Volume of Oriental Studies,*

It seems highly unlikely, however, that Marcello was also accompanied by Giàcomo de' Languschi, whose unusually graphic and succinct description of the twenty-two-year-old sultan was saved for us by Zorzo Dolfin in his *Cronaca*: "The sovereign, the Grand Turk Mehmed Bey, is a youth of twenty-six, well built, of large rather than medium stature, expert at arms, of aspect more frightening than venerable, laughing seldom, full of circumspection, endowed with great generosity, obstinate in pursuing his plans, bold in all undertakings, as eager for fame as Alexander of Macedonia. Daily he has Roman and other historical works read to him by a companion named Ciriaco of Ancona and another Italian. He has them read Laertius, Herodotus, Livy, Quintus Curtius, the chronicles of the popes, the emperors, the kings of France, and the Lombards. He speaks three languages, Turkish, Greek, and Slavic. He is at great pains to learn the geography of Italy and to inform himself of the places where Anchises and Aeneas and Antenor landed, where the seat of the pope is and that of the emperor, and how many kingdoms there are in Europe. He possesses a map of Europe with the countries and provinces. He learns of nothing with greater interest and enthusiasm than the geography of the world and military affairs; he burns with desire to dominate; he is a shrewd investigator of conditions. It is with such a man that we Christians have to deal."

And further: "Today, he says, the times have changed, and declares that he will advance from East to West as in former times the Westerners advanced into the Orient. There must, he says, be only one empire, one faith, and one sovereignty in the world."[39]

These remarks, which Mehmed must have made soon after the fall of Byzantium, throw a bright light on his underlying political aim: the subjection of the Occident to his scepter.

The next tasks confronting Mehmed were to restore the future capital of his empire to its old splendor and to strengthen his central administration. We are told that in the summer of 1454, at the spot where the tomb of Abu Ayyub, the Prophet's standard-bearer, was believed to have been

Presented to Professor E. G. Browne (Cambridge, 1922); reprinted in *A&A* I, 378–395.

[39] The work of Zorzi Dolfin is edited by G. Thomas in *Sitzungsberichte der königlich bayerischen Akademie der Wissenschaften, philos.-hist. Klasse* 2 (1868). A Turkish translation of the preceding was published by Suat and Samim Sinanoğlu as "1453 Yılında Istanbul'un Muhasara ve zapti," *Fatih ve Istanbul* I, part 1 (1953), 19–62. A part of Zorzi's *Cronaca*, including a more extensive quotation from Languschi (Langusto), is now available in Jones, *The Siege of Constantinople*, 125–130.

found during the siege of the previous year, Mehmed laid the foundation stone of a white marble mosque, in the simplest style, without columns, its dome sustained by four large pillars of masonry. Until fairly recently the mosque of Eyüp, like the enormous cemetery surrounding it, was a cult site forbidden to all non-Moslems. It was to become a kind of coronation mosque. Here the new sultan was girded with the sword of the Emir Osman by the superior of the Mevlevi dervishes; here holy relics of Islam, such as Mohammed's footprint cast in silver, were sometimes, in later years, safeguarded from the eyes of infidels.

The miraculous discovery of the tomb in a thicket not far from Eğri Kapı was long ago relegated to the realm of fable by serious scholarship. The story was a later invention; according to this legend, Mehmed, seeing that his army was losing heart, bade the dervish sheikh Ak Şemseddin look for Abu Ayyub's last resting place. His search was successful, the troops regained their courage and enthusiasm when they heard the news, and the city was soon taken. The fact is that this pious fraud is not mentioned in any contemporary source and that the story was not thought up until much later. None of the missives sent by Mehmed to the Moslem world, not even his letter to Mecca, contains one word about the Prophet's companion-in-arms.

Considerations of style and building technique make it seem unlikely that Mehmed erected the mosque as early as 1454 or, as elsewhere stated, 1458; it was probably built considerably later. Only the tomb of Abu Ayyub and a small part of the outer court can have been built in the fifteenth century. It is no less questionable that Mehmed was the first sultan to have been girded with the sword of his ancestor; in all likelihood, this ceremony, comparable to the Western rite of consecration and coronation, was not instituted until long after the conquest.[40]

The sultan seems to have decided in the same year to build a palace in Istanbul on the former site of the Forum of Theodosius, where Leo the

---

[40] While the present-day mosque at Eyüp is a late 18th-century reconstruction, it is generally agreed by architectural historians that Mehmed originally ordered its construction, probably five years after the conquest. For details, see Ekrem H. Ayverdi, *Fatih devri mimarisi*, 216–217. Following his lead are Aptullah Kuran, *The Mosque in Early Ottoman Architecture* (Chicago, 1968), 226, and Godfrey Goodwin, *A History of Ottoman Architecture*, 131. For the tradition of the Mevlevi role in the girding of the Ottoman ruler, see F. W. Hasluck, *Christianity and Islam under the Sultans* II (Oxford, 1929), 604–622. For the venerated Arab companion of the Prophet and the Turkish sheikh in Mehmed's entourage who reputedly found his tomb, see respectively: "Abu Ayyūb" (E. Levi Provencal, J. H. Mordtmann, Cl. Huart), *EI*² I, 708–709, and "Aḳ Šams al-Dīn" (H. J. Kissling), *EI*² I, 312–313; also Hasluck, 714–716.

Great had built the city's true capitol, the Palatium in Tauro. It has been supposed that this circumstance impelled Mehmed to choose this location for the palace that was to house his government. But this is pure conjecture. He was probably more influenced by the charm and magnificence of the location, which has few equals in the city.

The Old Serai took four years to complete. Its extensive grounds, surrounded by a high wall, included buildings of all kinds, which after a few years ceased to be used for their original purpose. In later years the Old Serai was used only to house the imperial harem, where the sultan ordinarily spent a few nights a week. The area of the palace was considerably reduced by Süleyman the Magnificent (1520–1566), Mehmed's great-grandson, who, taking a part of the grounds for the Süleymaniye Mosque and the Mosque of the Prince (Şehzade Camii), authorized his first viziers to build their palaces on another part of the grounds. In 1714 the palace went up in flames. Until the reign of Mahmud II (1808–1839) the buildings erected after the fire were again used for the harem housing the wives of dethroned or deceased sultans. Long after they were torn down in 1870 they were popularly referred to as the Old Serai (*Eski Saray*). Today the site is occupied by the University of Istanbul, whose buildings were previously used by the Ministry of War (*Seraskerat*). No vestige remains now to recall the first palace of the conqueror of Constantinople.

After the execution of Çandarlïoğlu Halil Pasha, in July 1453, the office of grand vizier remained unoccupied for over a year. All crucial decisions ordinarily within the province of the grand vizier were made by the sultan. When he decided to appoint a new grand vizier, Mehmed kept the presidency of the *divan*, the crown council, for himself, while the supreme command of the army was given to the first vizier. This state of affairs seems to have continued until the last years of Mehmed's reign. The *divan* met on four consecutive days, from Saturday until Tuesday; everyone had the right to appear before it and state his desire. Then the *divan* turned to its regular business, which remained in the hands of the viziers, whose number, under Mehmed, was increased from three to four. The first, or grand vizier, presided over the council as the sultan's representative and supreme head of all branches of the administration. He enjoyed special privileges, the most important of which under Mehmed were: custody of the imperial seal with which the doors of the treasury were sealed when the *divan* was in session; the right to hold a special afternoon *divan* (imperial council) in his own palace; the right to be escorted by a marshal, the so-called *divan bey*, and by all the state messengers (*çavuş*) from his own to the sultan's palace and back, and on

Friday during the procession to the mosque; the right to be waited on every Wednesday by the army judges (*kazasker*) and the treasurers (*defterdar*) wearing the same official turbans as at court; the right to be attended by the so-called lords of the imperial stirrup at the Monday divan. His remaining privileges had to do with ceremonial precedence and need not be listed here.[41]

Critoboulos alone tells us that Ishak Pasha held the post of grand vizier for a brief time. But in the summer of 1454, at all events, Mehmed conferred it on one of the most remarkable figures in Ottoman history, whose achievements and tragic fate are still remembered by the Turkish people. This was Mahmud Pasha Angelović. Apart from the Cantacuzeni, the most distinguished family of the Serbian despotate was that of the Angeli of Thessaly, descended from Alexius III Angelus Philanthropenus, Byzantine emperor (1195–1203), or his brother or son, Manuel Angelus, despot of Thessaloniki (1230–1240). Another branch of the Angeli had furnished the despots of Epirus (1204–1318). A late descendant, Michael Angelus, resided at Novo Brdo, where he married a Serbian woman; presumably about 1427, while fleeing to the Danube from her home, she was taken prisoner by Turkish cavalrymen and carried off to Edirne with others. One of her sons was taken into the service of the Ottoman court, where he soon attracted attention by his talents, converted to Islam, and became friendly with the crown prince Mehmed Çelebi. Not long after Mehmed became sultan for the second time, the young man was appointed governor of Rumelia. It was to this man that Mehmed now entrusted the imperial seal. Mahmud Pasha had a brother, Michael Angelović, who had stayed in Serbia; he too rose quickly to high state office and later, as we shall have occasion to see, played an important role as his brother's agent. Their mother, who remained a Christian, moved to Istanbul; for a time, at least, she enjoyed the sultan's favor and was rewarded with landed property.[42]

At the same time other changes seem to have been made in the cabinet. The second vizier, Saruca Pasha, the trusted favorite of Mehmed's father, appears to have been deposed and exiled to Gelibolu. Zaganos Pasha too, although his daughter had found favor in Mehmed's eyes and been taken

---

[41] For a discussion of the *divan* and its composition in the time of Mehmed II, see K. Dilger, *Untersuchungen zur Geschichte des Osmanischen Hofzeremoniells im 15. und 16. Jahrhundert* (Munich, 1967) 37ff.

[42] For an alternate interpretation of the chronology of grand viziers under Mehmed, according to which Mahmud Pasha did not reach this highest office until 1456, see Inalcık, "Mehmed the Conqueror," 413–415. Mahmud Pasha's ancestry remains uncertain. (Cf. Babinger's own remarks below, p. 196.) For references to the sources, see "Mahmud Paşa" (M. C. S. Tekindag) *IA* VII, 183–188.

into the imperial harem, fell into disgrace and was banished, along with his daughter, to Balïkesir, where he perhaps owned large estates. A mosque endowed by him and the tombs of his family have been preserved to this day. Zaganos Pasha's second daughter was married to the newly appointed grand vizier, Mahmud Pasha; to him she had borne a son, Ali Bey, whose only title to fame, despite his illustrious origin, was his endowment of pious works in the region of Edirne. He seems to have been the last of a glorious line, related even to the Comneni.

After the fall of Constantinople an extraordinary number of educated Byzantines succeeded in escaping to the West, particularly to Italy. The Italian courts were crowded with these learned refugees, who were at first received with enthusiasm but, with certain exceptions, gradually lost much of their prestige and popularity; many returned home to their native land, preferring the Turkish yoke to the lives of unappreciated schoolmasters under the Latins. For as they began to arrive in ever greater numbers, most of them without a farthing to their name, the veneration with which these supposed "descendants of the Homeric heroes and ancient Athenians" were at first received turned to aversion. Though owing their livelihood to the generosity of their hosts, they were unable to put aside their Byzantine arrogance; they became sullen and moody because, deprived of their accustomed comforts, they were obliged to wander from place to place, flattering the great. Their hosts were of the opinion that they would have done better to adapt themselves to the customs of their new home, to trim their silly beards, and to stop giving themselves such stupid airs (Georg Voigt). Furthermore, they showed a strange ineptness for learning Latin and the Italian vernacular. Only a few achieved any measure of proficiency in these tongues, and the Latins, who were making every effort to learn Greek in their eagerness to discover the treasures of Greek literature, regarded most of them as lazy and obstinate. "The sluggish Byzantine blood simply did not mix with the easy-flowing blood of the Italians" (G. Voigt).[43]

Of course there were notable exceptions, figures such as Cardinal Bessarion, Joannes Argyropoulos, Theodoros Gaza, Constantine Laskaris, to mention only a few. Along with other Byzantine scholars who had found a livelihood as teachers of Greek at Italian universities, they played a leading role in saving Greek culture and the works of classical Greek literature for humanity. Many of the fugitives, especially the poor Greek priests, whose ranks included a number of estimable scholars, made only

[43] Babinger refers to Georg Voigt, author of *Enea Silvio de' Piccolomini als Papst Pius der Zweite und sein Zeitalter*, 3 vols. (Berlin, 1856–63).

the barest of livings copying *exemplaria graeca*. Certain of them—as, for example, the learned Aristotelian Joannes Argyropoulos, the Cretan Joannes Rhosos, Demetrios Sgunopoulos, whose names we find at the end of their copies along with lamentations about their exile—were assuredly born to higher things than the copying of books. Pope Nicholas V, not to mention the courts of northern Italy, especially the Medici, and Naples as well, earned everlasting merit by employing more than one "victim of the Erinyes," as one of the copyists called himself at the end of a volume. Many manuscripts were carried to safety in Italy; Cardinal Bessarion alone valued at 15,000 ducats the library of 900 volumes which he bequeathed to the Venetian Republic. But little solicitude was shown for this precious heritage. Even in Venice, where most of the Greeks landed— so that Venice came to be looked upon as the natural intermediary between the Greek East and the Occident, a "second Byzantium"—we find plaints written as late as 1490 about manuscripts left to rot in their crates. Not until much later did the world-famous library of San Marco, whose nucleus was supplied by Bessarion's manuscripts, give this heritage the place of honor it deserves.[44]

Far more numerous than the scholars were the adventurers and soldiers of fortune who were driven to the West, especially to Italy, by the fall of Constantinople. Here there is no better source of information than the entries of the court treasurers. In the registers of the Kingdom of Naples, the strangest figures are listed as recipients of alms and assistance: David, the self-styled Ottoman prince, "a relative of the Grand Turk"; the Tunisian ambassador to Mehmed II, captured in the port of Syracuse; real or alleged chamberlains to the emperor of Byzantium, such as "misser Dimitri Caleba"; such scions of the Palaeologi as Manuel or "Paleolo, Grech; gentilhomen de Contastinoble [!]"; Giovanni Torcello, the shady courtier and nobleman, and his brother Manuel. Of all types and from all walks of life such men were quick to avail themselves of the initial generosity of the Italian princes.

While Greek scholars were disseminating Greek culture in Italy, Mehmed was busily engaged, with the help of Italian advisers, in amassing information about the Western world, its geography and political situation, its rulers, its faith, its quarrels, its art of war, and its armies.

---

[44] Steven Runciman provides a useful background sketch for this movement of scholars in *The Last Byzantine Renaissance* (Cambridge, 1970). For more details of the several figures mentioned, see Schwoebel, *The Shadow of the Crescent* (especially chap. 6); also the closing pages of Kenneth Setton's "The Byzantine Background to the Italian Renaissance," *Proceedings of the American Philosophical Society* 100 (1956), 1–76.

Immediately after the conquest if not before, he gathered round him a number of "Latins," who gladly offered him their services to this end. According to Giàcomo de' Languschi, whose testimony we have already cited, Mehmed studied the geography of Italy and possessed a map of Europe, on which the kingdoms and provinces were indicated. With the help of his Italian humanist advisers, he had built up a collection of classical works for use in his studies. Along with others which he may have found in Constantinople after the conquest, these books constitute the main body of the mysterious library of the serai, which for centuries fired the imagination of Western scholars; very mistakenly, they supposed it to contain the most precious treasures of classical antiquity, such as the lost books of Livy. Down to our times the naïve and sometimes touching romanticism of the European scholars who attempted, often amid the greatest difficulties and dangers, to penetrate this palace library has aroused vain hopes and speculations.[45]

The critical examination of those manuscripts in the serai which may plausibly be assigned to the Conqueror's library leaves no doubt concerning their purpose. If we disregard the classical source works, there remain a number of religious manuals, referring mostly to Christianity, Bibles, and so on, which clearly indicate Mehmed's interest—purely practical, no doubt—in Christianity as the religion of the Occident. His instructors in this field were probably for the most part Greeks; we possess, for example, numerous copies and editions of a Turkish translation done in 1455–1456 of a Credo written by the patriarch Gennadius, which unmistakably served to instruct the sultan. Ciriaco de' Pizzicolli seems to have been chief among the sultan's Italian teachers in the years before and after the conquest. Francesco Filelfo refers to him as the sultan's "secretary" in a despicable letter to Mehmed in which, writing from Milan on March 11, 1454, he asks for the release of his mother-in-law, Manfredonia Chrysoloras, and her two daughters. The letter abounds in fulsome adulation of the sultan and obscene vilification of those whom he accuses of enslaving his relatives, namely, the Jews—a view certainly not shared by the sultan.[46]

[45] Babinger discusses the palace library in his "Mehmed II., der Eroberer, und Italien," 128 and 136–145. See also E. Jacobs, "Mehmed II., der Eroberer, seine Beziehungen zur Renaissance und seine Büchersammlung," *Oriens* 2 (1949), 6–30.

[46] An English translation of the confession of faith written by Gennadius is given by A. Papadakis, "Gennadius II and Mehmet the Conqueror," *Byzantion* 42 (1972), 88–106. The article includes also a useful bibliography on Byzantine attitudes toward Islam. Cf. Aurel Decei, "Patrik II. Gennadios Skolarios'un Fatih Sultan Mehmet için yazdığı ortodoks i'tikad-namesinin türkçe metni," *Fatih ve Istanbul* 1 (1953), 98–116. For the letter of Filelfo to Mehmed, see the reference in Schwoebel, 151,

Reference has already been made to the consternation and despair aroused by the fall of Constantinople, especially in Italy, where the threat was felt most keenly. Setting aside all concern for the fate of the Occident and considering only its own advantage, Venice had been the first European power to enter upon negotiations with the young Ottoman ruler, so successfully indeed that the sultan had consented to the appointment of a *bailo* in Istanbul. Such was the general indignation aroused by this act of betrayal that the Signoria felt impelled to justify its conduct in a tortuous letter of apology to the pope (December 15, 1453).

Genoa, after Venice the Italian state most directly involved, was at first unwilling to believe the terrible news, which, however, was soon confirmed. Weakened by internal strife and the war with Naples and fearful of losing their Levantine and Aegean possessions, the Genoese tried to organize a concerted drive for peace among the Christian nations, but finally in their perplexity and despair could think of no better solution than to cede their Black Sea possessions by treaty (November 15, 1453) to the Uffizio (later Banco) di San Giorgio, whose importance at the time has aptly been compared to that of the East India Company. This enormous credit establishment, which had become a state within the state, seemed to exhausted Genoa to represent the last hope. But Kaffa (Turkish Kefe; now Feodosiya) on the Crimean Chersonese, Genoa's most important trading post on the overland trade route to Persia and India by way of Astrakhan, was not to escape unscathed. In the summer of 1454 a unit of the Ottoman fleet, reported to consist of fifty-six vessels, entered the Black Sea, unsuccessfully attacked Akkerman (Italian Moncastro, Romanian Cetatea Alba; now Belgorod-Dnestrovski), took Sevastopol (Sebastopol; the Tatar Aktiar) by storm, and finally on July 11 appeared off Kaffa. Haci Giray, the khan of the Crimea and an ally of the Ottomans, appeared before the walls of the city at the head of 6,000 mounted Tatars; he accomplished nothing, however, and had to content himself with hostages and a tribute payment of 6,000 *somme*, or 1,600 ducats. Now a messenger from the sultan demanded an annual tribute of 8,000 pounds, but was told that the decision in this matter rested with the Uffizio di San Giorgio. Soon thereafter, in any case before the end of the year, Kaffa did agree to pay an annual tribute of 3,000 ducats, in return for which the Genoese received permission from Mehmed to ship a

---

n. 13. A Turkish translation of the letter, as well as the eulogy by the same Filelfo, are given (together with the Greek texts) by Vl. Mirmiroglu, *Fatih Sultan Mehmet ve Francesko Filelfo* (Istanbul, 1956).

limited quantity of grain through the Bosporus. The land route through Poland and Hungary, used for messengers and mercenaries bound for Kaffa, was never satisfactory for commercial shipments.

Moved by blind hatred of Venice, Milan, under the *condottiere* Francesco Sforza, took advantage of the republic's dilemma immediately after the fall of Constantinople to invade the region of Brescia. Sforza's ally, the Florentine Republic, shared his feelings toward Venice and Naples; in fact, the Florentines were overjoyed at the setback incurred by Venice in the Levant. When in July 1453 Nicodemo Tranchedini, envoy of the duke of Milan, presented himself in Florence, he went so far as to declare, "I too hope that things will fare badly with Venice, but not in this way, not to the detriment of the Christian faith, and I have no doubt that you are of the same opinion."

As for Naples, King Alfonso declared grandiloquently in the spring of 1454 that he would step forward as the avenger of Christendom and personally take the lead in a crusade. He was widely regarded as the man for such an undertaking. His rule extended from Aragon, Catalonia, Valencia, and the Balearic Islands to Naples, Sicily, and Sardinia. With the exception of Corsica, which belonged to the Genoese, he controlled the whole western Mediterranean. By his example, Alfonso declared, he hoped to impel the princes of the West to make war on the Turks and drive the infidels out of Europe. But the crafty politician never went beyond these high-sounding words. Once the tranquillity of the next few months convinced him that there was no imminent danger, he grew more chary of his promises. The one thing the Aragonese sovereign was really interested in was maintaining his dynasty, and he had no intention of compromising its future by uncertain undertakings.

The situation to the north of the Alps was not very different. Concern over the threat to Christendom diminished with the distance separating a country from the Ottoman Empire. Christian I, king of Denmark and Norway, compared the Turks with the beast rising out of the sea in the Apocalypse and called upon God to witness his own eagerness to take up arms against the monster. Empty words! All the Western sovereigns professed their readiness to take part in a crusade against the Ottomans. But none took the decisive step from words to deeds. Nothing could be expected of the Scandinavian countries. King Charles VII of France did not so much as deign to reply to Francesco Filelfo's letter arguing in favor of a crusade; the war with England seemed far more important than the struggle against the common foe in the East. The appeals addressed by the Holy See to all the states of Christendom fell on deaf ears. Sick and bitterly disillusioned by the recent events, Nicholas V could offer little more than his powerless papal word. His treasury was exhausted, and the return of peace in Italy, prerequisite to any crusade, seemed further off than ever. In vain the papal legates tried to persuade the powers of Christendom to make peace among themselves and join in a common crusade against the Ottomans.

For a time it seemed as though Emperor Frederick III, whose first duty it was, according to medieval conceptions, to defend the common interests of Christendom, would take serious action. He had been deeply moved by the fall of the Byzantine Empire and the sad fate of the Palaeologi. Under the influence of his famous adviser, Enea Silvio Piccolomini, bishop of Siena, later Pope Pius II, the timid, irresolute emperor was prepared to act for the first time in years. When he received the news of the fall of Constantinople from Venice, he retired to his quarters, burst into tears, and spent several days in seclusion, praying and meditating on the uncertainty of human affairs. Enea Silvio, who was perhaps the man who stood closest to him at the time, gave a moving account of this incident to the estates of the empire. The bishop and imperial secretary, a man of keen intelligence and versatile mind, did his utmost to convince the emperor that he must take the lead in the war of the Christian world against the Turks. In this Piccolomini saw his own life mission, and to its fulfillment he attached the highest hopes for the restoration of Christian unity under the aegis of the pope. "Already Mehmed rules among us," the bishop wrote on July 12, 1453, to Pope Nicholas V.

Already the sword of the Turks hovers over our heads; already the Black Sea is closed to us; already Walachia is in the hands of the Turks. Thence they will invade Hungary and then Germany. Meanwhile we live in discord and enmity. The kings of England and France have taken up arms against each other. Seldom is all Spain at peace and the Italian states can never find peace in their struggle for hegemony. How much better it would be if we were to turn our weapons against the enemies of our faith! I can think of nothing that might be more to Your Holiness's desire, Holy Father.

To this appeal, only a few sentences of which are here reproduced, Emperor Frederick III, in a letter of almost the same tenor, added his promise to convoke all the princes of the empire and enlist their forces against the enemies of the "cross of salvation." Deeply impressed by these declarations, Nicholas V, some two months later, issued the strange bull in which he represents Sultan Mehmed as the precursor of the Antichrist and compares him to the red dragon of the Apocalypse, bearing seven heads with seven diadems and ten horns. In the style of previous encyclicals calling for a general crusade, he summons all the princes of Christendom to defend the faith with their possessions and their blood, and promises universal indulgence to all who, beginning February 1, 1454, should personally take part in the holy war or supply a substitute. Let every warrior, the bull continues, display the cross on his shoulder. The Church would contribute financially to the holy undertaking. The Apostolic treasury would set aside for the purpose all receipts from benefices large and small, archbishoprics and bishoprics, abbeys, monasteries, and convents. The cardinals as well as all officials of the Curia, down to the lowest ranks, were to be taxed one-tenth of their revenues. A general tithe was to be imposed throughout Christendom, and failure to comply would be punished by excommunication. Heavy penalties would be imposed on all those who should treasonably supply the infidels with arms, ammunition, or provisions. The states of Christendom, so the encyclical concluded, must make peace with one another, or at the very least a truce must be strictly observed. Recalcitrants were menaced with excommunication, or in the case of whole communities, with interdict.[47]

The pope's message to the Christian princes failed to produce the desired effect. Its principal weakness, as has often been pointed out, was its overemphasis on the financial aspect; by threatening the faithful in their pocketbooks, it turned their hearts away from the holy cause. It met with a paralyzing indifference and even Enea Silvio, despite his zeal for the Holy War, was none too enthusiastic about the tithe.

The relative calm of the months following the fall of Constantinople lulled many princes and nations into supposing that the danger from the East was not as urgent as had been feared under the first shock. Only Emperor Frederick III and Hungary remained on their guard. Having undertaken certain obligations toward the Holy See at the behest of Enea Silvio, the emperor could not simply relapse into his accustomed inactivity, which had once led the horrified bishop to remark that Frederick III hoped to "conquer the world sitting down." Accordingly, he convoked a diet at Regensburg for the spring of 1454 and issued a formal invitation to the Italian states and Philip the Good, duke of Burgundy. But he himself did not attend. The difficult situation in his hereditary states, the religious ferment in Bohemia, and the intrigues of the Hungarians were his excuses. The soul and guiding spirit of the diet was Enea Silvio, who headed the imperial delegation. The estates were extremely slow in arriving. Engaged at the time in negotiations with Mehmed, Venice arranged matters so that its emissaries had not even

[47] Further on the bull of Pope Nicholas and the appeals of Enea Silvio and the emperor, Schwoebel, 31 and 3, respectively.

reached the Bavarian border when the diet disbanded. Philip the Good of Burgundy, whose religious zeal Enea Silvio could not praise enough, was the only sovereign to appear. Anxious to avenge the disgrace that had befallen his house at the battle of Nikopol (1396), he offered to participate in the Turkish campaign provided that the emperor, the king of Hungary, or some other important ruler should take command of the armies; if not, he declared his willingness to send as many troops as the menacing attitude of Charles of France would permit him to spare. It was thanks to him, as Enea Silvio declared, that the diet, which convened in April 1454 and remained in session for some four weeks, was not entirely fruitless. No one questioned the necessity or urgency of a general crusade. But concerning ways and means no agreement could be reached. Deliberations were brought to a standstill by the demand for a five-year truce, held to be indispensable. It was generally agreed that the Italians must cooperate, that a fleet must be sent to blockade the Dardanelles and the Bosporus. In accordance with the time-honored method, it was decided to postpone further discussion until a second diet, which the emperor scheduled for Michaelmas (late September) of the same year, at Frankfurt on the Main.[48]

Discouraged by the mediocre results of the first diet, Enea Silvio expected nothing better of the second. In a letter of July 5, 1454, he wrote:

A new diet has been called. The king of Aragon, the Venetians, the Genoese, the Florentines, Count Francesco [Sforza], although he has not yet received the duchy of Milan in fief, the duke of Modena, even the marquesses of Mantua, Montferrat, and Saluzzo have again been invited. We shall see how much zeal our Italians exhibit. The kings of France, England, Bohemia, Hungary, Poland, Denmark, Norway, and Scotland have been invited in writing to send delegations. The princes and counts of Germany are expected to appear in person or to send representatives. You ask what I think of it, what I expect? On this score, I should like best to say nothing at all. I hope that my view of things may be utterly mistaken and that I shall prove to be a false prophet. . . . I am without hope that what I desire may come to pass. I expect no good.

Nevertheless, the imperial secretary repaired to Frankfurt at the appointed time. Once again the emperor failed to appear in person and vested his powers in the bishop of Siena. A papal legate had arrived in due time but did next to nothing. Most of the estates of the empire, as

[48] For the background to the attitude and role of Philip of Burgundy, see ibid., 82ff.

well as the especially invited foreign sovereigns, failed to appear. Many
had not even thought it worthwhile to send delegates. The resulting
mood of discouragement was reflected in a motion to annul the decisions
taken by the Regensburg diet, which had been meager enough, and to
leave matters as they were. But then Enea Silvio delivered a two-hour
address, insisting on the urgency of the projected campaign against the
Turks and assuring the assembly in the emperor's name of Frederick's
determination to keep his promises. In conclusion he praised the aged
heroes Alfonso of Aragon and Philip of Burgundy, citing them as models
to be emulated by the youthful princes of the empire. The Hungarian
delegates took advantage of the largely hypocritical applause to demand,
in the name of their king, that the estates send him at least an auxiliary
army for use against the Ottomans. The Turks, so the Hungarian delegates declared, had advanced once again to the borders of Hungary, and
if the Hungarian pleas should go unanswered, King Ladislas Posthumus
would be compelled to make peace with the sultan at any price. The
emperor's representatives supported the request without hesitation, but
the Electors did everything in their power to block, or at least to postpone,
a decision in the matter. In the end the emperor's party, thanks to the
eloquence of Enea Silvio, gained the upper hand. It was decided to send
an auxiliary army of 30,000 foot soldiers and 10,000 cavalry to Hungary,
on condition that the Hungarians should put an army of equal strength
into the field. If, it was prematurely concluded, the Italian states should
send a fleet of twenty-five galleys to the Levant, it would be an easy
matter to drive the Ottomans from Europe. But since no decisions were
taken concerning the equipment of the auxiliary troops or the time at
which they were to set out, another winter passed in inactivity. Everyone
had lost faith in the projects for a crusade. Rumors went round to the
effect that the pope and the emperor were merely interested in taking in
money. As such opinions spread among the people, enthusiasm for the
holy cause seeped away.

In February 1455 the emperor convoked a new diet, this time at Wiener
Neustadt. The dismal atmosphere prevailing in this assembly can be
gathered from the absurd quarrels over precedence that broke out among
the representatives of the estates when it came to choosing a chairman.
Precious time was wasted and when finally attention was turned to the
main business on the agenda, the news came from Rome that Pope
Nicholas V had died (March 24, 1455). The assembly was filled with
consternation. All further deliberations about a crusade or an auxiliary
army for Hungary were dropped. The diet disbanded without having

come to any decision, except that all outstanding matters would be settled the following year. On April 8 the aged Spaniard Alfonso Borgia was elected pope as Calixtus III.

During the year 1454 the situation in the Morea, where Constantine's two brothers, Demetrius and Thomas, shared the last remnant of the Eastern Empire, took an alarming turn. Unwilling to pay the annual tribute, the despots decided to seek safety in Italy and to embark as soon as possible. But their Albanian auxiliaries refused to obey them and a mutiny broke out. The brothers were obliged to abandon their plan of flight and hastened to promise the sultan payment of the tribute. Dissensions now arose among the Greeks themselves, in the course of which Manuel Cantacuzenus put himself at the head of the party that had fallen away from the two Palaeologi. Setting himself up as despot, he received the support of two influential Greeks who had escaped from the Castel Tornese (Chlomoutsi), where Thomas had imprisoned them. At the head of the rebellious Albanians and Greeks, they threatened to seize the Peloponnese. It would probably have been all up with the two despots if Hasan, commander of Corinth, had not come to their aid by asking the Porte to intervene. In October 1454, the aged Turahan Bey arrived on the scene of the rebellion, accompanied by his two sons and a considerable army. He summoned the two Palaeologi, who at once declared their willingness to make common cause with the Turks. The Albanians were defeated and Turahan Bey withdrew to the north, after admonishing the despots to maintain peace and harmony. As soon as he was gone, new revolts broke out and even a conspiracy to free the cities of the Morea from the despots. The rebels appealed to Hasan for help, but he refused to interfere, for the rebels were unable to pay the annual tribute. The two despots immediately offered to do so, whereupon the sultan, in a Greek document drawn up at Istanbul on December 26, 1454, granted the most noble families of the Morea a patent of immunity in which he solemnly swore "by his father's spirit, by the sword he was girt with, by the 124,000 prophets of the Moslems, and by the Koran" that no harm would befall them or their possessions and that they would be better off under his rule than ever before. The large landowners whose names are mentioned in this document had informed the sultan that they wished to depend directly upon the Porte, and no longer on the despots. The inevitable consequence of this defection of the Moreotic nobles was that the economic situation of the two brothers in the Morea became increasingly critical, and that the rule of the Palaeologi there, soon to end altogether, was reduced to a shadow existence. Mehmed had brought about this state of disintegration by a mere signed order, without striking a blow.[49]

Early in 1455, Mehmed was preparing another attack against the West. The unsatisfactory outcome of the Serbian campaign of the preceding year was for him reason enough to try the fortunes of war again. Isa Bey, son of Ishak Bey, who as march warden ruled over southern Serbia, seems to have spurred the sultan to this undertaking. As usual Mehmed rapidly assembled his army on the plain of Edirne and, seconded by Dayï Karaca Bey and the governor of Anatolia, put himself at its head. At the onset of spring he started westward, this time not, as usual, by way of Sofia but in a southwesterly direction by way of Kyustendil (Küstendil). In Kratovo, situated in the mountains to the west of Skoplje, he joined forces with Isa Bey, who advised him to attack the mountain city of Novo Brdo at once.

Novo Brdo, at that time the most important city in the interior of the Balkan peninsula, is situated in mountainous country between the field of Kosovo and the Morava River, some twelve miles southeast of Priština. The ruins of the castle of Novo Brdo, called Nyeuberge by the Saxon miners and Novomonte by the Italians, are still to be seen on the top of a high mountain (3,500 feet), some 1,000 feet above the floor of the neighboring valleys. At the foot of the castle lay the sizable town. But there were also numerous houses scattered about the nearby mines. The main trading post was that of the Ragusans, but there were also Italian, particularly Venetian, merchants in residence. Numerous Serbian noblemen had settled here. The city's commercial ties extended to Serrai and Thessaloniki, as far as Sofia, Edirne, and Istanbul, and to Italy in the West. Thanks to this active trade, Novo Brdo was always first to receive reliable news of events in southeastern Europe. After the city had surrendered to the Turks on June 27, 1441, the Ragusans remained there under Turkish rule (1441-1444), but the city began to decline. After his territories had been restored to him in 1444, George Branković tried to revive the city but failed.

Isa Bey reached the city walls in advance of the sultan with a battalion of troops and summoned its commander to surrender voluntarily. When he received a negative answer, the sultan moved up with the rest of his army. The siege was begun at once. It lasted forty days, until the walls

---

[49] See, for Mehmed's guarantee to the Greek nobles, Franz Miklosich and Joseph Müller, *Acta et diplomata graeca medii aevi sacra et profana* III (Vienna, 1865; reprinted Darmstadt, 1968), 290.

were demolished by heavy artillery fire. On June 1, 1455, the "Mother of Cities" surrendered to the Ottomans with all its gold and silver mines. The glory of Novo Brdo was ended forever. The treaty of surrender explicitly granted the inhabitants the right to remain in their city, but in the end this right was limited to the miners, whose work was indispensable. The notables of the city were executed; 320 young men were enrolled in the Janissaries. Among these were the sons of Michael Konstantinović of Ostrovica, and most notably Constantine Mihajlović, who later made a name for himself with his *Memoirs of a Janissary*, written in Poland, a trustworthy record of the events of the period. Seven hundred women of Novo Brdo were handed over to the army. The Church of St. Nicholas, commonly referred to as the Saxon church, was shorn of its roof and bells, but not taken away from the Saxons until 1466, when it was transformed into a mosque. In 1467 the rest of the population was carried off to Istanbul. The Ottoman colony established in the conquered city proved unable to halt its decline. As the site of an Ottoman mint, Novo Brdo preserved a certain importance until the reign of Murad IV, who still had coins struck there. The gold and silver mines, which until the conquest had yielded 120,000 ducats a year, gave out, and today there is not so much as a trace of the city's former importance and almost legendary wealth.[50]

After the capture of Novo Brdo, the whole southwestern part of the Serbian despotate was occupied in a few days, chiefly by Dayï Karaca Bey, who had been sent out to devastate and pillage the country. The locality of Taş Hisar (Stone Castle), mentioned along with Novo Brdo in the Ottoman sources, is most likely either Kamenica, northwest of Novo Brdo, or one of the two small castles, Prizrenac and Prilepac, which served to guard the widely dispersed mines and settlements of Novo Brdo. At certain points, such as Priština and Trepča, the Turks already had garrisons. Prizren (Prizrend) in the plain of Kosovo fell to the Turks on June 21. The mines surrounding Novo Brdo for a considerable distance were occupied by Isa Bey, while the sultan, presumably in September, marched to Thessaloniki by way of Kosovo, where he stopped to

---

[50] The Polish text, together with a Serbo-Croatian translation of Mihajlović's work, has been published by Djordje Živanović: *Konstantin Mihailovic d'Ostrovica, Mémoires d'un Janissaire ou chronique turque* (= *Srpska Akademija Nauka, Spomenik*, no. 107, Belgrade, 1959). There is a French résumé, 165–166. For more details on the city of Novo Brdo and mining operations, see Robert Anhegger, *Beiträge zur Geschichte des Bergbaus im osmanischen Reich*, 3 vols. (Istanbul, 1943–45) and Nicoară Beldiceanu, *Les actes des premiers sultans conservés dans les manuscrits turcs de la Bibliothèque Nationale à Paris* II: *Règlements miniers 1390–1512* (= *Documents et Recherches* VII, ed. Paul Lemerle; Paris, 1964), passim.

hold a funeral sacrifice in honor of his ancestor Murad I. After a few days in Thessaloniki, which he was visiting for the first time, he returned through southern Thrace to Edirne, where he must have arrived in the course of the early autumn. Here he spent the rest of the year, except for a holiday in the Balkan Mountains.

The fall of Novo Brdo, regarded as a bastion of Christianity, produced a devastating impression in Hungary and Italy. The despot George Branković received the terrible news on June 21 while attending the diet in Győr (Raab), Hungary, where great plans were being made for a campaign of the Christian powers against the Turks, to which the Serbian prince promised to contribute 10,000 horsemen.

It was at this diet that the eloquent Franciscan Giovanni da Capistrano (1386–1456), one of the most remarkable figures of the declining Middle Ages, first participated in the struggle against the Turks. Of small stature, lean and emaciated, all skin and bones, this monk wandered untiringly through the German territories at the pope's behest, revered by the people as a prophet and herald of the apostolic faith, if not as a messenger from heaven, hurling thunderous invectives now against the Hussites, now against the Jews. Day in, day out, twenty to thirty thousand people attended his sermons and listened, although hardly anyone understood him, for he spoke in Latin. He lodged with his fellow Minorites, visited the sick, whom he treated by the laying on of hands, and spent his nights in devotions and penitential prayers. Wherever he went he held the masses spellbound with his eloquence. After hearing his sermons, men and women would often gather their playing cards and dice, cosmetics, hair ornaments, and other articles of luxury and burn them in the marketplace. No one was better equipped than this man of almost seventy to champion the common cause of Christendom and preach a crusade against the Turks. In addition, he tried, at the diet, to win George Branković to the Catholic church, though without success. The despot replied that he had preserved the faith of his fathers down to an advanced age and that his people had always looked upon him as a reasonable, if unhappy, prince; that if he should now change his faith, they could only regard him as an insane old man. Disappointed by the diet, the despot went on to Vienna in the hope of receiving help, but returned to his capital city of Smederevo with empty promises. He was nearing the end of his life.

Only a few days after his return to Edirne from Serbia, Mehmed turned his attention to a new venture. This time it was a naval expedition. We have little reliable information about the Ottoman fleet before the fall of

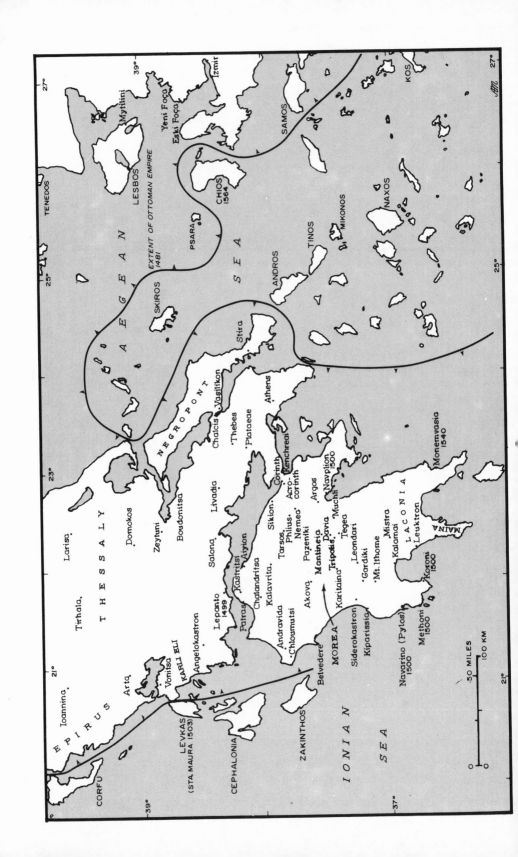

Constantinople. Only the siege and capture of the Byzantine capital seem to have convinced Mehmed of the need for a large and powerful navy with which to oppose the Western maritime powers, particularly Venice and Genoa, and to secure his territorial gains. Both his apologist Critoboulos and the contemporary Laonicus Chalcocondylas describe the sultan's haste in building the war fleet with which he hoped to gain control of the seas. It has not yet been established whether he chose the Byzantine fleet as his model or whether Westerners helped to build his warships. We do know that some of the petty Turkmen princes along the coasts of the Aegean and the Black Sea, such as the Aydïnoğlu dynasty, possessed small fleets with which they pillaged and terrorized the Aegean islands and even the Greek mainland. The Italian sources contain numerous gruesome reports of their depredations. Thus the new fleet may well have drawn on Anatolian models.

By way of explaining why Mehmed became interested in the Aegean islands at this time, it will be necessary to give a brief account of conditions in this part of the world. Most of the islands were under Venetian sovereignty. A number of small, independent communities had grown up, however, which for almost 200 years had experienced all manner of vicissitudes at the hands of warring Frankish princes but had been able to carry on a life of their own, unnoticed and hence unmolested by the outside world. The Duchy of Naxos and the Johannite community on Rhodes, under its grand master, were by far the most considerable of these small island states.

Guglielmo II, the aged duke of Naxos, had just acceded to power when Constantinople fell to the Ottomans. As a subject of Venice, he had himself included in the peace treaty which the Signoria concluded with the sultan immediately after the fall of Byzantium; he further succeeded in obtaining a special agreement with Mehmed whereby he was recognized as duke of the archipelago and called upon to live in peace and harmony with the Porte. He received the right to fly the lion banner of St. Mark in his duchy. As could have been foreseen, this state of peace lasted only a short time. A payment of tribute was soon imposed on Guglielmo and it was only by acceding to the sultan's demands that he managed to maintain his sovereignty up to the time of his death in 1463.

The Rhodiots showed far less political wisdom. Confident in their power to defend themselves, they had refused to pay tribute after the fall of Constantinople. Not until 1455 did envoys from the grand master, bearing rich gifts, appear at the court in Edirne to propose a commercial treaty on the basis of equal rights and certain mutual concessions. The treaty would have provided that the Knights of St. John be free to trade on the coasts of Caria and Lycia in Asia Minor, while the Turks would enjoy similar rights in Rhodes. When, on instructions from the sultan, the Ottoman negotiators again demanded an annual tribute from Rhodes after the example of other Aegean islands such as Chios, Lesbos, Lemnos, and Imroz, the envoys replied that they had no mandate to make any such arrangements. The Turks became threatening. Agree to the tribute, they said, or incur the wrath of the sultan with all its consequences. This had no effect. It was finally agreed that a Turkish plenipotentiary should accompany the envoys to Rhodes, where he might negotiate with the grand master himself. Jacques de Milly, the grand master, contemptuously rejected the Turkish demand, declaring that Rhodes belonged to the pope, who refused to pay tribute even to Christian sovereigns, not to mention adherents of foreign religions. The Rhodiots would be willing to send emissaries with gifts each year in token of their respect. If this did not satisfy the sultan, let him do as he saw fit.

Mehmed looked upon the grand master's refusal as a welcome pretext for war against the Knights of St. John. First he arranged for the mariners of the region of Aydïn, dreaded as pirates from time immemorial, to attack the nearby islands with some thirty ships. The fleet put out to sea at once and attacked Kos (Istanköy), also a possession of the knights, and Rhodes, devastated both islands, and returned to their hiding places laden with rich spoils in prisoners and cattle. Meanwhile, at the sultan's order, an impressive fleet of 25 triremes and 50 biremes as well as 100 small vessels was fitted out in Gelibolu. Under Admiral Hamza Bey, it put to sea. However, it headed not for Rhodes but for Mytilini (Lesbos) and anchored in the roadstead toward the end of June. The historian Ducas, secretary to Prince Domenico Gattilusio, was sent on board with impressive gifts to demonstrate his master's devotion to the sultan. The gifts consisted of precious silk and woolen garments, a carefully chosen selection of the island's finest products—horses, 20 oxen and 50 rams, 800 quarts of wine, two bushels of leavened and one of unleavened bread, more than ten hundredweight of cheese, a large quantity of vegetables for the ships' crews—and finally 6,000 silver thalers. Delighted at the gifts and the attitude they expressed, Hamza weighed anchor at the end of two days and sailed on to Chios.

The Chiots had purchased a tolerable relationship with the Porte by payment of an annual 6,000 gold pieces. Hamza was not received with honors, still less with presents—a mistake that was to cost the islanders dearly. On board the admiral's ship was Francesco Draperio, the wealthy alum merchant resident in Galata, who had long been on the best of terms with the Ottoman rulers, hence also with Mehmed. He had turned to the sultan for help in collecting a debt of 40,000 ducats for alum, which the Chiots had refused to pay. The sultan, to whom Draperio seems to have transferred his claim, instructed Hamza to demand payment. The plenipotentiaries from the island declared the claim to be without validity. The admiral, whose squadron apparently was insufficiently equipped with offensive weapons, had prudently kept clear of the harbor of Chios and anchored off the Anatolian shore. Here he began the negotiations, which soon broke off when the Chiots refused to make any payment whatever to the sultan or the Genoese merchant. Hamza put ashore a part of his troops, who devastated the nearby settlements with fire and sword. He was unable to make any headway against the city of Chios (Kastron), whose fortifications were manned by a strong garrison, consisting partly of Italians. At length Hamza persuaded the Chiots to send two of their most respected citizens, members of the Giustiniani family, to the fleet to work out a friendly settlement in the Draperio affair. En route they grew suspicious, fearing they were being lured aboard ship to be imprisoned and used as hostages. They turned back but were captured on the way by a Turkish patrol and held to answer for Draperio's claim.

Hamza weighed anchor and headed for Rhodes. But no sooner had he arrived than it became clear to him that he could take no action against the well-fortified city without a considerable army and adequate offensive equipment. Not wishing to have made the trip for nothing, he attacked the small island of Kos and proceeded to besiege the fortress of "Rachia"—probably the castle of Antimachia in the interior of the island rather than the desert island of Rachia to the west of Nisiros—to which the inhabitants of the abandoned city had fled. At the end of twenty-two days he was obliged to admit failure and sail away with considerable losses. On his way back to Gelibolu the admiral returned to Chios, meaning to suggest that the Maona, the trading company of the Giustiniani which since 1346 had enjoyed the mastic monopoly, send a delegation to Edirne to negotiate a final settlement in the Draperio matter. However, the Turkish landing party was received with hostility by the Chiots, and the ensuing brawl ended tragically. The repulsed Turks fled to the galley lying closest to the shore, which happened to be the admiral's ship, though Hamza was not on board. In a few moments the overloaded vessel tipped, shipped water, and sank with all aboard before help could come. The horrified Chiots paid an indemnity equal to twice the value of the sunken ship, but this did not help them evade the consequence of the sultan's wrath. Hamza, described as a mild, peaceable soul, sailed northward, stopping again at Mytilini, where Ducas received him with a sumptuous banquet. After an absence of two months he returned to Gelibolu without his finest vessel.

Mehmed was beside himself with rage at the lamentable outcome of Hamza's expedition. He summoned the admiral, reviled him in the crudest terms, and said he would have him flayed on the spot, had he not stood in such high favor with Murad II. A few days later Mehmed summoned him again. "Where," the sultan asked, "have you the galley that the Chiots destroyed?" Hamza, who had passed the incident over in silence at his first audience, now described the circumstances of the sinking, and tried to exonerate himself by pointing out that the vessel belonged to him and not to the sultan, so that he alone had been affected by the loss. This excuse seemed to satisfy Mehmed, but Hamza was removed from his post as admiral and sent to Antalya (Adalia) as governor. The sultan now turned to Francesco Draperio, who was present at the scene. "You owe me forty thousand ducats," said Mehmed. "I forgive you the debt, but I am taking over your claim against the Chiots, who are to pay me double the amount and an indemnity for the Turkish blood they have shed." Draperio kissed the sultan's hand in gratitude and in that same hour war was declared on Chios.[51]

Meanwhile, the situation on Lesbos had taken a dramatic turn and demanded the attention of the Porte. On June 30, 1455, just as the Ottoman fleet under Hamza was putting out to sea, Dorino I Gattilusio died. The lord of Mytilini, Eski Foça (near the ancient Phocaea north of Izmir) with its rich alum pits, Thasos, and Lemnos left his precariously held possessions to his eldest surviving son, Domenico. Domenico's younger brother Niccolò ruled Lemnos as his governor. A few weeks after taking power, Domenico Gattilusio sent the historian Ducas to Edirne to announce the change of ruler and pay his tribute, which amounted to 3,000 gold pieces for Lesbos and 2,325 for Lemnos. Ducas was given a friendly reception, permitted to kiss the sultan's hand, and remain in attendance until the sultan had finished his noonday meal. On the following day, when Ducas came to deliver the funds, the official who received him inquired, with a crafty smile, about his master's health. He replied that his master was well and sent greetings. The official then said he had been referring to the old prince. Ducas answered that the prince had been dead for forty days, that to all intents and purposes his successor had been in possession of the principality for the last six years, that in the

[51] An earlier English account of this and the following Turkish expeditions in the Aegean, based exclusively on Western sources, is William Miller, *Essays on the Latin Orient* (London, 1921; reprinted Amsterdam, 1964), 333ff.

course of this time he had made several visits to Edirne, to convey his respects and good wishes to the sultan. No one, said the official, had the right to take the title of lord of Mytilini—borne by Dorino until the time of his death—without first appearing at court and receiving it from the hands of Sultan Mehmed, his sovereign. "Go then," said the official brusquely, "and come back with your master! If he fails to appear, he knows what the future has in store for him."

Ducas hurried back to Mytilini and returned as quickly as possible with Domenico Gattilusio and an imposing retinue of Frankish and Rhomaic nobles. But Gattilusio did not find the sultan who, for fear of one of the terrible outbreaks of the plague which so frequently visited Thrace, had left Edirne for the pure air of the Balkan Mountains. They sought him vainly at Philippopolis and finally found him at Zlatitsa along with the grand vizier Mahmud Pasha. Mehmed permitted the prince to kiss his hand, but refused him an interview, and turned him over to Mahmud. Despite the lavish gifts he and the other dignitaries present had received, Mahmud did not hesitate to present the disconcerted Domenico Gattilusio with exorbitant claims on his master's behalf. First he demanded the cession of the island of Thasos, to which the prince, unable to help himself, consented. Next day Mahmud demanded that he double the tribute for Lesbos, to which the prince replied that he could not raise so much money and that the Ottomans should rather take the island instead. After protracted haggling—Ducas describes the incident with all the exciting details—it was agreed that the annual tribute for Lesbos be raised from 3,000 to 4,000 gold pieces. The prince further obligated himself to defend the Anatolian coast facing the island against the Catalan pirates by whom it was then infested, and to pay an indemnity for every Turk who suffered any harm there. The new agreements were sealed by a solemn oath, and a magnificent garment of honor, the brocade caftan, was bestowed on the prince, while his companions received silver garments. Then they returned in all haste to their island, where they gave thanks to their Creator, as Ducas says, for allowing them, at least this once, to escape the "monster" with a sound skin.

Meanwhile, in midsummer 1455, a squadron of ten triremes and as many biremes was made ready to sail in command of Yunus, who was soon to be appointed admiral and commandant of Gelibolu as Hamza Bey's successor. This man had a curious career behind him. A Spaniard or Catalan by birth, he had drifted into the service of the Porte and attracted Mehmed's attention by his exceptional beauty. He seems to have owed his swift rise to the rank of admiral more to his physical virtues than to his nautical ability. Off the Trojan coast his squadron ran into a storm and no less than seven of the twenty vessels were destroyed. It was only the skill of a compatriot, the Spanish helmsman, that saved Yunus and his ship. Making his way out of the storm, he finally anchored off Chios, while the other twelve ships sought refuge in the harbor of Mytilini. The admiral gave up any plans to attack Chios with his battered fleet. He contented himself with falling upon a Lesbiot guard ship which Niccolò Gattilusio, acting for his absent brother, had sent out to reconnoiter the Catalan pirates, so that actually it was employed in the service of the Porte. On board was a wealthy Greek woman from Chios, Domenico's mother-in-law. Yunus chased the ship into the harbor of Lesbos and demanded its surrender as a war prize, threatened the Lesbiots with the wrath of Mehmed in case of refusal. Then he sailed on to the Anatolian coast and on October 31 attacked Yeni Foça, where he pillaged the property of numerous well-to-do Genoese merchants and alum dealers and took them aboard ship as prisoners. On the rest of the population he imposed the head tax; in addition, he selected the 100 handsomest boys and girls as a gift to the sultan. After spending two weeks in the rich city and setting up a Turkish garrison, he returned to Gelibolu after the middle of November. The sultan's rage over the failure of the expedition against Chios was somewhat appeased by the gift which Yunus Pasha personally presented to him in Edirne.

After their return from Zlatitsa, Domenico sent the unfortunate Ducas once again to the Porte to make representations over the conduct of Yunus Pasha. His mission was hardly a success. On orders from the sultan, the new admiral, with whom Ducas was confronted, told him that his master must pay 10,000 gold pieces on the spot or prepare to be attacked. Meanwhile, Mehmed ordered the occupation of Eski Foça, one of the duke's possessions, an act which was quickly carried out. When he heard that the city was taken (on December 24, 1455), he sent Ducas, who had been detained until then, back to his island without further demands. Thus the Frankish possessions in the Aegean dwindled more and more. It was hardly necessary to strike a blow. Mere threats sufficed.

Soon after Ducas reported to his master on the sorry outcome of his mission, new clouds gathered over another Frankish possession in the Levant. The storm broke in January 1456. This time Mehmed's designs were directed against the younger branch of the Gattilusi, rulers of Enez on the Aegean for a hundred years. Enez was a prosperous harbor east of the estuary of the Maritsa (Meriç), then still navigable, and the site of a very profitable salt-panning industry yielding an annual income of

300,000 silver pieces. In addition the family held Samothraki (Samothrace) and, since Mehmed had granted it to them in 1453 in return for an annual tribute of 1,200 gold pieces, the island of Imroz. Palamede Gattilusio, lord of Enez and brother of Dorino I, had also died in 1455. His eldest son, Giorgio, had preceded him in death in 1449. Thus Palamede's estate fell to his younger son, Dorino II, and to Giorgio's widow and her children. In his lifetime Giorgio had been given all his father's possessions except some property on Lesbos which had been promised to Dorino II; and after Giorgio's death, his widow and children had retained certain rights of primogeniture. Defying these rights, Dorino II now seized the whole estate, and violent disputes broke out between the two parties. The widow tried to obtain a friendly settlement with her brother-in-law, lest she be obliged to ask the arbitration of the supreme overlord, the sultan. When her efforts proved vain, she sent her uncle to the Porte; her emissary painted Dorino II in the darkest colors and branded him a traitor who was trying to make common cause with the Italians and was at the same time amassing arms, enlisting men, and strengthening the garrison of Enez, with the intention of throwing off Ottoman sovereignty completely. The intrigant found an eager listener in Mehmed, who had long been waiting for a pretext to take possession of Enez, an inviting morsel in view of its Turkish hinterland and its prosperity.

Furthermore, the Turkish judges of Ipsala and Ferrai (Ferecik) had complained to the sultan of Dorino's high-handed treatment of the inhabitants of their towns and accused him of selling salt to infidels to the detriment of the Moslems. The sultan had every reason to take a hand and on January 24, 1456, he set out for Enez by the land route. A bitter cold winter had settled over the Thracian plain. At the same time Yunus Pasha sailed for Enez with a squadron of ten galleys and established a blockade. Dorino II was not in the city but on the island of Samothraki, where he was planning to spend the unusually severe winter in his father's palace. Enez and its inhabitants were left to their fate. They sent a delegation to the sultan's quarters at Ipsala, surrendering the city on condition that the inhabitants should incur no harm.

The sultan received the envoys graciously, promised to grant their plea, and commissioned the grand vizier Mahmud Pasha to take possession of the city. The following day the sultan appeared in person, seized all the gold, silver, and other valuables that he found in Dorino's palace, and looted the houses of Dorino's attendants, who were also away. After three days he returned to his winter residence, taking with him 150 children, the flower of the youth of Enez. A certain Murad was appointed prefect (*subaşi*) of the city. Yunus Pasha was instructed to take possession of Imroz and Samothraki.

After landing on Imroz, the admiral sent for Critoboulos, whose loyalty was known to him, and appointed him governor in the place of the imprisoned John Lascaris Rhyndacenos, who had hitherto represented Dorino II on the island. At the same time a ship was sent to Samothraki to take Dorino into custody. Distrusting the admiral, the prince preferred to travel to the Porte on his own account, after sending his beautiful daughter ahead with gifts. At first the sultan promised to return both islands but changed his mind after Yunus Pasha had described the discontent of the duke's subjects; instead he assigned him a possession far from the sea, at Zichne in Macedonia. Here Dorino soon found life unendurable. Quarreling with his Turkish "guard of honor," he had them massacred and fled to Christendom. First he settled on Lesbos, then on Naxos, where he married his cousin Elisabetta Crispo, daughter of the late duke Giàcomo II, and settled down for good.

Virtually without a struggle Imroz, Samothraki, and Enez had been incorporated into the Ottoman Empire. Impressed by these events, the Lemnians complained secretly to the sultan of the autocratic Niccolò Gattilusio, who enjoyed free rein on the island as his brother Domenico's representative; they even asked Mehmed to appoint a commander over the island. The sultan did not have to be asked twice, but sent the eunuch Ismail Pasha—the successor of Yunus Pasha, who had meanwhile fallen from favor—to Lemnos to install the former admiral Hamza as Ottoman governor. Before his arrival a battle had broken out between the inhabitants of the island and the sailors sent by Domenico Gattilusio from Mytilini under the leadership of Giovanni Fontana and Spineta Colomboto. Some of the intruders were killed and the rest taken prisoner. Ismail, who returned to Gelibolu in May 1456 as soon as his mission was carried out, brought these forty Lesbiots with him as a present to his master. In August, Ducas, on another of his trips to Edirne with the annual tribute, tried to obtain their release. His efforts were in vain; Mehmed, who had just returned from Serbia, wished to have them executed. They were on their way to the scaffold when he decided to spare their lives and have them sold as slaves. As for the proceeds of 1,000 gold florins, he kept them for himself.

The sultan would probably not have contented himself with this solution of the Gattilusi question had his attention not been taken up, since April, by a large-scale military undertaking against Serbia and Hungary. The willingness with which the despots of the Morea and the petty island rulers of the Aegean offered their submission one after another, the complete impotence of Genoa, and the Signoria's manifest desire for friendly relations with the Porte obviated all danger of a naval attack from the West. The only serious threat was in the north. As long as John Hunyadi lived, there could be no assurance that the northern neighbors would keep their treaties with the Ottoman Empire. After the campaigns of 1454 and 1455, Serbia had virtually lost its political independence, and Mehmed could easily have found a pretext for eliminating it altogether.

There remained Moldavia, whose prince, Petru III Aaron, had been called upon to pay an annual tribute of 2,000 gold pieces under such humiliating conditions that he hesitated to accept the sultan's demands without consulting his boyars. In September 1455, he obtained their agreement, and soon thereafter sent his logothete Mihail to Sultan Mehmed, whom he finally found in Zlatitsa in the Balkan Mountains. A Slavonic document guaranteeing the peace of Moldavia in return for punctual payment of tribute was drawn up on October 5 in Sarukhanbeyli (Saranovo or Saranbei; now Septemvri, near [Tatar] Pazardzhik). It reads:

> From the great sovereign and great Emir Sultan Mehmed Bey to the noble, wise, and estimable Ioan Petru, Voivode and Lord of Mavrovlachia. Receive friendly greetings, Your Excellency. You have sent your emissary, the boyar Mihail the Logothete. And My Highness has taken note of all the words he has said. If you send My Highness *harac* [head tax] in the amount of 2,000 gold ducats each year, let there be perfect peace. And I grant you a delay of three months. If [the head tax] arrives within this time, let there be complete peace with My Highness. But if it does not arrive, you know [what will happen]. And let God rejoice you! On the fifth day of October, in Sarukhanbeyli!

With this document the principality of Moldavia purchased its seeming independence in return for a tribute of 2,000 gold pieces. Actually Petru III Aaron, a weak prince, had every reason to be pleased, at least as long as the Turks contented themselves with the present tribute.

In June 1456, from his camp at Yeni Derbend (or Rudnik?), Mehmed wrote a second letter to the same Petru III Aaron, this one in Turkish, granting the merchants of Akkerman the right to trade unhindered in the Ottoman Empire on the strength of the peace recently concluded with Moldavia, putting an end to the previous state of hostility.[52]

---

[52] The firman from the sultan to Petru is the oldest of two dozen documents published in facsimile and edited and translated by Friedrich Kraelitz, "Osmanische Urkunden in türkischer Sprache aus der zweiten Hälfte des 15. Jahrhunderts,"

Mehmed had nothing to fear on the northeastern border of Rumelia; Walachia showed no sign of hostility and in any case its armed forces were negligible. Clearly Hungary was the only serious adversary, and so it was against Hungary that the sultan, in the summer of 1456, directed the first large-scale campaign after the conquest of Constantinople.

Obviously the first step would have to be the total subjugation of Serbia, which alone could provide a secure base for any further military operations to the northwest. And like his father, Mehmed attached the utmost importance to the annexation of Belgrade, the Hungarian fortress on the Danube [pl. XIV]. Once that was in his hands, he was quoted as saying, Hungary would be subjected in two months, and he would be able to eat his dinner quietly in Buda.

The preparations for the Serbo-Hungarian campaign had been in progress all winter. Every effort was made to keep them secret, but nevertheless the news had reached the West. The sultan's armies converged from all parts of the empire and were mustered on the plains between Istanbul and Edirne. As usual, the figures vary. The estimates of the Turkish fighting strength range from 150,000 to 400,000 men. All these figures are of Western origin and should no doubt be considerably reduced, although they are based in part on the calculations of eyewitnesses, who speak of at least 150,000 selected and fully equipped soldiers. It is more than doubtful that an army of such size could be moved and adequately supplied at that time. As on the occasion of the siege of Constantinople, the Western estimates of the Ottoman forces were grossly exaggerated. Such exaggerations were equally useful in the case of either victory or defeat.

Mehmed planned to invest the fortress of Belgrade simultaneously by land and from the Danube. He gave orders to build a fleet consisting allegedly of 200 light vessels, but perhaps only of 60, which moved up the Danube to Vidin, where they were assembled. The larger ships were to transport the heavy siege guns. In Kruševac on the Morava in central Serbia, the sultan set up a foundry, where mortars and cannon were manufactured by foreign artificers. At this time (1456), one Jörg, a Nuremberg gunsmith, was called to the service of "Duke Stjepan of Bosnia," from which he later transferred to the service of Mehmed, whose history he wrote in short, crude sentences. Large numbers of cannon founders,

---

Sitzungsberichte der Akademie der Wissenschaften in Wien, philos.-hist. Klasse, 197 (1921). For the Slavonic document of the preceding autumn, see the reference in Mihail Guboglu, *Paleografia și diplomatica turco-osmană studiu și album* (Bucharest, 1958), 131 (document 2).

particularly Germans, seem in those years to have left their homes for southeastern Europe, where they found employment to spare.[53]

In the course of June 1456, when, as John Thurocz wrote, the grain was beginning to ripen, the Ottomans gradually moved up from the south toward Belgrade in dense swarms. By June 9 the sultan, who had spent the winter and spring in Edirne, except for the brief campaign against Enez, was on Serbian soil. Nowhere did he encounter resistance. On Sunday, June 13, he pitched his imperial tent on a hill within sight of the fortress of Belgrade. The tents of his Janissaries were lined up around him as far as the eye could see. The much admired fortress, with its powerful walls and towers, made no great impression on the Italians of the time. One of them compared it to "any good castle in Italy." Toward the end of the month, the siege guns, 300 in number, including 27 giant cannon of enormous length and seven mortars, were put into position. According to Pietro Ranzano, the culverins were not manned by Turks or even by Moslems, but by Germans, Hungarians, Bosnians, and Dalmatians, while the siege machines were entrusted to Italians and Germans. It goes without saying that all these war machines had been fashioned by Occidentals, among whom North Italian technicians must have played a leading role. The catapults and other devices which had been invented and tried out only in the West could not have been used without the help of Western engineers.

In order to prevent the Hungarians from forcing a passage to the beleaguered city by water, Mehmed spanned the Danube, just above the fortress of Belgrade or at the confluence of the Sava and the Danube, with a line of ships fastened together by chains. Indeed, Hunyadi had succeeded in manning some 40 Danube barges with fighting men picked for that very purpose. Here again the figures vary widely. The estimates of the strength of the Hungarian flotilla range from 40 to 200, but it does not seem likely that there were more than 40 really serviceable craft. The Hungarian preparations for raising the siege of Belgrade seem to have been quite inadequate and to have been made very slowly. At the news that the Turks were approaching, King Ladislas, pretexting a hunting expedition, fled in the middle of the night from Buda to safety in Vienna. The Hungarian nobles were also unwilling to risk their skins. Only when the cannons of Belgrade could be heard as far as Szeged did the barons hasten to join Hunyadi, the sole source of hope, with their troops. Otherwise, no one in all of the West stirred a finger. In July 1456, when

[53] For details of the brief history of Jörg, see A. Vasiliev, "Jörg of Nuremberg. A Writer Contemporary with the Fall of Constantinople," *Byzantion* 10 (1935), 205–209.

Belgrade was already thought to be lost, Pope Calixtus III issued through his legate a plenary indulgence for those who should take part in the struggle against the hereditary enemy.

By the almost unprecedented secrecy of his war preparations, the sultan had gained a head start that could not be made up. While endless columns of camels and other beasts of burden had been hauling amazing quantities of siege material, ammunition, and provisions to Belgrade, Hunyadi had gathered an army of some 60,000 men. But it included few properly equipped soldiers. The bulk consisted of volunteers, peasants, and poor burghers with nothing to lose, discalced and mendicant friars, hermits, and students, not to mention adventurers of every class. Most were unarmed or had nothing but a sword; many had only cudgels, staves, and slings. There were scarcely any horsemen. If nevertheless these bands were not lacking in courage, sacred enthusiasm, and crusading spirit, it was largely due to the fervor and flaming eloquence of Giovanni da Capistrano, who had turned up with a few like-minded fellow Minorites and who, along with John Hunyadi and the papal legate Juan de Carvajal—three Johns, as Enea Silvio had noted—became the soul of the crusading army.

In the early days of July, as Hunyadi approached with his motley army, the siege had already begun. The fortress was bombarded day and night by a hundred cannon. The Turkish cavalry laid waste the country far and wide, taking what could be found for the camp. Giovanni da Tagliacozzo, a monk in the following of Capistrano, described the siege of Belgrade in all its stages, as did also another friar, Niccolò da Fara; Tagliacozzo gives a vivid account of the effect of the great boulders that were hurled against the walls and into the interior of the city. Actually, there was little loss of life. In the daytime at least, the besieged were able to escape destruction by posting observers who followed the trajectories of the boulders. When one was seen approaching, a bell was rung on one of the watchtowers. Everyone looked up and fled from the spot where the projectile, usually doing little damage, hit the ground. The bombardment of Belgrade had been in progress for some two weeks when the little Hungarian flotilla, which was supposed to clear the path to the fortress for the army, appeared on the Danube. The only way to pass was to break the line of Turkish ships. Forty small vessels and one larger one were manned with seasoned fighting men and sent down the Danube. With a part of his cavalry Hunyadi occupied the banks in order to cut off supplies and retreat of the Turks. Capistrano fired the warriors with courage.

In the night of July 13, 1456, the Hungarian flotilla made ready to attack. Beset by land and water, the Turks offered desperate resistance.

After a murderous battle lasting five hours—the waters of the Danube were said to have been colored with blood for miles—the Hungarians succeeded in breaking the chains and in scattering the Turkish vessels. The victory was brilliant and complete. Three Ottoman galleys were sent to the bottom with their crews. Four others fell with all their equipment into the hands of the victors. The remainder, battered and laden almost exclusively with the dead and dying, fled. To prevent their capture by the enemy, the sultan had them set on fire. More than 500 Turks were reported to have drowned.

This engagement decided the fate of Belgrade, bastion of Vienna. Hunyadi took advantage of the situation and with the best of his troops made his way into the fortress that had already been given up for lost. Capistrano followed him and revived the courage of the besieged with his impassioned eloquence. The fortifications that had been almost entirely demolished were repaired in all haste and the available artillery set up at suitable points. Beside himself over the defeat on the Danube, Mehmed was bent on vengeance. What remained of the city's walls and towers was subjected to unceasing cannon fire. The sultan in person rallied the vanguard of his troops before the walls, determined to carry the day by a full-scale assault. At several points the Turks pressed through the breaches in the outworks, but were always repulsed. Finally the Christians withdrew from these rubble heaps and concentrated on defending the fortress. The Janissaries set up Turkish flags on the outer walls.

On the seventh day after the battle of the Danube, in the late afternoon of July 21, the sultan gave the sign for a decisive attack. The Janissaries rushed to the inner city bridge, but were unable to dislodge the massed crusaders. In the very first onslaught, Dayï Karaca Bey, governor of Rumelia, who commanded the besieging army, was torn to pieces by a cannon ball. The bloody battle lasted all night. Toward dawn the Janissaries succeeded in scaling the wall at several points and in penetrating the fortress. Hunyadi had intentionally withdrawn his men from the walls and hidden them. At a concerted signal they fell upon the enemy, who had dispersed through the deserted streets in search of booty. The stratagem was fully successful. Suddenly the Janissaries' shouts of victory were drowned out by the battle cry of the Hungarians. Before the Turks could assemble, they were surrounded and cut down in small groups. Only a few were able to escape through the main gate to the bridge, where they fell into a new and even more murderous trap. Having seen the Janissaries press forward in small bands and doubting that he would be able to resist them, Hunyadi, perhaps on the advice of Capistrano, had decided on a desperate measure. During the night he had ordered his men to gather bundles of faggots and dip them in sulfur; in the morning the faggots were lit and thrown on the Janissaries camped in the ditches below the walls. The effect was terrible. All those in the ditches died in the flames; even those who tried to escape were caught in the blaze. A pitiful remnant withdrew behind the siege guns. The Christians' cries of rejoicing mingled with the hideous screams of the wounded and half-burned Ottomans. The ditches were filled to the brim with horribly disfigured corpses. Only sixty Christians were said to have lost their lives.

Afraid that the tide of battle might turn, Hunyadi did not wish to commit all his forces, but he was powerless to curb the enthusiasm of the crusaders, especially as Capistrano did his utmost to fire them on. Toward noon the Minorite, at the head of some 1,000 men, advanced against the enemy siege guns. Other troops pressed on behind him, so that Hunyadi himself was carried along. The Turks put up little resistance, abandoning their cannon to the Christians and retreating to the second line. When the second line was taken by storm, they continued on to the third, site of the sultan's camp, heavily fortified with trenches, bulwarks, and cannon. Wild with rage, Mehmed threw himself into the fray and repulsed the assailants wherever he appeared, until at last, seriously wounded—according to one version, by an arrow in the thigh—he was forced to abandon the field. The Janissaries, in whom Mehmed seemed to repose his last hope, were exhausted; their courage forsook them and they refused to obey. When the sultan violently reprimanded their chief, Hasan Agha, Hasan in despair threw himself into the thick of the battle; in a few moments he succumbed to his wounds within view of his master.

The victory of the Hungarians was now secure. Coming from the Danube, some 6,000 Ottoman cavalrymen, it is true, reached the battlefield late in the afternoon and threw the Christians back from the sultan's tent to the second battle line. But the sultan had lost heart and at nightfall gave the order for a retreat, which degenerated into a rout. Fearing that Hunyadi would pursue them with fresh troops and that the battle would resume the next day, the Turks took with them only as much as the men could carry. Tents, armaments, all the cannon, which on orders from Mehmed had hurriedly been spiked, were abandoned and fell with other rich spoils into the hands of the victors. The number of fallen Turks was estimated at 24,000, which is no doubt an exaggeration if it is true that only 3,000 to 5,000 Christians took part in the battle. A considerable number of Turks were reported to have met their death in the course of the retreat. If Tagliacozzo and Niccolò da Fara are to be believed, Mehmed in his fury struck down several of his generals and high officials with his own hand, or had them executed on his arrival in Sofia. For a long time the rumor went round that the sultan had died in battle or succumbed to his wounds. Most of the forty scouts whom the despot George Branković had sent after the fleeing Ottoman army brought back the report that the sultan had vanished without a trace.

If Pope Calixtus III, with his Spanish temperament, continued to pursue the struggle against the Ottomans with youthful vigor despite his age, there were other men, further to the north, who took a more sober and realistic view of the triumph of Belgrade. One of these was Bernhard von Kraiburg, chancellor of the archbishopric of Salzburg, later bishop of Chiemsee (d. October 17, 1477, at Herren-Chiemsee), who in a letter from Vienna on August 25, 1456, sent a vivid account of the events in Belgrade to Siegmund von Volkersdorf, archbishop of Salzburg. He had been informed of what had happened in Belgrade, he wrote, "by a reliable witness." His authority, no doubt one of the many soldiers returning northward in August, estimated the number of Turks at some 100,000 men; according to him, there were no more than twenty-one ships, which carried no troops but only "provisions"; the entire army had been moved by land. In the battle for the fortress, roughly 4,000 to 5,000 on both sides were "struck down." John Hunyadi and Giovanni da Capistrano had no more than 16,000 men in the upper castle, and only half of these took part in the battle. The Christian forces as a whole indeed numbered 70,000 men, but "none wished to go to defeat." Only thirteen cannon were captured, including "one large one and no more." Some of the Turkish ships were burned and others captured, while some escaped. The Turkish emperor was shot under the left breast, and because of this wound, and with God's help, the Turks fled. The city of Belgrade was "battered" only at one end by the Turks, and even there not very seriously. Two Turkish ships were attacked and captured on the Sava "by simple folk," who had run off from the sermon. It was a true miracle that only 8,000 "simple people" without arms routed a Turkish army of 100,000. "As to the fighting and how often it took place, and how the Turks were defeated and put to flight, much could be written." On his return home he would report in person to the archbishop.

In another letter, written the following day to Heinrich Rüger von Pegnitz, Bernhard von Kraiburg speaks of the discovery in Belgrade of two Venetian ships, "with crews and equipment," sent by the Signoria to help the Turks. Called to account, a few sailors and merchants related that six ships in all had been fitted out, two of which indeed, they regretted to say, had joined the Turks.

These unembellished reports seem to support the view long held that despite the ample records at our disposal, it is impossible to form a really coherent picture of the battle of Belgrade, because each of the two factions in the Christian camp, on the one hand the Hungarians and on the other the crusaders under Capistrano, contested the other's share in the victory. The most complete accounts are at variance in many points. The delivery of Belgrade, as has often been pointed out, is one of those historical events that remain inadequately known despite an abundance of source material, because from the very outset the eyewitness reports were used as partisan documents. Yet, for all the discrepancies in the Western sources, there is no reason to doubt that the Ottoman army suffered a serious defeat and was put to flight.[54]

The Christian world sighed with relief when the news of Hunyadi's brilliant victory reached the West. The rejoicing knew no bounds. The report of the crusaders' victory was echoed even in the local chronicles of the most distant cities. Certain reports were enormously exaggerated. In Rome the false rumor went round that Constantinople had been retaken. The cities of the Papal State organized magnificent festivities, while the great event was also celebrated in Florence and Venice. In Bologna the holy relics were carried about the city in great processions for three days running. Pope Calixtus described the liberation of Belgrade as "the happiest event of his life." He had the church bells rung in Rome, ordered processions of thanksgiving held in every church; bonfires were lighted and the glad tidings proclaimed to the people everywhere. The pope trusted that the Christian princes would now take a different view of his crusading efforts and would show greater willingness to sacrifice themselves for the common cause of Christendom. Had he not said and written a thousand times in the past year that Mohammed's infidel sect would be defeated and exterminated? And now, he declared, the victory at Belgrade had brilliantly confirmed his predictions. The pope was encouraged in this view by the reports sent him from Hungary by Hunyadi and Capistrano, assuring him that the Christian armies would reconquer not only the Greek Empire in Europe but Jerusalem and the Holy Land as well, provided only that the pope would send 10,000 to 12,000 well-armed horsemen, who could contribute more to the spread of the Christian faith than 30,000 men at any other time. Hunyadi wrote that the emperor of the Turks was so completely ruined and crushed that if the Christians

---

[54] Babinger appraises the sources on the struggle for Belgrade in "Der Quellenwert der Berichte über den Entsatz von Belgrad am 21./22. Juli 1456," *Sitzungsberichte der bayerischen Akademie der Wissenschaften, philos.-hist. Klasse* (Munich, 1957); reprinted in *A&A* II, 263-310.

were to rise up against him, they could easily seize the whole Ottoman Empire with God's help.

Small wonder that Calixtus III exhorted his legates and the Christian rulers to unite their forces and attack the Turks. He called for a great crusade to begin the following March, not only to reconquer Constantinople and to free Europe from the Ottoman yoke but also to drive the infidels from the Holy Land, and indeed to exterminate the whole species. He himself decided on immediate action in the Aegean to avenge the loss of the Gattilusi domains. For a year now he had been building a small fleet at the Ripa Grande shipyards in Rome; on December 17, 1455, he had appointed Cardinal Lodovico Scarampo captain general with orders to put to sea with the sixteen galleys then available. By reason of his energy and fighting spirit this prince of the Church was eminently suited to his post, yet no one could have been more reluctant to accept it. Rather than do battle in the Aegean, he would have preferred to continue his comfortable life in Rome, where he enjoyed a highly influential position. By a papal decree Scarampo was appointed legate for Sicily, Dalmatia, Macedonia, all Greece, the Aegean islands, Crete, Rhodes, Cyprus, and the provinces of Asia, and commissioned to govern all regions that he took from the enemy. Later than the impatient pope had hoped, the cardinal-legate put to sea in the summer of 1456 with a reported 1,000 seamen, 5,000 soldiers, and 300 guns. By August the cost of the expedition had already amounted to 150,000 ducats. Its mission was not only to protect the Christians of the Aegean islands, hard pressed by Mehmed, but above all to divide the infidel armies by an attack from the sea.

Clearly the sixteen vessels were inadequate to such a purpose. The prospects of success dwindled further when the Aragonese Alfonso of Naples, who had offered to fit out fifteen galleys, spent the money instead on paying his debts and on organizing sumptuous festivities. Lodovico Scarampo kept postponing the squadron's departure from Naples. Finally, on August 6, 1456, the crusading fleet, reinforced by a few vessels contributed by King Alfonso, put out of Naples. But the captain general stopped in Sicily and once again had to be admonished by Rome to betake himself to Greek waters. At last the pope's dream was fulfilled: in the autumn of 1456, the flag of St. Peter appeared in the Aegean Sea. The first stop was at Rhodes, where money, arms, and grain were delivered to the Knights of St. John. Then the fleet sailed on to Chios and Lesbos. Here Scarampo tried to persuade the inhabitants to withhold payment of tribute to the Turks, but without success. Fear of Mehmed and

145

his vengeance deterred them from supporting the Christian cause. However, the cardinal-legate drove the Turkish garrisons out of Lemnos, Samothraki, and Thasos, and finally set up headquarters in Rhodes.

The crusading squadron had not won any decisive victories, and in view of the small number of ships none could be expected. No one but the pope was interested in strengthening the fleet, and his treasury was exhausted. In vain did he raise his voice in behalf of a holy war. The princes of the West made no move to join forces with him. At this juncture, moreover, Europe was struck by a double catastrophe: the two heroes whose zeal had done most to arouse the pope's enthusiasm died soon after the liberation of Belgrade. On August 11, 1456, John Hunyadi was carried off in Zemun (Semlin) by a terrible epidemic, perhaps the plague, which was ravaging all southeastern Europe from Istanbul to Rome. On October 23, Capistrano, his aged comrade-in-arms, succumbed in turn at Ilok (Ujlak), exhausted by the excitement and hardship of the campaign. But it was the indifference of the Western powers that crushed all hope that the victory of Belgrade would provide new impetus for a holy war. Only the pope persisted in his efforts to combat the Crescent. In December 1456 he appealed for help to the Christian king of Ethiopia, and in the following year to the Christians of Georgia and Persia and even to Uzun Hasan, ruler of the White Sheep (Ak Koyunlu), who alone among Oriental princes was in a position to measure his strength with Mehmed II.

The unexpected death of John Hunyadi, who had barely reached the age of seventy, suddenly changed the situation in Hungary. In Belgrade his elder son, Ladislas, took command, and at the beginning of winter the Hungarian king, Ladislas Posthumus, not yet seventeen, repaired to Belgrade in person, accompanied by his uncle, Count Ulrich of Cilli, who was then ban of Croatia. The long-existing tension between the Cilli and Hunyadi parties now reached the breaking point. After the entry of King Ladislas, Ladislas Hunyadi ordered the drawbridge raised, so compelling the German crusaders and the king's army to remain outside. A stormy altercation ensued, in the course of which Ladislas Hunyadi treacherously had Count Ulrich murdered (November 9, 1456). A master of dissimulation and utterly devoid of courage, King Ladislas feared to avenge his uncle's death on the spot. It was not until the following year, when he became aware of the dangers threatening him from this quarter, that he caused Ladislas Hunyadi, who was trying to organize a campaign against the Turks, to be thrown into prison along with his brother Matthias. Ladislas was beheaded in March 1457, while his brother remained in prison.

Emperor Frederick III looked on these bloody intrigues as a welcome occasion to carry out at least a part of his own long-standing designs on Hungary. The struggle between him and Ladislas Posthumus over the possessions of the extinct house of Cilli, which by the terms of an old treaty were to fall to the Hapsburgs, became more and more envenomed. Pope Calixtus attempted, in a letter of solemn exhortation, to persuade Ladislas to give in. How should it be possible, the pope wrote, to win over Frenchmen and Spaniards, not to say Englishmen, who are all so far away, to a campaign against the Turks if Ladislas, who is closest to the enemy and bound to suffer the most at his hands, lives in perpetual strife, seeming to forget that the "infidel nation of Turks" never ceased to plot the downfall of Christendom? It was to be expected that King Ladislas's projected marriage to a daughter of King Charles VII of France would bring a change for the better, but before it could be celebrated Ladislas died unexpectedly in Prague on November 23, 1457. The planned diet of the princes of the empire did not take place. Two months later (January 24, 1458) Matthias Corvinus, the sixteen-year-old second son of John Hunyadi, mounted the throne of Hungary.

Another unexpected event had taken place in the Serbian despotate: on Christmas Eve, 1456, the eighty-one-year-old Serbian prince George Branković closed his eyes forever. He alone distrusted the good fortune of the Christian camp, and shortly before his death he had sent George Golemović on two successive missions to Edirne. Only three weeks after his death (January 15, 1457) Lazar, his son and co-regent, whom he had initiated into his Turkish policies, sought to obtain a friendly understanding with Mehmed by concluding a treaty and sending the annual tribute of 20,000 (according to other authorities, 40,000) ducats. The negotiations were carried on by two brothers, one in the Ottoman camp, the other in the Serbian. These were Mahmud Pasha, the grand vizier and governor of Rumelia, and Michael Angelović, the "Grand Čelnik" (a sort of count palatine) who had become grand voivode, holder of the highest Serbian court charge. The two brothers were always on the best of terms, and if the new despot obtained a peace favorable to himself, it was no doubt due in part in their influence, though Mehmed's intimate knowledge of the political situation in Serbia must have had a good deal to do with it.

After the deaths of Ulrich of Cilli and his father-in-law George Branković, the despot Lazar was on poor terms with the Hungarians. Michael Szilagyi, John Hunyadi's brother-in-law and commander of Belgrade, seldom let a day go by without harassing him in some way. Moreover, the late despot's children quarreled among themselves. While his widow Irene lived, she was able to keep the peace among them. But on May 3,

1457, she died at Rudnik. That same night the despot's eldest son, the blind Gregor, his sister, the late sultan Murad's widow Mara, and Irene's brother Thomas Cantacuzenus fled with all their belongings to the Turks in Edirne, where as might be expected, they were given a friendly reception. Only the blind Stjepan remained behind in Serbia.

Although Critoboulos describes Mehmed's thigh wound as trifling, the sultan did not personally engage in any military action during the year 1457. When local conditions permitted, he left military matters to his march wardens; during the recent Serbian campaign they had been aided by Mihaloğlu Ali Bey, who owned estates in and around Pleven (Plevna) and who, at least according to Critoboulos, was entrusted by the sultan with far-reaching powers. The Ottoman chronicles do not mention his name, and in general they devote few words to the vain siege of Belgrade and the shameful rout of the Turkish army. These same chronicles speak all the more profusely of the comet with two tails, one pointing eastward, the other westward (the periodic comet later named after Edmund Halley), whose appearance in 1456 aroused great excitement among the superstitious.

The sultan seems to have spent almost the entire year following the Belgrade campaign at his court in Edirne. On March 17 he composed a letter to Doge Francesco Foscari of Venice, inviting him to the circumcision ceremonies for his two sons Bayezid and Mustafa, and dispatched it to the Signoria by his "slave" Caracoxo (= Kara Hüseyn, Hasan?). Similar letters had previously been sent to the princes of the Orient, among them his brother-in-law Ismail Bey, the emir of Sinop. The letter to Venice, which has been preserved in an Italian translation, runs:

The great lord and grand emir Sultan Mehmed Bey. To the most excellent, most glorious, most noble, most prudent, most powerful, most praiseworthy and honorable; to our dearly beloved and revered father, Doge of the most illustrious Signoria of Venice. May Your Grace and his counselors as well receive fit, proper, and honorable greeting from My Magnificence. We wish to call it to Your Grace's attention that with God's help we are planning to celebrate the circumcision [nozze; literally, "wedding"] of Our sons. And by the peace and friendship that we observe with Your Grace! And since we are informed by Our slave here present that you harbor the same affection for us, we send hereby Our slave Kara Hasan ["Caracoxo"] to invite you to our rejoicings, according to our tradition. On the seventeenth day of March, 1457.

It was obviously expected, and Francesco Foscari seems to have realized it, that he should decline the invitation on any suitable grounds.

This did not detract from the splendor of the festivities held in the now completed palace on the Tunca island in Edirne. Neither of the two princes was yet ten years old. Bayezid had been residing in Amasya and Mustafa in Manisa. Now they appeared with their full retinues and possibly their respective mothers. The guests poured in from every corner of the far-flung Ottoman Empire: scholars of the law, judges, members of the clergy, and above all poets, commissioned to describe the festivities in rhyme. For later periods we possess many detailed descriptions of such circumcision ceremonies, some in Western languages. Thus far we have no independent account for the fifteenth century—except perhaps that of the Ottoman annalist Aşıkpaşazade, who attended the ceremony of 1457 and wove a description of it into his chronicle. The Tunca island was covered with tents; in the sultan's tent stood a throne. The first solemn assembly before the sultan was that of the scholars, to whom he was particularly devoted. Mehmed sat on his throne in full state. On his right side sat the mufti, the Persian Fahreddin, and on his left Mullah Ali from Tus in Persia, who had come from his homeland in the reign of Murad II and had taught first in Bursa. He enjoyed Mehmed's special favor and would later teach in the new capital. Before the sultan stood Hızır Bey Çelebi, the first judge of conquered Istanbul, and the Persian Şükrullah of Şirvan, a physician and historian. The sultan ordered certain Koran passages to be read and then commented on by the scholars present. Learned discussions followed. Then poems composed for the occasion were recited and stories told, and bowls of sweets and pastry set before the scholars and their assistants. Aşıkpaşazade relates that he was given a piece of precious fabric (*futa*), but left it for his servant. Heaped with gifts of money and garments of honor, the guests were dismissed. The next day the poor were invited; they too were lavishly entertained. Mehmed was said to have been in a particularly good humor. The third day was reserved for the nobles of the empire. There were exercises at arms, horse races, and an archery contest. On the fourth day money was cast among the people. All the dignitaries now brought the sultan presents. Those of Mahmud Pasha, the grand vizier, outshone all the rest.[55]

Thus the Thracian spring passed in joyous festivity. In the summer Mehmed sent Admiral Ismail Pasha on a punitive expedition against

[55] The chronicle of Aşıkpaşazade has been translated into German by Richard F. Kreutel under the title *Vom Hirtenzelt zur Hohen Pforte* (Graz, 1959). For the circumcision ceremony, see 208–210.

Lesbos to avenge the loss of Thasos, Lemnos, and Samothraki to Sca-rampo the previous year. The islands had not been handed back to the Gattilusi; they were retained by the pope. Nevertheless, Mehmed held Domenico Gattilusio, still lord of Mytilini, responsible for the loss. But the action failed. The Lesbiots resisted fiercely and Ismail was forced to retreat on August 9. The three islands were to remain in the pope's hands for another two years.

Otherwise, the sultan devoted himself to peaceful pursuits; he spent the greater part of the summer in his capital, making, so it seems, occa-sional trips to Istanbul to supervise the construction of his new palace as well as the work being done in the city. The previous year, Critoboulos tells us, he had had the roads leading into the city repaired and new streets laid out. Inns (caravansaries) were erected here and there at his expense, and the building of an enormous covered bazaar was begun, constructed not of wood but of brick faced with fine stone. Baths were built, and water conduits were laid out to supply numerous fountains. Moslems have always looked upon water as a symbol of life. The Koran verse "We made every living thing of water" (XXI:31) is inscribed on nearly all their large fountains. Baths and fountains, deemed necessary comforts, are abundant in every city, and their construction is regarded as a most meritorious service. Toward the end of the year, shortly before the sultan finally moved his residence to the newly built serai in Istanbul, an enormous fire seems to have devastated the old capital city of Edirne, a horrible symbol of its end as imperial residence. This was the beginning of that city's slow but sure decline.

Book Three

OTTOMAN CAMPAIGNS—ALBANIA, SERBIA, AND GREECE.
PAPAL EFFORTS AT WESTERN UNIFICATION.
THE LAST OF THE PALAEOLOGI.
EASTERN ADVENTURERS AND THE FALL OF TREBIZOND.
THE POPE AND THE SULTAN.
VLAD THE IMPALER.

AFTER the unexpected death of John Hunyadi, Mehmed confronted in all southeastern Europe no adversary strong enough to challenge his increasing power or impede his westward drive. But in the western part of the Balkan peninsula he still had to reckon with a serious enemy, one whose familiarity not only with Ottoman customs and institutions but also with Mehmed's mentality and intentions made him all the formidable: George Castriota, prince of Albania, known as Skanderbeg.

As we have seen, he spent his youth at the sultan's court as a hostage, but by 1443 he was back in Albania, ready to serve his country. In 1444 he inflicted a first defeat on the Ottomans in Lower Dibra. His struggle for his country's freedom and independence was off to a good start. He soon became a legendary figure in western Europe, where several biographies of him were written long after his death, one by a fabulist and another by an out-and-out swindler. We still have no account of his romantic existence based on the sources. Apart from his keen military judgment and his astonishing bravery and endurance, Skanderbeg was quite the equal of the Turks in guile and circumspection. Moreover, he possessed an invaluable ally in the terrain of his native country. Unable to make much headway against him by the usual methods, the Turks resorted on most occasions to ruse and intrigue. They succeeded in winning over to their camp such Albanian chieftains as Nicholas and Paul Dukagin. The Signoria of Venice, which looked askance at Castriota's appointment as "captain general of the king of Aragon" (January 1451), seems also to have intrigued against him. There is no doubt that he maintained close ties with the court of Naples, which constantly provided him with mercenaries, arms, food, and money by way of Durrës and Himarë (Chimara). Now and then Venice succeeded in stirring up Skanderbëg's relatives and weaker neighbors, who set up in opposition to him the elderly George Arianit as "captain of all Albania" from Shkodër to Durrës (1456), but in this clan warfare Skanderbeg usually had the upper hand. He defeated his uncle Moses (Musa) Komninos Golem and his Turkish auxiliaries toward the end of March 1456 and took possession of his territory of Dibra and of the lands of the Zenevisi and the Balsides as well. On April 5 he made his solemn entry into Krujë. Komninos fled to his nephew, professing his willingness to take up arms against the Ottomans, and Skanderbeg pardoned him. Skanderbeg followers ruled over Upper Albania, and all the chieftains on both sides of the Tomor Mountains were loyal to him.

We have little reliable information about the details of the fighting in Albania. Chalcocondylas tells us that during the campaign against Belgrade, an Ottoman army under Firuz Bey, former governor of Kruševac, and Mihaloğlu Ali Bey, who had been placed in charge of Albanian affairs, was sent westward, probably as a diversionary measure, and fought bitterly with Skanderbeg in the Albanian mountains for the possession of Krujë, Svetigrad, and Berat. In any event, the Turks seem to have occupied a number of Albanian valleys in 1457. Skanderbeg was driven back as far as Alessio in Upper Albania by Isa Bey and Hamza, Skanderbeg's nephew, who had been converted to Islam. On September 2, 1457, Skanderbeg won his bloodiest but most brilliant victory in Tomorrit (Tomoritsa), in southern Albania. He surprised Isa Bey's army in rest quarters. Those Turks who did not flee were cut down, and an enormous number of them—15,000 or, according to other reports, which are no doubt exaggerated, 30,000—met their death. Fifteen thousand prisoners, twenty-four horsetails of Ottoman commanders, and the whole camp with all its treasures fell into the hands of the victors. Among the prisoners was Hamza, whose life his uncle generously spared but who was sent to Naples, where he was held under close guard. Skanderbeg was even more outraged by this nephew's apostasy and betrayal of his country than he had been by the treason of Komninos.

Skanderbeg's military undertakings involved considerable expense, which the contribution of the king of Naples was not sufficient to defray. Pope Calixtus, to whom the "athlete of Christendom" had appealed for help, was in financial difficulties. The crusading fleet consumed enormous sums, and payments of the tithe proclaimed by the pope were niggardly and irregular. The pope could do no more than send Skanderbeg a single galley and a modest sum of money, promising more ships and larger amounts of money for the future. But Dubrovnik refused bluntly to release the funds which had been collected in Dalmatia for the crusade and which were to have been distributed in equal parts to Hungary, Bosnia, and Albania. The Ragusans went so far as to enter into negotiations with Mehmed. At the end of December 1457, Calixtus threatened Dubrovnik with interdict, and when his threat failed to produce results, repeated it in February 1458. After the victory of Tomorrit, Skanderbeg, whose country and Bosnia were the only remaining bastions between the Turks and Italy, appealed to the princes of the West for support, without which, he declared, he could not hope for success in his hard struggle. It was high time, wrote Skanderbeg, that they abandoned their petty quarrels and join forces for the freedom and security of Christendom. His pleas met with no more response than those of the pope. Only Naples agreed to send a few mercenaries. On December 23, 1457, to be sure, the pope appointed Skanderbeg captain general of the Curia in the war against the Turks, but once again Venice destroyed the prospects for a favorable turn in Albania by raising new claims. As his lieutenant in his native land, Skanderbeg appointed the duke of Levkas (Santa Maura), Leonardo III Tocco, whilom prince of Arta and "despot of the Rhomaeans," a figure virtually unknown except in southern Epirus.[1]

While Skanderbeg gradually welded the Albanian tribal chieftains together into a power capable of defying the Ottomans, at least for the present, internal strife and sectarian hatred in Serbia and Bosnia did much to favor Mehmed's plans of conquest. He was far from displeased at the family quarrel in the house of Branković. He promised to support Despot Lazar's brother and sister, Gregor and Mara, who had fled to the Turks, in a manner appropriate to their station, and in return reserved the right to claim their share of the Serbian shadow kingdom at any time. Lazar was approaching the end of his life. He died without male heirs on January 20, 1458, four days before Matthias Corvinus mounted the throne of Hungary, and the despotate fell a victim to the rivalry between Hungary and the Ottomans. At first (February 3, 1458) a regency was set up, composed of Lazar's widow, Helena Palaeologova (daughter of Thomas, the despot of Patras), the blind Stjepan, and Michael Angelović, the grand voivode of Serbia and brother of the grand vizier. The first two tried to unite the country to Hungary, while Michael Angelović, as agent and favorite of the Ottoman house, pressed its interests. But King Stjepan Tomaš of Bosnia was also interested in obtaining the inheritance of the Serbian Despotate. He invaded Serbia, occupied Srebrnica and

---

[1] The background to the Ottoman conquest of Albania under Mehmed is given in the article "Arnawutluk" (H. Inalcïk), EI^2 I, especially 653–656. See also there the bibliography of European and Eastern sources.

5. THE BALKANS

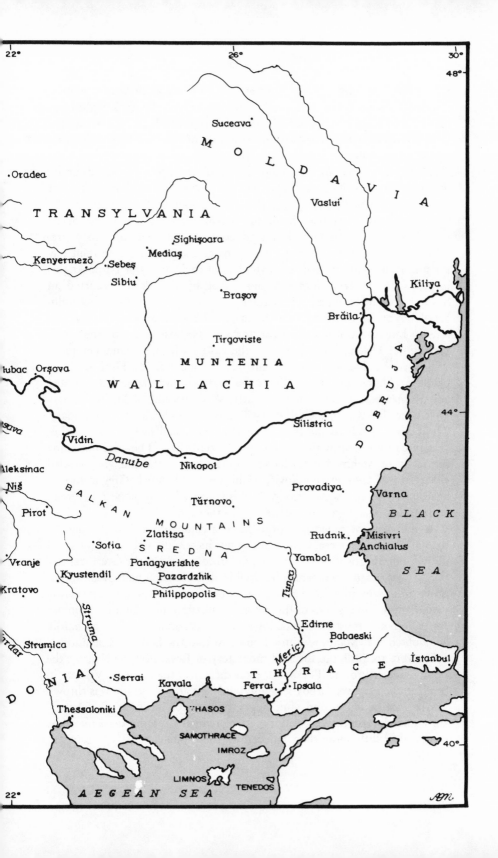

eleven fortresses of the region, and entered into negotiations for the marriage of his son Stjepan to Lazar's daughter Jelena; this took place later, on April 1, 1459. At the end of February 1458 the king of Bosnia concluded a peace with the sultan, undertaking, of course, to pay an appropriate annual tribute.

Hungarian claims to the despotate, papal attempts to place it under the protection of the Curia, and partisan rivalry resulted in a state of grave unrest. The Cilli party and the Serbian nobility did not take kindly to the prospect of Serbia's becoming a papal fief. Such was the Serbs' hatred of Catholicism, whose introduction they feared, that they preferred to throw themselves into the arms of the Turks rather than pay for uncertain Western help with the loss of their ancestral faith. At this juncture an incident, fomented no doubt by the Porte, occurred in Smederevo. Preferring to have a ruler appointed by a Turks, a few influential boyars of the city chose Michael Angelović as their leader and offered him the command of the fortress. He responded to their call, whereupon Helena lured him into the castle, which she and her party still occupied. He was thrown into chains and sent to Hungary as a prisoner (March 31, 1458). His estates were confiscated and distributed among members of the victorious party. What became of Michael Angelović is not known. In the fall of 1458 he was still in custody in Hungary. The despotate fell to the blind Stjepan, who ruled over it for another year in collaboration with his ambitious sister-in-law. They did not enjoy the favor of Mehmed, who looked upon Gregor, the likewise blinded eldest son of George Branković, as his man. In April, Gregor moved against Kruševac with a strong Turkish army, led by none other than Mahmud Pasha, eager to avenge his brother's fate.

At this time Mehmed was organizing a campaign against the last of the Palaeologi in Greece. Certain historians have supposed that if Mehmed did not put his grand vizier and favorite in command of the Greek expedition, it was because he feared that Mahmud Pasha as a half-Greek might prove untrustworthy in dealing with the Greeks. But this contention would apply equally well to the Serbian campaign, for Mahmud's mother was a Serb and must have ended her days in Istanbul. Thus, it can hardly be doubted that Mahmud himself chose to lead the Serbian expedition.

On May 10, 1458, the fortified monastery of Resava on the river of the same name fell to the Turks and soon thereafter the castle of Viševac in the Danube narrows. Žrnov was also taken. Nearby Belgrade was thrown into a state of alarm and after heavy fighting Golubac on the Danube surrendered (August 1458). The pitiful remnants of the despotate now consisted of little more than Smederevo, the capital.

The grand vizier's camp was at Niš. Here he was visited on several occasions by Ragusan emissaries; on the advice of Mara, the late sultan Murad's widow, and the blind Gregor, they had been sent to the sultan, who had referred them to Mahmud Pasha. The negotiations that Dubrovnik had sought with the Porte late in 1457 were the result of considerable pressure on Mehmed's part. Shortly after Murad's annexation of Serbia in 1439, Dubrovnik had been invited to send envoys to the sultan. Upon their refusal to pay tribute, however, the envoys were imprisoned and held until a charter was granted (1442) imposing annual payment of 1,000 ducats. Toward the end of 1457, in a communication to the senate of Dubrovnik, Mehmed threatened to arrest all the Ragusan merchants in the Ottoman Empire and invade the republic unless the senate sent a legation to the Porte forthwith and undertook to make punctual payment of 1,500 ducats a year. And still not content, he demanded payment of arrears. In their conversations with Mahmud Pasha the Ragusans managed, by using bribes, to have the ruinous payment of arrears cancelled, but they were unable to sidestep the annual tribute of 1,500 ducats. To this sum it was always necessary to add generous presents (*peşkeş*) for the viziers and state dignitaries. The resulting treaty renewed the rights and freedom of trade accorded the republic by Murad in 1442. But it did not renew the provision granting the Ragusans their own jurisdiction for disputes arising on Turkish soil. Thus ended the golden age of Dubrovnik, as well as her diplomacy of the *sette bandiere* (seven standards), which, adroitly administered, had thus far enabled her to avoid all conflict with the Porte. Not until October 23, 1458, however, did Mehmed send a letter from his camp in Üsküp (the Skopos, Skopoi of the Byzantines, in the Istranca Mountains east of Kïrk Kilise, the present-day Kïrklareli) to the council of Dubrovnik acknowledging receipt of tribute to the amount of 1,500 gold ducats and assuring the republic of his benevolence.[2]

When Mahmud Pasha returned eastward and why he did not take

---

[2] For the relations of Dubrovnik with the Ottomans see above, book 1, n. 12; especially Biegman, *The Turco-Ragusan Relationship*, 26 and 49, for details of the earliest charters. The expression *le sette bandiere* was applied to Dubrovnik because of the diplomatic policy which she successfully pursued under the protection of the seven powers: Spain, the Papacy, Naples, Venice, Hungary, the Ottomans, and the Barbary Deys. Cf. Carter, *Dubrovnik*, 333. Truhelka gives the text of Mehmed's letter in "Tursko-slovjenski spomenici," *GZMBH* 23 (1911), 15. Cf. the summary translation in *IED* 1 (1955), 46–47 (document 11). The identification of Üsküp is questioned by Inalcïk, who suggests the Upper Macedonian Skoplje rather than the Thracian Skopos ("Mehmed the Conqueror [1432–1481] and His Time," *Speculum* 35 [1960], 420).

Smederevo, or was not able to, are questions requiring clarification. When the Ottomans had crossed the Sava, plundered Srem (Syrmia), and burned down Mitrovica, King Matthias, accompanied by the cardinal-legate Juan de Carvajal, hurried to the spot and inflicted a defeat on the Turkish army (probably early in October 1458). A few days later Matthias entered Smederevo and imprisoned his uncle Michael Szilágyi, allegedly for conspiracy (October 15, 1458). In January 1459, the diet at Szeged agreed that the Serbian Despotate should be made over to Prince Stjepan of Bosnia, as the prospective husband of the late despot Lazar's daughter. King Matthias was recognized as overlord and Bosnia's alliance with Turkey was solemnly denounced. The king of Hungary assumed the task of defending Bosnia. But despite these agreements the end of Serbia was not far off.[3]

While Mahmud Pasha was trying, without clearly discernible results, to settle matters in Serbia, his master was preparing to complete the subjugation of Greece. Since the fall of Constantinople, the two despots, Demetrius in Mistra and Thomas in Patras, had quarreled incessantly with each other and maintained their positions thanks only to the sultan's protection. The perpetual disorders, in which the always rebellious Albanians in the Morea played a leading part, need not be considered in this connection. In 1457, after the two despots had failed to meet their tribute payments for several years, Mehmed, as Ducas tells us, sent them the following communication:

> How could you voluntarily promise an annual tribute of 10,000 gold pieces when I now see that you despise me and concern yourselves not at all with the treaties that were concluded? Now, of two things choose the one which seems better to you: either pay the tribute that is due, and then let peace prevail between us, or go away quickly and leave your country to my rule!

But even then payment was not forthcoming. Mehmed accorded the two brothers a period of grace in which to settle their quarrels, and when, as was to be expected, this too passed without result, he decided to intervene in person. He did not, as was customary in the West, take into account family plans or hereditary claims, but invoked only the naked right of conquest. Whenever he seemed to act in accordance with Western conceptions, it was only in order to gain time, to arouse false hopes, or to

[3] Inalcïk reviews the Ottoman campaigns in Serbia and gives a partial text in translation of the terms of surrender of the fortress of Golubac, "Mehmed the Conqueror," 415–421.

mask his intentions. After his second accession to the throne, he did not once deviate from his fundamental belief that, as Giàcomo de' Languschi put it, there must be only one empire, one faith, and one emperor on earth.

And so Mehmed set out from Edirne in April 1458, at the head of an army levied in Rumelia and Anatolia. A short time before he had received an envoy from the Bosnian king, bringing him a tribute payment of 9,000 gold pieces. By way of Thrace and Macedonia the vast army went to Thessaly, where the sultan decided to spend a few days and wait for the despots' plenipotentiaries. When they failed to appear, the column resumed its southward march, traversing all Greece. Nowhere did the Turks meet with serious resistance, for the Greek national spirit was dead, and above all there was no resolute common leadership. Shortly before the sultan reached the fortifications of the Hexamilion, which had long since been repaired, a legation arrived from the Palaeologi, bringing 4,500 gold pieces as part of the tribute due and hoping to obtain in return a treaty of peace and fealty. It was too late. The sultan accepted the money and replied scornfully that he himself would direct the negotiations on his arrival in the Morea. On May 15 the army entered the Peloponnese without opposition and camped near Corinth. An immediate assault seemed inadvisable in view of the city's powerful walls and fortress. Leaving a part of his Anatolian troops behind to besiege Corinth, in the hope of starving the poorly supplied city, Mehmed himself proceeded into the interior of the peninsula.

Tarsos, a mountain city in the region of ancient Phlius (Polyphengon), which was defended by native Albanians, fell after brief resistance and purchased the victor's mercy by delivering 300 young men to the Turks and accepting an Ottoman commander. As for Phlius, it was situated on an elevation and strongly defended. The Turks reduced it by cutting off the only source of water, which lay outside the walls. In desperation the garrison of Greeks and Albanians tried to bake bread by mixing flour with the blood of slaughtered beasts of burden, but was finally obliged to sue for peace. While negotiations were under way, the Janissaries discovered an unguarded point in the wall. Making their way into the city, they plundered it and mercilessly slaughtered almost the entire population. Next the town of Akribe (Akrivi) was taken by storm and Rupela (Rouvali), where many Greeks and Albanians had sought refuge with their families, was besieged. For two days the place defended itself with heroic courage. The sultan gave the order to withdraw. But then the inhabitants, fearing that the sultan would seek vengeance later, accepted their fate and surrendered. The city itself was spared, but the entire population, including women and children, was led away to distant Istanbul under strong guard. Only twenty Albanians, who had been given leave to withdraw freely from Tarsos but had broken their word and taken up arms again in Rupela, incurred the sultan's vengeance. He ordered their limbs to be crushed with iron balls.[4]

Continuing southward, the Turks invested the mountain citadel of Pazeniki (now Vlakherna). But the Albanian defenders possessed a secure escape route through a ravine situated behind the town, and even Manuel Cantacuzenus, who had led the Albanian uprising of 1454, could not move them to surrender. No sooner had Mehmed made his appearance in the peninsula than this crafty Greek had come to his camp and offered his services as a go-between. The sultan, however, regarded him as a two-faced scoundrel and had him sent away. Shortly thereafter Cantacuzenus fled to Hungary, where he ended his days. The sultan discontinued the siege and resumed his march into the interior. The despot Thomas had fled to Mantineia and his brother Demetrius to Monemvasia. The sultan's army camped near Tegea and proceeded to encircle the triple-walled city of Muchli, not far from present-day Tripolis. Demetrius Asanes led the defenders, but without success, for here again the Turks were able to force surrender by cutting off the city's water supply. Perhaps because of supply difficulties and the increasingly mountainous terrain, Mehmed decided in July 1458 to return northward and storm Corinth, the key to the entire peninsula, with his whole army.

The commander of the fortress was Matthew Asanes, who had succeeded with the help of Venice in bringing in a certain amount of provisions and reinforcements, chiefly by way of the port of Kenchreai. The sultan ordered enormous cannon to be cast on the spot. The projectiles, weighing several hundredweight, were made of marble taken from the ruins of ancient Corinth. Before giving the order to storm the city, he once again, in accordance with Islamic custom, summoned the defenders to surrender peacefully, though he did not, on this or any other occasion, demand that they adopt the Moslem faith. He sent word to Asanes that if he should surrender Corinth, he and all the inhabitants would be free to settle in any part of the Ottoman Empire they pleased, but that if he refused, he and all his followers were irrevocably doomed. Confident in the strength of the walls and the courage of the garrison, Asanes proudly

---

[4] While the identification of most of the sites named by Babinger in connection with the Morean campaigns is not difficult, uncertainty remains with regard to a few. In this connection see Kenneth Setton, *Renaissance News* 12 (1959), who identifies (p. 198) Akribe with Akova, near Karitaina; also useful is W. McLeod, "Castles of the Morea in 1467," *BZ* 65 (1972), 353–363.

declined the offer, replying that he well knew the power of the Turkish sultan, but that even he would not be able to storm the triple walls of Corinth, and that he, Asanes, preferred to die rather than abandon the city without a struggle.

Thereupon Mehmed set his culverins to work. In a few days the outermost wall, which was also the weakest, was leveled. When Asanes, after a sortie, withdrew behind the second wall, it too was breached at many points by the great marble balls. The food shortage in the city was critical, but even this would not have impelled the defenders to surrender if the bishop of Corinth, with the agreement of some of the city's notables, had not informed the sultan of the increasing distress of the population, so leading him to continue the bombardment. Mehmed now repeated his offer of surrender terms, and since the majority of the garrison was in favor of accepting, Asanes and Nicephorus Lukanes, termed by Phrantzes the "destroyers of the Peloponnese," repaired to the sultan's camp. As was to be expected, Mehmed's demands were considerable, including the surrender of all the lands through which he had passed, as well as Patras, Corinth, Aiyion, Kalavrita, and the surrounding country—in other words, roughly the whole territory over which the despot Constantine had ruled before mounting the throne of Byzantium. For the pitiful bit of land he left them, the despots were expected to pay an annual tribute of 3,000 gold pieces. Asanes hurried to Tripolis, where the two despots were at the time, to inform them of Mehmed's terms. Glad to save a part of their possessions, they both agreed to his demands. The peace was signed at once and both sides swore solemnly to observe it. The Greeks handed over the cities and territories "like garden vegetables" (Phrantzes). Like all the other fortresses and towns taken by the Turks, it received an Ottoman garrison consisting of Janissaries. While Turahanoğlu Ömer Bey, whose father had died in the middle of 1456 and been buried in Kirk Kavak near Uzun Köprü (Thrace), remained in the Morea as the sultan's governor, Mehmed (if Critoboulos is to believed), after conquering 250 Greek localities, hurried northward in forced marches. On his way, at Ömer Bey's invitation, he visited Athens, which had also been taken.[5]

Athens, an independent Latin duchy since 1204, and in the possession of the Florentine Acciajuoli since 1385, had been ruled by Duke Franco II. When Ömer Bey occupied the lower city in 1456, the citizens and their duke fled to the Acropolis, where the ducal palace was situated. For

[5] For an earlier narrative of Mehmed's Morean campaign of 1458 based exclusively on Western sources, see William Miller, *The Latins in the Levant* (New York, 1908), chap. 13, especially 426–435.

almost two years they bravely held out, until in June 1458 they surrendered. The duke, to whom a safe-conduct was granted, was allowed to retain Boeotia, including Thebes, as a vassal of the Porte. Now, in late August 1458, the sultan made his solemn entry into the city, thus inaugurating its Turkish occupation, which was to last almost 330 years.[6]

Mehmed, we are told by his apologist, Critoboulos, had a great predilection for the "city of the philosophers," as the Ottomans called Athens, and for its sights. As a "wise man and Philhellenist and great king," he admired the vestiges of classical antiquity, particularly the Acropolis. Chalcocondylas also relates that after visiting the harbor of Piraeus, the city of Athens, and the Acropolis, marveling at all these ancient glories, Mehmed cried out that he was deeply obligated to Ömer Bey for such a conquest. At that time the city, whose trade and other resources had been drastically reduced by the Ottoman campaigns and especially by the depredations of Ömer Bey, must have relapsed into a pitiful state such as Michael Choniates had described at the end of the twelfth century. Perhaps with some exaggeration, but assuredly on the basis of eyewitness reports, Pius II judged that Athens now had the appearance of a small fortress and owed its fame throughout Greece only to the Acropolis, with its magnificent temple of Pallas Athena. It seems highly unlikely that the city numbered 50,000 inhabitants in 1458, as was claimed.

Mehmed treated the Athenians with generosity and granted the wishes they presented to him. He confirmed the liberties which Ömer Bey had already conferred on them. A head tax was levied, but many families held patents relieving them of taxes and services. For the most part the inhabitants could avoid the levy of boys for the Janissaries by payments of money. The abbot of the monastery of Kyriani on Mount Hymettus, who had tendered the keys to the city, was also relieved of the head tax and had only to contribute one gold piece annually as a tax of homage. The population retained the right to be represented by a *gerousia* or council of elders (*vecchiades*) under the control of the Turkish governor. The Athenians derived particular satisfaction from the downfall of the hitherto prevailing Latin church and its priesthood. As compensation for the losses sustained by their church, the Orthodox clergy were quick to obtain favors and privileges by adulation of the Conqueror; it was a Greek abbot who had presented him with the keys of the city. Eager to win the Athenians, Mehmed accorded full tolerance to their religion, though without slighting the Catholic faith. The Acropolis was barred both to Greeks and to Latins. The chapels situated there were closed.

[6] For an alternative view of the length of the siege of the Athenian citadel, see Setton, 198–199.

The sultan spent four days in Athens. While Ömer Bey took up his residence in the castle of the banished Acciajuoli in the Propylaea, his master seems to have preferred to pitch his tents in the olive grove near the Academy or by the banks of the Ilissus.[7]

Then he continued on to Boeotia, visiting ancient Plataiai as well as Thebes, where he was humbly welcomed by Franco. Mehmed was curious to see nearby Negropont. Exclusive possession of this much contested island, over which Lombard barons had ruled for nearly 300 years, had passed to Venice following the peace guaranteed by Mehmed in April 1454. Especially since the fall of Constantinople, the Venetians regarded it as their "jewel in the Greek Sea" and their most important commercial colony. The sultan announced his visit to the *bailo* Paolo Barbarigo. At first the inhabitants of Negropont were terrified, but they came to meet him with palm branches when on September 2 he crossed the Euripos bridge with a thousand horsemen. He spoke amiably to the inhabitants, rode through the city, and no doubt surveyed it from the nearby hillside with a view to his military designs for the future. Another twelve years were to pass before he made his entry into the shattered city as a conqueror.

After this brief excursion, Mehmed returned to Thebes, whence he proceeded northward. A large train of prisoners took the same route; the artisans among them were to be resettled in Istanbul, all others in its environs. In the course of his journey, the sultan sent a messenger to the despot Demetrius, with orders to hand over his sixteen-year-old daughter Helena, famed for her beauty, for inclusion in the harem. On October 23, 1458, as is evident from the above-mentioned letter written on that date to Dubrovnik, Mehmed was in Üsküp in the Istranca Mountains. At this season he liked to enjoy the fresh air of the Balkan mountain regions. As the autumn drew to a close, he returned to Edirne. Here, immediately after his return, he received David Comnenus, the youngest brother of John IV, emperor of Trebizond, who delivered the annual tribute imposed on that city in 1456 after a brief siege by Hïzïr Pasha, which will be dealt with below.

By the spring of 1459, the desperate, self-destructive struggle between the two despots of the Morea had broken down all semblance of order in their domains. Energetic but untrustworthy, Thomas could not reconcile himself to the state of affairs created by his treaty with the sultan. It is

---

[7] Whatever privilege of exemption from the *devşirme* was granted the Athenians by Mehmed, it seems to have been revoked by the middle of the following century. (See *EI*[2] II, 211.) The end of Italian rule over the city is recorded by Miller, 435–443.

uncertain whether blindness or an excess of pride led him to break his oath. His evil spirit seems to have been the ambitious and restless archon Nicephorus Lukanes, who so fired his greed for power that he resolved not only to drive the Ottomans out of the Morea but also to seize the share of his sluggish and cowardly brother. In February 1459, Thomas and his adviser attacked the cities occupied by the Turks. Lukanes was to take Corinth by surprise, while Thomas had chosen to attack Patras. Both ventures failed, although Lukanes claimed to have obtained the connivance of the Corinthians. Only the sparsely garrisoned Kalavrita was cleared of Turks. The two rebels now called upon the whole population, Albanians as well as Greeks, to rise up; for the present, however, they waged war not on the Ottomans but on Demetrius, who in his distress sent his brother-in-law Matthew Asanes to Mehmed for help. The rebellion in the Morea soon assumed dangerous proportions. The entire peninsula was involved in the terrible fratricidal conflict. A number of places belonging to Demetrius, such as the fortresses of Karitaina, Bordonia, Kastritsa, Kalamata (Kalamai), Zarnata, and Leuktron, and almost all of the Maina (Mani), were taken by Thomas, partly by treachery and partly by force of arms. At length Demetrius summoned up the courage to resist; his generals Manuel Bochalis and Georgius Palaeologus seized his brother's capital city of Leondarion and a few other towns, but were compelled to withdraw with heavy losses when Thomas hurried to the spot. Meanwhile, the Albanians, the scourge of the Peloponnese traversed the country, pillaging and looting, changing sides according to the prospects for spoils, and, throughout the southern part of the peninsula, committing the most hideous crimes against the Greek population. Further to the north the Ottoman garrisons of Patras, Corinth, and Muchli devastated the surrounding territory, slaughtering or carrying off with them all those they found in their path.

The sultan, according to Critoboulos, spent the greater part of the winter in his island palace in Edirne, which at this date he seems still to have favored over the new serai in Istanbul. In any case, he had left a part of his harem in the old capital. We possess no authenticated information about his choice of residence in those years. We cannot be certain, for example, whether the charter, allegedly written not in Slavic but in Greek, which the sultan conferred upon the Ragusans on March 7, 1459, granting them full freedom to trade in the territories both of the sultan and of his vassals in return for an annual tribute of 1,500 gold pieces, was issued in Edirne or in Istanbul. A few weeks later Mehmed sent his stepmother Mara ("amirissa," "mistress of the Christian noblewomen," his "mother"—these are the terms employed in the text), a document concerning the convent of Hagia Sophia in Thessaloniki, which she had acquired. From this document, written in an encampment, we know that the sultan was already on his way to the west.[8]

By mid-March, his hostile intentions were indeed known at the court of Buda; toward the end of May a Milanese ambassador informed the court of Ferrara that, as he had learned from Hungarian sources, the sultan had made his appearance in Sofia on April 9. No one doubted that Mehmed was planning to invade Serbia and perhaps Hungary as well. The alarm was general. "The Christian cause is in the gravest peril," wrote Pietro Tommasi from Buda to the doge Pasquale Malipiero in Venice. The confused situation in the despotate made it seem likely that the sultan was going to intervene in person. Matthias Corvinus's attempt to unite Bosnia and Serbia under Stjepan Tomašević, who mounted the Serbian throne during Holy Week, on March 21, 1459, shortly after narrowly escaping from Turkish imprisonment in Bobovac, seemed unlikely to produce favorable results. On April 1, the first Sunday after Easter, his marriage with Jelena Branković, Lazar's daughter, was celebrated. The Turks looked upon the installation of the Bosnian prince as an unwarranted infringement on their rights, since the Serbian Despotate was a vassal state. On April 8, a few days after Stjepan's accession, the blind and helpless despot Stjepan Branković was overthrown by his own retinue and driven out of the country. He fled northward to Buda, then to Croatia, and finally, in fear for his life, by way of Dubrovnik to Albania. King Stjepan Tomaš of Bosnia attempted to divert the onslaught of the Turkish armies by laying siege to the fortress of Hodidjed (east of Sarajevo), which had long been in Turkish hands, but he did not succeed. At length he was obliged to appeal to the Hungarians for help.

Meanwhile Mehmed, meeting with no resistance, was approaching Smederevo with his army. No one thought seriously of defending the city. As soon as the Ottoman army was seen in the distance, the notables opened the gates, trooped out to present the sultan with the keys to the city, and implored his protection. On Wednesday, June 20, 1459, the famous Serbian city fell into the sultan's hands without a struggle.

The fall of Smederevo appears to have created almost as much emotion in the West as the capture of Constantinople. Enea Silvio Piccolomini, who at the death of the aged Calixtus III, on August 6, 1458, had mounted the chair of St. Peter as Pius II, aptly termed Smederevo "a gateway to

---

[8] For this document, see Babinger's "Ein Freibrief Mehmeds II., des Eroberers, für das Kloster Hagia Sophia zu Saloniki, Eigentum der Sultanin Mara (1459)," *BZ* 44 (1951), 11–20; reprinted in *A&A* I, 97–106.

Rascia" (Rascia or Rashka, the ancient name of Serbia). Both he and King Matthias put the full blame for its shameful surrender on the treachery of the Bosnians, the king, his brother, and his son. By way of punishment, all property of the Serbian Despotate on Hungarian soil was confiscated. Only Helena Branković, Lazar's widow, was allowed, in accordance with a previous agreement, to leave the country with her treasures. Stjepan Tomaš had fled shortly before. Helena and her daughters went first to Bosnia by way of Hungary and later to Italy, where they lived in various places. Helena died on November 7, 1473, as a nun on the island of Levkas (Santa Mavra).

The notables of Smederevo, who had been so helpful to the sultan, were richly rewarded with money and lands. Only the Hungarian garrison and those citizens who showed signs of recalcitrance were taken prisoner and led away. At the sight of the Ottoman banners, the smaller fortresses of northern Serbia surrendered without resistance. By the end of 1459 all Serbia was in Ottoman hands. Such was the ignominious end of a once proud kingdom. Metamorphosed into the monk Germanos, the blind Gregor vanished. He died on October 16, 1459, presumably in Chilandar on the sacred Mount Athos, where, in any event, he was buried. Only his sister Mara lived out her life in peace. Unmolested and on good terms with her stepson Mehmed, she resided at Ježevo near Mount Athos, surrounded by Serbian nobles and monks. She seldom went to Istanbul, but as "stepmother of the Grand Turk" (*maregna del Gran Turco*) was often called upon for help by Christians having business with the sultan. Not infrequently Western envoys on their way to the Porte made a detour to ask the advice of the pious *amirissa* in her residence, the ruins of which, including her violated and looted grave, are still to be seen. Her influence was to stand many of her fellow Christians in good stead. She was instrumental in the appointment and removal of more than one patriarch of Istanbul. Aged about seventy—rather than "over eighty-five," as most writers maintain—she died on Friday, September 14, 1487, and was buried by her faithful followers not far from her palace at Ježevo.[9]

In its downfall the Serbian Despotate lost the core of its Christian population. Some 200,000 Serbs, we are told, were enslaved and either

---

[9] Babinger gives further details regarding the establishment of Mara's resting place in his "Witwensitz und Sterbeplatz der Sultanin Mara" in *A&A* I, 340–343. Additional details on Mara's later life, with comments on her age at death, are given by I. A. Papadrianos, "The Marriage-arrangement between Constantine XI Palaeologus and the Serbian Mara (1451)," *Balkan Studies* 6 (1965), 131–138.

sent to the Turkish army or settled in remote sections of the Ottoman Empire. Little by little the devastated country was repopulated, in part by Ottomans, who introduced new institutions which soon destroyed the vitality and independence of the remaining Slav population.

Mehmed's itinerary after the fall of Smederevo cannot readily be reconstructed, although he seems to have returned to Istanbul toward the end of the summer. In any case, he left it to his generals, who were familiar with local conditions, to deal with the disorders in the Morea. He had no doubt been informed by Demetrius's envoys of the defection of the despot Thomas and of the mutinies on the peninsula. Seething with rage, he is reported to have sent orders to Hamza Pasha, governor of Thessaly, to hasten to the Peloponnese with all available troops and punish the guilty parties. The chief butt of his indignation was the governor of the Morea, Turahanoğlu Ömer Bey, whom he regarded as largely responsible for the disorders, though it seems unlikely that—as Chalcocondylas, among others, supposed—he suspected him of fomenting the rebellion. More probably, the sultan merely blamed his weakness and lack of energy for having allowed things to go so far. Ömer Bey was deprived both of his post and of his fiefs in Thessaly, and his son-in-law, the renegade Ahmed Bey, was appointed governor of the Morea in his stead. Along with Ahmed Bey, Hamza entered the Peloponnese in the middle of 1459.

Thomas, who saw disaster approaching, turned in despair to the pope, sending a delegation with sixteen Turkish prisoners who had presumably fallen into his hands at Kalavrita. Pope Pius II, who at the same time was trying to implement his plans for a crusade at the Congress of Mantua, was informed, "with true Byzantine braggadocio," that a company of Italian troops would suffice to drive the Turks from the Peloponnese. When the matter was discussed in the consistory, the pope expressed his doubts that so small a number of men would suffice, but the fanatical and impractical Cardinal Bessarion persuaded him to grant the request and Duchess Bianca-Maria Sforza of Milan supplied one-third of the promised levy. The Pope's misgivings had been well founded, however. The expedition was a lamentable failure: the 300 foot soldiers did not reach the Morea in time to help Thomas renew the siege of Patras. Hearing that Ottoman reinforcements were on their way, Thomas abandoned the venture and retreated in haste to his capital city of Leondarion. Here he gave the Turks open battle and incurred a severe defeat. Poorly distributed on the heights, his troops, including the papal contingent, were dispersed by the first charge of the Ottoman cavalry under

Yunus Bey, commander of the *sipahis*, and fled to the more southerly mountains in such haste that only a few were overtaken and killed by the pursuing Turkish *akincis*.

The Turks gained no immediate advantage from their victory. Hamza, who had encircled Leondarion, set out for Muchli, but his army, none too large to begin with, suffered considerable losses from disease and the shortage of supplies. Obliged to ask the sultan for reinforcements, he quickly withdrew to Thessaly, leaving a small auxiliary force behind him with Demetrius. Thomas took advantage of Hamza's departure to attempt a third siege of Patras, this time supported by the papal contingent. But since the despot did not know how to handle his siege guns and the papal troops proved a total failure, he was again unable to breach the powerful walls. When at Thomas's command the trumpeters sounded the signal to retreat, his troops scattered. After the manner of the Albanians, the Italians roamed the impoverished countryside, looting and pillaging, and finally vanished without a trace. The true masters of the battlefield were the Albanians under their powerful leader, Peter Bua, who dominated those sections of the peninsula that were not in Turkish hands.

At the southern end of the peninsula, in ancient Laconia, Thomas reassembled a part of his army. He was about to attack the coastal cities that still belonged to his brother, particularly Kalamata, when he suddenly decided to make peace with the sultan. Glad to end the confusion in this remote and troubled corner of Greece, Mehmed was inclined to agree, but exacted hard terms, demanding that the despot Thomas should remove his troops everywhere, evacuate all the cities he had taken, pay out 3,000 gold pieces on the spot, and furthermore that he appear personally in Corinth within twenty days to sign a treaty with the sultan's plenipotentiary. Thomas accepted all these demands and even expressed his willingness to become reconciled with his brother Demetrius. The two despots met in the church of the little city of Kastritsa, where the metropolitan of Mistra said Mass, not in the usual rich vestments but covered with sackcloth and ashes as a sign of repentance. Deeply moved, the brothers fell into each other's arms and swore to live in eternal harmony. But this "eternity" was to endure only a few weeks.

This time the breach of faith seems to have originated with Demetrius, who apparently counted heavily on the friendship and help of Mehmed. Such at least is the opinion of Phrantzes, who tries to give a faithful account of the events. In the course of the following winter, the war between the brothers was renewed with all its horrors, and as a result Thomas was unable to raise the promised tribute. Once again Kalamata and Demetrius's other possessions in Messenia were ravaged by guerrilla warfare. Turkish freebooters from Palaça in Anatolia plundered the Maina, destroyed the ships of the Mainots, and carried off numerous prisoners to Asia Minor. The whole of the Morea, even the Venetian settlements, was reduced to misery. In Navplion (Nauplia, Napoli di Romania) the treasury was so burdened with debt that the officials went unpaid and the citizens were without protection. It could easily be foreseen that Mehmed would not for long look on inactive at the disorder in the Peloponnese, but would soon intervene in person. Later in the winter of 1459–1460, he seems to have postponed his projected campaign in Asia Minor, with the intention of repairing to the Morea as soon as possible with all available forces.

The reports pouring in from southeastern Europe concerning the alarming and irresistible progress of the Ottomans had cast a shadow on the coronation of Pius II (September 3, 1458). Once installed in Rome, the new pope had but one thought: war against the Turks. In a long address delivered on October 12 to an assembly of cardinals, bishops, and prelates of the Curia, and attended by the foreign ambassadors to the Eternal City, he described the defeats which the Christians had thus far suffered at the hands of the Turks and proclaimed his determination to resist the furious enemy at last. In a bull issued on this occasion, the pope summoned all the princes of the West to a congress, where the measures to be taken toward a European crusade would be discussed. He described the oppression with which the supporters of the "false prophet Mohammed" and the bloodthirsty hordes of the "venomous dragon" threatened Christendom. This, the pope declared, was God's punishment for the sins of the fathers. God, he went on, had elevated him to the papacy to redeem the world from this affliction. Even the less important states, princes, and towns received urgent summonses to participate in the congress, which was to be held in Mantua.[10]

It was obvious that as long as harmony did not prevail in Italy itself, effective opposition to the Turks was unthinkable. Thus the pope's most urgent concern was to restore peace in Italy. First of all, it would be necessary to end the conflict with Naples which he had inherited from his predecessor. Pius set out for Mantua in January 1459. Shortly before his departure he founded a new chivalric order, on the model of the Knights of St. John in Rhodes, to defend the Christians in Greek waters against

[10] The papacy under Pius II is described in detail by Pastor, *The History of the Popes* III. A modern biography of the pope, covering the earlier years as well, is R. J. Mitchell, *The Laurels and the Tiara, Pope Pius II 1458–1464* (London, 1962).

the rising sea power of the Ottomans. But it is uncertain whether this order, which was to be named after the Virgin Mary of Bethlehem and to have its headquarters on the island of Lemnos, ever came into being.

Although Pope Pius and his retinue did not reach Mantua until May 27, 1459, none of the Christian kings and princes to whom he had sent repeated and urgent invitations arrived ahead of him; they had not even considered it necessary to send delegations. The worst fears seemed to be justified by such disrespect toward the pope, who had arrived before the appointed date. When the congress was opened on June 1, there could be no question of embarking on any business. The cardinals present complained bitterly of the pestilential air of Mantua, where there was no sound to be heard but the croaking of frogs. Did the pope imagine, they asked bitterly, that he could defeat the Turks alone? Let him return to Rome, for he had done as much as his honor demanded. Cardinal Bessarion, well acquainted with the Turkish peril from his own hard experience, was almost alone in remaining true to the pope. New letters were dispatched in all directions. Slowly, very slowly, a few ambassadors appeared. The indifference of the European rulers was directly proportional to the distance of their territories from the Turkish menace. Most deplorable of all was the attitude taken by Emperor Frederick III, who, according to medieval conceptions, should have been the protector of Christendom. Masking his true political intentions beneath shameful subterfuges, he sidestepped the duty of defending the West against the onslaught of Islam. His actual intentions were directly opposed to the pope's plan for a crusade against the Turks. His main concern was to overthrow the king of Hungary, when it should have been to defend this last bulwark of Austria and the entire West. Conniving with the Magnates' Party, which was hostile to Matthias Corvinus, he had himself proclaimed king of Hungary during the Congress of Mantua.

Pius II was horrified at the course of events. Once again he urgently implored the German emperor, whom he knew well, having served him for five years as an official in the imperial chancellery and later as adviser, even writing a history of him, to consider the needs of the day. All his efforts were in vain. The conflict between Frederick III and Matthias Corvinus burst into the open. At length the emperor sent some obscure plenipotentiaries to Mantua, but held out the prospect of a real imperial legation for the following autumn.

The other German princes, ecclesiastical as well as secular, showed equal indifference. The messages which the pope dispatched across the Alps were as voices crying in the wilderness. The few delegates who finally started out for Mantua were motivated neither by religious fervor nor by fear of the Turks.

Almost worse than the indifference of Germany was the overtly hostile attitude of France. King Charles VII was alarmed by the developments in Naples. King Alfonso had died on July 27, 1458, whereupon Pope Calixtus, during the few days left to him, had tried to make Naples a fief of the Church. Alfonso's bastard son Ferdinand (called Don Ferrante) had mounted the throne at once, however, and was soon recognized by the new pope, Pius II. Reviving the ancient claims of the house of Anjou to the throne of Naples, the king of France urged annulment of Ferrante's investiture and demanded papal concessions in the Italian controversy as the price of his participation in a crusade. Venice and Florence also used the Naples affair as a convenient pretext with which to veil their reluctance—resulting largely from mercantile considerations—to participate in a campaign against the Turks. Deaf to repeated admonitions, Florence, despite the proximity of Mantua, sent no emissaries.

Meanwhile, witnesses to the impending peril in the East arrived at Mantua. Messengers came from Albania, Dubrovnik, Rhodes, Lesbos, and even Cyprus. The legation sent by the despot Thomas has already been mentioned. At the end of July, Hungarian delegates arrived. Emissaries from Bosnia brought news of the fall of Smederevo. "Now," the pope lamented, "there is nothing to prevent the Turks from invading Hungary." Before the actual sessions could begin, the usual quarrels broke out over rank and seating order, to which the pope finally put an end by an adroit decree to the effect that no one should suffer disadvantage. In the middle of August a splendid delegation from the duke of Burgundy appeared. The duke himself was not present, but was represented by his nephew, Duke John of Cleve, with a retinue of 400 horsemen. Before solemnly committing himself to participate in the crusade, he too attempted to obtain political advantages in connection with the recent trouble in Soest. He did not remain at the congress for long, but left Mantua in haste after making a niggardly promise that Burgundy would send 2,000 horsemen and 4,000 foot soldiers to Hungary.

At the end of September, Francesco Sforza, duke of Milan, appeared in person. His retinue glittering with gold and the brilliant procession of Milanese aroused admiration and confidence. The vain Francesco Filelfo spoke, promising in the name of his master that he would do everything in his power to combat the "bloodthirsty infidels"—insofar as the situation in Italy permitted. Here again the Neapolitan question rose up in the background. Little by little, emissaries arrived from other states and cities.

At the end of September even the Signoria of Venice, though thoroughly disinclined to a Turkish campaign because of its Levantine trade, sent two delegates: Orsato Giustiniani and the famous jurist and diplomat Luigi Foscarini, whose departure had repeatedly been postponed in the hope that Pius II would ultimately give up hope and abandon his plan. Venice was unwilling to take the risk of giving up its profitable relations with the Porte, especially in view of the rivalry and hostility of the Florentines, who were on the best of terms with the sultan. Pursuing the self-seeking policy of Venice with meticulous persistence, the doge Pasquale Malipiero took no little pride in his friendly relations with Mehmed. In an address to the pope, Luigi Foscarini, an astute statesman and eloquent orator, gave his assurance that Venice was willing to take part in an all-European campaign. But in view of the negative attitude of most of the Christian powers, Pius was forced to doubt that all Christendom would join in the campaign. Perhaps nothing is more characteristic of the attitude of the Venetians than their violent opposition, for fear of provoking the dreaded enemy, to the pope's proposal of transferring the congress from Mantua to Udine. Their position was that if the great war was to be undertaken, it should be done with adequate resources, and rather later than sooner.

On September 26, 1459, the first session was held in the cathedral of Mantua. In a speech lasting two hours the pope described the losses thus far incurred by Christendom at the hands of the Ottomans.

Not our fathers, no, we ourselves allowed Constantinople, the capital of the East, to be conquered by the Turks. And while we sit at home in ease and idleness, the arms of these barbarians are advancing to the Danube and the Sava. In the Eastern imperial city they have massacred the successor of Constantine along with his people, desecrated the temples of the Lord, sullied the noble edifice of Justinian with the hideous cult of Mohammed; they have destroyed the images of the Mother of God and other saints, overturned the altars, cast the relics of the martyrs to the swine, killed the priests, dishonored women and young girls, even the virgins dedicated to the Lord, slaughtered the nobles of the city at the sultan's banquet, carried off the image of our crucified Savior to their camp with scorn and mockery amid cries of "That is the God of the Christians!" and befouled it with mud and spittle. All this happened beneath our very eyes, but we lie in a deep sleep. No, we are able to fight among ourselves, but let the Turks do as they please. For trifling provocations the Christians take up arms and fight bloody battles; but against the Turks, who blaspheme our God, destroy our churches, and seek to extirpate the very name of Christianity, no one is willing to raise a hand. Verily, all have withdrawn, all have become useless; there is none to do good, none. It is thought perhaps that these things are already done and can no longer be altered, and that from now on we shall have peace. As though peace might be expected from a nation which thirsts for our blood, which after subjecting Greece has already thrust its sword into the flank of Hungary, from an enemy such as Sultan Mehmed! Abandon this belief, for Mehmed will never lay down arms except in victory or total defeat. Every victory will be for him a stepping-stone to another, until, after subjecting all the princes of the West, he has destroyed the Gospel of Christ and imposed the law of his false prophet upon the whole world.

In the name of the college of cardinals, Bessarion, of all those present the most familiar with conditions in the Levant, replied to the pope's impressive arguments. His oration, delivered with Christian and classical eloquence, ended with an appeal to all the princes and nations of Christendom to take up the struggle against the infidels. Finally the assembly resolved unanimously to make war against the Turks. The ways and means of organizing the projected crusade by land and sea were to be taken up at the ensuing sessions. But when in conclusion the pope made the proposal that to defray the heavy costs of the undertaking the clergy over a period of three years should contribute one-tenth, the laity one-thirtieth, and the Jews one-twentieth of their revenues, it was precisely the wealthiest states, Venice and Florence, which presented the greatest obstacles. When those in attendance were asked to sign the papal decree concerning the distribution of the burdens involved in the war, the Venetians alone refused, making their signature contingent on conditions that could not possibly be met: Venice must have supreme command of the entire fleet and sole right to the anticipated spoils, its expenses must be reimbursed, the other participants must supply 8,000 men as crews for the Venetian ships, and an army of 20,000 foot soldiers and 50,000 horsemen must be assembled at the Hungarian border. Pius II protested vehemently:

Against the Pisans, against the Genoese, against emperors and kings you have waged great wars for your allies and subjects. Now that you are asked to fight for Christ against the infidel, you demand payment. You raise difficulties only in order that the war should not take place. But if it did not, you would be the first to regret it.

All the pope's words were in vain. Venice persisted in its determination to grant nothing.

The German delegation, led by the embittered, crude, and ruthless jurist Gregor von Heimburg, confronted the pope with one unpleasant surprise after another. Von Heimburg did his utmost to stir up discord among the Germans. In jeering speeches he attacked the pope and even his overlord, the emperor. At length the Germans promised to provide 32,000 foot soldiers and 10,000 horsemen. But the practical details were to be settled at two diets, one in Nuremberg, the other in Austria. Frederick III was appointed leader of the German crusading army, but with the express proviso that, should he be prevented from participating in person, he choose a prince of the Holy Roman Empire to take his place.

The congress failed because of the general faintheartedness and hypocrisy. There were no men resolved to surmount all obstacles and correct the political situation by committing themselves to the full. In Mantua the tune was called by men of mediocre talents. The shrill bickering of the Italians never died down. In the last weeks of the congress its true purpose, the crusade against the Turks, was overshadowed by the Neapolitan question.

Thus the year 1459 passed in Mantua. The delegates devoured the fat oxen which the duke of Milan had donated to the pope, and found them exceedingly tasty. Then they dispersed in all directions. Pope Pius II was the last to leave. On January 19, 1460, he set out from Mantua in a poor state of health. With new bulls and encyclicals as well as embassies, he kept trying to revive the flagging enthusiasm of the rulers of Europe and to put an end to their quarrels. The inevitable outcome of his efforts was more promises and more disappointment.

Meanwhile Mehmed, who, as there is good reason to suppose, was well informed by his Italian spies about the proceedings and meager results of the congress, was busy in his serai in Istanbul with new projects, presumably quite untroubled by the dubious Western plans to resist him.

Thasos, Lemnos, and Samothraki, the three islands seized by Scarampo in 1456, were left without protection after the papal fleet had returned to Italy in the summer of 1458. It was easy for Mehmed's friend Critoboulos as governor of Lemnos to reestablish Turkish sovereignty, for the Orthodox inhabitants were none too happy with the pope's rule. And in August 1459, Zaganos Pasha, the successor of Ismail Pasha as admiral, recaptured Thasos and Samothraki for the sultan.

On November 7, 1459, Mehmed acknowledged in Istanbul receipt of the Ragusan tribute of 1,500 ducats for the current year, which had been delivered by an emissary named Jaketa. A few days later, on November 18, Turkish patrols burned to the ground the famous old Serbian convent of Mileševa near Prijepolje on the Lim. On this occasion the Turks left unmolested the body of St. Sava, the Serbian national hero. It was only in 1594 that, by way of discouraging Serbian national sentiment, they removed it to Belgrade and publicly burned it on the Vracar.

On December 22, 1459, a third son was born to Mehmed. This was Sultan Cem, whose romantic and adventurous career was to be a source of interest to the courts of Europe long after his father's death and until his own, far from home, in Capua in southern Italy, a victim of slow poison (February 25, 1495).[11] Most historians claim that his mother was a Serbian princess, but this cannot be proved. According to more credible sources, she was a Moslem bearing the Turkish name of Çiçek Hatun.

Before setting out on his second expedition to the Morea, Mehmed replaced the deposed Albanian Hamza Zenevisi (not to be confused with Skanderbeg's nephew) by Zaganos Pasha, who, as husband of Murad II's daughter Fatima Hatun, had for a time been at once Mehmed's brother-in-law and father-in-law. The sultan had recalled him from exile in Anatolia and made him governor of Thessaly and the Morea. In March 1460, Zaganos Pasha appeared on the peninsula with the advance guard of the Turkish army. The sultan himself did not start for southern Greece with the main body of his troops until Easter Sunday (April 13, 1460), probably from Edirne.[12] At the beginning of May, after twenty days of marching, he was before Corinth, where he camped for three days. According to a previous agreement, the despot Demetrius was to present himself when the sultan's army arrived. But the despot, who had fled from Epidhavros (Epidaurus) to Mistra, preferred to remain in the background and to send his brother-in-law Matthew Asanes to the sultan's camp with lavish gifts. The sultan was infuriated. Holding Asanes as a hostage, he ordered the grand vizier Mahmud Pasha to march on Mistra, capital of the despotate. Mahmud complied and laid siege to New Sparta. The sultan's Greek secretary, Thomas Catavolenus (turned Moslem under the name of Yunus Bey), who had been employed successfully on various diplomatic missions, and Hamza Zenevisi were commissioned to negotiate with the encircled Demetrius. After some hesitation,

---

[11] For the second son of Mehmed see *EI²*, II, 529–531, "Djem" (H. Inalcïk). The honorific title "sultan" was accorded to princes of the Ottoman dynasty, preceding the given name. The same title was also given to highly venerated, popular figures, especially mystical teachers, in which case it followed the name. Mehmed's son Cem was thus known both as Sultan Cem and, especially after his death, as Cem Sultan.

[12] For a firman issued by Mehmed on April 26 see Elizabeth A. Zachariadou, "Early Ottoman Documents of the Prodromos Monastery," *Südost-Forschungen* 28 (1969), 7.

Demetrius agreed to leave his capital and surrender it to the Turks (May 30). On the next day, the sultan arrived with the van of his army, and united with the troops from Laconia. But instead of turning against the despot Thomas, he started at once for Venetian Argos. Demetrius was summoned to appear before the sultan. Critoboulos has given us a vivid and perhaps faithful account of the meeting:

> When Demetrius entered the sultan's tent, Mehmed arose from his seat, held out his right hand to him, and bade him be seated. Then he spoke with him of the peace existing between them, regaled him with gentle and friendly words, and comforted him when he became aware of his fear and anguish. He gave him hope for the future and the conviction that he could obtain from him anything he desired. Then he made him many rich presents of silver, garments of honor, horses, mules, and many other things, which were later of great use to him.

But Mehmed left no doubt that Demetrius was to consider himself a hostage and that it was all up with Greek rule in Mistra. At the same time the sultan reiterated his demand that Demetrius finally hand over his daughter Helena, who was then at Monemvasia with her mother. Hamza, recently out of favor, was appointed commandant of Mistra. Before being led away, Demetrius seems to have promised the sultan, with rather too much alacrity, to hand over his daughter and at the same time surrender the city of Monemvasia. Thereupon Isa Bey, son of the Macedonian march warden Ishak Bey, moved up to the fortress along with emissaries from Demetrius. The despot's family was given up to them without resistance; with the support of the population, however, Manuel Palaeologus, commander of the fortress, resolutely declined to surrender the town, declaring that he would do his utmost to hold it for Thomas, the rightful prince. The Turks withdrew, but in their stead came Lope de Baldaja, the Catalan freebooter, to whom Manuel Palaeologus had appealed for help. When he occupied the city, Thomas ceded it voluntarily to the pope. Overjoyed, Pius praised the Monemvasiots' zeal for the Catholic church, took possession of the city, and promised several Catalan corsairs lands in Greece if they should succeed in wresting the lands from the Turks. But the papal regime in Monemvasia was short-lived, for by 1462 the defenseless population had thrown themselves into the arms of Venice.[18]

[18] Paul Wittek reviews the place of Monemvasia in the Greek resistance to Ottoman attack, giving special regard to the transformation of its name in the Turkish sources, in "The Castle of Violets. From Greek Monemvasia to Turkish Menekshe," *Bulletin of the School of Oriental and African Studies* 20 (1957),

The Despotate of Mistra was destroyed. Mehmed spent four days in the city and started on his campaign against Thomas. Resistance was negligible. Everywhere the people swore allegiance to the sultan. First Bordonia fell, abandoned by its inhabitants, then Kastritsa after brief resistance. The city was easily taken and laid waste; it proved more difficult to capture the inaccessible citadel, and many Janissaries fell to their death while trying to scale its cliffs. Finally the garrison, consisting of 300 men, surrendered. Mehmed had them rounded up and slaughtered. Proinokokkas, the commander, was sawed in two. The next place to surrender was Leondarion, whose inhabitants had fled to the almost impregnable Gardiki. When this stronghold surrendered in return for the promise of safeconduct for the garrison, Mehmed did not hesitate to renew the blood bath of Kastritsa. Penned into a small area, 6,000 people were chained by their hands and feet and tortured to death. On this occasion not even the women and children were spared. Gardiki was a fief of the Bochalis family. Because the wife of Manuel Bochalis, Eugenia, an Albanian and a relative (stepsister) of Mahmud Pasha, brought her influence to bear, Manuel Bochalis and Georgius Palaeologus were able, thanks to a ruse, to withdraw unhindered to Corfu, whence they later continued on to Naples. Korkodeilos Kladas, the same who in 1480 was to arouse Mehmed's fury and provoke a sharp exchange of letters with the Venetian Signoria by fomenting a dangerous uprising in the Maina, surrendered the Frankish castle of St. George in Arcadia to the sultan. One town after another opened its gates to the invaders. Kiparissia, only recently the capital of the despot Thomas, Karitaina, Androusa, and Ithomi fell quickly into Turkish hands. No less than 10,000 people were said to have been taken from Kiparissia alone and carried off to Istanbul as slaves.

Thomas made no attempt to defend his despotate. On hearing that Mehmed had taken possession of Mistra, he had hastened to Mantineia on the Gulf of Messenia, from where it would be easy to escape if necessary. When he saw that all was lost and that only Venetian territory was left in peace, he fought his way to Pilos (Navarino). Meanwhile, the sultan visited Methoni and Koroni, the Venetian possessions in Messenia, whose authorities, for fear of diplomatic difficulties, put pressure on Thomas not to remain in Pilos. Two ships were put at his disposal, and the frightened despot fled to Marathos. As the sultan appeared within sight of Pilos, Thomas, accompanied by his wife and children and a few

---

601–613. Kenneth Setton proposes 1464 as the date of the Venetian occupation of Monemvasia, instead of 1462. (See his review of Babinger's book, *Renaissance News* 12 [1959], 198.)

nobles, put out to sea and sailed from nearby Porto Longo to Corfu, where he arrived on July 28. The Venetian *rettore* of the island welcomed the fugitives with great pomp. Venice hastened to renew its treaties of peace and friendship with him, which did not prevent the sultan's troops from devastating the whole countryside and killing a considerable number of Venetian subjects.

Meanwhile, the army under Zaganos Pasha was winning further victories in the northwest of the peninsula. The strongly fortified Chlomoutsi fell quickly into Ottoman hands. The city of Kalavrita, whose Albanian commander Doxas (or Doxies) as Phrantzes reports, was loyal neither to the despots nor the sultan, nor to God himself, was surrendered by its inhabitants. Doxas and his men were cruelly put to death. Only the fortress of Grevenon resisted bravely, compelling the besiegers to withdraw. But another Frankish castle, St. Omer (Santimeri), to which the nobles and the wealthy of the land had removed their treasures, supposing that they would here be in safety, fell into the hands of the Turks. Those of the inhabitants who escaped the blood bath were carried off into slavery. The cruelty of Zaganos aroused the resistance of the Moreots, who in the end preferred to die rather than to fall into his power. The sultan, who after visiting the Venetian possessions had arrived by way of Elis to join forces with Zaganos, was said to have been so incensed at his behavior that he ordered the prisoners of St. Omer set free on the spot. Even though Zaganos Pasha lost his post on this occasion and was replaced by Hamza Zenevisi, there is no doubt that this act of clemency was shrewdly calculated for its effect on the inhabitants, some of whom succeeded in escaping across the Gulf of Corinth.

Mehmed decided to remain in the Morea until Achaea should be subjugated. The castle of Grevenon, which had previously defied all assaults, was taken by Ishakoğlu Isa Bey, margrave of Skoplje. A third of the population were carried away prisoner. Other strongholds such as Aiyion, Kastrimenon, and Listraina soon changed hands. The powerful mountain fortress of Salmenikon, situated between Patras and Aiyion, was defended by Graitzas Palaeologus, who, though not of pure imperial blood, proved worthier of the name than the two despots. He refused to surrender in response to the sultan's summons. In vain Mehmed's culverins bombarded the fortress; in vain the Janissaries stormed the walls. Only after seven days, when the water supply was cut off, did the lower city, overcrowded with Greek and Albanian fugitives, surrender. Six thousand prisoners were taken; the sultan kept the boys for himself, while the rest were divided among his captains. But the citadel was still in the hands of Graitzas, who agreed to surrender only if the sultan himself should withdraw. Mehmed accepted this condition and returned to Aiyion, leaving the field to Hamza Zenevisi. But after the experience of St. Omer, the defender had little faith in Turkish oaths. He decided to put Hamza's honor to the test by sending out a part of the garrison, laden with baggage. Hamza fell upon the men and seized the baggage, so shamelessly breaking his commander's oath. Graitzas now declined any form of surrender. The sultan reinstated Zaganos Pasha as governor of Thessaly and the Morea, but the brave Salmenikon held out. Only after a year's siege (1461) did the heroic commander surrender, but now he was permitted to withdraw with all honor into Venetian territory. So great was the enthusiasm even of his enemies that the grand vizier Mahmud Pasha was said to have cried out, "I saw many slavish souls in the Morea, but he was a man." The Venetian senate honored the bold warrior by making him commander of their light cavalry.

From Aiyion, Mehmed proceeded to Corinth by way of Lake Pheneos and Phlius. In Phlius many Albanians had stored their possessions, which caused the Ottomans to seize the town in all haste and, despite their promise of forbearance, to slaughter the inhabitants without mercy. Mehmed left Zaganos Pasha in his rear, while he himself continued into the interior of the Morea to put things in order and to organize the administration. The first concern of the Ottomans in the Peloponnese was to install their own feudal system, which was probably not very different from the Frankish system. The majority of the Moreots were allowed to adhere to their old faith, and the political concessions that were made to the inhabitants soon after the Turkish occupation of the peninsula, consisting above all in the free administration of their communities, contributed greatly to the survival of Greek Christianity. Nevertheless, not a few nobles and burghers, chiefly of Frankish descent, espoused Islam in order, as later in Bosnia, to secure the possession of their property. In this region there were also secret Christians and others whose conversion did not go beyond superficial forms. The Turkish rule was to be least felt by the Mainots in their rough, inaccessible mountain country. From 1460 to 1821 the Mainot tribes engaged in constant uprisings against all foreign rule.

Mehmed destroyed all fortified places that struck him as dangerous and moved the inhabitants to the plains. A part were led away to Istanbul.

Toward the end of summer the sultan returned northward across the isthmus. Ömer Bey was reappointed governor of the Morea. The sultan was accompanied by the deposed Demetrius, whose wife and daughter had long since been sent ahead to Thrace. The booty in men and in treasures of all sorts was enormous.

On the way, Mehmed paid a second visit to Athens. On this occasion the Janissaries stationed in the Acropolis informed him of a Frankish conspiracy in favor of Franco II, who was then living in the ruined castle of St. Omer near Thebes and who seems to have harbored the vain hope of regaining possession of his former capital. It is not known whether his partisans in Athens were too inept to keep their conspiracy secret or whether the Janissaries invented it altogether; in any case, the reports infuriated Mehmed. At first he wanted to impose severe penalties on the whole city, but then he contented himself with seizing ten of the wealthiest citizens and sending them off to settle in Istanbul. Otherwise, the city was allowed to retain its privileges granted in 1458.

But Zaganos Pasha received instructions to forestall any such conspiracies in the future by putting the duke out of the way. Suspecting nothing, Franco went to the Morea, whither he had been summoned. He appeared in the tent of the pasha, who gave him a friendly reception and entertained him like a prince. A lively conversation continued until far into the night, when suddenly Zaganos Pasha informed the prince that his last hour had struck. Franco Acciajuoli was said to have asked the favor of receiving the death blow in his own tent and it was granted. A few moments later he succumbed at the hands of his executioners. Thus Thebes and the surrounding country, the last remnant of the Duchy of Athens, fell an easy prey to the Ottomans in the same year as the peninsula of the Morea.[14]

In mid-autumn Mehmed made a brief stay in Edirne, but spent the rest of the year and the whole winter in Istanbul. There he took counsel with the grand vizier Mahmud Pasha as well as Ishak Pasha—so Critoboulos tells us—and decided to grant the despot Demetrius the revenues from the islands of Imroz and Lemnos, estimated at 300,000 aspers, and parts of Samothraki and Thasos. He further gave him Enez, with its rich salt mines, in fief, and all the taxes and imposts that he had taken away from Dorino II Gattilusio. These yielded another 300,000 aspers. Still another 100,000 aspers were to be paid him in three annual installments from the Edirne mint, so that his annual income amounted to 700,000 aspers. Demetrius himself went to live in Enez, where he devoted himself to hunting and other pleasures. But in 1467 he was suddenly deprived of his revenues and moved to Dimotika. In accordance with the custom of the day, he had been accused of misappropriation, and it is said that only the intervention of Mahmud Pasha saved his life. Later the story was told

[14] The account of the second Morean campaign is given by Miller, 444–452, with references to the Greek sources.

that one day while hunting Mehmed caught sight of Demetrius, now a poor fugitive, and, touched by his misery, granted him the sum of 50,000 aspers from the grain tax, far less than he had previously drawn but in any case sufficient for his keep. Soon thereafter he became a monk under the name of David. He died in 1470 in a monastery in Edirne. His daughter Helena, however, may never have entered the harem, for the sultan feared she might poison him. She died before her father. Such was the miserable end of this branch of the Palaeologi.

Still on his guard, Mehmed made every effort to establish control over the despot Thomas, who had fled to Corfu. He sent him a messenger to suggest that Thomas should dispatch one of his archons to the Porte to negotiate a peaceful agreement and arrange for an annuity from the Porte. What induced him to do this it is hard to say. It has been claimed that Mehmed feared Thomas would stir up the Western powers against the Ottoman Empire. But everything we know about the sultan's attitude toward subjected states and their rulers, both before and after this incident, argues against such an interpretation. When the despot's messenger arrived at the sultan's court and in his master's name offered to exchange Monemvasia for another town on the coast, Mehmed had him thrown into prison and later set free to inform Thomas that he must either appear in person or send one of his sons. This, as might be expected, Thomas could not resolve to do. As a true son of the Church, he had meanwhile besought the help of Pope Pius II, and on November 16, 1460, he and his retinue sailed to Ancona, in response to an invitation from the Curia to bring to Christendom the head of St. Andrew; this had long been preserved as a precious relic in Patras, whence it had been removed at the approach of the Turks and taken along by Thomas. Christian princes had offered large sums for the precious relic, and Thomas had no difficulty in obtaining a considerable annuity from the pope in return for it. On March 7, 1461, the former co-ruler of the Morea, an imposing man in his middle fifties, clad in a long black coat and a white velvet hat—the statue of St. Paul which formerly stood in front of the Church of St. Peter is said to have borne his features—made his appearance in the Eternal City. The pope assigned him a palace, honored him with the order of the Golden Rose, and with the cardinals' help settled an annual income of 6,000 ducats on him. This Palaeologus, who even in poverty felt himself to be the ruler of Byzantium, later attempted to recover his lost possessions with the support of the Italian states. But all was in vain; bitterness and disappointed hopes undermined his health. He lost his wife, Catherine, in 1462, and he himself died, forgotten, on May 12, 1465, in the hospital of Santo Spirito in Rome. Apart from Helena, widow of the Serbian despot Lazar, Thomas left a second daughter, named Zoë, who lived under the protection of Cardinal Bessarion and, provided with a dowry by Pope Sixtus IV, married Grand Duke Ivan III Vasilievich of Russia in 1472. Thus the hereditary claim to the Byzantine throne passed to the czars of Russia. As for her two brothers, Andreas, whom the pope had appointed "titular despot of the Morea," forfeited all esteem by his marriage to a Roman harlot and died in poverty in 1502, while the second, Manuel, emigrated to Istanbul, where he may have become a Moslem. Pensioned by the Porte, he died in obscurity during the reign of Bayezid II. According to a Byzantine source, he was buried in the church of Sergentzion, probably the present-day Istranca (northwest of Istanbul) in the mountains of the same name.

This was the lamentable end of the Byzantine despotates in Morea and of the ancient imperial house of the Palaeologi. Phrantzes, the historian of this tragedy, had fled with Thomas to Corfu, resolved to share his fate. Here he became a monk and ended his sad and agitated life in a lonely cell in the monastery of St. Elias.

Ever since the Bosporus had been closed by the erection of Rumeli Hisarï, the Genoese were much hampered in their Black Sea trade, and their chief trading post on the southern shore, Amasra (Amastris), had begun to decline. It had become necessary to bring in troops and munitions over the difficult and insecure land route. The Genoese were all the more eager to recover complete possession of Galata, but failed in their attempts to persuade the sultan to return it amicably. Mehmed informed them that Galata had come into his hands not by force of arms but by peaceful treaties. He had injured no one by taking it and had done the Genoese more good than harm. Now, in the late summer of 1460, in order to forestall an armed intervention, which the Genoese contemplated at least for a time, Mehmed ordered Mahmud Pasha, his grand vizier, to proceed against Amasra both by land and sea, and so deal the death blow to Genoese power in the southern Black Sea.[15]

Amasra is peculiarly situated between two bays to the east and west, on two rocky, islandlike promontories which are connected by two narrow, sandy, and perfectly flat isthmuses [pl. V b]. Seen from the sea, the city looks like a group of islands; the inner bays contain two harbors, open to the north and southwest. The northern harbor is further protected by a rocky island; the southern one is bordered by the mainland beach. The southwestern side of the foremost peninsula consists of wild, almost

[15] An exhaustive study of Genoese commercial activity is Heers, *Gênes au XV*[e] *siècle*. See especially 363ff. for trade across the Black Sea.

vertical cliffs, which jut over the bay. Here is situated the fortress, which in later centuries was often used as a place of banishment for rebellious *beys* and for governors who had fallen out of favor. The now insignificant town would seem still more insignificant were it not for the ruins of the impressive buildings of the Genoese period, especially the castle, from which these merchants and navigators dominated the entire Black Sea trade. The Genoese had erected these walls and towers, which to this day surround the entire old and new cities, as is still attested by the blazons of Genoa and of various Genoese families over the gates. But even in earlier times, Amasra, the Sesamos of the *Iliad* (II, 853), was an important center of Black Sea trade. In the Christian era it became a diocese. One Church author refers to it as the pearl of Paphlagonia and indeed of the whole world. In the remote past it was the seat of the proud queen Amastris, who because of her lineage, her mastery over men, and her passion for architecture was termed the Semiramis of Asia Minor. On all sides the visitor perceives impressive and thus far little-studied vestiges of antiquity, particularly of the Byzantine period. The surrounding mountains, covered with the deep green of woods, give the whole landscape a picturesque and romantic aspect, typical of the region and perhaps excelled only by Sinop and its surroundings.

As we have seen, the whole of Amasra faces north and is connected with the mainland only by a narrow isthmus. Consequently, it was far more vulnerable to Ottoman attack by sea than by land. It is unlikely that the city put up a serious defense in September (or perhaps later in the autumn) 1460, for the peninsula surrendered unconditionally and two-thirds of the population, including the handsomest boys, who were selected as pages for the serai, were carried off to Istanbul. The rest of the population remained within the walls. It is highly improbable that the sultan personally took part in the capture of Amasra.[16]

Mehmed seems to have spent the remainder of the year in his palace in Istanbul. There on November 3, 1460, he received an emissary from Dubrovnik, who brought him the annual tribute of 1,500 ducats for the current year.[17] It must have been shortly after the sultan's return from

---

[16] An alternate chronology for the fall of Amasra is proposed by Inalcïk ("Mehmed the Conqueror," 421–422), according to which the city capitulated in 863 H. (1458/59).

[17] Sultan Mehmed's written confirmation of payment is given in text and discussed by Friedrich Giese, "Die osmanisch-türkischen Urkunden im Archive des Rektorenpalastes in Dubrovnik (Ragusa)," in *Festschrift Georg Jacob* (Leipzig, 1932), 46–47. Cf. the document given by Elezović, *Turski spomenici* I, part 1 (Belgrade, 1940), 26–27; I, part 2 (1952), 4.

the Morea that a strange meeting—perhaps the first—occurred between him and Benedetto Dei (1418–1492), the Florentine spy, adventurer, merchant, and chronicler. These conversations continued over a period of years, for from about 1460 to 1472 Florence and the Porte maintained close relations in which, as Dei put it, "pratiche e intelligenze" played a large part. During this period Florentines were constantly present in the camp of the Ottoman army, and the republic spent considerable sums on this espionage service. Of this meeting with the sultan, Benedetto Dei left us a vivid, though perhaps exaggerated account, in which he directly quotes the remarks of both parties. No sooner, he tells us, had he put ashore in Istanbul, assuredly supplied with ample letters of recommendation from influential persons, than the Grand Turk summoned him and submitted him to a kind of interrogation. Mehmed inquired in detail concerning political conditions in Italy and the situation at the various courts there. If his account is to be trusted, Benedetto Dei, whom Leonardo da Vinci had already put down as a fabulist after he met him at the court of the Sforzas, informed the sultan that Italy was comprised of several powers, four "possessing money, prestige, and arms"—the Duchy of Milan, Naples under King Ferrante, Venice and Florence—in addition to sixteen free states, whose names he listed, and finally, two considerable cities, Bologna and Perugia. And, so he went on, "if they wished, or were obliged, to make a major effort by sea and by land, the Italians of today would be able to do far better than their forebears of antiquity." The Grand Turk replied:

My Florentine, I have heard all you have said . . . and I believe it fully . . . but I answer you and say that Italy could no longer perform the great deeds it performed in the past, because in those days when it did wonders, the reason was the power of the Romans, who were then sole masters of Italy . . . but today you are twenty states and groups of powers in your country, and you are in disagreement among yourselves and bitter enemies . . . and I know many things which will all be of help to me in the plan I have made; and seeing that I am young and rich and favored by fortune, I intend to surpass Caesar and Alexander and Xerxes by far.

Having spoken these words, the Grand Turk turned away from Benedetto Dei and toward his canopied throne. But the crafty Florentine resumed the interrupted conversation, or so he claims, and began to describe Italy's awe-inspiring sea power:

Any time you should attempt to make war on Italy, you will see all the Christians stand up against you. If they have not helped the

Venetians, the reason is that the four nations of Italy are the enemies of that nation and would like to see it destroyed. But if you came to Italy, they would all move against you. Believe Benedetto Dei.

"So," he concludes, "ended my interview with him."

The mere fact that Dei, this archenemy of Venice, should have entered the service as treasurer or administrator of the wealthy Venetian lessor of alum mines Girolamo Michiel, resident in Pera, bears witness to his gift of simulation and to his political designs in favor of his beloved native city of Florence. All indications are that he was sent and expressly commissioned by Florence to carry on economic and political espionage and report faithfully to his masters. Mehmed's friendly attitude toward Florence, which Benedetto Dei enthusiastically confirms in a letter of August 6, 1460, was not to change for twelve years, and seems to show that the *pratiche e intelligenze* carried on during this period with the Grand Turk, as well as with his grand vizier Mahmud Pasha, were not without results. Benedetto Dei boasts explicitly that Florence continuously maintained agents at the Porte and spent 5,000 ducats a year for this purpose.[18]

As we have seen, Pius II, disillusioned and gravely ill, was the last to leave Mantua (January 19, 1460). After visiting the baths of Macerata and Petriolo in an attempt to cure his gout, he returned to his native city of Siena, where he was again thrown into a state of agitation by the continuing conflict over the throne of Naples and the unfortunate repercussions of this on the Papal State. While he had been trying to unite the princes of the West and particularly of Italy in a common crusade against the Turks, the conflict between the houses of Aragon and Anjou had assumed menacing proportions. King Charles VII of France gave his support to the Angevin party and in the autumn of 1459, while the Congress of Mantua was still in session, had not hesitated to throw the twenty-four galleys, which Cardinal Alain had assembled in Marseilles for the war against the Turks, into the battle against King Ferrante of Aragon. Combated not only by the old Angevin party but also by a number of powerful feudal lords, the house of Aragon was in dire straits. At this juncture, Francesco Sforza, duke of Milan, clearly aware that a French victory in Italy and French implantation in Naples would spell

---

[18] Further details on the activities of Benedetto Dei, with references to the sources, are given by Babinger, "Mehmed II., der Eroberer, und Italien," *Byzantion* 21 (1951), 151ff. Increased Florentine commercial interest in Ottoman waters is discussed by Michael E. Mallett, *The Florentine Galleys in the Fifteenth Century* (Oxford, 1967).

the end of all political independence in Italy, persuaded the pope to join him in support of Ferrante. Thus hostilities began in the spring of 1460, but in Italy and not, as the pope had hoped, in southeastern Europe. Here there is no need to follow these developments; suffice it to say that the bitter struggle over the Neapolitan crown gave rise to an indescribable reign of terror—murder, pillage, and rape—in the Holy City, necessitating the immediate return of the pope (October 1460). Dissatisfied with the pope's participation in the Neapolitan war, the rebellious population seemed to threaten the very existence of the Papal State. Under such conditions, a crusade against the Ottomans was unthinkable.

In April 1460, while Pope Pius II was still in Siena, he received the visit of a certain Moses Giblet, archdeacon of Antioch, a scholar famed for his thorough knowledge of Greek and especially Syriac literature. The Giblets were numbered among the most distinguished families of the Syrian nobility. The archdeacon came, so he said, not only as the emissary of the Greek patriarchs of Jerusalem, Alexandria, and Antioch but also of Ibrahim Bey, prince of Karaman, and of other Oriental rulers, all of whom hoped that Pius II would save them from the Ottoman yoke. Moses Giblet gave the pope letters from the above-mentioned sovereigns, in which they solemnly announced their adherence to the Florentine union. Pius II received the messenger from the Orient both privately and in public, and on April 21, 1460, had a document drawn up concerning this act of allegiance. This so-called Red Book, which was deposited in the archives of the Curia along with Latin translations of the patriarchs' and princes' letters, has come down to us. So far it has been impossible to establish the authenticity of these documents, because the originals are lacking. It is worth noting, however, that Pius II never subsequently referred to the incident. We know in any case that his confidence in Oriental emissaries was gravely undermined by another embassy, which made its fantastic entrance into the Eternal City shortly before Christmas of the same year.

In the Orient as in the West, a plan had taken shape to unite the most immediately threatened princes into a league against Mehmed, the common enemy. While in the West the popes, especially Calixtus III and Pius II, were the chief advocates of these projects, in the East John IV Comnenus (Kalo Ioannes), the emperor of Trebizond, tried to assume the leadership of all those who, in defense of their own realms, were eager to combat the Ottomans in Asia. Although we are without documentary records of this league, we do know that it was at least seriously projected and that some sort of understanding existed among the Karaman Ibrahim Bey, the sultan's own brother-in-law, Isfendiyaroğlu Ismail

Bey of Sinop, Uzun Hasan, the lord of the White Sheep in Diyarbakïr (the older Amid or Kara Amid), and the Christian princes of Georgia and Mingrelia. Uzun Hasan had formed close political ties with John IV, and in 1458 he married John's beautiful daughter Catherine (after her marriage generally known as Despina Hatun). But the emperor had died shortly before and his sickly brother David had become emperor as guardian of the former's son, John V, who was still a minor. If John IV had lived longer, his alliance with the powerful Uzun Hasan, whose grandfather, the "Black Leech," had also married a Comnena, the daughter of Alexius IV (1417–1429), might have become a serious threat to the Ottoman Empire, especially if it had been possible to synchronize the European and the Asiatic efforts. In a letter from Trebizond of April 22, 1459 (of doubtful authenticity, to be sure), Emperor David informed the duke of Burgundy of the existence of a league of Asiatic states directed against Mehmed and tried to arouse fabulous hopes concerning the assistance which this league with its alleged allies could give a simultaneous Western undertaking.[19]

By way of making contact with the potentates of the Near East, Popes Nicholas V and Calixtus III had employed a Minorite monk, Fra Ludovico da Bologna, as their plenipotentiary to Trebizond, Iberia, Georgia, Little Armenia, Karaman, and even to Uzun Hasan in Diyarbakïr, to enlist troops against the common enemy of Christendom. These endeavors go far back, for we know that immediately after the ascension of Calixtus to the Apostolic chair, when he was employing the greatest zeal in favor of a war against the Turks, Fra Ludovico returned to Rome from Jerusalem, Ethiopia, and India, where he had gone on a political mission for Nicholas V. He was reputed to have a thorough knowledge of the Orient, and the aged pope spent hours listening to his stories, which, it is safe to assume, were full of atrocious lies. Then Calixtus sent him back to the East to make contact in Gondar with Zara Jacob (1438–1468), the Christian king of Ethiopia, and also with certain Indian princes. Not until a year later did the Franciscan return to Italy from this second journey. If we consider the remoteness of the countries which he allegedly visited,

---

[19] For background to these events see Walther Hinz, *Irans Aufstieg zum Nationalstaat im fünfzehnten Jahrhundert* (Berlin, 1936); Turkish translation by T. Bïyïklïoğlu of the preceding: *Uzun Hasan ve Şeyh Cüneyd* (Ankara, 1948; as *TTK*: IV. seri, no. 5); Bekir Sïtkï Baykal, "Fatih Sultan Mehmet—Uzun Hasan rekabetinde Trabzon meselesi," *Tarih Araştirmalari Dergisi* 2 (1964), 67–81. See also "Aḳ Ḳoyunlu" (V. Minorsky), *EI²* I, 311–312. Reference to the emperor's letter is given by William Miller, *Trebizond, The Last Greek Empire* (London, 1926; reprinted Amsterdam, 1968), 98.

it is hard to say which is more astonishing, the aplomb with which he claimed to have championed the cause of Christianity in those distant lands, or the credulity of the three popes, who imagined that they could arrest the Turkish peril for a single moment by sending an adventurer and obvious charlatan to Abyssinia and India.

Even Pius II, author of a geography of Europe and Asia outstanding for his time, let himself be hoodwinked by Ludovico, whom on October 4, 1458, he appointed nuncio to the Orient and whom he confirmed in the privileges and benefits accorded him by Nicholas and Calixtus. In the Christmas season of 1460, Ludovico returned once more from the East. This time he was not alone, but was accompanied by several Oriental emissaries. So strange were their costumes and ways that the people pointed at them in the streets, while the children followed them in merry throngs. One was an imposing knight, who represented himself as the emissary of Emperor David of Trebizond. The envoy of King George VIII of Imeretia, who was termed king of the Persians, although his realm was limited to Khartli, had the appearance of a dignified old gentleman and attracted attention only by the fact that though purporting to be a knight, he wore a monk's tonsure. Prince Qwarqware II ("Gorgora"), duke of Zamtche—described, however, as "prince of Georgiana or Great Iberia"—was represented by an impressively large and powerful man, who was said to consume twenty pounds of meat a day. By far the most imposing member of the company, he wore a kind of double tonsure, with a great shock of hair in the middle, ear pendants, and a bristling beard like a marmot's. The lord of Little Armenia, called by many different names, had sent an affable knight, who played several musical instruments; wearing a broad cloak and a tall hat, he appeared in the midst of his retinue. Finally, there was a representative of Uzun Hasan, the "Little Turk," who offered to put 50,000 men into the field against the Grand Turk. A later arrival, it appears, was the envoy of the legendary Prester John, who was reputed to be a learned theologian and astrologer. According to Ludovico, these Orientals had traveled by way of Colchis, Scythia, the Don and the Danube, Hungary, Germany, and Venice. In October they had stood before the emperor, but on this occasion only Ludovico, the "Persian," and the "Georgian" are mentioned. They offered no less than 150,000 warriors for the war against the Turks, and Frederick III also promised to provide a powerful army. When the emperor refused to let the "Persian" envoy kiss his feet in the name of his master, the emissary declared that he would not dare to go home without having done so. Frederick III seems to have put faith in the Orientals, as may be inferred from a draft of an imperial letter to the "king of Persia," dated October 17, 1460, that has come down to us.

In Rome the outlandish guests were received like royal ambassadors. The prelates went out to meet them and a public banquet was held in their honor. In the consistory the representatives of the Christian rulers presented Pius II with the homage of their sovereigns. Then there was talk of the great Oriental league against Mehmed. The ambassadors themselves uttered only short, solemn formulas. Their eloquent interpreter and spokesman was Fra Ludovico, who, although he wished to be addressed as "Doctor," claimed to have forgotten the Latin language in the course of his long stay in the Orient. Since he would not have been understood had he spoken Greek or Persian, he preferred to express himself in plain Italian. In all the letters and speeches of the Oriental Ambassadors, it was duly stressed that the mighty Oriental league was the work of Ludovico. The princes sent word to the pope that in deference to him and his nuncio they had forsworn their internecine quarrels to unite against the common foe.

But the great Oriental league included a number of additional princes, who had sent no messengers to Rome. There was the Dadian Liparit, ruler of Mingrelia; there was Rabia, the lord of Abkhazia; there was Ismail Bey of Sinop. Finally, there was the lord of Karaman, whom on October 16, 1459, Pius II had reminded of the promises he had made to Pius's predecessor, Calixtus III, and who, in the pope's opinion, could muster 40,000 men if need be. Other princes of the league appear under such multilated titles and names that it is hard to identify them. The tribes of the Goths and Alans, whom it seems surprising to encounter in this context, wished to fight under the banners of the "Persian." All the states mentioned promised to provide enormous armies, obviously out of all proportion to their power and the extent of their territories. David of Trebizond, whose empire had for some time been reduced to his capital city, promised to raise 20,000 soldiers and 30 biremes, the lord of Imeretia and the still more insignificant Dadian of Mingrelia each promised 60,000 men and Uzun Hasan 50,000.

Thus, the Asiatics boldly undertook to crush all the Turks as far as the Black Sea if only the European powers under the pope's leadership would do their part in the West; the Turkish name would be wiped off the face of the earth.

How convenient it would have been if the princes of the Orient had united to save the West from the Ottoman menace! The idea had long been in the air. The promises from the East did actually sound more encouraging than those of the princes who had gathered reluctantly at Mantua or had merely participated at a distance. Nevertheless, Pius II could not resolve to proclaim a war against the Turks until the strangers had paid their respects to the king of France and the duke of Burgundy, without whose approval a crusade was hardly practicable. The envoys consented with alacrity, asking only that the pope should provide them with a suitable sum of travel money and appoint Ludovico patriarch over all Catholic Christians of the Orient. Pius II agreed to both provisions, stipulating only that the Franciscan should not assume the title of patriarch until the borders of his domain were exactly defined. Although the pope seems to have been skeptical of the Asiatic princes' high-sounding promises, he does not appear to have suspected at this time the sincerity of the missionary or the authenticity of his Orientals; in any event, he expressed no doubts. Even the Venetian senate, with its ample knowledge of the Orient, and the Signoria of Florence, which the emissaries visited in mid-December, had taken them for real Orientals. Before the legation left Rome in mid-January, 1461, Pius II provided Fra Ludovico with official credentials, representing him as his nuncio to the two rulers and instructing him to enlist them in the struggle for the faith by holding out the promise of divine reward and the favor of the Apostolic See.

When in May 1461 Ludovico appeared at the French court with his Asiatics, he was greeted with open distrust. To be sure, the strange figures were provided with maintenance and festivals were organized in their honor. Received by Charles VII in the presence of his crown council, they enthusiastically addressed him as the "king of kings" and assured him that his fleur-de-lis flag and a captain sent in his name would carry more weight than 100,000 soldiers. But with all their boasts of the wealth and military power of their rulers, the strange emissaries were unable to conceal the fact that they themselves were reduced to mendicancy.

To their misfortune, Charles VII died on July 22, 1461, and his son, Louis XI, displayed no serious interest in their fantastic offers and promises. Empty-handed, the ambassadors proceeded to the court of Duke Philip of Burgundy in the castle of St. Omer, where the Order of the Golden Fleece had just held a conclave, and where their arrival was welcomed as an occasion for further festivities. The emissaries presented a missive from the pope and letters from the three Oriental princes, the emperor of Trebizond, the "Persian," and the Georgian. The king of Georgia, a Comnenus, begged the friendship and favor of the duke of Burgundy, for, so he said, his most ardent desire was to die for the faith and he had heard that the Burgundian was of all men the most eager to save the Holy Land from the hands of the infidels. Comnenus promised that if this should come to pass, he would confirm the duke of Burgundy in his claim to the crown of Jerusalem. In all the letters, which are so much alike that they seem to come from the same chancellery, Ludovico is designated as patriarch. It is not known who made the Latin speech at the Burgundian court. In any event, it was neither the doctor-patriarch who had forgotten his Latin nor any of the Asiatics. After Philip of Burgundy had reiterated his determination to carry the old banner of Robert Guiscard and Godefroy de Bouillon across the Bosporus, Ludovico and his companions started on their return journey to Rome. Neither in France nor in Burgundy had the proceedings gone beyond the stage of preliminary negotiations.

Meanwhile, Pope Pius II had begun to doubt the authenticity of the Oriental venture. It had come to his ears that Ludovico, in disregard of his order, had taken the title of patriarch and that even before, in Hungary and Germany, had arrogated to himself rights to which he had never been entitled. On their return to Rome, the delegation, now looked upon as adventurers and charlatans, were refused the honors that had previously been shown them. Pius II gave them travel money and sent them away. He would have liked best to throw the shameless Franciscan into prison. When he learned shortly afterward that Ludovico was in Venice, sporting the title of patriarch, he ordered the patriarch of that city to have him arrested as an impostor. Warned by the doge, Ludovico escaped. We learn from Pius's well-known memoirs (*Commentarii*) that he heard nothing more of Ludovico and his ambassadors, but that from that time on he looked with suspicion on all reports from the Orient.[20]

This is the story of the league of Oriental rulers against Mehmed II and of the mountebank Ludovico da Bologna. If the letters had been authentic and the promises had been made in earnest, the princes would have been obliged to levy the entire male population of their countries. But, as the events of the ensuing year amply demonstrate, none of these Caucasian dynasts had any serious intention of making war on the remote Ottomans to defend the Comneni.

[20] Anthony Bryer, "Ludovico da Bologna and the Georgian and Anatolian Embassy of 1460–1461," *Bedi Kartlisa* 19–20 (1965), 178–198, takes up again the question of Ludovico's mission with particular attention to the role in the embassy's tour of Michael Alighieri, descendant of the poet and a Florentine merchant on the Black Sea coast. The *Commentaries* of the pope have been translated into English by Florence A. Gragg, with notes by Leona C. Gabell, and published as *Smith College Studies in History*, XXII, XXV, XXX, XXXV, and XLIII. For the Oriental delegation described in the preceding pages, see XXX, 371–374.

As though wishing to belie the real or alleged boasts of his Eastern neighbors, Mehmed decided in 1461 to turn his attention to the Black Sea region. For years he had been irritated by the behavior of Uzun Hasan and his Comnenus relatives. Now he finally decided to shatter this association of the Turkmen state with Trebizond before it could build up dangerous strength, and thus at one stroke to deprive the restless peoples of Greece and Anatolia of their last hope of liberation from the Ottoman yoke. In the lifetime of John IV, Mehmed already seems to have regarded the emperor of Trebizond as an annoying rival who—if not by the strength of his armies, then at least by his spiritual influence on the Greek peoples—could still hamper him in the full enjoyment of his power.

For some years, to be sure, the empire of the Comneni had ceased to be independent. In June 1456, while Mehmed was besieging Belgrade, Hïzïr Pasha, second governor of Amasya, received instructions to assault Trebizond by land and sea. The Turks advanced as far as the suburbs of the city, where the plague was raging at the time. In the hope of forestalling disaster and obtaining at least a breathing spell, the emperor consented to pay an annual tribute of 2,000 gold pieces, which the sultan increased forthwith to 3,000. The emperor's brother David, then bearing the rank of despot, repaired to the Porte with the tribute, to obtain the sultan's confirmation of the treaty. On this occasion he was able to observe at first hand not only the sultan's cast of mind but also the size and discipline of his army. No doubt David returned home with the impression that the danger facing his brother's shadow empire could be averted only by a miracle. As usual, the miracle failed to materialize.

When David himself became emperor in 1458, he put all his hope in the husband of his niece Catherine, Uzun Hasan in Diyarbakïr, although he had every reason to doubt that this Moslem prince, who seems to have regarded himself as the sole true descendant of Tamerlane, would go to any great lengths to save a Christian state. He asked the lord of the White Sheep to intercede with Mehmed, through an embassy, to have his tribute canceled. Before the end of 1459, the envoys of the Turkmen prince went to Istanbul, where they not only requested the annulment of David's tribute but also demanded in behalf of their master that Mehmed resume payment, suspended during the previous sixty years, of the 1,000 horse blankets, and as many turban cloths and carpets, which the sultan's grandfather, Mehmed I, was alleged to have sent each year to the White Horde; in addition, they demanded the surrender of Cappadocia, since Uzun Hasan had received this territory from the Comneni as part of the dowry of his wife Despina Hatun. Whether the lord of the White Sheep supposed that by presenting exaggerated demands he would obtain at least something, or whether, with old barbaric swagger, he wished to provoke the sultan, Mehmed's reply was obscure but distinctly menacing. In one version he is said to have responded that the Comneni would soon find out what they had to expect of the Ottoman emperor (Chalcocondylas), while in another, which seems more likely, he declared that the emissaries should return home in peace, for in the following year he himself would come to clear up the question of tribute (Ducas).

Beginning in the spring of 1461 the Ottoman squadrons in the harbor of Gelibolu, headquarters of the admiral (*kapudan paşa*), were over-hauled and reinforced; the news, as Ducas reports, terrified the inhabi-tants of the Aegean islands, who believed the preparations to be directed against them. Actually, however, Mehmed soon ordered the fleet, said to comprise a total of 300 vessels, in command of Admiral Kasïm Pasha, seconded by one Yakub, a veteran seaman, to set out for the Black Sea. He himself called up the land army and sent both foot soldiers and cavalry across the Dardanelles toward Bursa. The army is estimated at 60,000 horsemen and 80,000 foot soldiers, not to mention the artillery and supply train. Then, taking personal command of the Rumelian troops, the sultan crossed over to Anatolia. By the time he reached Bursa by way of Akyazï, the Anatolian troops were assembled there in full strength. Mehmed visited the tombs of his father and of his ancestors and then started eastward with the entire army, telling no one of his intentions. When the army judge had the audacity to ask where they were going, the sultan replied angrily, "If the hair of my beard knew my plans, I would pull it out and burn it." From Bursa the sultan wrote to his brother-in-law Ismail Bey, of the Isfendiyar family, emir of Sinop, calling on him to supply the fleet with food and, if necessary, with money from the revenues of the rich mines of the region. In a second letter, he de-manded that Ismail Bey should send his son, Hasan, the sultan's nephew, to meet him in Ankara. The Isfendiyaroğlu prince obeyed promptly. Hasan was already there when his uncle reached Ankara. He was graciously received, but was immediately sent back to his father in Sinop with the message: "Tell your father that I am burning with desire for his city of Sinop. I will give him the region of Philippopolis in return. If he is not satisfied, I will soon be on the spot in person." Thereupon a document was drawn up transferring the greater part of Ismail Bey's territory—namely, the region of Kastamonu—to his brother Kïzïl Ahmed Bey, who had incited the sultan against him.

Mehmed now moved up to Sinop and the grand vizier Mahmud Pasha made it clear to the lord of the city in writing and by word of mouth that all resistance would be futile, especially as more than half of his territory had already been made over to his brother. Ismail Bey resigned himself to his fate and appeared before his brother-in-law. When, in accordance with the traditional custom, he wished to kiss the sultan's hand, Mehmed declined and addressed him according to the court ceremonial of the Byzantines as "elder brother." Thus Sinop surrendered without a blow, although, defended as it was by nature and artifice, especially by 400 cannon manned by 2,000 artillerymen, it could certainly have held out for some time. At first the sultan indemnified the dethroned emir with Yenişehir, Inegöl, and Yarhisar in Anatolia, but soon thereafter gave him Philippopolis and vicinity instead. Here Ismail lived on his lands and wrote a widely read work on the ritual prescriptions of Islam entitled *Hulviyat-i Sultani*. He died in 1479 and was buried beside the now vanished Bey Mosque, which he had endowed. Ismail's son Hasan Bey, to whom Mehmed had first given Bolu in Asia Minor in fief, inherited his father's estate of Markovo near Philippopolis, while a second son, Mahmud Bey, received an estate near Edirne.[21]

Among the ships in the harbor of Sinop there was one of 900 *pilsoi* (tons?), which the sultan at once ordered removed to Istanbul.

The sultan left Sinop and marched in rainy weather, not along the coast but inland over the military highway leading to Erzurum by way of Amasya and Sivas. Apparently he wished to give the impression that he was headed not for Trebizond but for the territory of Uzun Hasan. East of Tokat, two days' march from Sivas on the road to Erzurum, lies the mountain castle of Koylu Hisar (or Koyunlu Hisar; now Koyul Hisar), which Uzun Hasan had wrested from one Hüseyin, its former owner, and established as a border fortress to protect his territories against invasion from Anatolia. The sultan commissioned Sarabdar Hasan Bey, governor of Little Rum, that is, the region of Amasya and Sivas, to take the castle or at least to lay waste the surrounding country. Both tasks were carried out and the sultan marched on eastward toward Erzincan. On his way he was met by Sara Hatun, Uzun Hasan's mother, probably an Aramaic Christian from the region of Diyarbakïr, accompanied by Sheikh Hüseyin, *bey* of the Kurds, and numerous Turkmen princes. She had been sent with rich gifts to negotiate a peaceable compromise in her son's name. Mehmed received the princess and the sheikh with special honors, addressed the one as "mother," the other as "father," and through them concluded a peace with Uzun Hasan, who was required to promise that he would give the Comneni no further assistance. Then, accompanied

[21] For Ismail Bey of Sinop see Yaşar Yücel, "Candar–oğullarï Beyliği (1439–61)," *Belleten* 34 (1970), 373–407.

by Sara and Hüseyin, he headed for Trebizond across the precipitous coastal mountains. Mehmed was obliged to climb the heights of Zigana largely on foot. "My son," said Sara to the sultan, "how can you undergo such hardships just for the sake of Trebizond?" "Mother," he was reported to have answered, "in my hand is the sword of Islam. Without this hardship I should not deserve the name of ghazi [warrior of the faith], and today and tomorrow I should have to cover my face in shame before Allah!" Sara Hatun's efforts to include the emperor of Trebizond in the peace treaty of Erzincan were no more successful than her wily attempt to discourage the sultan from marching against David by describing the dangers ahead—impassable mountains, impenetrable wooded ravines, and lack of supplies. David's doom was sealed.

During the negotiations the Ottoman fleet, coming from Sinop, hove within sight of Trebizond and began to besiege the city. The suburbs along the seacoast were burned without difficulty. The assault on the city proper, on which the Ottoman naval guns inflicted only little damage, had been in progress for thirty-two days when the grand vizier Mahmud Pasha arrived with the advance guard of the army and encircled Trebizond on the land side.

Built in the form of an amphitheater on the coastal hills, Trebizond was surrounded by a broad belt of garden country. Seen from the sea, especially in the light of the morning sun, the city with its proud palaces, domes, and towers seemed in those days the queen of the Pontus. In the period of the Comneni it possessed innumerable churches, arcades, marketplaces, and dwellings. At the foot of the hills and along the sea stood long rows of houses belonging to wealthy merchants, seafarers, and burghers. At first the ancient Greek city had consisted only of the section which in the imperial period was usually known as the Acropolis. This was a platform surmounted by a lofty castle. Around the Acropolis the Comneni, enthusiastic builders, erected great circular walls, deep trenches, and fortified towers. Within the walls there were narrow cobbled streets, with houses of many stories, on whose flat roofs orchards, flower gardens, and vine arbors were laid out. Along the seacoast, outside this fortified section, extended the long, wide avenues of the suburbs. Here, especially to the east of the castle, lay the bazaars and the houses of the merchants and artisans. At the city limits lay two fortresses, which had been built with the emperor's permission, one by the Genoese, the other by the Venetians, to safeguard their precious warehouses. The imperial castle, built above the platform into the cliff, towered over the Acropolis as well as the lower city. With its treasure house, archives, government buildings, and courtiers' quarters, it was protected by deep trenches, walls, towers, and iron gates. A tall flight of stairs led to the innermost "golden palace of the Comneni." Supported by white marble columns, the great imperial hall was floored with slabs of white marble and adorned with the portraits and coats of arms of the Comneni. It was surrounded by reception rooms, balconies, galleries, and terraces, which on all sides offered magnificent views of the plain and the mountains, the city and the sea. From this height one could see the surrounding country, traversed by romantic valleys; on every side there were pleasure groves, meadows, gardens, olive groves, vineyards, and shady woods cooled by abundant fountains and rivulets and traversed by footpaths, while on the southern slopes the most attractive spots were occupied by convents and hospices. Don Ruy Gonzalez de Clavijo, the Castilian ambassador, who visited Trebizond in 1404 on his way to Samarkand and observed the city, the court, and the activity of the local Italian merchants dealing in the most precious wares of the Orient, is probably the most faithful and impartial witness to that golden age of the city. A glowing description of the place has also come down to us from a native of the city, Cardinal Basil Bessarion (d. 1472 in Ravenna), who survived the unhappy fate of Trebizond by only a few years. He rightly looked upon it as a secluded paradise, rich with all the treasures of the earth.[22]

David Comnenus was not yet aware that his relative and closest ally, Uzun Hasan, had made peace with the sultan. Believing the Ottoman land army to be engaged in battle with the lord of the White Sheep, he confidently repulsed the attacks of the Turkish fleet, for the city was amply supplied with food and ammunition. But when news came that the sultan and his whole army were approaching through the mountains, clearly intending to encircle Trebizond from the land side, David lost heart and decided to save his life and treasures, if not the city, by negotiating. It would not have occurred to his weak and cowardly person that it was preferable to be buried, with his family and property, under the ruins of his empire rather than to purchase through a shameful peace the false glitter of a dishonored existence.

Consequently, when Mahmud Pasha, who a short time before had been wounded in the face by a Turkish would-be assassin and had been saved

[22] The account of Trebizond by the Castilian is found in *Narrative of the Embassy of Ruy Gonzalez de Clavijo to the Court of Timour, at Samarcand, A.D. 1403–6*, trans. with notes and introd. by C. R. Markham (Hakluyt Society, 1st series, XXVI, 1859; reprinted New York, 1963). See also A. A. Vasiliev, "The Empire of Trebizond in History and Literature," *Byzantion* 15 (1940–41), 316–373, and especially p. 365 for reference to Bessarion's work.

only thanks to the medical skill of Maestro Iacopo of Gaeta, the sultan's personal physician, called upon David to surrender, the emperor immediately declared his willingness to abandon the city under certain conditions. The grand vizier conferred with the treacherous *protovestiarius* George Amirutzes, who happened to be a relative (their mothers were cousins), and through him sent the following message, recorded by Ducas, to the emperor:

> To the Emperor of Trebizond of the imperial family of the Hellenes, Mehmed the Great King, declares: You see how great a distance I have traveled after deciding to invade your territory. If you now surrender your capital without delay, I shall make over lands to you, as I did to Demetrius, the Greek prince of Morea, on whom I bestowed riches, islands, and the beautiful city of Aenos [Enez]. He is now living at peace and is happy. But if you do not give ear to these proposals, know that annihilation awaits your city. For I will not leave this spot until I have leveled the walls and ignominiously killed all the inhabitants.

Terrified at these threats, abandoned by all his allies, the emperor David reiterated his willingness to surrender under the conditions he had stated, not without suggesting that the sultan should take his second daughter in marriage and should assign to him a territory from which he might derive as much revenue as from the empire of Trebizond. On receiving these proposals from Mahmud Pasha, the sultan wished at first to insist on unconditional surrender and decided to take the city by force, all the more so because it had come to his ears that the empress Helena had left Trebizond before the arrival of his fleet. Sara Hatun finally persuaded him to accept David's conditions, to make peace, and to confirm his undertakings by oath. The emperor was granted leave to depart with his courtiers and chattels, as well as his treasures of gold, silver, and precious stones. Along with his whole family and all the higher dignitaries of the empire, he was placed on shipboard and moved to Istanbul. The castle of the Comneni was occupied by Janissaries and the city by *azaps*. The supreme command was conferred on Kasïm Pasha, while Hïzïr Pasha was ordered to take possession of the rest of the country. The male population of Trebizond was enslaved; some were taken into the service of the Porte and others assigned to the personal service of the sultan's dignitaries. Eight hundred selected youths were enrolled in the Janissaries, while numerous families were sent to Istanbul as colonists. Thus on August 15, 1461, exactly 200 years after the final restoration of the old Rhomaic Empire under Michael VIII of Byzantium, the empire of the Comneni ceased to be.[23]

In two almost bloodless campaigns Mehmed had made himself master of the entire northern coast of Asia Minor from Ereğli to the borders of Armenia, including three of its most important and richest harbors, Amasra, Sinop, and Trebizond. If the last of the Comneni had been a warrior, the sultan could not possibly have subdued Trebizond so quickly. Without siege guns and with virtually no cavalry, he had been obliged to make his way for eighteen days through the steep and inhospitable mountains of Zigana. Defended by brave soldiers and effective artillery, Trebizond could not have fallen an easy prey to the Turks, if only because of its natural situation. The lack of supplies, expressly mentioned by both Byzantine and Ottoman chroniclers, who explain that this was why Mehmed was obliged to bypass many castles and fortresses on his inland march, would either have destroyed him and his army or driven them from the country. But apart from David's cowardice, the treachery of George Amirutzes had much to do with the surrender of the city. One of the first dignitaries of the empire, Amirutzes was able through his influence to paralyze all measures of defense and to spread discouragement.

Attempts have been made, especially in recent years, to exculpate George Amirutzes of treachery. The mere fact, however, that later he and his sons, probably alone of the dignitaries of Trebizond, enjoyed distinctions of all sorts at the Porte and that he glorified the sultan in fulsome panegyrics while the other nobles of the empire were put to death seems sufficient proof that he had earned a claim to the sultan's favor. In this connection we must also mention the far-reaching influence of the half-Serb, half-Greek grand vizier Mahmud Pasha, whose ties of kinship with prominent families throughout Greece enabled him to make himself extremely useful to the sultan. His mother, who must have come from Trebizond, seems to have gone to the Serbian court in the retinue of a Comnenus princess, probably a relative of the despot, who there married a noble or wealthy Serb. This alone would account for Mahmud Pasha's connections with remote Trebizond and his part in handing over the empire of the Comneni to the sultan.

[23] William Miller gives an account of the end of the Black Sea state of the Comneni, with reference to the Western sources, in his *Trebizond*. Cf. Babinger's own article, "La date de la prise de Trebizonde par les Turcs (1461)," *Revue des études byzantines* 7 (1950), 205–207; reprinted in *A&A* I, 211–213. Confirmation of the date 1461 for the fall of Trebizond, provided by the colophon in a Latin manuscript, was brought to light by Ernest H. Wilkins, "The Harvard Manuscript of Petrarch's *Africa*," *Harvard Library Bulletin* 12 (1958), 321–322.

There is no truth in the widely recorded belief that after the conquest of Trebizond, Mehmed spent the winter in that city, departing only in the spring of 1462. Actually he left the Black Sea coast before the end of summer 1461, perhaps with Sara Hatun, whom he was said to have rewarded with the most precious jewels from the imperial treasure house of Trebizond. It took him twenty-eight days to reach Bursa over the same land route; then he returned to Istanbul. Reliable evidence of this is provided by a letter from the humanist Angelo Vadio, then in that city, to his learned countryman Roberto Valturio in Rimini, stating that Mehmed had returned to Istanbul on October 6, 1461. He spent the rest of the year and the ensuing winter, however, on the Tunca island in Edirne, a spot which seems to have appealed to him beyond all others.[24]

If it is true, as certain Armenian historians claim, that the sultan transferred Joachim (Hovakim), the Armenian archbishop of Bursa, to Istanbul in 1461 and established him there with the title of patriarch (*patrik*) as supreme head of all Armenian Christians in the empire, it seems likely that this event occurred either in the course of the sultan's march to Anatolia or on his return from the Trebizond expedition. The rights and duties of the new patriarch seem to have corresponded exactly to those conferred and imposed on the Greeks. At least according to Armenian sources, Patriarch Joachim—concerning whose activities, or even the extent of his flock, little is known—held two terms of office ending in 1478. There seem to have been a considerable number of Armenians in Bursa, where they engaged in commerce. There were also some in the capital, especially in the Galata quarter, and many Armenian merchants reside there to this day. In the remaining territory of the Ottoman state, particularly in "Romania" (Rumelia), there were few Armenians outside of the larger cities, such as Edirne, Philippopolis, Varna, and certain seaports. They probably did not number more than half a million in the Ottoman Empire at the time of the Conqueror and the figure may have been a great deal smaller. The Byzantine Church of Sulu Manastir in the quarter of Psamathia was assigned to the patriarch as his residence; here the patriarchs resided until 1644, when their seat was moved to the Kumkapï quarter.

The news of the fall of Sinop and Trebizond reached the West by way of Venice at the end of September or, more probably, in the first days of October, 1461. It found the pope in the midst of the Apulian war, of

---

[24] For Angelo Vadio, see Babinger's "Mehmed II., der Eroberer, und Italien," 163, n. 3. On Valturio, see further below, pp. 201, 504.

disorders in Rome, and of the most crushing financial difficulties. No one made the slightest move toward an expedition against the Turks.

The emperor Frederick had, to be sure, convoked a diet in Vienna in September 1460. There had been much talk about the 150,000 ducats distributed by Pope Pius II, about the missives addressed to two hundred princes and states, about the mission to Hungary of Juan de Carvajal, cardinal of Sant'Angelo, and of other prelates to France, England, and Spain, and about possible allies for the struggle against the Ottomans. But there had been no visible result. The German representatives replied that the decisions of Mantua were not binding on the "Germanic nation" and, to justify their denunciation of the agreement they had previously made, cited the death of the archbishops of Mainz and Trier, the change of kings in Hungary, their distrust of their Latin and Eastern neighbors, and the lack of reliable information about the Turks. As late as October 11, 1460, the pope had invoked the "honor of Germany" in a letter to the emperor. Now he proposed as commander-in-chief the Wittelsbach count palatine, Frederick I. All was in vain. Meanwhile, court humanists in Ferrara, Rimini, and elsewhere wrote poems of admonition. Some, like "Tribrachius" of Modena in his fatuous *Carmen de apparatu contra Turcum*, stated preposterous views concerning "imperative" military measures, while others, after the manner of the "eccellente astrologo" Teodoro of Rimini, cursed the "wild beast" which seemed to be coming from the East to shed Christian blood, though thus far, to be sure, only that of vile schismatics:

> *Quel fiero animal che d'Oriente*
> *Par venga a spargere sangue cristiano*
> *Della meschina chismatica gente.*

Equally futile were the counsels which an individual with an empty head, but with the high-sounding name of Donato Belloria di Serravalle, gave the papal nuncio in France. It is hard to think of anything sillier or more degrading than the anti-Turkish literary exercises that the venal humanists of Italy turned out in those years.

Soon after the arrival of the terrible news from the Levant, Pope Pius II conceived the strange idea of attempting to convert the sultan. How this notion matured in his brain we can only guess. Quite certainly it had reached his ears that the patriarch Gennadius had presented the sultan, at his request, with an interpretation of the Apostolic Credo in twenty chapters. In this connection the legend arose that the sultan had begun to doubt the teachings of the Prophet Mohammed and to conceive an inclination for the Christian faith. Travelers from the East never wearied of relating that Mehmed was intensely interested in the Christian faith, for which his supposedly Christian mother had instilled a keen sympathy in him as a child, that he could recite the *Pater noster* by heart, and even that he had secretly forsworn Islam and been converted to Christianity. Such allegations appear even in the otherwise so sober and realistic *avvisi*, or reports of the Venetian diplomats. It is no accident that in 1461 the learned cardinal Nicholas of Cusa (1401-1464), who had remained in Rome as vicar general during the pope's absence at the Congress of Mantua, wrote an "Examination of the Koran" (*Cribratio Alchorani*), dedicated to Pius II, in which he pointed out ways and means of combating effectively the doctrine of Mohammed. And so, while the pope regarded it as the main task of his pontificate to set the whole Christian world in motion against Mehmed II, the archenemy of Christianity, he tried at the same time to convince him of the superiority of the teachings of Jesus over the beliefs of Islam. It has rightly been pointed out that these efforts involved very worldly aims, chief of which was to restore an Eastern empire under the spiritual sovereignty of the Holy See, partly at the expense of the other Western powers.

It cannot be determined exactly when the pope wrote his strange communication, which is more like a dissertation than a letter, to the sultan. Since the author sometimes takes over almost verbatim the learned apparatus employed by Nicholas of Cusa in his *Cribratio Alchorani*, the papal work must have been written after the summer of 1461—actually, since the conquest of Sinop and Trebizond is mentioned, not before the end of October. A few years ago the pope's manuscript draft came to light, but even this has not made it possible to determine the exact date. Although the letter was almost certainly never sent to Istanbul, it was, still in the lifetime of Mehmed, published several times, probably for the first time in Cologne about 1469, then later (Treviso, 1475) in a textually perfect version. It was included in the pope's collected letters and also disseminated in numerous manuscripts.[25]

In this letter Pius II assured the sultan that he did not hate him, since his Lord bade him love his enemies and pray for the persecutors. He went on to point out that it was a delusion to suppose that the sword of Islam could conquer the Latin world as easily as it had the Asiatics,

---

[25] The text of the letter with an Italian translation and introduction is given by Giuseppe Toffanin, *Pio II: Lettera a Maometto II (Epistola ad Mahumetem)* (Naples, 1953). See also the remarks of Pastor, *The History of the Popes* III, 256-257. For a broad historical perspective taking in Pope Pius, Nicholas of Cusa, and other representative figures of the mid-15th century, see R. W. Southern, *Western Views of Islam in the Middle Ages* (Cambridge, Mass., 1962), especially 83-109.

Greeks, Serbs, and Walachians—all infidels and heretics. But if Mehmed did wish to extend his rule among Christians and cover his name with glory, he needed no money, no weapons, no armies, no navies.

An insignificant trifle can make you the greatest, the most powerful, the most famous of living mortals. You ask what it is? It is not hard to find; there is no need to go far in search of it. It can be found everywhere: a little water [*aquae pauxillum*] with which to be baptized, to be converted to Christianity, and to accept the faith of the Gospel. Once you have done this there will be no prince on the whole earth to outdo you in fame or equal you in power. We shall appoint you emperor of the Greeks and the Orient, and what you have now obtained by violence, and hold unjustly, will be your possession by right. All Christians will honor you and make you arbiter of their quarrels. All the oppressed will take refuge in you as in their common protector; men will turn to you from nearly all the countries on earth. Many will submit to you voluntarily, appear before your judgment seat, and pay taxes to you. It will be given you to quell tyrants, to support the good and combat the wicked. And the Roman Church will not oppose you if you walk in the right path. The first spiritual chair will embrace you in the same love as other kings, and all the more so accordingly as your position is higher. Under these conditions you can easily, without war or bloodshed, acquire many kingdoms. . . . We should never lend aid to your enemies, but on the contrary call on your arm against those who sometimes usurp the rights of the Roman Church and raise their horns against their own mother.

The learned author of this long, carefully written letter goes on to relate the history of the Old and New Covenants and to expound the fundamental truths of the Christian faith. At the same time, using the ideas of Nicholas of Cusa, he endeavors to refute the doctrines of the Koran. The tantalizing notion of a correspondence between the foremost representatives of Christianity and Islam seems to have fired the imagination of many contemporaries, and no doubt accounts in good part for the "Turkish" craze in the literature of the time, which more than a hundred years later Cervantes, in the introduction to *Don Quixote*, still considered important enough to ridicule. Obviously the pope's letter would have brought no results if it had reached its destination. But—as other historians have pointed out—it was highly characteristic of the Christian reaction to the mounting power of Islam that Pius II, who was then seriously thinking of conferring the Albanian crown on Skanderbeg and restoring the kingdom of Jerusalem for the benefit of the duke of Burgundy, should at the same time offer to transform the sultan of the infidel Ottomans into a Catholic emperor of the Orient.

At approximately the same time, Sigismondo Pandolfo Malatesta (1417–1468), lord of Rimini, the most feared of all the Italian petty tyrants and perhaps the most terrifying figure of the early Renaissance, sent Mehmed a letter drafted by his secretary and adviser, the humanist Roberto Valturio. Apparently the sultan had asked Malatesta to send the painter Matteo de' Pasti, long a resident at Malatesta's court, to Istanbul to paint his portrait. Malatesta promised to send the court painter at once and at the same time a gift—namely, a magnificent manuscript of *De re militari*, an illustrated work on arms and military tactics by Valturio. In September 1461 Matteo set out, reportedly taking with him a carefully executed map of the Adriatic Sea (*el colfo designato*) for the sultan. Off Crete, however, he was captured by the Venetians, who hauled him along with his book and other writings before the Council of Ten. He was severely questioned and threatened with torture if he did not state the true purpose for which he was being sent to the sultan. The question of his guilt was put to a vote at the Signoria. There were ten votes in his favor, four against, and three abstentions. Thus he was pronounced innocent and released early in December 1461. But before he returned to Rimini he was informed that if he valued the favor of the Signoria, he should give up the idea of going to Turkey and abstain from all relations with the sultan. By January 18, 1462, he was back at Malatesta's court. But in Venice and wherever the news of his journey had become known, it was generally believed that Malatesta, who was capable of any treachery, was preparing to forge close political ties with the sultan. It was even thought that there was a plan afoot to invite the sultan to Italy and offer him Malatesta's services as *condottiere*. Pius II, whose army on July 2, 1461, had routed Malatesta, was probably not far from the truth when he accused the lord of Rimini of wishing to attract the Turks to Italy. Shortly before the departure of Matteo de' Pasti for the Levant in September of that year, it was asserted, Malatesta had declared that if King Ferrante of Naples sent for Skanderbeg, he, Malatesta, would send for the Turks. Giovanni di Pedrino of Forlì, a contemporary chronicler, reports that the supposed map of the Adriatic actually covered all Italy and indicated every detail that might be of interest to the sultan. Malatesta's attempt to send Valturio's treatise hardly argues in favor of the innocence of the undertaking. The magnificent manuscript, to be sure, did not reach the sultan, but fell into the hands of Pius II and is today in the Vatican library. The brave and crafty Sigismondo Malatesta, who was not infrequently favored by fortune and combined the qualities of the fox and the lion, so meeting Machiavelli's requirements for the perfect prince, does not seem to have made any further contact with Mehmed, whom he later combated in the field—"io servo che mi paga" ("I serve him who pays me")—although the presence in Istanbul at the time (October 1461) of Valturio's compatriot and friend Angelo Vadio might give ground for suspicion of closer relations between Rimini and the Ottoman capital.[26]

Before Mehmed moved against Trebizond, he received news that the hereditary chief of the raiders (akĩncĩs), Mihaloğlu Ali Bey, who left the Hungarians no peace with his raids into their Danubian border territories, had captured Michael Szilágyi, uncle of the Hungarian king, who with twenty-eight followers had penetrated Turkish territory on the Bulgarian bank of the Danube. The prisoners were taken to Istanbul, where, on the sultan's order, they were mercilessly executed. Szilágyi survived his companions by three days, during which Mehmed tried to obtain information about Belgrade and Hungary as a basis for his aggressive plans against these countries. Then he too was put to death.

Hostilities against King Matthias, who had recently become reconciled with his uncle, were inaugurated by these murders, although Matthias hesitated to retaliate for a new incursion of Ali Bey into the Temesvar Banat. He left it to his Walachian vassal Prince Vlad III—whose cruelty and the fiendish pleasure he took in having people impaled earned him the nicknames Țepeș, the Impaler, or Dracul, the Devil—to make trouble for the sultan on the Danube. Ever since his accession to power in 1456, Vlad had been the terror of his subjects, his neighbors, and sometimes even of the Ottomans. His refined cruelty and bestial blood lust were unparalleled even in those barbarous times. By the thousands, those who had aroused his anger were impaled, cut to pieces, or burned alive. Long after his death his fame lived on even in Western Europe, as can be seen

[26] For Matteo's unsuccessful journey and the treatise of Valturio, see Babinger, "Mehmed II., der Eroberer, und Italien," 164ff. See also his "An Italian Map of the Balkans, Presumably Owned by Mehmed II, the Conqueror (1452–53)," *Imago Mundi* 8 (1951), 10, n. 6 (= *A&A* II, 173, n. 5). Charles C. Bayley, in his *War and Society in Renaissance Florence* (Toronto, 1961), shows the debt of Valturio's work to the earlier treatise of Leonardo Bruni (216–218). For Sigismondo Malatesta, see Geoffrey Trease, *The Condottieri* (London, 1970), 301ff. A new full-length study of the Malatesta, but without reference to Mehmed or Turkey, is P. J. Jones, *The Malatesta of Rimini and the Papal State* (London, 1974).

Medal of the young Mehmed II, attributed to Matteo
de' Pasti and to a Burgundian artist, Jean Tricaudet

from the crude but impressive woodcuts to be found in incunabula printed in Augsburg, Bamberg, Nuremberg, and Strasbourg.[27]

His favorite sport was to dine with his court while a dense throng of freshly impaled Turks agonized nearby. He would order his henchmen to remove the skin from prisoners' feet, rub salt on the wounds, and bring in goats to lick it off. If an emissary from the sultan refused to bare his head when appearing before him, he would have three nails driven through the Turk's turban to make it all the more secure in accordance with tradition. One day he had all the beggars in the country invited to a banquet. After abundantly wining and dining them, he had the hall set on fire and all perished in the flames. He would have the heads of suckling babes impaled to their mothers' breasts. He forced children to eat pieces of their roasted mothers. He invented special devices for chopping people into hash, which would then be roasted or boiled. A monk whom he saw riding on an ass was impaled along with his mount. A priest who had preached that one should not lay hands on other people's possessions and who at table had eaten a piece of the bread that Vlad had cut for himself was impaled on the spot. When one of his concubines thought herself pregnant but was not, he cut open her belly with his own hand. One hot summer day, when Vlad was walking among the impaled, he was met by a worthy nobleman who asked him how he could bear the stench. Thereupon Vlad had the man impaled on the highest stake that could be found, in order to raise him above the stench. He was a lover of mass executions. Four hundred young men from Transylvania and Hungary, who had been sent to Walachia to learn the language, were burned all together; 600 merchants from Burzenland (Burzeland; Burcia) were impaled in the marketplace; 500 Walachian magistrates and nobles whom he regarded as suspect were impaled on the pretext that they could give him no satisfactory figures about the population of their districts.

As long as the Walachians had paid the annual tribute, inaugurated by Murad II, Mehmed had left them in peace. Indeed, he had helped Vlad to defeat a rival claimant to the throne, contenting himself with carrying off Vlad's younger brother Radu as a hostage to the Porte.

Once securely established, however, Vlad stopped paying the tribute and began to infringe on Ottoman territory and to direct his blood lust against the Turks. And in 1461 he wrote secretly to his relative, King Matthias of Hungary, proposing an offensive and defensive alliance against the Turks. Although Vlad had wrought constant havoc in Transylvania and other Hungarian territory with his raids, Matthias accepted

[27] The most recent Western study of Vlad is Florescu and McNally, *Dracula* (see above, book 1, n. 40).

the proposal. But even before the alliance was concluded, Mehmed, informed by his spies that Vlad was plotting open hostilities, decided to forestall his plans and if possible to capture him. His crafty Greek private secretary Thomas Catavolenus (known as Yunus Bey) invited Vlad to the Porte in the sultan's name, with the assurance that if he should appear and so demonstrate his allegiance and good faith, he would be received with honors and favored with rewards of all sorts. By way of proving his good intentions, Vlad was called upon to send 500 selected Walachians to serve at the Porte and to convey to Istanbul in person the annual tribute of 2,000 ducats, which now amounted to 10,000 in view of five years' arrears. In case Vlad should not, of his own free will, accept the invitation, Catavolenus had orders to capture him by trickery. To this end the Greek was to make arrangements with the *çakirci başi* (chief falconer), Hamza Pasha, then in command of Vidin and the Danube territories.

The attempt to trap the shrewd Walachian prince was a complete failure. Vlad informed the sultan's ambassador that he had the tribute in readiness, but that he would never condescend to send 500 young men or go to the Porte in person. He finally accompanied the Greek, but did not neglect to provide himself with a suitable bodyguard. When they reached the place where the trap was to be sprung, a sharp battle broke out in which Vlad and his partisans were victorious. The Turks fled, Hamza Pasha and Catavolenus were taken prisoner; their hands and feet were cut off and they were impaled. In view of his rank, Hamza Pasha was honored with the tallest stake.

Vlad gathered an army, put across the Danube, devastated the Ottoman territories far and wide, burned every last village to the ground, and massacred the defenseless population, including women and children. All prisoners, reportedly no less than 25,000 in number, were tortured to death by impaling. That Vlad had carried things so far as to lay hands on an envoy, ordering his turban to be nailed to his head, seemed so inconceivable to Mehmed that in his first surge of indignation he thrashed Mahmud Pasha, his grand vizier, who had brought him the news. "Blows," Chalcocondylas remarks, "are no disgrace at the sultan's court for the slaves whom he has raised out of the dust to the highest dignities." According to other sources, the victim of the beating was only a mounted messenger.

Once the sultan had become convinced of the truth of the reports, thoughts of vengeance left him no rest, and he resolved to move against Walachia the following spring. The crimes of the "impaler voivode," as the Turks called Vlad, must have taken place in the winter of 1461–1462.

Mehmed II sent out messengers in all directions to assemble an army, which in numbers and armaments must have been almost equal to that which he had employed for the siege of Constantinople. Ducas speaks of 150,000 men; Chalcocondylas adds another 100,000, telling us in support of this obviously exaggerated figure that the Danube shipowners paid 300,000 gold pieces for the privilege of transporting this army commanded by Mahmud Pasha and nevertheless made a good profit. In addition a supply fleet, said to consist of 25 triremes and 150 smaller vessels, was sent through the Black Sea and up the Danube, reportedly as far as Vidin. The sultan himself was on one of these vessels; he had left Istanbul on April 26, 1462.

The size of this army, which must have been very considerable even if the recorded figures are exaggerated, seems to suggest that Mehmed's intention was not only to bring about a change of princes but to take possession of Walachia as he had of Serbia and Greece. True, he took along Radu, who could if necessary serve as a compliant pretender to the Walachian throne, but what he had in mind seems to have been complete occupation.

This Walachian expedition was to be unlike all the Conqueror's previous wars. The Ottomans were accustomed to campaigns in territories with powerful fortresses and walled cities. Such strongholds were not always easy to capture, but once they had fallen into his hands, Mehmed could be sure of controlling the surrounding country for the time being. In Walachia it was a very different matter. The few cities, built for the most part by Saxons and Hungarians, were situated at the foot of the mountains. The plains were inhabited chiefly by peasants and shepherds, living in villages or scattered farmsteads occasionally protected by palisades or trenches against minor attacks. Under such conditions Mehmed was inevitably at a loss. Vlad, on the other hand, was able to make skillful use of his shepherds and peasants.

While the river-borne troops disembarked, devastating the Walachian countryside and burning Braila, then the country's chief port though it consisted almost exclusively of wooden houses, the land army set out from the plain of Edirne by way of Philippopolis. They crossed the Danube without difficulty, for neither on the banks nor in the utterly deserted plains nearby was the slightest resistance offered. Vlad had ordered the whole population to withdraw their cattle and movable goods to the dense and impassable oak forests, where he too sought cover with his army, which cannot have exceeded 10,000 men. He seems to have counted on help from the Hungarians but not from the Moldavians. Stephen the Great, voivode of Moldavia, had hastened to Kiliya (Kilia) in the Danube delta, which was in Hungarian hands. With good reason he regarded the possession of this fortress as a strategic necessity for his country. In June 1462, when he stood before its walls, Vlad hurried to the spot to defend the important port. Even before Vlad's arrival, Stephen, wounded in the foot, was forced to give up his designs on the city. Vlad established himself in Kiliya, and the Ottoman squadron which had entered the Danube to take possession of the estuary and fortress was forced to withdraw.[28]

Vlad now dispatched a letter in all haste to the king of Hungary, who was well aware of the threat to himself, but contented himself for the present with sending a special envoy to the pope and the Signoria of Venice with an urgent plea for help. As can be inferred from the reports of the Venetian ambassador at the court of Buda, the Hungarians were poorly informed concerning the events in Walachia. The reports reiterate the fear that after completing his campaign in Walachia, Mehmed would direct his armies against Belgrade.

Left to his own resources, Vlad did his best to harass the Turks by sudden sallies from the woods. In those oak forests and inaccessible passes, numbers lost their value: what counted was knowledge of the terrain. In the woods Mehmed insisted on keeping his troops in formation and forbade all deviations from the main line of march. For seven days he advanced through the deserted countryside without meeting an enemy. The news, brought him by his spies, that Hungarian reinforcements were not to be expected made him overconfident and careless.

One night Vlad and his men broke into the poorly defended and inadequately entrenched Turkish camp, where no one expected such an incursion. Only with difficulty were the Ottomans prevented from fleeing in disorder. The Asiatic cavalry was first to reassemble and tried to repulse the Walachian assault, but was put to flight. Amid the confusion Vlad attempted to break into the sultan's camp with his cavalry, but lost his way and came instead to the tents of the grand vizier and of Ishak Pasha, where he accomplished nothing. The entire skirmish, in which many camels, mules, and horses were killed, had no significant results. When the Janissaries and the rest of the Ottoman cavalry had re-formed their ranks, the tide seemed to have turned. Ali Bey set off in pursuit of the retreating Walachians, killed many, and brought some 1,000 captives back to the camp. Mehmed had them executed on the spot.

Ducas and Chalcocondylas both speak of a grave defeat for the sultan. Whether this assertion is in keeping with the facts is uncertain. Nor can

---

[28] The voivode Stephen was able to add Kiliya to his Moldavian domains in 1465. N. Beldiceanu gives the background to Ottoman attacks on Walachia, dating from 1368, in "Eflāk," *EI²* II, 687–689.

it be determined whether, as claimed in other sources, this surprise attack was actually the main reason for the Turks' hurried withdrawal from Walachia. It had no doubt been Mehmed's original plan to attack Tirgoviște, the Walachian capital, which was strongly fortified and protected by swamps. A large part of the population from the plains had taken refuge in this city. But when the sultan reached the walls, he found them stripped of defenders and cannon. The gates were wide open and the city was deserted. He went on at once, and shortly thereafter seems to have passed through the most gruesome of forests; for all of half an hour his road was bordered by the impaled corpses of some 20,000 Bulgarians and Turks, among them, on the tallest stake and clad in ceremonial dress, Hamza Pasha, the commandant of Vidin. Even Mehmed, or at least so the two Byzantine chroniclers tell us, could not repress a shudder.

Vlad pursued the Ottoman army, harassing it with minor skirmishes, but did not dare to make a decisive attack. At length he withdrew with a part of his army to Moldavia, leaving in Walachia only some 6,000 men to watch the enemy. On one occasion Turahanoğlu Ömer Bey, commanding the right wing of the army, came to grips with this detachment and wiped it out almost completely. He laid the heads of 2,000 Walachians at the feet of his delighted master. Thereupon he was reinstated as governor of Thessaly.

Although the remnants of the Walachian army were able to form their ranks again, they were now powerless against the Ottomans, who laid the country waste to the best of their ability. In addition to the numerous prisoners whom they carried off into slavery, they are said to have driven 200,000 head of cattle and horses with them on their southward march. Crossing the Danube, the sultan returned to Istanbul on July 11, 1462. Before leaving Romania, he appointed Mihaloğlu Ali Bey governor of Walachia with instructions to install Vlad's brother Radu as ruler, under the sovereignty of the Porte. In sharp contrast to his brutal and ungainly brother, Radu was a weakling and a voluptuary, famous for his beauty. He had spent years as hostage at the sultan's court, where he had won Mehmed's special favor. Chalcocondylas describes at length an incident which allegedly took place between them. The story is that Mehmed, whose passion for the boy is reliably attested, attempted to take liberties with him, whereupon Radu drew his sword and wounded the importunate lover. For fear of the sultan's vengeance, Radu climbed a nearby tree. In the end, however, he showed himself more amenable to the sultan's attentions and was taken back into favor. He even managed to remain in Mehmed's good graces and accompanied him to Walachia, where certain local nobles had chosen him as successor to the throne.

Radu had no difficulty in winning over those boyars who were still opposed to him. They abandoned Vlad and in August 1462, after some threats and remonstrance, recognized Radu as their ruler.[29]

Forsaken by all, Vlad took refuge in Transylvania. He made one more attempt to recover his country and above all to regain the sultan's favor. On November 7, 1462, from "Rhotel," probably the German Rauthel (Hungarian Rudaly), near Sighişoara, he wrote Mehmed a letter in the Slavic language which has come down to us in a free Latin translation, though its authenticity is contested, for no apparent reason, by recent Romanian historians. This letter, in which Vlad offered the sultan his assistance and promised to win for him not only Transylvania but Hungary as well, never reached its destination. Probably in Braşov, it fell into the hands of King Matthias of Hungary, who immediately had his relative seized and carried off to prison in Buda, where he remained until 1476. Up until that time, his brother, in return for an annual tribute of 12,000 ducats, carried on an uncertain shadow rule under Turkish sovereignty. Then once again Vlad became the scourge of his unhappy country, though only for two years.

Some time after the sultan's return to his Istanbul serai, severe restrictions were imposed on all correspondence addressed to foreign countries. At the end of July 1462, Domenico Balbi, the Venetian *bailo* to the Porte, wrote his government that he had been put to great difficulty and expense in sending his report from Istanbul, for very few persons were permitted to leave the capital either by the land or the sea route. All dispatches containing news of events in Turkey were forbidden, and the vigilance was so strict that no one dared to smuggle them out. At the same time, much to the dismay of the merchants, all copper, lead, and leather goods were confiscated. All this suggests either that Mehmed was planning a new campaign that he wished to keep secret, or that he was taking large-scale defensive measures against an expected attack.

It is certain in any case that the construction of the two fortresses of Kilid ül-Bahreyn (Key of the Two Seas) and Kale-i Sultaniye (Sultan's Castle, near ancient Abydos), the so-called Old Dardanelles on the European and Asiatic shores of the Hellespont, was begun by Mehmed in 1462 for the defense of the straits. The two structures were apparently com-

---

[29] For critical remarks on this account of the campaign in Walachia, see M. Guboglu, "A propos de la monographie du professeur Franz Babinger," *Studia et Acta Orientalia* 2 (1959), 225–226, where the Romanian historian discusses the question of tribute owed to the Porte as well as the character of Vlad, with references to the works of his colleagues.

pleted with remarkable speed, and the striking impression which these large and powerful forts make even on modern observers gives us an idea of how imposing they must have seemed at that time. With these two fortresses, it was an easy matter to bar access to Istanbul from the west through the Sea of Marmara, while Rumeli Hisarï and Anadolu Hisarï could lock off the Bosporus from the Black Sea whenever desired.

At the same time many ships were built, though it would seem that the greatest efforts in this direction were not undertaken until the winter of 1462–1463, just as the extensive harbor works, calculated to make Istanbul the chief anchorage of the Ottoman Empire, were probably not begun until the cold season. This new harbor for galleys (*kadïrga limanï*) was intended especially for large warships, several of which were built and launched in the course of the same winter. The immediate reason for adding to the fleet and building a naval base near the capital was the campaign against the island of Lesbos, which immediately followed the Walachian expedition.[30]

A pretext for the campaign against Lesbos was easily found. After losing Lemnos to the Ottomans in 1456, Niccolò Gattilusio took up residence in Lesbos, the last of the Gattilusi possessions, where his brother Domenico still was ruler. At the end of 1458, the ambitious Niccolò found occasion to accuse his brother of planning to hand over the island to the Turks; with the help of his cousin Luchino, he deposed Domenico, threw him into prison, and had him strangled. He himself became the ruler. Casting himself in the role of a divine avenger, the same Mehmed whose first sovereign act had been to murder his own brother took this crime as a pretext for intervention. The real reason for his grudge against the prince, however, was Niccolò's complicity with the Catalan pirates, to whom, in disregard of his obligation to the sultan to clear his waters of pirates and bar them from the nearby Anatolian coast, he accorded shelter in Mytilini harbor, exacting a considerable share of their spoils in return. To make matters worse, pirates from the Cyclades had joined forces with the Catalans. Together they plundered the Anatolian coast, carrying off the inhabitants as slaves to Lesbos.

At the head of a small detachment of Janissaries, Mehmed crossed over to Asia in August 1462. First he went to the plain of the Maeander (Men-

---

[30] Additional information on Ottoman naval preparations and the fortification of the straits is given by H. Inalcïk, "Gelibolu," *EI*² II, 983–987. Ayverdi deals with the Dardanelles' fortresses in his *Osmanli Mi'mārisinde Fatih Devri* IV, 790–804. A. C. Hess discusses the rise of Ottoman naval power in "The evolution of the Ottoman seaborne empire in the age of the oceanic discoveries," *American Historical Review* 75 (1970), 1892–1919.

deres), where he appears to have visited the ruins of Troy, notably the legendary hill of Achilles and the so-called tomb of Ajax. After the manner of the contemporary chroniclers, Critoboulos quotes in direct discourse an alleged oration of the Conqueror, praising the heroes of Troy and castigating the Greeks—the Macedonians, Thessalians, and Moreots—for the destruction of glorious Ilium. But his hand, so the harangue goes on, had punished the descendants of these peoples for the crimes committed by their ancestors against the "peoples of Asia." Here we feel the influence of his Italian preceptors, who had persuaded him that Teucros, first king of Troy and ruler over the Teucri, was his ancestor, for the Latinists of the time did not hesitate to designate the Turks as "Teucri." There is no doubt that in nearly all his campaigns his retinue included Italian humanists, who on this occasion regaled him with stories from the Homeric epics and described the past glories of Troy.[31]

Then he marched on by way of Baba Burnu (the Cape Lectum of antiquity), probably halting in the vicinity of Assos (near Behram Köy), facing the northern coast of the isle of Lesbos. Meanwhile, Mahmud Pasha seems to have put to sea in command of an Ottoman fleet, consisting of 60 galleys and seven smaller vessels (Ducas) or, according to other writers, 125 larger and smaller vessels. Siege machines, catapults, mortars, and some 2,000 stone balls were also embarked. Three days later, on September 1, the fleet reached its destination.

Mehmed now sent troops to the island who laid waste the countryside and carried off the few inhabitants they found to the ships anchored in the harbor of St. George. But his hope that such measures would frighten Niccolò Gattilusio into surrendering was disappointed. The sultan sent him word that if he should lay down his arms at once, he would be indemnified with a suitable possession elsewhere. Confident in the strength of his fortifications, the courage of the defenders, and the population's fear of Turkish slavery, the prince replied that he would go down in honorable defeat by the side of his people but would never surrender the city of Mytilini to his enemies. The garrison numbered over 5,000, including 70 Knights of Rhodes and 110 Catalan mercenaries, while the noncombatant population is estimated to have been 20,000. After four days of fruitless skirmishing, six giant cannon bombarded the city's defenses for ten days. The walls resisted the great stone balls, but at length the outer fortifications began to give way, and the defenders were forced back into the inner castle. Finally, panic broke loose in the city; even with

[31] Most recently on the Turks and the Trojans, see Steven Runciman, "Teucri and Turci," in *Medieval and Middle Eastern Studies in Honor of Aziz Suryal Atiya*, ed. Sami A. Hanna (Leiden, 1972), 344–348.

the large sums of money allotted for the purpose, it became impossible to repair the shattered walls. The soldiery broke into the enormous stocks of wine and looted the food warehouses; when at length the Janissaries penetrated the city, they met with no serious opposition.

Niccolò Gattilusio was forced to recognize his defeat. His enemies on the island seem to have helped Mahmud Pasha subdue the city quickly by leading the Turks to the weak points in the walls. Niccolò named only one condition for his surrender: that he be assigned a possession equal in value to his principality, from which he might draw an equivalent income. Mehmed, who had observed the progress of the siege and assault from the nearby mainland, now crossed over to the island, where he remained for four days.

Followed by the notables of the city, the prince brought the sultan the keys to the city, fell at his feet in tears, and begged for forgiveness and for the favor of the mighty lord of the Ottomans. Throughout his reign, he protested, he had always observed his treaties with the Porte. When slaves had been brought to Lesbos from Anatolia, he had always returned them to their rightful owners, and if he had sometimes allowed the Catalans to put into his harbor, it had been solely in order to save his island from the ravages and extortions of the pirates, and all assertions to the effect that he had helped the corsairs in their expeditions against the mainland were pure slander. Only the ignorance of his subjects was to blame if he had not surrendered the city at the sultan's first summons, for they had advised him against it. Now he offered the sultan not only his capital but the whole island. Mehmed upbraided the miserable creature violently for his foolishness, but finally a treaty was drawn up and sworn to by both sides. Niccolò was assured that despite his folly and delay in surrendering, neither he or anyone else should suffer loss of life or property. The sultan ordered Niccolò to surrender the other cities of the island, and so Niccolò made the rounds with the Turkish commanders, showed them the bulwarks, and everywhere recommended submission to the new masters. Everywhere the Turks left garrisons; 500 Janissaries and *azaps* were stationed in the capital, which the sultan entrusted to the Persian sheikh Ali al-Bistami, known as Musannifek (Little Author). Three hundred Italian prisoners were cut in half, allegedly because Mehmed considered this the most painful form of death and because, as he mockingly remarked, this was the most conscientious way of carrying out Mahmud Pasha's promise, which he himself had confirmed, to respect the life and property of the defeated.

Putting his own interpretation on the treaty of surrender, Mehmed caused the population to be divided into three groups. He allowed the common people, the poorest and most useless, to remain within the walls; the stronger and more able members of the population were given to the Janissaries, while all the noble and wealthy inhabitants were carried off to Istanbul as colonists. For himself he picked 800 choice boys and girls to serve at the Porte. He selected Maria, sister of Niccolò Gattilusio and widow of Alexander Comnenus (a brother of Emperor David of Trebizond), considered the most beautiful woman of the day, for his harem; her son Alexius was to serve in the serai as a page.

Soon the indemnification promised the prince was forgotten. He and his cousin Luchino reached Istanbul when the fleet returned on October 16, 1462; they were held captive, but were set free after they had been converted to Islam, circumcised, and vested in the turban and caftan. A few weeks later Mehmed, who had meanwhile returned to his court for the rest of the year, ordered Luchino to be thrown into prison again, ostensibly for participating in his cousin's crimes, but actually because it was the sultan's principle to put defeated princes out of the way. Soon Niccolò too was arrested and both were strangled with bowstrings. Some of the sources mention an incident that may have accounted in part for this death sentence. A page who had been abused by Mehmed had escaped from the sultan's palace and made his way to Mytilini, where he turned Christian and became Niccolò Gattilusio's favorite. Included among the boys sent to Istanbul after the conquest of Lesbos, he had been recognized and reported to the sultan. The episode may well have hastened, if it did not actually cause, the execution of the last prince of Lesbos.[32]

Leonard, archbishop of Mytilini, was also taken prisoner and moved to Istanbul, which he had helped to defend in 1453, but he managed to escape. In a letter to Pope Pius II he described the last weeks of the island and implored him to restore peace at last in Italy, so that a crusade might be undertaken against the "Cerberus" of the Orient.[33]

While the Turkish fleet lay in the harbor of St. George of Lesbos, Vettore Capello, the Venetian captain who a year later would publicly assail the lukewarm peace policy of the Venetian Republic and take the lead of the war party in his native city, was in Chios with a Venetian fleet. When Niccolò Gattilusio called on him for help, he sailed to Lesbos with no less than twenty-nine galleys. He could have destroyed the unmanned Turkish vessels virtually without a struggle, but refused to intervene, for the instructions of the Signoria were to avoid all provocation

[32] The conquest of Lesbos according to Greek and Western sources is given by William Miller, *Essays on the Latin Orient*, 340–349.

[33] For the archbishop Leonard, see Steven Runciman, *The Fall of Constantinople*, 69 and passim. Cf. above, book 2, n. 20.

of the sultan. Even when after the fall of Mytilini the men at the castle of St. Theodore implored him to take them under the protection of Venice, he declined. Genoa also took the "misfortune of Mytilini" in its stride. To his dying day Vettore Capello regretted his inaction on this occasion; he became the bitterest adversary of the republic's Levantine policy. But the harm was done and the situation degenerated rapidly. Sixteen years of war betwen the Venetian Republic and the Ottoman Empire were in the offing.

The easy victory over Lesbos was lavishly celebrated in Istanbul. The sultan invited the Florentines of Pera and Galata, his "good friends," to take part in the festivities, to light bonfires and organize entertainments. Even three Florentine ships which lay at anchor in the Golden Horn received express orders to take part. The families and household of the grand vizier Mahmud Pasha appeared and were clothed at the expense of the Florentine colony. According to Benedetto Dei, the Venetians and Genoese residing in Pera and elsewhere in "Romania" were highly indignant over this preference shown their rivals, costly as it was.

In the spring of 1463 Yakub Pasha, admiral and governor of Gelibolu, completed the two fortresses on the Dardanelles. The new harbor for galleys also neared completion in the course of the winter, which the sultan spent in his Istanbul palace. Ship building proceeded at a rapid pace; both Ducas and Chalcocondylas report that construction was begun on a number of large galleys, one of which, copied from Western or Trebizontian models, was particularly imposing. During the winter and spring, the sultan busied himself with impressive construction projects outside the city, as all the chroniclers note. A fortified tower was said to have been built near Skoplje, at the great bridge across the Vardar. A town situated north of Silivri and still known as Fener Köy (from the Greek *phanari*, "lighthouse") formerly harbored a watchtower, built by Mehmed, whose purpose it was to alert the garrison of Silivri with flares if bandits should appear on the scene or rebellion should break out among the Greek population. The palace on the Tunca island was also being fortified.

After the fall of Lesbos and the preparations which Mehmed was making on every side, obviously for a campaign against the West, it had become clear, especially to Venice, that drastic measures would have to be taken if the Ottomans were not to gain control over the seas and if the remaining larger islands of the Aegean, such as Rhodes and particularly Negropont, were not to incur the same fate as Lesbos. The sultan's intensive building of ships and fortifications during the winter of 1462–1463 made it seem likely that he was planning expeditions against the

Venetian possessions in the Aegean; the republic's peaceful relations with the Porte had long become uncertain. Once the sultan felt sufficiently powerful, he would, as usual, find a pretext for hostilities.

In the midst of all these preparations Mehmed also busied himself with the construction of his own mosque, after having transformed the largest and most magnificent churches of his capital into places of Moslem worship. According to Islamic law, only conqueror-sultans were allowed to build mosques; they were not authorized to spend the money of their own subjects, but only the spoils of war, tribute, ransom money, and so on. At the sultan's wish, the new mosque was to be built somewhat to the north of Emperor Justinian's old Church of the Holy Apostles, which in size and splendor was second only to Hagia Sophia. This was the burial place of Constantine the Great, builder of the original church, which had been totally remodeled by Justinian. Here too was the *heroön*, the imperial burial site, where the dead rulers of the Byzantine Empire rested in sarcophagi of porphyry, granite, serpentine, and multicolored marble. During Latin rule of the city (1204–1261) the graves of the emperors were broken open and desecrated, and the body of Justinian, after lying for more than 700 years in the underground vault of the church he had built, was disinterred and despoiled of all the jewels with which he had been buried. At this spot then, in February or March 1463, construction was begun of an enormous mosque, in conscious imitation of Hagia Sophia. The lines of the Byzantine dome were followed closely. We shall speak in greater detail of this mosque, its architect, and his tragic end on the occasion of its completion.

Book Four

THE SUBJECTION OF BOSNIA.
OUTBREAK OF WAR WITH VENICE.
PAPAL EFFORTS AT CRUSADE.
THE OTTOMANS ON THE ADRIATIC.
ANATOLIAN UNDERTAKINGS.
THE FALL OF NEGROPONT.
THE MOSQUE OF THE CONQUEROR.

BEFORE the end of March 1463, Mehmed was marching westward. Now, from an army camp in the Balkans, he issued a deed donating the monastery of St. John Prodromos in Petra in Istanbul to the grand vizier Mahmud Pasha's mother, who had remained a Christian.[1]

On Saturday, March 26, 1463, probably a few days before his departure, he gave orders that her kinsman David, the last of the Comneni, should be imprisoned in Edirne. David's niece, Despina Hatun, the wife of Uzun Hasan, was alleged to have written her uncle a letter inviting one of his sons or Alexander Comnenus's son Alexius to visit her. Authentic or forged, the letter fell into the hands of the sultan, who suspected David of secretly plotting with Uzun Hasan in order to regain his freedom and reestablish his empire. Theodoros Spandugino, whose grandfather was said to have been a brother of Emperor David's second wife, maintains, to be sure, in his history of the Turks, that the letter in question was a forged letter from Rome, informing the emperor about a projected crusade against the Turks. No matter what the letter was, its interception led to the end of David and most of his family.[2]

Immediately after the arrest of Emperor David the sultan seems to

[1] For this document, see Vl. Mirmiroğlu, *Fatih Sultan Mehmet II devrine ait tarihi vesikalar* (Istanbul, 1945), 89–93.

[2] A brief account of the life and work of Theodoros Spandugino (Spandounes) is given by Donald M. Nicol, *The Byzantine Family of Kantakouzenos (Cantacuzenus)* (Washington, 1968), especially xv–xvi and 232–233. His history of the Turks has been published by C. Scheffer as Theodore Spandouyn Cantacusin, *Petit traicté de l'origine des turcqz* (Paris, 1896).

have started out on his new campaign. Not counting the baggage train and the *azaps*, or light infantry, his army was said to have consisted of 150,000 horsemen; as usual, this figure is subject to doubt. Mehmed himself held the supreme command, while the grand vizier Mahmud Pasha commanded the advance guard. The aim of the campaign was kept strictly secret except from the leading dignitaries of the empire.

King Stjepan Tomašević of Bosnia had known for some time that the sultan's next campaign would be directed against him. Shortly before his ascension to the throne early in November 1461, he informed the pope through an ambassador that the "Turkish emperor was planning to attack him with an army the following year, and the army and cannon were already in readiness." He entreated Pius II to help him, declaring that he did not expect the moon and the stars, but wished his enemies as well as his compatriots to know that he did not lack the pope's favor. This, he said, would influence the king of Hungary and induce him to take the field with Stjepan.

The Turks have built several fortresses in my kingdom and are very friendly with the peasants. They promise that every peasant who joins them will be free. The peasants with their limited intelligence are unaware of the deception and suppose that this freedom will endure forever. It is quite possible that the people, misled by such lies, will rebel against me unless they see that I have your power behind me. Abandoned by the peasants, the magnates have been unable to maintain themselves for long in their castles. If Mehmed only demanded my kingdom and would go no further, it would be possible to leave my kingdom to its fate and there would be no need for you to disturb the rest of Christendom in my defence. But his insatiable lust for power knows no bounds. After me he will attack Hungary and the Venetian province of Dalmatia. By way of Krain and Istria he will go to Italy, which he wishes to subjugate. He often speaks of Rome and longs to go there. If he conquers my kingdom thanks to the indifference of the Christians, he will find here the right country to fulfill his desires. I shall be the first victim. But after me the Hungarians and the Venetians and other peoples will suffer the same fate. That is what our enemy is thinking. I am informing you of what I have learned lest it be said one day that you were not informed and lest I be accused of negligence.[3]

[3] For the context of these words of the Bosnian ruler, see *The Commentaries of Pius II, Smith College Studies in History* XLIII (1957), 740–742.

Pius II was not deaf to the Bosnian's plea; he bade his legate crown Stjepan Tomašević king and persuaded Matthias Corvinus to patch up his quarrel with him; in the summer of 1462 the king of the Hungarians agreed to do so in return for a considerable sum of money and the cession of a few Bosnian castles. But this did not diminish the internal disorders in the country; on the contrary, they were aggravated by the king's reinforced ties with the Holy See. In religious matters Bosnia had long been torn, divided into two inexorably hostile camps. On the one side stood the Catholic Christians, whose cause the king espoused as his father had done before him; on the other, the heretical Bogomils or Patarines. Many of these heretics, who had already been obliged to leave their homes under King Stjepan Tomaš, sought and found protection in Turkish provinces. Even many magnates, who merely feigned to profess the Roman faith for fear of losing their property, secretly kept Sultan Mehmed informed through Turkish intermediaries of what went on at the Bosnian court. There is a story that the sultan in person had one day gone to Bosnia, disguised as a merchant or monk, in order to gain firsthand information on the state of the country and its defenses, that he had fallen into Bosnian hands, and that King Stjepan had spared his life only for fear of Turkish vengeance. This is probably a myth, invented by the king's adversaries by way of showing his untrustworthiness.[4]

In any case, Mehmed heard through the Patarine nobles and his spies of the entente between the kings of Bosnia and Hungary and decided to find out for himself. He sent an embassy to the Bosnian king in Jajce, demanding payment of the tribute which the king's father had already paid and which had again fallen due. Chalcocondylas relates how Stjepan Tomašević led the ambassador into his treasure house and showed him the money that had been set aside for the tribute, but informed him he had no intention of parting with such a treasure to please the Ottoman emperor. If the sultan should attack him, he would need his money, and if misfortune should befall him and he should be obliged to leave Bosnia, it would enable him to live more comfortably abroad. The ambassador apparently reminded him of the sanctity of treaties and expressed the opinion that he would not enjoy his treasure for long.

Informed of the king's refusal, Mehmed, as we may surmise from what we know of his character, was intensely irritated. He appears to have postponed his vengeance for one year for the sake of the Walachian cam-

---

[4] The standard account of the Bogomils is Dimitri Obolensky, *The Bogomils. A Study in Balkan Neo-Manichaeism* (Cambridge, 1948).

paign, but then to have been all the more determined to make up for lost time. Naturally, his preparations for war could not remain a secret to Stjepan Tomašević, who hurriedly sent envoys to Venice with a message to the effect that the sultan, as he had learned from an official of the Porte, was planning, after the conquest of Bosnia and the regions of Hum and Dubrovnik, to invade Venetian territory by way of Istria. On February 28, 1463, the Signoria coldly rejected the proposed alliance with Bosnia and the king's request for arms, advising him to appeal to Matthias Corvinus, the Emperor Frederick III, and especially Pope Pius II. Dubrovnik also refused all support. In his despair Stjepan turned to the Porte itself, asking forgiveness and requesting a fifteen-year truce. Concerning this Bosnian embassy an eyewitness, the Janissary Constantine Mihajlović of Ostrovica, a Serbian renegade, has given us a vivid report, which does not seem lacking in plausibility:

At this time the King of Bosnia also requested from Emperor Mehmed a truce of fifteen years. And the emperor sent at once to his army, commanding it to be in readiness and march to Adrianople, but no one knew where he meant to go with this army, and the Bosnian ambassadors had to wait. And I too, not knowing why this army had gathered, happened to be in one of the cellars of the imperial palace, where the imperial funds and treasure were kept. I was there because the treasure had been entrusted to my younger brother and he could not absent himself. Being all alone, he grew afraid and sent for me to come and sit with him. I went to him without hesitation, but immediately afterward the first imperial counselors Mahmud Pasha and Ishak Pasha came to the same room, and only they alone. Noticing their presence, my brother informed me of it, and since I could not leave the room without being seen by them, I hid behind a chest. And when they came in, my brother spread out a carpet for them. They sat down side by side and began to confer about the Bosnian king. And Mahmud Pasha said: "What should we do? What reply should we give the King of Bosnia?" Ishak Pasha replied: "What else can we do? We shall give him a fifteen-year truce and immediately afterward, without loss of time, follow them [the ambassadors]. If we do otherwise, we shall never conquer Bosnia, for it is a mountainous country, and moreover, the King of Hungary will come to their help and the Croats too and other lords. And they will prepare so well that we shall be unable to harm them. Therefore grant them [the ambassadors] a truce, so that they leave here on Saturday. But we will follow them and enter Bosnia near the

Sitnica [Sjenica?]. And still no one will know where the emperor means to go from here!" And so they agreed upon this plan, left the cellar, and went to the emperor. On the following Thursday morning the emperor promised them [the ambassadors] a fifteen-year truce as they had requested, to be observed loyally and faithfully. And the following day I went to see them in their lodgings and said to them: "My lords! Have you a truce with the emperor or not?" And they replied: "Thanks to the Lord God! We have settled everything as we wished." And I said to them: "By my faith, you have no truce." The elder of the ambassadors wished to question me further, but the younger would not allow it, for he thought I was making fun of them. Then I asked them: "On what day will you leave here?" And they replied: "On Saturday." And I said to them: "And we will follow you on Wednesday and pursue you all the way to Bosnia. I am telling you the truth, remember that!" But they laughed, and then I took my leave of them.

This sample of the narrative of the so-called Serbian Janissary gives an impressive picture of the Porte's attitude toward its vassals, as reflected in a conversation between the first and second viziers of the realm. In a serious situation the most solemn promises meant nothing at all.[5]

The truce and the route by which Mehmed and his army started out seem at first to have dispelled the Bosnians' fears that the new campaign might be directed against them. The sultan headed west for Skoplje, then by way of the field of Kosovo to Vučitrn, across the Sitnica River to Mitrovica, and from there north to Bosnia over the old trade route of Sjenica. By then no one was in doubt concerning the goal of the campaign. The advance guard under the grand vizier Mahmud Pasha, allegedly consisting of 20,000 light cavalry, was followed by the sultan with the army proper. After crossing the Bosnian border, they first entered the Drina territory, where the feudal voivode Tvrtko Kovačević, the last of his blood, commanded a number of castles. He was unprepared for resistance and surrendered at once to the sultan in the hope of being spared. He was immediately beheaded. After occupying the region of Podrinje, Mehmed invaded Bosnia proper, or Upper Bosnia, the "king's country," as it is called by Constantine Mihajlović, who served in the Ottoman army throughout the campaign and accordingly speaks as an eyewitness. Here the strongest and most important fortress was Bobovac, where the royal crown was formerly kept; the ruins of this castle, once the first in the kingdom, can still be seen on a high mountain

[5] For reference to the account of the Serbian Janissary, see above, p. 127.

overlooking the confluence of two streams to the east of Sutiska. Thus
far its defenders had bravely resisted all Turkish attacks. On May 19
Mahmud Pasha's advance guard reached the walls of Bobovac, which
was defended by Knez Radak, formerly a zealous Patarine and now a
forced Catholic. On the following day the sultan appeared with the main
army.

Observing that a siege would be a long-drawn-out affair, Mehmed
resolved to break down the walls and had large cannon cast on the spot.
But on the third day of the bombardment Radak, to whom a reward had
been promised, surrendered the Bosnian bulwark. Bobovac fell and as
usual the sultan divided the population into three parts: he kept one part
in the city, gave the second to his pashas, and sent the third to Istanbul
to increase the population. The ambassadors who had been at the sultan's
court in Edirne were among the prisoners. Constantine of Ostrovica reminded them of his prediction, but by then it was too late. When Knez
Radak wished to pocket his reward, Mehmed upbraided him violently,
accusing him of betraying his overlord, and gave orders for him to be
beheaded. "If you could not keep faith with a lord of your own faith," he
is reported to have said, "how can you be expected to keep faith with
me, a Turk?" On the road from Sutiska to Borovica travelers are still
shown the enormous rock of Radakovica, where according to the local
tradition Radak was put to the sword.

At the news of the sultan's arrival at Bobovac, King Stjepan Tomašević,
taking with him his family and all his possessions, had retired to the
powerful royal castle in Jajce, where the Pliva empties into the Vrbas.
A large, ancient fortified town with square towers and battlements sur-
mounts a conical mountain. The castle walls with their fortified gates
wind down the slope at sharp angles. To the left is the deep rocky bed
of the Vrbas, to the right the Pliva and its lakes, one above the next,
all this framed by wooded pyramids, the mountain walls closing off the
middleground, and the bare chains of hills in the blue distance. On the
other side of the pyramid city the Pliva, after encircling it with an impassable moat, rushes downward in a thundering waterfall 60 feet wide
and 100 feet in height, its spray forming a rainbow in the sunlight, and
flows into the Vrbas River. This is Jajce, the old royal city, the scene of
bitter struggles between Mehmed the Conqueror and the last king of
Bosnia.

Here Stjepan planned to gather his army and, confident in the resistance
of Bobovac, await help from the West. He and his men were all the
more horrified and disheartened when news reached them that Bobovac
had fallen. When the king realized that he would be able neither to

assemble an army nor to offer serious resistance, he decided to flee either to Croatia or to the Dalmatian coast, which was under Venetian sovereignty. But even for this it was too late. Determined to destroy Bosnia completely by taking advantage of the general terror and confusion, Mehmed sent Mahmud Pasha with the advance guard to Jajce with orders to capture the city and above all to seize the king. But when the grand vizier reached Jajce, he learned that the king had already fled. He set out in pursuit and followed, close on the king's heels, past Dolnji Kraji, where Stjepan turned off toward Croatia. Finally the hunted king reached the fortified city of Ključ, with its lofty, picturesque citadel. The Turkish pursuers did not suspect that the king was within, but as they were preparing to pass around the walls, they encountered a man who in return for money revealed the king's hiding place. Mahmud Pasha surrounded the city and besieged it for four days. At the end of this time, despairing of taking it, he sent messengers to the king conveying a solemn promise that no harm would befall him if he surrendered. The grand vizier went so far as to give the king a document guaranteeing his life and freedom. Short of food and ammunition, Stjepan Tomašević finally decided to surrender himself and the garrison to the grand vizier, trusting in his document and in the sultan's forbearance. Thereupon Mahmud Pasha brought the prisoner, his uncle Radivoj, and his thirteen-year-old son Tvrtko before the sultan.

In the meantime, Mehmed had gone from Bobovac to Jajce. Seeing themselves forsaken by the king and his retinue, the inhabitants lost heart and quite understandably decided to do what they could to save themselves. They sent several nobles to the sultan's tent and threw themselves on his mercy, asking leave only to preserve their ancient customs and to administer their city as they had done in the past. Esteeming that by such a gesture he might bring the remaining cities of Bosnia over to his side without doing battle, Mehmed agreed. Jajce and its inhabitants were spared. The Conqueror only took the sons of the noble families prisoner, keeping a few for himself and distributing the rest among his viziers.

The fall of Bobovac, Jajce, and Ključ sealed the fate of the kingdom of Bosnia. When Critoboulos claims that Mehmed had captured nearly 300 Bosnian towns, he is exaggerating, of course. But the fact remains that Stjepan Tomašević, trembling for his life, now helped the sultan to conquer the rest of the country. He sent orders to all his commanders and castellans to surrender the cities and castles to the sultan. Within a week seventy Bosnian towns, large and small, fell into the hands of the Ottomans in this way. Mehmed left garrisons in the most important fortresses and cities. Constantine Mihajlović, for example, was put in command of the Janissaries sent to Zvečaj Grad, not far from Jajce at the end of the Vrbas chasm.

By issuing a document in the sultan's name guaranteeing the life of the Bosnian king, Mahmud Pasha seems to have caused the sultan a certain embarrassment. But the difficulty was soon overcome. In the present campaign the learned Persian Ali al-Bistami, whom Mehmed had put in charge of conquered Mytilini, was a member of the sultan's retinue, to which, it might be mentioned, the Florentine Benedetto Dei also claims to have belonged. Before leaving Bosnia (end of May 1463) the sultan sent for King Stjepan, who, surmising no good, took the grand vizier's document with him. But Mullah Ali delivered a legal opinion (fetva) declaring the document to be null and void, since a servant of the sultan had issued it without the sultan's knowledge. Thus the last king of Bosnia was condemned to death, whereupon the aged Ali al-Bistami himself was said to have drawn his sword and beheaded him. But according to Benedetto Dei it was the sultan in person who wielded the sword. It is by no means certain that the bones which were disinterred in 1888 in the so-called royal tomb on the Hum, to the southeast of the city, and placed in a glass coffin in the right aisle of the Franciscan church in Jajce are really those of King Stjepan Tomašević. To this day travelers are shown the hilly "emperor's field" (carevo polje) north of Jajce, where Mehmed is believed to have camped with his army. His tent is said to have stood beside a gurgling spring beneath a young oak tree, which is today gnarled and rotting with age. It is there, according to the legend, that Stjepan Tomašević was executed. Throughout Bosnia the name of the "emperor" stands like a monument of stone and bronze in the memory of the people.

The late king's brother Ban Radivoj and his young son met with the same fate. Stjepan Tomašević's little half brother and half sister, Sigismund and Katharina, aged seven and three, were carried away into captivity. Both were converted to Islam. Under the name of Ishak Bey, Sigismund became the sultan's companion at table and in his games, and often entertained him with crude jests. Later the Kiraloğlu, "king's son," as he was generally called, became governor (sancak beyi) of Bolu in Asia Minor, where he presumably ended his days. What became of Katharina is uncertain. Not far from Skoplje there lies a mausoleum (türbe) visible from far across the plain, which the people of the region call the "tomb of the king's daughter." It is here that Princess Katharina is thought to have found her last resting place. What sufferings she had previously undergone lie shrouded in darkness.

In order to subjugate all parts of the kingdom, Mehmed decided to continue the campaign and divided his army into three columns. The first he entrusted to Turahanoğlu Ömer Bey, governor of Thessaly, and the second to the grand vizier Mahmud Pasha; these he dispatched to the eastern and western parts of Bosnia. He himself with the main army moved southward and overran the territory of King Stjepan's father-in-law, Duke Stjepan Vukčić, in the intention of conquering Herzegovina and Dubrovnik. Whereas Upper Bosnia, Dolnji Kraji, and Usora had surrendered to the sultan with hardly a struggle, Duke Stjepan and his sons decided to resist. In his distress he turned to the council of Dubrovnik, which, however, was itself trembling in fear of a Turkish invasion. By June 6, 1463, the duke was planning to take refuge there with his whole family. The city made all possible preparations for a Turkish siege. The outer moats were hastily deepened, all the buildings, garden walls, and trees outside the walls were leveled and all the cisterns filled in. When toward the middle of June, Mehmed entered Herzegovina, the fortunes of war turned against him. The rugged mountain country with its fortified castles and steep cliffs caused the Turkish cavalry great difficulties. Open fields and fertile valleys were laid waste, but stony Herzegovina defied the Conqueror. The sultan's army was attacked by guerrilla bands in narrow mountain passes. The sultan saw that it would not be easy for him to subdue the country; finally he attempted a siege of Blagaj, the duke's fortified capital to the southeast of Mostar. But after several days of fruitless assaults, he withdrew eastward in disappointment.[6]

On the return march the sultan occupied the territories of several noblemen, among them the Pavlovići, and had these feudal lords ruthlessly massacred. By July 7 he pitched camp again in Sjenica, on July 17 in Skoplje. On the way he provided the Franciscans of the monastery of Fojnica with a patent of liberty, allegedly after a courageous monk by the name of Angelus Zvjezdović had called his attention to the threatening depopulation of the recently acquired region. By the terms of this document the Christians were guaranteed the free exercise of their faith.[7] Actually the bulk of the population, allegedly 100,000 souls, were carried off into Turkish captivity and settled partly in Istanbul and partly in the Asiatic provinces of the empire. No less than 30,000 young Bosnians were

[6] A broad view of the Ottoman subjugation of Bosnia and Herzegovina may be found in the article "Bosna" (B. Djurdjev), *EI²* I, 1263–66. For a recent survey of Bosnian history, down to early Ottoman times, by the Yugoslav historian Sima Ćirković, see the review of J. V. A. Fine in *Speculum* 41 (1966), 526–529.

[7] For a document issued on July 7 see Truhelka, "Tursko-slovjenski spomenici," *GZMBH* 23 (1911), 21. Cf. *IED* I, 49–50 (document 17).

incorporated into the Turkish army. Minnet Bey remained behind as first governor over the devastated region.[8] Only six fortresses were left standing and these were heavily garrisoned. All the other cities and castles were dismantled or razed. Dubrovnik came off with a bad scare. The city, like all those of the Dalmatian coast, was full of fugitives from Bosnia. Many crossed the Adriatic to Venice and some went as far as Rome. None of them ever saw their homeland again. Mehmed called upon the Ragusans to surrender the Bosnian queen mother Katharina, widow of King Stjepan Tomaš and daughter of Duke Stjepan Vukčić. Luckily she had already fled to Italy. In later years she lived, generously supported by the Holy See, in Rome, where she died on October 25, 1478, at the age of fifty-four and was buried in the church of Ara Coeli on the Capitol. In her last will she bequeathed Bosnia to the pope, unless her son Sigismund should abjure Islam and return to Christianity. Jelena, the young queen of Bosnia, known in Bosnia as Maria, appealed to Dubrovnik for help, but then repaired to the convent of St. Stephen outside the walls of Split (Spalato). In the end she went to the sultan's court, where she made herself unpopular by slandering and intriguing against her closest relatives.

When after his return to Istanbul the sultan again bade the Florentine consul in Pera see to it that his compatriots light bonfires in celebration of the victory, he may well have been inspired in good part by guile and malice. In any case, none of the Florentine colony in Pera refused to arrange festivities, to adorn their houses and the streets with wall carpets and silk hangings, to decorate their church, to light bonfires, and to display rockets and fireworks. The sultan in person appeared in the dwellings of the wealthiest Florentine citizens, such as the Capelli and the Capponi, and merrily joined in the festivities.

On June 10, 1463, the terrible news reached Venice "that a mighty Turkish army had invaded Bosnia and overrun the greater part of the kingdom and its most important cities and settlements, and that even the king himself had fallen into odious Turkish slavery."

The news spread like wildfire through Italy, everywhere arousing horror. On June 14, Venice dispatched a call for help to detested Florence. "Impelled by his lusts and his inexorable hatred of the Catholic faith, the bitterest and fiercest enemy of the Christian name, the prince of the

[8] For an earlier Ottoman *bey* who governed Bosnia only briefly, see Inalcïk, "Mehmed the Conqueror (1432–1481) and His Time," *Speculum* 35 (1960), 423.

Turks," wrote the aging doge Cristoforo Moro to the Florentines, "has carried his audacity so far that among the princes of Christendom there is virtually none willing or even daring to oppose his designs." After an account of the sultan's success in Bosnia, the letter continues: "Not content with such a triumph, he, as one demanding more and hoping for still greater conquests, has not hesitated to advance, arrogantly and with arms in readiness, to the coast of Segno [Senj], that is to say, almost to the gate and entrance of Italy." And in words of anguish the doge goes on to describe the dangers facing the Occident and especially Italy in case of a further Ottoman advance. He implores all Christendom to open its eyes to this danger and finally to join in resisting it. The Florentines replied evasively: they hesitated to become involved in a war with the Turks for fear that the Florentines residing in Turkish possessions would suffer mistreatment. But before Christmas they would send three large galleys to Istanbul, which, pretexting a commercial undertaking, would embark all Florentine citizens and their possessions, and carry them to safety. This was their only concession.

Cristoforo Moro's message to the Florentines was by no means dictated by the imagination of an aged man interested only in peace and his personal welfare. Ever since Mehmed had seized the Morea and Lesbos, his ulterior aims were clear to all. Having destroyed the kingdom of Bosnia, the last bulwark of Christianity before the gates of Italy, he was now determined to gain possession of the Aegean Sea. Thus Venice was confronted with a fateful decision. Her only alternatives were to fight or to abandon all her possessions in Greece and the Levant, which were the foundation of her power and especially of her prosperity. Of the coastal strong points which had formerly rimmed the peninsula at regular intervals from Dalmatia past the mouth of the Vardar, some had been lost years before, while the rest had long been endangered.

During the Bosnian campaign in the spring, hostilities had broken out in the Morea between Venice and the Porte. Their cause had been insignificant. By the peace of 1430 both parties had expressly undertaken to return each other's escaped slaves, but the sultan recognized this agreement only where Moslems were not involved. An Albanian slave from the district of Grisumpsa not far from Skarminga had been carried off prisoner in 1459 and taken into the household of the Ottoman governor of Athens. In March 1463 he stole 100,000 aspers from his master, and fled to Koroni, a Venetian possession. Girolamo Valaresso, Venetian counselor in the government of that town, received him and allegedly shared the stolen money with him. The slave's master demanded the return both of his money and of the fugitive. The Venetians refused on the ground that the slave had been converted to Christianity.[9] Thereupon the Turks moved on Argos, also Venetian at the time, and favored by the treachery of a Greek priest—the hatred of the Orthodox fanatics for the Roman church still outweighed their fear of the Ottoman yoke—captured it on April 3, almost without striking a blow. At the same time Turkish bands invaded and laid waste the Venetian territory around Lepanto and Methoni. Alvise Loredano, captain general of the Venetian fleet, was already in the Aegean with his nineteen galleys. He received strict instructions to demand the return of Argos. When this claim was refused, Loredano asked for troops with which to attack Lesbos. Thereupon the question of war was raised in the council of the *pregadi* in Venice.[10]

Vettore Capello, who headed the war party, bitterly attacked the desultory policies of the Signoria. It was perfectly futile, he maintained, to enter into negotiations with the sultan; the war must be waged with weapons, not with words. A new Venetian embassy to the Porte, he declared, would signify nothing other than an admission of inability to wage war. In occupying Argos, the sultan was clearly trying to see how far he could go. If Venice were to put up with such treatment, he would seize the remaining Venetian possessions in the Morea and even take Negropont, on which he obviously had designs. We must, Capello continued, at last show this barbarian our power. Thanks to our eternal procrastination, Constantinople, the Morea, and finally Bosnia have been lost. If we fear for our Levantine trade, we must accept the lesser evil. Moreover, we must not invite the shame of having it said all over Europe that Venice, for the sake of commercial advantages and vile gain, is abandoning the nations of the West with which she is united by close ties of faith, custom, and interest. We must enter into contact with the pope and with Hungary, reinforce our land and sea forces, stir up the already dissatisfied peoples of the Peloponnese against their Turkish oppressors. We must conquer the Morea and from there invade the Ottoman Empire, while the Hungarians do likewise from the north. If we fold our hands, Venice can look forward only to the eternal loss of her possessions and the enslavement of her subjects.

After this speech the peace party acknowledged defeat. Although when

[9] The dating of this minor incident, which here begins a sequence of events culminating in the prolonged Turco-Venetian war, is questioned by Setton, who places it a year earlier, in 1462 (see his review in *Renaissance News* 12 [1959], 199–200).

[10] For instructions to Loredano from early in 1463 see Thiriet, *Régestes des délibérations du Sénat de Venise*, 247ff. (nos. 3172ff.).

the matter was put to a vote the majority of the war party was not very considerable, war was declared on July 28, 1463. It was hoped that the Morea, with its 300,000 ducats' worth of commercial profits, would be the prize of victory. Since May, Loredano had been cruising among the Greek islands with his reinforced squadron, and when on August 1 he returned to Navplion the feared *condottiere* Bertoldo, margrave of Este, who had been appointed supreme commander of the Venetian land forces, was on hand with his troops. Feebly defended, Argos surrendered after brief resistance on August 5. Loredano's next goal was to be Corinth. In the first half of September the wall across the isthmus (Hexamilion), which had long been in ruins, was rebuilt. The new wall, some twelve feet high, was built without mortar from great blocks of stone found on the spot, and was equipped with 136 watchtowers. Deep ditches ran along both sides of the wall, and in the middle an altar was erected over which waved the banner of St. Mark. The work was said to have been completed in two weeks by more than 30,000 workmen. The siege of Corinth was now begun in earnest.[11]

On September 25, Turahanoğlu Ömer Bey, who had been dispatched from Bosnia, arrived from the north, advanced to a distance of some 300 paces from the gigantic fortifications, and quickly withdrew when two cannon balls landed in his immediate vicinity. The following days were marked by skirmishes between the Venetians and the Turks, nor far from Corinth. The decisive blow was planned for October 20, but the fortunes of war did not smile on the assailants, who lost their best troops, including their leader, Bertoldo of Este. Hit in the head by a stray bullet, he died two weeks later of his wound. The Venetians were obliged to raise the siege and withdraw their forces in part to the wall and in part to Navplion. The Turks remained masters of the field and of their positions. Ömer Bey sent to the sultan for reinforcements, whereupon the grand vizier Mahmud Pasha received orders to march to southern Greece with as much of the Rumelian army as could be spared in Bosnia and to break through the fortified positions on the isthmus. On this occasion, presumably for reasons of health, Mehmed, who had returned from Bosnia to Istanbul by way of southern Serbia, did not personally take a hand in the hostilities. Mahmud Pasha had come only as far as Larisa in Thessaly when Ömer Bey sent word that the isthmus was guarded

---

[11] For some of the sources for the history of the long war between the Venetians and the Turks, see V. L. Ménage, "Seven Ottoman Documents from the Reign of Mehemmed II," in *Documents from Islamic Chanceries*, ed. S. M. Stern (Oxford, 1965), 101. Avery D. Andrews studies the background to the Ottoman-Venetian war, on the basis of Western sources only, in an unpublished dissertation, *The Turkish Threat to Venice, 1453–1463* (University of Pennsylvania, 1962).

by more than 2,000 (!) cannon and defended by a powerful army. Declaring that it could not be taken and that it would be folly to pitch camp
nearby, he advised the grand vizier to come no closer. Mahmud Pasha
asked the sultan for reinforcements and meanwhile proceeded to Levadhia
(twenty-six miles northwest of Thebes). The Venetian generals—Bettino
da Calzina had replaced Bertoldo as supreme commander—were so discouraged and bewildered by the defeat at Corinth and the news that
fresh Ottoman troops were approaching from the north that they decided
to abandon the isthmus and embark as much as possible of their army,
whose strength had been seriously impaired by an epidemic of dysentery,
along with their cannon, provisions, and armament. The infantry fled in
disorder to Navplion.

These developments decided the fate of the Peloponnese. On the morning of the Venetian withdrawal from the wall, Mahmud Pasha appeared
at the Hexamilion and destroyed the fortifications in his path. His cavalry
and Janissaries pursued the fugitives, Argos was retaken in the first
assault, and the Turkish onslaught was halted only at Navplion, where
there were fresh mercenaries. A sortie took a heavy toll of the grand
vizier's troops, who were driven back to the isthmus. But this setback
did not deter Mahmud Pasha from marching on southward and penetrating the interior of the peninsula. Many castles which had indicated
their intention of going over from the Turkish to the Venetian side
quickly resumed their old submission. Without striking a blow the main
Turkish army reached Leondarion. Ömer Bey made raids on the territory
of the Venetian possessions, overran the region of Methoni and Koroni,
and even forced the Albanians in the mountains of Laconia and in the
Maina to submit. If winter had not set in, the hostilities would no doubt
have continued to take a course favorable to the Turks.

Chalcocondylas, who concludes his chronicle with the story of this campaign, relates the following incident, for the veracity of which he bears
sole responsibility. In the course of his raids in the vicinity of Methoni, so
the story goes, Ömer Bey had taken prisoner 500 inhabitants of a nearby
town and sent them to the grand vizier. Mahmud Pasha in turn had
sent them on to Mehmed in Istanbul. The sultan had them executed by
his favorite method: sawing in two. Suddenly an ox brought together
the two halves of a body, which had been lying at a considerable distance
from one another. The sultan, to whom the occurrence was reported, put
his own superstitious construction on it: he became convinced that great
good fortune awaited the nation to whom the executed man had belonged. It was uncertain, however, whether the man had been a Venetian
or an Albanian. Mehmed gave orders to bury the body and to receive

the ox into the well-stocked zoological gardens of the serai, where he was to be given the best of treatment.

On September 12, 1463, even before the military enterprise of the Venetians had taken so tragic a turn in the south of Greece, a defensive and offensive alliance against the Turks had been concluded at Petrovaradin (Peterwardein) between the Signoria and the king of Hungary. Both parties engaged to further the projected crusade by common action and Venice promised in addition to equip forty galleys. Previously, on July 19, Matthias Corvinus had entered into an agreement with Emperor Frederick III, with whom he had been at odds for years over his crown, and had sworn to employ all his armed forces against the Ottomans. After various setbacks and losses, the excessively proud and vain scion of John Hunyadi had abandoned his father's belief that one decisive action could deliver the Balkan peninsula of the Ottomans.

At the end of September 1463 he crossed the Sava into Bosnia at the head of little more than 4,000 soldiers and marched straight on Jajce. Nowhere in the open country had the Turks put up fortifications. He reached the old capital by forced marches, meeting with no resistance. On October 1, only four days after his arrival, the poorly defended lower city was taken at the very first assault, all the more easily as the inhabitants had immediately come over to his side. The storming of the citadel, to be sure, which was defended by a garrison of 430 Ottomans and offered stubborn resistance, proved to be a good deal more difficult. The Janissaries were under the command of a certain Harambaşï Ilyas Bey, who withstood a siege of almost three months, rendered doubly cruel by the cold season. On December 16, 1463, the starving garrison, too weak to resist the impending assault, was obliged to surrender to the king of the Hungarians. The prisoners were given their choice of joining the Hungarian army as soldiers or of withdrawing unarmed. Ilyas Bey was carried off along with 400 selected prisoners to Hungary, where King Matthias made his solemn entry on Christmas Day. The crowning event of the day was the procession of the Ottoman captives, especially decked out for the occasion. More than sixty open and fortified places had surrendered to the Hungarians in Bosnia. Everywhere the king caused the garrisons to be spared. The victory, celebrated as the restoration of the kingdom of Bosnia under Hungarian sovereignty, was everywhere greeted with rejoicing. On December 6, Matthias Corvinus had appointed his high treasurer, Ban Emerich of Zapolya, governor of the reconquered country and distributed a number of large fiefs among faithful vassals. In Herzegovina Duke Stjepan Vukčić, whose eldest son, Vladislav, was one of those to obtain fiefs, had retaken possession of his entire duchy immediately after the sultan's withdrawal. As a special favorite of the Hungarian king, Vlatko, the duke's second son, obtained parts of the territories of the feudal lords Kovačević, and Pavlović who had been killed by Mehmed. Except for the quarrel between Duke Stjepan's sons, which delayed distribution of the land, Herzegovina would then have been restored to its former state.

It could easily have been predicted that the foregoing events, especially the fall of Jajce and the loss, no sooner conquered, of the greater part of Bosnia, would drive the sultan half mad with rage and that he would never become reconciled to them. The first to feel the brunt of Mehmed's fury was the emperor David of Trebizond and the Comnenus family. On November 1, 1463, David, six of his seven sons, his brother Alexander, and the latter's son Alexius were executed in the Prison of the Seven Towers, construction of which Mehmed II had completed in the winter of 1457–1458. The sultan continued to persecute the Comneni even after death, giving orders that their bodies be left unburied, to be destroyed by dogs and birds of prey. Empress Helena, David's second wife, witnessed the slaughter of her family with steadfastness, watched over their corpses by day, and buried them little by little with her own hands. Then, we are told, she donned a hair shirt and withdrew to a thatched hut, where she lived in frugal piety and soon died.

David's youngest son, George, aged three, who was being raised in the Islamic faith, and his daughter Anna, whom her father had destined for the sultan's harem but who was never admitted, escaped the executioner. As a Christian, Anna Comnena was assigned to Zaganos (Mehmed) Pasha; later, she was compelled to profess Islam and was given in marriage to a son of Elvan Bey, presumably Sinan Bey. If the chroniclers are to be believed, she died in the sultan's women's quarters.[12]

Many sons and daughters of grandees vanished among the nameless throngs of slaves and soldiers, in the sultan's serai, and in the harems of prominent Turks in Istanbul. Only George Amirutzes and his two sons managed, thanks to their craftiness and perhaps to their kinship with Mahmud Pasha, to save their lives and retain the sultan's favor.

In the winter of 1463–1464, which Mehmed spent in his palace in Istanbul, he seems to have suffered his first serious attack of ill health. Though barely thirty-two at the time, the sultan was disfigured by a morbid corpulence. He had considerable difficulty in riding, and the hardships of war, to which he had mercilessly subjected himself year after year,

---

[12] For references to the sources pertinent to the end of the Comnenus dynasty, see Donald M. Nicol, *The Byzantine Family of Kantakouzenos*, 188–190.

had brought on a painful attack of gout, the hereditary ailment of the Ottoman rulers. His physicians, first and foremost Maestro Iacopo of Gaeta, made every effort to relieve or cure it, and apparently with some success, for by the following spring Mehmed was already able to face the exertion of a new campaign.

In the first days of June 1464, rumors reached Venice to the effect that the sultan had mustered his army near Edirne and sent it ahead to Sofia. Ammunition and war equipment of all kinds, especially gun metal and ore, had allegedly been assembled in enormous quantities. The goal of the new campaign could only be surmised, and in the West it was generally thought to be Hungary. Soon travelers from Istria and Zadar brought news that a *subaşi* with 40,000 men had invaded Bosnia and laid the whole country waste, and that the king of the Hungarians was not stirring a finger. As usual, the news was exaggerated and inaccurate. Later it was maintained that the entire army, which the sultan in person was once again leading against Bosnia, numbered only 30,000 but was equipped with every conceivable kind of siege machine.

The sultan seems to have marched directly to the walls of Jajce. The castle, defended by Emerich of Zapolya, was besieged from July 10 to August 24, 1464. Mehmed hoped to reduce it by means of mines and heavy guns. The final assault began on St. Bartholomew's Day (August 24) and continued for a day and a night, ending in defeat for the sultan. Many Turks were killed or wounded. When Mehmed saw that it would be impossible to take the fortress without enormous losses and a long, violent battle, and when scouts informed him that King Matthias, encamped by the Sava with large numbers of cavalry and infantry, was planning to join in the battle, he ordered five heavy siege guns, said to have been more than sixteen feet long and three palms in diameter, to be rolled into the Vrbas. They had been cast on the spot especially for the storming of Jajce. Jörg of Nuremberg, the founder, speaks of only four giant cannon, which according to him were hurled into the Drina. The baggage train was abandoned and the entire Turkish army fled. With great difficulty the Hungarians later raised the cannon out of the river and put them into position. The number of dead Turks was reported to have been so large that the inhabitants of Jajce, sickened by the smell of corpses in the summer heat, worked unremittingly from August 24 to 28, clearing the streets and throwing the dead into the headlong current of the Vrbas.

For the Hungarians the end of the sultan's campaign was not so favorable as the beginning. Only in September 1464 was King Matthias able to cross the Sava with 10,000 men, long after the sultan had broken camp and marched off to the southeast. After brief resistance Emerich of

Zapolya was able to take the castle of Srebrnica, famous for its rich silver mines and situated in a narrow valley framed by high mountains, but the siege of Zvornik (the Turkish Izvornik) on the lower Drina (ninety-three miles east of Jajce) did not end so well. The large fortress was stubbornly defended by the Turkish garrison. Emerich of Zapolya was called to the assistance of the besiegers, but, seriously wounded in the eye by an arrow, he lost courage. The onset of winter made it increasingly difficult to carry on the siege operations and to feed the disheartened troops.

At this juncture the news arrived that Mahmud Pasha was approaching with an army of 40,000 men. Particulars concerning the genesis of this undertaking are provided only by the Ottoman chronicler Neşri.[13] In the course of his return journey Mehmed stopped in Sofia and decreed a new levy of troops. Men came from all sides, were placed under command of the grand vizier, and were sent at once to Bosnia. These fresh troops, so Neşri maintains, had not yet reached Jajce when panic broke out among the Christians. This statement agrees exactly with the facts. At the news that an Ottoman relief army was approaching, the forces of the king of Hungary could not be held in check. The retreat across the Sava become a headlong rout. All the artillery and the larger part of the baggage train were abandoned. Many of the fugitives were cut down or taken prisoner by the pursuing Turks. Only with the greatest difficulty was King Matthias able in late November to lead the remnants of his army to safety in Syrmia. With the exception of Jajce, a few other strong points occupied by the Hungarians, and certain northern frontier districts, the entire country, which had been almost entirely devastated, remained in the hands of the Ottomans.

For sixty-four years, during which Hungary struggled with the Turks for the possession of Bosnia, Jajce, which in 1472 became the capital of the resurrected kingdom of Bosnia under Nicholas Ujláky, was to be the most important theater of Bosnian history. As long as Hungarian troops in Bosnia could endanger his withdrawal, Mehmed and his successors were unable to lead their armies into the heart of Hungary, much less to threaten Germany. The Ottoman campaigns against Jajce, renewed in rapid succession in the ensuing period, demonstrate the strategic importance of this place and the significance of the sultan's defeat in August 1464. Quite certainly the quick and lamentable termination of this campaign may be laid not only to fear of Hungarian superiority but

[13] For the Ottoman chronicler Neşri and an analysis of the place of his work in the early Ottoman historical literature, see V. L. Ménage, *Neshri's History of the Ottomans* (London, 1964).

above all to Mehmed's poor physical condition. After his return to his Istanbul court toward the end of summer, 1464, he became so ill that for the first time since his accession to the throne he spent over a year in his palace without leaving it.

The year 1464 was a time of misfortune for Mehmed. It brought but two events that must surely have given him pleasure. On August 4 or 5 his bitter foe and thus far his most dangerous enemy on Asiatic soil, Ibrahim Bey, the ruler of Karaman, died in the old mountain castle of Kevele (or Gevele; the Byzantine Kavalla [Κάβαλλα]) not far from Konya. And on August 15 Pope Pius II died, just at the moment when he was attempting to launch his universal crusade against the Ottomans.

In the course of sleepless nights, as he himself relates, Pius II had been conceiving a new plan for combating the Ottomans. Although sick and feeble with age, Pius II wished to be the leader in the Holy War. In March 1462, he confided his plan only to six trusted cardinals. He hoped that if he himself as vicar of Christ, "who is greater than any king or emperor," should take the field, all other princes of the West, even England, Spain, and Germany, but especially Burgundy and France, would be unable to withhold their support.

The fall of Bosnia had quickly put an end to the territorial quarrels of the Hungarians. By the peace of Wiener Neustadt (July 24, 1463) the emperor granted the Corvinus dynasty perpetual rule over Hungary; only in case Matthias Corvinus should die without legitimate heirs would the succession fall to the Hapsburgs. Though hardly with a view to defending the faith and moved solely by concern over the danger facing her Levantine trade, Venice had taken up the inevitable struggle with the Ottomans. But the participation only of Hungary and Venice in the crusade did not satisfy the pope. He considered it necessary to win over to his plan not only the emperor, France, and Burgundy but also all Italy. Louis XI of France, however, took a negative attitude, for he regarded the plan for a crusade as a mere subterfuge to distract attention from the Neapolitan question. Encouraged by the pope and Venice, Skanderbeg, who in 1461 had concluded a sort of truce with the Turks, now opened hostilities without hesitation.

In Italy the political situation at the time was decidedly favorable to a holy war. In Naples the dynastic controversy was ended, the unruly Sigismondo Malatesta had been humbled, and all Italy was at peace. Hungary and Venice had concluded a military alliance. Only wealthy Florence played a double game, intriguing against the pope's plans. The reason may be sought partly in the old hostility of the Florentines toward Venice and above all in the rivalry between the two states in the field of Eastern trade. The Florentines secretly hoped that Venice would gradually be bled white by its war with the Turks. For this reason alone they did not wish the war to become a common Western undertaking. The quarrel of Venice with the Porte, so the Florentines held, would be a long-drawn-out affair and would, for the greater good of Italy and the whole Christian world, bring both parties to their well-deserved downfall. The pope, to whom these views were communicated by the Florentine legate in a private audience, was horrified by such pettiness and expounded a plan, which he himself had devised, for the partition of Turkey, perhaps the first of its kind, in order to prove that in his intention Venice would not acquire the lion's share. She would obtain the Morea, Boeotia, and Attica, as well as the coastal cities of Epirus, Skanderbeg would receive Macedonia, but the Hungarians would be given Bulgaria, Serbia, Bosnia, Walachia, and all territory as far as the Black Sea, while other parts of the Byzantine Empire would be allotted to respected Greek nobles.[14]

In a secret consistory on September 23, 1463, the pope laid his plans before the entire college of cardinals. Most of the princes of the Church agreed with enthusiasm; only the French party raised objections. The discussion then turned to the question of armaments and funds. It was decided that the common operations against the infidel should be directed by a supreme commander and that the conquered territories should be apportioned according to the achievement of the participant states. Each of these should be prepared to set out the following May (1464), equipped with provisions for one year. By way of avoiding friction, it was decided that a fixed rate of exchange between currencies would be established. With the exception of Venice, all the legates gathered in Rome accepted the directives laid down by the pope. The Venetian reservations had to do with the ecclesiastical supreme command and with the division of the spoils. After endless negotiations, in which some of the participants put the pope off with evasions and empty promises, a general agreement was arrived at. The necessary funds, it was decided, should be provided by means of tenths, twentieths, and thirtieths levied in the Papal State. All superfluous Church treasures, chalices, and ritual objects for the Mass would be disposed of for the cause, all monasteries and convents subjected to a tax. On October 19, 1463, the pope and Venice concluded an alliance with the duke of Burgundy, promising to provide mutual assistance over a period of three years and to make peace only in common. In an encyclical of the same date, the pope made known his intention of fighting not with prayer but with the sword. He planned to inspire the Christian

[14] The exchange of views between the Florentine and the pope is recorded in *The Commentaries, Smith College Studies in History* XLIII (1957), 812–817.

world by his example, for who, what knight, count, duke, king, or emperor, would dare to remain idly at home when he, the successor of St. Peter, sick and frail as he was, had gone to war with his cardinals?

A few days later the crusade bull was read, promising spiritual benefits in abundance to all those who should perform war service at their own expense for one year or at least six months. It said in part:

> You Germans who do not help the Hungarians, do not hope for the help of the French! And you Frenchmen, do not hope for the assistance of the Spaniards unless you help the Germans. With what measure ye mete, it shall be measured to you. What is to be gained by looking on and waiting has been learned by the emperors of Constantinople and Trebizond, the kings of Bosnia and Serbia, and other princes, who have all, one after another, been overpowered and have perished. Now that Mehmed has conquered the Orient, he wishes to conquer the West.

Everywhere the initial misgivings over the crusade gradually gave way to confidence. The bull was dispatched to all countries; legates of the pope, preachers, and collectors of funds roamed Europe and were to be heard on every side. The Minorites were the most zealous advocates of the common cause. The princes and grandees proved far more reserved and lukewarm than the middle and lower classes, who, especially in Germany, were stirred to enthusiasm. In many places, even in the remote north of Germany, the agitation was so deep-seated that, as a Hamburg chronicle of those years reports, "people are running off to Rome from their wagons and plows to battle the Turks." "In consequence of the Christian sovereigns' indifference and neglect of duty," wrote Pius II in November 1463 to a representative of his native city, "I am compelled to take the lead in the crusade. If we allow the Turks to continue advancing as in the preceding years, we shall soon all of us be subjected to their yoke. What is in my power I will do. God will help me."

Early in 1464, Alvise Loredano, who was cruising in the Greek archipelago with his ships, made a successful raid on the island of Lemnos, thus trying to make up for the failures of the preceding year. The island was still held by Demetrius, but a pirate from the Morea had recently seized the city and the citadel from his officials. Realizing that he was not able to hold his conquest, the pirate assisted Loredano in annexing the entire island for Venice; it was to remain under Venetian rule for fifteen years.

The pitiful remnants of the Venetian land forces, quartered for the winter in Navplion, succeeded in fighting off Davud Pasha, the governor of Rumelia, who had hurried to the spot, but the climate, the shortage of provisions, and renewed Turkish assaults had destroyed them as a fighting force. Mahmud Pasha was able to win back all the rebellious castles and cities whose inhabitants had expelled their Ottoman garrisons and commanders on the arrival of the Latins. In the spring Orsato Giustiniano replaced Loredano in command of the fleet. Sigismondo Malatesta became governor of the Morea and commander of land forces, in short, captain general of the terra firma.

Naval actions, for which Giustiniano was able to muster a total of 32 galleys, were now directed primarily against the island of Lesbos, whose capital was besieged for six weeks in April and May, 1464. On May 18, Mahmud Pasha appeared with an Ottoman squadron of 150 sailing vessels, including 45 triremes, and compelled the Venetian admiral to raise the siege. Three hundred Turkish prisoners and a number of Christians carried to safety in Negropont were the sole benefit gained in the Aegean expedition. In June, Giustiniano once more attempted a landing in Lesbos, but without greater success. At the beginning of July he and his squadron sailed back to Methoni, where a few days after his arrival he died in bitterness and despair.

His successor, Iacopo Loredano, did not fare much better. In a sortie into Levantine waters he touched on Rhodes, Chios, Lemnos, and Tenedos (now Bozcaada), and he seems to have harbored a daring plan for an attack on Istanbul. As Loredano's ships rode at anchor not far from the new Dardanelles castles, one of his captains, Iacopo Venier, entered the straits with his galley and passed through under the fire of the coastal fortresses. The stone projectiles of the Turks cost him some fifteen men, but he nevertheless returned under cover of night and reached his starting point under full sail, amid the jubilation of the whole squadron. It is not known whether this bold feat was undertaken for purposes of reconnaissance. In any case, the Venetian fleet returned to Tenedos immediately thereafter.

On land as well, the fortunes of war were none too favorable to the Venetians. On August 8, 1464, the cruel, obstinate, and intractable Sigismondo Malatesta arrived at Methoni, where he found 1,400 of his own army, in addition to 400 mounted crossbowmen and 300 infantrymen. He was permanently at odds with the Signoria, complaining either that it asked too much of him or that it gave him insufficient support. But his greatest quarrel was with Andrea Dandolo, the *provveditore* of the Morea, with whom he could never agree. These circumstances made a successful outcome of the land warfare virtually impossible. Malatesta captured a few cities and finally launched a full-scale attack on Mistra. He managed to overrun the two outer walls, but despite all his efforts was unable to take the fortress proper, which was situated on a high rock. Fearing the trackless region and especially concerned over his supply route, the *condottiere* had raised the siege and hastened to safety in Navplion when he heard that Ömer Bey was on his way with 12,000 men to relieve the Turkish forces. Unwilling to leave the field without a struggle, a few of Malatesta's lieutenants gave battle to the Ottoman cavalry not far from Mistra. They and their troops were killed to the last man. This miserable failure brought the campaign to an end for the year 1464. In April 1466, Malatesta returned to Italy. His only booty consisted of the bones of Georgius Gemistus Pletho, who was buried in Mistra. Malatesta carried the bones with him to Rimini, where he had them buried beside the sarcophagus of Roberto Valturio in the Tempio Malatestiano, which he caused to be renovated for the occasion. Malatesta's anonymous secretary left detailed and daily notes on his master's Moreotic campaign, which appear to be trustworthy, though the more dismal aspects of the campaign are passed over in silence.

Cristoforo Moro, the doge of Venice, tried to put off his departure for the crusade on grounds of old age. But Vettore Capello, leader of the radical war party, gave him to understand that if he refused to board ship he would be put on board by force, because the interests of the Signoria carried more weight than his own person. Thus the doge was compelled to play the role of Enrico Dandolo, for which he was not at all equipped.[15] It is true that the whole world expected Venice to save Christendom and to encompass the speedy downfall of the Ottoman Empire. Francesco Filelfo, the scholar, once again a victim of his own boundless vanity and presumption, also took a hand in the course of events. In two long-winded letters, the one addressed to Alvise Foscarini, the famous jurist, the other to Cristoforo Moro (March 15, 1464), he expatiated on the favorable prospects for the crusade under Venetian leadership, thanks to which "the base and disastrous deeds of the infamous and criminal Mehmed will meet with their just punishment." Already he saw Constantinople in the possession of the Latins, but frankly expressed his fear that Pius II, whose nepotism was indeed undeniable, was planning to install "a Piccolomini in place of the Palaeologi" (*a Paleologis in Piccolominos*) as emperor of Byzantium. His political counsels reflect an elaborate technique of mendicancy and a frenzied desire to be remembered, to know that his name would pass down to posterity or live forever in the mouths of men. At the

---

[15] Dandolo, Venetian doge in the early 13th century, had played a leading role in the capture of Constantinople by the Latins during the fourth crusade.

end of 1463 the Venetians, through Cardinal Bessarion, had tried to persuade Filelfo to take up residence in their midst. He had replied that though science could never be paid for in terms of money, he would come if they gave him 1,200 *zecchini*. All his life Filelfo was ashamed to be poor, but never had any scruple about begging.

The preparations for the papal expedition proceeded at a dilatory pace. Meanwhile, the pope was driven to the brink of despair by bad news about developments in the Morea. But there was neither an overall plan nor unified leadership. Every day the princes brought forth new excuses, while from all countries an idle mob, avid for gain, flocked to Ancona, whence the ships with the crusading army were to set sail. Arriving penniless and finding no fleet ready, they behaved riotously and of course demanded pay and maintenance from the pope; finally, reduced to utter misery, they began to sell their arms and to desert in droves. Thereupon the pope sent the experienced but aged and feeble Juan de Carvajal, cardinal of Sant'Angelo, ahead to Ancona to start assembling and embarking the impatient crusaders.

After a solemn Mass at St. Peter's the pope left the Eternal City on June 18, 1464. The ailing old man was carried in a litter to the Ponte Molle, whence he sailed up the Tiber on the first leg of his journey eastward. Because of the intolerable heat and the pope's weakness, the journey proceeded slowly. In Spoleto the cortege was joined by the alleged half brother of Mehmed II, known as Bayezid Osman or Calixtus Ottomanus, in whose future role as Ottoman sovereign his godfather, Calixtus III (he had baptized the young prince on March 8, 1456), had set high hopes. We shall have occasion to say more of this strange figure and of his destinies in Italy, Hungary, and Austria. On the way the papal litter passed whole companies of crusaders bound for home. In order to spare the pope, a prey to intense physical and moral sufferings, the sight of these deserters who were threatening to become a plague throughout Italy, Iacopo Ammanati, cardinal of Pavia, carefully pulled down the curtains of the litter whenever a body of them came in sight. Exhausted and mortally ill, Pope Pius arrived in Ancona on July 19. The physicians warned him that if he boarded ship he would be dead in two days, but his decision remained irrevocable. The cardinals present had long since ceased to depend on the dying pope and busied themselves all the more zealously with the impending conclave. At the beginning of August a plaguelike epidemic broke out that took many victims, and only the spread of the contagion throughout the neighboring lands, indeed through all of Italy, prevented a wild flight.[16]

[16] For more on the would-be Ottoman sovereign, see below, p. 324.

The panic became still more alarming when the terrible news arrived from across the Adriatic that an enormous Turkish army was marching on Dubrovnik and that the city was threatened with total destruction if the tribute that had fallen due were not paid and if the galleys promised to the pope were indeed sent to him. Although this report brought by ambassadors from Dubrovnik was doubtless false and fabricated for a very definite purpose, the credulous pope immediately agreed to send his own bodyguard of 400 archers and a shipment of grain across the Adriatic. Four days later news came that the enemy had allegedly withdrawn. Such alarms, added to continual disappointments, kept the pope under a severe strain. But it was the attitude of Venice that provided the death blow. The Venetian galleys that were to embark the crusaders had not yet appeared. And though the doge had been obliged, after long urging, to put to sea on August 2, he did not sail directly to Ancona but went instead to Istria, to complete the equipment of his squadron. On August 12 the pope was finally informed that the ships were approaching. In the bishop's palace he had himself moved to a window overlooking the sea, and as the squadron put into port, he cried out, "Until this day I was without a fleet to sail with! Now the fleet will have to sail without me." And so it was. On August 15, 1464, in the third hour of the night, he was relieved of his spiritual and physical sufferings. So died Enea Silvio, demonstrating by his death, as it has been aptly remarked, how much the great plan he pursued had meant to him in his life. Four days earlier (August 11) his friend and adviser, Cardinal Nicholas of Cusa, had preceded him in death. Cristoforo Moro left Ancona in the night of August 18. When he reached Venice the order was issued to dismantle the crusading squadron at once.

The death of Pius II brought with it the end of his efforts in behalf of a universal crusade against the Ottomans, a project whose prospects and possibilities he had far overestimated in his almost unworldly enthusiasm. Not only his failure to appreciate the enormous strength of the Ottoman people and Sultan Mehmed's keen understanding of Western affairs, not only his vastly overoptimistic view of the character, intensity, and vigor of Christian faith in his time, but above all his inability to understand that such an undertaking had long been incompatible with the spiritual climate of the Christian world undermined his lifework and lent a profoundly tragic imprint to his activity as head of the Church.

But even in his time Cardinal Iacopo Ammanati (whose *Commentaria Jacobi Cardinalis Papiensis* may be regarded as the true sequel to the *Commentarii* of Pope Pius II, which end with the preparations for the campaign against the Turks) castigated those who, setting themselves up as prophets and judges after the fact, condemned the pope mercilessly for his unsuccessful plan for a crusade. Pius II was far too close to his time, a turning point in Western history, to perceive and take into account the change that had taken place in the minds of the potentates of the day. He overestimated his influence on the rulers of the West and set far too much store by his power to kindle their enthusiasm by his example. This fundamental error made hopeless from the very start his daring design to take up arms against such a despot as Mehmed II, who could and did dispose ruthlessly of the lives of his subjects.

Venice now pursued her campaign against the Turks alone and unsuccessfully. Paul II, the new pope, was a Venetian—Pietro Barbo, a wealthy, splendor-loving noble; Pope Eugenius IV had been his mother's brother —but his election was far from welcome to his native city. In 1459 Venice had bitterly opposed his appointment as bishop of Padua; now she was obliged to acclaim him as pope. As a cardinal, to be sure, Paul II had taken an active interest in the Turkish question, but as a practical man and a merchant's son he was determined to remedy the financial stringency before going ahead seriously with plans for a crusade. The receipts from the "Turkish tithe," from indulgences, and above all from the alum monopoly were to be used for the pursuit of the Turkish war and distributed by special commission of cardinals. (In May 1462 the Paduan Giovanni de Castro, who as director of a large dyehouse in Constantinople before its fall in 1453 had acquired an intimate knowledge of Levantine alum production, discovered enormous deposits of that mineral on papal territory not far from Civitavecchia, so increasing the income of the papal treasury by 100,000 ducats a year.) The funds were assigned primarily to Hungary, and no mention was made of Venice. Time and time again the Signoria was dismayed to learn how ill disposed their compatriot, the pope, was toward his native city. Early in September 1464, a Venetian embassy of ten men went to Rome to congratulate the son of their city on his election as pope but at the same time to obtain help against the Turks. A new tax levy on the Italian states was decided upon, in which the Curia and Venice should bear the heaviest burden, 100,000 ducats each; next in order came the king of Naples (80,000), the duke of Milan (70,000), Florence (50,000), and so on down to the margrave of Montferrat, who was to be taxed 5,000 ducats. No one was willing to hear of such expenditures, least of all the Venetians, who were prepared for anything except to pay out money. In despair the pope described the situation to the assembled college of cardinals. If Hungary did not receive sufficient support, she would have to make peace with the sultan. No different was the situation of Venice, to whom Mehmed had already offered honorable peace conditions, which the pope had seen with his own eyes. If these two champions should abandon the fight, the water and land routes to Italy would lie open to the enemy.

Fortunately for the Signoria, the sultan's court in the winter of 1464–1465 was the scene of strange happenings which seemed for the present to preclude any great threat from that direction. Critoboulos, who scrupulously avoids any denigration of his idol, reports that Mehmed, who spent the winter in the now finished and sumptuously decorated palace in Istanbul forging new war plans for the coming spring, had learned to his consternation that the army, long weary of the eternal hostilities, was in a state of extreme agitation. Even his own guards were rebellious, dissatisfied over the constant long marches and campaigns which kept them always away from home, beyond the confines of the empire, risking their possessions, their horses, their vehicles, and their very lives; in short, they were sick of the incessant campaigning. These few facts, which the chronicler records in the most cautious terms, make it clear that the sultan's armies—especially, no doubt, the always unruly Janissaries—were a prey to grave unrest. And since, as Critoboulos goes on, the sultan himself was tired in body and spirit, he set aside the year 1465 as a rest period for himself and the army. He demobilized most of his troops and made them presents in the form of horses, clothing, money, and so on. He was particularly lavish in rewards and gifts of honor to his bodyguard. Mehmed devoted his own attention, Critoboulos tells us, to the development of Istanbul, to increasing the population by bringing in new settlers, and even to philosophy.[17]

Reports from the capital, quite numerous for the year 1465, repeatedly stress the poor health of the sultan, who was said to be "dissatisfied and half in despair" (*malcontento a mezzo disperato*). The hostilities with Venice, which took place chiefly in regions where Turkish rule was far from fully consolidated, must also have been a source of grave anxiety to him, and there is no doubt that the Venetian declaration of war in 1463 had come too soon for his taste. The war in the Morea, where Sigismondo Malatesta had found considerable support among the Greeks and Albanians, so that he had seen fit to promise solemnly to reconquer the whole peninsula for the Signoria, was degenerating more and more into occasional surprise attacks, raids on the Turks, and skirmishes. No decisive progress was made on either side. Amid all these events, the Venetian fleet in the Aegean also remained virtually inactive and seems to have done little more than block the straits whenever word came that Turkish ships were preparing to leave their harbors. It may well be that Mehmed did not take the Moreotic war, which for Venice involved such enormous expenditure and the loss of her best fortresses, very seriously, and that it did not strike him as worthwhile to dispatch a vizier, much less take the field in person, for the sake of the few castles on the peninsula. But the

[17] See Kritovoulos, *History of Mehmed the Conqueror*, 207–209.

negotiations for an "honorable peace" with the Venetian Republic, which began in 1465 and dragged on for many months, were taken seriously—if not indeed initiated by the Porte—as may be seen from the repeated intervention of the grand vizier, and give an indication of the sultan's embarrassment and indecision at the time.

As early as January 1465 peace feelers were put out by the Porte through Skanderbeg. In June 1461, shortly before his expedition to Italy in support of Ferrante, Skanderbeg had not, as has sometimes been claimed, concluded a ten-year peace with Mehmed but at most a short-term armistice, which was followed by a formal peace treaty only in the spring or early summer of 1463. At the instigation of the Vatican, Skanderbeg denounced this "impium foedus," this godless alliance, only a few weeks or months later and resumed hostilities against the Turks. Although Sultan Mehmed made another attempt to preserve the peace after this breach of faith, it seems difficult to believe that friendly relations still prevailed between him and the "athlete of Christendom" at the beginning of 1465. But there is no doubt that by the end of April, at the latest, the Venetians were seriously discussing a peace with the Porte, for at that time the Council of Ten held a number of sessions at which the terms transmitted from Istanbul by the Venetian *bailo*, Paolo Barbarigo (who, it might be remarked, was not then in prison but still free), and by Leonardo III Tocco, duke of Levkas, were discussed at length. The prevailing sentiment in the council favored conciliation, for most of the members had long been weary of the "undertaking with the sultan," and were gravely concerned over the gigantic expenditures, primarily for the fleet, which were defrayed entirely by Venice, while the other "lords of Christendom" collected "Turk money" from their subjects but spent it entirely for their own purposes.

On February 13, 1465, Paolo Barbarigo wrote to the Signoria from Istanbul reporting that he had met the grand vizier and discussed the possibility of a peace. Mahmud Pasha, so he wrote, had found "humane words," but had clearly expressed his consternation that Venice should have initiated this war without provocation, adding, however, that the Porte nevertheless wished to make peace. The Signoria was not at a loss for an answer to the grand vizier's reproach: Venice had been challenged and compelled to fight not only by the events in Argos but by the constant depredations and acts of violence against the inhabitants of the Morea, who were under Venetian protection. Moreover, Venice was obliged to observe her alliance with Hungary. But all this did not prevent the Venetians from desiring a "good peace" (*buona pace*). In the early summer Jakob Bunić (Giàcomo de Bona), an alleged member of a well-known noble family of Dubrovnik, took a hand in the negotiations, though it was not at first evident at whose behest he was acting. He declared that he had spoken with the grand vizier in Istanbul and had then come to Venice. The Signoria assured him on July 3, 1465, of the Venetian desire for peace, but at the same time stated the conditions it held to be compatible with the honor of the republic: Venice must obtain all the Morea as well as Mytilini, while the rest of Bosnia must be ceded to Hungary. Bunić was promised 10,000 ducats should he succeed in obtaining an armistice. For the present he was given 100 ducats to cover his expenses and pay for his return to Istanbul. The Signoria declined, on the ground that this had never been its custom, to meet the grand vizier's request that an ambassador be sent to the Porte to carry on negotiations.

A few weeks later, at the end of August, it was bruited about in Venice that the sultan had sent a solemn embassy to Matthias Corvinus to arrange a peace but that the king of the Hungarians declined all presents or proposals, although the Turks were offering to return Bosnia and Serbia of their own free will. Still according to the rumor, the Turkish envoys had been sent home without having been granted an audience. More and more confused and alarming became the reports which reached the West from Istanbul almost simultaneously by a number of devious channels. The Grand Turk, it was said, was in poor health; he had grown so fat that he could not ride and was in no condition to endure hardship. But according to another rumor, Mehmed had taken to riding through the city accompanied by four horsemen and had resumed official receptions. On one occasion the doge related that the "Turk" could not go to war because of his corpulence and that he was suffering from gout in the legs; moreover, Turkey was in the grip of an "extreme famine"; this assertion is confirmed by other sources, from which we learn that Istanbul was suffering from grave shortages, especially of grain, though the situation had been somewhat alleviated by imports from Genoa. Not until Christmas did it become clear that both the Ragusan and Leonardo Tocco's messenger were in all likelihood Turkish spies. Both had come to Venice and had made the Signoria the same proposals, the most important of which was the supposed cession of the Morea to the republic. Both emissaries had been well received; one had even been promised that in case of success he would be made a Venetian nobleman with an annual income of 1,000 ducats. Neither of them was ever seen again. The prospects for peace became increasingly dim and Mahmud Pasha seems to have become more and more arrogant and high-handed in his dealings with the representatives of Venice and Hungary. He did not neglect to recall the fate of the king of Bosnia, who had been "put out like a candle." In the end the conversations came to nothing, probably because of the demands of the Signoria, which the Porte was never willing to accept, although, according to one report, the sultan was disposed to make peace with everyone, since because of his health he had no desire to make war. In addition the sultan was said to be grief stricken over his son Mustafa, who had eloped with the wife of the governor of Rumelia, carried her away to Anatolia, and refused to give her up.

In the middle of November 1465, the Signoria resolved to break off all peace negotiations with the sultan, "that treacherous enemy of the faith," but put high hopes in an embassy from the sultan of Syria and Egypt, which was then expected in Venice. This Sultan Hoşkadem (1461–1467), as we learn from Venetian sources, was an Albanian from the Morea, a former slave, who had risen to the rank of atabeg and minister of war and finally become a Mamluk sultan. Unfortunately, nothing is known of the purpose or background of this embassy, and thus far we have little information about the relations between Mehmed and the Mamluk court in Cairo. All we really know is that when Constantinople was taken, bonfires were burned for many days in Cairo to celebrate the fall of the Byzantine capital.[18] Critoboulos claims that the sultan of Egypt paid tribute to the Ottoman ruler for fear of becoming involved in a war with him, but thus far we have no proof of this contention. In any case, the relations between the two Moslem states must have deteriorated over the years. When Constantinople fell, the sultan in Cairo was still the octogenarian Çakmak, the brother-in-law of Mehmed's father. But Hoşkadem was bound by an alliance to Uzun Hasan, who required the support of the sultan of Syria and Egypt because of his quarrels with the rulers of the Black Sheep (Kara Koyunlu) and of the house of Dulkadïr. The prince of Karaman was also among the allies of the Mamluk prince, so that if nothing else the latter's close ties with these two archenemies of the Ottoman house must have seriously endangered Mehmed's relations with Cairo. We shall have more than one occasion to speak of these tensions. They did not result in open conflict until the reign of the Burjite Mamluk Qa'it Bay (1468–1495).

As it was reported in Venice in the fall of 1465, Mehmed then had in his council of state a few Italians, including Florentines, Genoese, and Ragusans, who gave him their advice. A meeting with these advisers may have been responsible for the establishment, toward the end of the year, of a Bosnian king chosen by the sultan. He is referred to as "King Mat-

---

[18] For the account, by one Mamluk chronicler, of the arrival in Cairo of the news of the fall of Constantinople, see Abu'l-Mahasin ibn Taghri Birdi, *History of Egypt, 1382–1469* A.D. (part 6, 1453–1461 A.D.), trans. William Popper (*University of California Publications in Semitic Philology* XXII, Berkeley, 1960), 38–39.

thias" in the communications from Istanbul. He was said to have been a "baron" under the last king of Bosnia but to have become a Moslem; his wife lived in Istanbul. There rumor had it that Mehmed, "full of every guile," had appointed this king because he had been unable to take Jajce the preceding year and could not keep a firm grip on Bosnia without possession of this fortress. For that reason, so the story went, he had ceded Jajce to this king under Turkish sovereignty, all the more willingly as the king was the natural enemy of Hungary. Such sidelights show that the king could not have been the son of Radivoj, the former pretender, but was in all likelihood a member of the Bosnian noble family of the Šabančići. "King Matthias" proved ungrateful to the sultan. Casting off Mehmed's sovereignty, he reverted to Christianity once more and appealed to King Matthias of Hungary for help against the Turks. Matthias Corvinus bore the anti-king no grudge. Much later when the Turks, eager to punish the Bosnian for his treason, besieged him in one of his castles, King Matthias sent Stephen Bathory to free him from his dangerous situation (1476). Nothing seems to be known of the subsequent destinies of "King Matthias."

As far as can be determined from the sources now available, this dubious act of king making was the only political measure taken by Mehmed in the year 1465, which, doubtless because of his critical state of mental and physical health and the alarming mood of the army, was otherwise devoted exclusively to his architectural designs and literary endeavors. Recent investigations show that the construction of the new palace was probably begun after 1465. In all likelihood the so-called New Serai (now termed Old Serai, or Topkapï Sarayï, from the now demolished Twin Cannon Gate at water's edge on Palace Point) was originally a mere summer palace which Mehmed had built himself on the airy hilltop previously occupied by the original settlement and the acropolis of ancient Byzantium. The present-day serai [pl. XV b], with its ring of walls, its extensive gardens, three courtyards, and numerous lead-roofed buildings, covers the whole of this hill and reflects the efforts of several sultans over a period of many years. Only a small part of what is preserved today dates from the period immediately after the conquest of Constantinople. Sultan Süleyman the Magnificent (1520–1566) was first to make the New Serai the actual seat of his court. During the entire latter part of his reign Mehmed worked on the New Serai and the buildings that can be traced to his efforts were completed only in 1479. As is shown by the inscription, which has been preserved, the so-called Imperial Gate (*bab-i hümayun*) [pl. XV a] on the south side of the extensive palace grounds was completed a year before (1478). There all the sultans lived until 1839, when Abdülmecid built and moved into the palace of Dolmabahçe on the Bosporus. In 1465 (870 H.) the sultan, with the help of an architect by the name of Kemaleddin, presumably a Persian, began work on the so-called Çinili Köşk, or faience palace [pl. XX]. This edifice, unique of its kind, derives its name from the mosaic and the green-and-blue tiles with which it was formerly trimmed both inside and outside; but originally it was called Sïrça Saray (glass palace). Magnificent remains of faiences, green tiles similar to those of Bursa, are still to be found in little niches in the halls of the köşk, today used as a museum of Islamic art. Its cruciform ground plan as well as the details of the two-story colonnade occupying the entire façade point clearly to the work of Persians. The building required a good seven years to complete (September 1472). While Western architects cannot have been involved in the Çinili Köşk, where Oriental influence is unmistakable, the activity of the former is evident in others of the Conqueror's buildings, especially his fortifications, although the names of the architects have been forgotten. Greeks and Armenians appear to have played no large part; the chief influence seems to be Italian. If it is true that Antonio di Pietro Averlino, known as Filarete, was planning in the year 1465 to go to Turkey to enter the sultan's service as an architect and that we find no trace of him from then on, we are tempted to speculate on his presence in Istanbul, where the Florentine sculptor and builder would have found ample occupation at the time.[19]

Perhaps even more than as a patron of architecture, Mehmed was active as a promoter of learning during his forced "creative pause" of 1465. Critoboulos speaks with enthusiasm of his philosophical endeavors. The sultan took particular pleasure in daily conversation with leading scholars, and seems to have shown a predilection for the stoics and peripatetics. To what extent these statements are in keeping with the facts we cannot determine. But since the sultan's Greek panegyrist expressly identifies his teacher as George Amirutzes of Trebizond, it seems possible that these efforts to initiate the sultan into peripatetic philosophy—or Neoplatonism, as seems more likely—were undertaken in the leisure hours of that summer.

The unstable, none too attractive figure of Amirutzes—as we have seen,

[19] For Mehmed's foundation of the present Topkapï Sarayï, see Goodwin, *A History of Ottoman Architecture*, 131–135; for the Çinili Kösk, ibid., 137–138. Fanny Davis, *The Palace of Topkapi in Istanbul* (New York, 1970), deals at length, and showing numerous photographs, with the development of the serai throughout the Ottoman period.

a cousin of the grand vizier Mahmud Pasha, to whose intervention he probably owed his life and that of his two sons—has been illumined from many sides. He died in 1475 of a heart attack while playing dice (*zar*). He has often been accused of unscrupulous conduct and complacent servility, though a number of scholars have tried to clear him of these charges. It is uncontestable, in any case, that Amirutzes, even if it is true that he himself did not espouse Islam, caused his two sons Mehmed and Skender to be raised in this faith and that in three panegyrics to Mehmed II he showed himself to be utterly hypocritical and devoid of character; on the other hand, his knowledge of philosophical and theological matters was outstanding for his time. In any event, he and his two sons survived all the Comneni, his former masters, and readily adapted themselves to the new conditions. The sultan formed an affection for this learned and servile man and drew him into his entourage. His sons, who seem to have quickly mastered the Arabic language and to have found full satisfaction in the spiritual life of Islam, were apparently even more active than their father in helping the sultan to read the Greek works that interested him.[20]

In the summer of 1465 the sultan devoted himself to geographical studies under the guidance of the elder Amirutzes. Among other things, he studied a manuscript of Ptolemy's diagrams, containing the so-called *periegesis* (description) and *periodos* (map) of the world. Because of the difficulty of obtaining an overall view from the many partial maps contained in this work, it seemed advisable to collate them. This arduous task was successfully performed by Amirutzes, who produced a single map representing the entire *periodos* of the *oikoumene*, the inhabited world. This *mappa mundi* must have been quite in keeping with the desires and the intentions of the would-be conqueror of the world. One of Amirutzes' sons entered the names of the countries, cities, and towns on the map in Arabic script. The map makers were royally rewarded and encouraged to prepare an Arabic translation of the manuscript, for which they were promised large financial and honorific rewards. The Arabic translation was actually completed and has been preserved in two copies. Soon thereafter we lose trace of the three Amirutzes. It is related, however, that one of Amirutzes' sons, probably Mehmed Bey, requested the future patriarch Maximos III (1476-1482) to prepare an exposition of the Christian faith for his master, explaining that the sultan wished to be converted to Christianity. He seems to have remained in the sultan's entourage and to have been commissioned by him to translate the Bible into Arabic. If this translation was ever made, the manuscript has been

[20] For Amirutzes, see Vacalopoulos, *Origins of the Greek Nation*, 226-228, and especially n. 77 for a reference to the poems of the Greek scholar.

lost; at all events, it has thus far not come to light. There is no doubt that the sultan took a keen interest in the doctrine of Christianity, but to infer from this that he ever thought of espousing the Christian faith is to misunderstand him completely. Essentially he was without religious ties; his son Bayezid, who must have known, went so far as to declare that his father had no faith at all. If he wished to familiarize himself with the principal articles of the Catholic faith, it was assuredly because he felt that an understanding of the Christian mind would help him to combat his Western adversaries more effectively. One source mentions that Mehmed's supposedly Christian mother taught him the *Pater noster*, but that he stubbornly rejected the Christian faith. Nowhere do we find the least confirmation of this story, which is obviously a fable. When Iacopo of Gaeta told the Venetian *bailo* that Mehmed had become a Christian, he had his own reasons for doing so. The sultan was a superstitious man, especially given to astrology. The ideas and conceptions of the most diverse cultures, epochs, and peoples seem to have blended in his mind. We shall have more to say of this later on.

At this time Mehmed also took a keen interest in Ptolemy's basic work on the cosmic system named after him, which under the title *Almagest* (that is, the Arabic definite article followed by Greek *megiste*, "greatest"; short for *kitab al-maghisti*) had been several times translated into Latin from the twelfth century on. However, it does not seem to have been Amirutzes who seconded him in this study, but another scholar—of doubtful learning, it might be added—George Trapezuntios (b. April 4, 1395), a Cretan from Trebizond, who demonstrably visited Istanbul at this time and established contact with the sultan. We know that in November 1465 he journeyed from Crete to Istanbul and from there to Rome on March 18, 1466. The real reasons for this strange and suspect trip are obscure. Ostensibly he undertook it at the behest of the pope, in order to investigate conditions in Turkey, but the documents found on him when he was arrested in Rome must have indicated that he did the exact opposite. It seems he informed the sultan on "developments in the West and the dissatisfaction of its people," encouraging the "Turk" to hasten his invasion of Italy. He already referred to the sultan, so it was claimed, as "emperor of the Romans and of the terrestrial globe" and indulged in many other "practices" at the sultan's court, where apparently he was much flattered and favored with rich gifts. In any case, the Cretan was arrested on his return to Rome and was four months a prisoner in the Castel Sant'Angelo, until released by Pope Paul II, his former pupil in the fine arts and grammar.

His judges seem to have been convinced that the charges against him were sufficiently borne out by the papers found on his person. Of this we cannot be certain, but we do know that he wrote Mehmed two letters, one dated from Galata on February 25, 1466, while the other must have been written in Rome shortly thereafter; whether they were ever sent, however, is not known. Both are revoltingly obsequious: he praises the sultan as infinitely greater than Cyrus, Alexander the Great, and Caesar, celebrates his military victories in the most fulsome terms, and exalts him high above all other sovereigns. As mere specimens of loathsome servility these "discourses" (*orationes*), as he called them, would not be worth mentioning, but they provide important information about the writer's work in the scientific field. At the end of the first letter he states expressly that at the cost of great pains and many sleepless nights he had prepared a Latin translation of the *Almagest* and dedicated it to the sultan. He was planning to show the sultan the book and later present it to him, along with his own commentaries. In the second letter he vaunts his own good fortune at having seen and spoken to the sultan. In Rome, he declares, he had informed the pope, the cardinals, and others of Mehmed's rectitude, intelligence, knowledge of Aristotelian philosophy, and learning in all the sciences. To all who knew Latin, he tells us, he had proclaimed that there was no man alive—that there never had been and, he ventured to say, never would be any man—who, with God's help, could lead the people of the whole earth into one faith and one church and build a single empire of all mankind more easily than Mehmed. And Trapezuntios goes on to speak in the most exalted terms of the mission that had fallen to the sultan since the conquest of Constantinople. "Let no one doubt that he is by right the emperor of the Romans. For he is emperor who by right possesses the seat of the empire, but the seat of the Roman Empire is Constantinople: thus he who by right possesses this city is the emperor. But it is not from men but from God that you, thanks to your sword, have received this throne. Consequently, you are the legitimate emperor of the Romans. . . . And he who is and remains emperor of the Romans is also emperor of the entire earth."

In the remainder of this second letter he describes his philosophical works to the sultan, beginning with a violent attack on Georgius Gemistus Pletho. It was hard to say whether Pletho had been more animal or man, but he had, in any case, been subject to the Platonic folly and had written a book attacking Aristotle. He, George Trapezuntios, so the letter goes on, knowing more Latin than Greek, had written three books dealing with a comparison between Plato and Aristotle: the last was devoted to the biographies of the two philosophers and the two others to their knowledge of nature, in which connection he had expatiated in particular on Plato's ignorance. These books too, he writes, he wished to dedicate to the sultan. As for the *Almagest*, he had already translated it into Latin but had not yet published his translation. Because of the length of these books and the difficulty of reproducing the diagrams, he had not been able to complete them as easily and quickly as he had hoped. Consequently he required "royal aid"—George Trapezuntios was a good friend of Francesco Filelfo, who wrote him a letter immediately after Trapezuntios's return from Istanbul—and should the sultan grant such aid, he would be profoundly grateful to him for the rest of his life. Meanwhile, as George Amirutzes had encouraged him to do, he was sending the sultan his Greek introduction to the *Almagest*. Finally, he relates, he had written a book about the differences between "Arabic" and Christian law, but in Latin, since his Greek was rather meager. The sultan, however, had near him in Constantinople a man exceptionally well versed in all the sciences, and above all so learned in the Greek language that he, Trapezuntios, could not say whether Hellas had possessed a greater scholar in the last thousand years. This man, George Scholarios, who also knew Latin, would be able to translate Trapezuntios's book for the sultan. Nevertheless, should any difficulty arise, Trapezuntios would write in Greek in future to the best of his ability.[21]

Setting aside the nauseating flattery and obsequiousness of this letter, which remind one of Francesco Filelfo, who had the barefaced audacity to offer as recompense to those who had done him favors the immortality of their names, we glean, if nothing else, the following facts: In the autumn of 1465 George Trapezuntios went to Istanbul, where he spent four months, became acquainted with the sultan, and, having discovered his openhandedness, tried to exploit his interest in Ptolemy for his own financial advantage. Apart from fragments of the *Almagest*, he apparently gave Mehmed nothing that could have furthered his studies, but merely held out promises for the future. His philosophical effusions, directed against Plato, Aristotle, and above all the Neoplatonist Pletho, can hardly have made any great impression on the sultan, and least of all his polemic on Islam and Christianity, in which he presumably repeated what he had already written in his Greek treatise "On the Truth of the Christian Faith," which he planned to send the sultan in July 1453, a few weeks after the capture of Constantinople. In this little treatise, which has been preserved in the original manuscript and which he wished to have translated into Turkish and submitted to Moslem scholars, he had undertaken

---

[21] On George Trapezuntios, see Vacalopoulos, op. cit., 257, and the sources cited there (nn. 7 and 8). Also Angelo Mercati, "Le due lettere di Giorgio da Trebisonda a Maometto II," *Orientalia Christiana Periodica* 9 (1943), 65–99.

to prove neither more nor less than that there was no fundamental difference between Islam and Christianity. The sultan, he declared, could easily
reconcile the two religions and would so be enabled to rule over all the
nations professing either faith.

On the whole the reports of happenings at the sultan's court which
reached Italy, and especially Venice, directly or by devious ways in the
course of 1465 were not such as to arouse great fears for the immediate
future. In the summer Girolamo Michiel, the wealthy Venetian holder
of the alum monopoly, who had formerly been very influential at the
sultan's court and in whose services Benedetto Dei had tried his hand
as a spy, was arrested at the sultan's order, because he was in arrears
with the tax on alum deliveries. He met a violent death, whether at this
time or later we cannot be sure. In general the state treasury had great
difficulty with the collection of taxes. Many Turkish collectors fled when
unable to make payments for want of receipts. Sometimes merchants
evaded the tax by fleeing to the West; even a few Florentines did this,
taking with them 50,000 ducats, although they had been much better
treated by the sultan than other merchants in Pera.

Early in 1466 the chancellor of the Venetian *bailo* Paolo Barbarigo,
who in the meantime had been imprisoned and had died in confinement,
set out for home by the land route in the company of a Jew, David, son
of Eli Mavrogonatos of Candia. They left Istanbul on February 25 and
had got no farther than Philippopolis when they encountered the sultan,
marching westward with his armies. The chancellor resumed his journey
on March 9, but had been unable to find out where the sultan was
headed. Some said Albania, some Negropont, and still others Belgrade.
Only one of those questioned suggested Bosnia. The Signoria immediately passed the news on to the Curia and on April 28 to its ambassador
in Buda, who was assured that the republic was on its guard but warned
that Hungary should also do everything possible to forestall possible
dangers. For in view of Mehmed's enormous preparations both by land
and on sea, a large-scale undertaking seemed imminent. In the middle
of May the Venetians still did not know what was in the offing. George
Trapezuntios, who returned to Rome from Istanbul at about this time,
was able to report that this latter city was "wonderfully" fortified and
that the "Turk," who was planning a campaign against Belgrade overland and by the Danube route, had begun to lose weight. It was mid-June
before the Venetians learned for certain that the attack was directed
against Albania and that the sultan had already arrived on the scene.
Francesco Venier, the Venetian ambassador to the Hungarian court, was

informed of these developments and of the measures taken by Venice to defend her Albanian possessions; he was also asked to find out, as diplomatically as he could, whether Matthias Corvinus was possibly in league with the sultan, and if so what sort of person or persons he was employing to this end. In the council of state all forty-six of those present voted the resolution, with the exception of one member, who had handed in a ballot marked with the words "dolere cogimur."

It seemed almost certain that Mehmed's agents had spread a rumor in Istanbul and elsewhere to the effect that his plans were directed against Belgrade and Hungary, in order to veil his real goal and prevent defensive measures from being taken. At the end of May the Romans had long been of this opinion, especially when news came from Dubrovnik that the "Turk" was approaching with 30,000 men. This is probably the figure most in keeping with the truth and the figures of 200,000 men for the sultan's army and another 80,000 for the advance guard in command of Balaban Bey prove, as usual, to be pure products of the imagination. Mehmed and his army had headed for the mountains of Albania by way of Monastïr (Manastir, Bitola). Against stubborn resistance the passes were occupied; the road to the interior lay open. The advance guard under Balaban, who despite earlier defeats had retained the sultan's confidence, pillaged and devastated the countryside far and wide, in the hope of intimidating Skanderbeg. Finally, probably as early as February, Balaban pitched camp outside Krujë in accordance with his orders. The mountain fortress was defended by 1,000 men. Gian-Matteo Contarini, the Venetian *provveditore*, received orders from the Signoria to direct the defensive operations in person. The commander in Krujë was Baldassare Perducci. In addition to Albanians and Venetians, a few mercenaries in the pay of the king of Naples probably participated in the defense.

When Mehmed reached Krujë with the main army, the siege began but made little progress. The strength of the walls and the courage of the defenders resisted all assaults, all the more so as Skanderbeg, who had occupied a fortified camp not far from the lower city, harassed the besiegers' rear by day and night. The Turks suffered considerable losses in men and war equipment, and from day to day it became more difficult to obtain supplies in the devastated region. By June the sultan abandoned the undertaking and moved off toward Durrës in a towering rage. We are told that he vented his fury at the failure of his campaign on the unfortunate inhabitants of Cedhin, who had surrendered and thrown themselves on his mercy, slaughtering 8,000 men and a large number of women and children. He had left Balaban outside Krujë with the order not to stir from the spot until he had reduced the fortress either by force of arms or starvation. But this too proved futile. A detachment that his brother Yunus tried to lead to his assistance was completely destroyed by Skanderbeg in a night attack, and both Yunus and his son Hïzïr were taken prisoner. Shortly thereafter, in a last desperate attack on Krujë, Balaban was severely wounded by a musket ball in the neck, whereupon the entire army was thrown into such terror and confusion that the siege had to be abandoned at once. Near Tirana, on its return march, the Turkish army was twice halted. After a delay of three days, driven by hunger and terror, it broke through the feebly defended eastern border of Albania and fled in disorder to Macedonia.

Before his withdrawal, Mehmed, in a period of thirty days during June and July, as is shown both by the Arabic inscription and by Western sources, built the stronghold of Elbasan in the interior of the country, on the site of the old city of Valma on the Shkumbi River, and razed the village of Chorlu built by Skanderbeg on the coast not far from Durrës. Critoboulos describes the building of Elbasan in considerable detail, while the Ottoman chroniclers, for want of a military event worth mentioning, cite the establishment of this fortress as the sole result of this Albanian campaign. But even if many hands were employed, it is safe to say that the construction of a fortress the size of the castle of Elbasan, whose foundations and a considerable part of the walls are still standing, cannot have been completed in so short a time. We can only assume that the builders made use of considerable remnants of an earlier structure. The news of this new bulwark of Islam soon reached the Christian world. As early as August 14, 1466, the Venetian senate called on Skanderbeg to attack the newly founded city in collaboration with the Venetian *provveditori* of Albania and raze it to the ground. As we learn from Ottoman sources, Skanderbeg acceded to the request the following spring, but without success. Although the lower city was laid waste, the citadel defied the assaults of the Albanians. After the withdrawal of the sultan, who carried off 3,000 Albanian prisoners, guerrilla warfare continued in every corner of this country so well suited to swift surprise attacks.[22]

Mehmed did not return to his capital over the route by which he had come. On the way he learned of a terrible plague that had broken out in Thessaly and then in midsummer spread throughout Macedonia and Thrace, sparing none of the cities, and finally extending to Asia. The

---

[22] Babinger deals with the establishment of an Ottoman fortress in Albania in his "Die Gründung von Elbasan," *Mitteilungen des Seminars für orientalische Sprachen*, XXXIV. Jahrg., II. Abt., *Westasiatische Studien* (Berlin, 1931), 94–103; reprinted in *A&A* I, 201–210.

devastating epidemic struck the entire coast of the Hellespont and the Black Sea; it was particularly severe in Bursa, depopulating the whole region. But also in Istanbul the Black Death occasioned untold sufferings. One victim after another died, some after four days, others after a week of excruciating torment. Because of the extreme heat the epidemic spread rapidly. Many of the sick were left without care, because everyone thought of himself or at most of his closest relatives; there were no priests to comfort the dying, and often the dead lay in the houses for two or three days. More than 600 bodies had to be buried each day and the gravediggers were no longer able to dispose of the corpses. The city became a desert. Those who could left; the rest shut themselves up in their houses for fear of contagion. Men lost their faith in Providence, writes Critoboulos, and resigned themselves to the course of events, as though blind chance had dethroned God. Their whole world was unhinged.[23]

Kept informed by express messengers who arrived daily from Istanbul, Mehmed headed for the mountains of northern Bulgaria with his troops. Having reached the salubrious region between Vidin and Nikopol, he decided to spend the autumn there. Only when winter set in and news came from Istanbul that the plague had died out did he start for his capital. As late as October 9, 1466, the meticulous Milanese ambassador to the Signoria reported from Venice that for fear of the plague Mehmed was planning to spend the winter in Sofia and not to return to Edirne or Istanbul, that he had established himself on a mountaintop, and that no visitor was permitted to come within a day's journey of his encampment.

No sooner had he returned to his capital after his unsuccessful campaign in Albania than he created an atmosphere of terror. Those most immediately threatened were the Venetian colony, but the highest dignitaries of the empire as well, including Mahmud Pasha, feared for their heads. Mahmud remained grand vizier, but as second vizier the sultan appointed a certain Rum (i.e. "Rhomaean," or Greek) Mehmed Bey (later Pasha), who acquired a disastrous influence in the ensuing years. The Ottoman chroniclers show a rare unanimity in condemning his cupidity and sordid intrigues. One might be tempted to suspect them of exaggeration were it not for the recorded events which soon reflected the second vizier's baneful influence. Next to nothing is known of his origin and early life. He seems to have begun his career as an official in the serai. Perhaps he came from the region of Dimotika, perhaps from Anatolia.

[23] There is no specific treatment of the plague in Turkey. Of several accounts of the great plague of the mid-14th century, see Philip Ziegler, *The Black Death* (New York, 1969).

The situation of the Venetians took a turn for the worse when Florentine spies or merchants intercepted certain letters in the harbor of Chios. Benedetto Dei, that archenemy of Venice, managed to get them into the hands of his consul in Pera and through him to the Porte. The sultan, to whom the letters were submitted and who had them translated by his Florentine advisers, summoned four respected members of the Florentine colony in Pera (Mainardo Ubaldini, Iacopo Tedaldo, Niccolò Ardinghelli, and Carlo Martelli) and discussed the situation with them. The four advised him to build the "Castello del Vitupero" (Castle of Shame) on the Dardanelles and to arm it with thirty mortars (*bombarde*). If Benedetto Dei, who provides this information, is to be believed, he himself was dispatched to Cairo as the sultan's official messenger to inform the Mamluk sultan of the Venetian plans. In addition, copies of the intercepted letters were sent to Florence. No mention of these events is made in Venetian reports from the same period.

Benedetto Dei tells us that the fury of Mehmed against Venice at this time knew no bounds. After his return from Albania, still according to Benedetto Dei, he had given orders that the Venetian captives imprisoned in the Seven Towers should be executed along with the "rulers from Trebizond and Mytilini," who shared the same prison. From the chronological point of view, this report, insofar as it concerns the princes, can hardly hold water, although the date given for the execution of the Comneni—Saturday, November 1—would be correct for the year 1466 and not for 1463 (Tuesday). The chronological contradictions in the *Cronaca* (Chronicle; 1453–1479) of the Florentine merchant and spy often make it misleading and subject to caution. Still, what Dei has to say about the fate of the Venetian victims of the sultan's fury and cruelty may well be true in substance. Their corpses were thrown into the middle of the street from the tower of the castle of Yedi Kule, and the sultan gave strict orders that no one should remove or even touch them. They remained unburied until only their bones were left. The flesh had been devoured by dogs, ravens, and wild beasts.

How quickly the times had changed. Before Venice declared war in July 1463, Mehmed had bestowed signal favor on the Venetians. As Benedetto Dei notes with envy, he had leased the alum mines of Foça to Venetians, entrusted them with the exploitation of copper mines, and put them in charge of soap production, coinage, and the collection of excise taxes. But immediately after the outbreak of the war, no Venetian in the entire empire was sure of his life. All those whom the vengeful sultan or his myrmidons could lay hands on were thrown into prison or simply executed without trial. Those who could escaped to safety in the West. But only a few rich merchants managed to get away. Among these were Bartolomeo Zorzi and Girolamo Michiel, owners of alum mines, who left behind them a gross debt of 150,000 gold ducats, payment of which was still being demanded of the Signoria by the Porte in 1479 and again in 1482. In Istanbul, Edirne, Gelibolu, Foça, and Bursa numerous Venetian commercial establishments collapsed, dragging a number of Florentine houses down with them in their ruin. The Venetian commercial colony in Istanbul dwindled away. But though it was clear that all was lost, a few staunch souls stuck to their posts. Even the sinister and now frequent spectacle of Venetian citizens from the interior or from distant Morea, being dragged to the capital to be publicly executed, could not shake their resolution. In constant view of death and terrible sufferings, they tried to carry on with their affairs. One of these men was Antonio Michiel, a leading alum merchant established in Pera, who not only pursued his once lucrative trade but looked after the local interests of the republic. The Signoria had forbidden all large merchant vessels flying the banner of St. Mark to enter the Golden Horn, so rendering impossible any imports from Venice. Slowly but inexorably Venetian trade with the Levant was dying out.

Small wonder, then, that peace efforts were intended seriously by the Signoria. In the preceding year Mehmed may have been interested in peace with Venice, but now he preferred to temporize, and when David Mavrogonatos reached Venice at the end of March or in April he brought a message from Mahmud Pasha, his employer, to the effect that the sultan was prepared to make peace, that the Venetians should send a negotiator to the Porte, and that in case the sultan were absent, they should instruct the Cretan David to apply to Iacopo, the sultan's personal physician, who would procure a safe-conduct for him from the sultan.[24] Antonio Michiel, the message continued, who was on good terms with Iacopo of Gaeta, should inform him that both the Signoria and the king of the Hungarians were willing at any time to cease hostilities, for it was indispensable that Hungary, as the ally of Venice, should be a party to any peace treaty. In April 1466 a party of the *pregadi* arranged to send two emissaries to Negropont to put out renewed peace feelers. But when in October 1466 Antonio Michiel was appointed vice-*bailo* of his native city, with an annual stipend of 300 ducats, the conversations still made no headway. All these initiatives were doomed to failure, because the republic could not resolve to make vital concessions and continued to press its claim to the Morea and Mytilini.

[24] See Babinger, "Johannes Darius (1414–1494), Sachwalter Venedigs im Morgenland und sein griechischer Umkreis," *Sitzungsberichte der bayerische Akademie der Wissenschaften, philos.-hist. Klasse* (Munich, 1961), 56ff.

Edirne and the Üç Şerefeli Cami. The mosque, built by Murad II between 1437 and 1447, and named for the three balconies on the towering minaret, is considered a turning point in Ottoman architecture. Edirne was the second, and European, capital of the empire (until 1453). The excellent possibilities for hunting in its surroundings made it a favorite residence of the sultans

Bursa. The first major conquest by the Ottomans (1326) and their original capital, the city remained a major religious and commercial center even after the fall of Constantinople. On the near ridge, right, the *türbe* (mausoleum) of Mehmed I, and at left, his mosque

I

Mosques of Manisa. One of the principal residences of Ottoman princes, Manisa is richly endowed with religious architecture. Shown here are the Sultaniye mosque (1522) and, in the background, the Muradiye mosque (1586)

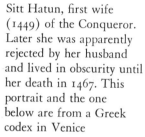

a

Sitt Hatun, first wife
(1449) of the Conqueror.
Later she was apparently
rejected by her husband
and lived in obscurity until
her death in 1467. This
portrait and the one
below are from a Greek
codex in Venice

Melik Arslan, brother of
Sitt Hatun and successor
to his father Süleyman
as ruler of the Turkmen
dynasty of Dulgadir, in
southeastern Anatolia
(1454–1465)

b

III

a

Smederevo. These immense fortifications, east of Belgrade on the Danube, erected by George Branković (1428–1430), were destroyed in the Second World War. Smederevo, capital of the last medieval Serbian state, fell to the Ottomans first in 1439 and finally in 1459

b

Mistra. Built by the Crusaders in the 13th century and later the center of a despotate under the Paleologi. The Morea, or Peloponnesos, first subjected to Ottoman rule by Murad II, was finally conquered by Mehmed in 1460

a

Amasya. On the Yeşil (Green) River, in northeastern Anatolia, the city was a principal residence of Ottoman princes in the 15th century

b

Amasra. The ancient Amastris, built on a narrow peninsula jutting into the Black Sea, was one of Mehmed's first Asian conquests

Golubac, on the Danube. The loss of this Serbian fortress to the Turks in 1427 was partially compensated for by the construction of Smederevo (IV a). It was regained briefly by George Branković but fell into Ottoman hands again soon after the conquest of Constantinople

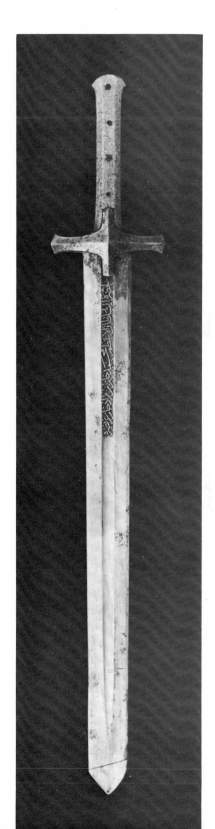

Ivory-hilted sword
belonging to Mehmed.
Now approximately
32 inches long, it has
apparently been shortened
from its original length

a   The fortress of Anadolu Hisari (reconstruction by A. Gabriel). Built in 1395 by Mehmed's great-grandfather, Bayezid I, on the Asian side of the Bosporus. The much greater size of Mehmed's fortification (below) suggests his determination to carry out the conquest

b   The fortress of Rumeli Hisari (reconstruction by A. Gabriel). The first major fortification carried out by Mehmed in connection with his siege of Constantinople, it was rapidly built in the summer of 1452. Rumeli Hisari and the older fortress diagonally across the narrow strait (above) together gave Mehmed control over the waterway to the Black Sea

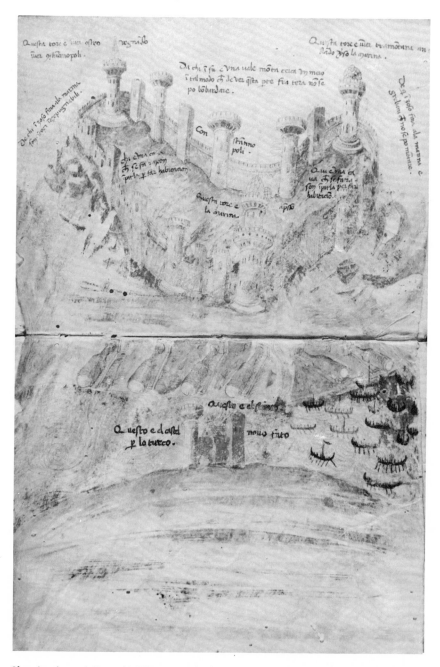

Sketch plan of Rumeli Hisarï, made by a Venetian spy around the year 1453. The plan, which is in a codex in Milan, is apparently the oldest of Mehmed's fortress that we have, and suggests an appearance somewhat different from that in Gabriel's reconstruction (VIII b)

a   "Verily they will conquer Constantinople. Truly their commander will be an excellent one. Truly that army will be an excellent one!" From the body of sayings (*hadith*) attributed to the Prophet Mohammed

b   The land walls of Constantinople. They were built by the Byzantine emperor Theodosius II (408–450) and marked the final geographical expansion of the Byzantine city proper, which they successfully defended against numerous attackers. The height, from moat bottom to tower tops, was over 100 feet

X

a

Cannon of Mehmed the Conqueror. Now known as the "Dardanelles Gun" from its later location, it was cast in 1464. The breech and barrel are separate parts to facilitate loading. The shot was a stone ball weighing approximately 650 pounds. The cannon was brought to England in 1868 and is now at the Tower of London

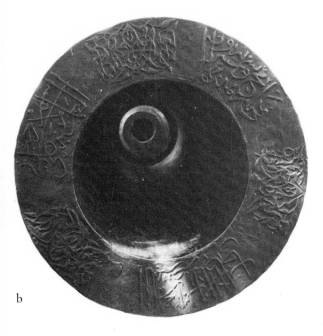

b

Inscription on the "Dardanelles Gun": "Help, O God, Sultan Mehmed Khan son of Murad. The work of Munir Ali in the month of Rejeb in the year 868 H. [March 10–April 8, 1464]"

Istanbul in the 16th century. A Turkish view of the city by Matrakçi Nasuh, from a contemporary manuscript. The artist accompanied Sultan Suleyman on his eastern campaign of 1534–1536 and painted more than a hundred pictures to give a topographical description of the army's route

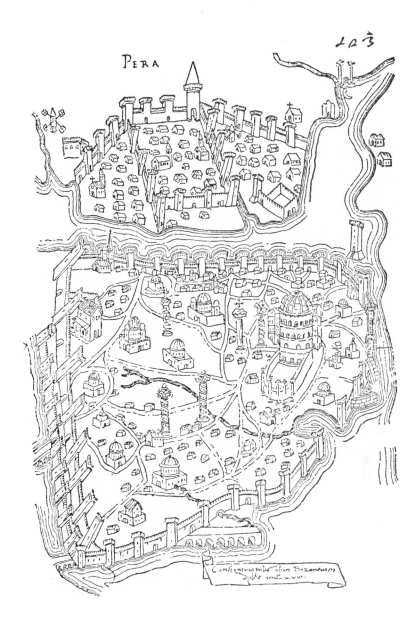

PERA

123

Constantinopolis olim Bizantium
jbb anno xvIII.

Byzantine Constantinople (c. 1422). From a manuscript by Cristoforo Buondel-
monti. The Florentine traveler left several different plans of the Byzantine
capital after his visit in 1420

Turkish siege of Belgrade, 1456. A little-known rendering, in a contemporary Turkish manuscript, of Mehmed's unsuccessful attempt to take the city. Belgrade, at the confluence of the Danube and Sava rivers, holds the key to the Hungarian plains beyond

First gate—the Imperial Gate (Bab-i Hümayun)—to Topkapĭ Palace. This
engraving from a travel memoir by the Comte de Choiseul-Gouffier, French
ambassador to the Porte in the late 18th century, shows the entrance to the palace
grounds at that time. The upper story was subsequently destroyed by fire

The former Ottoman imperial palace, Topkapĭ Sarayĭ. The hills of Asia Minor
are visible in the background, across the Marmara Sea

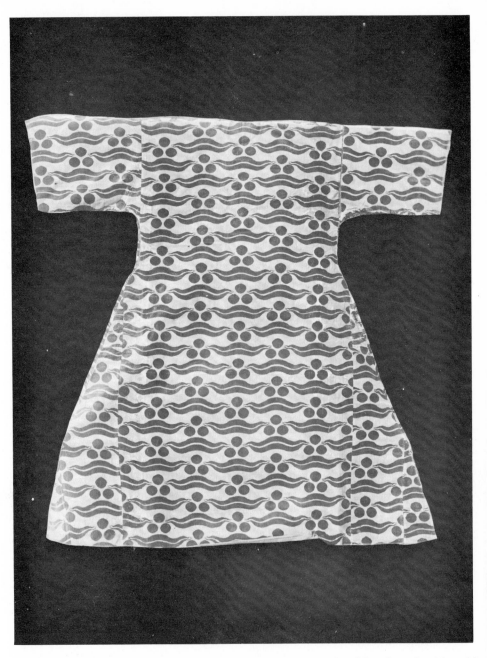

Robe (*kaftan*) of the Conqueror. The brocaded garment is lavishly adorned with gold

Ottoman iron helmet with silver inlay, 15th century. The fluting imitates the folds of the Turkish turban

a   Tile pattern from Mehmed's mosque. This 15th-century panel in blues, yellow, and white, over a courtyard window, is inscribed with the opening line of the Koran: "In the name of God, the Merciful, the Compassionate"

b   The Conqueror's mosque as it appears today. Heavily damaged by earthquake in 1766, it was substantially redesigned at the time of reconstruction

Mosque of Mehmed the Conqueror (Fatih Camii), dominating its surroundings from the crest of the fourth of Istanbul's seven hills. The mosque is shown here in the sketch of Melchior Lorichs, who visited the city in 1606

Mausoleum (*türbe*) of Mahmud Pasha, the grand vizier who served Mehmed for the longest period of time. Mahmud Pasha fell from favor through the intrigue of a rival and was executed in 878 H. (1473/1474). The inscription over the door shows that the *türbe* was built in the same year

XIX

Tiled pavilion (Çinili Köşk). One of the oldest buildings on the imperial palace grounds. This structure still stands, restored nearly to its original appearance as in the 15th century

opposite:
Carved doors from the Conqueror's mosque complex. Now in the treasury (*hazine*) of the Topkapï Palace Museum

XXI

a   Janissary.
b   Young woman.

The sketches are
attributed to Gentile
Bellini, who visited
Istanbul at the indirect
invitation of the sultan
late in Mehmed's reign.
The drawings may equally
well be the work of one
of Bellini's students

Bellini's portrait of the Conqueror. Heavily painted over, this work served as a model for later artists. It is now in the National Gallery, London

Mehmed II and an unidentified boy. The double portrait has been attributed to Bellini, a claim so far unsubstantiated

At the end of October, Iacopo Venier, the "captain of the Adriatic" (*capitano del golfo*) was instructed to repair to Istanbul as soon as the safe-conduct arrived, to present his credentials, and enter into negotiations for an armistice. If he encountered difficulties, he should return to Lemnos (Stalimeni, still in Venetian hands) or Negropont on pretext of asking for new instructions. He received thirty ells of gold cloth to take as a present and was bidden to bring each of the pashas crimson velvet as a gift from the Signoria, in addition to the usual salutations and offerings. He was told above all to take with him two reliable interpreters, one well versed in Greek, the other in Turkish, in order that he might know under all circumstances what was being said. But it soon became clear to the Venetian plenipotentiary that no one at the Porte wished to hear anything of an armistice. He noted a distinctly hostile attitude toward Venice and reported that the Genoese and Florentines in Galata and Pera were agitating against Venice and trying to persuade the grand vizier that Venier had come to Istanbul with designs other than to make peace. Subjects of both states, but in particular the Florentine consul, had blocked any understanding between Venice and the Porte; moreover, by the sultan's order two respected Venetian merchants, Domenico Veglia and Antonio Trevisano, were being held prisoner in the house of the Florentine consul.

In April then, Mehmed rejected all proposals, though in the end Venice seems to have asked for nothing more than continuance of the territorial status quo. He demanded the return of the islands of Lemnos and Imroz (recently taken by Venice) and in addition an annual tribute. "You have come here to drink fresh water," the sultan roared at Giovanni Capello, the Venetian *oratore*. "Your government gave the king of Hungary enormous sums of money and he did nothing." He knew in advance, of course, that proud Venice would never consent to such terms, and it is more than questionable whether the negotiations that were carried on through all conceivable channels—in the end even the governor of Rumelia took a hand as mediator—were ever taken seriously by the Porte. It seems more likely that the Turks merely took advantage of the negotiations to obtain as much reliable information as possible about the war weariness of the Venetians, which was unquestionable, and the extent of the concessions they were willing to make.

The events in the theaters of war in the year 1466 make it clear that Venice would have gladly accepted any peace offer halfway in keeping with her honor. The burden of the hostilities with the Ottomans had thus far rested entirely on the shoulders of the republic. Barriers to trade had reduced Venetian receipts to barely a million ducats a year. And neither on sea nor on land were the fortunes of war particularly favorable to the republic. At the beginning of 1466, to be sure, Vettore Capello, the unswerving champion of resistance and leading advocate of the war against the Turks, had replaced Iacopo Loredano in the responsible post of captain general of the sea, which brought him an annual salary of roughly 100 ducats, and naval activities, which had been virtually paralyzed, were resumed. But even under his command the fleet was unable to carry out any decisive action. Capello set out for Negropont with twenty-five galleys and took the islands of Imroz, Thasos, and Samothraki by surprise attack, captured a few Turkish vessels with precious cargoes, and even undertook a successful raid on Athens, which he occupied, though he did not succeed in dislodging the Turks for good. But all these undertakings did not bring about a decisive turn.

On land the situation was even worse. Iacopo Barbarigo, the *provveditore* of the Morea, assumed supreme command over the land troops after Malatesta's departure. Early in the summer of 1466 he attacked Patras with a force of some 2,000 armed men. But Turahanoğlu Ömer Bey, who knew the region well, came to the assistance of the besieged garrison. The city walls were on the point of collapse after long bombardment when Ömer Bey appeared, prevented the Venetians from entering, and hurled them back into the sea. Many were drowned; the forty ships that were supposed to help the land forces were powerless. The Turks took about 100 prisoners, and 600 Venetians fell in the battle. Ömer Bey first withdrew to Corinth, then proceeded with his prisoners to Istanbul, where he was received with favor and privileged to look on as all the prisoners were mercilessly executed. Iacopo Barbarigo himself had fallen into the hands of the Turks, who dragged him off to Patras and impaled him. Capello, who wished to avenge the disgrace, landed some troops and attacked the Turks. But the murderous battle that developed cost him many of his men, allegedly 1,200, and he barely succeeded in escaping to Negropont with the rest of his crew. There he died of a broken heart in March 1467.

On November 2, 1466, the council of Dubrovnik decreed that three noblemen should go out to meet the "illustrious lord" Skanderbeg (*illustri domino Schenderbegh*) and request him not to enter the city's territory, "for reasons of expedient caution" (*ob bonum respectum*). In other words, they feared Turkish retribution should they receive the hero of Albanian freedom within their gates. At roughly the same time, on November 29, it was deplored in Venice that since the repulse of Skanderbeg only

Krujë, with its defenders paid by the republic, represented Christian sovereignty in the region. Skanderbeg therefore decided to go to Italy and plead for help, especially with the pope. On December 12 he arrived in Rome, where he was received with great pomp by the Curia. An eye-witness writes: "He is a man advanced in years, past sixty; he arrived with a few horses; it seems that he is poor and wishes to ask for help." Apart from a subsidy of 5,000 ducats he obtained no help in protecting his hard-pressed country from further Turkish attacks. He would have to help himself as best he could, wrote Francesco Gonzaga, cardinal of Mantua, on January 12, 1467, to Marquis Ludovico, his father. A few days later it was learned in Venice that Balaban was gathering great strength in Albania, that he was laying the countryside waste day after day and had encircled Krujë.

In the meantime Skanderbeg had gone to Naples, to call on King Ferrante, who granted him a small subsidy and some supplies. Then he returned to Albania. At the end of March an official messenger arrived in Naples from the "pasha of Albania," probably from Vlorë (Valona, Avlona), suggesting that an emissary be sent to Istanbul, because the Porte had things to communicate that would undoubtedly meet with ap-proval. The Aragonese court agreed to send the secretary Bernardo Lopez (Lopis), presumably a Spaniard, to the sultan's court. He started out at the beginning of April, went first to the pasha of Albania to thank him for the gifts that his emissary had sent King Ferrante in Naples, and, provided with "good advice" and an escort, continued his journey to Istanbul. Unfortunately, nothing has thus far become known about the result of this journey, probably the first Neapolitan embassy to the Porte, but the mere fact that it was undertaken seems to indicate that Ferrante was eager to establish contact with the sultan.

At the end of May, Venice learned that in an attempt to relieve the fortress of Krujë, Skanderbeg had killed Balaban, that the Turks had suffered great losses, and that Krujë had been liberated. Immediately thereafter came the news that the "Turk" in person was once more on the march toward Albania. From the construction of the fortress of Elbasan in the preceding year it was inferred that Mehmed would now do everything in his power to take Durrës, in order to establish himself on the Adriatic and gain a strong base opposite the Italian coast (Durrës to Brindisi = 75 nautical miles, or 90 statute miles) for operations against the peninsula.

But in the first week of June, it would seem, the sultan was not yet on Albanian soil as the Venetians supposed. On July 8, 1467, large num-bers of refugees—men, women, and children, who arrived in Brindisi penniless and in rags from across the Adriatic—reported that on July 3, a Friday, Mehmed, at the head of an enormous army, had reached a river named "Argenta" (i.e. the Erzan; the "Arsenta" of the medieval sources), which flows into the sea nine miles north of Durrës. The sultan's encampment was five miles from this city. On the following day (July 4) he was expected before Durrës, which was well supplied but whose inhabitants had fled in droves. No fewer than nine ships full of desperate fugitives had reached Brindisi. Dreading the vengeance of the "Turk," convinced that he was utterly merciless, they had abandoned their homes and possessions, content if they could save their skins. Not without reason, an outbreak of contagious disease was feared in Apulia.

Durrës was almost deserted. The inhabitants of the nearby villages had fled to the mountains. The Turkish troops pretended to withdraw, but when the peasants and shepherds returned to their homes, they were mercilessly cut down or carried off into slavery. Everywhere the bronze bells had been carried away to safety lest they provide the Turks with metal from which to cast cannon. Increasingly grim reports reached the West concerning the flight of great masses to the mountains and the butchering of all those who fell into the hands of the enemy; no one over seven years of age was spared. The Signoria was aghast, especially over the fate of the coastal cities, first and foremost Durrës, because from there the "Turk" would be able to cross over to Italy. At the end of July, however, Mehmed seems to have been outside Krujë, where he was said to have spent two weeks. On July 8 Skanderbeg had written the Venetian council from Shkodër, pleading for help. He received a reply to the effect that the Venetian *rettori* had been instructed to give him all possible assistance and that 1,000 foot soldiers and 300 horsemen were being dispatched to the threatened zones. At about this time Bernardo Lopez returned from his mission to Istanbul, and reported in Naples that Mehmed (to whom he had probably spoken before the sultan's departure for Albania, and not in that country) had said that he "very much hated the Signoria of Venice and that if he found a suitable harbor in those parts of Albania, he would carry the war into its territory." For the present, however, Durrës did not seem to be in danger. The sultan had sent 12,000 horsemen into the harbor region, but from the reports reaching the Signoria we must conclude that the attack on Durrës and its environs failed and that the Turkish cavalry was prevented from taking the city by the stubborn resistance of the troops still within its walls. The horsemen then moved off toward Krujë. There was a rumor in Venice to the effect that Skanderbeg was to surrender Krujë to Mehmed through the mediation of the king of Naples, who was in league with the "Turk."

The Ottomans, however, seem to have withdrawn eastward without having taken Krujë.

A nephew of Skanderbeg (the son of one of his sisters) who had turned Moslem was left behind by the retiring Ottomans to safeguard their interests; he ensconced himself at Cape Rodoni north of Durrës. One night he was attacked from the sea by Venetian ships and overland by Skanderbeg. Taken aboard the captain's ship, he was beheaded by his uncle's own hand. According to a report that reached Venice at the beginning of August, Skanderbeg had by then regained power over all his territories. If the communication of the Venetian *provveditore* of Shkodër to the Signoria is to be believed, Balaban, whose death had so often been reported, had really lost his life shortly before, and Skanderbeg was wearing the dead man's ring as proof that he had killed him and many of the Turks. The popular tradition still has it that death came to him in the village of Hekali (not far from Priska) and that he was buried in a *türbe* which still exists on the outskirts of Petrelë.

By midsummer the second Turkish campaign against Albania, in which the sultan had participated only hesitantly and infrequently, came to an unsuccessful end. The whole country breathed easier and those who had fled or been driven away returned to their homes. Giosafat Barbaro (1413–1494), the celebrated and widely traveled Venetian diplomat, was appointed *provveditore* of Albania in Shkodër; we shall encounter him later performing important missions in Persia.

At about the same time Leonardo Boldu, *rettore* of Shkodër, was chosen as Venetian ambassador to Istanbul. He was expected to journey by way of San Sergio, the Venetian port in Upper Albania, to Drisht (Drivasto) and then eastward and inland to find the sultan in the headquarters he occupied at the time; Boldu was instructed to obtain a safe-conduct from Alexius Span, an Upper Albanian feudal lord, who had offered his services as intermediary between the Porte and Venice. This plan, however, was not put into execution immediately, either because the Porte failed to give its consent or because Alexius Span had overestimated or exaggerated his influence with the Porte. Only at the end of January 1468 was Leonardo Boldu able to set out.[25]

More than ever before, the Signoria needed peace with the Turks, for the war was cutting off the entire Levantine trade and disaster threatened on every hand. Local Turkish commanders in Bosnia were now making raids as far as the Dalmatian coast. In mid-September 1467 a cry of alarm went out from Dalmatia: the Turks were only a day's journey from Zadar

[25] Ibid., 58–59.

and Šibenik (Sebenico), they had carried away men and cattle, and the entire country population had fled. The Signoria was urgently informed "that the aforesaid Turks have come within two days' journey of Italy and that they are not far from Pula [in Istria, no more than sixty miles from the Italian border]. It seems almost as if the Christians were unaware of their ruin and as if they, the Turks, were coming closer each year."

The situation was not much better in the south, especially in Herzegovina, then ruled by Duke Stjepan Vukčić. Taking advantage of the continuing feud in the ducal family, Isa Bey, son of Ishak Bey, had passed unhindered through the "Herzog's country" in 1465 and approached the Ragusan frontier. Dubrovnik brought her peasants to safety in the coastal strongholds and on the islands; the numerous fugitives were forbidden to enter the city itself. Then the Hungarians, to whom Vlatko, the duke's second son, had appealed for help, took a hand. They occupied the territory of the lower Neretva (Narenta) with picturesque Počitelj, lowered the banners of St. Mark, and were to remain there for more than twenty years. As Venice for her part had occupied the region of Krajina near Makarska as well as the Neretva estuary in October 1465, old Duke Stjepan vacillated distrustfully between the Hungarians and the Venetians. The sultan, he lamented to the Signoria in the spring of 1466, had conquered almost his entire domain, and it was his oldest son, Vladislav, who had led the Turks into the country. A little later, on May 22, 1466, death relieved him of his sufferings and his two older sons went on fighting over possession of their father's territories, insofar as the Ottomans permitted them to do so. Stjepan, the youngest, was to go over completely to the sultan's side. Born in June 1459, presumably the son of the Bavarian princess Barbara of Landshut, herself probably illegitimate, he was to have a brilliant career. Under the name of Hersekoğlu Ahmed Pasha, he became the son-in-law of Sultan Bayezid II, for whom and for whose successor, Selim I, Stjepan held the highest office of the realm, the grand vizierate, no less than four times.[26]

Now the Turks were making themselves more and more at home in Bosnia and Herzegovina. Their Bosnian governor officiated in Sarajevo, while the military governor (*sancak beyi*) of Herzegovina had his headquarters in Foča on the Drina. From their base in Bosnia, the Ottomans kept raiding northern Dalmatia and Croatia unhindered.

Dubrovnik, which had so far met its tribute payments punctually, was

[26] For the grand vizier of the late 15th and early 16th centuries, see "Hersek-zade Ahmed Pasha" (H. Sabanović), *EI²* III, 340–342. Cf. Erdmute Heller, *Venedische Quellen zur Lebensgeschichte des Ahmed Pasa Hersekoghlu* (Munich, 1961).

spared for the present, although the Ottoman fortifications along its borders, built in 1464, were a source of frequent clashes and friction was now constant. In 1467 a message came from the sultan increasing the annual tribute payments from 1,500 to 5,000 ducats.[27] Although Dubrovnik took good care not to become involved in the anti-Turkish policies of the West, Mehmed demanded more and more tribute. Toward the end of his reign, it amounted to 10,000 ducats "for the current year," to which were added 2,500 ducats for customs duties (*gümrük*), burdens to which the city's finances were no longer equal. By way of raising at least a part of the required funds, the republic was compelled to increase its import and export duties and internal taxes, and to reduce the wages of officials.

In a terrifyingly short time the Ottomans had become neighbors of Italy, from which, in Dalmatia, they were separated only by the narrow Adriatic (75 to 110 miles). In addition to the port of Vlorë (Turkish since 1435) they could use the new fortress of Elbasan on the Shkumbi River, which was still navigable at the time. Thus they were virtually masters of the Adriatic, which they could close to Venetian ships at any time. This situation is reflected almost a hundred years later by Joachim du Bellay, the poet of the Pléiade, who wrote in connection with the *Sensa*, the famous Venetian festival celebrating the marriage of the doge with the sea:

> *Ces vieux cocus vont espouser la mer*
> *Dont ils sont les maris et le Turc l'adultère.*
> (Those old cuckolds are going to marry the sea.
> They are her husbands and the Turk her lover.)

Of course there is a good deal of Gallic malice in these verses, but they faithfully reflect the increasing threat of Ottoman sea power.

Toward the midsummer of 1467 Mehmed, probably in the company of the grand vizier Mahmud Pasha, who was said to have accompanied him on this campaign, withdrew from Albania. But in Macedonia and Thrace a plague had again broken out, which deterred him from hastening his return to Edirne or Istanbul. This time he seems to have spent the entire winter in the Balkan Mountains, for only toward March 1468 did news reach Venice that the "Turk" had gone to Istanbul because the plague had died down. On March 28, 1468, the sultan's presence in his capital palace was reliably reported in Venice. Still greater silence

---

[27] Biegman, *The Turco-Ragusan Relationship*, 49, dates the tribute increase to the following year, 1468.

surrounded Mahmud Pasha during that year. We should be without any reliable evidence of his activity in 1467 were it not for a letter in Slavonic that has been preserved. Written in Sazli Dere (near Edirne), where his feudal estate of Hasköy was situated, it was dispatched on April 15 (1467), "from the Pasha and Grand Vizier and ruler of all Western lords," as its arrogant salutation runs, to the *rettore* and senate of the Republic of Dubrovnik. In this strange letter he gives thanks for the three medical manuscripts procured for him by the council of Dubrovnik and asks for three more then famous medical works, in particular the two Latin commentaries on the *Kanun fi't-tibb* [*Canon of Medicine*] of Avicenna, and also for certain copper, silver, and gold objects, probably the work of goldsmiths, which it has thus far been impossible to identify. All this was intended for his "emperor": the medical books for Iacopo of Gaeta, the metal objects for the sultan himself, who took special pleasure in such things. It had taken over a year to obtain the manuscripts, for the initial request had been addressed to Dubrovnik in the spring of 1466. There is little doubt that Iacopo desired them as a source of wisdom for the treatment of his sick master and it seems no less likely that by procuring them Mahmud Pasha wished to reestablish his precarious credit with the sultan.[28]

The second campaign against Albania had not turned out as the Ottomans wished, and beyond a doubt that mountainous country with its freedom-loving inhabitants would soon have called Mehmed to new and difficult tasks if once again fate had not come to his assistance: taken with a malignant fever, Skanderbeg died on January 17, 1468, in the castle above Alessio in Upper Albania after a brief illness. On his deathbed, so it seems, he commended his orphaned country to his "most loyal and powerful" ally, the Venetian Republic, and his minor son, John, to the protection and wisdom of the Signoria. His grief-stricken compatriots buried him in Alessio, in the Church of St. Nicholas, which was long ago destroyed. But his remains were not destined to lie in eternal peace. When Mehmed took possession of the city in 1478, at the time of the siege of Shkodër, he had the vault opened and the remains of the man he had once so greatly feared publicly displayed. Marino Barlezio, in this case perhaps a reliable witness, claims that more than one Moslem took a bone, had it set in gold or silver, and carried it with him as a talisman, thinking to steel his courage by contact with this relic of a brave, persevering, and well-nigh unconquerable hero.

[28] For the document see Ciro Truhelka, "Tursko-slovjenski spomenici," GZMBH 23 (1911), 26–27 (document 23); summary Turkish translation in *IED* I (1955), 51–52.

We must certainly assign to the realm of myth the story that when Mehmed II heard of the death of Skanderbeg, he cried out, "At last Europe and Asia are mine! Woe to Christendom! It has lost its sword and its shield." But it is safe to assume that the death of George Castriota came to him as very good news.

With the death of Skanderbeg the defense of Albania became the burdensome legacy of the Republic of Venice. Soon the country was in a state of complete chaos. First the Upper Albanian feudal lords—the Musachi, the Spans, the Dukagins, the Skuras, the Zaccarias—tried to recoup their losses by seizing lands. Then the Ottomans penetrated to every corner of Albania, to the gates of Shkodër, Alessio, even Durrës, and dragged away thousands of people. "In all Albania we see nothing but Turks," ran a dispatch of the period. The chieftains quarreled with one another and some went over to the Turks, attaining, as in the case of the Skuras and Dukagins, positions of honor in the Ottoman state. Only Krujë held out, for Venice took this chief citadel of Skanderbeg under her wing and appreciably reinforced the garrison. And Montenegro, whose freedom and independence the Crnojevići had bravely defended against the infidel, was still able to hold its own. But in Epirus the situation of the despot Leonardo III Tocco (1448–1479) was becoming more and more desperate. Since March 24, 1449, when the Ottomans incorporated Arta into their empire, the duchy (despotate) of "Little Greece" (Akarnania) or Karlĭ Eli, "land of Carlo [Tocco]," as the Turks called it, had consisted only of Angelokastron, Vonitsa, and Varnatsa on the mainland of Epirus, and of the islands of Levkas, Cephalonia (Kefallinia), and Zakinthos (Zante). In the end Leonardo Tocco could hope for assistance only from the Venetians. As their spokesman, he tried from time to time to intercede in their behalf with the Turkish pashas of Vlorë, until at length even the last remnant of his shadow despotate fell a prey to the Turks (1479).

Before preparing to strike a new blow, the sultan, probably in the first days of March, granted an audience to Leonardo Boldu, the Venetian plenipotentiary, who brought him rich gifts, including four pieces of beautiful gold-embroidered silk. The emissary was received with special honors, or so at least he wrote to Venice, from which the Signoria rather prematurely inferred that the sultan was interested in embarking on serious peace negotiations. But no such negotiations ever materialized, and Gherardo de Colli, the shrewd Milanese diplomat, probably came very close to the truth in a letter written on March 26, 1468, to Duke Galeazzo Sforza. "If only the Turk did not grant him safe-conduct and invite him to come in order to lay his hands on those pieces of gold cloth and to inspire a good opinion of himself, as he has done in the past!" Since Leonardo Boldu's departure from Shkodër, the letter continues, two months had passed, and it hardly seemed likely that Mehmed, whose aim was domination of the world (*monarchia del mondo*), would involve himself in peace conversations. On the following day Gherardo de Colli had an interview with the doge Cristoforo Moro, who informed him that he had received reports from three different sources, by way of Dubrovnik and Novo Brdo (whose last remaining inhabitants had been moved to Istanbul in 1467), to the effect that peace had been made with the Porte. To be sure, the doge had added, little credence was given to such reports. But letters had also come from Buda, according to which Matthias Corvinus had spoken of Venice to a Turkish emissary who had arrived in Oradea (Grosswardein, Nagyvarad) with 400 horsemen to take up peace negotiations. The Turkish agent had replied that he was not empowered to discuss this subject, but that he had every reason to hope that Leonardo Boldu would conclude a peace with the Porte within the next few days. An eyewitness to the conversations in Oradea had the following to report after arriving in Venice: the differences of opinion between the Turks and Hungarians were slight; Mehmed insisted on possession of Jajce, which he regarded as his property, while the Hungarian said it was his by right of conquest. In return, the sultan was willing to cede Smederevo, the important base on the Danube, but this seemed hardly credible, for that city numbered more than 3,000 houses, was strongly fortified, and moreover was a "thorn in the side of Belgrade." It seemed more likely that the "Turk" was demanding Jajce because it belonged to Bosnia and not to Hungary, and above all because possession of it would give him free access to Istria. In furtherance of his "diabolical designs," the "Turk" was trying to drive a wedge between the Signoria and Hungary; the news from Novo Brdo did not emanate from Venetian circles, but from the Turkish prefect (*subaşi*) of the city. Finally, this same eyewitness expressed the opinion that the emissary of the Signoria was being detained in Istanbul to prevent Venice from raising an army or strengthening the defenses of Albania.

All this proved to be perfectly true. The "Turk" had persisted in "his usual obstinacy and effrontery," and after a few days Leonardo Boldu had returned empty-handed from Istanbul to Shkodër; the Signoria so informed Francesco Diedo, its ambassador at the court in Buda (May 2, 1468), and enjoined him to press the Hungarian king to have Venice included in any armistice with the Turks. The "Turk," so the message continued, would be all the more willing to do this once he knew that peace prevailed throughout Christendom and that, as Pope Paul II had expressly announced at the feast of St. Mark (April 25, 1468), the danger of an Italian war had definitely been averted. A few days later (May 12) Francesco received further instructions: he should insist that the treaty include the explicit stipulation, hitherto customary in such cases, that the Ottoman fleet must in no event leave the straits. In the name of Venice he should reject definitely any treaty not including this provision.

The Turkish negotiator in Oradea would not easily have obtained the consent of the Porte to such an agreement, but he was spared the embarrassment of suggesting it. The sultan agreed to an armistice with Hungary no more than to a peace with Venice. Indeed, he had little reason to do so, for on March 31, 1468, Matthias Corvinus, at the insistence of the Curia, had declared war on Bohemia. While the sultan's *çavuş*, his messenger of state, was still on Hungarian soil, he himself, accompanied by Mahmud Pasha, had embarked on a new campaign, this time in Anatolia.

The situation in Europe, on the northern and western boundaries of the Turkish Empire, was not at all unfavorable to such an undertaking, which the situation in Karaman demanded. Pope Paul II, to be sure, was doing his best to promote the war against the infidel by his own resources, but with him it was not a consuming passion as it had been with his predecessor, who had given his life for the crusade. The funds accruing from the "Turkish tithe" went almost exclusively to Hungary, and a considerable share of the alum tax was also diverted in that direction; in 1465 alone, the sums of 80,000 and 57,500 gold florins were made over to Matthias Corvinus.[29] If in sending Mehmed's supposed half brother, Calixtus Ottomanus, to the court of Buda (June 1465), Paul II cherished the hope that the strange prince might be useful in stirring up disorder in the Ottoman Empire, this shows how little help he must have expected from the Hungarians in combating the Turks. And indeed Matthias Corvinus soon excused his failure to engage in an offensive war on the ground that the mercenaries he had engaged were gobbling up too much money. In Italy the situation was no better. Venice was trying by every means at her disposal to arrive at a friendly agreement with the Porte. Milan and Naples (the latter had already begun, though only occasionally, to exchange embassies with the Ottomans) wished on no account to endanger their relations with the Turks. Florence and Genoa were eager to inherit the Levantine trade of their fallen Venetian rival. Paul II made considerable offers of money to Venice to forestall a peace with the sultan. For over a year Cardinal Juan de Carvajal, who had spent his whole life zealously promoting a war against the Turks, en-

[29] See Pastor, *History of the Popes* IV, 83.

deavored, as papal legate in Venice, to dissuade the Signoria from making peace. In Germany a diet had been held in Nuremberg in 1466, largely at the behest of the pope, in order to discuss the question of the Turkish war. Ulrich von Grafeneck, one of the companions of John Hunyadi from the days of the siege of Belgrade, offered his services as a new commander for the salvation of Hungary, and in the Holy Roman Empire, where internal peace was to be proclaimed for five years, it was decreed that every hundredth man should be enlisted for the crusade for a period of three years. Envoys of King Matthias, who as early as the fall of 1466 had ordered a squadron of twenty-four Danube ships (which, to be sure, was never to encounter the Turks) built in Regensburg, declared their king's readiness to provide 5,000 warriors, to issue a gold and silver coinage celebrating the Holy War, and for the duration of the war to turn a number of castles on and near the Danube over to the commander. Three times a week, it was decided, prayers should be said in every church for the success of the great undertaking, and in the spring of 1468 hostilities should finally begin. The customs duties of the empire were to be set aside to cover the costs of the war. German princes of the empire, such as Otto of Bavaria, Eberhard of Württemberg, Albrecht and Friedrich of Brandenburg, offered to participate in the campaign, some of them in person. As representative of the pope, Fantino de Valle, archbishop of Crete, declared that the Holy See had already paid out 140,000 ducats to Hungary. Even King George Podiebrad of Bohemia (1420–1471), whom Paul II had twice excommunicated as a Hussite heretic, had caused his Italian favorite, the imaginative and superficial Antonio Marini, to work out a plan for a crusade and submit it to the pope for his approval. A second diet, which the emperor had called for June 15 of the following year, concerned itself with the size of the contingents to be provided by the various participant states. On May 20, 1467, the feeble Frederick III ordered that all internal quarrels should be suspended and called a new diet in Regensburg. Certain of the Hungarian delegates were quite justified in declaring that one diet merely prepared the way for another (*semper dieta dietam parat*). In Italy peace was proclaimed by Paul II on St. Mark's Day, 1468. After an unsuccessful diet in Nuremberg in the spring of 1468, there was talk of a new diet to be held on October 1 of the same year.

Meanwhile George Podiebrad, the Hussite king, had endeavored, unsuccessfully of course, to make his private conflict with Rome over the question of the Bohemian church into the common cause of the secular powers. Finally King Matthias Corvinus, as the ally of the pope and the Bohemian Catholics, declared war on George on March 31, 1468, invaded

Bohemia, conquered the larger part of Moravia, Silesia, and Lusatia, and had himself elected and proclaimed king of Bohemia (May 3, 1469).

Mehmed, well informed of events far beyond his borders by an excellent secret service, knew he had nothing to fear from the Hungarian king. The weakness, helplessness, disunion, and mutual jealousy of the Christian world were, as usual, Mehmed's best allies. The states of Italy vied for his favor, the king of Hungary was in Bohemia, involved in a war that was to keep him busy for some time, while in Albania Skanderbeg was no longer alive. Furthermore, during the year 1468—toward the end of which Emperor Frederick III received the holy sword from the pope and, as a sign that he would valiantly defend the Church, made it vibrate three times on receiving it—Isa Bey's pillaging bands reappeared in Bosnia as well as near the Venetian possessions of Zadar, Split, and Skradin (Scardona), took numerous Dalmatian slaves, and finally appeared at the gates of Šibenik. At about the same time Turkish freebooters attacked Andros and killed Giovanni Sommaripa, the lord of this island.

Thus quite secure in the rear, the sultan crossed the Bosporus at the latest in the first days of April 1468, for on April 13 he was encamped at Gebze, not far from the Gulf of Izmit, where his army gathered for the Anatolian campaign. Here he issued a receipt to the Ragusan envoys Stjepko Lukarević and Vlahusa Gundulić for the annual tribute of 5,000 ducats for the year 1468. On May 6, in a Slavonic letter written in Afyon Karahisar, he called on the Ragusan council to see to it that the residual debt of a Ragusan citizen, amounting to 3,000 gold pieces, was paid. From here the sultan and the vanguard of his army moved straight to Akşehir and Konya, the old capital of the Seljuks and now capital of the princes of Karaman.[30]

After a stormy existence that marks him as one of the most remarkable, though sadly neglected, figures in all medieval Islam, Ibrahim Bey, ruler of Karaman, had died early in August 1464. By his marriage with a sister of Murad II he had six sons: Pir Ahmed, Kasîm, Karaman, Nure Sufi, Alaeddin, and Süleyman. Even during his lifetime they had quarreled with their father, as well as among themselves, because he had singled out another son, Ishak, the child of a slave woman, for his special favor. Shortly before his death he had given the Mediterranean city of Silifke (Seleucia Trachea) with its treasury to Ishak, and the indignant legitimate sons had shut Ibrahim Bey up in Konya in the hope of making him

---

[30] For the documents of the spring of 1468, see Kraelitz, "Osmanische Urkunden," 48–50 (document 3), and Truhelka, 27–28 (documents 24 and 25); cf. *IED* I (1955), 52.

change his mind. After a brief siege he managed to escape and took refuge in the castle of Kevele on Mount Takyeli (Takkeli). There he soon died, but his death stirred the quarrel among the brothers to still greater violence.[31]

Taking possession of Konya and the northern and best part of the kingdom, Pir Ahmed, the eldest, exiled his half brother Ishak to rocky Cilicia. Two of his legitimate brothers, Süleyman and Nure Sufi, whose rights were equal to his, appealed for help to their cousin, Sultan Mehmed, who settled fiefs on them. Kasïm fled first to Syria, then to the court of the Mamluk sultan in Cairo. Ishak alone proved to be a dangerous rival. He turned to the powerful lord of the White Sheep and promised that if Uzun Hasan sent troops, he would provide a large sum for their maintenance. Ishak went to meet his protector, who had left Erzincan for Karaman by way of Sivas, and led him and his troops into the country. When Uzun Hasan soon after withdrew to the east, he left behind Isfendiyaroğlu Kïzïl Ahmed, the former lord of Kastamonu, the same man who had first encouraged Mehmed to depose his own brother in Sinop but who, having been rewarded by receiving Yenişehir as his fief (now vacated by Ismail Bey), had fled in the end to the ruler of the White Sheep.

Since Ishak had gained power with the support of a sworn enemy of the Ottomans, he wished to obtain the sultan's recognition of his crown and to this end sent one of the most cultivated men of Anatolia, Ahmed Çelebi, son of Mullah Sarï Yakub, to the Porte. Through him he offered Mehmed the cities of Akşehir and Beyşehir on condition that his two stepbrothers who were living at the sultan's court should receive them as appanages. Mehmed's only answer was an order to cede all territory as far as the river Çarşamba immediately to the Ottoman Empire. To offer such gifts, he informed Ishak through Ahmed Çelebi, was tantamount to freeing a hunchbacked slave. If he wished to have nothing to fear from his two stepbrothers, he should restore the old boundary between the two states fixed under Sultan Bayezid I. Ishak rejected this demand with indignation, whereupon Mehmed instructed the former admiral Hamza Pasha, now governor of Antalya, to invade Karaman. A battle was fought at Ermenek (the Germanicopolis of the ancients) or, according to other

---

[31] For the mountain fortress, see Babinger's "Kávalla (Anatolien)," *Der Islam* 29 (1950), 301–302; reprinted in *A&A* II, 90–91. Cf. I. H. Uzunçarşilï, *Anadolu beylikleri*, 30, n. 2. More information on the family of Karaman, with references to the Ottoman sources, is given in the latter work, especially 28–38. For further details on Ibrahim and his successors with reference to the Eastern sources, see M. C. Şehabeddin Tekindağ, "Son Osmanlï-Karaman münasebetleri hakkïnda araştïrmalar," *Tarih Dergisi* 13 (1962–63), 43–76.

6. ANATOLIA

sources, at Dağ Pazari, north of Mut, and Ishak was defeated. He fled, leaving his wife and child defenseless in Silifke. Pir Ahmed, who had accompanied Hamza Pasha and his border troops, magnanimously gave this city to the young son of the defeated Ishak. For himself Pir Ahmed kept the rest of the country, with the exception of the two cities Akşehir and Beyşehir, which Ishak had offered the sultan, and the castles of Ilgun and "Saichlan" (Saklan?), the keys of which he sent to his cousin Mehmed. As can be seen from an inscription in Kayseri (870 H. = 1466), Pir Ahmed regarded himself as an Ottoman vassal. But soon he too showed stirrings of the spirit of independence characteristic of the Karamans, and it became evident that eventually the sultan would have to eliminate this source of danger.[32]

All this had happened in the years 1464 and 1465, at a time when Mehmed, perhaps too ill to engage in military campaigns, spent well over a year in his serai in Istanbul. In the two following years he and Mahmud Pasha had their hands full with the Albanian campaigns and could not possibly have concerned themselves with affairs in Karaman. As usual, the sultan had no difficulty in finding a pretext. To him the mere fact that Ishak (like himself, the son of a slave woman) had turned for protection to Uzun Hasan, his most dangerous enemy on Asian soil, and that the latter had willingly taken part in the hostilities was sufficient reason to invade Karaman. An aggravating circumstance was that Pir Ahmed had kept up the secret relations of the princes of Karaman with the Western powers, especially Venice and the pope, and that these ties with the West were beginning to assume more menacing forms. For a century and a half the principality of Karaman had been a dangerous rival of the Ottoman Empire and the two states had been embroiled in frequent wars, most of which had ended in dubious peace, thanks to kinships on the distaff side. Mehmed felt that a new uprising could not be tolerated on any account.

After taking the mountain fortress of Kevele, the sultan entered Konya without resistance and immediately built a fortress (inscription 872 H. = 1468). He sent Mahmud Pasha to Laranda, i.e. Karaman, from which Ishak had fled. Here a violent battle ensued, in which the Bey of Karaman was defeated but not taken. Mehmed vented his rage at Ishak's escape by ruthlessly executing all the prisoners. Mahmud Pasha then received orders to exterminate the Turgutlu, a heretical Turkman tribe in the vicinity of Karaman. The grand vizier pursued the fugitives across the Bulgar Mountains (in the Taurus range, also known as Bozoğlan

[32] For the inscription of Pir Ahmed, see Albert Gabriel, *Monuments turcs d'Anatolie* I (Paris, 1931), 28.

Dağları) to the vicinity of Tarsus; here he located the survivors and sent them in chains to his commander who, in the language of the old Ottoman chronicles "settled his account with them," that is to say, had them put to death.[33]

Next he received orders from the sultan to round up all the artisans and artists in the cities of Konya and Laranda and lead them off to Istanbul as colonists. For centuries these cities had been the homes of masters in the arts of ceramics and architecture, carpet weaving and miniature painting, calligraphy and applied art. Mehmed was undoubtedly very eager to settle them in his capital. This order gave rise to an incident fraught with consequences. In selecting those to be deported, Mahmud Pasha evidently concentrated on the poor and spared the wealthier members of the community. For this his envious rival Rum Mehmed Pasha, the second vizier, who was also present, denounced him to the sultan. Mehmed immediately put the matter into the hands of Rum Mehmed Pasha, who carried out the sultan's orders with a ruthlessness and severity which provoked general indignation. In the contemporary rhymed and prose chronicles of the Ottomans this incident is related with expressions of the deepest contempt for Rum Mehmed, the Greek, who allegedly wished by his brutal and inhuman selection of the most respected and well-to-do Moslems to take vengeance for the conquest of Constantinople. This accusation occurs over and over again. The fact of the matter is that, alleging them to be artists and artisans, the second vizier indiscriminately condemned the more respected citizens of both cities to deportation, destroyed their houses, and confiscated their possessions. He was even on the point of dragging off Ahmed Çelebi, a direct descendant of the famous sheikh and poet Mevlana Celaleddin (Jalāl al-Dīn) Rumi, when the sultan heard of it and sent the poor man home again with presents and apologies.

But Rum Mehmed Pasha had attained his principal aim: Mahmud Pasha was deposed from his post as grand vizier. A strange ceremony, presumably of old Turkish origin, was enacted: the sultan arranged to have Mahmud Pasha's tent suddenly collapse over his head. The imperial seal was conferred on the renegade Rum Mehmed Pasha, while the governorship of Karaman Eli was given to the sultan's second son, Mustafa Çelebi. The former grand vizier was banished in disgrace to his estate in Hasköy, some seventeen miles east of Edirne. So for the present ended the brilliant career of this statesman and general, without whose devotion

[33] For the inscription on the fortress at Konya, see Ibrahim Hakkï Konyalï (*Abideleri ve kitabeleri ile*) *Konya tarihi* (Konya, 1964), 110.

and creative genius his master would never have achieved his greatest triumphs.

Ishak Bey had fled to Uzun Hasan, and all Karaman, with the exception of Silifke, where Ishak's wife and son lived on even after Ishak Bey's death, was incorporated into the Ottoman Empire.[34] In November 1468, the campaign was concluded and at the end of the month Mehmed made his entry into Istanbul despite the plague that had broken out. On December 20 the Persian Fahreddin, who had been mufti for many years, died in Istanbul, possibly of the plague, and was buried in Edirne. Mullah Husrev, the sultan's tutor and adviser, took his place. The new grand vizier made all manner of changes in the high administration: Köpelioğlu Muhyiddin was dismissed as army judge and his position given to Vildan Mehmed. Mullah Sinan, the sultan's teacher; Hass Murad, a descendant of the Palaeologi and a special favorite with the sultan; Gedik Ahmed and Ozguroğlu Isa Bey, a descendant of the Albanian Skura, all received the rank of vizier and accordingly the title of pasha.[35]

The Venetians had been very happy when news came at the end of June 1468 that the sultan had gone so deep into Asia that it would take him six months to return. But the West had no information about the aims of the Karaman campaign. On August 2, 1468, it was reported in Venice that Mehmed, who for five years had engaged in no important warlike actions against either Venice or Hungary, had decided to attack Syria. Rumor had it that the Syrian crown had changed hands three times in March and April, each successive ruler driving his predecessor from the country, and that in consequence the sultan had sent his army to Karaman and Alanya (Alaiye; Italian Candeloro); further, that he had wrested Little Armenia from the Bey of Karaman; and finally that he had destroyed a Mamluk army near Aleppo. When the sultan of Syria and Egypt had heard the news, still according to the same rumor, he had rent his clothes, thrust his sword into the ground, and undertaken to march on Syria, but the Turk had already withdrawn. On August 10 word was received in Venice that Mehmed had taken possession of Syria.

[34] On the basis of a contemporary Arabic chronicle, Inalcïk suggests a somewhat different interpretation of the events taking place between the Ottomans and Karamanids during these years ("Mehmed the Conqueror," 423–424).

[35] Babinger deals in more detail with the vizier Hass Murad in his "Eine Verfügung des Paläologen Châss Murâd Pasa," in the *Festschrift* for R. Hartmann: *Documenta Islamica Inedita*, ed. J. Fück (Berlin, 1952), 197–210; reprinted in *A&A* I, 344–354.

All these exaggerated or false reports show that the Venetian intelligence service in the Levant was not functioning very well at the time. Nor was it very successful in keeping track of Mehmed's whereabouts after his return from Anatolia, and throughout the year we have virtually no record of his activities.

The plague, which for years had been haunting southeastern Europe and was becoming more and more widespread, seems finally, in the course of the winter, to have driven the sultan from his capital to the Balkan Mountains. In Venice, at least, it was believed at the beginning of February 1469 that Mehmed had fled by way of Sofia to Nikopol on the Danube.

But the Venetians were excellently informed about the terrifying events taking place on the eastern coast of the Adriatic. In January 1469, Turkish freebooters, under Isa Bey, *sancak beyi* of Bosnia, once again invaded Dalmatia and advanced as far as the harbors of Zadar and Šibenik. More than 6,000 Turks were said to have looted the region; numerous inhabitants were carried away to replace those who had died of the plague in Istanbul and Gelibolu; others who were able to escape in time fled to the islands off the coast. The raids were all the more devastating in that they were completely unexpected. On the Pentecost (May 21) a large body of raiders, allegedly 10,000 horsemen, suddenly appeared near Metlike (Möttling) in Carniola, where they camped for a week. But when no enemy appeared, they split up into numerous small bands and devastated the entire region as far as the gates of Ljubljana (Laibach). Market towns and villages were burned, the inhabitants massacred or carried away prisoner. Only when a general levy was decreed against them, in which every household was obliged to provide one armed man, did the raiders withdraw and vanish across the border as fast as they had come. This first Turkish incursion into the interior of Austria had lasted only two weeks, but Carniola was the poorer by 20,000 to 24,000 men. The damage to property was unanimously described as enormous. Venice and Rome were alarmed. Everywhere, in Croatia, Istria, and Dalmatia, even deep into Austria, people no longer felt secure against the raids of Ottoman bands. Emperor Frederick III ordered that the fortifications of the cities be reinforced. The unfortunate policy of the Curia, which had set the Hungarians, who alone would have been able to resist the Turks, to fighting the Hussites was bearing bitter fruit.

All the wilder was the rejoicing in Venice when news came from the Levant of a victory over the Ottomans. For three days the bells were rung throughout the territory of the republic; everywhere processions and festivals were organized. Bonfires were lighted on the tops of towers and in the squares. The whole city burst into jubilation at learning that serious damage had at last been inflicted on the detested Turk. But what had happened? When early in the summer Niccolò da Canale, the new *provveditore* of Negropont, a man "born to read books but not to be a sailor," arrived in Negropont, then the Aegean base of the Venetian fleet, he immediately attacked the Macedonian coast with twenty ships, devastated and pillaged the Turkish coastal settlements, especially in the region of Thessaloniki, and after adding six ships to his squadron made for Lemnos and Imroz. On the morning of July 14, 1469, he attacked Enez, near the mouth of the Maritsa River. No sooner had his sailors scaled the almost undefended walls and battered the gates in than they unleashed a frightful massacre, in which even the Christian population found no mercy. Atrocities were committed that gravely harmed the Christian name. But since Niccolò da Canale could not remain forever in Enez, he set the city on fire after his men had thoroughly looted it, and transformed it into a desolate heap of ashes. Along with an enormous amount of booty, 2,000 prisoners and 200 Greek women, including many nuns, were carried off to Negropont. Many others had died in battle. Immediately thereafter a like fate befell the Anatolian port of Yeni Foça, after da Canale had incurred considerable losses in the course of an unsuccessful attack on Eski Foça. The *provveditore* now sailed around the Morea, put into Koroni and Methoni, then turned north and occupied Aiyion in the Bay of Patras, which the Turks had already abandoned and which he immediately fortified. Turks who had hastened to the scene to repel the Venetians were thrown back with losses, and six galleys remained in the waters of Patras for defensive purposes.

These events in Greek waters, which of course were without lasting effect and merely raised the sultan's rage to the point of frenzy, were the occasion for the Venetian rejoicings.

In August, Niccolò da Canale was instructed by the Signoria to send a messenger to Uzun Hasan to inform him that the republic was overjoyed at his recent victories (within the last two years he had increased his power tremendously by defeating the Black Sheep confederation and adding all of Persia to his empire), to encourage him to make war on the Ottomans, and to remind him that his wife, daughter of the Comnenus emperor, was a relative of the duke of Naxos and the king of Cyprus, both of whom were *nobili* of Venice.

Only a short time before, the Venetians had once again cherished the hope of arriving at an understanding with the sultan. This time it was Countess Catherine, commonly called Cantacuzena, widow of Ulrich of Cilli, who from her home, presumably in southern Macedonia—for it was there that she died about 1487 and was buried in the convent of Konča near Strumica—had written to the Venetian council suggesting that it purchase the garment of Christ, then in the possession of the Turks, and other relics, and through her sister Mara enter into peace negotiations with the sultan, Mara's stepson. The College of Sages (*Savi*) was enthusiastic about both suggestions and recommended that the countess send "her" monk to her sister as usual, to induce her to do everything in her power to dispose the sultan to make peace. For the present, at least, the whole plan went up in smoke, as had those preceding it. Nothing had ever so infuriated Mehmed as the Venetian attack on Enez. The naval undertakings of the Signoria were becoming more and more of a thorn in his flesh, and for this reason he concentrated all his attention on the enlargement and equipment of his fleet, which he manned, apart from the Turks, chiefly with Greeks, the most accomplished sailors of the day, and Jews. As supreme commander of the fleet the sultan appointed Mahmud Pasha, the former grand vizier, whom he called back from exile in Thrace.

The enormous loss of life caused by the plague of 1469, especially in Istanbul, confronted the sultan once again with a difficult task of repopulation. The Florentine colony in particular had suffered alarming losses. Hardly a household was exempt from the contagion, and the list of the dead that has come down to us includes the names of many respected merchant families settled in Pera. Among the victims was Mehmed's friend Vermiglio, the son of Francesco Capponi.

In general, the Florentine settlement was now going through a period of grave crisis. In 1466, when Benedetto Dei played intercepted Venetian letters into the sultan's hands, its merchants, in collaboration with the Genoese of Galata, had begun to exploit the hostility of the Porte toward Venice, and were, as we have seen, none too particular about the methods employed. The relations between the Florentine colony and the sultan became increasingly close, to the great displeasure and detriment of other Italian states, who rightly feared serious damage to their own trade. The reaction in Italy was so violent that in the fall of 1467 the commune of Florence forbade its ships to go to Istanbul and recalled the heads of the commercial firms in question, who hastily called in their credit and boarded Anconitan ships with all their possessions. Off Methoni the ships were captured and thoroughly pillaged by Venetian vessels. Of course the Signoria had no difficulty in finding a justification for this action. It declared that the Florentine merchants had provided the sultan with arms for his war on Venice. This accusation was probably unfounded. The maritime trade between Florence and Istanbul fell off sharply and continued to do so until 1472. Only in that year were two Florentine merchant vessels to set sail again for the Golden Horn.

The sultan was extremely indignant over the inexplicable cessation of trade. But in answer to his remonstrances he was told that not only the Florentine colonies in Turkey but also the ports used by the Florentine ships had been hard hit by the plague. Actually the lapse in trade proved to be only temporary. Undoubtedly the Florentine colony in Pera, which was always administered by hard-working consuls (to September 1472, Mainardo Ubaldini; to April 1476, Carlo Baroncelli; after September 1477, Lorenzo Carducci) was alarmingly reduced by the plague and other events; many Florentine citizens fled, leaving their property behind them. Ample measures were taken to protect this property, especially as many business establishments continued to operate. In 1469 Mainardo Ubaldini, then consul, reported no less than fifty Florentine commercial firms in the Ottoman Empire. During the absence of the directors who had been recalled, the substitutes who handled their affairs apparently were not very scrupulous, for on March 22, 1474, the commune of Florence was obliged to call on the *Gran Turco* for help.

In the course of the disorders, which seem to have occurred in 1469, even the Florentine consul fell under grave suspicion. On April 29 of that year his home government assured him of its special confidence. At the same time it urged him to take measures against insubordinate persons and to make sure that the disorder, which seems to have diminished by that time, did not spread. In spite of this difficult situation the prospect of large and rapid profits continued to attract Florentine citizens to the Ottoman Empire, and at no time did they forfeit the sultan's favor. Precisely in 1469 Mehmed appears to have granted them important commercial privileges. For on numerous occasions the commune expressed its "undying gratitude" to the sultan and praised him as a "benefactor."

In Turkey, if we can trust the statements of Domenico Malipiero, the Venetian captain and historian, who witnessed or gained firsthand information concerning many important events in the course of his frequent military and diplomatic missions, the entire year of 1469 was taken up with feverish naval preparations.[36] The sultan constructed a large number of vessels, evidently intended to transport an army. In December

---

[36] The author of the *Cronaca* compiled also the *Annali Veneti*, detailing events of the years 1457 to 1500, published in *Archivio storico italiano* 7 (Florence, 1843).

1469 the production of ship's biscuit was so accelerated and increased as to drain the market of flour, leaving the population without bread. The infuriated populace protested outside the Porte and received assurance that their needs would be met. In Bursa quantities of charcoal were prepared for gunpowder. On January 29, 1470, a messenger from Gelibolu arrived in Chios, and communicated to the Maona an order from Admiral Mahmud Pasha to send to Gelibolu sixty caulkers as well as all the oared vessels in the region. A large number of *azaps*, one out of every five, were enrolled in the navy. Letters from Pera reported intensive efforts to prepare the Ottoman fleet for action: 100,000 men were said to have been enlisted. Large food depots were set up. The terrified Maonesi quickly took defensive measures on their island and sent an emissary to the Porte with tribute. Fearing an attack, because they had already expected one the previous year, they hurriedly put the fortifications in order, armed the population, dug trenches, and strengthened the damaged walls.

The Chiots had indeed every reason to take defensive measures and to be prepared for the worst. During the year 1469, Mehmed had apparently tried to gain possession of the island by intrigue, though the background of this affair has not been fully clarified. The sultan made use of a Venetian resident of Pera by the name of Callimacho Romano, who worked hand in hand with a certain Marcantonio Perusin on Chios. The sultan circulated the rumor that he was fitting out a squadron of 250 sailing vessels, including 120 galleys, for action in the Black Sea. News of these preparations reached Chios, where it provoked great consternation. All available ships were detained, and no one was allowed to leave the island. One day a ship anchored in the roadstead with letters from Pera; supposing them to be from its envoy, the Maona sent a cutter to receive them. It soon turned out, however, that they were not from the envoy, but that Callimacho Romano was trying to smuggle these letters into Chios. They were handed back to him, and he was questioned about their content. The Chiots thus discovered his stratagem and the sultan's intentions. Marcantonio Perusin and his accomplices were put to the torture. They made a full confession and were hanged. A certain Galeazzo Giustiniani, who was also involved in the plot, was arrested and torn to pieces by the populace. At the news that his plan had failed, the sultan, so the source maintains, withdrew his ships and abandoned the whole undertaking. If we could know for sure to which of the numerous branches of the Giustiniani family this Galeazzo belonged (possibly the Giustiniani-Longo, among whom the first name is frequent), it would perhaps throw more light on the conspiracy, in which a member of the house of Giustiniani must have played a leading part.

As is only to be expected in such times of anxiety and uncertainty, all manner of rumors and contradictory reports reached the West by the most divergent, sometimes dubious channels. Often the wish was father to the thought, as when news came from Anatolia that numerous tribes had joined forces with Uzun Hasan, the traditional enemy of the Ottomans, with a view to retaking Trabzon (Trebizond). Another story: Mehmed's first-born son, Prince Bayezid, governor of Amasya and in command of the border troops, had been compelled by his father to execute his teacher (*lâla*) Hayreddin Hïzïr Pasha, commandant of the city of Amasya, because the latter had received emissaries from Uzun Hasan; they had appeared in Amasya with sumptuous gifts to arrange a marriage between one of Uzun Hasan's daughters and the Ottoman prince, Bayezid Çelebi. Mehmed was furious, because he had not been kept informed and because the presents of the lord of the White Sheep had not been passed on to him. According to another version, the sultan had commanded Hïzïr Pasha to poison his own son because Mehmed harbored a "certain suspicion" against him; when the suspicion proved to be unfounded, he had retracted the order, made over the city of Trabzon to Bayezid Çelebi, and called on him to take up arms against Uzun Hasan, while Hïzïr Pasha was put to death. All that can be inferred from the very meager Ottoman sources in this connection is that Hïzïr Pasha disappeared from Amasya at that time. It is also a well-attested historical fact that a short time later Uzun Hasan threatened Sivas and Tokat and gave the Ottomans ground for extreme vigilance in Anatolia. A number of incidents that took place in Amasya during the governorship of Prince Bayezid show clearly that his relations with the sultan were permanently strained. When, some time in 1476, to cite only one example, Bayezid Çelebi received an order from his father to kill the scholar Muayyedzade, who had incurred disfavor, he informed the mullah of the danger, provided him with money, and helped him to escape. Father and son were so essentially different in character that fruitful collaboration between them was unthinkable. There is little doubt that the friction between them burst into the open during the last years of Mehmed's life and almost certainly at the time of his sudden death.[37]

Along the coast of Rumelia the sultan's war preparations were proceeding so rapidly and on so large a scale that no one doubted the imminence of an important naval undertaking. The Venetians had long foreseen the

[37] Further on the relations between Bayezid and his father, see below, pp. 404ff. Cf. H. J. Kissling, "Aus der Geschichte des Chalvetijje-Ordens," *Zeitschrift der Deutschen Morgenländischen Gesellschaft* 103 (1953), 245–251.

danger of an attack on Negropont, the "glory and splendor of Venice," which contemporary German city chronicles describe as "four times better than Constantinople." News soon trickled out that enormous cannon were being cast in Thessaloniki, clearly indicating that the sultan was planning a "campaign against Europe." As his preparations neared completion, Mehmed threw secrecy to the winds. The Venetians were well aware that if Negropont were lost all their remaining Levantine possessions would be in great danger.

The Signoria had kept well informed about the Turkish naval preparations. As early as 1466 Antonio Michiel, holder of the alum monopoly, had sent information from Pera and in the winter of 1469–1470 every effort was made to reinforce the republic's sea power. The squadron wintering in Negropont was increased to 35 triremes. One day news came that more than 100 Ottoman triremes had gathered off Tenedos and were being joined by additional vessels each day. Niccolò da Canale, the new captain general of the sea, was soon able to ascertain through scouts that the Turkish fleet was already off Imroz and had taken on such proportions that it was no longer possible to count the vessels. "The sea is like a forest. To hear this said seems incredible, but to see it is terrible," wrote a seaman in a letter home. To check on the truth of these reports, the Venetian admiral first sent ten ships to Aegean waters, but with orders to give battle only if the enemy force should number no more than 60 triremes, in which event he would immediately follow with the rest of his squadron. A swift sailing vessel that was sent ahead soon confirmed the statements of the islanders and at the sight of this gigantic forest of ships the Venetians quickly took flight. The Turks pursued the ten galleys as far as the island of Skiros east of Negropont, where they stormed a coastal fortress. Without resistance the Ottoman triremes, with which the Venetian unit dared exchange only a few shots from the distance, reached Negropont and reduced to ashes several coastal cities, such as Stira and Vasilikon, in the vicinity of Chalcis, the capital.

These preliminary skirmishes, which already extended to the island of Euboea and endangered this vital Venetian base, showed that large-scale operations were to be expected as soon as the main Turkish fleet, which for the moment was still in the eastern Aegean, should appear. Reduced almost entirely to her own resources and short of funds, Venice was placed in a desperate situation by the sultan's gigantic preparations. According to one report from the islands, the sea was covered with Turkish ships over a stretch of six miles.

Early in June 1470, Mehmed's army and the main squadron of his fleet started westward. While the sultan in person was leading an enormous army through Thessaly to Boeotia, his grand admiral Mahmud Pasha put out of the Dardanelles and on June 5 landed on Imroz, whose *rettore*, Marco Zeno, died in the ensuing battle. Three days later Mahmud Pasha stormed Lemnos but was unable to take either that island or Skiros, which he attacked on the Pentecost (June 10). On June 15 the Turkish fleet sailed unhindered into the Euboic Sea. Niccolò da Canale, who had at his disposal 36 galleys and six freight vessels, was obliged to risk battle with 300 ships—450, according to other accounts—including 108 large galleys. He anchored off Cape Mandili (Mandhelo) at the extreme southern tip of Euboea.

More than 70,000 landing troops were said to have been aboard Mahmud Pasha's ships and the sultan was reported to have brought 120,000 men to the vicinity of Negropont by the land route. As usual the figures are undoubtedly very much exaggerated, but the vast numerical superiority of the Ottomans cannot be questioned.

The siege of Negropont, the capital (the Chalcis of antiquity, now Khalkis), soon began. The city was strongly and extensively fortified, especially on the sea side, and the Venetians had put its defenses into excellent condition. The resolute and adequate garrison was well supplied. The supreme command was held by Paolo Erizzo, the *bailo*—the title borne here too by the highest administrative official. To help him the Signoria had only a short time before sent Captain Alviso Calbo, who shared command of the land troops with the recently recalled Giovanni Badoer, both men of great circumspection and personal courage. The subaltern commanders, as we shall soon see, were far less reliable.

As soon as he arrived, the sultan built a bridge of ships across the channel separating the island from the mainland. For only from the west was it possible to attack the island, which runs like a long bulwark along the east coast of Greece. The harbors are all on the west side, while the eastern side consists almost entirely of steep cliffs. Unfortunately the captain general took his squadron to Candia (Herakleion) on Crete for provisions and possibly for new troops while the bridge was being built.

Two Ottoman assaults on June 25 and 30 were thrown back with heavy losses—reportedly not less than 16,000 men and thirty galleys—for the assailants. No more successful were subsequent assaults on July 5 and 8, which again were said to have cost the Turks thousands of lives. Although every preparation had been made for stubborn resistance, the besieged were exhausted by their untold exertions and no longer equal to the situation. All hoped for help from the squadron of Niccolò da Canale, but this was absent at the decisive moment. He alone would have been capable of averting the doom of Negropont, for the fresh ships fitted out in

Venice at the news of the Turks' appearance were far too late in setting out. When at last the besieged saw their home fleet, increased by a few Cretan vessels, approaching with full sail, and when on July 11 fourteen Venetian triremes and two freight ships sailed to within a mile of the city, the defenders thought the worst of their troubles were over. They believed that Niccolò da Canale would now destroy the bridge of ships and so prevent the Turks from bringing supplies from the mainland. He did nothing of the kind. The captain general remained at anchor with his ships off Santa Chiara. In despair the defenders signaled to him from the walls. A black flag was hoisted on the highest tower of the citadel. All in vain. When even his own captains urged him to take action, da Canale replied that he could do nothing until he had gathered the rest of the fleet. Thereupon one of his ships, commanded by Antonio Ottobon, dashed into the mass of enemy vessels and safely reached the harbor, though of course his feat of daring could not relieve the situation of the hemmed-in defenders. When the Cretan ships wished to follow him, the captain general gave strict orders that no one should move until the whole squadron was assembled. With this order "Messer Niccolò da Canale, Dottor" sealed the fate of Negropont.

Mehmed was discouraged by the failure of his assaults and by the heavy losses he had incurred. At the sight of the Venetian fleet, the size of which he no doubt greatly overestimated, he thought of abandoning the siege. The urgent pleas of Mahmud Pasha decided him to attempt a last assault. It began on July 11 and ended on the morning of July 12 with the capture of Negropont. Here again treason was at work. Conspiracies had long been afoot, and only a few days earlier a captain by the name of Tommaso Schiavo, a Dalmatian, and his friend Luca from Curzola, had been surprised by a vigilant woman as they were trying to admit the Turks to the city. Both were immediately hanged and their corpses were displayed outside the *rettore*'s palace as a warning. A Florentine accomplice fled to the Turks in time. On the day of the final assault the weakest point in the city walls was pointed out to the Ottomans by another captain of the garrison, one Fiorio di Nardone.

As usual, Mehmed had offered large rewards to those who should be first to scale the walls. The whole population took part in the desperate battle that now developed. Old men, women, and children had taken up arms. Heaps of dead women were later found among the fallen. The butchery continued for all of five hours, and when early on July 12 the Janissaries entered the chained-off streets through the Porta Giudecca and the Porta Burchiana, they had to pay for every step forward with streams of blood. When finally the decimated and weary garrison threw itself on the mercy of the conquerors, they were cut down without quarter. Paolo Erizzo, Alvise Calbo, and Giovanni Badoer all met their death. The Turks sliced the *bailo* through the waist after informing him that they had promised to spare his head but not his flanks.

Those of the Italian defenders who had come through the battle alive were ruthlessly massacred. The Greeks were taken into slavery and carried off to Istanbul. After the fall of the capital the whole island and the lesser islands round about were soon taken by the Ottomans. Among the few to survive was Gian-Maria Angiolello from Vicenza, whose brother was killed in the battle. He was dragged off to Istanbul over the land route in the sultan's train, a circumstance to which we owe a straightforward account, incomplete but in many respects unequaled, of those stormy times in the Ottoman Empire.[38]

When news of the conquest of Negropont reached the Morea, the entire population was seized with terror. Aiyion, which had been occupied by the Venetians shortly before, was evacuated and humbly pleaded for mercy. At the sight of the crescent flags on the walls of Negropont, the Venetian fleet had beat a hasty retreat. A Turkish attack on Navplion was unsuccessful.

The confusion in Venice knew no bounds when news of the fall of Negropont arrived on July 30. Solemn processions were organized, prayers offered up, and on the public squares speeches were made in an effort to encourage the desperate population, which thought the end of the republic was at hand. The council of *pregadi* decided to continue the war with the Turks under all circumstances and by all possible means, but to relieve Niccolò da Canale of his command and bring him to trial. They unanimously appointed Pietro Mocenigo to replace him as captain general of the sea. Mocenigo, it was hoped, would revive the confidence of the subjects and allies of the Signoria, which had been dangerously shaken. He received orders to take his post immediately and, in accordance with a decision of the Council of Ten, to throw his predecessor in chains and bring him back to Venice. Once again entering on the scene, Francesco Filelfo attempted in two letters (September 1470 and May 1471), addressed to Bernardo Giustiniani and Alvise Foscarini, to defend his friend Dr. Niccolò da Canale against the popular vengeance, but was unable to save him. The former captain general paid for his cowardice and pusillanimity with lifelong banishment to Portogruaro (in the region of Friuli). Indeed, the Venetian squadron had played an inglorious role. On its flight from Negropont, it hid in the harbors of Methoni and Koroni

---

[38] Babinger refers to Angiolello's *Historia turchesca* (see above, book 1, n. 47).

and a number of the sailors threatened, for want of pay, to desert to the Turks.

On August 7 Gherardo de Colli, the Milanese ambassador to the Signoria of Venice, wrote to his duke that he had seen the proud *nobili* of the city in tears as though their own women and children had been killed. "All Venice," he wrote a few days later, "is in the grip of horror; the inhabitants, half dead with fear, are saying that to give up all their possessions on the mainland would have been a lesser evil." "The glory and prestige of Venice are destroyed," wrote the chronicler Domenico Malipiero. "Our pride is humbled."

After losing its most important, wealthiest, and most profitable possession in the Levant and a distressing number of its best commanders on land and sea, after almost seven years of war with the Ottomans, which devoured roughly 700,000 gold ducats a year and gave promise of ever greater expenditures and losses, the republic had not the slightest hope of bringing this crippling war to a victorious conclusion. It was not show trials, or the absurd imprecations of the humanists against the blood-thirsty Grand Turk, or calls for a universal crusade of Christendom that could help the Signoria in those days of disillusionment and despair. The sultan was still alive to the lure of Italy with Rome and its priests. But, as we read in a letter sent by the commune of Florence to the pope on August 8, 1470, what ultimately interested him was "dominion over the globe and not only over Italy and the Urbs [Rome]." A sage observation, which was not translated into the slightest activity, although, if Benedetto Dei is to be believed, Florence alone lost 700 of her citizens and 400,000 florins to her Turkish friends by the fall of Negropont.[39]

Mehmed did not immediately turn his back on Negropont. On the day after its capture he gave orders to bring before him all prisoners bearing beards, some 800 in number. According to the eyewitness Gian-Maria Angiolello, whose captor presented him to the sultan as a slave, Mehmed had them all kneel down in a circle with their hands bound. Then they were beheaded. Women and girls, as well as boys over eighteen, were sold, given away as presents, or exchanged by their captors. On the second and third day after the conquest every hiding place in the city and throughout the island was searched for fugitives and valuables. On July 16 the sultan gave orders to clean up the whole countryside; the dead

[39] Further details of the fall of Negropont with references to the primary sources are given by V. L. Ménage in "Eğriboz" (the Turkish name of the island), *EI²* II, 691. For the response of the pope to the siege and capture of Negropont, see Pastor, *History of the Popes* IV, 174–183. See also Schwoebel, *The Shadow of the Crescent*, 157–159 and 167–168.

were thrown into the sea, the ditches were cleared, and the damaged city walls repaired. No one dared resist the order. Iskender Bey, perhaps a Mihaloğlu, was left behind with adequate forces as commander of the island.

On July 26 the army moved off to northward. The crimson tent of the sultan, which had been pitched near the Church of Santa Chiara, was taken down. Angiolello gives a detailed account of the return journey, in which he participated. Each day, so he tells us, the army covered some twenty miles, whereas on the way to Negropont the sultan, who wished men and horses to arrive in good fighting condition, had kept the daily marches down to eight or ten miles. The army stopped at Thebes (July 28–29), Athens (July 29–30), Levadhia, Salona (today Amfissa), Bodinitza (Mendenitza; August 1). After passing through Zeitun (today Lamia) and Neopatras (today Badra), Mehmed camped on the plain of Thermopylai; on August 3 he marched to the castle of Dhomokos (Domoko) and from there, on the following day, to the Thessalian plain. On August 5 he stopped at the castle of "La Phersa" (Farsala, Pharsalos?), reached Larisa on August 6, Küstenje on the next day, camped in Platamona on August 9, on August 10 in Kitros, and was outside Thessaloniki on August 11. On the following day the Turks marched by way of Mount Bodanos, where they camped, to Serrai (August 13), then continued in view of the Holy Mountain, for which the Turks had "great reverence," to Filibecik, the ancient Philippi (August 15), and to Kavalla (August 16). On August 19 they passed through Gümülcine (Komotini) and arrived in Dimotika on August 22. In the old Byzantine castle there lived, so Angiolello relates, a sister of Sultan Mehmed, whom he had banished. Much later Charles XII of Sweden was to stay there for almost two years (1713–1714) when he evaded his pursuers. According to Angiolello, Mehmed's sister was a sadistic madwoman who once had twenty slave girls beheaded in order to see whether they would remain alive.

Even now she wished to have [heads] cut off, in order to measure her power with her brother's. She was also a harlot and bought young slaves who satisfied her desires. Then she had them killed lest they accuse her. If the Grand Turk had known it, he would have had her killed; even her father, the sultan Murad, had disregarded her in his last will, and she had to hold her brother in honor and remain obedient to him. After the Grand Turk had won his victory of Negropont, some of his lords reminded him of her, and she so cajoled him that he released her from her prison and married her to one of his slaves called Esebeg [i.e. Isa Bey], who was a relative of the Palaeologi, the emperors of Constantinople.

In view of the large number of renegades belonging to this widely rami-
fied family, it is impossible to determine what scion of the Palaeologi, if
any, achieved this doubtful honor. Far more important for the light it
might throw on Mehmed's psychological heredity is the question of
whether the princess was a true sister or only a stepsister.

Mehmed did not remain in Dimotika for long, for on August 24 he
was already in Çirmen and on the 25th on the plain of Edirne, where
he seems to have rested for a few days. On August 30 he arrived in Havsa,
where a characteristic event took place. Some books had been stolen from
a foreign resident of the city. The thief was caught and impaled, but all
the inhabitants of Havsa, men and women, big and little, were driven to
Istanbul in a body; the town remained uninhabited until the sultan had
new settlers brought in from Karaman. On September 1 he stopped in
Baba Eski, on the next day in Sütlüce, and on the third in Karĭştĭran. In
this last place a new incident aroused one of the sultan's sudden rages.
He had one of his first commanders, a certain "Nasufbeg," i.e. Nasuh Bey,
an Albanian, virtually unmentioned in other contexts, brought before him
with his hands tied behind his back. Nasuh Bey, allegedly a man of
great reputation, possessed lands in eastern Anatolia not far from the
domain of Uzun Hasan. Someone had accused him of planning to rebel
against the sultan and to desert to Uzun Hasan. The mere accusation
sufficed to make Mehmed give the order that Nasuh Bey be cut to pieces
in his presence and that of the whole army. Seized by the hands and feet,
he was butchered with a short broadsword.

On September 5, the sultan marched to Istanbul by way of Çekmece.

Before the year 1470 drew to a close, Mehmed "settled his accounts" with
the grand vizier Rum Mehmed Pasha. The exact date is not established
but can be approximately inferred from the fact that, while the sultan's
main army was marching on Negropont, a raid was made on Karaman
for the purpose of stifling a rebellion stirred up by Kasĭm Bey. Kasĭm,
who had fled to Cairo, made attempts, so the story was, to regain Karaman. The grand vizier was charged with crushing the rebellion. He
shamelessly plundered and persecuted the two cities of Laranda and
Ereğli. When the inhabitants of Laranda besought Mehmed Pasha to
spare their mosques and schools, pointing out that they and their property
constituted a pious foundation (*vakif*) dedicated to the Arabian city of
Medina, the burial place of the Prophet, he had the petitioners butchered.
Then his greed led him against the Turkmen tribe of the Varsak Eli.
In the stony passes of Cilicia his cavalry was ambushed by nomads in

command of Uyuz Bey, a Varsak chieftain, who cut down more than half of the Ottoman troops. The survivors were obliged to withdraw northward, leaving the whole of their Karamanian booty behind them.

Indignant over the conduct of Rum Mehmed Pasha, the sultan deposed him, perhaps in the autumn of 1470, and had him executed. He was buried in a *türbe* beside the small mosque endowed by him but probably completed only a year after his violent death, not far from the landing in Üsküdar (Scutari) across from Istanbul.[40]

Apart from his cruelty and greed, the Ottoman chronicles tell us next to nothing about the official activity of Mehmed Pasha, the Greek. He appears to have been a financial expert who introduced a system of tax farming (*mukataa*), which proved to be profitable but naturally aroused keen resentment among its victims. Immediately after the capture of Constantinople, when the Conqueror was bringing new settlers to the deserted city from all sides, he had levied a tax on the houses assigned to the new arrivals. The consequence was that many of the Moslem immigrants moved out again. The sultan subsequently abolished this house tax, but Rum Mehmed Pasha reintroduced it during his grand vizierate. In so doing, he pleased the sultan, who was always avid for gain, but certainly not the recent settlers affected by it. This property tax seems to have remained in force after the death of Mehmed Pasha.

In the Moslem year 875 (June 30, 1470, to June 19, 1471) the sultan minted new silver coins (*akçe*). For the year 1470 a Venetian register copied from Ottoman tax rolls lists 29,000 houses subject to taxation in Europe, a small number if we consider that less than half a century later 3,000,000 taxpayers were listed, though to be sure in the entire Ottoman Empire.[41]

Ishak Pasha, the former grand vizier under Murad II, who had been forced to marry one of Murad's widows, been banished to Anatolia, and been alternately shunned and consulted by Mehmed, was now called back to Istanbul from his exile in Inegöl (southeast of Bursa) and entrusted

---

[40] Details of the career of the grand vizier are given in "Mehmed Paşa, Rūm" (M. C. Şehabeddin Tekindağ), *IA* VII, 594–595. For the mosque see Ayverdi, *Fatih devri mimarisi*, 219–222.

[41] For estimates of the population of the Ottoman Empire in the late 15th and 16th centuries, see Ömer Lutfi Barkan, "Essai sur les données statistiques des registres de rencensement dans l'empire ottoman aux XVe et XVIe siècles," *Journal of Economic and Social History of the Orient* 1 (1957), 9–36. Cf. the same author's "Research on the Ottoman Fiscal Surveys," in *Studies in the Economic History of the Middle East*, ed. M. A. Cook (London, 1970), 163–171. For more on the *mukataa*, see below, p. 451.

with the imperial seal. In view of his age this solution gave little promise of permanence.[42]

"All Italy and all Christendom are in the same boat" (*In eadem navi, ut ajunt, omnis Italia et omnis Christianitas est*), wrote Cristoforo Moro, doge of Venice, in a letter dated August 22, 1470. With these words, which must have been almost proverbial at the time, the writer implored Galeazzo-Maria Sforza, duke of Milan, to consider the terrible situation of all Christendom since the fall of Negropont. "We are all in the same danger," the letter continues, "and there is no coast, no region, no place in Italy which, however remote and secluded it may seem, can be considered more secure than any other. This pestilence and this conflagration are spreading continuously, and perhaps there is no part of the body of Christendom that they will not seize hold of and infect, unless measures are taken immediately." Words of such persuasive power might have been expected to bring results. But Sforza would have liked best to reply by invading the republic's terra firma; a strong party in his entourage was pressing him to benefit by the misfortunes of Venice to win back the territory that Milan had ceded in 1454. An incursion of Milanese troops was already feared in Bergamo, Cremona, and Brescia. Fortunately for the Signoria, King Ferrante of Naples advised the Milanese envoy that in view of the Turkish peril he refused to participate in a campaign against Venice. But less than ever could Venice hope for help from the other Italian states or from Hungary.

On August 25, 1470, Pope Paul II informed all the Christian powers of the fall of Negropont and painted a gloomy picture of the dangers menacing from the East. He pleaded urgently for help and tried to appease the feuds of the Italian states, especially Venice and Milan. On September 18 he invited all the rulers of the peninsula to send delegates to Rome as quickly as possible to discuss an alliance against the Turks, whereby each of the Italian states might preserve its independence. These negotiations, which dragged on for several weeks and several times threatened to founder, culminated on December 22, 1470, in the establishment of the League of Lodi, a general offensive and defensive alliance against the Turks. Public prayers of thanksgiving and bonfires were prematurely ordered in Rome. But the pope's joyous expectations ended in bitter disappointment. Milan and Florence, which had never seriously intended to participate in a campaign against the Turks, were to blame. Galeazzo-Maria Sforza carped at the text of the treaty

[42] The completely different chronology of the grand vizierate proposed by Inalcïk ("Mehmed the Conqueror," 414–415) should be kept in mind.

and withheld his confirmation. The Florentine ambassador actually left Rome without signing the treaty. Neither of the two powers wished to become involved in a difficult and expensive adventure.[43]

The situation was no better in France and Germany. King Louis XI was hostile to Paul II and unwilling to enter into negotiations of any kind with him. In Germany no action could be taken before the "Great Christian Diet," which was to meet in Regensburg at the end of June 1471. As his legate the pope sent the cardinal Francesco Piccolomini, a nephew of Pius II, whose memory was still revered at the imperial court. The Regensburg diet came to no agreement on the Turkish question. Four weeks of haggling brought no more results than the previous diets. The imperial idea had long since paled to a shadow and was powerless to withstand the selfish separatist policies of the estates. Mehmed, whose spies kept him closely informed of developments at the Regensburg diet, the largest within memory of man, was reported to have said that the Germans were indeed a warlike race, but that the crusade would come to nothing.

On July 26, 1471, Pope Paul died unexpectedly. Cardinal Francesco della Rovere took his place as Sixtus IV (1471–1484). Under him the idea of a crusade assumed world importance for the last time.

If the sultan really believed there was no danger that the Christian powers would unite after the fall of Negropont, there would be no reason to take seriously his supposed attempts to make peace with Venice in the first half of October 1470. But the fact remains that Mehmed engaged the services of his stepmother Mara and also of her sister Catherine, who had been in touch with Venice the preceding year. Early in October two envoys from the two Serbian women presented themselves to the Signoria. Each declared independently that before the sultan had marched on Negropont the ladies had tried on their own initiative to influence him in favor of peace, because they were Christians and as such devoted to all Christians, but especially to the Signoria. Mehmed had answered that the time was inopportune, because he had incurred enormous expense for a military venture. After the capture of Negropont they had repeated their plea to the sultan and learned that he was prepared to make peace if Venice should send negotiators to the Porte. On the strength of these communications the senate decided to send Niccolò Cocco and Francesco Capello to Istanbul and to demand nothing less than the return of Negropont. If the sultan consented, Venice was willing to pay as much

[43] References to the pope's several letters are in Pastor, *History of the Popes* IV, 178.

as 250,000 gold ducats in five annual installments, but only on condition that the islands still in Venetian possession be guaranteed against an Ottoman attack. The grand vizier, for his part, stipulated two conditions for peace: Venice must cede Lemnos and the other Aegean islands, and further pay an annual 100,000 ducats in head tax. The two Venetian plenipotentiaries replied that the republic would rather lose the entire terra firma than pay tribute to anyone. Niccolò Cocco left Istanbul disappointed and outraged at the Turkish pretensions; his companion Francesco Capello had just died in the Ottoman capital. Cocco took a fishing bark to Lemnos, where he boarded a galley bound for Venice.[44]

In the middle of all these negotiations Venice received a strange offer from Mesih Pasha, commander of the fleet in the Dardanelles. A son-in-law of Alexius Span, who had taken part in negotiations with the Porte before, communicated to Venice Mesih Pasha's offer to surrender the Dardanelles and the Turkish fleet under his command in return for 40,000 ducats, but the Council of Ten informed the Turkish traitor, who aspired to become ruler over the Morea, that 10,000 ducats ought to be enough. Thus Mesih Pasha's attempt to use his power against the sultan and obtain for himself a secure position in the West came to nothing.

But Venice was not at all above making use of traitors. After negotiations with the Porte broke down, the Council of Ten resorted to a less innocuous means of dealing with the sultan, namely, poison. In this they were not alone among Italian states, but it was they who showed the greatest ingenuity and perseverance. The records of the time make this very clear. From April 1456 to July 1479, Venice set in motion no less than fourteen plots to poison the sultan, though none ever reached the stage of execution. In the course of these twenty-three years the Ten left no stone unturned in their effort to put the sultan out of the way, and spared no expense. No reward was too great and no prospective assassin was rejected as unfit. Indeed, the most fantastic adventurers offered their services to murder the sultan: a seaman from Trogir (Trau), a Carthusian monk, a Florentine nobleman by the name of Francesco Baroncello, a Pole from Cracow, a Catalan, an Albanian barber, and now the sultan's Jewish physician and financial adviser, Maestro Iacopo of Gaeta, who succeeded for three whole decades in retaining the sultan's otherwise so fickle favor and even in becoming a pasha with the rank of vizier.

[44] The chronology of events surrounding the mission of Cocco and Capello to Istanbul is laid out by V. L. Ménage, "Seven Ottoman Documents from the Reign of Mehemmed II," 82–83 and 101–106. The first of the documents, a letter of May 24, 1471, in Italian from the sultan to the Venetian doge, demands the return of Lemnos, the region of the Maina in the southern Peloponnese, and Krujë. There is no specific mention of annual cash payments.

The influential position of Maestro Iacopo at the sultan's court had long been known in Venice. He seems to have been born in Gaeta between 1425 and 1430. What led him to leave his Italian home we do not know. But if we consider the situation of the Jewish physicians of Italy in the middle of the fifteenth century, when Pope Nicholas V deprived the Jews and "Saracens" of all professional privileges and forbade Catholics to accept treatment from Jews lest their sons be perverted, it does not seem so surprising that the young maestro, who had probably studied medicine in Italy, should have sought his fortune abroad. Under Murad II he became court physician in Edirne and was retained in the same capacity by Mehmed. He accompanied the sultan to Istanbul, where he soon seems to have made a name for himself, thanks to his financial as well as his medical skill. He became first chamberlain to the sultan and accompanied him on his campaigns. In Istanbul he seems never to have left Mehmed's side. Iacopo remained in constant touch with his Italian compatriots, especially with the Venetians, who as early as 1457 sent him thirty-two ells of the finest crimson velvet, in order that he might intercede for them at the Porte. He frequented the houses of the *baili* in Pera and must have been the source of many of the reports they sent to the Signoria. He was no great stickler for the truth: witness his communication to the *bailo* in the autumn of 1465 to the effect that Mehmed had turned Christian. Benedetto Dei also made contact with him and even journeyed overland with him to Dubrovnik, probably in 1468. There Maestro Iacopo tried to procure medical books, namely, Latin translations of basic Arabic works, to help him in his treatment of the ailing sultan.[45]

It was in 1471 that Venice first approached Maestro Iacopo with the suggestion that he put Mehmed out of the way by poison. The intermediary seems to have been one Lando degli Albizzi, a political refugee from Florence. He was a member of a great noble family, then suffering extreme persecution as enemies of the Medici. Lando seems to have fled to Istanbul, where, finding himself short of money, he cast around for a source of income. (At about the same time another Florentine, Francesco Baroncello, brother of Carlo Baroncello, the Florentine consul in Pera, offered to set the sultan's war fleet on fire, for which service he asked the very modest reward of 400 ducats, payment to be guaranteed by a bank.) Sent by Maestro Iacopo, Lando degli Albizzi arrived in Venice in the middle of September 1471; there he went into hiding at the house of the ambassador of the duke of Mantua and got in touch with

---

[45] For recent studies on Iacopo, see above, book 2, n. 15. For the assassination plots, see especially Babinger's "Ja'qub Pascha, ein Leibarzt Mehmeds II," *Rivista degli Studi Orientali* 26 (1951).

the Council of Ten. Through Lando the sultan's physician had pledged himself to make an attempt on Mehmed's life in the course of the period from March to May 1472. For this he demanded outright 10,000 ducats, which were granted him unanimously and without hesitation, plus an additional 25,000 ducats if the murder were successful, because he would have to abandon all his belongings in Istanbul and set himself up elsewhere. Lando degli Albizzi was promised 500 ducats a year if the plan should succeed and 1,000 ducats if he should bring the news of the murder to Venice in person. The Signoria also held out a promise that it would intercede with the Florentine government, and in particular with Lorenzo de' Medici, to allow Lando to return to Florence and recover his confiscated property. Lando's conversations with the Council of Ten went on for some time, and the council showed increasing generosity. In the end Maestro Iacopo was promised a security of 260,000 pieces of coined gold in the event that the Venetians should not fulfill their obligations within a month of the successful murder, Venetian citizenship for himself and his descendants, and exemption from all taxes. In addition to the above-mentioned rewards, the Florentine go-between was guaranteed the rights of a Venetian citizen. Both Iacopo and Lando were to receive letters written and sealed by the doge, Cristoforo Moro. Their wording has come down to us. These documents constitute one of the last official acts of the doge—he died on November 10, 1471—as well as the last known trace of Lando degli Albizzi. Whether he ever reached Istanbul or whether he was captured on the way by the sultan's paid agents is a mystery that has not thus far been elucidated. All we know for certain is that Maestro Iacopo did not—any more than another Jewish physician by the name of Maestro Valco (Vlaco) at a later date (1475)— succeed in carrying out the Venetian plot, if indeed he had any intention of doing so.

The sultan spent almost the whole of 1471 in his capital. In all likelihood it was chiefly his physical condition that deprived him of his freedom of movement. Presumably in the summer, the large "new mosque" that bears his name was completed [pl. XIX a]. As we have seen, construction was begun in the spring of 1463 after Mehmed had taken the collapsing Church of the Holy Apostles away from the patriarch and torn it down, along with the neighboring church of Constantine Lips. Over a period of roughly eight years the mosque was built a short distance to the north of the ruins of the two churches by an architect of Christian origin, allegedly named Christodoulos, later in any case known as the "freedman" (atik) Sinan. In response to his employer's ambitious desires, the archi-

tect succeeded, thanks to his own talent and the sultan's money, in building an edifice magnificent for those times. The structure reflects the
transition from Byzantine to Ottoman art or, one might say, the posthumous renaissance of Byzantine architecture. In this mosque, which
probably more than any other was to serve as a shining example to all
subsequent Turkish builders, we find reminiscences of Christian architecture at a time when Hagia Sophia had already been remodeled in
accordance with the requirements of the Islamic cult.

The Mosque of the Conqueror (Fatih Camii) with its numerous dependencies forms an enormous rectangle. It is situated in the center of
a large park, today traversed by several streets. In front of it lies a rec-
tangular courtyard, which seems to have preserved its original form. The
eighteen columns of granite and marble, of varying thickness but all
without exception antique, support twenty-two cupolas. Above the barred,
marble-trimmed windows of the courtyard is a frieze, in which is grace-
fully engraved the first *sura* of the Koran, regarded as a symbol of the
power of Islam. In the interior, to the right of the main entrance, there
is a marble tablet, framed in lapis lazuli, which in golden letters traced
by a master of Islamic calligraphy bears the words (of doubtful authenticity) of the Prophet: "They will conquer Kostantiniya. Hail to the
prince and the army to whom this is given." The interior of the mosque
is of almost overpowering puritanical simplicity. The unobscured light
enters through numerous windows ordered in six superimposed rows.
The imitation of Hagia Sophia is obvious. But in the magnificence of
its plan, in the deliberate execution of the underlying idea, and in its
simplification on a scale a third smaller, the Conqueror's mosque, in the
opinion of connoisseurs, is superior even to the most famous of Istanbul
mosques. Around it lie numerous benevolent institutions established by
the sultan. The whole occupies a large area: the two courtyards, eight
colleges (*medreses*) with dormitories for students, the garden of the
tombs with its octagonal mausoleum and the catafalque of the Conqueror,
the *türbe* of his wife Gülbahar, the hospital and almshouse, the kitchens,
and a bath give the edifice an impressive, almost unique stamp.

Concerning the first architect, who allegedly bore the Christian name
of Christodoulos, numerous rumors and legends, almost all of them patent-
ly false, have been in circulation for centuries. As a reward for his work,
Mehmed was said to have made him a present of Küçük Cafer Street
and the Church of the Blessed Virgin Muchliotissa, both situated in
upper Fener. According to another tale, the sultan, enraged that the architect had made the new mosque lower than Aya Sofya and had sawed
off two of the largest and most beautiful columns, had his hands chopped

off, whereupon the cripple haled the sultan into court. Fortunately, an almost contemporaneous Ottoman chronicle gives a more truthful account. On September 12, 1471, Sinan was put to death at the sultan's order. His tomb has been preserved to this day in the courtyard of Kumrulu mosque, not far from the mosque of Nişancỉ Mehmed Pasha. Actually, two columns brought from a great distance at enormous expense seem to have proved too long, so that they had to be sawed off. When, not long ago, the large square in front of the Conqueror's mosque was paved with stone flags, the two truncated columns came to light. The old Ottoman chronicle does not tell us whether or not the architect was punished for mutilating the columns. But with a frankness unusual for those days the chronicler expressed sinister suspicions about the enormous expenditure incurred in the construction of the "new mosque":

> How the columns were then brought from distant lands and what sums were spent in transporting them, God alone knows. Who can indicate the sums expended in Istanbul for the new mosque, especially in view of the fact that all the columns and stones were ready and prepared. Merely to transport them from one place to another so much money was spent that God alone knows how much. . . . In those days [referring to former times] building was not done by means of coercion. All work was paid for. If today we wished to erect a building, we would collect money from all the provinces and cities and we would transplant architects and artisans by force from all the provinces. And none of those who have been transplanted, whether architect or artisan, ever returns to his home. We give the architect and workman building material and wages for supposedly three months and make them work for five or six months, in order that the funds may thereafter be squeezed out of the population; architect and workmen may be transplanted by force. . . . The Lord be praised, you have seen with your own eyes how Sultan Mehmed after long punishment imprisoned Sinan the builder, who had built the new mosque, eight *medreses*, almshouse kitchens, and hospitals. Was his sin so great that he deserved to die in such a way? Well, you have heard how many garments of honor were formerly given the masters. Now you can see what sort of "garments of honor" are bestowed today.

These reflections, written toward the end of the fifteenth century in a state where every inhabitant trembled before the unlimited power of the ruler, show an astonishing frankness and almost suggest modern social criticism. The chronicle makes it clear in any case that the architect of the Mosque of the Conqueror incurred the sultan's anger (we may assume, immediately after completing his unique work) and was put to death after having been maimed and imprisoned. That he was originally a Christian, or in any case a non-Moslem, is adequately proved by the name Sinan, which was then in principle adopted only by converts. The most celebrated of Ottoman architects, Sinan ibn Abd al-Mennan, who has been termed the "Michelangelo of the Ottomans," was a Greek or more probably an Armenian from the region of Kayseri in Anatolia. The presumed successor of the older Sinan—namely, the freedman Iyas ibn Abdullah, who began his activity under the Conqueror but, according to his tombstone, which has been preserved, died in Istanbul at the end of March 1487 in the reign of Bayezid II—was also of Christian descent, born, if we may so interpret his testament of April 1475, in Afyon Karahisar in Anatolia.

Three centuries later, on the evening of May 22, 1766, the third day of the Moslem sacrificial feast (*kurban bayramĭ*), the Conqueror's mosque was in large part destroyed by a terrible earthquake which shook all Istanbul. Sultan Mustafa III (1757–1773), it has been maintained, caused the ruins of the mosque to be razed and entrusted an architect by the name of Haci Ahmed Dayezade with the task of rebuilding, which went on from 1767 to 1771. The vestiges of fifteenth-century architecture still discernible in the courtyard and also in the ground plan of the mosque lead us to doubt this contention. Be that as it may, a large part of the edifice was rebuilt [pl. XVIII b]. Older descriptions and drawings by sixteenth-century travelers, especially Melchior Lorichs of Holstein and Wilhelm Dillich (1606, 1609), show that the mosque possessed a central cupola and two rows of four smaller cupolas on either side of the central axis. On the east the mosque was prolonged by a prayer niche (*mihrap*) covered by a half-cupola.[46]

As the first preacher (*hatip*) in the new mosque its builder appointed not a Turk but a Persian, Mullah Siracuddin, concerning whose origins and activity nothing is known and who deserves mention only because of the sultan's preference for a Persian. We shall have occasion to speak later of the unusual role played under the Conqueror by the poets, writers,

---

[46] For the Mosque of the Conqueror, see Goodwin, *A History of Ottoman Architecture*, 121–131; also Ayverdi, *Fatih devri mimarisi*, 125ff. For the problem of the identity of the mosque's chief architect, see, in addition to the above, especially I. H. Konyalï, *Azadli Sinan (Sinan-i Atik): vakfiyeleri, eserleri, hayati, mezari* (Istanbul, 1953).

and above all theologians who had poured into the Ottoman Empire from Iran. The preacher Siracuddin was one of the few who lived quiet, inconspicuous lives; he died in obscurity in 1492 or 1493.

Far more important than the position of Friday preacher was an institution which the Conqueror attached to his mosque, namely, the foundation consisting of eight *medreses*, or Koran schools. In special buildings (*tetimmat*) adjoining the eight schools, additional students (*softa*) were provided with board and lodging. Their curriculum embraced complete courses in ten sciences: grammar, syntax, logic, rhetoric, geometry, astronomy, and the four legal-theological disciplines, dogmatics, jurisprudence, the "traditions" of Mohammed, and Koranic exegesis. Once a student had completed his studies, he received the title of *danişmend* and went to work in a lower school, where he taught beginners the fundamentals of the branches of knowledge he had just mastered. The eight superior schools, the "paradise of learning" attached to the Mosque of the Conqueror, paid their teachers fifty to sixty *akçe* a day, and carried more prestige than any other school in the Ottoman Empire, even the famous old *medreses* of Bursa and Edirne. Near the Eyüp mosque Mehmed had previously founded a *medrese* where the teachers received the same wages. By the Aya Sofya mosque he had founded still another *medrese*, whose teachers received as much as sixty *akçe* a day. Pay and rank of the teachers depended on the importance of the work on which they lectured. The establishment of the hierarchy of scholars, the teachers of law and theology (*ülema*), which cannot be described here, were the work of the grand vizier Mahmud Pasha, who took a special interest in the classification and placement of scholars.

Few Ottoman rulers in those early times were so concerned with the welfare and progress of scholars and poets as Mehmed, who particularly favored their company. He kept a list in which the qualities and weaknesses of every candidate for a teaching position were carefully noted. With its help he himself made appointments "from declension to Isfahani," that is, from the teacher of the ABC's to the celebrated paragon of all philology. Often enough the sultan paid a surprise visit to one of the eight schools to listen to the lectures and test the teachers' knowledge and pedagogic ability. Many attempts were made, almost always in vain, to exploit the sultan's well-known generosity toward scholars and poets. One day, for example, a dervish appealed to him for alms in the name of the 124,000 prophets. "Very well," said the sultan mockingly, "name them. I will give you one *akçe* for each one." The dervish was able to name only ten or twelve even of the twenty-four named in the Koran, and the sultan was rid of him for that many silver pieces. But toward men of true creative genius Mehmed showed a generosity which fully justifies his fame as a patron of the sciences.

His generosity extended to those aged and retired scholars who were able to retain his favor. When there was no campaign afoot or when his physical ailments prevented him from campaigning, he gave the scholarly community his full attention, and the year his own mosque and the schools connected with it were completed found him especially disposed to promote the intellectual life of his new capital.

Apart from these occupations, the sultan seems in the year 1471 to have experienced an inner crisis which, even on his return journey from Greece, was reflected in arbitrary measures and repeated outbursts of rage. And he must have been increasingly irritated by the diplomatic negotiations then in progress between East and West. For many years, as we shall soon see, Uzun Hasan had exchanged embassies with Venice; now he was also in touch with the Holy See and Naples, Hungary, and Poland. Mehmed was of course aware of these activities; they must have convinced him that he would not be able to conquer the West as quickly as he had hoped and as his victories had perhaps led him to expect. Angiolello (and after him Paolo Giovio, historian, physician, and bishop of Nocera) had once called the sultan *re della fortuna*, the "king of fortune." The power-hungry potentate, already gravely ill, may now have begun to doubt the feasibility of his plans for world conquest; perhaps, with only himself and a handful of truly devoted followers to count on, he would not attain his goal, and if an alliance between the West and Uzun Hasan should succeed in taking him in a pincers movement, all hope would be lost of extending his Western conquests. It may well have been such considerations which in the early summer of 1471 led Mehmed, perhaps in response to the urging of his stepmother Mara, to make another attempt to arrive at a peace with Venice. This alone can account for the astonishing fact, reported on July 3, 1471, by Gherardo de Colli, the Milanese ambassador to the Signoria, in a letter to his duke, that a light galley accompanied by a fast sailing vessel, a *fusta*, had quite unexpectedly put into the harbor of Venice that very morning, with a Turkish peace emissary on board.

The presence of this emissary from the East was kept strictly secret, but the news spread like wildfire. It soon became known that the envoy had been sent by the sultan's stepmother to persuade the Signoria to accept the new peace conditions proposed by the sultan. Mehmed demanded Navplion, Krujë in Albania, Crete (Candia), Corfu, Lemnos, as well as certain small Aegean islands, among them Andros and Tinos, and finally an annual head tax (*harac*) of 50,000 Venetian gold ducats. According to Gherardo de Colli, the Venetian desire for peace was so great that the Signoria was inclined to accept Mehmed's demands if only he would drop the humiliating tribute.[47] In another letter of July 18, the Milanese ambassador wrote that the "Turk" was asking far more, but that the Venetians had declared their willingness to make peace if they could keep Krujë and Monemvasia with the Braccio di Maina. Krujë, so Gherardo de Colli explained in a letter of August 3, must remain in the hands of the Signoria, because its only other possessions on the terra firma were Alessio and Durrës on the seacoast, which the "Turk" was no longer eager to capture and which, if he had wished, he could have taken ten times over. The Venetians, the letter continued, were all aware that if Mehmed had a firm foothold in Albania in addition to "Valma" (Elbasan), he would easily be able to seize the remaining territory by means of the raids (*scorrerie*) which he regularly undertook even in peacetime; if demonstrations were made over these raids, he always replied that his pashas, not he, had been responsible. Gherardo de Colli's reports do not make it clear how the negotiations ended, but it is certain that they brought no result. "Everyone hopes for and desires peace" (*cadauno spera e brama pace*), Gherardo de Colli had written in May.

By the end of June the Venetians received word of the humiliating treatment accorded their ambassadors who had arrived at the Porte on March 12. When they asked to be admitted to the sultan, they were told that he received no "enemy emissaries" but would deal with them only through intermediaries. The high-handed claims submitted to them exceeded their worst fears, so that the ambassadors wished to leave Istanbul at once. The Venetians must have been all the more startled at the arrival of a peace emissary from the sultan a few days later, especially if they believed his move to be sincere and not a mere sham to spy out conditions in Venice and determine its war potential after seven years of hostilities. In view of the sultan's inflexible and exorbitant claims, it was clear from the very start that he had far overestimated the Venetians' willingness to make concessions. But conceivably his aim in sending an emissary to Venice had been precisely to find out how far the Signoria was prepared to go in its desire for peace. Venice revived her hopes of a military agreement with Uzun Hasan. The Rialto was full of rumors concerning the military strength of the Turkmen prince.

Early in April 1471, "Re Costanzo de Zorziana" (Georgia) also sent ambassadors to Venice, who reported that their sovereign had concluded

---

[47] For this peace feeler, see the reference (n. 44 above) to the document published by Ménage, and especially his comments there, 103, n. 12.

a close alliance with Uzun Hasan, his blood kinsman, and that the lord of the White Sheep had taken the field against Mehmed with 30,000 horsemen. The historical fact is that Uzun Hasan undertook no less than five campaigns against Georgia (1458, 1463, 1466, 1472, and 1477), that he was never on good terms with its rulers, and that none of these bore a name remotely resembling Costanzo (Constantius). No doubt another charlatan from the Orient had found a way of obtaining a temporary livelihood at the expense of credulous Westerners. Once these conversations begin to bear fruit, wrote Gherardo de Colli hopefully in a letter to Milan on April 12, 1471, it will be a great thing (*une grande faccenda*).

Throughout 1471 Mehmed received no delegations from any Western state other than Dubrovnik. Twice Ragusan envoys came to the Porte, bringing the annual tribute, which had meanwhile been increased to 9,000 ducats. From existing documents in the Slavonic language (April 24 and May 15) we learn that the sultan spent the spring in Istanbul, but that in the late fall (November 30), perhaps to evade a new outbreak of the plague, he was in Vize southeast of Kirklareli, enjoying the pure air of the Istranca Mountains. This region had long been a favorite resort of the sultans, who had built a serai in the town of Istranca and on their visits devoted themselves chiefly to the hunt. In the ensuing years Mehmed returned frequently to these parts when in need of rest.[48]

When and where, in the course of the same year 1471, the circumcision, mentioned in only one of the old Ottoman chronicles, of the three princes Cem, Abdullah, and Şehinşah was celebrated is thus far unknown, which is all the more surprising when we consider that hitherto such festivities had always been marked by considerable pomp and the participation of the entire population. The princes Abdullah and Şehinşah were the two eldest sons of Bayezid, hence grandsons of Mehmed, who arranged that they be circumcised at the same time.

It is exceedingly difficult to establish the chronological order of the Karaman campaigns before the final conflict of 1472, but it would seem that still in 1471, after the unsuccessful venture of Rum Mehmed Pasha, Ishak Pasha, his successor in the grand vizierate, undertook a campaign against Karaman. At that time Kasïm Bey was stirring up the population in behalf of his house, and the new grand vizier was sent to quell the disorder. A battle was fought near Mut in the Taurus Mountains. Kasïm Bey was put to flight; Ishak Pasha repaired the fortifications of

---

[48] The documents testifying to the sultan's residence during the year are given by Truhelka, "Tursko-slovjenski spomenici," 32–33; Turkish translation in *IED* I (1955), 55–56.

Mut and Niğde and then captured the presumably rebellious castles of Varköy, Uc Hisar, and Orta Hisar, and the city of Aksaray, the entire population of which, on the sultan's express order, was carried off to Istanbul, where they were settled in the quarter which is known to this day as Aksaray.

If Domenico Malipiero was not mistaken, another campaign in southern Anatolia took place in the same year (1471), against Alanya, the seaport on the Gulf of Antalya. Also known as Alaiye, the settlement took its name from its founder, the Seljuk Alaeddin Kaykobad (ca. 1220), who walled and fortified it. Still earlier there had been a castle which, because of its enchanting situation, was called Kalon Oros (Beautiful Mountain), from which the medieval name of Candeloro (or Scandeloro) derives. Long after the fall of the Anatolian Seljuk empire the descendants of the founder maintained themselves in the city. The last of these was Kılıç Arslan, whose fate was now to be sealed.[49]

The sultan put the vizier Gedik Ahmed Pasha in charge of the raid. He arrived at the gates of the city, in whose high citadel Kılıç Arslan had taken refuge with his family. The vizier persuaded him to surrender peacefully and sent him with his wife and son to Istanbul. The sultan took pity on him and sent him to Gümülcine on the southern slope of the Rhodope Mountains.

In this connection Domenico Malipiero mentions a pathetic incident. When in 1471 Scandeloro (that is, the fortified city of Alanya) was besieged by the Turks, the king of Cyprus, then James II of Lusignan, sent 300 crossbowmen to the help of Kılıç Arslan from his nearby island. But even if they reached their destination, they were unable to help the last Seljuk prince. Later King James sent a special envoy to Mehmed in a vain attempt to obtain the prisoner's release. His plea was disdainfully rejected.

Concerning the further destinies of this prince, who was probably the last authentic scion of the Anatolian Seljuks, it is recorded that one day, pretexting a hunting expedition, he fled to Egypt, leaving his wife and son behind. From there he proudly sent back to Gedik Ahmed Pasha a costly jewel which Mehmed had given him on the occasion of a visit to his treasure house. The vizier, who was expected to return it to the donor, put the jewel in with many others, representing the whole as a jeweler's display. The sultan, a shrewd connoisseur of jewels, was said to have recognized it at once as his present to Kılıç Arslan. The fugitive's

---

[49] For the strongly fortified coastal city, see "Alanya" (F. Taeschner), *EI*[2] I, 354–355. An excellent study is Seton Lloyd and D. S. Rice, *Alanya ('Ala'iyya)* (London, 1958).

wife and son remained in Gümülcine, where both ended their days (the son in 1508) and were buried; their tombs, of course, have long since disappeared.

We have already noted that after having been driven from his country, Ishak Bey of Karaman sought refuge with Uzun Hasan. He does not seem to have lived long thereafter, for, probably before the end of 1471, his widow in Silifke appealed to the Ottoman sultan for mercy for herself and her little son Mehmed Bey. It was most likely in the spring of 1472, and not during his campaign against Alanya, that Gedik Ahmed Pasha received orders to seize the castle of Silifke. First the vizier appeared before the castle of Mokan, to which the family of the fugitive Pir Ahmed had withdrawn, and took for his sovereign not only the treasures stored in the castle dungeons but also the Karaman princess, noted for her extraordinary beauty. Then he captured the castles of Alara, Manavgat, and Lula (the Loulon of the Byzantines, possibly the *Hisn al-saqaliba*, Slavs' Castle, of the Arabs), some of whose defenders he caused to be cut down and the rest hurled from the walls. Only the approach of Uzun Hasan prevented him from continuing his cleanup of southwestern Anatolia. Gedik Ahmed Pasha was now obliged to seek safety in Konya.

Book Five

UZUN HASAN IN LEAGUE WITH THE WEST.
WAR IN THE EAST WITH UZUN HASAN.
THE FALL OF MAHMUD PASHA.
DEATHBLOW TO GENOA'S LEVANTINE TRADE.
OTTOMAN RAIDERS AT THE GATES OF VENICE
AND AUSTRIA.
MEHMED IN WALACHIA AND MOLDAVIA.
THE ŚIEGES OF KRUJË AND SHKODËR.

THE ANATOLIAN expeditions mentioned in the last chapter were the prelude to a showdown between the Grand Turk and Uzun Hasan, his bitterest and, since the fall of Karaman, most dangerous enemy. Uzun Hasan (Hasan the Long), originally a tribal chieftain, lord of the White Sheep, had conquered vast territories in recent years and was now king of Persia, with his residence in Tabriz. He was by far the most powerful eastern neighbor of the Ottomans, and direct conflict with him was in the long run unavoidable. Mehmed might have preferred to postpone it in order to secure and extend his conquests in the West, and more than likely the decisive impetus came from Uzun Hasan. His increasingly provocative attitude is no doubt explained by his confidence in his own strength and reliance on strong support from the West. The sultan's intrigues against Uzun Hasan's Karamanian "cousins," one after another of whom had been put out of the way, and the successes of the Ottoman armies in eastern Anatolia, must have goaded him to attack the sultan.

The diplomatic traffic between Persia and the West can hardly have remained a secret from Mehmed. The pope and Venice had carried on negotiations with Uzun Hasan for many years—we shall soon have occasion to consider the Venetian efforts in detail—but they had been largely explorative and noncommittal. Some time in 1471, however, a more serious understanding about a grand alliance against the sultan seems to have been reached. Unfortunately, we still lack documented studies concerning the nature and extent of the agreements concluded at this time between Uzun Hasan on the one hand and the pope and Venice on the other. According to Niccolò della Tuccia, the chronicler of Viterbo, even the Grand Karaman played a part in these negotiations through an embassy to the pope. But on this score reliable information is lacking.

The widespread hope of striking a decisive blow against Mehmed, thanks to this unexpected help in his rear, revived the idea of a grandiose, world-embracing venture. In a secret consistory held on Christmas, 1471, Pope Sixtus IV appointed five legates *de latere*, all cardinals, with the mission of arousing the entire Christian world to the need of defending the faith against the "accursed Turk, the enemy of the name of Jesus," as we read in the minutes of the proceedings. The aged Bessarion was to visit France, Burgundy, and England; Rodrigo Borgia, Spain; Angelo Capranica, Italy; Marco Barbo, Germany, Poland, and Hungary; while Oliviero Caraffa was chosen as commander of the pope's naval forces. Whether Sixtus selected the right men is open to doubt, for even at the time his choice provoked ironical comment. Some, such as the learned Bessarion, were much too old; indeed, Bessarion never returned to Rome, but died on the way in Ravenna on November 18, 1472, aged seventy-seven. Others were too comfort-loving to endure the hardship of long journeys and unaccustomed tasks. None of them succeeded in firing the countries they visited with enthusiasm for a Turkish war. A few days later the pope issued a solemn bull in which he vividly described the measures taken by the Turks to force Christendom to its knees and called on all to take up arms against them. This appeal was once more in vain.[1]

The inner disorganization of the European family of nations defied all appeals for unity. Emperor Frederick III, as usual slow and hesitant to reach a decision, offered the overzealous and overconfident cardinal Marco Barbo no hope of obtaining his support. The self-seeking greed of the ecclesiastical and secular estates in Germany surpassed all bounds. As if by common accord they closed their eyes to the danger threatening from the East and coming closer and closer to the borders of Germany.

Not discouraged by the deplorable experience of his legates, Sixtus IV continued to work for peace in Italy and did everything in his power to fit out a fleet. When he had begun his pontificate on August 9, 1471, the papal treasury was found, to the general consternation, to contain only 7,000 or even, according to other sources, 5,000 gold ducats. Nevertheless, the account books show that in 1471 and 1472 Sixtus spent a total of 144,000 gold ducats for the construction of his warships; the participation of Venetian and Neapolitan contingents in the expedition was mutually

[1] See Pastor, *History of the Popes* IV, 219–224, for more details of the undertakings of the legates.

agreed upon. It was clear that everyone set the highest hopes on naval warfare. The idea of waging war by land was entertained only by such eccentrics as the aging Francesco Filelfo, who never wearied of calling attention to himself by fiery missives. At the end of 1471 he gave the doge Niccolò Tron the advice to abandon these fruitless maritime undertakings and "win an easy victory" by a land war, man to man, against the Turks.

After the first year of his pontificate, Sixtus's fervor began to peter out. He was able to launch his ships in the summer of 1472, but then he confined himself to costly gestures and hollow proclamations. On June 1, 1472, he blessed the marriage by proxy (*per procurationem*) of Princess Zoë, niece of the last Byzantine emperor, with the Russian grand duke Ivan III; he had arranged this highly political marriage and provided a handsome dowry in the hope of gaining in the grand duke a powerful champion in the war against the infidel and of bringing about a union of the Roman and the Russian Orthodox churches, but his expectations were to be disappointed soon after the bride and her imposing Russian retinue had left the Eternal City. Once in Russia, Zoë returned to the Orthodox faith.

When Pietro Mocenigo succeeded Canale as captain general of the Venetian fleet after the disaster of Negropont, he first repaired the battered ships and cruised the Aegean visiting allies and making quick, inconsequential raids on Ottoman possessions. No encounters with the Turkish fleet took place. Instead of rousing himself to serious action, Mocenigo accepted the offer early in 1472 of a Sicilian, Antonello, who had fallen into Turkish slavery at the capture of Negropont and who now professed his willingness to blow up the arsenal near the harbor of Gelibolu, which Mehmed had had strongly fortified long before. At the time this arsenal housed the arms and ammunition for more than 300 galleys and a large quantity of inflammable materials such as tar, hemp, and pitch. Antonello offered to set all this on fire. Thoroughly familiar with the region, the foolhardy Sicilian asked only for a lighter and six daring companions. After loading his vessel with supposed merchandise, among which the fuel and implements needed for his venture were hidden, he sailed through the Dardanelles unhindered on February 13, 1472, broke the locks of fifteen warehouses of the poorly guarded arsenal in the dead of night, and set fire in several places. Before the Turks were aware of the disaster the whole arsenal was in flames. In a few hours it was reduced, with all its contents, to a smoking rubble heap. The fire could not be checked and continued for ten days. The total damage amounted to 100,000 gold ducats. The intrepid incendiary, however, did not escape his fate. As he was trying to get away a sack of powder on his boat caught fire and the boat sank. Antonello and his men reached land but were caught and dragged before the sultan. Without torture he freely confessed the deed, which wrested admiration even from the sultan. "And with great courage," reports Domenico Malipiero, the Venetian chronicler, "he added that he, the sultan, was the plague of the world, that he had plundered all his neighbor princes, that he had kept faith with no one, and that he was trying to eradicate the name of Christ. And that was why he had taken it into his head to do what he had done. . . . The Grand Turk," so the account goes on, "listened to him with great patience and admiration. But then he gave orders to behead him and his companions."

This coup against the naval arsenal in Gelibolu had no telling consequences, perhaps because the main arsenal had already been moved to the Bosporus. Still, it might have helped the Venetian fleet, which was then not far from the Dardanelles, to force the straits if it had taken quick action.

A fortunate accident has helped to throw light on the diplomatic ties between the Signoria and Uzun Hasan; the *relazioni* of such leading Venetian ambassadors as Lazzaro Querini, Caterino Zeno, Ambrogio Contarini, Giosafat Barbaro, Paolo Ogniben, providing in large part an excellent record of Venetian diplomacy, have been preserved either in manuscript or in print. A glance at them will give us a general idea of what was done in those momentous days to free Christendom from the Ottoman threat.[2]

Relations between the lord of the White Sheep and Venice go back to the winter of 1463–1464. On December 2, 1463, the senate agreed to consider an alliance and soon thereafter sent Lazzaro Querini as its first envoy to the court of Tabriz. Twice during the many years of Querini's absence ambassadors from Uzun Hasan appeared in Venice; certain agreements were reached, but no actions were taken. It was only after the fall of Negropont that the Signoria abandoned its hesitation.

In February 1471, Lazzaro Querini returned from Persia to Venice with one Murad, an emissary of Uzun Hasan. Querini was the first to

[2] The accounts of Contarini and Barbaro appear in English as *Travels to Tana and Persia* by Josafa Barbaro and Ambrogio Contarini, trans. W. Thomas and S. A. Roy; ed. Lord Stanley of Alderley (Hakluyt Society, 1st series XLIX; London, 1873; reprinted New York, 1963). Zeno's account is the first given by Charles Grey (ed. and trans.), *A Narrative of Italian Travels in Persia in the Fifteenth and Sixteenth Centuries* (Hakluyt Society, 1st series XLIX, part 2; London, 1873).

provide the Signoria with reliable information about conditions in Uzun Hasan's empire. His Turkmen companion brought a letter from his master, in which the lord of the White Sheep spoke boastfully of his past victories and informed the Signoria that he had resolved to take up arms against Mehmed but was counting on the support of the West and particularly that of Venice. By 148 votes against 2, the senate decided to send an ambassador to Uzun Hasan's court. After two of the men proposed, Francesco Michiel and Giàcomo Medin, had declined, the choice fell on Caterino Zeno, perhaps because his wife, Violante, was a niece of Uzun Hasan's wife, who in turn was a daughter of the late emperor John IV Comnenus of Trebizond. The three other daughters of this Comnenus princess (the sister of Despina) and her husband, Niccolò Crespo, the duke of the archipelago, had also married Venetian noblemen of the Cornaro, Priuli, and Loredano families, so that Uzun Hasan was united with Venice by ties of kinship.

Before Caterino Zeno started for the East, a second emissary arrived, who had crossed the Black Sea from Trebizond to Akkerman and proceeded by way of Poland, where he had been joined by an envoy of King Casimir IV. He first negotiated with the Signoria, which promised him "help for help and offer for offer," and then he went on to Rome, hoping that the pope would help him to gain the support of Christendom for his master's warlike venture. Here, too, he was well received, put off with promises, and finally sent home in the company of a Franciscan monk.

Caterino Zeno was thoroughly familiar with the ways and customs of the Orient, having spent years in Damascus with his father, Dracone. This as well as his ties of kinship with Uzun Hasan made him particularly well suited to the task. His departure, however, was repeatedly postponed. First Venice wished to make sure that it would not be possible to negotiate a peace with Mehmed. When the negotiations (which were discussed above) foundered, the Signoria finally decided to play the Persian card. It was autumn (1471) by the time Caterino Zeno started off in the company of Murad. He carried with him rich gifts, including gold cloth for Despina Hatun. He was not at a loss for an explanation of why the republic had first entered into negotiations with the sultan. He was to say at the court in Tabriz that the sultan had asked for them and that the Venetians were without reliable information about Persia. Such information was what he had come for. On his return home he would report on Uzun Hasan's power (*potenza*), his age, his revenues, the frontiers of his country, his neighbors, in short, on everything that was set down tersely but exhaustively in the *relazioni* which he addressed to the Signoria.

And so Caterino Zeno set out from Venice, spent a few months on Rhodes, crossed over to Karaman, and after no end of perils arrived at his destination of Tabriz no later than April 30, 1472. There every possible honor was shown him; he was immediately presented to the queen, who received him as her nephew, to lodge in the palace and dine at the royal board. Despina Hatun regarded herself as a kinswoman of the Venetian Republic and promised its representative all conceivable help. On May 30, Caterino Zeno wrote to Captain General Pietro Mocenigo in Rhodes bidding him attack the Ottomans on the Anatolian coast. He also asked the admiral to grant passage to Venice to another envoy from Uzun Hasan.

At the end of August, indeed, a certain Haci Muhammad arrived in Venice with a plea for artillery, of which Uzun Hasan had none. He brought the Signoria a costly gift which is still one of the most magnificent items in the Tesoro di San Marco. It is a bowl hollowed out from an unusually large turquoise (diameter: nine inches), encased inside and out in a jewel-studded setting. No sooner had Haci Muhammad acquitted himself of his mission than another emissary arrived by the overland route via Kaffa, this time a Sephardic Jew. But he seems only to have announced that his master was on his way west with an enormous army and would not leave Anatolia until he had defeated the sultan of Istanbul. The envoy then continued on his way to Rome and Naples, allowing himself to be baptized and accepting lavish gifts on the way.

Caterino Zeno proved an adroit negotiator. He did his utmost to establish contact with Uzun Hasan's other allies in Asia Minor (including a nephew of the last emperor of Trebizond), who had fled to the Persian court with what was left of their hopes. This Comnenus, it seems, was the first to believe that his hour had come. In May 1472, with the approval of Uzun Hasan and the Georgians, he invaded the region of Trebizond and allegedly began to besiege the city. A shortage of provisions, violent Turkish resistance, and finally the arrival of nine Ottoman galleys and twenty-five sailing vessels led him to abandon his project. The plan to reconquer Trebizond collapsed, the unsuccessful undertaking having served only to alarm the sultan.

In the meantime, the ships of the pope and of King Ferrante having been made ready, both units sailed off separately to the Aegean, where they joined the Venetian fleet in June 1472. The combined fleet now assembled off Samos consisted of eighty-five galleys: forty-eight from Venice (including twelve from the cities of Dalmatia), eighteen from the pope under Oliviero Caraffa, seventeen from the king of Naples, and two from the Knights of Rhodes. The captain general, a brave warrior but hardly a naval hero, was provided with two very capable *provveditori*, Luigi Bembo and Marin Malipiero (the father of the chronicler). With a view to establishing communications with Uzun Hasan the fleet moved to Rhodes; no contact was made with the Ottoman navy, which did not leave the Dardanelles. Instead, a council of war, in which the battle-tried *provveditore* Vettore Soranzo participated, decided to storm the well-defended port of Antalya on the coast of the region of Karaman. The soldiers, who were put ashore in August 1472, burned the suburbs, plundered the storehouses full of Oriental spices and precious stuffs, but, unable to pass the outer walls, were finally obliged to return to Rhodes.

Here Mocenigo was met by still another emissary from Uzun Hasan, who brought word that his master was adequately supplied with cavalry adept in handling the lance, the sword, and the bow, but that he lacked everything needed to attack the enemy from a distance and to capture cities. He reiterated his plea for heavy guns, crews to man them, and ammunition. He urged the captain general to attack. But the raids subsequently carried out by Mocenigo's Albanian mercenaries along the coasts of Lycia, Caria, and Cilicia were nothing more than piracy in the grand style. They were finally crowned on September 13, 1472, by the cruel attack on Izmir, which was protected only by a crumbling wall and scarcely defended. The city was pillaged and, after a murderous battle with the Ottoman garrison, set on fire. In a few hours the city was reduced to an ash heap. Two hundred and fifteen Turkish heads were brought to the ships as trophies. The Ottomans feared that the hour had struck for Istanbul. The sultan, as we shall see, had just begun to prepare for a campaign in eastern Anatolia; at this moment a thrust through the Dardanelles to the capital would have been a most effective way of collaborating with his Persian enemy, who was moving west fast. Nothing of the kind was done. Soon after the sacking of Izmir, the fleet moved to winter quarters in Navplion. The Neapolitan contingent had sailed home at the end of the summer, and at the onset of cold weather (January 1473), the papal legate returned to Italy with his squadron. As a trophy of the campaign, he brought back to Rome pieces of the iron chain that had blocked the entrance to the port of Antalya. It was hung up in the sacristy of St. Peter's and may still be seen over the door leading to the archives; it bears a high-flown Latin inscription presenting a weirdly distorted picture of the naval operation.

In the meantime, on August 24, 1472, orders were dispatched from the Venetian senate to Mocenigo to move the bulk of his fleet to Cyprus and occupy all important points. Uzun Hasan's allies began to press forward in eastern Anatolia. In order to stem the assault Mehmed had appointed his second-born, Prince Mustafa, who was governor of Karaman, commander of the troops. The letter of appointment, issued in Istanbul toward the middle of July 1472, has been preserved. In it express mention is made of certain insulting missives which Uzun Hasan had addressed to Mehmed, who had not deigned to reply. Mahmud Pasha, the commander of the fleet in Gelibolu, criticized this appointment, though it is uncertain whether the objection was motivated by dislike of Mustafa or by doubts concerning his military ability. In any event he persuaded the sultan to entrust the aged and reliable Davud Pasha with the defense of Karaman against the hordes of Turkmen bandits, especially the Varsak Eli, who were threatening it. Davud was dispatched to Karaman and Mustafa informed of this imperial order.

Meanwhile, the brothers Pir Ahmed and Kasïm Bey of Karaman, in league with Yusufça Mirza, a cousin of Uzun Hasan, and under the supreme command of Uzun Hasan's vizier Ömer ibn Bektaş, devastated the Karaman territories. Estimates of the strength of this army vary between 50,000 and 100,000 men. The first figure emanating from Caterino Zeno, an eyewitness, is probably the more reliable. The vizier Ömer soon returned to Diyarbakïr, while Yusufça Mirza with the two Karamanids turned toward their former territory. Davud Pasha and Prince Mustafa, allegedly in command of an army of 60,000 men, were sent to counter this advance. On August 19, 1472, the contending armies met near Kireli (Carallia) on the lake of Beyşehir, the Caralis of antiquity, according to Prince Mustafa's so-called message of victory to his father. Yusufça Mirza was taken and sent to Mehmed, who imprisoned him. The two Karamanid princes saved themselves by flight, Pir Ahmed hastening to Uzun Hasan and Kasïm Bey establishing himself in Silifke in Cilicia.

In the summer of 1472 the plague once again had devastated Istanbul, and Mehmed left with his court for the Sweet Waters of Europe at the northeastern end of the Golden Horn. On August 25 he returned to Istanbul in spite of the plague and caused a wooden dock to be built at Beşiktaş (*alle Colonne*) on the Bosporus, across from Üsküdar, to facilitate the loading of troops onto the cutters that would carry them to the Asian shore. A council was held on the next day and the sultan discussed the situation with his viziers. The following night the disgraced former grand vizier, Mahmud Pasha, was hastily recalled from his post in Gelibolu and consulted. His recommendation was not to cross over to Asia for the present but first to wait for more detailed news from eastern

Anatolia. Numerous reports came in during the ensuing days, but all to the effect that Uzun Hasan was still moving within his own frontiers. Early in September the news became more alarming. First came rumors that all the Grand Turk's neighbors had joined Uzun Hasan and that no less than 60,000 cavalrymen had appeared outside Tokat. By September 5 it became definitely known that Kïzïl Ahmed, former lord of Kastamonu, and the Karamanoğlu Kasïm Bey had captured the city and laid it waste. The entire population had been taken prisoner and sent to Erzincan, where the lord of the White Sheep had his headquarters at the time. The Ottoman frontier guard had also been wiped out, so that the eastern borders of the empire were dangerously exposed.

At this point the sultan was obliged to take action. The imperial seal was once again entrusted to Mahmud Pasha, and messengers were sent to all European provinces with orders that the Rumelian army should assemble outside Edirne on September 20, on which day the soldiers were to receive their pay. By September 7 it was known at court that the enemy had raided Amasya, where Crown Prince Bayezid resided as governor. Prince Bayezid sent an urgent plea for reinforcements. The new grand vizier took advantage of the opportunity to raise the pay of the Janissaries by one to ten *akçe*, according to their rank. He also caused other sums of money and new clothes to be distributed among them in order to keep them in a good humor and to make sure of their cooperation in the war that was now inevitable.

Kïzïl Ahmed and Kasïm Bey were not content with their success in Tokat. According to reports from the East, they had divided their cavalry into two equal parts. Kïzïl Ahmed was planning to press forward to his old fief of Kastamonu, while Kasïm Bey planned an invasion of Karaman. According to the same message, Uzun Hasan was at Erzincan preparing to take the field with an enormous army, allegedly 100,000 strong, which was being joined by another 100,000.

These alarming measures by the enemy were the signal for vast preparations in the Ottoman camp. On September 11, the sultan gave orders that all ships, large and small, should be confiscated in his name and held in readiness. On the following day Mehmed caused 2,000 loads (*gordeni*) of *akçe*, corresponding to 1,200,000 ducats, to be taken from his treasury and distributed among all those who wished to join in his campaign. On the same day he issued a further order that every village in "Greece" (*Grecia*) must supply two men for the impending operations.

On September 13, two emissaries from Uzun Hasan who had been on their way to Hungary with letters for King Matthias Corvinus were brought before the sultan. The sultan promised to spare their lives if they answered his many questions. Reportedly they declared that Uzun Hasan was determined to make war on Mehmed "under any circumstances," that he had a secret understanding with the king of the Hungarians and with the Venetian Signoria, and that all three powers would set out at the same time to destroy the sultan.

The rumors reaching Istanbul from Anatolia became more and more confused. Kïzïl Ahmed and Kasïm Bey were said to have invaded Kara-man with their cavalry and to have inflicted heavy losses on the Ottomans. Early in October it was learned that in the course of their invasion of Karaman the two landless princes had occupied the region around Kayseri and pitched their camp in that city. The Ottoman commander and his army had been captured and massacred.

Meanwhile, troops poured into Edirne from all parts of Rumelia. They were given three months' pay, lavish premiums, and gifts of velvet. The author of a letter written from Pera on October 27, 1472 (to which we owe all these interesting details), was present in the sultan's camp on October 3 when 100 loads (*gordeni*), or 19,000 *akçe*, were paid out to the agha of the Janissaries to be distributed among his troops over and above their increased pay.[3] These repeated gifts to the Janissaries and to the army as a whole are an eloquent indication of the extent to which even then the success of a campaign depended on the good will and combative-ness of the troops, whose loyalty could never be taken for granted.

On October 5, 1472, the first bodies of troops were ferried across to Üsküdar on the Anatolian shore. A week later, at dawn on Monday, October 12, the sultan himself crossed over to Asia with his retinue. This hour had been chosen on the advice of his court astrologers, whom he consulted regularly. As we shall soon see, Uzun Hasan was also guided by astrology in his most important decisions.

The news from the scene of hostilities was bad. The entire region of Ankara had been devastated by the enemy and nothing remained but the bare earth. On October 24, a great storm broke out over the Bosporus which lasted for four whole days and caused enormous damage. Wind and incessant rain destroyed a large part of the sultan's camp and many ships were sunk in the Black Sea, among them five large vessels bearing barley for the troops. During the storm, supply shipments were halted and the army, all of which had by then been ferried across to Anatolia, suffered cruelly from hunger. Prices rose. What had formerly cost one *akçe* was now scarcely obtainable for ten. If the downpour had continued a quarter of the army would have perished of hunger and hardship in two days.

[3] See the *Monumenta Hungariae Historica* (*Hungarian Academy of Sciences, Historical Section* IV, part 2 [Budapest, 1877]), 239–244 (document 170).

This unfortunate beginning was widely interpreted as an evil omen indicating that Allah was hostile to the undertaking. Not a few hesitated to follow the sultan any further for fear of divine punishment. What, they wondered, would happen when the cold weather set in? Would it be possible to keep the troops supplied amid the ice and snow of eastern Anatolia? The price of barley had already risen from three to ten *akçe* a measure and was still going up. Uzun Hasan's hands had burned the granaries of Tokat, Amasya, Ankara, and Karaman, and everyone thought with foreboding of the hard winter ahead. Finally, on October 28, the storm abated. The supply ships were able to sail and more than eighty cutters were sent out with provisions. Their crews had meanwhile appropriated houses, from which they had to be removed and taken to their ships by force.

In Istanbul, Mehmed's son Cem,[4] a boy of twelve, had remained behind with reliable advisers as his father's representative. Princes Mustafa and Bayezid stood ready in Anatolia to join their father's forces.

Where the sultan spent the winter cannot be determined with certainty from the Turkish and Western sources. Gian-Maria Angiolello, who writes as if he had been present in the sultan's camp, gives the impression that the Ottoman army wintered not far from Amasya on the enormous Plain of Geese (Kaz Ovasi). It is there, in any case, that all the levies of troops appear to have been concentrated. Bayezid Çelebi and his brother Mustafa were also summoned there.[5]

The army was divided into five columns. The first, numbering 30,000 men, was under the command of the sultan himself. The second, also of 30,000 men, was entrusted to Prince Bayezid. Prince Mustafa commanded a third column of 30,000, of whom 12,000 were Walachians under a certain Basarab; this column took up a position next to the sultan. The fourth column was led by the governor of Rumelia, the young Hass Murad Pasha, a scion of the Palaeologi, who owed his rapid rise in the administration to the sultan's special favor. Because of Hass Murad's youth and inexperience, the grand vizier Mahmud Pasha was assigned to him as an adviser. This column was said to have numbered 60,000 men, among them many Christian Greeks, Albanians, and Serbs. They occupied a position in front of the sultan. Finally, behind the sultan, Davud Pasha, now

[4] For Sultan Cem, see above, book 3, n. 11.

[5] Angiolello's account of the Ottoman campaign against Uzun Hasan comprises the first chapters of the "Short Narrative of the Life and Acts of the King Ussun Cassano" in Grey, 73–138. It may be compared with the account of Zeno in the same volume, 21–26.

governor of Anatolia, took his place with the fifth column, numbering 40,000 infantry and cavalry. Thus, Mehmed and his army were in the middle, surrounded by four columns; the total strength, according to the figures just cited, would have been 190,000 men. Its actual fighting strength amounted to hardly more than 100,000, the remainder consisting of auxiliaries and supply troops. This gigantic army was drawn up on the Plain of Geese in the exact prescribed order. To it were added the *akincis* under Mahmud Ağa. The task of supplying this enormous army was entrusted to the two "barley commissioners" (*arpa emini*).

The army seems to have spent the greater part of the winter, always severe in eastern Anatolia, in this camp near Amasya, unmolested by the enemy. If Angiolello is to be believed, the remoteness of the sultan's camp from the capital resulted in a strange but typical incident in Istanbul. Communications were irregular, to say the least. When Prince Cem had been without reliable news for forty days, his advisers convinced him that the sultan's army had been destroyed. Whether on his own initiative or at the behest of his advisers, Prince Cem now attempted to win the support of the military and civilian commanders and to set up a regime of his own. These advisers, including a certain Nasuh Bey and Süleyman Bey of Karıştıran, who had grown old in the sultan's service, were ruthlessly dismissed by the sultan on his return. What proportions this first usurpation of Prince Cem assumed is not clear. The circumstances of a second one later on are much better known and show what groups were behind this strange figure. In any event, the incident makes it plain that Mehmed could not count on the absolute loyalty of his home administration, which obviously included enemies who were looking only for an opportunity to end his rule.

In February or March 1473, the sultan's army finally left its winter quarters. The entire force marched by way of Tokat in a northeasterly direction to Niksar (Neocaesarea, Pontus), and from there via Koylu Hisar to Şebin Karahisar (also Kara Hisar). Finally, the sultan with his army reached the plain of Erzincan where a halt was made. The commander of the *akincis*, Ali Bey of the Mihaloğlu family, sent ahead with the advance guard, sacked Kemah on the Euphrates southwest of Erzincan. In the course of their expedition the raiders came to an Armenian church, in which was sitting an elderly priest deep in his manuscripts. The soldiers called out to him and when he failed to reply or to stir from the spot, they killed him and set fire to his church. This incident, which must have been one among many similar cases, is deserving of mention because the sultan flew into a towering rage when he learned that the murdered priest had been a great scholar.

Uzun Hasan had already set out with his army when, on July 11, he bade Caterino Zeno, who accompanied him, write letters to the emperor and to the king of Hungary enjoining them to "set fire and flame to the European territory of the Ottomans, because with God's help he was about to achieve certain victory over the sultan and wished the sultan to be attacked from all sides, so that he would never recover from the defeat and his name would be extinguished for all time." It is not known whether these letters ever reached their destinations, but it is certain that neither King Matthias Corvinus nor the Emperor Frederick III offered to raise a finger against the Ottomans.

At the end of July 1473, Uzun Hasan arrived in the region of Erzincan and selected the mountains on the left bank of the Euphrates as his base. From there he saw the Ottoman armies and, as has been reported in several sources, cried out in Turkish, "Vay, kahboglu, ne deryadir!" (Woe, thunderation, what an ocean!) When, reportedly on Wednesday, August 4, Hass Murad Pasha crossed the river in his youthful exuberance, he and his army were surrounded by Uzun Hasan and wiped out. The Ottoman losses were set at 12,000 men. The governor met his death in the raging river. The sultan was infuriated at the setback and especially at the death of his favorite Murad Pasha, for which he never forgave his grand vizier, accusing him of failing to rush to the young governor's assistance and of letting him perish in the waters of the Euphrates. At the time, circumstances prevented him from calling Mahmud Pasha to account, as he assuredly would like to have done.

The defeat, it seems, led Mehmed briefly to abandon the campaign and to return to Istanbul in all haste. He gave orders to evacuate the battlefield in the region of Tercan (above Erzincan) and head for Trabzon (former Trebizond), bypassing Bayburt. From there, it would seem, the Ottomans intended to continue westward.

In the meantime, however, Caterino Zeno and his aunt urged Uzun Hasan to proceed swiftly against the Ottomans. Before taking action, Uzun Hasan sent a messenger to the sultan's camp to inform him that the lord of the White Sheep demanded the immediate return of Trabzon, which belonged to his father-in-law, and also of Sinop, which was the property of his nephews, his sister's sons. Finally, the territory of the Karamanoğlus, his "cousins," must be returned to them. Should Mehmed refuse these demands, he would regard the sultan as his enemy. In order to make it clear that he possessed the power to enforce his demands, he caused his envoy to give Mehmed a sack of millet with the remark that should the sultan wish to take up arms against him, his troops would have to be at least as numerous as the grains. The sultan made no reply but in the presence of the Turkmen messenger ordered the millet poured out before a flock of chickens, who quickly consumed it. "Tell your master," he said imperiously, "that as quickly as these chickens have devoured the sack of millet my Janissaries will deal with his men, who may be skilled at herding goats but not at fighting." The inevitable outcome was a declaration of war.

While the Ottomans were still encamped in the region of Üç Ağïzlï, probably in the mountains north of Erzincan, Uzun Hasan suddenly appeared with his army on the heights of Otluk Beli, on the Ottoman right flank. The Ottomans gave battle and, again on a Wednesday, August 11, 1473, defeated the prince of the White Sheep near Başkent. Uzun Hasan had chosen Wednesday, which he regarded as his lucky day and always set aside for his most important affairs of state, as the date of battle, but on this occasion luck forsook him, and the sultan, thanks chiefly to his use of firearms, won a brilliant victory, whose consequences were to be far-reaching. Uzun Hasan's younger son, Zeynel, had commanded his left flank and his elder son, Uğurlu Mehmed, his right. Facing them in the Ottoman order of battle were Mehmed's two sons, Prince Mustafa with Davud Pasha and the Anatolian army and *akïncïs* on the left wing, and Prince Bayezid with the European troops and Janissaries on the right. Mustafa flung himself boldly at the enemy's right wing and Zeynel lost his life in the fray. Mahmud Ağa, the leader of the *akïncïs*, laid Zeynel's head at the feet of the prince, who dispatched it to his father. Bayezid threw back the enemy's left wing. The entire Turkmen army was thrown into confusion. Uzun Hasan himself fled on an Arab palfrey. The battle lasted eight hours. The Ak Koyunlu were said to have lost 10,000 men, while Ottoman losses were set at only 1,000. The entire enemy camp and baggage train were taken. The sultan spent three days on the battlefield butchering the prisoners. Only a few important scholars —as a patron of the arts and sciences, Uzun Hasan always had several in his retinue—were spared. Three thousand Turkmen met a particularly cruel fate. They were taken along on the return march and 400 of them killed each day. The artisans and scholars taken prisoner were transferred to Istanbul.[6]

But instead of pursuing Uzun Hasan and fully exploiting his victory, Mehmed was persuaded by his grand vizier Mahmud Pasha to start home. This advice was sound, for it would certainly have been very difficult to hold the conquered territories. The further westward he marched, however, the more the sultan regretted his decision and worked himself up against his grand vizier.

[6] For the battle of Otluk Beli, cf. Angiolello, 89–93, and Zeno, 27–30.

In the course of the march, Darab Bey, commander of the Turkmen fortress of Şebin Karahisar, surrendered it to the passing sultan; he was rewarded with the appointment as governor (*sancak beyi*) of Çirmen near Edirne. At the same time, the unusually rich spoils were divided. In addition, the sultan forgave his troops the advance against their wages which had been paid out at the beginning of the campaign. He also freed all his slaves of both sexes, some 40,000 in number. From Şebin Karahisar the usual victory reports were sent to Sultan Hüseyin Baykara, the lord of Khorasan, and to Mehmed's son Cem, and orders went out to the governors and bannerets of the empire to organize victory celebrations. But the most interesting letter sent from Karahisar by the sultan was the *yarlik* [decree] of August 30, 1473, addressed in the Uighur language to the inhabitants of Anatolia, informing them of his victory over Uzun Hasan and describing details of the battle.[7]

Shortly before his departure from Istanbul, Mehmed had sent an agent named Hasan Bey to King Matthias of Hungary in Buda, bearing word that the sultan was eager for a friendly agreement with Hungary, that the two states had been at odds for too long, and that their quarrel must be settled once and for all. Matthias Corvinus, the message went on, should send an ambassador to the Porte to discuss further arrangements. King Matthias immediately sent one of his barons to whom, at the sultan's bidding, every conceivable honor and service was shown en route. When he arrived in the capital, Mehmed had long since left for Anatolia and there was nothing for the ambassador to do but, pursuant to the sultan's express invitation, to follow him. The sultan, he was told, had eagerly awaited his arrival, but the warlike measures of Mehmed's enemy Uzun Hasan had obliged him to start the campaign sooner than he had expected. When the Hungarian baron crossed over to Üsküdar, the sultan was already in eastern Anatolia, eight days' march away. The Hungarian hastened his journey. When he reached Ankara, he learned that Mehmed had assigned forty noblemen as his guard of honor and had given orders that he be entertained in every possible way. When he was finally admitted by the sultan's representative, not a word was spoken about a peace treaty, but the Hungarian received rich gifts, costly horses, saddles, and so on, and an invitation to accompany the court to Sivas. There hunts and displays of falconry were arranged in the guest's honor. He was told

---

[7] The letter is given in facsimile, transcription and modern Turkish translation by Rahmeti Arat, "Fatih Sultan Mehmed'in 'Yarlığı'," *Türkiyat Mecmuası* (Istanbul), 6 (1936–39), 285–322.

that the sultan would return to Sivas shortly, but he waited three whole months.

Meanwhile, Uzun Hasan had been defeated. The Hungarian baron witnessed the victory celebrations, the acts of vengeance against the prisoners, and the return of the sultan's armies. The envoy was now permitted to enter into negotiations with the sultan's viziers. He made the mistake of demanding in the name of his king two fortresses not far from Belgrade, namely, Žrnov and Golubac. The response was what might have been expected. Not only did Mehmed refuse to give up either of these fortresses but demanded others from King Matthias. Jajce, for example, it was maintained, belonged to the sultan, for he had driven out the king of Bosnia. The discussions came to nothing, but the sultan's political shrewdness had achieved its aim. During Mehmed's absence in eastern Anatolia it would have been easy for Matthias and his allies to attack Rumelia, which had been virtually stripped of troops and could not have offered serious resistance. Indeed, even Istanbul with its fortifications could not have been defended for any length of time. By temporizing with the Hungarian ambassador throughout the campaign, Mehmed had averted the danger from the north. Matthias had also sent an envoy to Uzun Hasan, but we have no knowledge of what became of him.

Probably the sultan did not return to his capital until close to the end of the year. His route took him through Amasya, where he appears to have spent four weeks, Ankara, and Kütahya. Apparently he hesitated whether to spend the winter in Bursa or in Istanbul but decided in favor of the latter. His sons, whom he heaped with honors—especially Mustafa, his favorite—returned to their posts in Amasya and Konya. In Istanbul stern punishment was meted out to the dignitaries who had tried to usurp the power for Prince Cem. With a part of the army the grand vizier Mahmud Pasha had remained six days' march behind the sultan. On the third day after his arrival in Istanbul he incurred an outburst of his master's rage. The episode will be detailed on a later page.

The favorable moment, the period of the sultan's absence, during which his European territories and even his capital could have been wrested away from him, had been allowed to slip by. The sultan himself had fully expected such an invasion, as is proved by the defensive measures hastily undertaken in Istanbul. When news of the defeat at Tercan reached the capital, the city gates were quickly walled over. Only three were left open. According to Domenico Malipiero, 10,000 workmen were employed to build walls and dig trenches. Enormous chains were forged, one of which was used to block the straits between Asia and Europe and prevent any enemy ships from sailing in to Istanbul and the Golden Horn. Near St. Demetrius, at Cape Serai (Saray Burnu), a wall twenty paces in length was erected and furnished with fourteen bombards. All along the shore of Galata, mortars were installed, and new walls built around this quarter. All Greeks were removed from Negropont and 150 Greek families were transplanted to Istanbul. The fears proved totally groundless, although a Venetian attack was planned in the summer of 1473.

Girolamo da Mula, a member of the college of the five *Savi agli Ordini* and a man reputed for his shrewdness and experience, proposed, against the opposition of his colleagues, an adventurous plan by which, he believed, Pietro Mocenigo could capture Istanbul. The Venetian fleet, so he explained in the council, had been reinforced by 100 galleys, Uzun Hasan was approaching the borders of Turkey, and southeastern Europe was virtually undefended since the sultan had sent every available man into the field; in short, the time had come to strike a blow at the Ottoman capital. His plan was that the captain general should set fire to a ship laden with 200 or 300 barrels of powder and send it ashore at the entrance of the straits, near the Castello della Grecia (Eski Hisarlïk). The heat, so Girolamo da Mula believed, would make the fortress cannon go off of their own accord. Then the Christian fleet would be able to enter the Hellespont unhindered, since the blaze would prevent the Turks from reloading quickly enough. His proposition was actually accepted by the senate on June 25, 1473. Pietro Mocenigo was sent orders to proceed accordingly, provided the papal legate and the captain of the Neapolitan squadron agreed, but by the time Mocenigo received the letter off Rhodes on July 24, 1473, news came that the king of Cyprus was dead. The adventurous project was abandoned at once and Mocenigo hastened to Cyprus.

Even after the victory over Uzun Hasan, the situation in Rumelia was not regarded as secure. At the end of October 1473, spies who had left Edirne reported details of the fighting in eastern Anatolia to the rector and council of Dubrovnik. In order to pacify the population, so they said, the sultan had sent messengers to Serbia and Bosnia to inform them of his brilliant victory. Indeed, it can be gathered from various reliable reports of those days that during the campaign, for which all young men capable of bearing arms had been enlisted, Rumelia was at times in a state of dangerous ferment. Bands were raiding the countryside, pillaging towns and villages, creating confusion, and terrorizing the old men to whom the defense of their country had been entrusted. Although counseled by the crafty and experienced Ishak Pasha, the boy Cem, as regent of Rumelia, was unable to check the disorder. But when before the sultan's departure Ishak Pasha had asked him what he should do if the enemy invaded the country, Mehmed replied, "Here there are merchants and artisans. You can defend yourself with them. I must take all the rest with me."

At the request of Haci Muhammad the Venetian senate had resolved on September 25, 1472, to assure Uzun Hasan of its continued support, to promise the requested artillery, and to order Mocenigo to put himself and his fleet at Uzun Hasan's disposal. It was necessary to send an ambassador to Tabriz with the news, and on September 27 the senate decided to send Giosafat Barbaro, with an annual wage of 1,800 ducats and an escort of ten men. The choice seemed fortunate, for Barbaro had long been Venetian consul in Azov (Tana; Turkish Azak) on the Black Sea, then commander (*provveditore*) of Albania, and had ample knowledge of Oriental languages. On January 11, 1473, the senate agreed to send Uzun Hasan six large mortars, ten of medium size, and thirty-six small ones. Other war material was also to be delivered, not to mention presents of costly fabrics. Giosafat Barbaro was given open and secret instructions. On the way he was to visit Pietro Mocenigo and exhort him to attack; he was also to call on the king and queen of Cyprus and on the Knights of Rhodes to solicit cooperation of their ships. The secret orders said that the Signoria was resolved never to make peace with the sultan unless he agreed to abandon the whole of Anatolia to Uzun Hasan, to give up all his territories beyond the straits and the whole coast opposite Greece, and to obligate himself never again to build a fortress along his coasts, so that the route to the Black Sea would remain open to the Venetians for purposes of trade and travel. If, on the other hand, Uzun Hasan should make peace with the sultan, he must include his ally, the Venetian Republic, in the peace and demand the return of the Morea, Mytilini, and Negropont, or at least of Negropont and Argos.

Whether the Signoria actually hoped to obtain even a part of these immoderate demands is not clear. But it is obvious that all these claims could never have been realized unless a joint campaign had completely crushed the Ottoman power. With this mission Giosafat Barbaro left Venice on February 18, 1473. Haci Muhammad accompanied him. In Zadar he met the envoys of the Curia and the court of Naples. They continued on together by way of Corfu, Methoni, and Koroni to Rhodes and Famagusta on Cyprus, where they arrived on March 29.[8]

Here their journey was unexpectedly interrupted. Giosafat Barbaro was obliged to remain on the island for over a year because the Ottomans

---

[8] For Barbaro's account of his travels, see *Travels to Tana and Persia*, 37ff.

had occupied the coasts of Anatolia and blocked the land route to Tabriz. The time passed in conversations with Pietro Mocenigo, who hesitated to give the dethroned prince of Karaman more active aid, and with King James II of Lusignan, who, because of the situation of his island, seemed to be more favorable to the Ottomans than to the Christians even though his queen, Caterina Cornaro of Venice, was related to Uzun Hasan's wife. From Karaman, Kasĭm Bey sent urgent pleas for help which finally moved the Christian fleet to take action. During June and July the fortresses of Sighino, Korykos, and Silifke were captured and handed over to Kasĭm Bey. He conveyed his thanks by means of a leopard, a magnificent charger, and an abundance of silver plate.

On June 8, 1473, Giosafat Barbaro wrote Uzun Hasan from Korykos that he, along with Haci Muhammad and emissaries from the pope and the king of Naples, was awaiting his bidding and that the Christian forces were willing to attack even Constantinople. The Turkmen prince caused the glad tidings to be proclaimed throughout his army and the name of Venice was cheered to the sound of trumpets and cymbals.

On July 6, King James II of Cyprus died, leaving a nineteen-year-old widow and an infant son. The king had been ailing for some time and his death was to be expected. His widow, Caterina Cornaro, Venetian by birth and a "daughter of the republic," became regent. Under the circumstances everybody suspected Venice of having designs on the island, and both the pope and Naples jealously watched the situation. This was the reason why Mocenigo shied away from decisive action, confined himself to quick raids on the nearby coast, and otherwise stayed close to the island. Upon receiving the news of the king's death, he gave up the attack on the straits at once and hastened to Cyprus. By summer the squadrons of Naples and the pope had returned to eastern waters, but now they were not under the supreme command of Mocenigo; they preferred to be independent and keep an eye on his movements and the developments on Cyprus. No one paid much attention to Uzun Hasan's pleas for action. Soon after his defeat at Başkent, Venice, menaced by Ottoman raids in Friuli, recalled the fleet with the provision that the Cyprus question be settled first. Thus Mocenigo did not sail into the Adriatic until the following summer, after having secured Caterina's reign as queen (her infant son James III died at the age of two in 1475, thus terminating the line of Lusignan) and installed Venetian governors in the key cities. Caterina was able to hold out against the Turkish threat and Venetian pressure for some time until, in 1489, she yielded and transferred sovereignty over the island to Venice.

Uzun Hasan, although beaten, did not abandon hope of a change of fortune. The greater part of the enormous territory over which he ruled was hardly aware of his defeat. He turned at once to the Signoria with the proposal that they should "ride against the Ottomans together." At the same time he sent Caterino Zeno back to Venice to convince the princes of Christendom that he had not abandoned the field but would raise a powerful army the following spring and continue the struggle, provided the Christians did not deny him their help. The ambassadors from Poland and Hungary were also sent home. But most Western princes had by now lost what little interest they had had in a common crusade, and only the Holy See and the Signoria continued to bank on an alliance with the lord of the White Sheep.

Stripped of all earthly goods and in a pitiful frame of mind, Caterino Zeno first reached Kaffa, whence he sent a report to the Signoria about Uzun Hasan's plans. As Giosafat Barbaro had still not reached his destination with his shipment of armaments, the senate, on receiving Caterino Zeno's report, decided to send Paolo Ogniben to Tabriz to inform Uzun Hasan that Venice would remain loyal to its alliance with him. Shortly before Christmas (December 10, 1473) another envoy, Ambrogio Contarini, was chosen, and on December 20 a letter went out to Giosafat Barbaro, telling him to complete his journey. Ambrogio also received two sets of instructions, open and secret, which, to prevent their falling into enemy hands, he had to learn by heart. They were a repetition of earlier messages. The senate promised once again to commit its fleet. Uzun Hasan was authorized to begin hostilities where and when he pleased, but enjoined to haste.

While Paolo Ogniben and Ambrogio Contarini were on their way to Persia, Caterino Zeno returned home, making a detour through Poland. King Casimir, who was at war with Matthias Corvinus, received the Venetian envoy hospitably, made high promises, and knighted him (April 20, 1474). From Venice, Zeno went on at once to Rome and Naples, to report on his experiences to the pope and King Ferrante.[9]

Deserted by the papal and Neapolitan envoys, Giosafat Barbaro and Haci Muhammad started out from Cyprus disguised as pilgrims on February 11, 1474. From Korykos they traveled by way of Silifke, Tarsus, Mardin, Hasankeyf (Hissn Kaifa), and Siirt (Tigranocerta). Then they entered the territory of Kurdish bandits, who attacked them and robbed them mercilessly. Only Giosafat Barbaro, thanks to his swift horse, suc-

[9] Zeno gives the account of his trip home in *A Narrative of Italian Travels in Persia*, 30ff.

ceeded in escaping. His companions were butchered. When he finally reached the court in Tabriz on April 12, 1474, he found Uzun Hasan, then fifty years old, in dire straits. His own son Uğurlu Mehmed had rebelled against him (Uğurlu Mehmed later took refuge with Bayezid II, married one of his eight daughters, and became governor of Anatolia) and Uzun Hasan was bitterly disappointed at the indifference of the Christian world. To make a long story short, a new campaign was out the question.

Paolo Ogniben returned to Venice on February 17, 1475. Ambrogio Contarini, who had met Giosafat Barbaro in Isfahan, where Uzun Hasan was then residing (November 1474), left Persia in June 1475; he crossed the Caspian Sea to Tatary, then continued on by way of Moscow, Lithuania, Poland, and Germany, and reached Venice on April 9, 1477. The last to return was Giosafat Barbaro, who set out for home only after Uzun Hasan's death on January 6, 1478. He joined a caravan going to Beirut, where he boarded a Cretan ship to Venice.

Pietro Mocenigo returned home in 1474 and was chosen doge on December 15. He died on February 23, 1476, and was glorified in his epitaph for having laid waste Asia from the Hellespont to Cyprus with fire and sword and having reestablished the rule of the kings of Karaman, allies of Venice, who had been oppressed by the Ottomans (. . . *qui Asia a faucibus Hellesponti usque ad Cyprum ferro ignique vastate, Caramanis regibus, Venetorum sociis, Othomano oppressis, regno restituto*).

These claims—truthful as far as they go, although somewhat exaggerated—hide the lack of real significance in Mocenigo's feats. In 1473 it would have been possible to strike a mortal blow against Mehmed's empire and such a blow was, as we have seen, expected by the Porte. While Hungary and Germany failed to invade Rumelia, the principal blame must be imputed to Venice, whose policy was guided solely by commercial considerations. During all these months the captain general studiously avoided any encounter of his large fleet with the enemy. Over a period of almost a century and a half, from the battle of Gelibolu (May 29, 1416) to the battle of Lepanto (October 7, 1571), the Ottomans remained undefeated on the seas.

It goes without saying that Filelfo's advice to the doge to undertake a land war against the Turks was easier to give than to put into practice. Venice's land army consisted of mercenaries. Even to promise them a share of the spoils in the Turkish manner would not have kept up their fighting spirit. The state treasury, which had suffered dangerously from the interruption of the Levantine trade, barely sufficed to maintain the fleet. By herself, Venice was not in a position to wage a land war on the

Ottomans, and the indifference of the Western world precluded any joint plan of campaign. Instead, it was the sultan's raiders, the *akĭncĭs*, who took the offensive and hardly let a year pass without carrying their devastating raids almost unhindered into the unguarded frontier territories of the Holy Roman Empire. Ineluctably, like a raging torrent, Islam advanced against the divided West. The dreaded Turkish incursions into Carniola, Styria, and Carinthia began in 1469 and were renewed every year for the remainder of Mehmed's reign. After that they occurred at intervals well into the first half of the sixteenth century.

These frightful raids, which assumed larger and larger proportions and brought death and misery to the populations, seem to have been carried out systematically in conjunction with the sultan's military undertakings. As leaders, Ottoman sources mention Mihaloğlu Ali Bey, the hereditary commander of the *akĭncĭs,* Malkoçoğlu Bali Bey, who had his headquarters in Smederevo, and Ishak Pasha himself, the governor of Bosnia.

Styria was first raided at Pentecost, 1471. But the terrible reports which reached the Regensburg diet in the summer, along with urgent pleas for help, produced no effect; no one thought seriously of resisting the Ottoman hordes. Everywhere churches, monasteries, and settlements went up in flames; men and cattle were carried off by the thousands; no one was sure of his life. The raiders appeared in the remotest valleys; not even high mountains could stop their incursions. Nor was Hungarian territory spared, and finally the robber bands, whose numbers have been variously estimated and sometimes set, perhaps exaggeratedly, at 40,000 horsemen, came within sight of Venice. Their leaders, especially Malkoçoğlu Bali Bey, drove innumerable prisoners off to the southeast. A source worthy of belief relates that in order to demonstrate the success of his Hungarian expedition, he displayed countless sacks full of heads, noses, and ears at the Porte.

In 1470 and 1471, by way of providing fixed bases for large and small incursions to the north and northwest, the march wardens built new bastions, the most important being at Šabac (Turkish Bögürdelen) on the Sava, thirty-eight miles west of Belgrade; it was built so quickly under the protection of allegedly 20,000 men that King Matthias Corvinus, busy fighting the Bohemians in the north, was unable to interfere. The army which he finally sent to the Sava made desperate attempts to harass the Turkish workmen, but without success, for the Turks were able to entrench themselves behind the high earth bulwark on the far shore of the river. No sooner was the bastion completed than the first swarms of Ottoman horsemen, led by Ishak Pasha, poured through Croatia to Carniola as far as the walls of Ljubljana, transforming the flourishing but undefended countryside into a desert and carrying many thousands off into slavery. These wild raids cost countless people their freedom each year. Priests and officials, for the most part eyewitnesses, have left a number of heartrending accounts describing the cruelty of the Turkish hordes and the sufferings of the population.[9a]

By and large, the Ottoman threat to a weary and divided Christendom was undiminished. It required no great political acumen to conclude that as soon as the sultan had rid himself of Uzun Hasan, his one truly dangerous enemy in the East, and had secured his eastern frontiers, he would turn his arms with redoubled violence against the West. There was little talk of serious and sustained resistance, least of all in the German countries. No further mention was made of the "imperial aid" announced in Regensburg.

It was around this time, perhaps in 1473, that Emperor Frederick III drew to his court Calixtus Ottomanus, that strange alleged half brother of Mehmed II, who was then at the court of Matthias Corvinus in Buda. "Emperor Bayezid Osman," as he was called at least for a time, traveled through the provinces with his imperial patron marveled at by the populace, to whom he was displayed as the rightful Ottoman sultan, turban and richly embroidered robes serving to identify him as such. At many imperial diets he was presented to the amazed crowds, who were told that thanks to this strange hostage, Emperor Frederick had the Ottoman throne in his power.[10]

At a banquet on the occasion of the diet of Trèves (1473), where the emperor and Charles the Bold of Burgundy met to arrange the marriage between their children, Mary of Burgundy and Maximilian of Hapsburg, the Turkish prince poured water for the emperor, whom he then accompanied on all further journeys through the empire. Calixtus was still with the emperor when he campaigned against and besieged the duke of Burgundy at Neuss. Through the influence of Pope Sixtus IV an armistice was concluded between the warring parties on May 28, 1475, and the emperor was finally able to return to Vienna, still accompanied by Calixtus.

In Austria he was made lord successively over various fiefs such as Perchtoldsdorf, Baden near Vienna, and Rauhenstein on the Schwechat.

[9a] For references to some of the sources see Jorga, *Geschichte des Osmanischen Reiches* II, 156–159.

[10] Babinger deals with the Ottoman pretender in his "Zur Lebensgeschichte des Calixtus Ottomanus," *KPHTIKA XPONIKA* 7 (Heraklion, 1953), 457–461; and "'Bajezid Osman' (Calixtus Ottomanus), ein Vorläufer und Gegenspieler Dschem Sultans," *La Nouvelle Clio* (Brussels, 1951), 349–388 (reprinted in *A&A* I, 326–328 and 297–325, respectively).

But from then on his life became more uneventful. He was long engaged to Lucia von Hohenfeld, an impoverished noblewoman famous throughout Austria for her beauty, but they were never married. When Matthias Corvinus occupied Austria in 1481, Bayezid Osman sided with him. After the death of his "brother" Mehmed in the same year, he sent a message to the grand master of the Knights of St. John in Rhodes, asking his help in mounting the Ottoman throne. In 1490, King Matthias died and Calixtus went over to King Maximilian of Germany, whom he accompanied on his travels through southern Germany. Then he seems to have settled in Vienna. For a few weeks he held the Prugg Castle in Bruck on the Leitha, but lost it again shortly before he died in the fall of 1496, ignored and forgotten.

We will never know the true facts, but the version current in the fifteenth century in Europe and in part derived from statements of Pope Calixtus III is of some interest. According to this, Bayezid Osman was born in 1448 to Murad II. Afraid that the boy might be killed, his father sent him to Constantinople, where he was raised secretly by a "certain cavalier." After the fall of the city, the cavalier and his ward were sold as slaves, and after some adventures redeemed by the pope and brought to Rome. Circumstantial evidence indicates that this "cavalier" was Giovanni Torcello, who was on the papal payroll for three years to educate the boy. Thus Calixtus became a pawn in the hands of kings, emperors, and popes.

Hard pressed by almost all his neighbors, Frederick III was obliged to entrust the defense of the empire in the southeast to his noblemen and the local estates who, with their improvised companies and bands of peasants, were decimated in the unequal struggle with the Turkish robber hordes. Nothing bears more eloquent witness to the emperor's terrifying indifference to the fate of the West than his attempt, noted by Domenico Malipiero in his *Cronaca*, to force the diet of Regensburg to deny Uzun Hasan all aid in order that the "Turk" might be more successful in his struggle against the Signoria. The Venetian chronicler's assumption that Galeazzo-Maria Sforza and the Florentines had something to do with this requires a word of explanation. Both were indignant that of all the Italian states only Venice should have an ambassador with Uzun Hasan's armies, and that should Greece actually be conquered, Venice alone would take possession of it. Not much better was the attitude of Hungary, whose crafty and calculating ruler thought only of his personal advantage. When his war with Bohemia was concluded, Matthias Corvinus might have been free to send his army against the Ottomans, whose fort of Šabac, with a standing garrison of at least 5,000 men, was a permanent threat to his frontiers. He saw plainly that his empire would never be at peace as long as Šabac was in Ottoman hands. Charles the Bold of Burgundy, to be sure, had undertaken to proceed in common with Venice, the Curia, and Naples, but in the end his passionate efforts to extend the power of Burgundy and his designs on the crown of France, for whose accomplishment he needed the emperor, made him look on the Turkish peril as a secondary concern. Indifference to the threat increased with the distance from the seat of danger. France and England were utterly indifferent to the plight of Christendom.

Italy was no less divided. One political alliance followed another in breathless and aimless haste. "This perpetual change of ties, this faculty of being friend and enemy in one, this inability to understand clearly at every moment the situation of every state—these are becoming more and more the hallmarks of Italian political life." It cannot be denied that Sixtus IV was animated by the desire to unite the armies of Christendom against the Crescent. But it is questionable whether he possessed the power necessary for so vast an undertaking. The zealous defense of the West that marked the beginning of his pontificate was increasingly obscured by the fantastic favors which he heaped almost promiscuously on his numerous and largely unworthy relatives. Rome was the scene of banquets which for wild extravagance exceeded anything the sybaritic age of the Renaissance had hitherto witnessed. One of these, given during the carnival of 1473 by the pope's nephew, the splendor-loving cardinal Pietro Riario, who was then twenty-seven years old, deserves mention in this connection.

This fantastic banquet was attended by four cardinals, by all the ambassadors and prelates present in Rome, and by the sons of the despot of the Morea, who had been driven out of Greece by Mehmed II. The walls of the banquet hall, so writes Giovanni Arcimboldi, bishop of Novara, in a letter to Galeazzo-Maria Sforza, were adorned with the most precious carpets. In the center, on a dais, stood a table at which sat the sumptuously clad "king of Macedonia." On all sides torches illuminated the lurid banquet. The meal, at tables overloaded with silver, went on for three full hours. Before every course a seneschal appeared on horseback, each time in a different costume, and music was played. After the meal a Moorish dance was performed, followed by other entertainment. At the end a Turkish envoy appeared with credentials from the sultan and an interpreter, complaining that Cardinal Riario had given the Grand Turk's empire to the king of Macedonia. If, he declared, the king did not cast off his usurped emblems of dignity, he would challenge him to combat.

The cardinal and the king accepted the challenge. On the following day, accordingly, a tournament was held on the Piazza dei Santi Apostoli. The outcome was that the Grand Turk was taken prisoner by the king of Macedonia's general—Uzun Hasan!—and dragged through the Eternal City in chains.

Full light cannot be thrown on the role of the various Italian states in the struggle against the Ottomans. Jacob Burckhardt has already pointed out that, great as their fear of the Turks and great as the actual danger may have been, there was scarcely a state of any importance which was not prepared at one time or another to enter into an agreement with Mehmed II and his successors against other Italian states. "And even when it was not done, each suspected the others' intentions." To cite only one example from the period under consideration: while Venice, the Curia, and Naples with their squadrons were staging at least a semblance of a crusade against the Ottomans, the city of Florence addressed two letters (September 3 and November 5, 1472) to Mehmed II, praising him for his humanity and his enduring good will toward the Florentines in the Levant and commending the new consul, Carlo Baroncello, to his benevolence. Much as one may be tempted to regard such turns of phrase as mere formulas, involving no commitment, it is certain that after the fall of Negropont, Florence managed to remain aloof from the struggle, while representing itself as the companion in fate of Venice and encouraging the republic to answer the "Turkish fury" (*furor turcus*) with "Venetian bravery" (letter of August 30, 1470). We shall soon see what consequences this shrewdly pursued policy of nonintervention was to bring forth in Mehmed's lifetime. It was perfectly clear that the Venetians could not count on the active assistance of their rivals on the Arno.[11]

When, in the late fall of 1473, Mehmed returned to Istanbul from his victorious campaign in eastern Anatolia, cruel punishment was immediately meted out to the guilty and the innocent alike. The grand vizier Mahmud Pasha was one of the first to fall a victim to the sultan's capricious vengeance. He had been in the capital only three days when his master summoned him to a council. The topic under discussion was said to have been the conditions among the Janissaries. When the conference was over, Mahmud Pasha was detained, arrested, and thrown

[11] For the context of Burckhardt's remarks see *The Civilization of the Renaissance in Italy*, trans. S. G. C. Middlemore (London, 1950), 59. Babinger gives bibliographic details for the Florentine letters in his *Spätmittelalterliche fränkische Briefschaften aus dem grossherrlichen Seraj zu Stambul* (= *Südosteuropäische Arbeiten* 61, [1963]), 9–10.

into the Prison of the Seven Towers. One version was that he stayed there for six whole months in uncertainty over his fate, another that he spent this period in his country estate of Hasköy and was only then taken to the capital and locked up in the Seven Towers, where Sinan, the bailiff of Istanbul, aided by a few of his henchmen, strangled him with a bow-string. The day of his death, July 18, 1474, is established with certainty. Some sources attribute his execution to his failure to save the Palaeologus Hass Murad Pasha, the sultan's favorite, from drowning in the Euphrates; others to his having deterred Mehmed from completing his victory at Başkent by swift pursuit of Uzun Hasan. A connection was also seen between the sultan's act of vengeance and the sudden death of Prince Mustafa a few weeks earlier. Of this we shall speak presently.

However he met his end, it is unlikely that the real reasons for the execution of Mahmud Pasha, probably the greatest statesman of the Conqueror's reign, will ever come to light. The common people, who to this day tell countless tales about this illustrious man, have adorned his life and death with legend. The chapbook of Mahmud Pasha, "the saint" (*veli*), which was first circulated in innumerable manuscripts and later in lithographic prints, has not yet lost its appeal although, strangely enough, the legends of Mahmud Pasha were transferred in the course of time to Sultan Mahmud I (1730–1754) who, like the grand vizier, was accredited with supernatural wisdom as well as a knowledge of the language of the animals and the secrets of the earth. Not only did this outstanding statesman and general, who twice occupied the highest position in the land, earn the gratitude of his people by his many pious foundations, among which a mosque with his *türbe* [pl. XIX b] is still preserved near the covered bazaar of Istanbul. He also merits remembrance for his patronage of scholars and artists and for poetry in Persian and Turkish, which he wrote under the name Adni (the Eden-like). Once a week, on Friday at the noonday meal, he received the students of the superior school he had endowed. On these occasions golden peas were mixed into the pilaf—the grand vizier's way of letting chance rather than merit allot the prizes. He was known and feared for the frankness with which he spoke to everyone, even the sultan. The story goes that one day he asked Mullah Ahmed the reason for the decline of his native Crimea. The blame, replied the mullah, lay entirely with the last khan's vizier, through whose fault "the palaces are falling into ruins given over to hooting owls, ravens live in the window frames, spiders spin their webs in the halls, and the stars and the moon shine through the cracks in the dome." "Do you see?" remarked the sultan to Mahmud Pasha. "The viziers are the cause of the downfall of empires." Mahmud Pasha was bold enough to reply, "The fault is not, as the mullah maintains, with the vizier, who was a righteous man and a shrewd statesman, but with the khan, who did not know how to govern." Such outspokenness, together with his popularity with the people, might have aroused Mehmed's jealousy and distrust and have been the ultimate cause for the grand vizier's downfall.[12]

Thanks to a fortunate accident, we possess a graphic account of the events connected with the sudden death of Prince Mustafa, the sultan's favorite son. Gian-Maria Angiolello was in the prince's immediate entourage and wrote a faithful account of his last illness, his burial, the fate of his family, and the impact of his death on his almost inconsolable father.[13] During the year 1474, for which only two documents (July 8 and September 24) attest the probably continuous presence of the sultan in his capital, the sultan did not take part in any military campaigns.[14] The background and consequences of the family tragedy in the house of Osman, which might in some way be related to the hasty elimination of the grand vizier Mahmud Pasha, are unknown to us, chiefly because the cause of death remains a mystery. When his stepbrother Bayezid returned to Amasya, his place of office, Prince Mustafa and his retinue had journeyed from the battlefield by way of Kayseri, Aksaray, Niğde, and Bor to Konya, his residence as governor of Karaman. Toward the end of September 1473, he arrived in the best of health and devoted himself to falconry and other entertainment. He had a sailboat on the lake of Beyşehir, and he often spent his time with friends fishing, hunting, and enjoying the wine grown by the Greeks and Armenians of the region. His amusements were not exactly to the taste of the Christian population, for when drunk he was prone to all sorts of mischief. Three months later, at the end of the year, he commissioned one of his officers, a certain Koçi Bey, to take the mountain castle of Develü Karahisar (twenty-eight miles southwest of Kayseri), which was still held by partisans of the Karamanid Pir Ahmed and, along with the other fortified places in so-called Taş Eli, resisted the Ottomans. After the departure of Koçi Bey, Prince Mustafa

[12] The article "Mahmud Paşa" (M. C. Ş. Tekindağ), *IA* VII, 183–188, is the closest thing to a monograph study of Mehmed's grand vizier. The continued popular appreciation of this "saint" is testified to by the publication of the latest "chapbook" biography, N. Ahmed Banoğlu, *Mahmud Paşa hayati ve şehadeti* (Istanbul, 1970). The vizier's mosque and *türbe* are treated by Goodwin, *A History of Ottoman Architecture*, 109ff. (See also the index there for other buildings constructed in his name.)

[13] Angiolello's account is given in his *Historia turchesca*, 62–71.

[14] The documents are given by Truhelka, "Tursko-slovjenski spomenici," *GZMBH* 23 (1911), 38–40; Turkish translation in *IED* 1 (1955), 59 (documents 40 and 41).

suddenly fell ill. The physicians prescribed medicines which brought relief, soon followed by a relapse brought on by the prince's usual dissipations. His illness lasted with ups and downs for six months. The captain in command of Develü Karahisar refused to surrender the fortress to Koçi Bey, declaring that he would negotiate only with Prince Mustafa himself. His limbs virtually paralyzed, the prince set out and reached his destination at the end of twelve days. Meanwhile his condition deteriorated and his followers agreed to take him back to Konya; at the same time they would inform the sultan of the military situation and ask for help. Mehmed immediately sent Gedik Ahmed Pasha, who at the time enjoyed his special confidence, to Karaman with an army of allegedly 30,000 men and at the same time dispatched his personal physician, Maestro Iacopo, to attend his son. In the mild air of Niğde the physicians expected Mustafa's health to improve, but after a week the prince and his retinue started for Konya, where they hoped to find Maestro Iacopo. When they reached Bor after a two-day journey, the prince took a hot bath, after which he felt still worse than before. Fever set in and he died at midnight. The prince's entourage decided to keep his death secret. On the pretext that the prince thought the night air would do him good, they raised the camp. Previously, so Angiolello reports, they removed the dead man's entrails, filled his body with honey and barley, sewed it up, and put him in a coffin, which was sealed. The entrails were washed and put in a box filled with salt. So the funeral procession proceeded to Konya. In the wagon that carried the mortal remains of the prince there were two men, one a dwarf by the name of Nasuh ("Nasuf"), the other, larger in stature, named Ismail, who was instructed to imitate his master's voice. From time to time a member of the retinue, who knew of the prince's death, approached the wagon and began to speak; Ismail answered from inside the wagon. And so all believed that Mustafa Çelebi was alive and in possession of his strength. After six days, the procession reached Konya, where meanwhile news of the governor's death had spread. It was feared that the population, which was far from supporting the new Ottoman overlords, would rebel. The prince's mother had not been informed of his death, and when the wagon with her dead son stopped outside the palace, she and the women of her train began to wail. Mustafa's only child, a daughter of about fourteen by the name of Nergiszade, shared her grandmother's grief, and the lamentations went on endlessly. Soon Gedik Ahmed Pasha and his army camped in Meram, the garden suburb of Konya at the time inhabited exclusively by Greek Christians, only a few of whom, however, knew Greek; they spoke almost entirely Turkish and their religious books, so Angiolello reports, were Turkish written in Arabic script. Mustafa's body was laid out in a mosque and a mounted messenger sent to Istanbul to announce the mournful news to the sultan.[15]

When the messenger reached the capital, he was afraid to break the news to the sultan. Indeed, no one was able to summon up the courage except for Hoca Sinan Pasha, the sultan's old confidant and teacher, who had often incurred the sultan's rages but was better able to deal with him than almost anyone else. Hoca Sinan put on black mourning garments and went to the sultan. When the sultan saw him, he knew at once what had happened and stepped down from the dais on which he had been sitting. Picking up the carpets that were spread over the floor, he burst into loud lamentations, mourning his son's fate in the true Oriental manner. He gathered the dust from the cracks in the floor, strewed it on his head in token of his grief, beat his face with his hands, then his chest and thighs, all the while emitting loud sighs. According to Angiolello, he spent three days and nights in this state of despair. Then he stopped lamenting and gave orders that all the shops in the capital should remain closed for three days. "The entire city was filled with loud lamentation because Mustafa was especially beloved of his father and of all those who had dealings with him."

If Angiolello's dates are correct, Prince Mustafa died in June 1474. If we recall that the grand vizier Mahmud Pasha was executed on July 18, we are tempted to see a connection between the two events. Mustafa, so we are told by writers worthy of credence, did not always respect other men's harems, and as early as 1465 a report reached Venice to the effect that he had taken liberties with the wife of the then governor of Rumelia. The wife of Gedik Ahmed Pasha, a daughter of Ishak Pasha, also found favor in the prince's eyes and was therefore divorced. It was also said that Mustafa had approached the wife of Mahmud Pasha, who was governor of Rumelia for a time. Thus, a rumor connecting the prince's death with Mahmud Pasha sprang up, although, as Angiolello shows, the deposed vizier was perfectly innocent. According to another rumor, Mahmud Pasha, who was still living at his estate of Hasköy at the time of the prince's death and went to Bursa only for the funeral, had earned the sultan's mortal hatred by unseemly behavior during the period of mourning: he had worn a white robe while playing chess instead of the black garment prescribed for the entire court.[16]

Three weeks after the sultan had received the news of his son's death,

[15] For the Turkish-speaking Christian community, see Vryonis, *The Decline of Medieval Hellenism*, 452–462.

[16] For a cause of bad relations between the grand vizier and Prince Mustafa, see I. H. Uzunçarşïlï, "Fatih Sultan Mehmed'in veziri azamlarından Mahmud Paşa ile Şehzade Mustafa'nïn aralarï neden açïlmïştï?," *Belleten* 28 (1964), 719–728.

the prince's burial was ordered in Bursa. At the same time Gedik Ahmed Pasha received orders at last to subdue the rebellious region of Taş Eli. The mother, with her dead son and her entire retinue, repaired to the old Anatolian capital, where the prince was laid to rest in the burial place of his ancestors. His father was not present. Mustafa's mother, who had no doubt lost the sultan's favor, was ordered to reside thereafter in Bursa. Most of her retinue was transferred to Istanbul. The women were as usual moved into the old serai, and only a few days later the marriageable among them were married to courtiers and others. Mehmed's granddaughter Nergiszade was married to her cousin Ahmed Çelebi, the firstborn of Prince Bayezid, who was invested with the *sancak* for the occasion. The governorship of Karaman was conferred on Prince Cem, Mehmed's third son.

Gedik Ahmed Pasha had meanwhile pitched camp in Laranda, whence he invaded the surrounding territory. It took him approximately two months to arrive at a satisfactory understanding with the chiefs of the various tribes of the region and to make them into the sultan's compliant subjects. Before returning to Istanbul the vizier arranged a gathering with equestrian games, and invited all the nobles of Karaman. While they were seated at table, expecting no evil, Ahmed Pasha had them seized from behind; almost all were killed. He dragged innumerable men, women, and children of the region off to the north with him. They were settled partly in Thrace, partly in Serbia and Bosnia. In this way Karaman was immunized against further uprisings for many years to come, and from this time on bore the Conqueror's fetters without resistance.

And so the year 1474 passed without important military undertakings. In the interior of the empire, where Mahmud Pasha had done so much to insure stability, the sultan took more power into his own hands. None of the highest dignitaries played a prominent role, and it is typical of this period that the identity of the executed vizier's successor cannot be determined with certainty. It is usually held that Gedik Ahmed Pasha assumed the supreme office, but none of the Western sources so far available mentions him in this position. It is not infrequently maintained that the vizier Hoca Sinan Pasha, son of Hïzïr Bey (the first judge of Istanbul), took over the grand vizierate and held it for two years. If he really held the imperial seal, he made no name for himself during his term in office, whereas, as we shall soon see, Gedik Ahmed Pasha was spoken of on more than one occasion.

One measure which, according to an Ottoman source, was taken by Mehmed before the end of 1474 should be mentioned here because it undoubtedly has a bearing on the political legislation and institutions to which the sultan largely devoted the next years of his reign. He decreed that when a fief (*timar*), large or small, was conferred, not only the name of the enfeoffed, as before, but also a transcript of the deed listing the incomes from each village must be entered in the feudal registers of the treasury. As a natural consequence of Mehmed's far-flung conquests, a steadily increasing number of soldiers were rewarded with fiefs for their service in battle. The decree in question was designed to counteract certain abuses resulting from the large numbers of vassals. In the Rumelian territories epecially, the feudal administration appears to have been marked by irregularities and errors which must have offended the sultan as much as neglect of the five daily prayers, an observance strictly enforced, particularly among recent converts to Islam. Whenever Mehmed traversed the subjected territories at the head of an army, his officers reported on any abuses, which he was determined to correct immediately. In this connection, a story reported by several chroniclers shows that he sometimes took measures that strike us as absurd. While Mehmed was marching through Bulgaria on his way to Moldavia, Davud Pasha, the governor of Anatolia, who was riding beside him, informed him that at Tavşanlï (today Tavşantepe), five miles northwest of Yambol, a dozen wool carders had surprised a fox in their workshop and chased it but had not succeeded in catching it. As punishment for their incompetence, Mehmed decreed that the wool carders of Tavşanlï must henceforth pay a fine of five aspers to the local police captain. Centuries later, so a traveler tells us, this regulation was still in force.

Before the end of 1474 Mehmed, then forty-two years of age, suffered severe attacks of gout brought on by the hardships and exertions of the east Anatolian campaign. In the ensuing years his hereditary predisposition to gout, encouraged by his plethoric, obese physique and his pleasure-loving ways, was to result in alarming disorders in almost every part of his body. In 1474, in any case, his illness deterred him from campaigning in person. He spent his time in the palace, whose large, irregular structure had been extended in September 1472 by the completion of the so-called Sïrça Saray. There he hatched plans for new campaigns, the execution of which was entrusted to persons enjoying his special favor.

It had been perfectly clear to those most directly involved, especially to the Venetians, that the sultan would transfer his attentions to the Western world after defeating Uzun Hasan. And in Italy there were few who doubted that Albania, which had so long evaded Mehmed's arm, would be one of his first goals. Moreover, the conviction had gradually taken root that Albania, the last bulwark to the east of the Italian coasts, would have to fall before Italy's turn could come. Accordingly, the Venetians were determined to defend Albania at all costs. The principal task of the Venetian fleet was to protect its coasts and to screen off the mouths of the larger rivers, above all the Drin and the Bojana (Buenë). Since Pietro Mocenigo was immobilized by the situation on Cyprus, the Signoria designated as his successor Triadan Gritti, the eighty-four-year-old scion of a family which, in the following decades, was to play a part more than once in negotiations with the Porte. Early in May 1474, Gritti sailed to Albanian waters with six galleys. By summer Pietro Mocenigo was at last able to leave Cyprus, after having secured Caterina Cornaro as queen. On the way home he received orders near Corfu to sail the fleet to Albania and there to collaborate with Gritti in taking the necessary measures. At the same time the important post of *provveditore* of all Albania was conferred on Leonardo Boldu, who was well acquainted with the country and had proved himself in the course of important diplomatic missions. Antonio Loredano, one of the bravest and most steadfast Venetians of his day, was made commander of Shkodër in Upper Albania, which, both because of its situation and because of its fortress, the key to its defense, was regarded as the chief city of the country. Shkodër, however, was garrisoned by only 2,500 men, whose situation would have been desperate in the event of a strong Turkish attack.[17]

The Venetian precautions soon proved to be only too justified. The spies of the Signoria had noted the vast preparations for an Albanian campaign, an undertaking which, if successful, would enable the sultan to extend his conquests across the Adriatic to Italy.

The execution of the campaign was entrusted to a man who enjoyed Mehmed's special favor—Hadïm (i.e. eunuch) Süleyman Pasha, the governor of Rumelia. A Bosnian by birth, he was, according to some sources, taken prisoner as a boy, castrated, and, being beautiful, abused by Mehmed. Subsequently, he had spent many years in the service of the serai. He had long been devoted to the sultan, who in turn cherished and trusted him. It was believed that eunuchs, being without family ties, were less likely than other men to pursue selfish aims and for that reason they were often appointed to responsible posts in the government. Süleyman Pasha not only had proved an able governor of Rumelia but also had shown military abilities.

He received the supreme command over an army of 80,000 men, in-

[17] More details of the life of Loredano, who captained pilgrim vessels to the Holy Land before embarking on a military career, are given by R. J. Mitchell, *The Spring Voyage* (New York, 1964), 54–55, 58, and 128–129.

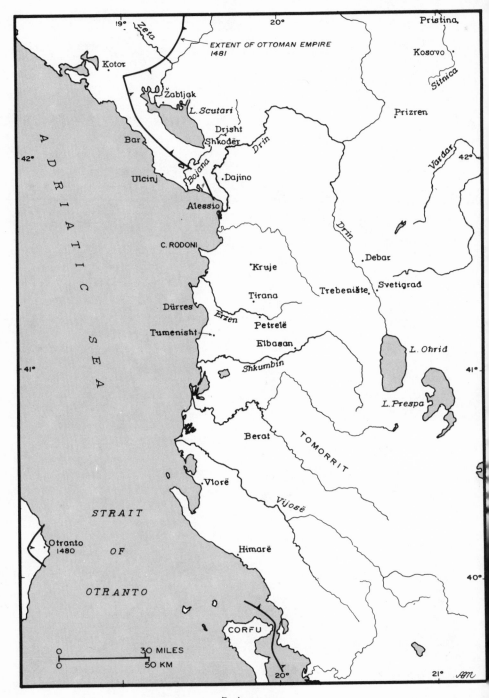

7. ALBANIA

cluding 8,000 Janissaries. The inclusion of the Janissaries in itself bears witness to the importance the sultan attached to the Albanian campaign. No less than 500 camels were needed to transport the metal for cannon. Mehmed had been in the habit of casting his cannon under the walls of the fortress to be attacked. As usual, many skilled cannon founders were with the army. Meister Jörg of Nuremberg, known for his forthright though too summary *Geschicht von der Turckey* (Memmingen, ca. 1482–1483 and several times reprinted), seems to have been a member of Süleyman Pasha's retinue.[18]

Crossing Serbia and Macedonia, the Turkish commander entered Albania through the mountains without meeting resistance and pitched his camp outside Shkodër early in May. He surrounded the city from all sides and prepared the siege. He built a bridge across the Bojana near the sea and placed it under guard to prevent the city from being supplied by the Venetian ships that were cruising off the coast. In a few days four large cannon and a dozen small ones were ready on their carriages. An uninterrupted hail of stones poured over the walls of the citadel. The fortress, situated on a rock dome some 450 feet high and accessible only from one side, had defended the city since the remotest times.

The Venetian fleet was ranged along the Albanian coast in accordance with a careful plan. Four galleys lay off Kotor (Cattaro), five more at the mouth of the Drin to protect Alessio and the large island formed of silt on which the inhabitants of the open country often took refuge in times of danger. Four galleys anchored off Durrës, others off Budva, Bar (Antivari), and Ulcinj (Dulcigno). The remaining ships with the two admirals put into the Bojana but were obliged to anchor near the Benedictine monastery and the Church of Sts. Sergius and Bacchus on the southern bank, eighteen miles from the mouth and six miles from Shkodër. From Lake Shkodër the Venetians tried to keep the fortress supplied with the help of seventy fishing boats. Venice's ally Ivan Crnojević, whose ancestors had long been voivodes over the territory (smaller than the future Montenegro) between Lake Shkodër and the Gulf of Kotor, was, with his intrepid followers, to protect the Venetians' communications between sea and lake.

In the battles during the siege, which lasted from July 15 to August 28, 1474, the situation of the castle of Shkodër became increasingly desperate. During the murderous but indecisive skirmishes at the mouth of the Bojana, old Triadan Gritti and his *provveditore* Luigi Bembo had come down with malaria. They were removed to Kotor, where they died. Under cannon fire from two platforms, a large part of the walls of

---

[18] For Jörg and his brief chronicle, see above, pp. 138f.

Shkodër had already collapsed. But the besiegers' guns were powerless against the high earthworks. Süleyman Pasha sent a message to Antonio Loredano offering favorable conditions and a large reward if he would surrender the fortress. The Venetian commander declined with proud indignation. He was not a Turkish slave, he replied, but a Venetian nobleman of an old family; loyalty and love of country meant more to him than all the sultan's treasures; if Süleyman was really the man he thought himself, he would know how to take the city whose walls had long been in ruins.

Thereupon Süleyman attempted for eight hours to storm the bulwarks of Shkodër. But in the end the Turks, who were said to have been driven forward with iron clubs, had to abandon their efforts. Seven thousand men (6,000 or 3,000, according to other sources) lost their lives, while a considerably larger number were wounded. Fourteen captains were killed. The pasha did not dare to repeat his disastrous attempt, all the more so as his troops were sorely tried by disease and the shortage of water. But the inhabitants of the city also complained of the shortage of food and fresh water and began to speak of surrender. In this critical hour, while the people were clamoring for the end of hostilities, Loredano saved the situation by a harangue in which he gave a vivid picture of Turkish slavery. After that even the most fainthearted thought it preferable to await the hour of deliverance. On August 28, at the false news that a Venetian army was on its way under Leonardo Boldu, Süleyman Pasha raised the siege. The cannon were broken into pieces and the metal removed on camelback. On the march to Prizren, Süleyman Pasha destroyed the castle of Dajino (called Dagno by the Venetians) surmounting a bell-shaped hill on the southern bank of the Drin. Its ruins, like those of the ancient Church of St. Mary below it, may still be seen. Dubrovnik was subjected to an increase of its annual tribute from 9,000 (1471) to 10,000 ducats. The reason given was that two Ragusan officers had helped in the defense of Shkodër.[19]

The rejoicing in Shkodër at the raising of the siege and the enemy's withdrawal was indescribable. The parched population rushed out through the gates to the Bojana to slake their thirst. Many were seized with the "mortal tremor" and died from drinking too much water.

The Venetian fleet, which had been sorely tried by fever in the marshy estuary of the Bojana, withdrew at once to the north. Seriously ill, Pietro Mocenigo hurried ahead to Venice by way of Dubrovnik.

In Venice, the saving of Shkodër and Albania was celebrated as a bril-

[19] A document confirming receipt of the payment is given by Elezović, *Turski spomenici* I, part 1, 167–168, and I, part 2, 44 (document 21).

liant military action. In the Church of St. Mark a golden banner with an appropriate inscription was hung up to commemorate the loyalty and bravery of the inhabitants of Shkodër. The Signoria voted Antonio Loredano's daughter 1,000 ducats for her dowry, in gratitude for her father's achievement, while Loredano himself was made captain general to succeed the deceased Triadan Gritti. Pietro Mocenigo, then seventy years of age, survived his elevation to the rank of doge by only fourteen months.

The rejoicing at the happy turn of events was somewhat clouded, to be sure, by the consideration that the purpose of the bitter struggle had hardly been achieved with the temporary withdrawal of the Turks from Upper Albania. No one dared to hope that the defeat at Shkodër would move the sultan to abandon his Albanian plans. The Venetians were convinced that Mehmed would soon try to avenge the disgrace his arms had suffered. New reports of the Ottoman's military preparations were received, and the Signoria was especially alarmed by news of feverish activity in the Turkish shipyards. The sultan, as it was reported, was about to leave the Dardanelles with 300 ships. The Venetians decided to increase their fleet to 100 galleys. The new ships were built partly in the Dalmatian ports, partly on Crete. The squadrons were to meet in the harbor of Navplion and if necessary prepare to strike a decisive blow. As far as possible, the possessions of the Signoria in the Levant were provided with troops, ammunition, and funds, to make them self-sufficient for a time in case of Turkish attack.

With each passing year the Venetian Republic found itself less able to bear the full burden of the protracted war, which drained its treasury and threatened to cut off its entire Levantine trade. In the late fall of 1474, the Signoria looked about for additional allies. It happened that at the same time Lorenzo de' Medici, forced to reconsider his policy toward the pope, was interested in a northern alliance and approached Venice. Venice was aware of Lorenzo's motives and, despite its difficult position, seems to have been reticent at first. Holding itself to be bound by its anti-Turkish alliances with Naples, and especially with Pope Sixtus IV, who had sent the besieged population of Shkodër money and supplies, the Signoria replied that Venice had a treaty with the Curia and Naples which other parties were free to enter at any time. Negotiations were carried on in Rome and once more Sixtus IV nourished high hopes of an alliance of all Italian states against the Crescent. An agreement satisfactory to all parties had already been arrived at when King Ferrante of Naples suddenly withdrew his support. Thereupon, on November 2, 1474, Venice, Florence, and Milan concluded an alliance for twenty-five years whereby all undertook to participate in the war against the Ottomans. The pope, the king of Naples, and the duke of Ferrara were invited to join. Only the last agreed to do so. The pope declined, setting forth his reasons in detail: he regarded the pact as a conspiracy directed against the Holy See, an attempt to encircle him and to make him a "docile instrument of the selfish policy of tyranny." Instead, he concluded an alliance with Naples. As a result of the new alliance in the north, Milan had to make over the sum of 30,000 ducats to the Venetians for the equipment of ten galleys.

Venice was profoundly indignant at the outcome of the discussions with the pope. It recalled its ambassador from Rome "in order that the world may know what manner of shepherd it is who looks calmly on as his flock is being devoured and does not come to its help." The hope of persuading the king of Hungary to join the alliance came to nothing in spite of the many embassies that were sent him during that period.

Hungary was then in a difficult position. Apparently its turn had come to incur the assault of the Ottomans. On St. Dorothea's Day, February 6, 1474, Malkoçoğlu Bali Bey, march warden of Smederevo, had invaded Hungary and plundered the entire territory as far as Oradea, burned the tomb of St. Ladislas, killed the inhabitants, beheaded the old people and small children, and carried the boys and girls across the Danube into slavery.

But this raid deep into Hungary was not all. At the beginning of June hordes of Turkish horsemen from Bosnia broke into Croatia, pressed on as far as Križevci (Körös, Kreutz), Koprivnica (Kapronca, Kopreinitz), and Varaždin (Varasd, Warasdin), and even appeared outside Ptuj (Pettau) and Metlike. Emperor Frederick sent a summons to the estates of Carinthia to arm, to join with the Carniolans and Styrians in defending the boundaries of their provinces, and especially to guard the approaches to Carinthia. Even in the interior of Austria fortifications, stone and earth bulwarks (called *tabor, taber,* from Turkish *tabur*), were hastily thrown up, fortresses were built or repaired, and a system of signal fires (*Kreutefeuer*) laid out by which to spread the alarm. In August 1474 a large body of horsemen, allegedly 10,000 strong, crossed the Danube from Serbia and invaded the Hungarian low country as far as the Körös River. A Hungarian battalion opposed and defeated the Turks. In the late fall, Croatia and the coast were again raided from Bosnia.

In November the constant threat to his kingdom and the insistence of his dissatisfied subjects that he devote his energies to combating the Turks led Matthias Corvinus to conclude a several years' truce with King Casimir IV of Poland and to interrupt his war with Bohemia. Even the most zealous Hungarian patriots had come to disapprove of his struggle for the Bohemian crown and were demanding that the king defend his frontiers against the enemies of Christianity. King Ferrante of Naples and Aragon, who soon (autumn, 1476) would give his natural daughter Beatrice (1457–1508) to the Hungarian king in second marriage, was also not without influence on his future son-in-law's political designs. In the fall of 1474 and again in the spring of 1475 the diet in Buda voted very considerable funds for the defense of the country, but with the express stipulation that they might be used only against the Ottomans. Preparations were begun at once, but the propitious moment had long passed.

In 1473 Stephen, surnamed the Great, the warlike voivode of Moldavia, had taken advantage of the sultan's absence in remote Asia to invade Walachia. For some years the weakness of the effeminate Radu the Fair (*cel frumos*) had tempted the ambitious prince to seize one piece of territory after another. Radu was defeated at Cursul Apei (Rimnicu Sărat) on November 18–20, 1473, and in his place Basarab, also called Laiotă, was placed on the Walachian throne. An attempt of the Ottomans on November 28 to regain the crown for Radu, the sultan's favorite, was a lamentable failure. In the battle joined by Mihaloğlu Ali Bey and his *akincis*, the Turks incurred heavy losses and fled across the Danube. But four weeks later Laiotă's regal glory was at an end. Some 17,000 Turks appeared in Moldavia and on December 31, 1473, pitched camp near Barlad (Birlad). They drove out Stephen's protégé, laid waste the entire countryside, but avoided engagements and returned across the Danube. In the spring of 1474 Laiotă mounted the throne once again and it seemed as though the Moldavian prince would now be able to carry out his plans. But in June, Laiotă decided to go over to the sultan and turn his back on his shadow kingdom. Even then, however, Stephen did not abandon his efforts to install a prince favorable to him in Walachia. He helped a certain Basarab the Younger, also called Țepeluș (i.e. "little impaler"), who had ensconced himself in Transylvania, to take power in Walachia, though his reign lasted only a few weeks. On October 5, 1474, a battle was fought between the two "Basarabs." The older Basarab won the scepter, but Voivode Stephen drove him out two weeks later (October 20).

These absurd dynastic squabbles would hardly be worth mentioning if they had not provided the prelude to a war between the sultan and the prince of Walachia. As usual, a pretext for intervention was quickly found. An emissary from the sultan to Stephen demanded several years' arrears of tribute and the return of the southern Moldavian port of Kiliya, which thanks to its sheltered situation on an island in the lower Danube had been an important shipping center from time immemorial. Both demands were rejected out of hand, reason enough to begin hostilities immediately against the presumptuous lord of Moldavia (Kara Bogdan).[20]

Despite the Albanian defeat, Süleyman Pasha had not forfeited the sultan's favor and affection. After such a failure any other dignitary would surely have fallen into disgrace and have been exiled at best. But in the early fall of 1474 the eunuch received orders to embark on a campaign beyond the Danube.

The winter was to prove unusually severe and the flow of supplies for the large army (the chronicles speak of 100,000 or even 120,000 men, but these figures are doubtless exaggerated) was irregular. Such considerations, however, were not allowed to interfere with the campaign.

Accompanied by Laiotă and a number of lesser captains, Süleyman Pasha crossed the Danube into Walachia in January 1475. Prince Stephen lured them on through the dense forests to the vicinity of Vaslui at the confluence of the Barlad and Racova rivers. There he had massed his entire army, reinforced by Polish auxiliaries and contingents of Szeklers, the warlike tribe of southeastern Transylvania. The wild country, with its numerous hills, dark forests, deep rivers, and swamps, and the dense fog made it impossible for a stranger to get his bearings. By way of starving the invader, "everyone had destroyed his own house" along the Turkish line of march. At dawn of January 10, 1475, the Moldavians poured a shower of arrows on the approaching Turks from an invisible entrenched camp. The Ottomans were at a great disadvantage on the unaccustomed terrain. They quickly gave way and fled, but only a few were able to reach safety. Most died on the battlefield or in the waters of the Danube, whither the Moldavian cavalry pursued them. Their exhausted horses were unable to bear the Turkish cavalrymen either in battle or on their flight. Stephen then ordered the corpses on the battlefield to be burned, and most of the prisoners were impaled. The prince of Moldavia celebrated his hard-won victory with his peasants by a strict four days' fast on bread and water and by a solemn oath to build a new church in honor of God, the Lord of Hosts and King of Battles. Three hills on which crosses were erected marked the graves of the fallen Christians. Four pashas had remained on the field and some hundred banners were taken. Stephen sent four Turkish captains and thirty-six banners to the Polish king Casimir in gratitude for his help. He also sent prisoners and banners to King Matthias Corvinus, and even to the pope. In a letter to

[20] R. Rosetti, "Stephen the Great of Moldavia and the Turkish Invasion (1457–1504)," *Slavonic and East European Review* 6 (1927–28), 87–103, is still useful.

Christendom, written in Suceava on January 25, 1475, he imparted his triumph "at the gates of Christendom," announced that the sultan in person was planning to cross the Danube the following May to avenge the defeat, and called on all to summon up their forces to meet the threat.[21]

All the strong points and frontier posts between Moldavia and Bessarabia, which had been formerly taken by the Ottomans, were now deserted by their garrisons. The Moldavian prince took possession of them without striking a blow. Such a victory, Stephen proclaimed, was not the work of man but the decree of God. The countries of Christendom joined in his prayer of thanksgiving, but failed to learn from his victory that the sultan was not invincible and would be still less so if his enemies united.

In the spring of 1475 an urgent appeal for war against the Turks was carried to various Western potentates and especially the pope by Ladislas Vetesius (László Vitez), an emissary from the king of Hungary. It was immediately printed and also widely distributed in manuscript form. The document claimed that Mehmed had decided to invade Italy, and already his soldiers were crying out, "Alala Machmet, Machmet, Roma, Roma!" (*Lâ ilâha illallâh; Muhammad rasûlullâh, Roma, Roma.*) Venetian sources also bear witness to this battle cry combining the profession of faith with the name of the Eternal City.

At that time, of course, Mehmed was trying to propitiate Venice and to arouse hopes of peace. Through his stepmother Mara he granted Girolamo Zorzi (Giorgi), a Venetian envoy, a safe-conduct to Istanbul to engage in peace negotiations with the Porte. Zorzi was received on March 24, 1475, but was unable to meet the demands of the sultan, who claimed not only payment of an old debt of 150,000 gold ducats but also the return of all places occupied by Venice since the beginning of the war and the surrender of the mountain fortress of Krujë in Albania.[22] Girolamo Zorzi was neither empowered nor willing to make such concessions. Before he left Istanbul empty-handed, he was shown the gigantic preparations for war on Venice and orally—Mehmed expressly refused to give him a written statement—granted a six months' truce, during which the Signoria should make up its mind. The truce was accepted

[21] For more details on the Moldavian-Ottoman clash at this time, and relations between Stephen, Vlad, and Matthias Corvinus, see Florescu and McNally, *Dracula,* 111–118.

[22] Babinger writes later that Zorzi reached Istanbul on March 27 and was not personally received by Mehmed, who was sick: "Johannes Darius (1414–1494), Sachwalter Venedigs im Morgenland und sein griechischer Umkreis," *Sitzungsberichte der bayerische Akademie der Wissenschaften, philos.-hist. Klasse* (Munich, 1961), 81.

and the captain general was given orders to avoid all hostilities. But the peace proposals were rejected as dishonorable. This six months' truce gave the shrewd warrior in Istanbul the certainty of not being attacked by Venice during the spring and summer. It was clear from the start that his exaggerated demands would not be met, and in all likelihood the sole purpose of the peace negotiations was to give him a breathing spell, which was also welcome to the Venetians. At this very time Sixtus IV was making repeated attempts to obtain support for the Turkish war from the Italian states; on April 16, 1475, he urged the Florentines to receive a new emissary from Uzun Hasan, in whom the West still set high hopes. There was no hope of obtaining help from the north, where the Burgundian war had aroused dangerous tension among the states of Central Europe.[23]

The sultan had spent the whole winter and spring in his palace in Istanbul, still suffering, no doubt, from the gout that had been tormenting him since his return from eastern Anatolia. His presence in the capital is still attested for April (April 21).[24] A few weeks later the Black Death broke out once more, and the court removed to the mountains. In May the sultan was sick with gout in Edirne, probably on the island where he had built his summer palace. Western spies reported that he was on the point of leaving for Moldavia to avenge the disgrace of the previous winter. Süleyman Pasha, the governor of Rumelia, was also in the old capital, reportedly mustering the Rumelian army of 40,000 horsemen. An indication that the sultan distrusted the Western powers and felt it necessary to take precautions against a surprise attack is that he reinforced the garrisons of the Dardanelles fortresses, especially the Eski Hisarlïk, and sent 5,000 men to Krithia near the tip of the Gelibolu peninsula. The alarming state of his health prevented him from carrying out his decision to invade Moldavia in person. He became so weak that he had to be carried back to Istanbul, and the projected campaign was abandoned for good. By various channels news of the sultan's illness quickly reached the West, where already people began to count on his death. On June 23, 1475, Francesco Maletta, the Milanese ambassador at the court of Naples, wrote home that he had heard of the sultan's serious condition from King Ferrante himself. In Istanbul, the letter continued, Mehmed was generally believed to be in his death throes; the populace was grumbling and had moved on the palace with the intention of looting it, but the disorders had been rapidly quelled when, under pressure from his en-

[23] For the efforts of the pope, see Pastor, *History of the Popes* IV, 285.
[24] Truhelka, "Tursko-slovjenski spomenici," 42; Turkish translation in *IED* 1 (1955), 60 (document 44).

tourage, the "Turk" had appeared at the window, so showing the mob that he was still alive. The Signoria's ambassador in Naples reported that he had received a message from Trogir to the effect that two Venetian ships were on their way home; one was bearing an envoy from Uzun Hasan, the other an ambassador from the "Turk's son," who in the belief that his father was dying wished to take up peace negotiations with Venice. "From all sides," the report concludes, "comes confirmation of the Turk's death."

But while the plan for a Moldavian campaign went up in smoke, another undertaking was initiated which was to end the long-precarious existence of Kaffa, the famous old Genoese settlement on the northern shore of the Black Sea. The position of Kaffa had become untenable. Its maritime trade with Genoa had been virtually halted when the Turks closed the Bosporus, and once Amasra on the Anatolian shore of the Black Sea had fallen to the Turks, supplies could be brought in only over the difficult land route. It had probably long been Mehmed's intention to extinguish "this remnant of Western shopkeeper rule beyond the Darda- nelles" and to turn the economic importance of the Genoese settlement to his own account.[25]

Again Mehmed was at no loss for a pretext to intervene. The Genoese administration was involved in a dispute with the neighboring Tatar khan. The Tatars living in Kaffa and the surrounding country were subject to the jurisdiction of one of their own officials known as a *tudun* (governor), whom the khan of the Crimea always appointed after con- sultation with the Genoese consul. In 1473 Mamak, the influential holder of this office, died and was replaced by his brother Eminek. Eminek's sister-in-law, Mamak's widow, however, tried to have her son Sertak appointed as her husband's successor and, unfortunately for the Genoese colony, the relations between the two parties soon degenerated into bitter hostility. In the course of the negotiations Oberto Squarciafico, one of the four members of the Uffizio della Campagna, with which the final choice of *tudun* rested, played an increasingly despicable role. The committee finally persuaded Mengli Giray, khan of the Crimea and the son of Haci Giray, to accept the appointment of Sertak on the grounds that Eminek was in league with the Turks. Then, at the last minute, the khan declared that his choice was not Sertak but a certain Karai Mirza. When he tried to install Karai Mirza in Kaffa, however, he encountered strong

---

[25] For the Genoese in the Black Sea see Heers, *Génes au XVᵉ siècle*, 364ff. The work of Georges Bratianu, *La Mer noire* (Munich, 1969; *Societas Academica Dacoromana–Acta Historica* 9), deals with the Ottoman conquest only briefly in its concluding chapter.

resistance and Oberto Squarciafico, to whom Sertak's mother had promised 2,000 gold pieces, was one of his most violent adversaries. He put
pressure on the khan by threatening to release his brothers, who at the
time were being held under arrest in Sudak (Soldaya). Mengli Giray
finally agreed, and Sertak became *tudun*. But this was not the end of the
quarrel. Most of the Tatar notables favored Eminek and finally asked
Mehmed to settle the dispute. Needless to say, he jumped at the invitation.

As new commander of the naval forces, Gedik Ahmed Pasha received
orders to sail from Istanbul on May 19, 1475. Though as usual the figures
vary, his fleet seems to have consisted of 180 galleys, 3 galleons, 170 freight
ships, and 120 vessels bearing horses. It first halted off the lighthouse at
the mouth of the Bosporus, but then turned northward into the Black
Sea. On June 1, it anchored before the walls of Kaffa, which then numbered some 8,000 houses and 70,000 souls. Ahmed Pasha set up his ample
artillery before the walls and on June 2 the bombardment began. The city
resisted for only three days, for the majority of the Tatars led by Eminek
sided with the Turks. Abandoned by his supporters and fearing that he
would be unable to hold Kerkri, his capital, Mengli Giray had removed
to Kaffa with 1,500 loyal horsemen. On June 6 the besieged threw themselves on the enemy's mercy. Ahmed Pasha promised to spare their lives,
provided they paid the head tax. The foreigners in Kaffa—Walachians,
Poles, Russians, Georgians, Circassians—were the first to encounter the
arbitrary cruelty of the victors. Their entire wealth, evaluated at 250,000
gold ducats, was seized; they themselves were sold as slaves or thrown
into chains. On June 9 and 10 all other inhabitants of the city, Latins,
Greeks, Jews, Armenians, and so on, were instructed to make out detailed
statements of their personal and family circumstances as well as their
property. This information, so the Turks claimed, was necessary for
determining the head tax. In the following days a tax of 15 to 100 aspers
a head was imposed. On June 12 and 13 all the young girls and boys
were led before the Turks, who chose those suited for service in the
sultan's palace. Fifteen hundred persons—according to other sources,
3,000 or even 5,000—were mercilessly torn from their families. Just as the
Kaffans were beginning to think that they might now return to their
customary occupations, a new order was received: each man must surrender one-half of his declared wealth within three days. Those unable or
unwilling to obey were subjected to terrible tortures. Finally, on July 8,
all people of Latin origin were ordered to take their belongings and board
ships that had been set aside for the purpose. On July 12 the ships set out
for an unknown destination. A mutiny broke out on one of the vessels.
The mutineers put the crew to death and sailed away with their property.
They landed in Kiliya—or, according to other sources, near Akkerman—

but the commander of the city relieved them of their baggage and carried them off to Suceava as slaves.

When the other ships bearing the prisoners and the enormous spoils approached Istanbul on August 3, 1475, they were prevented from unloading by the plague still raging in the capital. The Italians and Armenians on board were first taken to Üsküdar, then after the plague had subsided they were assigned to their new homes in a previously uninhabited quarter between the present Edirne Gate and the Golden Horn. They occupied 267 houses (as we know from the census of 1477). The Byzantine churches of the Blessed Virgin (now Odalar Camii) and of the Manuel Monastery (Kefeli Cami) were given to the newcomers.

Oberto Squarciafico, who was largely to blame for the whole wretched business, soon met his fate. He was executed a few days after landing, presumably at the behest of Eminek. Mengli Giray was pardoned at the last minute and even sent back to the Crimea as the sultan's vassal.

There the Ottomans had meanwhile extended their conquests without incurring great losses. Sudak was besieged and starved out. The same fate befell the famous Mangup (Theodoros), where the last scions of the Trebizontian Comneni had maintained their rule, limited to a castle and several nearby towns totaling 30,000 houses. Alexander Comnenus, who shortly before had returned from a visit to the Moldavian court—his sister Maria was Prince Stephen's wife—had tried to defend Mangup. He was able to hold out until Ahmed Pasha departed, but soon thereafter he was defeated by treachery (December 1475), and the conquerors dealt mercilessly with him, his family, and his Moldavian bodyguards. Not even the women were spared but were carried off to the sultan's harem in Istanbul. The destruction of Genoese power in the Crimea was completed by the capture of Azov, where, however, a few Genoese families such as the Spinolas may have survived. Other pitiful Genoese remnants held out for a time in the vicinity of Bakhchisaray (Bahçe Saray) near Kaffa. This was the end of Genoese grandeur in the Crimea. An indication of their former wealth is provided by the enormous spoils, particularly the warehouses, which fell into Ottoman hands. All that remained of the Genoese possessions in the Levant were the settlements on the island of Chios and the nearby coast of Anatolia.[26]

---

[26] For the campaign against Kaffa, see Angiolello, *Historia turchesca*, 72–83. For letters between Mehmed and the Tatar Khans see Fevzi Kurtoğlu, "Ilk kirïm hanlarïnïn mektuplarï," *Belleten* III (1941), 641–655; Inalcïk studies the origins of Ottoman overlordship in the Crimea in "Yeni vesikalara göre kïrïm hanlïğïnïn osmanlï tabiliğine girmesi ve ahidname meselesi," *Belleten* VIII (1944), 185–229. Cf. Akdes N. Kurat, *IV.–XVIII. yüzillarda karadeniz küzeyindeki türk kavimleri ve devletleri* (Ankara, 1972).

While these events were taking place, the sultan was absent from his capital. He seems to have spent more than three months, beginning in June or July, in seclusion on a hill between Edirne and Kïrklareli to escape infection. When the summer was over, he went further west, first to Philippopolis and later to Sofia, where he spent the whole month of October. At the onset of winter he went to Vize in the pure air of the Istranca Mountains. Here the entire court camped in tents and, despite the cold weather, waited for the Black Death to subside before returning to Istanbul.

For many years the route by way of the Mediterranean, Syria, and Egypt had ceased to be the sole link between west and east; the development of the Black Sea route had made Kaffa a leading commercial center. The products of Western and Central Europe did not always reach the Black Sea via the Dardanelles; they also passed through Vienna and Buda, along the Danube and through the Carpathian passes, or over the much traveled route through Poland and Moldavia. The importance of this trade route for the development of the precapitalist and early capitalist economy of the West has often been stressed. The economic unity of Europe, which had withstood all manner of internal conflicts, was shattered by the Ottoman seizure of the Crimea. The increasing barriers to trade in the eastern Mediterranean and the transformation of the Black Sea into a Turkish lake, a development foreshadowed by Mehmed's closing of the Dardanelles, were to have profound repercussions in Europe, as many historians have pointed out. The appearance of large landed estates in the sixteenth century, the increase in numbers of the peasantry, and the sudden interruption of the growth of the towns may be attributed in part to the Turkish occupation of the Black Sea coast. Its effect on all Europe has been compared to that which Henri Pirenne found in Western Europe after the Arab occupation of the Mediterranean, or that of the Kuman and later the Tatar incursions on Russia, demonstrated by Alexander Eck. By closing the Black Sea and obstructing trade in the eastern Mediterranean, the Ottomans paralyzed some important western trade routes and destroyed others altogether. Genoa and Venice lost a number of their most important commercial centers, especially in the Levant. It is no exaggeration to say that even the discovery of the new Atlantic trade routes, with its crucial consequences for the economic life of the West, resulted in part from Ottoman expansion in the Black Sea area. The voyages of discovery to the New World were undertaken in the hope of creating a new, substitute route to India and Central Asia.[27]

[27] For an overview of the importance of the Black Sea trade area to the Ottomans see Carl Max Kortepeter, *Ottoman Imperialism during the Reformation: Europe and the Caucasus* (New York, 1972), 3–13.

Before the year 1475 was out, the rural population of Croatia and the border regions of Carniola and Carinthia were again to suffer grave losses in life and property at the hands of Turkish horsemen. In August the *akincis* from Bosnia raided Croatia, overran and pillaged the countryside without meeting appreciable resistance, and advanced as far as Ptuj, where they did enormous damage. Only when the captains of Styria and Carinthia hurried to the help of the stricken population did the Turks return to the valley of the Sava by way of Lemberg. Near Brežice (Rann) they met the Carniolans, and on August 24, 1475, Sigismund of Polheim, captain of Radkersburg, with three companies of 450 men each, attacked at Kaisersberg on the Sotla. But the battle went against the Christians. Thirty-one nobles were counted among the fallen. The brave Sigismund of Polheim and other nobles were taken prisoner.

While the Turkish bands were devastating Croatia, King Matthias Corvinus was making large-scale preparations for war on the Ottomans. Never chary of words, he informed the Venetian *oratore* Sebastiano Badoer that he had resolved to set up an army of 60,000 men, supported by 1,000 wagons and 100 ships. He gave orders to cast heavy guns and to build siege machines (he took a special interest in such devices and seems to have studied Italian manuscripts on the subject). The Hungarian king was so convinced of his strength that when two emissaries from the sultan appeared at his court, presumably at the end of November 1475, to discuss a truce, he dismissed them out of hand. Under what conditions the sultan was prepared to accept a truce or perhaps even a peace is not known. But he would seem to have been willing to make important concessions to Matthias Corvinus if it is true that he had offered in 1473 to cede all Bosnia should Hungary grant him free passage to Germany. Now Mehmed's purpose in sending his two agents became clear: he wished to secure his left flank for his projected Moldavian campaign. After rejecting the sultan's proposals, Matthias Corvinus expressed the hope that his Moldavian neighbor, Stephen, would immediately begin hostilities against the Turks.

He left no room for doubt concerning his own plans. By October 12 he had informed the ambassadors accredited to his court of his determination to make war and mentioned Šabac as his principal goal. There the Turks had steadily strengthened their fortifications and accumulated large stocks of arms and ammunition. Soon the king marched southward with a part of his army consisting of 10,000 men and divided into four columns. By December he pitched camp in Belgrade, and in the first days of January 1476 he appeared outside Šabac, where preparations for the siege began at once. The fortress was provided with moats fed by the Sava, behind which rose steep earthworks covered with faggots. The small walled citadel served as a second line of defense. There was no lack of artillery; the garrison consisted of 1,200 men.

The bombardment of the bulwarks brought small results, the projectiles inflicting little damage on the faggot covering. Moreover, a Turkish relief battalion had arrived and pitched camp nearby, but hesitated to attack the Hungarians. The relief troops had so little confidence that they soon withdrew, leaving the besieged to their fate. This episode encouraged the assailants to redouble their efforts under the personal leadership of the king. Disguised as a simple soldier, Matthias is said to have approached the fortress in a skiff to ferret out its weakest point. He himself led his ships into the castle moat. The garrison fought desperately and inflicted heavy losses but finally weakened and on February 15, 1476, opened the gates. The siege had lasted thirty days. The enormous stocks of ammunition he found there decided Matthias Corvinus not to raze the fortifications but to have them repaired. A ditch was dug from the Sava, so that Šabac lay on a well-nigh inaccessible island. With the main body of his army he then marched down the Sava and the Danube, destroying all Ottoman installations, and finally arrived before the turreted walls of Smederevo. Lack of siege equipment and heavy artillery made it seem inadvisable to attack this strongly fortified place. As though to proclaim his intention of storming Smederevo later on, the king had three wooden forts built nearby (at Omoljica or Kovin?), surrounded by a trench, a triple line of earthworks, and numerous rows of stockades. He garrisoned these forts with an observation troop.

Matthias Corvinus saw to it that the fall of Šabac should be speedily made known to all Christendom. In Rome and Venice public prayers of thanksgiving were offered up in all churches. The Signoria and Sixtus IV sent special embassies to the king of the Hungarians, bearing not only their congratulations but also 93,000 gold ducats to help him pursue the war against the Turks. "But what can hundreds of thousands avail a poor king against the mighty ruler of Asia and a good part of Europe?" wrote Cardinal Iacopo Ammanati a year later (March 1477), and no doubt he was right. Matthias actually used the unexpected funds scrupulously to continue the war on the Danube. At Regensburg, as far as possible from enemy spies, he built a small fleet of twenty-four ships equipped with all sorts of siege machines procured in Germany, especially bombards, which he planned to use in his subsequent undertakings, chiefly against Smederevo. He had asked Frederick, with whom he was not yet at war, to permit the duty-free passage of his ships and arms; this was refused him. Indeed, the emperor remained inactive while German robber barons harassed the northern frontier districts of Hungary. The Hungarian's bitter complaints to the Vienna court brought no results, for Frederick could not forgive the king of Hungary his projected marriage to Beatrice of Aragon. The consequence of this pettiness was that the ships were moved much too late and did not reach Smederevo in time to be used.

The loss of Šabac and the devastation wrought by the Hungarians along the Danube naturally aroused the Turkish march wardens. Yet King Matthias did next to nothing to stop their raids during the summer of 1476. His quarrel with the emperor, his attempt to draw the pope into an alliance against him, and especially his plans for marriage—the wedding was scheduled for October—drove the war against the Turks from his mind. The consequence was inevitable. The brothers Ali Bey and Iskender Bey of the Mihaloğlu family crossed the Danube near Smederevo with some 5,000 raiders and overran the Banat of Temesvar. The local captains Albert and Ambrose Nagy joined with the commander of Belgrade and certain other captains (including the brothers Ferenc and Peter Dóczy) from the region and drove back the invaders, who were totally defeated southeast of Bela Crkva (Weisskirchen) on the mountain slope of Pojejena on the Danube. Both Ali Bey and Iskender Bey escaped across the Danube. The prisoners dragged along by the raiders took advantage of the situation and attacked their camp. The spoils were so considerable that even mounted women and children were able to drive an additional loaded horse ahead of them. Two hundred and fifty prisoners and five banners were sent to King Matthias in Buda.

Nonetheless, the Turks continued their raids on the southwest border of Hungary. Early in June 1476, some 4,500 men from Bosnia invaded Croatia and entered Carniola. When they were unable to cross the Sava at Brežice, they marched up the Krka (Gurk) valley, swung over to Postojna (Adelsberg), and followed the valley of the Vipava (Wippach) to the vicinity of Gorizia. Turning northeast, they proceeded by way of Loka to the outskirts of Ljubljana, where they burned down the Church of St. Peter. Then they returned to Croatia.

In the meantime, a second detachment had crossed to the left bank of the Sava near Krško (Gurkfeld), pillaged and laid waste the region of Montpreis (Planina), Rogatec, Krapina, and Zagreb between the 15th and the 25th of July, 1476, and turned back up the Sava valley as far as Sevnica, where it joined the first troop on its way back from Carniola. Both detachments returned to Croatia by way of Kočevje and the Kulpa valley without meeting with any resistance.

This was not the end of it, for on October 10 the raiders once again invaded Carniola. They did not stay long, but moved on to Carinthia by way of Bela Peč (Weissenfels). After boldly crossing the mountains, which had been thought to be impassable for horsemen, they appeared in Tarvis (now Tarvisio) and Arnoldstein to the consternation of the population. One detachment then passed through Villach and entered the Krka valley by way of the Ossiacher See, while the other skirted the Wörther See to Klagenfurt, where the invaders set the suburbs on fire; they continued on as far as St. Paul and St. Andrä in the Lavant valley. For five days Carinthia was pillaged and laid waste. Then the raiders, laden with booty of all kinds, hurried back to Croatia and Bosnia by way of Slovenjgradec (Windischgrätz), Celje (Cilli), and Krško.

Next to nothing was done by the emperor or the estates of the interior of Austria to defend the frontier territories. The people of the plains, the peasants who were unable to take shelter in fortified places, became so embittered at the inactivity of the lords and estates that they accused them of being in league with the Turks and banded together against the nobles. In a few villages in the Glan valley the peasants revolted against the authorities. And in Croatia, where Matthias Corvinus should have taken defensive measures, no more was done than in the emperor's territories.

There would seem to be a connection between this second Turkish invasion and the journey to Hungary of Princess Beatrice of Aragon. On October 2, 1476, she and her retinue had boarded ship in Manfredonia. The original plan of landing in Dalmatia was abandoned because of the Turkish horsemen who infested the coast at the time. After long wanderings the ship landed on the eastern coast of Italy, where the journey was continued through Venetian territory, Carniola, and Styria. The Turkish raiders soon got wind of it and tried to capture the nineteen-year-old princess. They raided the regions through which the cortège would have to pass and the princess witnessed a gruesome spectacle: the fleeing multitudes of men and cattle, burned churches and monasteries, shattered altars, murdered priests. Filled with terror, she made her way through charred villages and fields of corpses until finally, in the first days of November, she reached Ptuj and soon thereafter the Hungarian border.

The wedding and coronation were celebrated (December 15, 1476) in Székesfehérvár and in Buda with unprecedented pomp, although the kingdom was groaning under a staggering burden of taxation. The new queen did her utmost to transplant the artistic splendor of the Italian Renaissance courts to the residence in Buda, sparing neither trouble nor expense. Before the year was out, while the Hungarian capital was busy with banquets and other festivities, the sultan in person appeared on the banks of the frozen Danube and demolished the wooden forts which Matthias Corvinus had just built. Mehmed had apparently recovered from his illness.

At the end of March 1476, the Conqueror with his whole court moved to Edirne, where he spent some forty days on the island until his army was in readiness. Soon the host was drawn up on the broad plain of Sofia. A Polish emissary, who had made a last vain attempt to settle the sultan's quarrel with the prince of Moldavia, found it on May 22, near Varna, marching northeastward. Shortly before, some 100 prisoners sent by the *sancak beyi* of the Morea were brought before the sultan; the men were immediately beheaded. Two hundred Janissaries, who had escaped at the fall of Šabac and had tried to join the sultan's army in Edirne, met no better fate. They pleaded for mercy and explained the circumstances under which Šabac had fallen to the Hungarians. The viziers interceded for them, but Mehmed knew no forgiveness for their flight. He had them all tied and thrown into the river with stones attached to their necks.

From Varna, where the heaped-up bones of those who had perished in 1444 could still be seen, the army moved northward along the Black Sea coast and a week later reached the Danube. On the march through the Dobruja the troops had suffered intensely from the water shortage and from great swarms of grasshoppers which descended on the horses and covered them to the ears, so that the men were obliged to shut themselves up in their tents by day and to march by night. The sultan halted for three days on the Danube, where meanwhile barks had arrived from Vidin and Silistria to help in the river crossing. He was one of the first to cross to the Walachian shore. The voivode Stephen had employed the same methods as in the previous year: he caused the whole countryside to be laid waste and, along with the peasants and townspeople, himself took refuge in the impassable oak woods. Near Akkerman, he had recently put to flight a Tatar horde of 10,000 men that had invaded Moldavia from the east.

From his hiding places Stephen struck a number of hard blows at the slowly advancing Ottomans. Finally, on the afternoon of July 26, 1476, not far from Cetatea Neamtzului in the so-called White Valley (Valea Alba, also Paraul Alb), he was hemmed in on all sides and forced to engage the enemy in what was to be known to history as the battle of Răsboieni. The Ottoman advance guard was commanded by Hadim Süleyman Pasha, who despite all his defeats had not yet lost the sultan's favor. He was again defeated, but the main army, led by Mehmed in person, stood fast. Shield in hand, the sultan spurred his charger into the woods and by his example revived the spirits of the Janissaries, who had thrown themselves to the ground, disheartened by the cannon fire from the thicket. Until the sultan put himself at their head their commander, Seğmenbaşi Mehmed Ağa of Trebizond, had been unable to restore their courage. The voivode was obliged to flee, although he had lost only 200 of his alleged 20,000 men. The Turks were said to have left 30,000 on the field, but this figure is no doubt grossly exaggerated. Mehmed was unable to follow up his victory, for in this inhospitable country he was helpless against a more powerful enemy—hunger; the small transport fleet that was to carry food and war material up the Danube from the Black Sea had been almost entirely destroyed by a storm.

The skulls of the dead were set up in pyramids, the spoils distributed among the troops. As the Ottoman chroniclers inform us, the large herds of unclean pigs were left to the Walachians who had fought under the sultan's banners with Laiotă Basarab. The whole countryside was laid waste. Not far from the northern border of Moldavia, the fortress of Khotin and that of Suceava, which was almost deserted, were stormed in vain. Hungarian help arrived too late. When the Hungarians entered Muntenia, they did little more than to set the monstrous Vlad Țepeș on the Walachian throne, though for only a short time, and to drive out Laiotă (November 16, 1476).[28]

On the Danube, meanwhile, provisions ships had arrived bringing bread, flour, barley, and wheat for the hungry troops. The army did not return through the Dobruja, but went further west by way of Nikopol (where it crossed the Danube), Telish, and the Balkan Mountains. In accordance with old custom, the army should have been disbanded on its arrival in Edirne. But when the sultan learned that the king of Hungary had invaded Serbia, evidently preparing to storm Smederevo, and had built and armed three forts for this purpose, he decided to take counter-measures immediately. Men and horses were half starved and in urgent need of rest, but after a pause of only ten days they were on the move again.

He himself took command of the army, which marched westward by way of Çirmen; here, to keep up the men's spirits and reconcile them to a winter campaign after so brief a rest, he distributed gifts of money. Some of the men had protested. Mehmed's only response was to have the grumblers laid out on the ground and flogged. Then he informed them that he expected them as a matter of course to serve in the present campaign without pay. The disgruntled army went by way of Konus and Philippopolis to Sofia, where the cold weather had already set in. Nevertheless, the northward march continued via Niš to Kruševac and the Danube River, which was by now frozen over and could be easily crossed. As soon as the garrisons of the wooden forts caught sight of the enemy, they fled. Only one fort resisted, but it was soon taken. When the Hungarians saw no possibility of defending the redoubts, they sent

[28] For this campaign also against Moldavia, see the article cited in n. 20 above.

emissaries to Mihaloğlu Iskender Bey, *sancaḳ beyi* of Nikopol, who promised the 600 men a safe-conduct to Belgrade and actually kept his promise. Sultan Mehmed seems not to have been present on the battlefield. This may be inferred not only from the humane treatment of the Hungarian garrisons but also from the fact that on December 12, at or near the castle of Bolvan northeast of Aleksinac, he received two Ragusan envoys, Jakov Bunić and Paladin Lukarević, who had brought the annual tribute of 10,000 ducats.[29] The castle of Bolvan is situated on a high hill in the wildly romantic gorge of the Moravica River. In the Middle Ages, together with another castle on the opposite side of the river, it dominated the narrow valley, which does not open out until near Kraljevo (now Rankovićevo). As late as 1860, Felix Kanitz saw the remnants of a "considerable city," consisting of crumbling mosques and other buildings at the foot of Mount Ozren to the right of the gorge.[30]

Ten days later, on December 22, 1476, the sultan made his entry into Istanbul after an absence of a year and a half.

Concomitantly with the northern campaigns, the Ottomans resumed their assaults on the outlying possessions of Venice soon after the six months' truce with the republic expired in the autumn of 1475. In May 1476, the governor of Rumelia—as though the fortunes of war had always smiled on him—was sent to Greece, reportedly with 40,000 men, to take Lepanto on the Gulf of Corinth, the strongest and most important Venetian bastion in Greece. Antonio Loredano, the captain general of the sea, who had been harassing the Anatolian coasts from his base in Navplion, appeared on the scene with eleven galleys and provided the threatened city with the necessary provisions and ammunition. The Ottoman fleet did not arrive until three days later. After several fruitless assaults on the walls of Lepanto, Süleyman Pasha was obliged to withdraw once again (July 25). This time he did earn the sultan's disfavor, although in a mild form, for immediately after his return he was imprisoned for a short time in the castle of Rumeli Hisarï. Later he was made to exchange governorships with the Albanian renegade Davud Pasha and to serve briefly as governor of Anatolia.

A little later a projected Turkish attack on the fortress of Kokkinos on the island of Lemnos was abandoned when Antonio Loredano landed troops on the small neighboring island of Psara (Psyra). At the same time, however, Ottoman galleys devastated the island of Naxos, seat of

[29] See Elezović, *Turski spomenici* I, part 1, 173–174; I, part 2, 48 (document 25). And compare Truhelka, 46 (Turkish translation: *IED* 1 [1955], 62), document 51.

[30] For the travels of Kanitz see his *Serbien* (Leipzig, 1868), especially 269ff. for the exploration of the Moravica valley.

the duke of the Cyclades, a vassal of Venice, but they did not dare to occupy it permanently. In Chios the Ottomans collected the arrears of tribute.

The situation of the Venetians in Albania was not promising. In the late spring of 1476, 8,000 men led by Gedik Ahmed Pasha attempted to reduce the mountain fortress of Krujë, but Pietro Vetturi, the *provveditore*, held out until Francesco Contarini, governor of all Albania, hastened to the rescue and threw the Turkish besiegers back into the nearby mountains. Thereupon the Venetian mercenaries, among them Albanians led by Nicholas Dukagin, fell on the camp abandoned by the Turks. At nightfall, however, the Ottomans returned and attacked the looters; many Italians were killed and only the Albanians, who were well acquainted with the region, were able to escape. Francesco Contarini with eight of his officers was taken prisoner and cut down. The siege of Krujë was resumed and although the fortress held out, it could not be relieved as the 3,000 cavalrymen of Francesco Michiel, the newly appointed *provedditore* of Albania, were being used to defend the adjoining country.

The enormous exertions of Mehmed's last campaigns now necessitated a protracted period of rest. Apart from a brief stay on Büyük Ada (the island of Principo) in May 1477, he seems to have spent the whole of the year in Istanbul devoting himself exclusively to domestic politics and to the enlargement and embellishment of his capital.

Almost twenty-five years had passed since the conquest of Constantinople. Thanks to constant transplantations and to the return of fugitives, the population had increased to somewhere between 60,000 and 70,000. Chance has preserved a census of 1477, taken by Muhyiddin, the city judge. It gives the following figures: 9,000 houses inhabited by Turks, 3,000 by Greeks, 1,500 by Jews; 267 were inhabited by Christians from Kaffa, 750 by persons transplanted from Karaman, and only 31 by Gypsies (probably from Balat in Anatolia). A total of 3,667 shops is listed. Assuming that a house lodges four to five persons, we arrive at the above figures for the population, which was kept down by frequent earthquakes, fires, and epidemics. Thus far the demographic growth amounted to little more than a repopulation of the Byzantine capital of 1453, which appears to have housed 40,000 to 50,000 souls. This work of repopulation proceeded rapidly during the reign of Mehmed II and reached its peak under Süleyman the Magnificent in the next century. Since each quarter (*mahalle*) centered around a mosque, whose *imam* had certain juridical prerogatives, we can determine the density of the population with fair certainty on the basis of the number of mosques built in the course of the fifteenth century, of Christian churches transformed into mosques, and of churches and synagogues retaining their original function. The density was greatest along the Golden Horn, diminishing toward the center and edge of the city. For the Christian quarter in Galata (Pera), the following approximate figures can be advanced for the same period: 535 Turkish and 572 Christian houses, in all 1,781 shops, hence a population of roughly 6,000.[31]

The Conqueror's capital was hardly a place of splendor. In the final phase of its isolation, shortly before its fall, Byzantium could boast magnificent churches and palaces but was visibly on the decline in other respects, and this had been the case since the thirteenth century, when the barbarism of the Latin conquerors had set its mark on the city. The old colonnaded streets had been largely replaced by rows of trees, and in the fourteenth century the population had so diminished that whole quarters, abandoned by their inhabitants, had been taken up by large monasteries and convents with gardens and vineyards. On the present-day Palace Point (Saray Burnu) there was even an olive grove, which was cut down when the sultan's palace was built. In 1403, half a century before the fall of the Byzantine Empire, Ruy Gonzalez de Clavijo saw gardens, vineyards, and even grainfields in Constantinople. Only the narrow strip along the shore of the Sea of Marmara and the Golden Horn was densely populated. Other quarters were characterized by ruined churches and the large estates of high government officials, which in turn included chapels, houses for the children of state dignitaries, workshops, and gigantic parks with ponds and vineyards. The former imperial palace, the hippodrome, and the large forums were gradually falling into decay for lack of maintenance. "Once the city of wisdom, now a city of ruins," the patriarch Gennadius had said of the dying Byzantium. The Ottoman conquest brought no esential change in this distressing picture; for one thing, the state funds were largely absorbed by the sultan's increasingly expensive campaigns.[32]

[31] The repopulation of the capital is discussed by Inalcïk, "The Policy of Mehmed II," *DOP* 23-24 (1969-70), 231-249; see there 238, n. 42, for reference to the census document of 1477. For the city as it was inherited by the Turks, aside from the works cited above (book 2, n. 18), see Ali S. Ülgen, *Constantinople during the Era of Mohammed the Conqueror, 1453-1481* (Ankara, 1939); Turkish edition: *Fatih devrinde Istanbul, 1453-1481.*

[32] For the description by the Spaniard of Constantinople at the turn of the century, see the *Narrative of the Embassy of Ruy Gonzalez de Clavijo*, trans. C. R. Markham, 29-49 (cf. above, p. 194). Of the countless books on the capital of the Byzantines and the Turks, David Talbot Rice's well-illustrated *Constantinople: From Byzantium to Istanbul* (New York, 1965) is one of a few which deal seriously with both traditions.

The city walls, which must have enclosed a territory of roughly five square miles, had been severely damaged by the conquest, especially on the land side, and only scantily repaired. When danger threatened from the west or northwest, the sultan had the breaches filled in as far as time and funds permitted. The walls seem to have undergone major repairs for the first time in 1477, though the statements of the old Ottoman chronicles refer only to the walls of the "new palace," which were also built in that year. The chief material employed in this work was provided by the ruins of Byzantine buildings, which were also used for the construction of mosques. There is no evidence whatever to support the romantic notion that Mehmed took measures to preserve the vestiges of antiquity. Any such assertion is refuted by the meagerness of the remains from Byzantine, let alone Hellenic, times to be found in the city; this cannot be attributed wholly to fires and earthquakes, or to the vandalism of the knights who took part in the fourth crusade. Apart from the wall on the land side, the churches that were transformed into mosques are the only monuments of preconquest times to have been preserved. Compared to the cities of Western Europe, Istanbul has few relics of the Middle Ages to offer. But whereas Rome, which is of roughly the same age, experienced only one great upheaval, the transition from paganism to Christianity, during which the monuments of pagan antiquity were willfully destroyed or at best treated with indifference, Constantinople lived through two such changes of faith; a thousand years after its conversion to Christianity, it was transformed into an Islamic city. Moreover, there had never been a rediscovery of, and revival of interest in, classical antiquity such as occurred in Italy, because the Palaeologi were utterly incapable of such ideas. As for the Conqueror's attitude toward the monuments of art found in the city, the words of the Frenchman Pierre Gilles (Gyllius) are as applicable to the time of Mehmed as to the mid-sixteenth century when he was resident in Constantinople: "From the marble gods they make limestone; the bronze figures are recast into cannon; the bronze pedestals of the statues are made into coins; the lofty columns are cut up into building stones with which to erect new mosques or tile the floors of Turkish baths. . . . The Turks believe they are building something better. They wish to give the city a new, Mohammedan face." If Mehmed saved the famous Plataean votive offering, the so-called column of the snakes in the hippodrome, from destruction by having a mulberry tree that was growing through its pedestal burned out with a hot iron, this should be attributed not to any enthusiasm for antiquity but rather to a superstitious awe of this mysterious and, to him, inexplicable work. Nothing so distorts the personality of this sultan as an attempt to make him into a Renaissance prince, determined to save the heritage of the past and to make his people the repositories of Roman and Greek antiquity. In the fifteenth century the rebirth of the ancient world was limited to Western Europe. We shall have more to say of this below.[33]

The battle of Răsboieni and the hasty withdrawal of the Turks across the Danube had been celebrated in the West as a victory, one that was actually ascribed, at least partly, to the king of Hungary, whose skirmishes near Smederevo had supposedly helped to hasten the Ottoman retreat. This was the quite mistaken interpretation of Pope Sixtus IV, who, conjointly with various Italian princes, sent Matthias Corvinus his congratulations and 200,000 ducats in special aid. The truth would seem to be that King Matthias, especially in the year of his marriage to Beatrice, had no desire to become involved in an arduous and expensive war with Mehmed, whom he later was to call his "elder brother and blood kinsman." He had none of his great father's chivalrous spirit or Christian enthusiasm and was certainly without the political wisdom of the Angevins, who occupied the throne of Hungary in the fourteenth century. His vacillating policy of "chasing petty triumphs" made it imposible for him to conceive a farsighted military plan. The documents emanating from his pen or from his entourage in those years when the West was so gravely threatened by the Ottomans paint a portrait of a vain, boastful, and inconstant man. Mehmed must have been well aware that this was no very dangerous adversary, and it seems unlikely that a war against Hungary played any great part in his well thought-out plans for expansion. Time and time again, he showed that he attached far more importance to Venice, whose Albanian bastion formed the last barrier to his westward advance. He was determined that Venice and its possessions should know no peace until his armies had won a decisive victory.

On St. Leonard's Day, November 26, 1476, Istria had suffered a surprise attack by Turkish hordes, who had advanced as far as the city of Koper (Capo d'Istria) and carried off large numbers of the population. Now in September 1477 disaster descended on Friuli, which had belonged to Venice since 1420. Quite some time before, measures had been taken against Turkish cavalry incursions: a line of earthworks had been thrown up from the mouth of the Isonzo (Soĉo) near Aquileia to Gorizia, and

---

[33] Gyllius's description of the monuments of the city, observed during a six-year residence in the capital, was published in English as *The Antiquities of Constantinople* (London, 1729). His observations and judgments have recently been given new life and reappraised by Hilary Sumner-Boyd and John Freely, *Strolling through Istanbul* (Istanbul, 1972).

two fortified camps had been built at Fogliana and Gradisca. These defenses proved unequal to the powerful thrust of autumn, 1477. The expedition was led by Iskender Bey, *sancak beyi* of Bosnia. Iskender Bey's father was an Italian from Genoa, his mother a Greek woman from Trabzon. While a brother of his, a Genoese merchant in Pera, was a Christian, and married to the daughter of another Genoese merchant, he himself had become a Moslem, rising from one important position to another in the Ottoman Empire, to attain considerable wealth.

Along with Turahanoğlu Ömer Bey, he had already taken the bridge at Gorizia before word of the Turkish approach had reached the camp at Gradisca. Some 1,000 horsemen crossed the Isonzo under Ömer Bey and lay in ambush. The Venetian captain, Girolamo Novella of Verona, accepted the proffered battle. Despite his father's warnings, Girolamo's son set out in pursuit of the Turks, fell into the trap, and was routed. A wild flight ensued, both Novellas fell in battle, and numerous prisoners were taken by the Turks, among them Count Antonio Caldora, Count Iacopo Piccinino, and Filippo da Navolin of Mantua. The Ottoman horsemen then scoured the plain between the Tagliamento and the Isonzo. Woods, castles, barns, and houses went up in flames that could be seen as far as Udine. The Turks now crossed the Tagliamento without meeting serious resistance. A vast sea of fire raged between the Tagliamento and the Piave. The flames could be seen clearly from the campanile of St. Mark's in Venice. Finally, on November 2, all the available armed forces of Venice marched out under Vettore Soranzo to drive away the enemy, who was in sight of the city. But before the mercenaries and the small flotilla reached Friuli, the robber hordes had vanished with enormous spoils and numerous prisoners. In Istanbul a bitter fate awaited the captives. Iskender Bey, who was well informed, had acquainted Mehmed with the circumstances of every single one. The sultan ordered a list drawn up showing the "purchasing power" of each prisoner. Those who were unable or unwilling to pay a ransom of 100 ducats or over were beheaded, thirty-five in all. The rest were thrown into prison, where they remained awaiting their redemption.

"The enemy is at our gates!" cried Celso Maffei to Andrea Vendramin, the doge. "The ax is at the root. Unless divine help comes, the doom of the Christian name is sealed." These words must have expressed the general sentiment of the Venetian people. But tired and forsaken, hemmed in by its relations with other Italian states, the republic continued to wage guerrilla warfare for petty spoils. No one offered serious assistance. Instead of actively combating the Ottomans, Matthias Corvinus, driven by hatred and immoderate ambition, embarked on a war against the emperor, his pretext being the conflict over the throne of Bohemia. It is highly unlikely that, as his apologists claim, Matthias hoped, by making war on the Hapsburgs and extending his kingdom westward, to strengthen Hungary for a war against the Turks. All negotiations initiated by the pope or Venice to settle this disastrous quarrel were fruitless, because Matthias persisted in his extravagant demands. In early August 1477 he invaded Lower Austria and soon had the entire province in his power, with the exception of a few cities. But in December, after Sixtus IV and the Signoria had threatened to withdraw all financial aid unless Matthias made war on the Turks, the king and emperor, possibly frightened by the Turkish raid on Friuli, concluded a peace; it, however, was to be short-lived. Matthias evacuated the Austrian territories, whereupon in February 1478 the diet in Buda granted him unprecedented taxes and the right to mobilize the Hungarian army against any conceivable enemy should the need arise. No one was to suffer less from this decision than Mehmed the Conqueror.

Probably late in 1477 or early in 1478, Matthias Corvinus's father-in-law, King Ferrante of Naples and Aragon, made peace overtures to the sultan. The inside story is obscure, for details are provided only by the Venetian chronicles, which are subject to caution in this connection. Nevertheless, we seem to be able to infer one plain fact from them, namely, that the king of Naples opened his ports to Ottoman ships which were to be used exclusively against Venice. It would be interesting to learn with whom this idea originated. In any event, King Ferrante received an ambassador from the sultan and confirmed the agreement he had made with the Porte. A Neapolitan emissary then repaired to Istanbul with rich gifts. In Venice, where this shift in Neapolitan policy toward the Turks could not remain a secret, it was feared that Ferrante's son-in-law, Matthias Corvinus, would conclude a similar pact of friendship with Mehmed. There is no definite proof that he did so, apart from the fact that he allowed every opportunity for an offensive against the Turks to slip by and contented himself with purely defensive measures on his frontiers.

The situation of the Signoria became more difficult from day to day; it could not bear the enormous burdens of the war alone and, in view of the tensions rending all Italy, was without reliable allies. Needless to say, it desired peace with the Porte, even at the cost of heavy sacrifices. But pride forbade the Serenissima to initiate peace negotiations, for it was obvious that the Turks would set humiliating conditions. The Venetians waited for the sultan to take the first step, and he actually did so. A Jewish emissary from the sultan appeared before Krujë with his instructions. Antonio Loredano provided him with a galley and safe-conduct to Venice. He never reached his destination but died off Koper. As for the sultan's demands, all that seeped through was that he attached the greatest importance to the surrender of Lepanto. Long discussions ensued in the senate; finally the war party was defeated, and it was decided to tender peace proposals.[34]

On pretext of expressing the republic's sympathy over the sudden death of the sultan's emissary, Tommaso Malipiero, *provveditore* of the fleet, left for the Porte early in January 1478, with extensive powers. He was authorized to offer the sultan not only the return of all the places taken by Venice since the beginning of hostilities (1463) but also the island of Lemnos off the Dardanelles, the whole mountainous territory of the Maina, Krujë, and a settlement of 100,000 gold ducats against the arrears of the alum tax. As soon as these broad concessions made it clear to the sultan that Venice urgently desired peace, he increased his demands and insisted, over and above his previous conditions, on an annual tribute of 10,000 ducats and a return to the status quo ante bellum. Malipiero's powers did not allow for the acceptance of such demands. He requested two months' time for reflection and a truce while he reported to the Signoria. These were granted and on April 15 Malipiero left the Ottoman capital. On May 3 he arrived in Shkodër by the land route through Kyustendil (Bulgaria) and Serbia; immediately he continued on to Venice. He was not unaware that the sultan was planning a campaign against Albania, that Mihaloğlu Ali Bey was already on his way from Serbia with his *akincis*, that the governors of Rumelia and Anatolia had been ordered to mobilize the army, and that the sultan in person was assuming supreme command. The matter was debated for two days in the Consiglio dei Pregadi, which finally decided that there was no way out but to accept the sultan's terms (May 5). Malipiero set out a second time with the necessary instructions and with rich gifts for the sultan and his viziers. Peace seemed to be assured.

But Tommaso Malipiero never reached his destination. Three days before expiration of the truce he met Mehmed at the head of a powerful army marching on Albania. The Venetian emissary informed the sultan that the Signoria had decided to accept his demands and that he had instructions to sign a peace under these conditions. The sultan replied that since his proposals had not been immediately accepted, he had changed his mind. The situation was modified, and he had received in-

[34] The progress of the peace negotiations between Venice and the Porte from this point forward is discussed by Ménage in connection with the documents which he published and analyzed (see above, book 4, n. 11).

formation of matters previously unknown to him; there was no point in offering him Krujë because the fortress was virtually in his hands; but if the Signoria wished instead to surrender Shkodër, Drisht, and Alessio, he was willing to make peace. Of course, Malipiero was not empowered to accept such a proposal. He returned to Venice empty-handed.

Meanwhile, Mehmed sent an express messenger to Iskender Bey, the *sancak beyi* of Bosnia, instructing him to invade Friuli. The order was obeyed at once. The Italian renegade entered Friuli, reportedly with 20,000 horsemen. This time he met with violent resistance, ably led by Count Carlo da Braccio. Before withdrawing to Bosnia, the Turkish bands nevertheless did enormous damage and carried away large numbers of men and cattle. Despite these constant threats and the plague that was raging in Venice, the Signoria did not condescend to accept the Conqueror's new peace conditions. It was determined, above all, to hold Shkodër. Malipiero was instructed to return once again to the sultan and to tell him that Venice would make peace only under the conditions previously agreed to. It was much too late for this, and Malipiero never had the embarrassment of facing the sultan. Again Venice had to try its luck, though no one could doubt the outcome of the struggle.

Mehmed's entire army had moved westward, resolved at last to wrest Shkodër from the Signoria. Once before the Ottomans had been masters of the region, but only for a short time. When Serbian power disintegrated during the reign of the last king of the house of Nemanja in about 1360, Albania fell under the rule of the Balšići family. In 1392 the Turks took George II Balšić prisoner and did not release him until he had ceded Shkodër to them. Şahin, the Ottoman commander, held the fortress for the next three years. In 1395 he was driven out by George Balšić, who was obliged, however, in the following year to pawn Shkodër, Drisht, Dajino, and St. Sergius to Venice, and was never able to redeem the pledge. The banner of St. Mark flew over the castle of Shkodër (Rosfa) for eighty-three years, after which the Turks held it for more than four centuries until 1913.

Despite its critical situation, Venice was unwilling to relinquish this last bastion in the East without a struggle. At the news that the enemy was approaching, soldiers, townspeople, and the crews of the galleys that had put into the Bojana worked day and night, repairing the tumbledown walls and throwing up earthworks. It was high time, for on May 14 some 8,000 raiders under Mihaloğlu Ali Bey appeared, pillaging and burning the villages in their path. The smoke could be seen far and wide from the citadel of Shkodër. The raiders were followed by Iskender Bey with 4,000 horsemen and Malkoçoğlu Bali Bey, governor of Smederevo, with 3,000. The male population was divided into three parts: one manned the fortifications, one worked on the entrenchments, and the third, including the priests, remained inside the walls. Children and old people had been removed to nearby coastal cities. But the 8,000 *akïncïs* and 7,000 light horsemen were only the advance guard of the Ottoman army.

The sultan had commissioned Evrenosoğlu Ahmed Bey and Turahanoğlu Ömer Bey to improve the roads and to build bridges. According to Gian-Maria Angiolello, the supreme commander of the besieging forces was Gedik Ahmed Pasha, who had fallen into disfavor shortly before and perhaps had been replaced as grand vizier. The dates of his grand vizierate cannot be determined with precision. In May 1476, we hear of one "Sinan Bey" as "commander over the Grand Turk's other commanders," possibly Hoca Sinan Pasha, who was married to a sister of Mehmed II. If this Sinan Bey actually was grand vizier, his term of office must have veen very brief, and Gedik Ahmed Pasha must have succeeded him. Before the siege of Shkodër, in any event, Gedik Ahmed Pasha was without a post and a prisoner in Rumeli Hisarï, allegedly because he, who knew the terrain better than anyone else, had aroused the sultan's anger by commenting on the difficulty of Albanian campaigns. While the army was on its way to Albania in May 1478, he appears to have been released from prison and to have been appointed *sancak beyi* first of Thessaloniki, then of Vlorë in Albania. The Ottoman chroniclers tell the story as follows: When Mehmed marched west he was obliged because of the poor state of the roads to travel a considerable distance on foot. Angered at this state of affairs, he remarked to Hersekoğlu Ahmed Bey, the imperial banner-bearer who was sitting beside him during a brief halt, that such hardships would have been spared him if he had had a vizier who knew his business, whereupon Ahmed Bey had dropped the name of Gedik Ahmed Pasha. The sultan thought the matter over and finally sent a dispatch to Istanbul, freeing the prisoner and appointing him governor of Vlorë.[35]

At this time the grand vizierate was assumed by a direct descendant of the great mystic Celaleddin Rumi, namely, Karamani Mehmed Pasha, an utterly unwarlike but intellectually eminent man who was to play an important role as adviser, as organizer of the administration, and as legislator—a career brought to a sorry end by his sordid political intrigues. He was the last grand vizier of Mehmed the Conqueror, whom he outlived by one day.

The sultan first went to Krujë, temporarily entrusting the command over the troops drawn up before Shkodër to the Albanian Davud Pasha,

[35] For Gedik Ahmed, see below, book 6, n. 15.

now governor of Rumelia. The mountain fortress of Krujë had been encircled for a whole year and the situation of the inhabitants had become intolerable. Hunger had compelled them to eat dogs, cats, rats, and mice. When the sultan himself appeared on the mountain slope, all hope of salvation was gone. On June 15 the besieged sent emissaries to Mehmed to arrange an amicable settlement. He allegedly sent them a written promise to spare their lives and allow them to withdraw with their possessions unless they preferred to go on living in Krujë under Ottoman rule. Imprudently, the majority chose the safe-conduct and surrendered to the Ottoman commander. But no sooner did they reach the plain than they were thrown into chains and brought before the sultan. The wealthiest and most prominent among them, including the *provveditore* and his family, were released in return for a heavy ransom; the rest were mercilessly beheaded. The sultan then received the keys of the fortress, which from that time on was no longer called Krujë but Ak Hisar (White Castle) and which did not change hands again until 1913.

This matter having been settled, the sultan turned the full force of his fury and his arms against Shkodër. Davud Pasha had reached the city's walls on May 18. On June 12, the new governor of Anatolia, Mesih Pasha of the Palaeologus family, a brother of Hass Murad Pasha, marched up with his Anatolian army. On June 22 the siege began; the artillery, which had been transported with great difficulty by camel, opened fire. On July 2 the sultan arrived from Krujë with his entire retinue and pitched his camp on the plain of Drisht, sheltered from enemy artillery fire by the so-called Monte Santa Veneranda, on the slopes of which Davud Pasha was encamped. The second siege of Shkodër has rightly been termed one of the most remarkable episodes in the struggle between the West and the Crescent, partly because of the unusual methods employed in the defense and, perhaps still more so, because of the desperate resistance the fortress was able to offer.

As usual, various figures were given for the strength of the besieging army. The governor of Rumelia, who occupied the vicinity of the fortress and the neighboring heights, was said to have been in command of 300,000 men, including the 30,000 who had arrived with Mesih Pasha, governor of Anatolia. Even if the new bands that arrived each day and the entire baggage train are included, this figure must have been vastly exaggerated. No less than 10,000 camels and innumerable mules were said to have been used in transporting tents, baggage, cannon, and siege machinery. In accordance with the Ottoman custom, the heavy cannon were cast on the spot. Reportedly they hurled stones weighing from three to thirteen hundredweight at the walls. There were eleven cannon of enormous caliber. Incendiary rockets, balls of rags impregnated with wax, sulfur, oil, and other inflammable materials, were used for the first time. The siege of Shkodër was described by a priest, Marino Barlezio, in *De Scodrensi Obsidione*, a Latin work in three books. Although much admired at the time, this account has long been regarded as untrustworthy because of its bias and the high-flown speeches which, in the classical manner, it puts into the mouths of protagonists who could never have spoken in such a way. It deals at great length with the nature and emplacement of the Ottoman siege machines, providing information that can be appraised only by experts in the history of weapons. The fireballs, which set fire to everything they touched and obliged the besieged to remove the roofs from all the houses and to organize fire brigades, were highly effective—more so, no doubt, than the mortars and heavy guns, which were poorly manned and did less damage than they were expected to. Finally a deep breach was made in the walls, but still the Ottomans were unable to enter the city. An all-out attack made on July 22, allegedly with 150,000 soldiers, was a failure. The siege guns had enabled the assailants to advance through the shattered outer fortifications to the inner walls, where they set up their crescent flags, but the defenders threw them back at the decisive moment and restored the banners of St. Mark and of the city's patron saint, St. Stephen. This undertaking cost the Ottomans 12,000 of their best troops, while the garrison was said to have lost only 400 men.

Five days later came the second attack (July 27), which began in the early morning and continued until noon of the following day. Not only the two parts of the garrison, which continued to relieve each other every six hours, took part in this desperate battle but the entire population, including the women. The Dominican Fra Bartolomeo of Epirus, a second Giovanni Capistrano, who had already proved himself as a warrior and preacher under Skanderbeg, and Niccolò Moneta, commander of the cavalry, dashed through the city, keeping up the courage of the population and organizing the defense. The tide of battle surged back and forth. Finally the enraged sultan directed eleven giant cannon at once against the main gate of the fortress, unconcerned over the effect this might have on the Turks who had already pressed through the gate. Immense confusion ensued and the besiegers withdrew in haste with enormous losses—allegedly a third of the entire army.

Three days after the repulse of this second attack the sultan held a council of war. Gedik Ahmed Pasha was said to have advised cessation of the bombardment, so falling in with the sultan's wishes. It was decided that only a part of the army should remain on the spot to encircle the city

and cut off all supplies. Then several detachments marched off to take possession of nearby strongpoints. The castle of Žabljak on a steep cone in
the marshy estuary of the Morača, where Ivan Crnojević (1465–1490),
"lord of the Zeta," had established his court, surrendered to the governor
of Rumelia almost without a blow. Drisht, however, the main fortress of
the region, six miles east of Shkodër in the valley of the Kjiri, resisted
bravely for sixteen days and when finally defeated had to pay for its
courage with the doom of its entire population. Three to five hundred
of its inhabitants were dragged in chains to the walls of Shkodër and there
on a hill executed within sight of the city as a warning that the same fate
would soon befall the people of Shkodër if they continued to resist. Abandoned by all, Alessio, where Skanderbeg had died, was set on fire. Only
Bar, courageously defended by the *podestà* Luigi da Muta, was able to
withstand the enemy attack.

Disappointed at the outcome of his Albanian campaign, Mehmed
started the return journey by torchlight in the night of September 7,
1478. With him went 40,000 men. In the same month the governor of
Anatolia followed. At the beginning of December the Rumelian army, disinclined to winter in inhospitable Albania, raised camp and set out eastward. Only Gedik Ahmed Pasha stayed behind with 10,000 men—or
40,000, according to other versions—to keep up the blockade of the starving city.

The hardships of the besieged were inconceivable. Their only suste-
nance was bread and water, for all animals, including rats and mice, had
already been eaten. The urgent messages of Antonio da Lezze, *provveditore* of Shkodër, that provisions would soon be exhausted and the city
forced to surrender, resulted in a decision by the Signoria, on November
18, to send 6,000 horsemen and 8,000 foot soldiers to Albania to raise the
siege and to recall to Albanian waters the squadron which had been sent
that summer to protect Cyprus. But four days later, after a stormy session
in the Consiglio dei Pregadi, the decision was annulled.

The plague, which at the time was devastating large parts of southeastern Europe, had broken out in Venice and was carrying off some forty
persons daily. It had begun in the early summer and reached its peak in
the fall. But even with the coming of winter it did not entirely die down.
Most of the well-to-do citizens had fled to the mountains. The city was
almost deserted, and if the *pregadi* still met twice a week, on Monday
and Tuesday, it was only because nonattendance was severely punished.
The wherewithal for new war preparations had long been lacking. The
tension dating from the two treaties of 1474—the one between Venice,
Florence, and Milan, the other between the pope and King Ferrante of

Naples—had deepened. This internal Italian conflict precluded any effective help. Once the danger of an alliance between Burgundy and Venice had as good as subsided, Louis XI of France had agreed, in response to the representations of Domenico Gradenigo, the Venetian ambassador, to a pact of friendship and trade with Venice (January 9, 1478). Since no serious help was to be expected from Venice's allies, Milan and Florence, however, this brought the Signoria no relief. All efforts to move the pope and the king of Naples, both engaged in a bitter conflict with Florence, to take a more active part in the struggle against the Ottomans were in vain. Nor was there any further help to be expected from Persia since the death of Uzun Hasan, Venice's last hope, on January 6, 1478.

Albania was almost entirely occupied by the Ottomans and it seemed doubtful whether the feeble army then available could succeed in breaking through the encirclement of Shkodër. Venice's power was at the breaking point and the few opponents of peace with Mehmed, proud men animated by the memory of a brilliant past, were unable to convince their fellows, for they themselves could hardly close their eyes to the sad fact that, stifled as it was by lack of funds, the republic could no longer hope for military success against the sultan.

The Venetians were also haunted by the fear of looking once again from the campanile of St. Mark's upon fires lit in the nearby valleys of the Tagliamento and the Isonzo by the Turkish "sackers" (*saccomanni*). Their fears were well founded, as became clear shortly before harvest time in the summer of 1478. A large body of Ottomans, reportedly 30,000 raiders, led by Iskender Bey, appeared on the Isonzo after crossing Carniola, Carinthia, Styria, and Friuli. No one dared resist the unruly horde. The defenders remained immobile in their two fortified camps, traces of which can still be distinguished today, allowed the invaders to wreak their terrible havoc for several days, and watched them ride off through the valley of the Canale. On July 26 they crossed the Predil Pass and, apparently losing their way, doubled back to Bela Peč on July 28 before reaching Tarvis. The raiders entered Carinthia, where they spent several weeks laying waste the valleys of the Gail and the Upper Drava. They roamed through the Krka and Metnitz valleys as far as Friesach, returning by way of the Zollfeld and the Wörther See, and finally made off through southern Styria, Celje, and Croatia to Bosnia. There, near Jajce, Peter Zrinyi, the ban of Croatia, fell upon the returning horsemen and almost wiped them out—a feeble consolation for the people of the regions that had just been plundered.

One is amazed at the knowledge of the country and population which the raiders revealed on nearly all their expeditions. Austrian accounts relate how, with their horses, they climbed the steepest slopes of the Loibl Pass in the Carinthian Alps. The network of Ottoman spies extended nearly to the heart of Germany; they were remarkably audacious and their work was extremely effective. No important occurrence in the countries bordering on the Ottoman Empire escaped the knowledge of the Porte. No diet could meet on German or Hungarian soil without Turkish agents sending detailed reports to Istanbul.

By way of demonstrating his indispensability to the Venetians, Matthias Corvinus removed his garrisons from the western frontier fortresses of Croatia. He was bitterly censured for leaving the Signoria to its fate and doing next to nothing to combat the Turkish threat to the neighboring countries. But he found ample justification in his strained relations with Venice and Sixtus IV, who used his conflict with the emperor as a pretext for withholding their financial aid. Least of all could he be expected to defend the hereditary territories of the emperor.

In the late fall Mehmed arrived at his New Serai, on the south side of which the Imperial Gate (*bab-i hümayun*) had been completed that year. Despite the unsatisfactory outcome of the siege of Shkodër, he was without fears for the immediate future. His intelligence service kept him excellently informed about everything that was going on in the West. At the end of December 1478, he was able to devote himself to such trifles as addressing a firman to the judges of European Turkey, bidding them to lay hands on a Ragusan by the name of Marin for robbing a Ragusan tax collector, to confiscate his property, and to return the stolen goods to the injured Ragusans.[36]

In the year 882 of the Hegira (April 15, 1477, to April 3, 1478) the sultan for the first time struck a gold coin in Istanbul (Kostantiniya). On one side it bears the proud inscription "Sultan Mehmed, son of Murad Khan / Glorious be his victory!" and on the other: "The Coiner of Gold / the Lord of Power and Victory / on Land and Sea." But possibly this gold coin was struck only the following spring, when suddenly the whole situation changed in favor of the Porte and the peace treaty with Venice provided an unexpected supply of gold. In any case, the emission was repeated in 883 H. (April 4, 1478, to March 24, 1479) and 885 H. (March 13, 1480, to March 1, 1481).

There can be no doubt that even in the days of Murad II "Turkish gold ducats" coined "in the Venetian mint" (*in istampa veneziana*) were in circulation in the Ottoman Empire. This is mentioned by Giàcomo da Promontorio, *olim* de Campis, who tells us that in 1475 the minting of these coins brought in 3,000 ducats. It goes without saying that the Otto-

---

[36] See Kraelitz, "Osmanische Urkunden," 62–64 (document 9), for the firman.

man silver coinage, which depreciated year after year, could be used only for internal commerce. Payments to foreign countries, especially those of the West, were made exclusively in gold. As formerly in the fourteenth century, certain small Turkmen princes in western Anatolia were in the habit of counterfeiting the Neapolitan *gigliato* for the purposes of trade with the Christian countries, so, from the end of the fourteenth century on, the Venetian *zecchino* was imitated by various emirates, and above all by the Ottomans. Under Murad II there was a genuine "Turkish ducat" bearing the imprint of the *zecchino*, a dubious procedure which was maintained down to the last years of Mehmed's reign. Until recently we had no exact knowledge of these vital financial matters. We now know that Mehmed confiscated all the gold in his empire, inflicted heavy punishments for infringement of his monetary regulations, and maintained in Edirne and in the capital special mints for the counterfeiting of Venetian ducats. It is very much to be hoped that full light will soon be thrown on the Conqueror's financial policy, for it unquestionably constitutes the background for many important political decisions and economic measures.[37]

Venice was now determined to put an end to its disastrous war with the sultan at any price. Before the year 1478 drew to an end, one of the republic's most capable statesmen, a man well acquainted with the Ottoman Empire, the Cretan Giovanni Dario, then secretary of the senate, a man well versed in languages and jurisprudence, who had been in the service of the Signoria since 1464, was dispatched to the Golden Horn with unlimited powers. It was known that the sultan would agree to make peace if the necessary concessions were made. Giovanni Dario was instructed to defend the interests of the Venetian Levantine trade as well as he could, but in other respects to accede to all the Grand Turk's demands. Never in the history of Venice had a peace negotiator been given similar powers, but never perhaps in the history of the republic had the Signoria found itself in so terrible a situation, constrained to abjure all dignity and forget the glory of the past.

[37] The gold coins are described by Pere, *Osmanlilarda madeni paralar*, 90 (#79, 80, and 81); and see plate 7. See also the following articles by Babinger: "Reliquienschacher am Osmanenhof im XV. Jahrhundert. Zugleich ein Beitrag zur Geschichte der osmanischen Goldprägung unter Mehmed II., dem Eroberer," in *Sitzungsberichte der bayerische Akademie der Wissenschaften, philos.-hist. Klasse* (Munich, 1956); "Zur Frage der osmanischen Goldprägung im 15. Jahrhundert unter Murad II. und Mehmed II.," *Südost-Forschungen* 15 (1956), 550–553; "Contraffazioni ottoman dello zecchino veneziano nel XV secolo," *Annali dell'istituto italiano di numismatica* 3 (1956), 83–99. The latter two are republished in *A&A* II, 110–112 and 113–126.

Book Six

PEACE AT LAST WITH VENICE.
OTTOMAN LANDING IN SOUTHEASTERN ITALY.
UNSUCCESSFUL ATTACK ON RHODES.
MEHMED'S LAST CAMPAIGNS AND DEATH.

ON JANUARY 25, 1479, a peace treaty was concluded between the Porte and Venice. Harsh conditions were imposed on the republic. The main points covered by the treaty are as follows:

Venice ceded Shkodër and environs, the island of Lemnos, and the mountainous region of Maina (Braccio di Maina) to the Porte, and relinquished all claims to Krujë and Negropont. All territories taken by Venice in sixteen years of warfare were to be returned within two months, but the Signoria was free to remove garrisons, guns, and ammunition. Mehmed, for his part, was to restore all towns and territories he had occupied in the Morea, Albania, and Dalmatia. Both parties were to appoint an arbiter to define the prewar boundaries between the two states.

Within two years the Signoria was to pay the sultan 100,000 gold ducats toward its alum debt of 150,000 gold ducats. Venice was to pay the Porte 10,000 gold ducats per annum for the privilege of moving its wares duty-free into and out of all towns and ports of the Ottoman Empire. The Signoria was authorized as in prewar times to maintain in Istanbul an ambassador, or *bailo*, endowed with civil jurisdiction over all Venetians in the Ottoman Empire. Included in the treaty were all subjects and supporters of both parties as well as those under their protection. In addition, all cities and ports which chose to hoist the banner of St. Mark were permitted to do so, but on condition that they had flown it before the declaration of war and were not part of a territory already under Ottoman rule.

The Greek text of the treaty along with a Latin translation are still to be found in the state archives in Venice. On January 25, 1479, the sultan swore to it in the traditional manner, "by the God of Heaven and earth, by our great Prophet Mohammed, by the seven copies of the Koran

369

which we Moslems possess and profess, by the 124,000 prophets of God, by the faith which I believe and profess, by my soul and the soul of my father, and by the sword with which I am girded."[1]

Giovanni Dario was then dismissed with all honors and a gift of three ceremonial garments (*ḳaftan*) of gold cloth. The few particulars of his life (he was born in Crete in 1414) that have become known to us suggest that he must have spent considerable time in Turkey and been thoroughly familiar with conditions there. The only monument to his memory today is his palace on the Grand Canal in Venice, bearing the characteristic inscription: VRBIS GENIO IOANNES DARIVS (To the tutelary spirit of the city, Giovanni Dario). He continued for many years to serve the republic, which on March 7, 1487, honored him with the post of secretary to the Council of Ten, and he performed a number of important missions in 1485, 1487, 1490, and 1493 that took him as far east as Persia, where he died on May 13, 1494. On his return from Istanbul in 1479, the Signoria made his natural daughter Marietta a gift of 1,000 ducats for her trousseau. But it was not until 1492 or 1493 that she married Vincenzo Barbaro, son of Giàcomo and probable owner of the nearby palace in the San Vio quarter. The male line of the Dario family died out with Giovanni.[2]

At Giovanni Dario's behest the *provveditore* Pietro Vetturi, who had been taken prisoner with his family at the surrender of Krujë, was released. He remained in Istanbul and became the first *bailo* of the Signoria at the Porte, but was replaced that same year by Battista Gritti. On April 25, when news of the peace reached Shkodër, its inhabitants were offered the choice of remaining in the city under Turkish rule or of leaving freely with their belongings. All without exception chose to emigrate. Of the 1,600 souls who had remained within the walls at the inception of the siege, only 450 men and some 150 women were left. After more than eleven months of inconceivable hardship, they departed from Albania, led by the *provveditore* Antonio da Lezze, taking with them their household goods, arms, and church vessels. At the mouth of the Bojana they were embarked on Venetian vessels. In Venice the Signoria received them with honor, conferred pensions or benefices on them, and after they had

---

[1] For the Greek text of the treaty see Franz Miklosich and Joseph Müller, *Acta et diplomata graeca medii aevi sacra et profana* III, 295–298. Cf. Vl. Mirmiroğlu, *Fatih Sultan Mehmet II devrine ait tarihi vesikalar* (Istanbul, 1945), 19–24, with Turkish translation.

[2] For the Venetian representative in the negotiations, see Babinger, "Johannes Darius (1414–1494) Sachwalter Venedigs im Morgenland, und sein griechischer Umkreis," *Sitzungsberichte der bayerische Akademie der Wissenschaften, philos.-hist. Klasse* (Munich, 1961).

declined an offer to move them to Cyprus, settled most of them in the vicinity of Gradisca. A few obtained suitable occupation in Venice.

The *provveditore* Antonio da Lezze fared far worse than the inhabitants of Shkodër. In consideration of his services he had received the rank of knight (*cavaliere*), a garment of honor, and a gold chain worth 100 ducats. But then certain of the emigrants from Shkodër accused him of having grossly neglected his duties and of having concealed the fact that he had sufficient provisions for a longer siege. The Council of Ten ordered an investigation, which seems to have borne out the charges at least in part. Antonio da Lezze was obliged to return the gifts of honor, to renounce his knighthood, and to pay a heavy fine; he was imprisoned for a year in the arsenal (*camera dell'armamento*), then sent to Capo d'Istria for ten years. The harsh sentence also deprived him of the right to hold any office or post of honor for the rest of his life.

The Signoria chose Giovanni Dario to defend its interests in connection with the towns which the Ottomans had agreed to transfer to Venice and the prisoners they had undertaken to release—a provision covering only those who professed Christianity, to the express exclusion of all who had been converted to Islam. In view of the prevailing custom of the Porte of selling and resettling prisoners, it is certain that only a very limited number were ever released. The territories of Navplion, Monemvasia, Koroni, Methoni, Lepanto, Corfu, Durrës, Kotor, Budva, Bar, Ulcinj, and Split were not transferred to Venice until 1480, and here again Giovanni Dario carried on the negotiations for the Signoria.

On April 16, 1479, Giovanni Dario returned to Venice with the Ottoman negotiator, one Lutfi Bey, who was accompanied by a retinue of twenty and bore a letter in Greek, written in Istanbul on January 29, 1479, and accrediting him to the doge Giovanni Mocenigo (1478–1485).[3] In the name of his sovereign, Lutfi presented the doge with several costly gifts, among them a woven belt that had been worn by the sultan. He was empowered to receive confirmation of the peace from Mocenigo. The belt was bestowed in pledge of the agreement between the two powers and in token of the close ties of peace that would now unite them, on which occasion the Turkish emissary did not forget to remark that the doge should wear the belt "for love of his master." The dress and attitude of the Ottoman delegation are described in contemporary documents. The populace were as much amazed at the guests from the Orient as they had been at their first elephant, which had been brought to Venice from India a short time before. From all accounts, the messenger of peace

---

[3] For the document see Miklosich and Müller, 298. Cf. Mirmiroğlu, 27–28.

behaved with unusual arrogance, deeming it beneath his dignity to respond politely to the honors shown him by the doge and the members of the council. During the reception ceremony he remained seated, condescending only to taste some wine in a little golden goblet he carried with him and then to present it to the head of state and the twelve first senators —strange behavior for a pious Moslem.

By the treaty Venice had regained free passage on the seas and so secured its Levantine trade. Some writers refer to the annual payment of 10,000 ducats as tribute, while others maintain that it entitled the Venetians to trade only in the Black Sea. The wording of the treaty shows these assertions to be unfounded. The 10,000 ducats amounted simply to a flat tax on Venetian trade in the Ottoman Empire; moreover, this tax was collected only for a few years and then discontinued by Bayezid II on January 12, 1482.

Venice was now able to move freely on the seas and gain a new foothold in Istanbul. At the same time the sultan obtained unrestricted rule over Albania, whose old families, such as the Arianiti, the Dukagins, the Castriotas, the Musachi, and the Topias, were obliged to take refuge in Naples, Venice, or northern Italy, except for those who preferred to espouse Islam and who were in future to provide the Porte with some of its foremost statesmen and generals.[4] As for the Albanian towns assigned to Venice in the treaty, namely, Bar, Budva, and Ulcinj, their continuance in Venetian possession (with the exception of Ulcinj, which fell to the Turks on April 17, 1501) was small consolation for the loss of Shkodër, which the Turks had been unable to capture and which the Signoria had never wearied of referring to as the last bastion of Christianity. In the summer of 1480 the Ionian islands of Cephalonia and (though only for a short time) Zakinthos passed into the hands of the Ottomans. Along with Turkish possession of the important port of Vlorë, this increased the threat to the Venetian position in the Adriatic.

The peace treaty of 1479 has with good reason been regarded as a turning point in the policy of the European powers toward the mortal enemy of the Christian name. Hitherto religious enthusiasm had guided the Western attitude toward the Ottomans. Now particularistic worldly aims gained the upper hand, and even in Mehmed's lifetime the princes and statesmen of Christendom began to feel not only that it was preferable to remain at peace with the common enemy but also that close ties with

---

[4] For more details on one of these Albanian families, see Babinger's "Das Ende der Arianiten," *Sitzungsberichte der bayerische Akademie der Wissenschaften, philos.-hist. Klasse* (Munich, 1960).

him could yield them certain political advantages. The example of Venice, which had been bled white in a long, hard struggle with the Ottomans and received no effective help from the Christian powers, exerted a lasting influence on the mood and attitude of the other states, especially those of Italy. Everywhere the Istanbul peace was looked upon as a disaster for Europe; the Venetians were condemned for accepting such harsh terms and for not having held out longer. But even Pope Sixtus IV, who at first bitterly reproached the Venetians for forsaking the Christian cause, finally had to admit that the Signoria had been obliged by prolonged and terrible sufferings to subscribe to such "harsh and reprehensible conditions." Most indignant of all against Venice was Matthias Corvinus, if only because of his justifiable fear that the sultan's wrath and the might of his arms would now be turned against him. He let it be understood that if he had chosen the same way out as Venice, he could long ago have arrived at a profitable understanding with Sultan Mehmed, who for the last three years had pressed him with the most attractive peace offers, asking nothing in return but free passage through Hungary for his troops. As a good Christian, he, Matthias Corvinus, had rejected all these offers, hoping of course that the other Western powers would follow his example; the Grand Turk, who had been able to impose so ignominious a peace on the Venetians, was well aware that he was now in a position to attack him, the forsaken king of Hungary, and quickly destroy him; if the sultan succeeded, there would be no further barrier to the spread of his power in the north and west.

The cardinals in Rome addressed a long letter to King Matthias in which they made every effort to appease his anger against Sixtus IV and to justify the pope's attitude toward Venice, pointing out that it was as a loving father that he had taken to his bosom his repentant sons who had suffered so terribly from the Turkish war, but who now perhaps would condescend to join the league of Italian princes against the infidel.

The Hungarian king's fears were confirmed even sooner than expected. That same summer, while Ottoman bands were overrunning Carniola, others invaded the Hungarian plain.

In late August 1479 (possibly on the 24th), while a fair was being held at Nedeljanec near Varaždin, a band of Turkish cavalry coming from Bosnia appeared, fell upon the assembled countryfolk, and stormed a watchtower serving as a customs house and garrisoned with fifty men. Then below Ptuj they crossed the Drava to Ljutomer, which they burned, crossed Carniola to Hungary, and advanced as far as the river Raab. There the plundering horde was pursued, and a detachment of some

3,000 men was overtaken and defeated. Meanwhile, the larger body of invaders had escaped southward with thousands of prisoners, fording the Drava and Sava, which were nearly dry at that season.

This Turkish incursion was as nothing beside the trials to which the Hungarian territories, especially Transylvania, were subjected shortly thereafter. A number of prominent commanders took part in a subsequent expedition which reportedly involved an army of 43,000 men. The principal goals of this large-scale campaign must have been the rich gold and silver mines and the salt deposits of Transylvania. The troops assembled near Smederevo and were allegedly commanded by twelve pashas: the two Mihaloğlus, Ali Bey and Iskender Bey, the Evrenosoğlus Hasan Bey and Isa Bey, and Malkoçoğlu Bali Bey[5]; the names of the remaining seven "voivodes" are not given. The efficiency of the army was considerably diminished by this plethora of commanders, who were often at odds. Ali Bey, commander of the raiders, put over the Danube at Orşova near the Iron Gate and moved on Transylvania by way of Varhely and the Iron Gate Pass. Plundering on their way, the raiders moved so quickly through the valleys of the Hatszeg Mountains and the river Strel (Streiul), over the Broos plateau, and up the Maros (Mareşul) valley that Stephen Bathory, voivode of Transylvania, had barely time to gather the militia at Şibiu. Paul Kinizsi, ban of Temesvar, who had learned of the Turkish invasion, promised Stephen Bathory his support and set out immediately for Transylvania with his army. The fame that preceded him made the enemy tremble. Formerly a journeyman miller, Paul Kinizsi had attracted the attention of King Matthias by his extraordinary physical strength and was taken into the army; thanks to his bravery and ability, he rose rapidly, becoming first commander of the fortress of Belgrade, then count of Temesvar and supreme commander of the southern districts of Hungary. Finally, owing to his perspicacity and ruthless cruelty, he was promoted to the position of highest magistrate, although he could neither read nor write. As Bathory was approaching by way of Şebeş Alba (Mühlbach; Szaszsebes), Ali Bey was retracing his steps with abundant spoils and many prisoners, apparently unaware that Kinizsi was approaching through the Maros valley.

Ali Bey had pitched his camp on the so-called Field of Bread (Kenyermező), a large fertile plain on the Maros, roughly halfway between Broos (Szaszvaros) and Şebeş Alba, to the west of the Cugir rivulet, when on the morning of October 13, 1479, the feast of St. Koloman, Bathory's army appeared on the heights beyond the brook. To cover his with-

[5] For the several families of raiders, especially the last named, see Babinger's "Beiträge zur Geschichte des Geschlechtes der Malqoč-oghlus," *A&A* I, 359–360.

drawal and above all in order to evacuate his booty, Ali Bey was obliged to stand fast. Stephen Bathory ordered his troops to give battle, setting up the Transylvanian Saxons, some 3,000 men strong, near Ballendorf, with their right flank to the Maros River. They were supported by a second line of Transylvanian Walachians. The Hungarians held the left flank. In the center stood Stephen Bathory himself with his heavy cavalry.

Disagreement between the many Ottoman leaders delayed the Turkish preparations for battle. After three hours of idle waiting, Bathory, confident that Paul Kinizsi would arrive any minute, gave the order to attack. The Saxons opened the battle, but were unable to withstand the violent assaults of the Turks and took flight. The Walachians gave way too, and many were killed or wounded on the field or drowned in the Maros. Bathory's left wing also gave way with considerable losses and, outflanked by the Turks, retreated toward the center. Now the Hungarian commander with his heavy cavalry started to the rescue of his menaced flanks. As he gave spur to his horse, it fell with him. His companions interpreted the incident as an ill omen and advised him either to turn back or to withdraw to the mountains. Ignoring their pleas, Bathory, at the head of his cavalry, flung himself at the enemy with such violence that the Turkish front lines crumpled. Ali Bey now hurled his large body of horsemen against the enemy center. A furious battle ensued and went on for three hours. Bathory was bleeding from six wounds; his horse had been killed under him. He was surrounded by a wall of corpses. Help was nowhere in sight. An Ottoman victory was scarcely in doubt when at last Kinizsi's army appeared on a hill in the enemy's rear. Leading a detachment of heavy cavalry, Kinizsi, followed by numerous courtiers of the king and some 900 Serbs under Demeter Jakšić, charged down the slope and fell on the unsuspecting Turks with terrible shouts and a clamor of drums and trumpets. Bewildered at the unexpected attack, the Turks allowed themselves for a time to be butchered almost without resistance. Furiously, the gigantic Paul Kinizsi, blood spattered from top to toe, flung himself at the enemy. In the confusion he tried to call out to Bathory, his companion-in-arms, whose doom already appeared to be sealed. Finally, Kinizsi saved him by a new charge, reviving the flagging courage of Bathory's companions with wild shouts of victory, and in the course of a murderous onslaught turning the tide in favor of the Hungarians.

When the Turks saw that they were being assailed from all sides, they abandoned their camp and all their spoils. A terrible slaughter ensued. The victors pursued them in all directions. Those Turks who had not lost their lives on the Field of Bread fled into the mountains and were

375

massacred by the population. Those alone were spared whose appearance suggested that an ample ransom might be obtained for them. Ali Bey himself, who knew the language of the country, put on peasant clothes and escaped to Walachia. Some 30,000 Turkish corpses were said to have covered the battlefield, but the Hungarians had also lost some 8,000 men, and approximately 2,000 Saxons and Walachians had died in the waters of the Maros. Their bodies were not recovered until later. The Turks' prisoners, freed from their shackles, participated in the looting of the Ottoman camp. The onset of darkness put an end to the pursuit. The two commanders decided to spend the night on the battlefield and to restore their army with food and drink, large quantities of which were found in the enemy camp. Since there was no lack of wine, all were soon in high spirits. Within a circle of soldiers using heaped-up Turkish corpses for benches, a song rang out. When his companions in arms asked him to dance, Kinizsi put on a performance worthy of those days of barbaric battles. Leaping into the center of the circle, he picked up a dead Turk with his teeth and danced to the wild applause of the onlookers. On the following morning Stephen Bathory and Paul Kinizsi entered Alba Iulia (Weissenburg, Karlsburg). Previously, most of the dead Christian warriors had been buried on the spot where the battle had been most violent. The chapel built by Stephen Bathory in commemoration of the battle fell into ruins in the course of the centuries and finally vanished altogether. The Requiem Mass endowed in 1479, which was supposed to be sung every year on St. Koloman's Day, has long been forgotten, and the memory of the battle on the Field of Bread has survived only in folk songs.

The victory was most welcome to King Matthias. In accordance with the custom of the day, some of the numerous Ottoman banners and insignia that had been brought to Buda were sent to friendly sovereigns. Pope Sixtus IV also received his share, accompanied by a long, high-flown letter from the Hungarian king, stressing his zeal for the Christian cause and openly accusing the sovereign pontiff of doing more to foment internal strife in Italy than to free Christians from the Ottoman yoke. It is true that Matthias obtained only promises and no actual help from the pope and accordingly decided to go his own way in the future. His first step in this direction was to renew his war against Emperor Frederick III.

Mehmed spent the entire year 1479 in his new palace in Istanbul. It was completed in January 1479, except, perhaps, for the interior decoration of the large buildings. The extensive grounds had meanwhile been surrounded by a high wall, which hid the precinct of the serai from the eyes of the world and guaranteed the security of its inhabitants. Here the sultan, no doubt gravely sick, spent his days.

In recent generations the members of the house of Osman had been short-lived. In the last hundred years hardly one had lived to be fifty, and perhaps Mehmed had put a greater strain on his physical powers than any. He had early been afflicted by the gout hereditary in his family, and he seems also to have been a prey to other ailments. In his *Mémoires*, a mirror for princes, Philippe de Commynes (Comines, 1445-1509), an acute observer and a brilliant diplomat, speaks of his contemporary Mehmed, whom he classed with Louis XI and Matthias Corvinus as the greatest rulers of the last hundred years. Mehmed, he tells us, had over-indulged in "les plaisirs du monde"; no carnal vice had been alien to this immoderate voluptuary; consequently, from a relatively early age he had been assailed by disease. Now he was afflicted by a strange abscess in the leg which had set in at the beginning of summer, taken on an unusual form, and finally subsided without opening. None of his surgeons had been able to explain it, but had looked upon it as divine punishment for his great gluttony (*grande gourmandise*). This disorder, so Commynes goes on, had kept him in his palace, showing himself in public as little as possible, lest anyone see what a state he was in and look upon him with contempt. This account of Mehmed's leg abscess, in support of which Philippe de Commynes invokes eyewitnesses, is corroborated by Ottoman chroniclers.[6]

His increasing desire to withdraw from the eyes of men and to avoid public life may have contributed to his decision to decorate the palace in full accordance with his tastes. One of his favorite occupations—so we read in an account referring precisely to the year 1480—was tending a certain garden within the palace grounds. He amused himself with handicrafts, such as the fashioning of bow rings, scabbards, knives, and the embroidering of girdles—a traditional custom in the house of Osman. He took a particular interest in painting and when the serai was completed the mural decoration of the rooms may well have been one of his chief concerns. At any event, in 1479, the year of the peace with Venice, he decided to invite an outstanding Western painter to Istanbul. Giovanni Dario may have encouraged him in this project during his recent stay in Istanbul.

It would be difficult to find another explanation for the visit to the Conqueror's court of Gentile Bellini (1429-1507), the famous Venetian

[6] For Commynes and his book, see the translation by Michael Jones, *Philippe de Commynes: Memoirs* (London, 1972).

master, a visit which began in September 1479 and probably extended to the middle of January 1481.

On August 1, 1479, one of the Jews whom Mehmed favored for semi-official embassies arrived by the land route in Venice, which shortly before (July 23) had been shaken by a violent earthquake. He carried an invitation to the doge Giovanni Mocenigo to attend the circumcision of one of the sultan's grandchildren and at the same time transmitted the sultan's request that the Venetians send a "good painter" (*un buon pittore*) to his court. The Signoria's choice fell on Gentile Bellini, who for the last five years had been busy repairing the Hall of the Great Council in the Palace of the Doges, where the murals had suffered greatly from humidity and age. This work was transferred to Gentile's younger brother Giovanni, and on September 3 the painter set out for Istanbul aboard Melchiorre Trevisano's galley. The sultan's letter to the doge had also asked for a sculptor and a bronze-caster. This proved to be far more of a problem. Bartolomeo Vellano (d. 1492), a pupil of Donatello, was taken under consideration. The cautious, timid artist proceeded to make his will, but he hesitated to set out and apparently never did. Two of his helpers, however, left with Bellini, who also took along two helpers. All traveled at government expense and seem to have arrived safely at the end of September. The clearest indication that Bartolomeo Vellano did not accede to the invitation is that on January 7, 1480, the sultan sent another letter to the Signoria, requesting that a bronze-caster and an architect be sent as soon as possible. The letter, written in Greek, was conveyed by the Ottoman ambassador Hasan Bey, who arrived in Venice on March 8, 1480, to negotiate with the Signoria on the subject of frontier difficulties in "Slavonia," Albania, and Greece arising from the previous year's peace treaty. The discussions did not bring the desired results, and it was decided to send Giovanni Dario to Istanbul along with Niccolò Cocco, who had been appointed ambassador to the Porte on April 3, 1480. Whether the sultan's request for the two artists was ever met is still unknown, but it seems unlikely that any Italian artist other than Gentile Bellini went to Mehmed's court in the last years of the sultan's life.

Concerning the master's stay in Istanbul, we possess only anecdotes whose veracity can scarcely be checked. Some of these stories originate with Gian-Maria Angiolello, an eyewitness, others with Vasari, who wrote many years later and can only have learned them from hearsay.[7]

---

[7] See Angiolello's *Historia turchesca,* 119ff. Giorgio Vasari (1511–74) is the Florentine artist and writer; for his remarks on Bellini's visit to Turkey see the edition of E. H. and E. W. Blashfield and A. A. Hopkins, *Lives of Seventy of the Most Eminent Painters, Sculptors and Architects* II (New York, 1902), 159–162.

Bellini's work consisted not only in painting portraits of the sultan and the members of his court but also in decorating the inner chambers of the palace with erotic and probably obscene paintings, which indeed are explicitly characterized as "cose di lussuria" (objects of lechery). Only a small portion of these works was saved by chance; the rest fell a victim to the pious, iconoclastic zeal of Sultan Bayezid II, who, on his accession to the throne, had all the many paintings in his father's palace sold cheaply in the Istanbul bazaar. In this way the famous portrait of Mehmed [pl. XXIII], which according to its inscription was completed on November 25, 1480, came into the possession of a Venetian merchant in Pera and was later brought to Venice. There it was acquired by Sir Austen Henry Layard (1817-1894), British ambassador to the Sublime Porte (1877-1880) and discoverer of Niniveh; his widow donated it to the National Gallery in London in 1917.

A second portrait, most probably by Gentile Bellini or at least his atelier, came to light in 1933. A Russian dealer who had brought it from his homeland sold it in Paris to an American collector. It is a panel of small size (21 x 16 cm). The unusual position of the head, which is turned over the left shoulder, suggests that it may have been painted not from life but rather after Bellini's return to Venice.

Recently, the late Swiss Orientalist Rudolf Tschudi discovered still another portrait in a private collection in Switzerland. It shows the Conqueror in left profile facing a young man of about twenty, who appears in right profile [pl. XXIV]. An old label on the back of the wooden panel identifies the painter as Gentile Bellini and his subjects as "Maometto Secondo i suo Figlio." It is, however, impossible to identify the young man. One son, Mustafa, had died in 1474, and during Bellini's stay the two other sons, Bayezid and Prince Cem, were, as far as we know, at their posts in distant Anatolia.[8]

The anecdotes woven around Bellini's stay in Istanbul do perhaps indicate that the sultan showed him special favor and encouraged him to speak frankly. If the tales are to be believed, Bellini made frequent use of this permission. We shall have more to say of this in a different context. Though the Latin letter of Mehmed, dated January 15, 1481, in which

[8] Babinger discussed the Bellini portraits in several articles, among them "Ein Weiteres Sultansbild von Gentile Bellini?," *Sitzungsberichte der Österreichische Akademie der Wissenschaften, philos.-hist. Klasse* CCXXXVII, part 3 (Vienna, 1961). Earlier articles in English include Basil Gray, "Two Portraits of Mehmet II," *Burlington Magazine* 61 (1932), 4-6, and A. Sakisian, "The Portraits of Mehmet II," *Burlington Magazine* 74 (1939), 172-181. Cf. Esin Atïl, "Ottoman Miniature Painting under Sultan Mehmed II," *Ars Orientalis* 9 (1973), especially 110-113. An older study is L. Thuasne, *Gentile Bellini et Sultan Mohammed II* (Paris, 1888).

he discharged the Venetian painter and confirmed his appointment as count palatine and knight must be looked upon with grave suspicion in view of these impossible honors, the date is perfectly credible.[8a] It must have been at this time that Bellini left for home. A golden chain of honor, given him by the sultan, was still preserved by the family in the sixteenth century, probably the only remaining souvenir of the master's activity in Istanbul.

Apart from the panel portraits of the sultan, a medallion, and seven pen-and-ink drawings [pl. XXII] showing Bellini's interest in strange Oriental costumes and types, none of the work done during his fifteen or sixteen months in Istanbul has survived. There is no ground whatsoever for supposing that the Venetian painter established a school during his relatively short stay or that he was able to instruct even one native artist in the Western technique of painting. Only a thorough investigation can show whether traces of Bellini's murals may have been preserved under the plaster of the inner chambers of the palace, although it is quite improbable that any considerable portion of the buildings erected by Mehmed and used by him has been preserved.

Although it is unknown whether any bronze-caster ever went to the sultan's court, one is tempted to suppose that this role was filled by Costanzo da Ferrara, who not only seems to have boasted of receiving from the sultan such honors as Bellini did—namely, titles unknown to the Ottoman Empire at that time—but who also lives on in the history of art as the creator of a medallion commemorating Mehmed II and perhaps a portrait done in watercolor.[8b]

It is safe to assume that Maestro Costanzo, who called himself "da Ferrara" because his wife was a woman of Ferrara and he had resided there for many years, actually spent some time at the sultan's court. All indications are that he was sent by King Ferrante of Naples, to whom the sultan had applied for an artist. The same reliable source informs us that Costanzo was dubbed knight (*cavaliere*) by the Grand Turk and that he spent "many years" (*molti anni*) at his court. The relative absence of gaps in the known dates of Costanzo's career does not seem to leave room for a very protracted stay. If he went to the Golden Horn at the

---

[8a] Such honors were in fact accorded the artist by the emperor Frederick III.

[8b] In the 1961 articles cited in n. 8, Babinger suggested the attribution to Costanzo da Ferrara of the watercolor miniature portrait of Mehmed II reproduced as the frontispiece of the present volume. The opinion persists, however, that the miniature was the work of a native Turkish painter known as Sinan; cf. articles in the *Encyclopedia of World Art* by Albert Gabriel, vol. X (1965), col. 869, and B. M. Alfieri, vol. XI (1966), col. 502.

same time as Bellini, Mehmed's sudden death makes it appear highly unlikely that he stayed there longer than the Venetian painter.

But before we go into the medallion and its story, let us deal briefly with the other events of the year 1479. On January 9, Dubrovnik had hastened to send two emissaries to Istanbul bearing the annual tribute of 12,500 gold ducats for the coming year.[9]

After the peace with Venice left the sea open to the Turkish squadrons, the Knights of St. John on the island of Rhodes, aware of impending danger, were making all possible preparations for a Turkish invasion. Grand master Pierre d'Aubusson (1476–1503), who a few years before had replaced Giovanni Orsini (1467–1476) in office, strengthened the fortifications and wrote solemn missives to all the grand priors of the order calling on them to defend this bastion of Christendom. In the summer of 1479 he had received the visit of an emissary from Prince Cem, governor of Karaman, who, apparently at his father's behest, offered the knights a lasting peace on condition that they pay an annual tribute. This emissary, a Greek renegade by the name of Dimitrios Sophianos, descendant of an old family of Euboean nobility, was probably supposed to investigate the situation of the Order and to report his observations to the Porte. But Pierre d'Aubusson had been apprised of the sultan's intentions by his agents in Istanbul. In order that the knights who had been summoned from the West might have time to reach the island in safety, he pretended to put faith in the emissary, asked to be exempted from the tribute, and requested a three months' period of reflection on the ground that he must first consult the Vatican and the Western powers. Dimitrios Sophianos came to Rhodes a second time and reiterated his demand for an annual payment, which, however, he now represented not as a tribute but as a gift. Once again the grand master staunchly refused. A truce was concluded, freedom of trade was granted, and the agreement was confirmed by a second Turkish emissary. It was perfectly clear to the Knights of Rhodes that the Ottomans' sole purpose in staging these supposed negotiations was to gain time in which to prepare their army and fleet for an attack. The grand master quickly concluded a peace treaty (October 28, 1479) with Qa'it Bey, the Mamluk sultan of Egypt, and made an agreement with Abu Amr Osman (1435–1488), the ruler of Tunisia, to secure the duty-free importation of grain in case of need. The assembled chapter of the Order, considerably increased in numbers

---

[9] For the document confirming receipt of payment, see Truhelka, "Turskoslovjenski spomenici," *GZMBH* 23 (1911), 52–53 (document 60); Turkish summary translation in *IED* 1 (1955), 65. Cf. Elezović, *Turski spomenici* I, part 1, 178–179, and I, part 2, 51.

by new arrivals from the West, entrusted Pierre d'Aubusson with dictatorial powers over the island. As his chief subordinates, his *capitaines de secours*, he chose the admiral, the administrator of the hospital, the chancellor Guillaume Caoursin, and the treasurer of the Order. Rudolf von Wallenberg, the grand prior of Brandenburg, was appointed general of cavalry, while Pierre's elder brother Antoine d'Aubusson, Vicomte de Monteil, became supreme commander of foot soldiers. The outer fortifications of the powerful citadel were disengaged by the razing of two churches situated on hills outside the city. Nothing was neglected that could contribute to successful resistance.[10]

Of course, these measures on Rhodes had not escaped Mehmed. In Istanbul, Gelibolu, and Anatolia he vigorously pressed preparations for a campaign against the Knights of St. John. To avoid the cumbersome business of ferrying the army across the straits, he had his land forces assemble near Üsküdar across from the capital and gradually moved southward. Sixty galleys were made ready in the port of Gelibolu, the remainder in the main harbor of Istanbul. In all, the fleet consisted of 160 sailing vessels of various sizes. While the land army moved from Üsküdar by way of Izmit, Bursa, Bergama, Manisa, and Alaşehir to the Bay of Marmaris (Fisco), the Palaeologus Mesih Pasha, who had been appointed admiral of the fleet and commander of all forces, put to sea with his fleet (December 4, 1479).

The city and fortress of Rhodes, which were regarded as impregnable, were provided with provisions for three years. A garrison of 7,000 men, for the most part knights with their shield bearers, took charge of the defense. Women, children, and the aged, in short, the noncombatant population, were for the most part moved inland to the castle of St. Peter (Castello). In the harbor the defenders had hidden fireships, with the help of which they planned to destroy the enemy fleet. Mesih Pasha landed on the northwest coast of the island near the castle of Fane (Phanaes) and put a few men ashore, but was obliged to reembark them when they were attacked by the grand prior of Brandenburg. He then attempted a landing to the northwest of Rhodes on the small island of Tilos, which belonged to the Rhodiots, who also defended it. Unable to overrun the fortress of this island, Mesih Pasha returned to the Bay of Marmaris, which offered his fleet ample shelter. Here he decided to await the spring, when naval reinforcements would arrive from Istanbul. The first attempt to take Rhodes by a surprise attack had failed, but Pierre d'Aubusson's astuteness, fortitude, and courage had not yet been put to the final test.

[10] For the Knights of St. John and background to the first Turkish siege, from a Western point of view, see Eric Brockman, *The Two Sieges of Rhodes 1480–1522* (London, 1969).

Fortune was far less favorable to another island commander, Leonardo III Tocco, lord of Levkas, Cephalonia, and Zakinthos in the Ionian Sea. Since 1353 these islands had been in the possession of the despots of Arta in Epirus, who had received them in fief from Robert II of Taranto (1346–1364), the titular Latin emperor of Constantinople. A Leonardo Tocco—the Christian name was handed down from father to son for an entire century—had at that time assumed the title of count of Cephalonia and duke of Levkas. But fortune had not smiled on the Toccos for long. During the reign of Mehmed II they had been obliged to pay a tribute to the Porte as the price of preserving their pitiful sovereignty. The treaty providing for this tribute included the odd provision that whenever a new *sancak beyi* of Ioannina (Ottoman since 1431) stopped at the town of Arta, a present of 500 ducats must be made him as a kind of viaticum. This tiresome tax was the cause of violent disputes and led finally to a breach with the Porte.

One day a new *sancak beyi* of Ioannina passed through. To make matters worse, he was related to Leonardo III Tocco: he was assuredly a cousin, that is, one of the five bastard sons of Leonardo's uncle Carlo I Tocco (d. July 4, 1429), who had gone over to the Turks and who under the name of Karlïzadeler long played a part in Turkish politics. Instead of 500 gold pieces all he received from the despot of Arta was a shipment of choice fruit. Indignant at this treatment, the former pasha, who had incurred the sultan's displeasure and so been demoted to the rank of *sancak beyi*, reported the incident to the Porte. His complaint was taken as a welcome pretext for war against the prince, who had long been in the sultan's bad books. The same *sancak beyi* was also reported to have informed the sultan that during the recent war with Venice, Leonardo had provided the Signoria's stradiots with a refuge on Zakinthos and so facilitated their raids on Ottoman territory. Moreover, Mehmed had an old grudge against Tocco, who therefore had not been included in the peace with Venice, allegedly because he had failed to secure the sultan's permission before taking the Neapolitan princess Francesca Marzano of Aragon as his second wife (1477). His first wife (1463), Milica, daughter of Lazar Branković, sister of Maria, the last queen of Bosnia (d. 1474 on Levkas), and niece of George Branković's daughter Mara, had died in 1464. Now the measure was full, and in the summer of 1479 Gedik Ahmed Pasha, the new *sancak beyi* of Vlorë, received orders to set sail for the Ionian islands with a squadron of twenty-nine vessels. News of this expedition aroused keen indignation in Venice, and a rupture between the republic and the Porte was only narrowly averted. The Signoria, itself at odds with Leonardo Tocco, had landed 500 horsemen on Zakinthos and occupied the island. Antonio Loredano, the captain general, who was

cruising nearby and closely observing the Ottoman operations, was instructed to demand at least that the garrison be permitted to leave before
the Turks landed. The question was referred to the sultan in Istanbul,
who, thanks to the adroit intercession of Benedetto Trevisano, the new
bailo, not only allowed the 500 horsemen to withdraw freely but also
permitted the Venetians to transport as many of the inhabitants as they
wished on their vessels. Many thousands left the island and were settled
under the protection of St. Mark in the Venetian possessions in the Morea.

Leonardo Tocco had no thought of serious resistance. No sooner had the
Ottoman squadron arrived than he set sail for Naples with his family,
his court, and his treasure. On his arrival King Ferrante, his new relative,
assigned him the fiefs of Calimera and Briatico. He had not lost by the
exchange, for his extortions had long earned him the hatred of the Ionian
islanders. But a hard and undeserved blow struck the entire population.
The Turks butchered all the despot's officials on whom they could lay
hands, while the remaining inhabitants, men and women, were carried off
to Istanbul and settled on the islands of the Sea of Marmara, where—if the
none too trustworthy Theodoros Spandugino "Cantacuzino" is to be believed—they were forced to intermarry with Abyssinians. Mehmed wished
allegedly to experiment with a racial mixture and employ the products
as slaves.

Anxious to regain possession of their paternal heritage, the three
brothers Leonardo, Antonio, and Giovanni Tocco appealed to the pope
and were received with special distinction; Leonardo persuaded Sixtus to
grant him a present of 1,000 ducats from the papal treasury and an
annual pension of 2,000 ducats, with a promise of more in better times.
In 1480 Antonio Tocco invaded and briefly occupied Cephalonia and
Zakinthos with an army of Catalan mercenaries, but he was soon driven
out by the Venetians and finally murdered on Cephalonia.[11]

We have seen that in the West, and particularly in Italy, Venice was
severely reproached for making peace so quickly with the Turks and that
soon the Signoria was openly or secretly accused of complicity with the
Turks. In view of the vastly increased power of the Porte, it is not surprising that Western powers found it more and more advantageous to
make concessions to the sultan. The next to do so was apparently the
Florentine Republic.

On the Sunday before Ascension, April 26, 1478, Giuliano de' Medici

---

[11] See Babinger's "Beiträge zur Geschichte von Qarly-eli vornehmlich aus osmanischen Quellen," *A&A* I, 370–377; and cf. William Miller, *The Latins in the Levant*,
483ff., with references to the Western sources.

was assassinated in the Florence cathedral, and his hated brother Lorenzo, against whom the conspiracy of the Pazzi was directed, escaped only by chance. The murderer was Bernardo Bandini Baroncello, who was captured but succeeded in giving his guards the slip and in escaping to Istanbul, where he had close relatives. One, Carlo Baroncello, had served as Florentine consul in Pera for four years (1472–1476), and at the beginning of 1471 his brother Francesco had made the Venetians an offer to set the sultan's fleet on fire in exchange for 400 ducats and a bank guarantee. All were members of a Florentine patrician family, at least a part of which had become involved in the political turmoil of the Medici period and had emigrated.

Bernardo's hiding place in Istanbul was soon known. In the spring of 1479 Mehmed had the murderer apprehended, and news of the arrest reached Florence by the middle of June. When Lorenzo Carducci, the Florentine consul, had confirmed the arrest (May 8), the republic decided to send an emissary with a request that Bernardo be extradited. The sultan had promised to hold him until the middle of August. Antonio de' Medici was chosen for the task. Laden with gifts for the sultan, "the most illustrious prince," who had always shown the Florentines his "love and immeasurable favor," he set out for the Golden Horn on July 14 by the overland route. He carried written instructions (dated July 11, 1479) prescribing his behavior during his audience with the sultan, with whom he was to enter an urgent plea for the surrender of the prisoner. Antonio de' Medici was received and Bernardo Bandini was handed over to him. Antonio reached Venice on December 7, and returned to Florence on the 24th. What had detained him in Venice for two whole weeks we do not know. A few days later the murderer of Giuliano de' Medici was hanged from a window of the Bargello, the palace of the *podestà*.[12] Leonardo da Vinci has left us a pen-and-ink sketch of the hanging. Lorenzo the Magnificent was absent at the time, negotiating a peace treaty with Ferrante of Aragon in Naples, which was signed only on March 13, 1480. When Lorenzo received news of the success of Antonio's mission, he decided to express his gratitude to the sultan in a very special way—by issuing a medallion in his honor. The commission was entrusted to Bertoldo di Giovanni, an otherwise little-known Florentine sculptor and medalist. The medallion, 7.4 inches in diameter, is generally believed to have been copied from Gentile Bellini's. This seems doubtful, although there is a certain resemblance between the two busts of the sultan wearing a turban, but

[12] For a near contemporary Florentine view of the cathedral assassination and the political rivalries behind it, see Francesco Guicciardini, *The History of Florence*, trans. M. Domandi (New York, 1970), especially 29–36.

the possibility that both were based on a common source cannot be excluded. Far more important than this portrait, which shows Mehmed in left profile wearing a crescent suspended by a chain over his chest—a pure invention on Bertoldo's part, proving that he was never in Istanbul and never saw the sultan—was the reverse of the medallion. (See illus. facing.)

On May 11, 1480, the commune of Florence wrote an official letter thanking the sultan for surrendering Bernardo Bandini, and on the following day another letter was written to Lorenzo Carducci, the Florentine consul in Pera. Both documents were entrusted to an emissary from Mehmed who immediately thereafter returned to Istanbul by the overland route. Presumably, he also carried a letter from Lorenzo de' Medici to a prominent Ottoman by the name of Ishak Bey, who had made him a present of an ornamental saddle. None of the letters say anything about the Turkish emissary's mission in Florence. The letter to Mehmed makes no mention of him, while that to the consul speaks of him only in the most general terms. This discretion, it has been pointed out, was intentional. From the letter of May 12, 1480, it can be gathered that the unnamed "honorable emissary" conveyed letters from Lorenzo Carducci to Florence and orally reiterated the request from the sultan communicated in these letters. In its answer, the commune expressed its willingness to meet this request. It goes on to relate that the emissary had spent some days in Florence, that the Florentines had welcomed him and had treated him graciously, that he was now returning with this letter, and that the sultan would learn from him personally what he had accomplished.

We should be reduced to conjectures on the purpose of the Turkish envoy's mission were it not for Benedetto Dei, who, as we have seen, had lived in Istanbul and the Near East from 1462 to 1468 as a political agent, spy, and merchant, and had had dealings with Mehmed. At the end of the remarks on the Turkish embassy in Florence contained in his chronicle he provides certain details. The sultan's messenger, so he says in substance, had come to Florence to ask the republic for masters in the arts of woodcarving and inlay, as well as for bronze-casters. His chief mission, however, had been to bring news of the sultan's "large-scale military preparations" (*grande apparecchio*) and to sound out Lorenzo's attitude. These military preparations were indeed in full swing at the time of the Turkish envoy's stay in Florence. No documentary source tells us what Lorenzo de' Medici replied to the sultan when he heard about them. It may be presumed that for reasons of security his reply was never committed to writing but was entrusted orally to the Turkish emissary. Recently, it has been suggested that the medallion which Bertoldo made for his master might furnish a clue.

Medal of Mehmed II by Bertoldo di Giovanni (1480)

The obverse shows Mehmed's head in profile, but the reverse shows the nude form of a triumphant victor riding a chariot drawn by two horses. The galloping horses are led by the running war god Mars, who is shouldering a trophy. Carried on the chariot behind the victor are three nude feminine forms symbolizing three conquered empires; each one bears a five-pronged crown and all are encircled by a rope whose end is held by the victor. Their names are clearly inscribed: Asia, Trebizond, Greece (ASIE TRAPESVNTY GRETIE). But when we examine the inscription on the obverse, we read: Mehmed, emperor of Asia and Trebizond and Greater Greece (MAVMBET ASIE AC TRAPESVNZIS MAGNEQVE GRETIE IMPER-AT[OR]). In triumph, as sovereign over three subjected empires, Mehmed is obviously riding out to conquer a fourth empire, the symbol of which, an empty throne over a garland of flowers held by the maws of two lions, adorns the lateral surface of the chariot. Below are two nude forms, one male bearing a trident, the other female with cornucopia, symbols of sea and land.

The victorious Mehmed is looking toward a figure which he holds in his left hand, a striding boy, the god Bonus Eventus, Success. His left leg forward, the boy hurries on, holding a bowl in his raised left hand and pouring out an offering. Thus, the accent in this *trionfo* is success in new battles. That is the hope of Mehmed and of Lorenzo de' Medici, the donor, as well. Few prints of this medallion were struck—those presumably in April or May, 1480—and fewer have been preserved; one was in Goethe's collection in Weimar.

This reading of the medallion was accomplished by Ludwig Deubner and Emil Jacobs. In a special monograph the latter developed the theory that Lorenzo knew of the forthcoming Ottoman landing in southern Italy because the sultan had notified him of his intentions, and that the inscription on the reverse of the medallion anticipated neither more nor less than a Turkish victory in Italy. "Magna Gretia," he claims, refers to southern Italy, as it did in antiquity. It is virtually certain, however, that the medallion had nothing whatever to do with the impending Ottoman invasion of Apulia. To suppose the contrary would imply that the ruler of Florence did not scruple to anticipate a Turkish landing in Italy as a fortunate turn of fate, as a *bonus eventus*. The "grande apparecchio" of Dei's chronicle refers rather to the Ottoman campaign against the island of Rhodes, which was then in full swing. Accordingly, "Magna Gretia" refers not to southern Italy but to "all Greece," that is, Rum-eli. The "Magna Gretia" mentioned on the medal along with Asia and Trebizond can refer only to greater Greece as opposed to little Trebizond, hence to Byzantium and its enormous hinterland, which, it seems evident, would otherwise have had to be mentioned in its usual form, Gretia. Thus, on sober scrutiny, the medallion must be regarded as a gesture of thanks to the sultan for his extradition of the "tanto nefario parricida."[13]

There is good reason to suppose that the medallion of Costanzo da Ferrara, of which we have two versions, one bearing the date 1481, was fashioned at the behest of King Ferrante of Aragon at roughly the same time as the Florentine medallion. On the obverse it shows a bust of the sultan in left profile, wearing a turban. The reverse shows Mehmed in left profile, mounted, holding a whip in his right hand. To the left and right behind him we discern two defoliated trees, and further in the background barren hills; on the central hill stands a building, perhaps a mosque. In the one version the inscription on the obverse reads: SVLTANI·MOHAMMETH·OCTHOMANI·VGVLI·BIZANTII·INPERATORIS·1481; in the other, SVLTANVS·MOHAMETH·OTHOMANVS·TVRCORVM·IMPERATOR. On the reverse the one version has: Mohameth·Asie et Gretie·inperatoris ymago·eqvestris·in exercitvs, and the other: Hic belli fvlmen popvlos prostravit et vrbes. The only feature worthy of note is the use of the title Ochtomani vgvli ("Osman-oğlu," descendant of Osman), which must have been suggested by someone familiar with Turkey and its language, perhaps Benedetto Dei. As for the verse Hic belli fulmen populos prostravit et urbes (Here [or now] the thunderbolt of war has laid low peoples and cities), it is hard to tell in what sense it should be taken. Belli fulmen can be employed metonymously for "irresistible warrior." We have the impression that the two different versions of Costanzo's medallion served, or were meant to serve, different purposes. (See illus. facing.)

On February 9, 1480, Mehmed wrote a letter from Istanbul in German, with his seal affixed, to Leonhard (a nephew of Catherine of Cilli), the last count of Gorizia, who for fear of enemy incursions spent his idle life far from his country in the castle of Bruck in Lienz, where he died on April 12, 1500. The letter was transmitted by a man named Simon, a Jewish diplomat in the service of the Porte—Domenico Malipiero refers to him solely as orator Judeo—who had gone to Venice on a mission for the sultan. It dealt with a real estate transaction going on in Friuli. Leonhard was interested in redeeming a large, tumbledown castle, the Castello Belgrado, not far from Udine, which he had pawned to his aunt in 1465. He had informed the sultan of his intention through a courtier, the "noble and honorable Kossach," that is to say, Stjepan Kosača, now known as Hersekoğlu Ahmed Bey. The sultan instructed Count Leon-

---

[13] See E. Jacobs, "Die Mehemmed-Medaille des Bertoldo," Jahrbuch der preussischen Kunstsammlungen 48 (1927), 1–17.

Medal of Mehmed II by Costanzo da Ferrara (1481)

hard to deposit the agreed purchase price of 5,400 Venetian gold ducats with Ayas Bey, military governor of Bosnia, in return for which Leonhard would receive the deed. The entire correspondence which has survived shows plainly that Mehmed or his adviser had simply doubled the purchase price, so making it impossible for the impecunious count to redeem his pledge. Probably not on his own initiative, Simon now proceeded with the consent of the Signoria, the feudal overlord of Gorizia, to sell the castle to a third party for only 3,200 gold pieces. It is scarcely conceivable that the sultan did not in some way profit by the deal. For some reason he was interested in this Castello Belgrado; at the end of 1477 he had been in communication with Dubrovnik about the sale of the property.

Late in the fall of 1480 the countess Catherine, who, persecuted by the sultan, was living out her old age in Ježevo in Macedonia with her sister Mara, complained in a letter to her nephew Leonhard about Mehmed's cruel treatment of her. Written in Serbian, the letter had to be sent to Venice for translation since no one could decipher it. She was, so she wrote, abused, tormented, and beaten, and had no other desire than to leave Turkey and die in her far-away home. Now she was doubly alarmed because her nephew, instead of using a trustworthy messenger, had written several letters to the sultan, and Catherine feared, perhaps with reason, that the two were plotting against her life. Although the Porte had given her permission to leave the empire, she spent the rest of her life in fear and misery far from the land of her birth. She died about 1487 and was buried in the convent of Konča near Strumica.[14]

Venice had saved itself from the storm in 1479—though with grave wounds that were never to heal—but soon all Italy was to feel the consequences of the Venetian defeat. Once the Ottomans had taken possession of the Ionian islands belonging to the former despotate of Arta, the idea of turning their arms against torn and helpless Italy was even more tempting. The chief stimulus to such a campaign may well have been Venetian jealousy of the king of Naples, who, it was widely believed, was planning nothing less than to make himself master of all Italy. There were many who held that a Venetian empire—a possibility of which scarcely any of the republic's political leaders lost sight—would be far more conducive to the welfare of Italy than the Spanish domination of southern Italy. The extension of such foreign rule to the north of the peninsula was especially unacceptable to Venice, which could only look upon such an eventuality as a grave menace to her own political existence. Thus, it was only natural to suspect that the Signoria had promised the

[14] Further see Babinger, "Le estreme vicende di Paola di Gonzaga, ultima contessa di Gorizia," *Studi Goriziani* 20 (1956), 8–19.

Grand Turk its assistance and naval support and had even summoned him to Italy. It is certain that when, in the summer of 1479, the Ottomans proposed an alliance with Venice, the Signoria declined in extremely courteous terms which may well have suggested a secret willingness to enter into such a pact, and equally certain that immediately after making peace with the sultan the republic hastened to lend assistance to its old enemy Florence. From Venetian sources worthy of credence (e.g. Andrea Navagero) it can be inferred that the Signoria, through Battista Gritti, its new *bailo* in Istanbul, gave the sultan to understand that he would be quite within his rights in seizing Brindisi, Taranto, and Otranto, because as Greek colonies these territories were part of the former Byzantine Empire, which was wholly subject to him as emperor of Constantinople. Of course, it is impossible to say to what extent such declarations contributed to Mehmed's decision to carry out his long-standing plan for a landing in Italy. All we know for sure is that he now acted quickly and resolutely.

Early in the summer of 1480, Gedik Ahmed Pasha, former governor of Vlorë, who, it would seem, had meanwhile been promoted to the post of grand admiral (*kapudan-i derya*), received orders from the sultan to cross the straits of Otranto from Vlorë to Apulia, only some forty-six miles distant. He was reportedly accompanied by a brother named Mehmed, by the governor of Rumelia, by the agha of the Janissaries, and by one Hayreddin ("Ariadeno"), *sancak beyi* of Negropont, and was at the head of a fleet consisting of 140 vessels—40 galleys, 60 one-masters, and 40 freight ships—and bearing an army of 18,000 soldiers (exaggerated to 100,000 in some accounts) and 700 horses. The devastating invasion is described in every conceivable detail in native Apulian sources. Gedik Ahmed Pasha is described as a "man of slight stature, with a brown complexion, a large nose, a sparse beard, of medium height, extremely cruel and niggardly, debased, and corrupt"—probably the only existing description of this powerful man—who had been promoted to pasha in jest, because he had formerly been a servant or page (*staffiere*).[15] We are told that the army destined for the Italian campaign had been brought overland to Vlorë, where it arrived in the first days of June, and that the freight ships had joined them bearing a thousand horses, numerous cannon, and a large supply of ammunition. A Venetian observation squadron of 60 vessels lay peacefully off Corfu and made no move to prevent the Ottoman fleet from crossing. For the sake of appearances— so scrupulous a chronicler as Marino Sanudo informs us—the Venetian

[15] For this Ottoman general and sometime grand vizier, see "Ahmed Pasha Gedik" (H. Inalcïk), *EI²* I, 292–293.

ships followed the Turkish armada a few miles, but then, when they heard of the landing in Apulia, returned quietly to Corfu.

The original plan was for a landing in Brindisi. Having heard, however, from a merchantman captured on his way from Otranto to Durrës that virtually no coastal defenses had been set up farther south. Gedik Ahmed Pasha decided to make his main landing near Otranto. First, on the morning of Friday, July 28, a squadron of cavalry was put ashore unobserved near the castle of Roca and poured through the countryside as far as Otranto, capturing many inhabitants and cattle. A sortie undertaken by a part of the Otranto garrison led to a violent skirmish with the Turks near the fishpond of Alimini, in the course of which many Turks were killed and many prisoners set free. Gedik Ahmed Pasha had sent an interpreter as a negotiator into the city, demanding as usual that it surrender without a fight. In this case the inhabitants were promised their choice of withdrawing unhindered or of remaining unmolested in the city. The offer was rejected, and the infuriated pasha threatened "fire, flame, ruin, annihilation, and death," which were not long in coming. The cannon brought ashore by the Ottomans went into action and showered the walls and the interior of the city with a hail of stone balls, some of them astonishingly large and effective. Many years later such projectiles were still seen lying about inside and outside the city. Thus, on the morning of Friday, August 11, Otranto, weakly defended, without artillery, and depending only on the courage of its citizens and small garrison, fell into the hands of the Ottomans. After hand to hand fighting at one of the outer walls had brought no results, the victors entered the defenseless city through a breach in the walls. The entire male population was killed, and of 22,000 inhabitants, only 10,000 survived. Francesco Burlo, defender of the citadel of Otranto, and his son were killed. The archbishop Stefano Pendinelli, a man of eighty who was just preparing to lead his entire clergy in a solemn procession to implore divine protection, met the same fate at the main altar of the cathedral. On Monday, August 14, 800 inhabitants of Otranto were chained by the pasha's order, dragged off to the nearby hill of Minerva (today Hill of the Martyrs), and put to death after they had refused to profess Islam. The corpses were left for the dogs, birds, and wild beasts. In the eighteenth century the victims were canonized as martyrs by Pope Clement XIV.

In possession of Otranto and its powerful citadel, the Turks laid waste the countryside for miles around. Everywhere the men of age to bear arms had taken flight and only women, children, and old men remained. Raids were made on Lecce and Brindisi to northward and Taranto in the west. All these measures seemed to indicate that the Turks planned to extend their conquests and establish themselves permanently. The sultan had reportedly promised to give the conquered territories in fief to Gedik Ahmed Pasha, who appears to have been responsibile for the timing of the invasion if not for the plan of attack. The invaders made alluring promises in an attempt to persuade the fugitive population to return. No one who submitted voluntarily, said one proclamation, would be molested in the practice of his faith, and all would enjoy freedom from taxes for ten years. Such promises, however, did not prevent the conquerors from immediately introducing a tax of one gold ducat for every family head and from ordering that all bells should be removed from the belfries for the casting of cannon. Some 8,000 persons were loaded on board ships and carried off to Albania as slaves.

The inhabitants of Otranto and vicinity did not respond to the Turks' blandishments. The situation of the occupying troops deteriorated from week to week as provisions failed to arrive and the rural population of the inhospitable region refused to help feed the infidels even for good money.

Meanwhile, in Naples, King Ferrante had somewhat recovered from the consternation into which the invasion of his kingdom had thrown him. He mustered a considerable army, which left Naples on September 8, 1480. His son Alfonso, duke of Calabria, had withdrawn from Tuscany with his troops, and at the end of the month he too set out for Otranto. Though the Neapolitan army was not able to take the offensive until winter, its presence in the immediate vicinity of Otranto prevented the Ottomans from moving westward. In October the Turks retired behind the walls of Otranto. Here they maintained an army of only 6,500 foot soldiers and 500 horsemen, commanded by Hayreddin (Mustafa) Bey, *sancak beyi* of Negropont, a crafty and intrepid Greek who knew Italian. All the remaining troops were precipitately shipped back to Vlorë and might well have come to grief on the way if adverse winds had not prevented King Ferrante's fleet from reaching the Apulian coast on time. But the commander of Otranto, whose arrogance had been increased by the arrival of reinforcements and provisions, refused to enter into negotiations of any kind with the king of Naples, who demanded the surrender of the city and payment of 800,000 gold ducats in compensation for the damage incurred by his kingdom. The Turkish commander not only refused to pay but demanded Brindisi, Lecce, and Taranto as well as Otranto as the price of peace, adding that if Ferrante should reject this proposition, the sultan in person would appear the following spring with an army of 100,000 troops and 18,000 cavalry, well equipped with artillery, and seize all Italy.

The reinforcement of the Turkish garrison and the fresh supply of provisions, reportedly sufficient for three years, may well have been the outcome of an interview between the sultan and Gedik Ahmed Pasha, who had been called to Istanbul to report on the situation. Arriving from Vlorë by the overland route, he had, we are told, found Mehmed gravely ill.

The news of the sultan's alleged threat spread like wildfire throughout Italy, and soon gave rise to the totally unfounded rumor that Mehmed was already in Vlorë with an army of 200,000 men, planning to land in Apulia and Sicily in November. In Rome, according to Sigismondo de' Conti, the humanist and historian, the consternation was no less than if the enemy had pitched his camp under the walls of the Eternal City. The terror and confusion were so general that even the pope was considering flight. The agitation of the king of Naples was perhaps even greater. He appealed at once to the pope and the Italian powers for support, going so far as to announce that if he did not receive active assistance immediately, he would accept all Mehmed's conditions to the detriment of everyone else. "Sixtus IV," wrote the same humanist, a loyal supporter of the pope, "would have viewed the downfall of his treacherous ally with equanimity if Ferrante had been confronted by any other enemy. But since the enemy of Christendom, the destroyer of the faith and its holy places, had set foot on Italian soil and, if not quickly expelled, might well destroy the papacy and the very name of Rome, Sixtus undertook with all zeal to help Ferrante. First, he sent as much money as he could spare, authorized the collection of tithes from the entire clergy of the kingdom of Naples, and promised all Christians who would fight the infidel under the banner of the Cross forgiveness of all their sins." How strained the relations between the pope and the king of Naples must have been for Sigismondo to express his indignation so openly![16]

Shortly before the Turkish landing in Apulia, the pope had addressed letters to all the Italian states—Florence, for example, received such missives on July 27 and August 5, 1480—and after the landing he sent out still more urgent appeals, calling the faithful to arms. In the face of the danger threatening Italy, an alliance was actually concluded on September 16, 1480, by which the Holy See, the king of Naples, the king of Hungary, the dukes of Milan and Ferrara, and the republics of Genoa and Florence committed themselves to the common defense. Venice too was exhorted to participate, but the Signoria immediately declined, declaring that it had fought the Turks for over fifteen years without so

[16] Pastor, *History of the Popes* IV, 333ff., gives additional details and references to the Western sources.

much as a single Christian state coming to its assistance, that it had made peace at considerable loss to itself, and could not now be expected to violate its treaty with the Turks. Early in November, the Italian states were summoned to send delegates to a council in Rome. Only Venice remained aloof, explicitly instructing its *oratore* Zaccaria Barbaro to stay away from any deliberation on the subject of a campaign against the Turks.

Sixtus IV set a good example by reconciling himself with Florence. From then on, according to a papal ordinance, All Saints' Day should be set aside throughout Christendom for prayers for divine aid. Steps were taken toward the building of a fleet: twenty-five galleys were commissioned, some in Genoa, others in Ancona. By way of replenishing the exhausted papal treasury, a tax of one gold ducat was imposed on every "hearth" in the entire Papal State. For two years a tithe was levied on all churches, monasteries, and convents. New indulgences were also granted all those who participated in the war effort. An indication of the exaggerated hopes aroused in certain quarters by these efforts is provided by the pamphlet *Glossa super apocalipsim* (Gloss to Revelation) by Giovanni Nanni, a Dominican monk from Viterbo, who in this strange little work of forty-eight folios, soon published in numerous editions, praised King Ferrante of Naples as the hero of the crusade and anticipated the conquest of Constantinople by the Christians. The year 1480 is rich in such pamphlets designed to revive the flagging spirits of the Western world; many were written by fortune-tellers and practitioners of the black arts, including Antonio Torquato, the Ferrarese physician and astrologer, and certain Dominican monks. The pope did not limit his efforts to Italy but attempted to unite all the princes of the West against the Crescent. While the reactions in England, where the autocratic Edward IV flatly refused to participate in a campaign against the Turks, or in Germany, where the fruits of imperial aid were meager in the extreme or were largely negative, Louis XI of France appeared to be willing to join the crusade. But the negotiations carried on in Vendôme at the end of August 1480 between the king of France and the papal legate Cardinal Giuliano della Rovere, the future pope Julius II, have no bearing on the present situation, and their final outcome is beyond the scope of this book.

In view of these far-reaching Western preparations for war, the Turkish hopes of using Otranto as a bridgehead for the conquest of all Italy proved more and more illusory. Ottoman resistance to the Neapolitan army and the Hungarian auxiliaries of 500 foot soldiers and 300 horsemen led by Blasius Magyar soon weakened and on September 10, 1481, collapsed altogether. But by this time Mehmed was dead, and the Western powers let well enough alone; the campaign against Vlorë, which Sixtus

IV and Ferrante had agreed upon, was never attempted. The Ottoman wave which had threatened to submerge the West now receded.

It will never be possible to establish with certainty whether Venice was directly to blame for the Turkish invasion of Italy. There can be no doubt, however, that Venice laid itself open to this grave suspicion. We definitely know that several Venetians took an active part in the Otranto venture on the Turkish side. Venetian ships transported the Turkish reserves from Durrës to Otranto, and Venetian ships towed the returning Turkish galleys, a service for which the captain general of the sea, who held the supreme command in those waters, was more than once severely reproached. It is also an uncontested fact that Niccolò Cocco, the Venetian *bailo*, saw fit to inflame the Porte against the political enemies of Venice, though this brought him a stern reprimand from the Signoria. Thus there is nothing surprising about the rumor that Venetian ships had brought supplies to the Ottomans in Otranto. The Venetians did not in so many words invite the Turks to invade Italy, but they did nothing to dispel the belief that such an invasion would be welcome to them. This was the official attitude of the Signoria. When in August 1479 an emissary from Gedik Ahmed Pasha informed the Signoria that the sultan was prepared to attack Naples or the pope if Venice so desired, he received an answer worthy of the oracle at Delphi. On August 23 he was told that the cause of the war which was devastating Italy had already been explained to the sultan, who was accordingly in a position to judge the situation: Mehmed could rest assured that Venice attached the greatest importance to full and sincere peace with him. Gedik Ahmed Pasha, it seems, took this reply as an invitation to attack the territory of Naples, but in a letter of May 15, 1480, to the sultan the Signoria emphatically denied any such intention. On the same day, however, Niccolò Cocco was informed that if the Signoria had not simply replied in the negative to the sultan's inquiry of the previous year, it was only because the Venetians, wishing on no account to be suspected of inconsistency, did not want to contradict earlier statements, and that Cocco should persuade the sultan to renounce his design or at least not to involve the possessions of the Venetian Republic in the campaign. For fear of antagonizing Mehmed the Venetians confined themselves to empty words and platitudes; the entire diplomacy of the republic in that period shows that it feared to provoke the anger of the Porte. When Federigo III, duke of Urbino, a *condottiere* as powerful as he was cultivated, asked the Signoria if he should take command, as he had been asked to do, of a Neapolitan army that was besieging Otranto, the Signoria, rather than give him a definite answer, told him to act according to his own lights. Even after the reconquest of Otranto, Venice was very cautious. On September 21, 1480, Domenico Contareno, the Venetian consul in Apulia, received orders to congratulate the king of Naples on his success in the name of the Serenissima, but was instructed to do so by word of mouth and to burn without delay the letter containing the order for fear that it come to the knowledge of the Turks.[16a]

Early in May 1480, even before a considerable part of the Ottoman fleet was immobilized on the Apulian coast and in Albania by the Italian undertaking, a scarcely less imposing squadron put out of the Dardanelles and appeared off Rhodes in the middle of the month. Once again, the supreme command was held by Mesih Pasha. The strength of the fleet was estimated at from 86 to 100 vessels. In the early summer of that eventful year the entire Turkish fleet must have left its home ports. The only naval power capable of interfering was Venice, from which at that time no opposition was to be feared.

The troops which had been wintering on the Anatolian coast were quickly taken on board, and on May 23, 1480, the siege of the city and fortress of Rhodes began; it was to continue for eighty-nine days. The various phases of this memorable episode are known to us in every detail from contemporary acccounts. Those which received the widest attention at the time and are still accepted as the principal sources were written by Guillaume Caoursin, chancellor of the Order, one appearing as a printed pamphlet (1480) and another in letter form, which was distributed throughout the West.[17] Three deserters, two Greeks and a Saxon from Meissen, played a sorry role in the attack on the island. The first, already mentioned, was Dimitrios Sophianos of Negropont, an eccentric who is reported to have busied himself with magic and other occult sciences; the second, his compatriot Antonios Meligalas of Rhodes, scion of a prominent family who had squandered his inheritance and now hoped to reestablish his position with the help of the sultan. The third was the German cannon founder known as Meister Georg, who had formerly lived on Rhodes but had then entered the sultan's pay and removed to Istanbul with his wife and child. He was a compatriot and homonym of the cannon founder Jörg of Nuremberg, whom Mehmed had just sent to Alexandria in Egypt with instructions to "take a look" at the country and find out how it might be conquered. The sultan hardly suspected

---

[16a] Further background to the Ottoman campaign in Italy is given by A. Bombaci, "Venezia e l'impresa turca di Otranto," *Rivista storica italiana* 66 (1954), 159–203.

[17] For an English translation of Caoursin's account see Brockman, 2.

that his agent, with the help of some Franciscan monks, would make his way directly to Rome, where he took up service with Pope Sixtus IV as a gunsmith.

All three repeatedly expressed the opinion to the sultan, and perhaps to his admiral Mesih Pasha as well, that the conquest of Rhodes could offer no particular difficulty, that the fortifications were in ruins and poorly defended, and that there was a grave shortage of food and ammunition. The German, Meister Georg, provided what was held to be the best map of the island fortress; it was used in drawing up the plan of attack, based as usual on the use of gigantic guns. Despite the violent opposition of the garrison, the fleet was able to land troops and artillery west of the city of Rhodes at the foot of Mount Santo Stefano (today called Mount Sidney Smith after the British admiral who owned a house there). The Turks entrenched themselves on the mountain slope, and two days later three enormous cannon were put into position outside the walls, near the Church of St. Anthony. The German was in charge of them. The two other traitors were already dead. Meligalas had died on shipboard of spotted fever, while Dimitrios Sophianos was killed in a skirmish outside the walls in the first days after landing. In the mask of a repentant deserter, the Saxon appeared outside the walls and asked admittance. It was granted, and he was brought before the grand master, to whom he confessed his apostasy and gave assurance of his sincere change of heart, without neglecting, however, to give a terrifying account of the Turkish war machine. The besiegers, he declared, had some sixteen enormous cannon, and their army numbered 100,000 men. Indeed, the effect of the great stone balls fired by the giant cannon from the land side against the outer bulwarks and especially against the main outwork of the fortress, the tower of St. Nicholas, was devastating; no fewer than three hundred of these terrible projectiles were hurled at the Christian bastion within six days. It trembled to its foundations, and the city would probably have been lost if some 1,000 workmen had not succeeded in blocking off the damaged tower with a trench and earthworks. Thus, the first Turkish assault was thrown back with a loss of some 700 men.

A second attempt cost them even more dearly. The tower of St. Nicholas stood at the head of a mole running about a quarter mile out into the sea and protecting the entrance to the harbor. The Turks lay on the opposite shore. The besiegers now built a pontoon bridge, which was intended to connect their side of the shore with the tower. In order to draw the bridge across the intervening stretch of water, they wedged an anchor in the rocks at the foot of the tower and fastened a strong cable to it. But an English sailor by the name of Gervas Roger—"wel experte in swymmynge," as John Kay's translation of Caoursin's account says—plunged into the sea at night and detached the cable from the anchor. When they began to pull the cable, the Turks discovered that they were foiled. Finally, they eased the bridge over to the tower with boats and on the night of June 19 launched their attack. But the bridge collapsed under the weight of the cannon and siege machines. All those who were on it vanished in the waves. Twenty-five hundred Turks were said to have lost their lives in a few hours.

After this defeat no new attempt was made to attack on this side. Mesih Pasha now directed the full power of his guns against the so-called Jewish quarter, where the city seemed most vulnerable. An enormous new catapult was put into position by the defenders and huge rocks, which the Rhodiots mockingly called "tribute," were flung down on the Ottomans. But the assailants too operated their cannon day and night and 3,500 stone balls were reported to have been fired against the walls and into the city. Efforts of all kinds were undertaken to repel the attackers. As a last resort, the defenders hauled sulfur, pitch, and other fuels, sacks full of gunpower and iron fragments, and stone rollers to the top of the crumbling walls of the fortress. In these desperate hours Pierre d'Aubusson summoned Meister Georg, who offered to operate a new catapult, but when the projectile hit the walls of the fortress instead of striking the enemy bulwark, he was suspected of treason. Put to the torture, he confessed, and whether innocent or guilty in this particular case, he was hanged. Another deserter, who declared under torture that he had been sent by Mesih Pasha to poison the grand master, was beheaded.

In these days a Greek emissary was sent into the fortress to make the usual offers in return for surrender. This was in keeping with Ottoman military law, which required that before a fortress was stormed the adversary be given an opportunity to profess Islam. But in the case of the Palaeologus Mesih Pasha, another consideration played a part. He calculated that if the Knights of St. John should lay down their arms, the rich spoils of the city would not fall into the hands of the army and that he would be able to claim them for the sultan and himself. When the emissary came back empty-handed, the admiral's rage knew no bounds, and he immediately gave the order for a new assault. The Turks had already provided themselves with sacks in which to collect booty and with ropes with which to bind young girls and boys, and also reportedly with 8,000 stakes on which to impale the enemy soldiers. All night the Turkish camp resounded with cries of "Allah ekber!" (Allah is supreme) and rejoicing over the imminent looting of the city. During the day the cannon had pounded the walls of the Jewish quarter, and there was no hope of repairing them quickly enough. On Friday, July 28, just as the Turkish fleet was casting anchor off Apulia, a mortar shot at dawn gave the signal for attack on the fortress. Irresistibly, the dense ranks of Turks made their way through the ruins of the walls. The entire Ottoman army of roughly 40,000 men swarmed over the trenches and beaches to surround the besieged city. Avid for spoils, the Janissaries pressed through the breaches. The first assault was successful. The Rhodiots were thrown back and the grand admiral's banner, with its fringes of gold and silver, was planted on the captured wall. The grand master and his men were grouped around the great banner of the Order with the picture of the Savior. Hand-to-hand combat had been in progress for two full hours when a disastrous order of Mesih Pasha suddenly reversed the situation. He had criers proclaim from the walls that looting was forbidden and that the treasure of Rhodes belonged to the sultan's exchequer. The consequence of this measure was immediate. Scorning to fight under these conditions, the assailants rushed back to their camp. More than 3,000 Turkish corpses covered the walls and filled the trenches. Many more were killed by the pursuing knights. Turkish losses were set at 9,000 dead and 15,000 wounded, while the Knights of St. John also paid a bitter price for victory and freedom. After this new failure Mesih Pasha did not have the heart to continue the siege of Rhodes, and gave the order to raise camp and to burn the siege installations. As he was about to ferry his troops to the Anatolian shore, two Neapolitan ships sent by King Ferrante to help the hard-pressed Rhodiots clashed with the Turkish squadron at the entrance to the harbor. The Turks tried to bar the passage of the Neapolitan galleys, but one of them, though damaged, fought its way through, while the other succeeded in doing so the following day.

The remnants of the Ottoman army were carried to the Bay of Marmaris, whence they were obliged to return home to Istanbul by the overland route. On the way, Mesih Pasha attacked Bodrum (the ancient Halicarnassus, in the hands of the Knights of St. John since 1402), vainly attempting to storm the powerful castle of San Pietro, which the knights had built with the stones of the famous Mausoleum. He then returned to the Golden Horn, where he was soon to feel the full weight of the sultan's fury over his failure to take Rhodes. Shorn of his rank, he was sent to Gelibolu as a simple *sancak beyi*. On the accession of Bayezid II, however, his fortunes revived and he was appointed governor of Rumelia (1493) and later, on his return from a pilgrimage to Mecca in 1499, was made grand vizier. What plans Mehmed the Conqueror may have forged in order to make up for the disgrace of his arms on Rhodes is not known. To replace Mesih Pasha, Manisa Çelebi was named vizier, an occurrence

worth mentioning because he had been army judge of Rumelia and Anatolia at the same time. Now, perhaps as a precautionary measure, the two
offices were separated. The new army judge of Rumelia was Mullah
Muslihuddin Mustafa, surnamed Kesteli (from Kestel, east of Bursa), a
celebrated theologian and jurist. It was at this time that Mullah Husrev,
the famous teacher of the law and also sheikh al-Islam, died, soon to be
followed by his master.

Before the year 1480 was out, Carniola, Carinthia, and Styria were once
again to feel the scourge of the Turkish raiders. While Emperor Frederick III and King Matthias Corvinus were waging war in the interior of
Austria and the population was suffering equal oppression from both
parties, 16,000 raiders rode with scarcely a halt through Croatia and almost
all of Carniola. On July 29, 1480, they laid waste the region of Cerknica
and Logatec southwest of Ljubljana, and on August 5 they crossed the
Sava and entered Carinthia. Fording the Drau near Möchling, they moved
north to Neumarkt, which had been occupied by 1,500 Hungarians. The
imperial and Hungarian troops made a truce in all haste, but the Turks
avoided contact and rode from Neumarkt (August 6) to the valley of
the Mur, pitching camp at Judenburg (August 7), where they divided
into three bands. One turned southward, devastating Carinthia; the second followed the Mur toward Leoben; and the third passed through the
Hohe Tauern and, by way of Rottenmann and Wald, probably rejoined
the second in Leoben. Thence the Turks continued down the Mur valley
to Bruck and Graz and disappeared by way of Radkersburg. Still another
band seems to have marched southward from Judenburg into Carinthia
(August 17), plundering the valley of the Drau and then crossing into
Carniola near Möchling, whence it returned through Croatia to Bosnia.

On this occasion 500 priests were included among the numerous prisoners. A Turkish deserter, who had lived a long while in the Ottoman
Empire as a Janissary, reliably reported that the invasion had begun
with an army of 50,000 men, 16,000 of whom had entered Carinthia while
the rest had been set aside for an invasion of Friuli. A full-scale invasion,
however, never materialized, and it seems reasonable to suppose that
34,000 men were held in readiness to be used in case of Venetian interference in the Turkish campaigns of 1480. In any event, it is reliably attested that a large body of Turks entered the Carso (Kras) plateau and
parts of Friuli at this time and advanced as far as the Canale valley, and
also that Iskender Bey, the Bosnian *sancak beyi*, plundered Dalmatia as
a warning to the Venetians that they had better respect their treaties. It
is possible that the 34,000 men may have been employed in these undertakings.

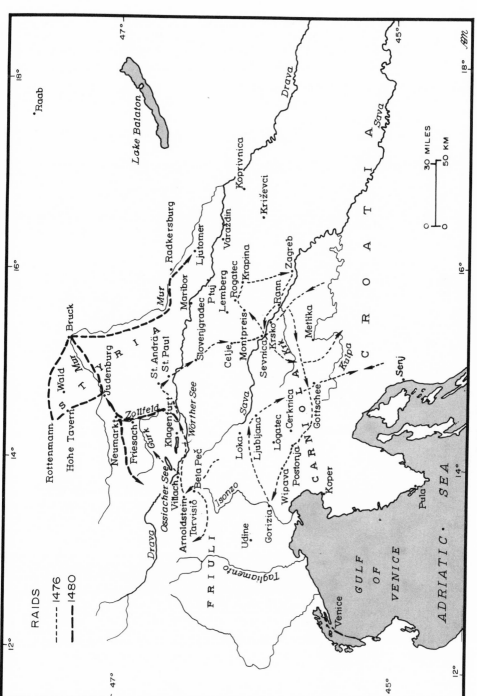

8. THE TURKISH RAIDS, 1476, 1480

The political acumen of the Ragusans was sorely tried at this time. The Ottomans continued to expand their fortifications on the southwestern frontier of Herzegovina and in doing so made no attempt at all to avoid inroads on Ragusan territory. In May 1479, after a year of uncertainty, Dubrovnik had received Mehmed's imperious demand that, apart from the city proper, the entire territory of the republic, including the islands along the coast, must submit to the military governor (*sancak beyi*) of Herzegovina, a native renegade by the name of Iyas Bey. Early in 1480, after this demand had been resolutely rejected, Yunus Bey, commander of the *sancak beyi*'s troops, invaded the Val Canale (Konavle valley) and returned laden with spoils. This fertile, densely populated valley, where the Ragusan nobility possessed flourishing estates, had long been a favored hunting ground of Ottoman raiders. By accepting a new increase of 2,500 ducats in their tribute—as the price of sparing the rural districts of Dubrovnik—the senate succeeded once again in averting doom.[18]

It is only much later that the Ottoman chronicles first mention, and then in very general terms, two further campaigns which must have been undertaken in the year 1480. Karamani Mehmed Pasha, the grand vizier at the time, notes in his far too concise chronicle that Mehmed had instructed his son Bayezid, then governor in Amasya, to move into Georgia with a small army and take two fortresses. Nothing can be said of their situation because of the badly garbled names (Torul, Turul?; Matsahilit, Mačahel?); more than likely, they were not in the distant Caucasus but on the border near Sivas. The lords of these castles had probably incurred the sultan's anger by siding with Uzun Hasan in his war with the Ottomans. What is far more interesting is the grand vizier's statement that a second army was sent to the land of the Circassians to punish the tribes of the Kuban and those around Anapa. In view of the enormous distance from Amasya to the steppes of the Kuban, we should be inclined to doubt that such an expedition ever took place were it not reported by the grand vizier himself.[19]

These actions fade into insignificance beside a campaign carried out in the course of 1480 at the sultan's behest. Its goal was southeastern Ana-

[18] On the basis of written receipts Biegman asserts that the increase in tribute to 12,500 ducats took place in 1478 and that the payment demanded reached a high of 15,000 two years later (*The Turco-Ragusan Relationship*, 49; this contradicts an earlier statement, however, ibid., 27). The rise to 15,000 ducats is not recognized by Carter or Krekić, who, however, date the 2,500-ducat increase to 1481.

[19] For the Ottoman vizier and his chronicle, see Franz Babinger, "Die Chronik des Qaramani Mehmed-Pascha, eine neuerschlossene osmanische Geschichtsquelle," *Mitteilungen zur osmanischen Geschichte* 2, 242–247; reprinted in *A&A* II, 1–5.

tolia, where, thanks only to its remoteness, the principality of Dulkadïr was still carrying on a shadow existence. It will be remembered that the rulers of Elbistan and Maraş were united with the house of Osman by multiple ties of kinship. In 1449 Mehmed had taken a princess from El-bistan as his wife. In 1467 her niece, Ayşe Hatun, had married Prince Bayezid. Mehmed's father-in-law, Süleyman Bey, a lover of women and fine horses, had passed away in 1454 after a peaceful reign of some twelve years and was succeeded by his four sons one after another. First, Arslan Bey ruled peacefully (1454–1465) until his brother Shah-budak had him murdered at his prayers in the mosque of Maraş. Shah-budak, who enjoyed the favor of Hoşkadem, the Mamluk sultan in Cairo, whither he had fled, was installed as prince by his Egyptian patron. The nobles of the country, however, rejected the fratricide, demanded his brother Shah-suvar as their ruler, and turned to his brother-in-law Mehmed, who supported their plea and dispatched a writ (dated December 4, 1465), formally investing Shah-suvar as lord of the tribes of Dulkadïr and Bozoklu. Expelled from the country, Shah-budak returned to his ally in Cairo. Skirmishes took place between Egyptian troops and those of the Dulkadïr. The Mamluk sultan finally sent a legation to the sultan in Istanbul, and there followed an exchange of diplomatic views which, however, did not turn out in favor of Shah-suvar. In 1470, abandoned by his followers, he fled to the fortified castle of Zamanti (Tsamando, today Aziziye), from where he was removed by the Egyptians and sent to Cairo. At the bidding of Sultan Qa'it Bay he was hanged from the Zuvele Gate. Mehmed would hardly have been perturbed over the execution of his brother-in-law if the Mamluk sultan, whose army had settled down in the territory of the Dulkadïr, had not once again established Shah-budak as prince. Mehmed now supported the fourth brother, Ala al-Dawla (Ayşe's father), and some time in 1480 sent an army to back up his demands. It is not known who commanded the troops sent against the Dulkadïr. Once again driven from his country, Shah-budak returned to Egypt and Ala al-Dawla now occupied the throne, thanks to his brother-in-law's intervention, a favor for which he showed the Ottomans little gratitude. He waged open warfare against his son-in-law Bayezid II, and his grandson Selim I, in the course of which he finally lost both his throne and his life (1515).

Insignificant from the standpoint of world affairs, these events would hardly be deserving of mention if they had not led to a serious conflict between Mehmed and the sultan in Cairo. The first indications of the Ottoman sultan's hostile attitude had appeared presumably some fifteen years earlier, when he offered to have the water conduits on the road to Mecca repaired at his own expense for the benefit of pilgrims.

It is possible that this apparently pious and disinterested offer concealed nothing more than a desire to establish a protectorate over the holy places of Mecca and Medina. Essentially, this would have meant that Mehmed, who now regarded himself as the supreme head of the Islamic world, was demanding a privilege which had been enjoyed by the Mamluk sultans for centuries and which, of course, they would not cheerfully renounce. In any event, whatever the reasons for this offer, it was rejected by Hoşkadem, who pointed out that the pride of the rulers of Syria and Egypt did not allow them to renounce the honor of maintaining these pious foundations. The incessant incidents on the borders of the empire in southern Anatolia were bound to lead to further conflicts and tensions which would someday inevitably culminate in war. This moment was now approaching.

Mehmed, however, was not well. He spent the winter quietly at his serai in Istanbul. Gentile Bellini stayed on for a few weeks after his completion in late November of the portrait now preserved in London [pl. XXIII].

At the approach of spring, the sultan seems to have improved sufficiently to begin his last campaign. His horsetail banners were hoisted on the Anatolian coast across from Istanbul. As everyone knew, this was the signal for a march into Asia. But no one, not even those closest to the sultan, knew the goal of the new expedition. The Rumelian army crossed the straits at about the same time as the supreme commander; the Anatolian army had received orders to assemble in mid-May on the broad plain near Konya. The size of the army suggested a large-scale undertaking, directed to all appearances southward against the territories of the Mamluk sultan. It was also feared, especially in the West, that Mehmed was planning to take the field in person against the Knights of St. John on Rhodes.

On April 25, a Wednesday, Mehmed crossed over to Üsküdar and the march began. A halt was made on Emperor's Meadow (Hunkâr Çayïrï) near Gebze, not far from the place where Hannibal was buried. Here, on May 1, the sultan was stricken with intense abdominal pains and the physicians were summoned. In addition to his old ailments, gout and rheumatism, new ones had set in. The first of the sultan's physicians to try his hand was the Persian Hamiduddin of Laristan, hence surnamed al-Lari. His role during the last days of the Conqueror's life was more than suspect. In fact, he had so little success in dispelling the widespread doubts concerning his trustworthiness that when he died four years later (February 22, 1485) in Edirne, where he had taken up residence and begun to build a mosque (completed in 1514), local legend attributed his death to an overdose of opium forced on him by Bayezid II. The version most favorable to al-Lari is that he merely gave the sultan an inappropriate medicine by mistake. Thus, it must be supposed either that the purpose of doing away with al-Lari was to eliminate an undesirable witness to a possible attempt to murder the sultan or that he was actually responsible for Mehmed's death.

When al-Lari failed, the sultan's old confidant, Maestro Iacopo, was called to the sultan's sickbed. He declared, however, that there was nothing he could do, because his predecessor had used an unsuitable medicine, the effects of which he could no longer combat. The pain became excruciating; the potion administered to the dying sultan seems to have blocked his intestines. At the time of the afternoon prayer, or about four o'clock, on Thursday, May 3, 1481, Mehmed the Conqueror, then aged 49, gave up the ghost. Mars governed the hour, as the Ottoman chroniclers expressly note.

We cannot be absolutely sure about the cause of Mehmed's death. The large number of his enemies and certain circumstances attending his death make it seem likely that he was poisoned. A week before the end, Mehmed had set out on a new campaign. In the previous year, and also on earlier occasions, when his old ailments made it difficult for him to move, he had entrusted important campaigns to his viziers. We need only recollect the attack on Rhodes or the landing in Italy, which had been led by two renegades. Thus, it must be assumed that the state of his health was satisfactory when he left his capital on April 25, especially in view of eyewitness reports that the fatal intestinal pains set in suddenly on the following Tuesday. These considerations favor the hypothesis that he was poisoned immediately after his departure and that no medicine could have saved his life. If he was poisoned, we do not know who was behind it. In view of the fact that a dozen previous attempts by the Venetians to murder the sultan had been lamentable failures, it seems relatively certain that the Venetians had nothing to do with it. The sultan's son Bayezid seems a far more plausible candidate. The relations between the freethinking father and the mystical, bigoted son had never been cordial. Indeed, many believed the sultan was now heading for Amasya, where Bayezid was governor. The sultan's conflict with his son seems to have become more and more violent and to have reached new heights at this very time. In the first half of April 1481, Prince Bayezid in Amasya had received letters from Istanbul informing him that the grand vizier Karamani Mehmed Pasha had in all seriousness and with apparent success persuaded his master to do away with the legitimate heir to the throne and to appoint Prince Cem as future sultan in his place. It would therefore not be surprising if Bayezid, with the help of the Halveti dervishes, had plotted at least against the life of the grand vizier, and his designs may just as well have been directed against his father. This view is supported by the pointed words of Muhyiddin Mehmed, nephew of the great astrologer Ali Kuşci and sheikh of the Halveti, who died in the odor of sanctity in 1514 in Iskilip (northeastern Anatolia). Shortly before the Conqueror's death, he went on a pilgrimage to Mecca; in Amasya he took his leave of Bayezid (who later as sultan accorded him very special favor) with the significant words that by the time he returned, the prince would have become sovereign in his own right. The mysterious remark was later interpreted, according to the custom of the dervishes, as proof of the sheikh's gift of divination and hence sanctity. As for Bayezid, he more than once expressed the opinion formulated in the Arabic saying "There are no ties of kinship between princes" (*La arhama baina 'l-muluk*). Thirty-one years later he himself was to fall a victim to the same harsh code: he died on May 26, 1512, on a trip to his native Dimotika, of a poison administered to him by a Jewish physician at the behest of his son and successor, Selim. In any event, it is safe to say that while Mehmed the Conqueror may have been suffering from the gout, he was not fatally ill when he set out on a campaign which, to judge by the scope of the preparations that had been made, must have been a large-scale undertaking.[20]

No one in the camp apart from the dead sultan's immediate entourage learned of his death. The grand vizier Mehmed Pasha and those close to him spread the rumor that the Conqueror, overcome by a violent attack of gout, had been obliged to return to Istanbul. The corpse was immediately carried in a litter to Üsküdar, whence it was ferried across to the capital.[21] The army received orders not to leave the Anatolian shore. No ship was permitted to cross the Bosporus to Istanbul. The grand vizier, who, in agreement with his former master, wished at all costs to prevent Prince Bayezid from mounting the throne, sent three riders in all haste to Prince Cem in Konya, whom he called upon to claim the throne as quickly as possible. Meanwhile, however, news of the sultan's death had

---

[20] On the sultan's death see the article by Babinger cited above, book 2, n. 15. A Turkish translation, with additional material, was published by Feridun N. Uzluk, *Fatih Sultan Mehmed zehirlendi mi eceli mi öldü?* (Ankara, 1965). Strongly critical of Babinger's verdict of poisoning in the death of the sultan is M. C. Şehabeddin Tekindağ, "Fatih'in ölümü meselesi," *Tarih Dergisi* 16 (1966), 95–108. Cf. also the remarks of Kissling concerning the involvement of the Halveti dervishes (see above, book 4, n. 37). And cf. Tahsin Yazici, "Fetih'ten sonra Istanbul'da ilk halveti şeyhleri: Çelebi Muhammed Cemaleddin, Sünbül Sinan ve Merkez Efendi," *IED* 2 (1956), 87–113.

[21] For a document regarding the treatment of the dead sultan's body, see I. H. Uzunçarşili, "Fatih Sultan Mehmed'in Ölümü," *Belleten* 34 (1970), 231–234.

spread, causing intense agitation. The military, especially the Janissaries, were in turmoil and assumed a threatening attitude. They ran to the shore, seized fishing boats, and crossed to the European side. With wild cries they demanded to see their master. When he failed to show himself, they forced the gate of the serai and caught sight of the sultan's lifeless body. Their fury turned at once against the grand vizier, whom they murdered on the spot, probably along with Maestro Iacopo. They carried the head of Karamani Mehmed Pasha through the streets spitted on a lance. The aroused populace attacked dwellings and shops, especially those belonging to Jews and Christians. The well-filled storehouses of the Venetian and Florentine merchants were plundered.

The three horsemen sent to Cem Sultan had no luck. All three were arrested. Bayezid had two sons-in-law in the army. The first was the agha of the Janissaries; the other was governor of Anatolia. In all likelihood, it was largely thanks to them that their father-in-law was kept abreast of events and induced to leave for Istanbul without delay. After the gruesome death of the grand vizier and the failure of his attempt to summon Cem Sultan, it was only too easy a matter to win the support of the populace for the eldest son of the deceased sultan. Sinan, the Janissary agha, promised to double the pay of his mutinous troops once Prince Bayezid should be seated on the throne. Thereupon, according to eyewitness reports, all cried out, "Long live Bayezid!" Meanwhile, Ishak Pasha, the former—and future—grand vizier, had seized power and allied himself with Sinan Ağa. With Sinan's agreement, he proclaimed Prince Bayezid sultan and appointed the latter's young son, Prince Korkut, who happened to be in Istanbul, regent until his father should arrive. The boy was led through the streets in triumph amid the cheers of the people.[22]

With a bodyguard of 4,000 horsemen, Bayezid reached Üsküdar on May 20. There he was welcomed by the exultant Janissaries, who even on that occasion did not forget to demand an increase in pay. In black garments, with a black head cloth (*šaš*), the new sultan made his entry into the capital. There he solemnly buried his father. The funeral ceremonies were directed by Sheikh Mustafa, better known as (Ibn) Vefa, a dubious figure, who at first was one of the resolute partisans of the grand vizier Karamani Mehmed Pasha, but after his death lost no time in going over to the new sultan. Sheikh Vefa, who belonged to the Zeyniye order of

[22] The attempts by Cem to gain control of at least part of the empire, which lasted several years into the reign of his brother, are discussed by Sidney N. Fisher, "Civil Strife in the Ottoman Empire 1481–1503," *Journal of Modern History* 13 (1941), 448–466. See also the same author's *The Foreign Relations of Turkey 1481–1512* (*Illinois Studies in the Social Sciences* XXX, no. 1; Urbana, 1948).

dervishes, had amassed great wealth, though all his life he termed himself a friend of the poor and needy, and had erected in Istanbul a mosque including a *medrese*, in front of which he was buried in 1491.

Clad in mourning, Bayezid II took turns with the dignitaries in helping to carry the coffin to the mosque which the Conqueror had built. It seems probable that Mehmed's remains were not removed to a special *türbe* until later. Bayezid then took possession of the throne for thirty-one years.

We possess an interesting, though not entirely credible, account of the exciting events which took place after Mehmed's sudden death. It is a Middle French manuscript of some twenty-four pages which, once in the possession of two English princesses, Elizabeth and Cecily, the daughters of Edward IV (1461–1483), ultimately found its way, after numerous changes of hands, to the Princeton University Library. Entitled *Testament de Amyra Sulthan Nichhemedy Empereur des Turcs*, it is in reality a French translation of an Italian letter, dealing with events in the Ottoman capital before and after the succession of Bayezid, written on September 12, 1481, and addressed to one Giovanni (Jehan), a friend of the author. We have no way of knowing whether this is the "testament" briefly mentioned by Philippe de Commynes in his *Mémoires*. It starts out with the alleged and none too plausible testamentary dispositions of Mehmed II concerning his succession, his burial, his slaves, and his subjects. The description of the funeral by night, which 20,000 persons are said to have attended, arouses the impression that the author, especially in the matter of numbers, gave free rein to his imagination. According to him, no fewer than 2,000 dervishes took part in the funeral ceremony, which went on until dawn.[23]

It was two to three weeks before news of the sudden death of the mortal enemy of Christianity reached the West. By the end of May a rumor had sprung up in Rome that Mehmed was no longer among the living. At about the same time the Venetian Signoria had received reliable information from Istanbul, from its ambassador, Niccolò Cocco, and the *bailo* Battista Gritti, and forwarded it to the Vatican. Cannon were fired and bells rung to announce the glad tidings to the inhabitants of the Eternal City. By way of thanking God for His providence, Sixtus led a solemn procession to the Church of Santa Maria del Popolo; the college of cardinals and all the ambassadors, this time not excluding the *magnifico*

---

[23] The document is given in facsimile, printed text, modern French and Turkish translations by A. Süheyl Ünver, *Fatih Sultan Mehmed'in ölümü ve hadiseleri üzerine bir vesika* (Istanbul, 1952). Commynes wrote that Mehmed had "made a will and I have seen it" (*Memoirs*, 417).

messer Zaccaria Barbaro of Venice, were also present. As night fell, fireworks were set off on all sides, and on June 3 magnificent processions of thanksgiving were held, in which the pope personally participated. The Italian chroniclers report similar celebrations in all Italy. The rejoicing knew no bounds. Matthias Corvinus was more cautious in appraising the consequences of the sultan's death. In a long letter to Sixtus IV he tried to prove that Mehmed had conceived a definite plan of invading Hungary toward St. John's Day (June 24), 1481, to take terrible revenge for his recent defeat at the hands of the Hungarians. His thesis was not borne out by subsequent events, but this did not deter the king of Hungary from his efforts to acquaint Christendom with the costly key position of his kingdom.

"Fù fortuna della Cristianità e dell' Italia, che la morte domasse il feroce ed indomabile Barbaro," wrote Giovanni Sagredo, the knight and procurator of St. Mark in Venice, more than two hundred years later. "It was fortunate for Christendom and for Italy that death checked the fierce and indomitable barbarian." This was undoubtedly the first feeling that took hold of the West. *La grande aquila è morta!* (The great eagle is dead) was the cry of rejoicing with which, on May 19, 1481, an emissary tried to startle the Signoria. No thought was given to the future, and nothing is more characteristic of the mood prevailing in Europe than the fact that the crusading zeal which had barely been awakened died down almost everywhere. Pointing out that the "Turkish tyrant" was now dead and that there was consequently no further need to pay out the promised financial aid, the Bolognese promptly threw off their obligation. From that time on, it is true, Italy was spared the threats and intimidations of the Turks. There was no serious danger from the Conqueror's son Bayezid, who was cautious and distrustful in all his undertakings. His son Selim I directed his arms against Persia, Syria, and Egypt, and it was not until the reign of Selim's son, Süleyman the Magnificent, that the Ottomans again cast covetous eyes on the West. Hungary fell into his hands and was occupied by the Ottomans for over 150 years (1541-1699). His army appeared before the walls of Vienna (1529) and threatened the heart of Europe. These conquests seeped away in the course of time, and only those territories and islands of southeastern Europe which Mehmed II had incorporated into his empire were retained until the nineteenth century. Only his Asiatic conquests have endured to this day.[24]

---

[24] For a Latin composition on Mehmed's death, see Babinger's "Eine Lateinische Totenklage auf Mehmed II.," in *Studi Orientalistici in onore di Giorgio Levi della Vida* I (Rome, 1956), 15-31; reprinted in *A&A* II, 151-161.

Book Seven

THE PERSONALITY AND EMPIRE OF
MEHMED THE CONQUEROR.

I. THE RULER AND THE MAN

However we may judge the part played by Mehmed the Conqueror in
the history of his own people and that of the Western world, it cannot
be denied that he was one of the most outstanding figures produced by
the Middle Ages. Our estimate of his personality as a ruler and also as a
man changes radically according to whether we consult Western sources
or confine ourselves to the accounts of the Ottoman historians. In Western
eyes, as can be gathered from numerous contemporary and even later
accounts, he was all his life the destroyer, the monarch who shed blood
on a monstrous scale, the archenemy of Christianity, the Antichrist.
When at the news of his decease the Christian West sighed with relief
and the rejoicing at the death of this most resolute of all enemies seemed
to take no end, Guillaume Caoursin, the shrewd and farsighted vice-
chancellor of the Order of St. John, informed a gathering of the Knights
of Rhodes that Mehmed was not in his grave and that the mighty earthquake which had occurred at the time of his death had been brought
about by the descent of his entrails from chasm to chasm to the very center
of hell. He went on to list all the horrors and crimes that the sultan had
perpetrated against mankind. Among the Turks, on the other hand, the
Conqueror is to this day represented as the greatest among all the sultans,
a figure unparalleled in the history of the world. And the further removed
the writers on Mehmed II are from him in time, the more glowing become
the colors in which he is set before the eyes of his compatriots. In our day,
when normally the events and figures of the distant past should pale
before the achievements of the present or recent past, Mehmed the Conqueror is presented to the Turkish people in numerous publications as
the most brilliant and blameless figure in its whole history—a phenomenon which can be explained only by virulent nationalism. Though
psychological interpretations may be adduced for this flight into past

409

history, a thoughtful observer of historical events cannot content himself with such explanations.

What makes an unbiased appraisal of Mehmed II so exceedingly difficult is the absence of reliable documentation concerning his personality. For the fifteenth century we are entirely lacking in the type of reportage which the Venetian *relazioni* provide for the sixteenth century and later periods. The succinct descriptions which such men as Giàcomo de' Languschi or Niccolò Sagundino composed on their trips to the Porte during the early years of the Conqueror's reign throw a certain light on him at least as ruler. They show that his plans for playing an active part in world history were already patent at that time. In his unconfined ambition to emulate and indeed to outdo Alexander the Great and Julius Caesar, he aspired to create an empire, a stable world power, and to govern it from his newly founded capital of Istanbul, which would be its center. His drive to rule, to reduce the whole world to his power, knew no bounds. Alexander of Macedonia, so he said, had marched into Asia with a smaller army; now the times had changed, for he was marching from East to West, whereas formerly the Occidentals had campaigned in the East. The universal empire, he said, could be only one, one faith and one rule. To achieve this unity, no place was better fitted than Constantinople; with this city in his power, it would be possible to subject the Christians. He was bound, so he proclaimed, by no law; God alone was great. The Venetian informant, whose account must refer to the period immediately after the capture of Constantinople, does not forget to add that Mehmed had derived this view from his father.

In this connection it will be well to clarify as far as possible Mehmed's attitude toward the Islamic faith: a difficult undertaking. His special predilection for everything that was Persian and hence heretical—"Every man who reads Persian," says an old Ottoman proverb, "loses half the religion"—the obvious leaning toward heterodox Shiite doctrines and freethinkers which he began to display even as a boy, his frequent association with heretics such as his librarian Mullah Lutfi show that at least during certain periods in his life he inclined toward religious opinions that were directly at variance with strict Sunnite theology. At times the sultan endeavored to inform himself of the principles of Christianity. As manuscripts found in his library bear witness, he caused his humanistic advisers, and especially the patriarch Gennadius, to instruct him in the history and doctrine of Christianity, and more than once strange reports reached the West to the effect that the sultan had been converted to Catholicism. It was even maintained that his Christian mother had taught him the Pater Noster and other popular prayers, but that he had forgotten them in later life and turned away from Christianity. Such tales cannot be taken seriously. More important perhaps is the "profession of faith" of Gennadius. This document has been preserved in its original Greek text and in a Turkish translation by a certain Ahmed Bey, judge in Karaferia (Thessaly). More than likely this credo was prepared at the Conqueror's bidding. But it would be a mistake to infer that Mehmed ever contemplated conversion. The conquest of the Byzantine capital and the Ottoman occupation of vast territories inhabited by Christians made it necessary for the sultan to inform himself about the religion of his new subjects, for it was evident that the administration and defense of the Ottoman state could no longer be entrusted exclusively to the Ottoman upper classes and a sprinkling of converts, but would have to be shared by all those in the newly conquered regions who by abjuring their Christian faith showed their readiness to be integrated in the sultan's political machine.

We know that in his private associations Mehmed had considerable sympathy for heretical ideas. But it is equally certain that as chief of state he strictly and undeviatingly enforced the Sunnite brand of Islam, which he himself publicly observed. In addition, his religious moods may in the course of the years have assumed different colorations, and it is assuredly something more than court gossip when Gian-Maria Angiolello, who spent years at the sultan's court, quotes Bayezid II as saying that "his father was domineering and did not believe in the Prophet Mohammed." Indeed, Angiolello continues, it was so, and for that reason all say that this Mehmed professed no religion of any kind. Even if we may be permitted to attribute the son's severe judgment of his father in part to Bayezid's narrow bigotry, which branded any deviation from the rigid forms of Islam as heresy, it certainly contained a good deal of truth. On the other hand, Theodoros Spandugino, who it must be admitted is not always a reliable observer, claims that shortly before his end, Mehmed became a great worshiper of Christian relics and always kept many candles burning in front of them.

It is certain that he was in the habit of accumulating in his palace relics taken from the treasures of the Byzantine churches, which he used for purposes of bargaining with Christians. When the Venetians offered him 30,000 ducats for the stone on which Jesus was supposed to have been born, he refused this sum with scorn, saying that he would not sell such a relic even for 100,000 ducats. His son Bayezid II fell heir to these treasures, of which we still have a partial catalogue, and tried to make use of them, offering them to Charles VIII of France in return for the extradition of his half brother Cem Sultan. During the lifetime of his father, and particularly during his (Bayezid's) own reign, many of the relics amassed in the serai found their way to the West as a currency of exchange.

There can be no doubt about Mehmed's religious tolerance. If even a part of what Isaac Sarfati wrote from Turkey in his circular letter of 1454 to the Jews of Central Europe about the favorable situation of his coreligionaries under the Crescent was true, Mehmed's empire must have been a paradise for non-Moslem subjects (*reaya*), especially Jews. Turkey, Sarfati wrote, was a country where nothing was lacking. Every man could spend his life unmolested under his fig tree and his vine.[1] In judging this letter with its invitation to emigrate to the Ottoman Empire, we must not, of course, forget that the situation of the Jews in Central Europe in the middle of the fifteenth century was particularly wretched, that they were subject to incessant persecution, and that measured by these conditions, Turkey, where no one was molested for his faith, could promise a truly blissful life. It must also be borne in mind that in his commercial undertakings and his fiscal policy, Mehmed preferred to rely on the help of Jews, including his physician Maestro Iacopo, whom he sometimes, to the dissatisfaction of the Moslems, employed as his financial adviser. But also in Christian quarters, as it is more than once confirmed, each man could "seek salvation in his own way," complete religious freedom prevailed, and no one incurred serious difficulties because of his faith. There can be no doubt that the Christian inhabitants of places far from the seat of government were often oppressed and unjustly treated, but it is equally certain that this was not the work of the supreme authorities. The truly magnanimous treatment of non-Moslems in the Ottoman Empire under Mehmed can in large measure be attributed to his indulgence and mildness in religious matters, qualities which were in all likelihood closely related to his own liberal ideas on religion.

In one respect, however, Mehmed was intolerant, though evidently less for religious than for political reasons. One is struck by the frank hostility he developed toward the orders of the dervishes, which earlier in the fifteenth century had spread triumphantly through the Ottoman territories and were well established in Rumelia and even as far as Albania, enjoying great consideration among the people and undoubtedly exerting a certain political influence. They owed their high popular prestige, so feared by the sultan, to their extreme unorthodoxy, which brought them closer to the Anatolian masses still very much under the influence of Shiism. The

---

[1] For an abridged translation of Sarfati's letter see Franz Kobler (ed.), *A Treasury of Jewish Letters* I (London, 1952), 283–285.

less fortunate among the sultan's subjects were impressed both by their rule of poverty and by their pastoral talents, which had a place neither in the teachings nor the practice of Orthodox Islam and its clergy. The Orthodox religious leaders were often spiritually arid. Remote from the common people, they had no consolation to offer but irrelevant dogmas and legalistic quibbles (*hiyal*). The dervishes were glad to replace them as the intermediaries between this world and the next. The mystical character of their rites and customs, often reflecting vestiges of older beliefs, held a strong appeal for the common people, whom the rationalism of Orthodox Islam simply failed to satisfy. The cult of saints, which had always been frowned on by Orthodox Islam and often bitterly combated, was particularly favored by certain orders of dervishes. It offered the little man far more than the complex, and to the layman largely unintelligible, edifice of the religious law. Finally, we must not forget the charitable work done by the dervishes in their monasteries. The substantially pantheistic character of the dervishes' beliefs enabled them to take a more liberal attitude toward non-Moslems and won them a certain affection even among the Christian subject population, so much so that Christians and Moslems occasionally joined in the cults of identical saints.[2]

It is well known that Mehmed's father showed the order of the Mevlevi in Konya great sympathy, that he built them a magnificent monastery beside his mosque in Edirne, and presumably was himself a member of the order. Whether Murad II used this order as a counterweight to the Bektaşi dervishes, who had close ties with the Janissaries, is not certain, nor can the special attachment of Bayezid II to the extremely powerful order of the Halveti be easily explained, though an alliance for common political goals is not inconceivable.

Early in life Mehmed seems to have had a less hostile attitude toward the dervishes and their sheikhs. In his youth he sought the company of Persian heretics and lodged them in his palace, and some events before and during the conquest of Constantinople are brought into relation with sheikhs, whom, we are told, he received with particular honor. We have mentioned the case of Ak Şemseddin, the discoverer of the tomb of Abu Ayyub. It is hard to dispel the impression that later enthusiasts, wishing

---

[2] H. J. Kissling gives a brief overview of the place of the orders in his "The Sociological and Educational Role of the Dervish Orders in the Ottoman Empire," in *Studies in Islamic Cultural History*, ed. G. E. von Grunebaum (= *The American Anthropologist* 56, no. 2, part 2 [April, 1954], memoir no. 76), 23–35. See also Gibb and Bowen, *Islamic Society and the West* I, part 2, 179–206. The transference of shrines from Christian to Moslem environment is documented by F. W. Hasluck, *Christianity and Islam under the Sultans*, especially I, 3–118.

to stress the sheikh's role in the capture of Byzantium, enriched the biography of the spiritual heir to the famous Sufi sheikh Suhrawardi (d. 1234 in Baghdad) with certain legendary elements. Strangely enough, he is represented as having opposed Mehmed's autocratic behavior and kept his distance in an attempt to teach the young sovereign to overcome his pride. The story goes that at last he did go to see the sultan in his tent before the walls of Constantinople and pressed him so close in the darkness that Mehmed "trembled and almost fell"; he did not release the sultan but held him in his arms until the nervous tremors subsided. The consequence of this strange encounter was supposedly that the sultan's previous dislike of the world-removed mystic changed to deep affection.

In later life, however, Mehmed viewed the popular influence of these mendicant monks with suspicion bordering on fear. He was dismayed to see them flooding the land and settling everywhere, and he did his best to restrict or repress their activity. Occasionally, we find it mentioned in the sources that he confiscated property of the orders. Toward the end of Mehmed's reign, the sheikh and chronicler Aşıkpaşazade complained and protested to the grand vizier about this repression, though without results. The more popular a sheikh was, the more resolutely the sultan avoided any contact with him; because of their fanaticism, their crack-brained behavior, and the flaunted poverty of their attire, he declared the sheikhs to be mad and often banished them from his empire.

Biographical sketches of some of these men confirm such observations. Almost without exception, they deal with members of the Halveti order, whom the sultan looked upon with special distrust, either because of their close ties with his son Bayezid in Amasya or because of their popularity and their meddling in political affairs. During Mehmed's reign this brotherhood had not yet built up a rigid organization with monasteries throughout the empire, but had achieved influence only in eastern Anatolia and the eastern frontier territories. It was only under Bayezid, and to a greater degree later still in the sixteenth century, that the Halveti dervishes were able to consolidate their extraordinary influence. But precisely because of their concentration in Asia Minor at that time and because of their connections with the East, particularly Baku and Tabriz, Uzun Hasan's capital, they may at least for a time have aroused the sultan's fears.

In Bursa, for example, a certain Halveti sheikh named Alaeddin was known for his ecstatic states, which he had the power of communicating to those he touched or even looked at. One day he went to the capital. Apparently, this gift of his was thought to have curative virtues, for large numbers of people, including dignitaries and members of society, came to consult him. Irritated by the sheikh's sudden popularity, the Conqueror ordered him to leave the country. He emigrated to Karaman and finally died in Laranda, where his tomb could be seen for many years. His younger brother was Sheikh Ömer of Aydïn Eli, surnamed Ruşeni. The sources seem to confuse his career with that of his fellow townsman, the musician Mullah Şemseddin, but it is definitely established that Ruşeni also turned his back on the Ottoman Empire, going first to Şirvan and then to the court of Uzun Hasan, where he was well received. He is thought to have died in Persia in 1487. Ruşeni was also a Halveti and as such, if for no other reason, suspect to the sultan.

To the same order belonged another sheikh, Alaeddin, surnamed al-Arabi (i.e. "the Arab"), who had gone to Anatolia from the region of Aleppo and settled in Bursa, where he entered into contact with his homonym, whose disciple he became. His asceticism and psychic powers won him a large following, and people thronged to him for advice. When stories about him reached the court, Mehmed banished him too, apparently at the same time as the other sheikh Alaeddin. He first went to Manisa, where the prince Mustafa Çelebi was then governor and won the confidence of the young prince, who persuaded his father to grant the sheikh a teaching position at a *medrese* there.[3]

When a dervish was reputed to possess special powers of blessing (*baraka*), the sultan for all his free thinking sometimes tried to benefit by them. On his campaign against Uzun Hasan, he met such a dervish in Bursa, Mullah Muhyiddin Mehmed ibn Hïzïrşah, a teacher at the Sultaniye *medrese*. The mullah went about in a threadbare woolen cloak and showed the utmost simplicity in his bearing. The common people believed him to be one of those whose prayers are heard. As the sultan rode past, the mullah greeted him and went his way. Mehmed, who knew of his reputation, called after him, asking if he were not the dervish Mehmed. The grand vizier Mahmud Pasha, who was riding beside the sultan, replied in the affirmative, whereupon the sultan ordered him to ride after the mullah and bid him pray for his sovereign. His supposed sanctity, which manifested itself in all manner of odd behavior, did not save the sheikh from death when one day he fell off the roof of a house.

When Ibrahim, son of the executed grand vizier Halil Pasha and grand vizier under Bayezid II, incurred the wrath of Mehmed himself, he joined the dervishes, probably out of conviction, and went through the streets in a hair garment. On the strength of his strange costume, one of his enemies denounced him to the sultan as a dangerous madman. One

[3] For the influence of the Halveti order during Mehmed's lifetime, see the articles cited above in book 6, n. 20.

day after his return to Istanbul from Bursa, where he had consorted with the wonder-working sheikh Haci Halife, Ibrahim met the Conqueror, who was going through the streets on foot, accompanied by four servants. Ibrahim dismounted and stood respectfully to one side. The sultan saw him and inquired if he were not Ibrahim, son of Halil Pasha; the answer was yes. The Conqueror congratulated him that Allah had relieved his madness and bade him appear before the *divan* the next day. Here he was asked at the sultan's bidding what position he desired. When he replied that he would like to be judge in Amasya—where Prince Bayezid was residing as governor—he was asked to repeat his request, which the viziers then carried to the sultan, who was no little astonished. "Now I know for sure that he will leave us no peace with his madness. If he had asked for one of the highest posts in the state, I should have granted it." This story shows how little understanding Mehmed, at least in his later years, had for the dervishes and their conduct. Ibrahim actually did go to Bayezid in Amasya and had later no cause to regret his move. For directly upon his accession, Bayezid II appointed him grand vizier. At that time more than 600 dervishes were fed from Ibrahim Pasha's kitchen.

Mehmed regarded himself with good reason as heir to the Byzantine emperors, for from the ruins of the Byzantine state he had succeeded in forging a unified empire, subservient to his will and extending from Mesopotamia to the Adriatic. For a period of several centuries the old Byzantine states were once again welded into a political unit, thanks to him and a few of his successors. The old dictum of the Byzantines, stated as early as the eleventh century in the *Strategikon* of Kekaumenos, that he who holds Byzantium holds the empire, lost none of its validity under the Ottomans. In possession of Constantinople, the Ottoman state fell heir to the policies of the East Roman Empire and hence to its claims to domination of the Mediterranean basin. We pointed out earlier that under Mehmed the borders of the Ottoman Empire coincided strikingly with those of the Byzantine Empire at its height, just as the decline of both empires was marked by a similar crumbling away of border territories. Before the Ottoman Empire took possession of the Arab world in the sixteenth century, the Balkan peninsula and Anatolia, on either side of the straits, formed its two wings. Since the Ottomans made no attempt at denationalization in the states they conquered, the populations, notably in southeastern Europe, were able to preserve their language and national sentiment throughout nearly 500 years of Turkish rule, even where, as in Albania and Bosnia, large numbers were converted to Islam. Undoubtedly this policy, already in practice under Mehmed II, provided the seeds of the decline and ultimate collapse of Turkish power in the peninsula. Here we find a strange recapitulation of the history of the Byzantine Empire, where under the influence of Christianity all Asia Minor had been at least superficially Hellenized, while in the Balkan peninsula this process had been limited to those peoples who were closely related to the Greeks, that is, the Macedonians and Thracians. Whereas in Greece itself, the immigrant Slavic population had been absorbed by the Greeks, Byzantine rule had virtually no effect on the Slavic heartlands of Bulgaria, Macedonia, and Serbia. Here again Mehmed showed himself to be the heir of the Byzantines.

The Western world was well aware of the Conqueror's claims and of the extent of his power. Pius II's strange letter to the sultan, bidding him have himself chosen "legitimate emperor of the Greeks and the Orient by means of a little water [*aquae pauxillum*]," implies the admission that Mehmed had already acquired this sovereignty without the consent and cooperation of the pope. And perhaps this Western insight is expressed even more clearly in the message from the Signoria. Brought to the sultan in 1480 by Battista Gritti (according to Andrea Navagero), the message recognized Mehmed's right to the ancient Greek colonies in Italy.

It can easily be imagined that to guide the destinies of so great an empire, acquired within a few decades, the memories and customs of the old nomadic days, which were in part preserved in the official protocol down to the fifteenth century, would no longer suffice and that consequently many civil and political institutions had to be borrowed from the Byzantine heritage. The customary law (*adet*), which had attained an elaborate development in the court and bureaucracy of the Palaeologi, lived on in the Ottoman Empire after the conquest, producing fruits of various kinds. We shall speak of it again in another context.

Just as after the conquest of Constantinople the sultan's court gradually adopted the forms of the old Byzantine court, so too the character of Mehmed's rule underwent a distinct change. The almost chivalric old customs, practiced for many years, vanished. The unostentatious court ceremonial which had prevailed under Murad II and which filled Western observers with admiration, seems to have lingered on for a while before it was abandoned by his son.

Murad II had signed his decrees simply with the title *beg*, a word employed in the oldest monuments of the Turkish language—the inscriptions of the eighth century A.D.—to designate any noble in distinction to the mass of the people (*budun*). His son, besides using "sultan," adopted the use of "great lord" (*megas afthentis*; *efendi* later developed from *afthentis*), and "great prince" (*megas amiras*). At first Mehmed also

retained *beg* (modern *bey*), but he dropped it, at least in Greek documents, after the conquest of Constantinople. This old-fashioned title, no
longer considered adequate to the heir of the East Roman Empire, was
from then on confined to the nobles of his empire.

The old, simple ways that were soon to disappear are strikingly illustrated by the *Tractatus de moribus conditionibus et nequitia Turcorum*
(Treatise on the customs, conditions, and iniquity of the Turks) written
by Brother George of Mühlenbach after his twenty years in Turkish
captivity (1438–1458). This work, editions or translations of which were
put out by Erasmus, Martin Luther, and Sebastian Franck, gives a candid,
unadorned account of life in the Ottoman Empire during those years.
After assuring the reader that amid 100,000 horses one could scarcely
hear the sound of a single horse—an observation corroborated by other
contemporary observers, such as the Burgundian knight Bertrandon de la
Broquière, who describes the utter silence in a Turkish army camp—
he continues:

> Saddles and harness are of the greatest simplicity. There is no sign of
> vanity or superfluity. Nothing is simpler than the gear of the horses.
> No one bears arms unless he is leaving the camp. They are kept in
> sacks. No little dogs or mules are seen scampering about. No one
> bustles about on horseback or makes noise, as is customary among
> Christians. The great lords and princes display such simplicity in
> everything that they cannot possibly be singled out from the crowd.
> I saw the ruler, followed only by two young men, on his way to the
> mosque far away from his palace. I saw him going to the baths in
> the same way. When he returned from the mosque to his palace, no
> one would have dared to join his followers, no one would have made
> bold to approach him and to cheer him as is done in our country, to
> burst into the cry: "Long live the king," or other such applause as is
> customary with us. I have seen the sultan at prayer in the mosque.
> He sat neither in a chair nor on a throne, but like the others had taken
> his place on a carpet spread out on the floor. Around him no decora-
> tion had been placed, hung, or spread out.
>
> On his clothing or on his horse the sultan had no special mark to
> distinguish him. I watched him at his mother's funeral, and if he had
> not been pointed out to me, I could not have recognized him. It is
> strictly forbidden to accompany him or to approach him without
> having received express permission. I pass over many particulars that
> have been related to me about his affability in conversation. In his
> judgments he shows maturity and indulgence. He is generous in
> giving alms and benevolent in all his actions.

The Franciscan brothers living in Pera have assured me that he came to their church and sat down in their choir to attend the ceremonies and the sacrifice of the Mass. To satisfy his curiosity, they offered him an unconsecrated wafer at the elevation of the Host, for pearls must not be cast before swine.

Brother George's observations are confirmed by Bertrandon de la Broquière and also by the so-called Serbian, but probably Greek, Janissary Constantine, son of Michael Konstantinović of Ostrovica. In his *Memoirs of a Janissary*, written or dictated in Polish, one of the most important sources for the story of the Conqueror, he gives a vivid picture of conditions in the Ottoman Empire during the eventful years of his stay.[4]

It was Mehmed himself who made all the important decisions in both foreign and domestic policy. For three decades he was the sole determining power, to all indications uninfluenced by those whom he himself had raised to positions of prominence in the serai, the army, and the corps of officials. In his reign we find no sign of the harem regime which often played a determining role in later years, particularly in the seventeenth and eighteenth centuries. Apart from his stepmother Mara, we hear of not a single woman exerting, or even attempting to exert, an influence on the sultan. Nor is there any indication that public opinion ever checked his despotism in an appreciable degree. The one force in the state which Mehmed at least occasionally took into consideration in forming his plans was the corps of Janissaries, of which we shall have more to say. There is virtually no record of any opposition considerable enough to endanger the state among the high officials or generals, on whose loyalty and reliability he was increasingly dependent as his empire expanded. And when anything of the kind occurred or seemed to occur, punishment and vengeance were not long in coming.

Murad II had fought the Christians in pitched battles, in which individual prowess could still play a decisive role. To him war was an annoying interruption of his efforts to insure the peace and well-being of his people. Under Mehmed it became the raison d'être, the central occupation of Ottoman society, for he compelled everyone to support the war effort in one way or another. The sultan's main concern was now to subjugate foreign countries permanently and to incorporate them in his empire, to govern them and divide his territories among his trusted warriors. This radically different type of warfare made it necessary to reduce fortified

---

[4] For Brother George and Broquière see above, book 1, nn. 18 and 25, respectively; for the Janissary Constantine's *Memoirs*, book 2, n. 50. There is now an English edition: B. Stolz, S. Soucek, *Memoirs of a Janissary, Konstantin Mihailović* (Ann Arbor, 1975; Michigan Slavic Translations).

cities and castles quickly and ruthlessly, and above all to capture and destroy foreign rulers.

At the beginning of his career Mehmed subjected all conquered provinces and islands to the payment of tribute. The amount depended on the wealth, size, and productivity of the place in question. There were numerous gradations ranging from 1,000 to 30,000 gold ducats. If the tribute was paid on time and suitable presents were made to the sultan and his viziers, the provinces and islands were allowed to retain their form of government, civil institutions, and even their dynast. But at the first sign of laxity the sultan sent a stern reprimand, accompanied by a threat to occupy the place and expel its overlord. If the arrears were not promptly paid up, the threat was made good. But many other reasons or pretexts were found for putting a sudden end to such sovereignties. A chance whim or personal dislike on the part of the unpredictable sultan, slander spread by enemies, the strategic position or wealth of a given territory, all this could result, quite unexpectedly, in the deposition or expulsion of the prince or his removal to Istanbul, where he would first be held in honorable confinement and then, as a rule, be put to death without the pretense of a hearing. At best, the sultan might promise the deposed dynast compensation in some city or rural district, promises which were often enough not kept at all or were observed only for a short time. Hardly any of the expelled princes enjoyed a peaceful old age. Even those who had enjoyed the sultan's favor in their youth found no mercy in the long run. The successors or heirs of a deceased dynast had to report personally to Istanbul, bringing ample gifts, and to receive the sultan's investiture from the hands of the grand vizier. In the course of these receptions the new tribute was established, often at a higher figure, and in conclusion the vassal received a garment of honor. Of course, the procedure was very different if the province, city, or island had been conquered, if submission had not been voluntary. Then no mercy was shown: the entire existing government would be removed and a high Ottoman official would reorganize the administration on the traditional Turkish model. But the population did not always lose by the exchange. Often enough, the political and civil condition of the community and the treatment of the subjects were no more oppressive than under the Palaeologi or the various petty dynasts, not to mention the Frankish feudal lords in Greece. The notion that even under Mehmed II the Christian inhabitants of the Ottoman Empire were always and everywhere worse off than they had been under their native dynasties is a myth, or, to speak with Voltaire, a *fable convenue.*

Mehmed the Conqueror has been described as "an Oriental of markedly tyrannical nature" (J. W. Zinkeisen). Such an assertion is true only with certain reservations. In all Islamic states the close bond between religious and secular principles is reflected in the inextricable interpenetration of church and state. Probably for this reason, political power based entirely on conquest almost always degenerated, in Islamic countries, into total despotism. Moreover, anyone who has even a superficial knowledge of Western history in the late Middle Ages, that of the Italian city-states, for example, will have no difficulty in recalling tyrants who show an astonishing resemblance to the Conqueror. When, for example, in his treatise *De magnanimitate* (On Magnanimity), based on Aristotle's *Ethics*, Giovanni Pontano, the Neapolitan humanist, set out to describe the antithesis of the ideal, perfect man, he may have derived his strongest colors from Aristotle's analysis of the tyrant's character, but beyond a doubt the living reality of his time provided him with much of his material. Side by side with dissolute vice, hideous cruelty, bloodthirstiness, unrestrained sexual lust, and bestial intemperance, we find all the qualities of the vengeful, violent, arbitrary ruler that Pontano was in a position to observe day in and day out in his own sovereign, Ferrante of Aragon. Jacob Burckhardt called Ferrante the most terrible of all the princes of his day, a demonic nature, who concentrated all his faculties, including a relentless memory and an infinite power to dissemble, on the annihilation of his enemies. He reveled in tortures, rubbed his hands with glee at the thought of his dungeons and their well-guarded prisoners tormented by uncertainty; after the Conspiracy of the Barons, he experienced the most fiendish delight in putting his adversaries to death one by one. Apart from Cesare Borgia in a later day, there is probably no Italian who in the practice of politics so well anticipated Machiavelli's theory as Ferrante of Aragon. But the period offers numerous other examples. We need only recall the petty Italian tyrants of the quattrocento, especially Sigismondo Pandolfo Malatesta in Rimini, that monster in human form who once tried to draw Mehmed to Italy. That traitor, voluptuary, and bestial criminal, who in times of peace replaced the excitement of warfare with courtly festivities, tournaments, hunts, and association with scholars and poets, was cruel, fierce, and godless, recognizing no moral barriers and shunning no crime. The history of the Visconti and several of the smaller city dynasties provide numerous examples.

Thus, it seems quite out of place to regard Mehmed, in whom we find many of the qualities observed among his Italian contemporaries and no doubt elsewhere, as an Oriental tyrant unparalleled in his time. Altogether it seems absurd to dissociate Mehmed, the ruler and the man, from his times, and to suppose that those qualities in him which repel us today were to be found only outside of Christendom.

Finally, the extraordinary violence of the clash between such radically antagonistic forces as Christianity and Islam, Europe and Asia, accounts in some degree for the ferocity linked with the Conqueror's name.

As Mehmed's conquests expanded, the dangers threatening his person from all sides increased. The affable sultan of the early days became reserved, distrustful, almost misanthropic, and even abandoned the old Ottoman custom of sitting at table with his viziers. He dined alone and took every possible precaution to avoid being poisoned. The desire to secure the succession to the throne induced him to legalize fratricide. At first he presided over the *divan*, or imperial council, in accordance with the time-honored custom; toward the end of his reign, he left his viziers to carry on these sessions by themselves. There is a story to the effect that one day a ragged Anatolian Turkman appeared in the council chamber, which at that time was open to all, and infuriated the Conqueror by asking in the crude dialect of his tribe: "Which of you is the fortunate emperor?" (*Delvetlü hunkâr kangunuzdur?*) On the strength of this incident, so the story goes, Gedik Ahmed Pasha advised the sultan to safeguard his sanctified person from such humiliations by leaving the affairs of the *divan* to his viziers, and Mehmed accepted the proposal. Even if, as seems plausible, this incident actually occurred, the Conqueror in all likelihood merely took it as welcome pretext for withdrawing as much as possible from contact with the world. From a barred window built into the wall of the council chamber behind the grand vizier's chair, the sultan could listen unseen to the deliberations. Strange to say, the law which forbade all those who approached the sultan to bear arms and prescribed, moreover, that each visitor be held by two chamberlains, one at each side—a regulation with which Western ambassadors had to comply until well into the nineteenth century—was introduced not by the Conqueror but by his son Bayezid II after a wandering dervish had attempted to murder him in a ravine between Monastïr and Prilep in southern Serbia (June, 1492). It was only in exceptional cases and as a special sign of favor that anyone was permitted to wear a saber when admitted to Mehmed's presence.

Even more than his unwarlike and popular successor, the Conqueror would have had ample reason to take such measures for the protection of his person. The Signoria of Venice alone, as we have seen, organized a good dozen attempts on his life. He owed the discovery of these plots to a highly developed secret service, whose ramifications must have extended far beyond the confines of the Ottoman Empire. We possess little reliable testimony concerning this institution, but enough to show that it must have been an enormous espionage and surveillance apparatus, whose undeniable success can be accounted for only by the complicity of well-paid foreign agents. Especially in the Italian states, Mehmed undoubtedly had numerous agents, whose espionage activities extended to the highest spheres of government. Rumors of these activities aroused hysteria even farther north. It is on record that in such remote places as Wasserburg and Sachrang in Upper Bavaria, perfectly innocent native persons were suspected of being Turkish spies and persecuted accordingly.

In view of such precautionary measures, the Conqueror's life must have been relatively secure against assassination. As long as the state of his health permitted, he walked through the streets of Istanbul accompanied by a number of slaves. Sometimes he rode through the capital followed by two mounted guards, now and then approaching an acquaintance to inquire after his health. These walks or rides were gradually abandoned in the course of the years as his gout and other complaints increased. He hid behind the high walls of his palace and appeared more and more rarely in public.

It is even more difficult to obtain a reliable portrait of Mehmed the man than of Mehmed the ruler. Any attempt to derive a complete picture of his character and personality from the statements of contemporaries and chance observers is a hazardous undertaking. Nearly everything that was said of him in his lifetime reflected either boundless, slavish admiration and deification or hatred and contempt. His compatriots do not agree even in their descriptions of his appearance, and the flowery language in which they are couched leaves little room for actual information. In his *Şamailname-i Al-i Osman* (Personal Descriptions of the House of Osman), written, to be sure, after the Conqueror's death, Seyyid Lokman, court poet of Murad III (1574–1595), describes him as follows:[5]

> His eyebrows were black, bushy, and long; the eyes with which he viewed the world were the light of the world and like pupils gave light to the eyes of the noble. He had a sheep-like nose and a yellowish red and white complexion; his chin was round and well shaped. The hair of his just-grown youthful beard was entwined

[5] Babinger discusses Lokman and his works in *Die Geschichtsschreiber der Osmanen und ihre Werke* (Leipzig, 1927), 164–167.

like gold wire; his hero's mustache was like fresh basil over a rosebud, his lips were pistachios, his shoulders broad, his neck long, his arms strong and warlike, his manner of sitting in the stirrups heroic, with proudly upraised head.

Far soberer are the words of Gian-Maria Angiolello's description, referring presumably to the last decade of the Conqueror's life:

This emperor Mehmed, who as I have said was known as the Grand Turk, was of medium height, fat, and fleshy; he had a wide forehead, large eyes with thick lashes, an aquiline nose, a small mouth with a round, copious, reddish-tinged beard, a short, thick neck, a sallow complexion, rather high shoulders, and a loud voice. He suffered from gout in the legs.

Italians such as Giàcomo de' Languschi or Niccolò Sagundino, who saw him shortly after the conquest of Constantinople, accord in describing him as "well built, of large rather than medium stature, a man who seldom laughed" (*di poco riso*), or "of melancholy nature and mood, of medium stature and rather distinguished mien, with frank, open features." All this refers to the Conqueror in his period of good health. Later, especially in the last years of his life, he was bowed and hideously disfigured by his illness and dissolute life. Philippe de Commynes, the French diplomat and historian, who was an excellent observer with far-flung connections, draws an almost gruesome picture of the sick Conqueror:

Men who have seen him have told me that a monstrous swelling formed on his legs; at the approach of summer it grew as large as the body of a man and could not be opened; and then it subsided. No surgeon was able to say what it was, but it was said that his bestial gluttony had a good deal to do with it and that it must be divine punishment. Lest people notice his sorry state and his enemies despise him, he seldom allowed himself to be seen and remained secluded in his serai.[6]

Bellini's famous portrait in London, completed five months before the sultan's death, shows the aquiline nose hanging down over the upper lip, "a parrot's beak resting on cherries," as the Turkish poet put it. But it can no longer be considered a faithful character study of the sultan. Basil Gray has pointed out that the portrait is in rather poor condition and was heavily overpainted. X-ray photographs taken in 1935 revealed

[6] In the translation by Michael Jones (see above, book 6, n. 6) the discussion of Mehmed is at 414 and 416–417.

that next to nothing beyond the turban remains of the original. If the double portrait in Basel is an authentic likeness, it hardly tells us more than that Mehmed looked unwell.[7]

As his corpulence increased and as the hydropic swellings and lymphatic occlusions, to which his illness can probably be attributed, began to hamper his movements, he rode out less frequently and spent more and more of his time in his palace with poets, scholars, and persons of whose affection he felt sure. In these periods of illness he was obliged to refrain from warfare and to devote himself to occupations connected with his plans for the future, to studies of the past or concerning foreign countries which had thus far evaded his arm. What Giàcomo de' Languschi said of him in about 1453—that nothing gave him greater pleasure than the study of geography and military questions—was also true of his mature years. "He burns with the desire to rule, an astute student of events." Thus the Venetian observer concludes his description, and adds on a note of warning: "So constituted is the man with whom we Christians have to deal."

We should have a far better insight into the nature of Mehmed the man if we knew something about the origins and character of his mother and her influence on the child. In accordance with the custom of the house of Osman, he was removed at an early age from his father's court and sent with his mother to the Anatolian hinterland, where he spent his childhood years, first in Amasya and later in Manisa. The turbulent, unruly prince was assuredly a great trial to those entrusted with his upbringing. We have mentioned the trouble it took to teach him the rudiments of good conduct and of the culture of those days.

Since his mother was unquestionably not a Turk or of Moslem origin but a Greek, Slav, or perhaps even an Italian—in any case, a product of the Christian West—we may presume the presence of Western elements in his early training. It is also safe to assign to his youth his first meetings with Italians, later association with whom must have done much to mold his ideas about the Christian world. The years between his deposition in 1446 and his definitive accession to the throne in February 1451 must have had a decisive effect on his character, and it would surely throw a significant light on his development if we could learn more concerning these years than is communicated in the notes of Ciriaco de' Pizzicolli. His autocratic leanings and passion for grandiose historical deeds, his determination to establish a world empire with Constantinople as its center, must have matured during those five years.

[7] For the article of Basil Gray, see above, book 6, n. 8.

425

It can readily be imagined that dealings with an autocrat almost impervious to outside influence must have been exceedingly and increasingly difficult for his viziers and other dignitaries. As time went on, he became more and more unpredictable and almost pathologically moody; to approach him was to take one's life in one's hands. No one, not even his grand vizier, was secure against his vengeance once his distrust had been aroused. He never forgot a wrong done him or neglected to exact retribution. The gruesome example of his grand vizier Halil Pasha or of a man who had done as much for the empire as Mahmud Pasha offers sufficient proof of his relentless and unforgiving nature.

His religious liberalism must also have matured in those years. In this it seems certain that Italian influence played a part. Another factor was his leaning to the supernatural, a superstitious streak which became apparent in later years and even affected important military decisions. He liked to have his fortune told, especially according to the stars, and to this end employed Persian astrologers, who took good care never to draw up a horoscope at variance with his hopes and desires.

In defiance of his court clergy, he boldly transgressed the Islamic prohibition of images, and yet he could not look upon the paintings of Western artists without an anxious, almost eerie feeling. All his life it seemed incredible to him that a mortal man such as Gentile Bellini should possess the supernatural, nearly divine power to conjure up living beings. He looked upon his own portrait, when Bellini had finished it, as a miracle. It may have been pressure from the Orthodox Moslem clergy that led to Bellini's sudden departure, though other explanations have been suggested.

Little light can be thrown on the Conqueror's private life, which was well hidden from the eyes of the world. Of his relations with the women who bore his sons, we know nothing at all. As Ernst Kantorowicz said of Emperor Frederick II, this was a monarch who avoided every semblance of domestic intimacy or tenderness. He did not create an atmosphere in which a woman could live at her ease. "In that rarefied air charged with tensions, no one other than himself could breathe; not a friend much less a woman."[8]

We have some definite information about one of his legitimate wives, Sitt Hatun, the princess from remote Elbistan whom his father had imposed on him. He suffered her presence in his palace for a brief time; later, if he did not repudiate her, he at least sent her away to Edirne, where

---

[8] Cf. E. Kantorowicz, *Frederick the Second 1194–1250*, trans. E. O. Lorimer (New York, 1957), especially 334 and 407.

the childless woman ended her joyless days in works of piety. His ties with Gülbahar, the mother of his eldest son, Bayezid, may have been closer, though this should by no means be deduced from the fact that her tomb was placed near his own *türbe*. She survived him by some years, and it was most likely her son and not her husband who built her tomb. As for Çiçek Hatun, who may have been the mother of Cem Sultan, we know neither where she came from nor what became of her. Angiolello's account makes it seem highly improbable that the mother of Mustafa, his favorite son, enjoyed the sultan's favor after Mustafa's death. The aging woman seems to have lived close to her son and after his sudden death apparently spent the rest of her days in mourning.

We have no even halfway credible indication that Mehmed loved any woman for very long, much less fell under her influence. He looked upon women, and boys too, as we know, as a pastime and source of pleasure. There is no ground whatever for supposing that he was ever capable of higher feelings. He was altogether a coldly calculating man, whose attitude toward others was determined exclusively by their utility for his own purposes. The only exception seems to have been his Jewish physician Yakub Pasha (Maestro Iacopo).

Gian-Maria Angiolello, who was at the sultan's court at the same time as Bellini and has a certain amount to say about the painter's activity in Istanbul, provides a few examples of the sultan's cruelty, brutality, and inhumanity, qualities which, as we have pointed out, he shared with other contemporary tyrants. A few of these examples are worth relating.

By way of illustrating the blood lust that sometimes overcame the Conqueror, Angiolello tells the famous story, whose credibility has often been doubted, of the fair Irene. At the capture of Constantinople, an exceedingly beautiful Greek girl of sixteen or seventeen was among the numerous prisoners taken. She was brought before the Conqueror, who fell in love with her and so neglected the affairs of state on her account that his advisers made representations to him. Far from taking offense at their audacity, the sultan undertook to prove that he was still master of himself. Summoning his dignitaries to the hall of his palace, he himself, accompanied by the radiant and sumptuously clad Irene, came to meet them. Turning to those around him, he asked whether they had ever encountered more perfect beauty. When all replied in the negative and vied with one another in lauding the sultan's choice, Mehmed cried out, "Nothing in the world can deter me from upholding the greatness of the house of Osman!" Thereupon he seized the Greek girl by the hair, drew his dagger, and cut her throat.

The story is told in the form of a novella by Matteo Bandello, who may have taken his material from Angiolello. The Piedmontese Boccaccio, to be sure, fails to tell us that the sultan fell sick with sorrow over his crime, but that little by little his horror at his deed subsided, and he overcame his love for the woman he had idolized. The episode shows a striking resemblance to a legend that has found its most familiar expression in the relatively late folk ballad about the Cossack chieftain Stenka Razin (d. 1671). Consequently, its historicity is rather open to doubt. The gruesome episode might conceivably have occurred in 1455, when on his return from the battlefield, Mehmed, as the sober and conscientious historian Mustafa Ali tells us, "spent many nights in debauchery with lovely-eyed, fairylike slave girls, and his days drinking with pages who looked like angels." "Mehmed," the historian adds with subtle irony, "was only seemingly engaged in debauchery and wantonness; in reality he was working, guided by love of justice, to relieve the oppression of his subjects in the land."[8a]

The Conqueror had a special love for gardens and liked to raise vegetables on the extensive grounds of the new palace. In his gardens he found distraction from the business of state. He planted cucumbers and lovingly followed their growth. He conceived a special affection for one particular cucumber and forbade his *bostancĭ*, or gardeners, to touch it. One day the sultan looked for his cucumber, and it was no longer there. He asked the men who had been working in the garden shortly before which of them had eaten it. To discover the truth, Mehmed had the belly of one of the young gardeners slit open; luckily for the others, the remains of the cucumber were found in it.

Carlo Ridolfi, known for his biographies of the Venetian painters and sculptors (1648), gives a late account of another occurrence connected with Gentile Bellini's stay at the sultan's court, which may have had something to do with the great painter's precipitate departure. One day Bellini showed the sultan a painting representing the beheading of John the Baptist. The sultan looked at the painting a long while and praised the master, but then informed him that he had made a mistake, for the beheaded man's neck protruded too far. Under such circumstances, he explained, the neck contracted. To prove his point, the sultan had a slave dragged in and beheaded before the painter's eyes. According to Ridolfi, Bellini was so horrified that he returned to Venice at once. This

---

[8a] Mehmed's earlier biographer, Guillet de Saint-Georges, tells the story of Irene in his *Histoire du regne de Mahomet II* I, 295–298. The section of Mustafa Ali's chronicle, *Kunh al-Ahbār*, dealing with Mehmed's reign is unpublished.

story too, it must be admitted, reflects a *topos*, for Seneca relates a very similar episode in connection with the Greek painter Parrhasios, the rival of Zeuxis, and the story is even told about Michelangelo, though in a very dubious source.[9]

After Gian-Maria Angiolello, perhaps the most trustworthy Western chronicler of events in the Ottoman Empire under the Conqueror is the Genoese Jacopo de Campi(s), who later became known as Jacopo de Promontorio. He spent some twenty-five years as a merchant in the Ottoman Empire, eighteen under Murad II and seven under Mehmed II, and set down his observations in a book, *Governo ed entrate del Gran Turco* (c. 1475). He describes the punishments inflicted by Mehmed II in a vivid account, which seems worth quoting at this point, though even so cool-headed a merchant as Don Jacopo may have been guilty of occasional exaggeration. Certain of these punishments, such as the cutting off of hands and feet, were sanctioned, in case of theft for example, by the then prevailing religious law and by Ottoman legislation; but this hardly detracts from the horror of Jacopo's picture.[10]

Diverse and horrible are the punishments, injustices, and cruelties of the Grand Turk. The most usual death he metes out to anyone he pleases, whether guilty of any crime or not, is to make the man he wishes to punish lie down on the ground; a sharp long pole is placed in the rectum; with a big mallet held in both hands the executioner strikes it with all his might, so that the pole, known as a *palo*, enters the human body and, according to its path, the unfortunate lingers on or dies at once; then he raises the pole and plants it in the ground; thus the unfortunate is left *in extremis*; he does not live long.

Another horrible cruelty is inflicted on graver offenders: The victim stands erect with his hands tied. He causes a two-pronged fork equipped with barbed hooks and affixed to a wooden pole to be rammed into his neck from behind just below the chin, in such a way that the windpipe is not touched and that the pole is at the victim's back. Usually, the prongs protude by four or five hand's breadths near the ears. Then his hands are untied. Eager to save his life, the unfortunate raises himself with both hands to escape from the hooks. For a moment suspended at the highest point, he invariably falls back.

[9] For the questionable story told by Ridolfi see the remark of the editors of Vasari, *Lives of the Painters* II, 161, n. 2.

[10] See Babinger's "Die Aufzeichnungen des Genuesen Iacopo de Promontorio-de Campis über den Osmanenstaat um 1475," in *Sitzungsberichte der bayerische Akademie der Wissenschaften, philos.-hist. Klasse* (Munich, 1950).

This continues and sometimes the unfortunate spends the whole day or even as much as two days in this torment. Then he dies a horrible death.

For still greater severity, as though he were a butcher, he has certain persons hung up by the legs like sheep. A long heavy beam is passed between his bound hands, so that he cannot move. Then he has the whole thickness of his skin removed all the way to his head. He then causes the neck and the hands to be cut loose. All this is done in such a way that head and hands remain attached to the skin. Then he has the skin washed and stuffed with straw and the feet attached to it. The whole then looks like a normal unharmed man, who is now impaled on a lance head and lifted up. This he does out of special contempt for such unfortunates.

There are hardly any traitors whose heads he has not had cut off despite the promises he had made them, after winning whole provinces, regions and castles through their wiles and machinations. Similarly, he has always massacred all enemy soldiers, even when they were taken on the strength of an agreement, and he had promised to spare their life and property, arguing that he was fully entitled to avenge Moslem blood.

When in the course of naval campaigns, unfortunate Christians attempted to flee, he had them placed in a bark filled with wood and nailed by their hands and feet to the benches and gunwales. Then the bark would be set on fire.

Others according to their offense he has spitted on forks.

In some cases he has the hands cut off, in others the feet, and in still other cases both hands and feet. Sometimes he has the eyes put out or the nose or arms cut off. In some cases he has the face mangled.

If a man has leased something from him but is unable to make his payments on time, he has that man hanged without mercy. In the case of lesser offenses or when he happens to be in the mood, he puts the offender on an ass in such a way that the tail serves him as a bridle and has him driven around the countryside with a filled animal's stomach on his head. Then he is laid on the ground and receives fifty or a hundred whip lashes.

Many claim that the sultan has people buried alive or even devoured by elephants and other wild beasts. But Master Iacopo says he has never seen such acts of cruelty. The worst, however, is the following: for the special punishment of those whom he particularly hates, he keeps among his executioners three or four perfect beasts, whom he pays well and whom, when he wishes to avenge himself on someone, he causes to eat the person in question in his presence until he gives up the ghost. That is the most hideous death that has ever been mentioned.

He need only suspect a lord, vizier, captain, soldier, or ordinary subject, of committing a fault, and he kills him without mercy, regardless of what a great lord he may be. When he sends a slave with a letter to the judge of a town, however remote, and the letter is given to the judge, the judge, without further investigation, has the persons decapitated who are mentioned in the letter, even if they are of the highest rank.

In short, if ever a ruler has been feared and dreaded, ruthless and cruel, this one is a second Nero and far worse.

It may be worth noting that this passage is immediately followed by the previously told story of the cucumber. Thus, that episode, related by various narrators, may actually have taken place. Otherwise, it too was borrowed from legend. It does indeed recall a familiar fairy-tale motif.

We have no way of knowing how much truth is contained in such reports of individual cases. But we do know, on the basis of numerous reliable sources, that Mehmed did not hesitate to extinguish thousands of human lives when he was so inclined or when the welfare of the state seemed to require it. In this, however, he was by no means unique. All the classes of sinners with which the fourteenth century peopled Dante's Hell are amply represented in the following centuries. We need only recall once more the insatiably vengeful Ferrante of Aragon.

Theodoros Spandugino claims that Mehmed was responsible for the death of 873,000 persons. How this figure was arrived at, Spandugino, who is often given to exaggeration, does not say. But if we allow for thirty years of almost unremitting war, it is probably not too far from the truth, for it would amount to an annual average of 29,000. This figure does not take into account the terrible havoc wrought by the Black Death which followed in the wake of the Conqueror's campaigns and depopulated whole sections of his empire. If the sultan's activities in the interior of his empire, where he devoted his organizational talents to public building, the establishment of pious and benevolent foundations, the development of theology and science, and the improvement of his government and administration, did not speak in his favor, the destructive violence which he coldly and unswervingly unleashed on all sides as long as he lived would quite suffice to mark him as one of the most terrible figures of the entire Middle Ages. His powerful personality, comparable perhaps to Napoleon's, not only altered the face of large areas of Europe but profoundly influenced the attitudes of his contemporaries toward man and the world. He was one of those historical figures presenting the enigma of the so-called demonic personality. In him, as in many great men, one is tempted to see a "natural force," which operates in accordance with laws of its own. Since it is not he who acts but rather this force that acts in him and through him, it is pointless to apply ethical standards to such a man. "In reality"—the half-truth is Goethe's—"only the observer has a conscience; the man of action is always without one." But if, as Hegel says, the individual's knowledge of his purposes constitutes the true content of ethics, a Western observer of Mehmed as a historical figure is inevitably confronted by the contradiction, running through all history, between the view that exonerates genius from all ethical consideration and that other view which makes the highest ethical demands on genius. In evaluating the role assigned to him by destiny, Mehmed the Conqueror would assuredly have recognized only the first view.

In his lifetime Mehmed was regarded as a bloodthirsty tyrant, not only by the Christian world but by a good part of his subjects. This is not the image, however, that has survived in the minds of the Turkish masses. With the passage of time, the common people came to endow him with the features of a holy man (*veli*). Outside the window of his tomb one sees even today simple folk, especially women, who look upon Mehmed as a wonder worker and beg him to intercede with Allah in all the trying situations of life.

II. State and Society

Like nearly all Oriental states, the Ottoman Empire was a military theocracy. The Koran, the sacred book of the Moslems, in which the discourses pronounced by the Prophet at different periods in his life and interpreted as divine revelation are gathered together, was regarded substantially as the supreme and immutable law governing political as well as religious life. The sultan sat enthroned high above his empire, bound by nothing but the word of the Prophet. His forebears of the house of Osman had founded their empire in Anatolia on the ruins of the Seljuk state, and now, by taking Constantinople and destroying the remnants of the Byzantine Empire, Mehmed built the Ottoman state into an edifice far exceeding its former limits and extending from Persia to the Adriatic. Obviously, the administration of so enormous a territory made the highest demands on its ruler's political acumen. Murad II had begun to work out a system of legislation, but it remained for his son to amplify it and adapt it to entirely new conditions. The commandments of the Koran were inadequate, even as supplemented by the *sunna* of Mohammed, that is to say, the practice followed by the Prophet in word, deed, and omission. This practice was transmitted in the *hadith*, the traditional sayings which enjoyed equal status with the Koran. In the Ottoman territories the *hadith* formed the foundation of regulations known as *ḳanun* (from the Greek κανών), which under Murad I had already been compiled into a body of state laws. The changes that had taken place in the last hundred years, the increasing complexity of the administrative apparatus, called not so much for confirmation of the old legislation as for wise innovations, which when effected were set down in the so-called *ḳanun-name*, or lawbooks. A comparison of the laws introduced by Mehmed toward the end of his reign with those promulgated by his great-grandson Süleyman the Magnificent, whom the Ottomans call the legislator (*ḳanuni*), shows that Süleyman was obliged to abrogate or amplify much of the Conqueror's legislation.

Immediately after a new conquest a land survey (*tahrir*) was made and subsequently renewed every thirty or forty years. This formed the basis of an administrative reorganization, in which existing property relationships were largely respected.[11] But the assimilation of new territory was not always free from crises and, in view of the increased intensity of overall economic activity, it is not surprising that certain branches developed far more rapidly than others. Especially commerce found unhoped-for possibilities of growth, largely because the expansion of the empire had swept away numerous borders and customs barriers and given rise to an enormous low-tariff zone.

C. J. Jireček has pointed out that in the early days of the new Moslem empire, the highways of nearly all southeastern Europe were far less dangerous than under the Old Serbian and Bosnian robber barons.[12] In the days of the Conqueror one almost had the impression that the security of the glorious Byzantine past, the *pax romana*, had returned and that all might benefit by it. The old manners and customs were everywhere left intact, and no one had to fear harm for not being a Moslem. Four times a year, so the so-called Serbian Janissary relates, the *çavuş* (very much like *missi dominici* of the Merovingians or Charlemagne's *missi camerali*) traveled through the vast territory of the *reaya* to supervise the

---

[11] For the pattern of Ottoman incorporation of conquered lands, see Inalcïk, "Ottoman Methods of Conquest," *Studia Islamica* 2 (1954), 103–129.

[12] Jireček deals especially with the main northwestern route from Istanbul in *Die Heerstrasse von Belgrad nach Constantinopel* (Prague, 1877).

administration and see to it that the people were not oppressed. At least under Mehmed II, the Ottoman ruling class was scarcely seen in the conquered countries. Only in the castles and fortified places were the Byzantine commanders replaced by Ottomans.

In Serbia and Bosnia the whole demographic picture underwent a change. The pre-Ottoman cities had been laid out in accordance with military considerations. As a rule, the burghers' dwellings were situated in the lower city (Serbian *varoš*; Hungarian *város*), grouped around the citadel, which was usually on a rise and well defended. For the purposes of the Ottomans, these fortresses were superfluous. Some they razed, others they allowed to fall into ruins, and the population of many of these towns was evacuated to the plain and resettled near the communications routes. Nearly all the larger towns in inhospitable regions had grown up around mines; in Bosnia, for example, there were few inhabited places above 3,000 feet. Of fifteen settlements at an altitude of between 3,600 and 4,000 feet, three were in the region of Foča and the remainder in the mining district of Vareš. The policy of the Ottoman administration was everywhere to leave the peaceful Christian inhabitants unmolested; more importance was attached to their punctual payment of the head tax and other levies than to a meaningless show of authority on the part of Turkish officials.

There was indeed no need for it. Wherever the sultan's army conquered new territories in Europe, the victor found a population torn by virulent national hatreds and religious passions. It was perfectly true that, as Heinrich von Treitschke puts it, the Greeks hated the Serbs even more bitterly than the Turks, and that the sight of a Latin altar over which Christ hangs on the cross with one foot on the other rather than both side by side was more offensive to an Orthodox son of the Eastern church than that of a Moslem turning toward Mecca in prayer. Such sentiments on the part of the *reaya* provided the foundation of the shrewd system of fostering opposition between peoples and creeds, to which the ruling Ottoman minority owed its security.[13]

But Treitschke was expressing an arbitrary and rather exaggerated view when he termed this tolerance of the Ottomans toward the Christian *reaya* an "art of enslavement," the success of which, he goes on to say, is explicable only by the inclination to servitude of the subjects of the Byzantine Empire and by the most ancient traditions of Oriental political life. Since the Near East, so he argues, knows no national states but

[13] See Treitschke's remarks in his *Politik* (Leipzig, 1913); English edition, *Politics* II, trans. B. Dugdale and T. de Bille (New York, 1916), 33–40.

only a mixture of national fragments welded together by force, the policy of "divide and rule" here achieved a perfection almost incomprehensible to a Westerner. While Christendom burned its heretics, under the Crescent everyone was permitted to live in his own faith. But in reality, still according to Treitschke, this widely vaunted tolerance of the Turks proves only how ingeniously they had perfected their system of enslavement: the Turks did not desire the conversion of those they had subjected, for only if the *reaya* remained "infidel dogs" could the Moslems be their absolute masters. While in other countries a rigid class structure held the common people down, on the Bosporus the meanest slave could hope, through force of character and good fortune, to rise to the highest offices in the state. In sixteenth-century Europe, accordingly, the villeins welcomed the approaching banner of the Prophet with rather the same feelings as later the armies of the French Revolution. But this perfect social equality, which everywhere forms the foundation of Oriental despotism, existed only for the master race of the faithful. Between it and the *reaya* there yawned an enormous gulf.

It is true that even at the time of the Arab caliphate a relationship approaching Treitschke's conception had developed between the ruling Moslem class and the non-Moslem population. Thus, with certain reservations, it may also apply to the Ottoman Empire. Indeed there is documentary evidence to show that the *reaya* enjoyed no more freedom of movement than slaves or serfs. Unauthorized movements, especially for purposes of evading the corvée, were severely punished. Where large numbers were involved, the penalty could be as drastic as removal to the interior of Anatolia and the incorporation of sons of military age in the sultan's bodyguard. In every district the feudatory or lessee and the community at large bore equal responsibility for maintaining the *reaya* and slaves in their places of work. But if the *reaya* paid their taxes punctually and avoided conflicts with Moslems, they were hardly worse off than before; indeed, their sufferings had often been more acute under native rulers. The peasants on their land and the burghers in the towns went peaceably about their business.

In accordance with the system prevailing among the master nations, the heads of the Christian churches were endowed with jurisdiction and police power over those of their own faith and at the same time were held responsible for the taxes of their flock. Thus, within the Ottoman state the Orthodox under their patriarch formed a subservient Greek state, in which the bishops were able to rule arbitrarily over their communities and even their priests. Without becoming dangerous to the Turkish masters, the high clergy often managed to feather their own nests very nicely.

There was one restriction, however. The Christians were forbidden to build new churches, to repair old ones, or to make use of church bells. In Rumelia during the early days of Turkish rule church services were announced solely by the hollow sound of a wooden gong (Greek *simantron*, whence Turkish *şamandïra*, Romanian *geamandură* or *toaca*). This prescription does not seem so very harsh when we consider that the English church forbade the Catholics to use bells until the nineteenth century and that Protestants are still forbidden to make use of them in Spain and Chile.

In the Conqueror's time, the religious heads of the Greek "nation" (*Rum milleti*) were not all of Greek origin; in any event, they were not capable of playing a political role, much less of performing a cultural and national function. Only a small number of otherwise unoccupied metropolitans and monks were available to the patriarchal church. For a considerable period few scions of noble families had offered their services to the Church; there were not many archons and merchants capable of filling its high offices, of acting as *logotheti* and *skevrophylaki* (administrators). Aside perhaps from Mara, daughter of George Branković and widow of Murad, none of the Orthodox nobles of the past who had been deposed or exiled by Mehmed was able or willing to step forward in Istanbul as a protector of the "great church" (*megali ekklisia*). Under such conditions it was quite impossible for the Church in that period to assume the least political importance.

Mehmed's installation of Gennadius as patriarch has recently been characterized as incompatible with Islamic law, on the ground that Constantinople did not surrender voluntarily but was taken by force (*cebren*). In this view, Mehmed's protection of the Greeks and their church was one of several instances in which he disregarded the law. By his tolerance, the argument continues, he hoped to prevent the growth of any possible crusading movement on the part of the West. It is perfectly possible that in pursuing a policy of indulgence, Mehmed looked beyond the situation of the moment; it is equally possible that his purpose was to hasten the repopulation of the deserted city at a time when Moslems, despite official encouragement, were showing no great eagerness to move to Istanbul. Quite conceivably his choice of Gennadius, known for his hostility to Rome, was intended to discourage any thoughts of church union, which would surely have been unwelcome to the sultan. There is no doubt that the rights granted the patriarch were very considerable and amounted to the establishment of a Christian state within the state. But it is certain that here Mehmed committed no offense against Islamic law.

First and foremost, the conquest of a Christian state by force of arms did not constitute an obligation to forgo all mercy but only a right to do so, and this right ceased with the end of hostilities, for then the conquered territory became a part of the *dar al-islam*, of Islamic territory. There is nothing in Islamic law to the effect that a right must be exercised. No limit was set to mildness of interpretation. In this connection, the so-called inference by analogy (*kiyas*), one of the basic principles of Islamic law, has a special relevance: the law concerning slaves of Islam is, in practice, one with the law concerning prisoners of war. Because a slave is regarded as a thing, a Moslem may theoretically kill him without reason, but the law explicitly disapproves such conduct. Nor is the principle of *dhimma* (the protection accorded to members of other revealed religions) invalidated by the law of war and spoils. Of course, in matters of jurisprudence, practice often deviated from theory, but this is not peculiar to the Moslem world. It would certainly be a mistake to attribute Mehmed's tolerence to humanitarianism. What impelled him to install Gennadius was cold and calculating *raison d'état*. But in so doing he committed no breach of the *şeriat* (*sharia*), the religious law.

Almost all the other patriarchs during Mehmed's reign were insignificant figures who owed their brief and precarious terms in office either to chance, to intrigue, or to the payment of considerable bribes. From the first, or in any case beginning with Symeon (1472-1475), the Greek patriarch paid to the treasury an annual tribute, or *peşkeş* (*peskession*), varying from 1,000 to 2,000 ducats. In addition, anyone who wished to become patriarch was obliged to make the customary gift of not less than 500 ducats to influential officials of the Porte. The sultan did not permit the heads of the Church to dispose of their estates as they pleased; the sultan's treasurer (*defterdar*), the convert Iskender Bey, son of George Amirutzes of Trebizond, not only confiscated the entire estate of the patriarch Symeon, who died intestate in 1475, but also sequestered church property to the value of 3,000 ducats. When the new head of the Church chose a nephew of Symeon as his heir, he was dismissed and three monks who had witnessed his will had their noses cut off. Woe to the patriarch who was unable to procure the sums he was called upon to pay: he was subjected to the most degrading humiliations and punishments. As a chronicle of the patriarchate relates, a favorite of Mara, the Serb Raphael, who on the occasion of his investiture had paid 2,000 ducats to the sultan and 500 more to the grandees of the empire, was reduced to wandering about the streets of Istanbul as a beggar with a chain around his neck. He died finally in the prison reserved for unfaithful employees and traitors to the state. The bribes paid by a prospective new patriarch were all-important in influencing the sultan's decision. A chronicle of the patriarchate of Dionysius (1467–1472) relates the circumstances of his nomination. Mara, who supported his candidacy, brought her stepson a silver platter with 2,000 gold coins, and the two held the following dialogue: "What is it, Mother?" the Conqueror asked. "I demand," she replied, "that you choose one of my monks as patriarch. Between the two contestants a third will succeed." "I thank you," replied the sultan; "do what you wish, Mother." In this manner Dionysius of the Morea, the metropolitan of Philippopolis and spiritual adviser to Mara, mounted the patriarch's see in place of Mark Xylokarabes, who was removed from office and sent as archbishop to Ochrida. But fortune did not long smile on Dionysius. His adversaries, who were of course numerous, soon accused him of having been circumcised as a Christian slave; it was only thanks to the intercession of his royal protectress that he was permitted to return to the monastery of Kosinitza at the foot of Mount Pangaios in Macedonia, there to end his days. This fiasco did not deter Mara from continuing to interfere in the elections of the patriarchs. As we have seen, she helped her fellow Serb Raphael to attain the supreme dignity of the Church. But the Greeks detested this patriarch "of foreign language": his miserable end has been related above.

If the inhabitants of the Balkans were fairly secure as far as their physical survival and their faith were concerned, Greeks and Bulgarians, Serbs, Bosnians, and Albanians, proud peoples with a long and glorious past, were now condemned to an existence without history. The brilliant deeds of their ancestors lived on only in their tenacious memories and in the heroic poetry that they managed to preserve. The flower of their youth was carried away from them by the "levy of boys" and impressed in the sultan's service. Removed from their home and country, these Christian boys grew up in the service of the serai and the Porte, wholly assimilated by the foreign nation and forgetting the homes to which there was no hope of returning. Under Mehmed the levy of boys (devşirme), introduced or revived by Murad II, took place every five years; it was restricted largely to the European parts of the empire (Bulgaria, Macedonia, Greece, Serbia, Albania, Bosnia and Herzegovina), while the islands and certain cities, e.g. Istanbul and Navplion, were excepted. As soon as the sultan's order went out to collect the tribute in boys, the officer of Janissaries selected for the purpose, followed by a number of "drovers" (*sürücü*), went to the territory assigned him and in each town commanded the eldest (*protoieros*) to bring before him all boys between the ages of ten and fifteen. Those fit for service (totaling, according to the sources, somewhere between 2,000 and 12,000) were carried off to Istanbul and there distributed. Those who were especially handsome, strong, intelligent, or otherwise gifted were assigned to the sultan's palace, where they were educated in special schools or trained to work in the imperial gardens. The rest were farmed out to the pashas and other dignitaries, to landowners or artisans. After a few years, when they had acquired the language, faith, and customs of the Turks, they were reassembled and sent to barracks to learn the use of arms. After completing their training, they were assigned to the Janissaries. The cream of those who had been raised in the serai were transferred to court as pages and trained for the personal service of the sultan or for high court offices. Once graduated from the palace, they were employed in the administration, and their ranks provided countless viziers and dignitaries of the Ottoman Empire. Apart from the Çandarlizadeler, the old Ottoman family of viziers, there was no high-ranking state official or general from the time of Mehmed II until well into the sixteenth century who did not owe his career to the human tithe. All served to bring fresh blood into the Ottoman nation. In this way Mehmed as well as his immediate successors were able to compensate for the enormous loss of life resulting from their incessant campaigns. It was above all the Janissaries whose ranks were continuously replenished by the levy of boys.[14]

Theirs was probably the hardest lot, for they were subjected to merciless discipline, condemned to celibacy and in general to an almost monastic life, with no hope other than to rise from rank to rank in the service according to their talent and achievement. These impetuous warriors, who constituted the core of the Ottoman army and fought blindly for the cause of Islam, were reluctant to accept native Turks in their ranks. In this connection it should be mentioned that Mehmed sternly forbade foreigners to trade in Moslem slaves in his empire. The Venetians, for example, were not allowed to transport Moslem slaves through any part of his territory, passage being granted only to dealers in Christian slaves. These provisions seriously hampered the lucrative slave trade, and as early as 1459 bitter complaints were heard in the Venetian senate about the scarcity of slaves.

[14] For the training of boys in the serai: Barnette Miller, *The Palace School of Muhammad the Conqueror* (Cambridge, 1941; reprinted 1973).

The drastic concentration of all power was the principal aim of Ottoman policy in the Conqueror's day. This was accomplished largely through the administrative apparatus, which Mehmed consolidated in the course of his reign by introducing various civil and political institutions probably derived from the Byzantine heritage and by rigorously defining the duties, privileges, and emoluments of the different ranks in the administrative hierarchy.

It has rightly been pointed out that the entire protocol was originally based on memories of the old nomadic days. For a long time, for example, the sultan presided over the *divan*, the assembly of the grandees of the empire, and it was only toward the end of his reign that he delegated this function to his grand vizier. The four branches of the administration were known as the "four pillars of the empire" after the four posts that supported the emir's tent. In the fundamental law of the empire (*ḳanun-name*) compiled around 1477 on the sultan's order by Leys-zade Mehmed ibn Mustafa, secretary for the signature (*nişancî*), the ranks of the high dignitaries (*ayan-i devlet*) and of the supports of the empire (*erkân-i devlet*) were established. In the same codex the various state functions and usages and finally the emoluments and penalties connected with every office are exactly defined. The true director of all government affairs, in secular matters the sultan's unlimited plenipotentiary and representative —that is, the vizier to whom all branches of the government administration are subordinate—is the grand vizier. He is the holder of the imperial seal and entitled to display five horsetails, unquestionably a holdover from the nomadic days of this nation of horsemen. Like the three other viziers, he received a wage of 2,600,000 aspers. The "second pillar" is the army judge (*ḳazasḳer*), who had the power to give ultimate decisions in all legal matters and whose prerogatives included the appointment of city and provincial judges and of priests. Originally, there was only one army judge; then, toward the end of his reign, Mehmed instituted separate judges for Rumelia and Anatolia. Their annual wage was 600,000 aspers. The "third pillar" is the chief bookkeeper of the chamber of accounts, or treasurer (*defterdar*), who enjoyed a favored position as the highest financial and fiscal authority of the realm. Under Mehmed there was one such treasurer, mainly concerned with Rumelia. A second *defterdar* for Anatolia was added by Bayezid II. Each drew an annual wage of 600,000 aspers, but in addition received gifts and favors of all kinds. Lastly, the chief official of the state secretariat (*nişancî*), the "fourth pillar," issued the sultan's commands and drew his stylized signature (*tuğra, nişan*) on all decrees. His annual income amounted to 400,000 aspers. These "four pillars" occupied the foremost places in the crown council (*divan*). To the right of the grand vizier sat the other viziers, to his left the two army judges, below the latter, at a right angle the treasurers, and opposite them, below the viziers, the secretaries for the signature.[15]

Both at court and among the officials there developed a ceremonial, undoubtedly deriving from Byzantine models and defined in every point by Mehmed II. The office and rank of each official could be recognized by the color of his dress, including the lining, the cut of the sleeves, and fur trimming, and above all by the shape of his turban (from *tülbent*) and the cut of his beard. The costumes differed summer and winter. In the cold season they were richly trimmed with fur. Special importance was attached to the headdress, which in the Orient was regarded as the characteristic emblem of the Moslem. Mehmed wore a round, white, spiral-shaped turban, embroidered with gold, over a cap (*taç*) similar to a scholar's cap (*mücevvese*), and it is thus that he is shown in all his portraits.

A dignitary could be recognized from far off by the color of his dress. The mufti, for example, wore white, the viziers green, the chamberlains scarlet, the *ülema* purple, the mullahs light blue. Dark green was reserved for the master of the horse (*imrahor*). The shoes, too, varied in color. The officials of the Porte wore yellow shoes, the court officials light red ones.

The turban was and has always been restricted to Moslems; non-Moslem subjects wore a cap, which in the case of Franks and Greeks could be red, black, or yellow. Under Mehmed II their footgear was probably also distinguished from that of Moslems. Greeks, Armenians, and Jews wore black, violet, and blue slippers or shoes.

The sultan's household consisted of the outer and the inner services. The outer service included all those offices catering to the person of the

---

[15] For a discussion of the Ottoman *kanun–names*, see F. Kraelitz-Greifenhorst, "Kānūnnāme Sultan Mehmeds des Eroberers," *Mitteilungen zur osmanischen Geschichte* 1 (1921–22), 13–48. Babinger published the text of the *kanun–name* in facsimile, together with an introduction, in *Sultanische Urkunden zur Geschichte der Osmanischen Wirtschaft und Staatsverwaltung am Ausgang der Herrschaft Mehmeds II., des Eroberers. I. Teil: Das Qānūn-nāme-i sultānī ber müdscheb-i 'örf-i 'osmānī* (= *Südosteuropäische Arbeiten* 59; Munich, 1956). For a transcription of the text, see Robert Anhegger and Halil Inalcïk, *Kānūnnāme-i sultānī ber müceb-i 'örf-i 'osmānī* (Ankara, 1956; as *TTK*: XI. seri, no. 5). More recently, cf. Nicoara Beldiceanu (ed.), *Code de lois coutumières de Mehmed II: Kitāb-i qavānīn-i 'örfiyye-i 'osmānī* (Wiesbaden, 1967). For the latter consult also the review of V. L. Ménage in *Bulletin of the School of Oriental and African Studies* (London), 32 (1969), 165–167. The regulations of secular criminal law (*kanun*) and their rela-

sultan; the inner service comprised the women's quarters, the "house of felicity" (*dar-i saadet*), whose precinct began at the third gate of the serai.

The head of the outside service was the chief of the white eunuchs (*ḳapu ağasï* = agha of the gate). He was the majordomo, master over the pages and the entire household, and in addition controlled numerous pious foundations, from the administration of which he drew considerable profit. He was the intermediary between the sultan and the outside world; no visitor had access to the sultan without his consent. He lived permanently in the serai. The entire household in his charge consisted of 340 persons, all of Christian origin, who had been kidnapped in the course of campaigns and raids. The boys employed at court were never more than eighteen years of age. They were educated by two experienced teachers, who taught them to read and write and instructed them in manners and customs. The service personnel included butlers, druggists, gardeners, bakers, launderers, cooks, and so on, whose wages were precisely fixed.

The inner service was directed by the agha of the girls and women, the chief of the black eunuchs (*ḳizlar ağasï*). All the women servants in the inner serai worked under him. He was also administrator of the mosques. During the day he could leave the palace for three to four hours, but he had to spend the night there. He had another twenty eunuchs under his orders. In Mehmed's time there were some 300 women and girls in the serai, all without exception of Christian origin. Each drew four *aḳçe* a day. The *ḳizlar ağasï* scarcely ever left the sultan's presence and enjoyed his special confidence.

The use of eunuchs at the Byzantine court is an established fact and their employment at the sultan's court has repeatedly been traced back to this model. But despite opinions to the contrary (Alfred von Kremer, for example), it seems likely that the Byzantines themselves had taken over an Oriental institution. The eunuchs were all imported from Christian countries, for Islam strictly prohibits the emasculation of any living creature. In the old Ottoman Empire many of the harem guards came from Ethiopia, Syria, Georgia, and so on. The trade in eunuchs and the slave market in general was largely in Jewish hands under Mehmed the Conqueror. But it had long been flourishing, ever since the Umayyad period of the caliphate, when Verdun, in Carolingian times, was one of its main centers.

Mehmed's *ḳanun-name* regulated not only the succession to the throne

---

tion to the religious law are discussed by Uriel Heyd, "*Ḳānūn* and *Sharī'a* in Old Ottoman Criminal Justice," *Proceedings of the Israel Academy of Sciences and Humanities* III (1969), 1–18. A posthumous publication by the same author is *Studies in Old Ottoman Criminal Law*, ed. V. L. Ménage (Oxford, 1973).

but also the etiquette of the sultan's table, which the Conqueror had modified, and that of the *divan*. Whereas his forebears had dined with the viziers, he wished to eat with no one except for persons of "imperial blood." Only the first treasurer (*baş defterdar*) was permitted to dine with the grand vizier. The other treasurers and the secretary for the signature sat at the table of the other viziers. The two army judges had to eat alone at a third table. There was even an express regulation prescribing what was to be done with the leavings from the various *divan* tables.

The sultan gave public audience on four successive days from Saturday to Tuesday. The order of reception was regulated by the *divan bey* in his quality of chief pursuivant (*çavuş başi*). On the other days the army judge was admitted first to audience and reported to the sultan on the affairs of his office. As we have seen, the post of army judge was divided only in the last year of Mehmed's reign. When this dignitary had departed, the four viziers and the treasurer appeared. The treasurer acquitted himself of his duties first; when he had received his orders, he made way for the viziers, who remained alone with the sultan to discuss secrets of state.

The complex organization of the court personnel is described in detail by Gian-Maria Angiolello. Here we cannot discuss it at length, but it will be worth our while to say a few words more about certain categories which are mentioned most frequently in the chronicles. A special role was played by the so-called *müteferrika*, or supply personnel, a body of some 200 persons of the most diverse origins and professions. Sons of subjugated ruling families were sometimes assigned to this group and not a few of them were favored with the sultan's company. We have already mentioned Sigismund, the half brother of the last king of Bosnia, who became a Moslem under the name of Kïraloğlu (son of the king) Ishak Bey; because of his wit, he was often called upon to entertain the Conqueror at table and seems to have enjoyed his special favor. The *müteferrika* included physicians, "philosophers," astrologers, soothsayers of various kinds, artists, engineers, painters, jewelers, and goldsmiths. They received daily remuneration of from 20 to 400 aspers, according to their rank and importance. Some even received gifts of lands comprising one or two villages. When the sultan left on a campaign, they rode ahead of him at some distance.

The gatekeepers (*kapuci*) also enjoyed special consideration. They were divided into two troops, each of 200 men. When the *divan* met, their two chiefs (*kapuci başi*), each bearing a staff, stood at the gate to the council room, announced the dignitaries as they arrived, and obtained

443

the sultan's permission to admit them. The gatekeepers held watch day and night at the gates of the palace.

No less important were the *çavuş*, who formed a separate body. On audience days their chief stood with staff in hand before the viziers; his duty was to meet and escort each person announced. His daily wage was sixty aspers. Under him were ten corporals, each of whom received twenty-five aspers; the rest, some thirty men, got fifteen to twenty aspers daily. When the sultan went to war, the *çavuş* had to cry out a few words in his praise every time he mounted his horse. Some writers have seen a connection between this cry of blessing (*alḳiş*), *Allah ömerler vere efendimize!* (God give our lord [long] life), to which the viziers were also entitled, and the Byzantine *polychronizein* (wishing of long life), but the relation is by no means certain.

In addition to the court *çavuş*, there were many other civil and military *çavuş*, who had nothing in common with the court officials. Their duty consisted in the performance of important missions for the sultan. We have already mentioned that they periodically visited the lands of the *reaya*. They were also the custodians of the seed. Above all, they carried messages to foreign chiefs of state. Under Mehmed II, as in earlier times, no ambassadors were sent to Christian governments, but only *çavuş* or an occasional chamberlain (*ḳapucĭ başĭ*). A certain importance also attached to the tasters (*çeşnegir*), who were twelve in number. On audience days when the sultan dined in public, they waited on his table. They served the viziers, army judges, and treasurers when they dined at court.

Since the organization of the army is closely connected with that of the Ottoman Empire, it will be well to devote a few words to it. According to Moslem law, the world is divided into war territory (*dar al-harb*) and territory under Moslem rule (*dar al-islam*). "War territory" comprised all non-Moslem countries whose subjection was ordained by the Koran, in other words, the Moslem's theater of war. Theoretically, the Mohammedan state was permanently at war with the entire non-Moslem world; its foremost aim was to wage holy war (*cihad*) and transform the non-Moslem world into Moslem territory. This view put the state under obligation to organize its Moslem population on a war footing and to develop its army to the utmost. Accordingly, military needs determined the regional divisions of the Ottoman Empire, which in many respects resembled the *provinciae* of Republican Rome. The function of the Ottoman regional governors has rightly been likened to that of the satraps in the late Persian Empire or of the Roman proconsuls.

The two parts (*eyalet*) of the empire, Anatolia and Rumelia, were ruled over by governors (*beylerbeyi*) with two horsetails. To these were subordinated the banner-holders (*sancak beyi*) with one horsetail, each of whom commanded a *sancak* (banner). A *sancak* in turn broke down into several *kılıç* (sabers). In the Conqueror's day the empire had forty-eight *sancaks*. Twenty of these were in Asia: Trebizond, Amasya, Sinop, Kastamonu, Iznik, Kayseri, Niğde, Karaman, Konya, Antalya, Teke, Ankara, Kütahya, Menteşe, Aydïn, Saruhan, Mytilini, Biga, Izmit, and Bursa; twenty-eight were in Europe ("Grecia"): Istanbul, Vize, Malkara, Silistria, Kaffa, Vidin, Nikopol, Smederevo, Bosnia, Herzegovina, Shkodër, Vlorë, Karaferia, Arta, Levkas, Angelokastron, Morea, Athens, Ochri, Tirhala, Negropont (Eğriboz), Thessaloniki, Gümülcine, Skoplje, Sofia, Philippopolis, Edirne, and Gelibolu. The banner-holders led the armed forces of their districts, commanded the police, provided for public safety and for the regular collection of taxes.

The number of *sancaks* began to increase under Bayezid II. Felix Petancius (Petančić), probably of Šibenik, who was well acquainted with Ottoman affairs at the time and long an adviser of King Matthias Corvinus and his successor Ladislas II (1490–1516) at the court in Buda, speaks in his informative little book on Turkish military power (published by Konrad Adelmann von Adelmannsfelden, the Augsburg canon and humanist) and in his hitherto unpublished "Genealogia Imperatorum Turcorum" of twenty-five Rumelian *sancaks* with 4,500 fiefs (*timar*) and 22,500 armed men (*loricati*; Turkish *cebeli*) and of thirty-six Anatolian *sancaks* with 5,500 fiefs and 37,500 "armor-bearing men," or a total of 10,000 fiefs and 60,000 *sipahi* (and not, as Petancius reckons, only 50,000).[16] All these figures, to be sure, give an impression of being rounded out. After Bayezid II the number of *sancaks* continued to grow, so that at the time of its greatest extension under Süleyman the Magnificent, the Ottoman Empire numbered no less than 250; at that time there were twenty-five governors.

This strict organization, thanks to which the empire was excellently defended within and without and always in readiness for new conquests, was closely connected with the feudal system which had been steadily perfected since the days of Osman, the founder of the dynasty. As we have seen (pp. 332f.), Mehmed set forth new regulations covering the conferring of fiefs.

Each *sancak* was divided into a certain number of large and small fiefs (*ziamet* and *timar*), the latter providing an annual income of 20,000 aspers or less. The *sipahis*, the native Turkish horsemen, who with the Janissaries provided the striking power of the Ottoman army, were

[16] For two published works of Petancius (Felice Petanzio) see Carl Göllner, *Turcica* (Berlin, 1961), 97 and 319.

appointed feudatories by imperial decree. They received newly conquered territories in fief with the right to exercise jurisdiction over the peasants inhabiting it, most of whom were bound to the soil, and to take for themselves all or a part of the taxes levied. Those who had owned the land before the conquest forfeited their property rights to the state, but were left in actual possession of the land, which they were now obliged to cultivate for the benefit of the new Ottoman feudatories, to whom they delivered a part of their yield (from one-third to one-fifth). Apart from the *sipahis*, land could legally be conferred only on a few high officials immune to military service. This land consisted of particular domains (*hass*) belonging to the Porte. As a rule, these domains, upward of a specified size, were connected with a particular office and not, like other fiefs, with the person of the feudatory.

The chief obligation of a *sipahi* was to take up residence on his fief and to be prepared at all times to rally, armed for battle, to his banner-holder's flag on the sultan's order. According to the income of his fief, every *sipahi* had to raise a fixed number of armed horsemen (*cebeli*), who followed him on campaigns. A feudatory with an income of 3,000 aspers had to provide the Porte with one horseman and an additional horseman for every additional 5,000 aspers. It was reckoned that a large fief could provide fifteen horsemen and a small one at least two. Neglect of these obligations was punished by temporary or permanent loss of the fief. To gather an army the sultan had only to send out an order to the governors, who passed it on to their *sancak beys*, who in turn transmitted it to their feudatories.[17]

These fiefs were not hereditary as in the West; thus, the institution could not give rise to a hereditary nobility dangerous to the sultan. When a feudatory died, his son or brother was occasionally favored for his succession, but the fief was first taken back by the state. Thus, even if in practice the fief was subsequently made over to his son, the law recognized no hereditary right of succession. As a rule, the sons even of large feudatories received only small fiefs with incomes of 5,000 aspers or less

---

[17] For additional details on the provincial administration, see Inalcïk, *The Ottoman Empire, The Classical Age 1300–1600*, 104–118. Cf. Gibb and Bowen, I, part 1, 137ff. Archival documents detailing land holdings under the Ottoman administration have received increasing attention in recent years. See, for example, the series of texts published by the Oriental Institute of Sarajevo as *Monumenta turcica. Historiam slavorum meridionalium illustrantia*. The most recent (1972), *Oblast Brankovića. Opsirni katastarski popis iz 1455. Godine*, 2 vols., ed. H. Hadzibegić et al., contains a facsimile and Serbo-Croatian translation of the register (*defter*) for the province of Vlk from the year 1455, together with an English summary (II, v–xiv).

and had to work themselves up to more considerable possessions by their military achievements.

In accordance perhaps with a traditional custom, Mehmed seems not infrequently to have conferred military fiefs on certain Christian subjects who in his opinion had distinguished themselves. The beneficiaries were probably for the most part petty native noblemen, but also included others who had proved their worth. They became Christian *sipahis*, a strange phenomenon which shows that Mehmed set political expedience as he understood it above all other considerations. It is completely in keeping with his freethinking and autocratic ways that he should have offended quite openly against the principles of the religious law when the circumstances seemed to warrant it. Especially in chronically insecure territories such as Albania and Serbia, the number of Christian *sipahis* seems to have been not inconsiderable, though obviously it cannot have exceeded that of their Moslem counterparts. The sultan's distrust of the possessors of latifundia (*mülk*) and of the beneficiaries of the pious foundations (*vakif*, plural: *evkaf*; *wakf*), i.e. the clergy, may have contributed to this state of affairs.[18] In order to check the power and influence of these groups, Mehmed always did his best to transform *mülk* and *vakif* holdings into military fiefs, which at least in the case of *vakif* was a gross infringement of Islamic law. It is not without significance that the *sipahis* had not only to provide military contingents but also to collect the head tax in their territories.[19]

This military aristocracy of the Ottoman Empire was complemented in wartime by irregular mounted troops, provided by the less well-to-do masses of the people. These included the so-called raiders, or *akincis*, command of whom was hereditary in the Mihaloğlu family. They lived from the spoils of their raids, and their name, as we have seen, aroused terror far and wide, even in distant Austria.

The *azaps* were another irregular militia. They formed a part of the group which in wartime was exempted (*müsellem*) from taxes. This

[18] For the Christian *timar* holders see Inalcïk, "Stefan Duşan'dan osmanlï imperatorluğuna," in *Fuad Köprülü Armagani*, ed. Osman Turan et al. (Istanbul, 1953), 207–248; revised version in Inalcïk's *Fatih Devri*, 137–184.

[19] Mehmed's conversion of the legal status of land holdings is dealt with by Nicoara Beldiceanu, "Recherches sur la réforme foncière de Mehmed II," *Acta Historica* (4 (1965) (*Societas Academica Dacoromana*), 27–39. And see further below, p. 453. Muhammed Ahmed Simsar gives an English translation of an Ottoman Turkish deed of foundation (*vakfiye*) from the early 16th century in *The Waqfiyah of 'Ahmed Pāšā* (Philadelphia, 1940). The founder of the *vakif* in question is the Ahmed Pasha discussed by Babinger above (see p. 262).

provincial militia, whose members did duty as foot soldiers, as builders of earthworks, or as oarsmen, was long a dangerous rival of the Janissaries, with whom they were almost always at loggerheads.

Along with the feudal cavalry, the Janissaries, or "new troops" (*yeni çeri*), constituted the chief force of the army. As we have seen, they were recruited from the levy of boys (*devşirme*). The origins of the corps of Janissaries have not been adequately elucidated. It would seem to have been connected from its inception with the Shiite order of Bektaşi dervishes, but here again our information is incomplete. In both organization and dress the Janissary corps resembled a fraternal organization. The headdress of the Janissaries suggested that of the Bektaşis. Like the latter, they wore a white felt cap, but theirs was adorned with a wooden spoon. The Janissary corps, known as *ocak* (hearth), was under the supreme command of an almost all-powerful agha of Janissaries, who had his own palace and a special chancellery in the capital. In addition, he held the office of police captain, responsible for the maintenance of order in Istanbul. As to the number of Janissaries, a wide range of figures has been given. It is certain, however, that under Murad II they did not exceed 3,000 men and that under Mehmed II the number increased to 5,000 and later (ca. 1472) to 10,000. Toward the end of the Conqueror's reign, they numbered only 8,000.

Joseph von Hammer-Purgstall has quite correctly pointed out that among the Janissaries love of country, home, and family was replaced by religious frenzy, fanatical obedience, and lust for spoils and handsome boys. These substitutes for patriotism brought results "which equaled the greatest deeds of the Roman generals and armies in scope, though not in nobility of motives." Without parents or relatives, alienated from their homes and countries, these native Christians knew no purpose in life other than warfare, no duty other than unconditional obedience to their superiors. Their unity of will made not only the enemy but even their own sultan tremble; on numerous occasions the fate of a ruler, or indeed of an entire dynasty, depended on their whim or on the amount of the gift that a threatened sovereign was constrained to bestow on them. In view of their relatively small numbers, the influence they wielded, especially between reigns and in other political crises, seems amazing. As the only regular troops in the capital, against which no other force could be mustered, or at least not quickly, the Janissaries often abused their inordinate power. Under Mehmed II their pay was no more than three to five aspers a day. In addition, to be sure, they were each year allotted by law five ells of blue cloth, thirty-two aspers for collars, fifty ells of linen for their turbans, a woolen caftan, a shirt made to measure, and thirty aspers for bow and arrows. Other rewards were ordered from time to time by the sultan.

On campaign each squad of ten was commanded by a corporal and had its own packhorse, tent, and treasury. The orderliness of their camp was famous. Morally, they were assuredly superior to all their adversaries. Swearing and quarreling were strictly forbidden, and extreme cleanliness was one of their duties. Their faith not only imposed the usual ablutions but also kept them sober, for wine and spirits were forbidden. Gambling was unknown to them, and they had no truck with harlots. They were well fed, for the sultan attached the utmost importance to the supply of food and ammunition. Their officers took their titles from the departments of the kitchen, e.g. "head of the kitchen" (*asçi başi*), "head of the soup cooks" (*çorbaci başi*). The most important possession of the entire troop was the kettle (*kazan*), around which they gathered at council meetings as well as meals. To overturn the kettle was the signal for mutiny.

Mehmed was probably the first Ottoman ruler to take a special interest in artillery. We have spoken repeatedly of the foreign cannon founders who entered his service. The effectiveness of their work first became apparent at the siege of Constantinople and was a characteristic feature of all his subsequent battles. Most of his cannon founders were probably Germans or Transylvanians. The names of only a few have come down to us, but there can be no doubt that the sultan made use of foreign artillery specialists throughout his reign.

Foreign influence can also be presumed to have been at work in the attempts to develop his war fleet. In the space of a few years, Mehmed expanded his navy considerably, but it seems that he never regarded it as a striking force of its own. Its field of action eventually extended to the coasts of Italy. And so great a sea power as Venice certainly lived in fear of the Turkish fleet.

The approximate strength of the Conqueror's navy is known to us thanks to the Genoese Jacopo de Promontorio, though his figures probably apply only to the last years of the Conqueror's reign (ca. 1475). According to Don Jacopo, who was well informed in naval matters, the Ottoman fleet consisted at that time of roughly 500 large vessels, including numerous galleys. In the conquest of Kaffa (1475) some 380 ships were employed, 120 of them being galleys. This figure, however, includes all the Greek galleons which the sultan impressed into the undertaking against the will of their owners, who received no payment. The Genoese chronicler characterizes the Ottoman galleys as "unfit for naval warfare" and adds that "four such galleys manned by such incompetent sailors are not worth one of ours." The sultan used them only to transport his troops

449

to the places he wished to conquer. Although Turkey possessed "fine large forests well suited to ship building," Mehmed did not, according to Don Jacopo, attach special importance to the development of the fleet. The Genoese attributes this reluctance to the alarming lack of reliable sailors. In "all Turkey and Greece"—i.e. Anatolia and Rumelia—there were no more than 2,000 families (*case*) of Turks (an obvious *lapsus calami* in the manuscript) and rarely did one of these have more than one son. By Turks he means only those "born of a Turkish father and mother." All the rest, according to him, are mixed and descended from Christian converts. He attributes the sparseness of this genuinely Turkish population to the "infinite lechery of various slaves and young boys to whom they give themselves." About 1475 all the sultan's armies (*il suo preforzo*) numbered, still according to Don Jacopo, no more than 76,000 men, to which, "in a dire emergency," could be added another 20,000 men unfit for combat. This would account for the lack of able seamen and the sultan's aversion to sea warfare. And indeed not a single naval battle of any importance can be cited in the thirty years of Mehmed's reign. "The truth," says Don Jacopo, "is that he always shuns naval warfare."

From these observations Jacopo de Promontorio draws obvious conclusions in regard to the struggle against the prime enemy of Christianity. "If," he writes, "his innumerable Christian subjects were only to see some greathearted lord or captain sent to those parts, they would immediately take up arms to throw off their servitude and would drive the sultan from all Greece and adjoining provinces; these Christians are truly the shrewdest and most warlike people in those countries. And the truth of the matter is that he never takes them with him when he goes on campaign, because he distrusts them and fears the smallest incident."

One is inclined to agree with Don Jacopo that the Western naval powers would have had the best chance of defeating the Conqueror; their combined fleets were more than a match for the ineffectual Ottoman navy.

Thus far, no one has been able to investigate the state finances of the Conqueror's empire, because only the barest fragments of the requisite documents have come down to us. In any event, it would be nearly impossible to arrive at a reliable figure for government receipts, because the constant acquisition of new territories must have produced continuous fluctuations during the three decades of the Conqueror's reign. Since native Turks as well as converts paid no taxes of any kind—all the state demanded of them was a tenth of their property in case war should be carried to their own district—the state derived its chief income from the head tax of the *reaya*, from the lease of crown lands and mines, from harbor duties, state monopolies, and so on.

The head of every family among the *reaya* had to contribute one ducat (ca. forty aspers). Altogether this yielded a sum of roughly 900,000 ducats. A Venetian catalogue drawn up in 1470 after a Turkish original lists in Europe 29,000 households of Christians and Jews subject to the head tax; half a century later we find three million taxpayers in the entire empire. If a town on the seacoast, in a mountain pass, or in a forest was of importance for the safeguard of the European borders, its inhabitants (known as *voynuk*), chiefly Bulgarians, were exempted from all taxes. Their obligation was limited to the guarding of passes, the care of forests, the maintenance of roads, and similar activities contributing to the welfare of the state. In case of war they had to serve the *sipahis* as laborers, drivers, or stablemen, in return for which they received regular maintenance.

The tithe payable on beasts of burden of all kinds—horses, oxen, mules, and so on—brought in no less than 300,000 ducats a year. The grain tithe also yielded considerable sums. Rice plantations were taxed and even beehives.

As numerous documents show, all occupations and economic activities were subject to a strict monopoly and rigid regulations suggesting the authoritarian regimes of modern times. The state, that is, the sultan, attached special importance to such commodities as salt, sesame, and particularly rice, the growing of which had been a Moslem prerogative ever since the conquest of the Balkans. Economic offenses were covered by an elaborate body of ordinances and subject to heavy punishment. In addition to penalties ranging from flogging to mutilation and capital punishment, much use was made of the *teşhir*, exposure to public ridicule. The offender was paraded through the streets in a humiliating way before being subjected to the appointed punishment. The regulations on the subject fully reflect the sultan's cruel nature. We read of offenders being led by a cord passed through their noses, made to sit backward on a horse or ass, having their heads shorn or beards cut off, being smeared with soot, and so forth.

One of the chief sources of government income was the system of farming-out (*mukataa*) which attained its full development under Mehmed II. The name applies to three types of lease: the leasing of state-owned enterprises and installations, the farming-out of the collection of taxes, customs duties, and anchorage and weighing fees, and the concession of monopolies. In certain regions private persons could acquire, in return for payment of a fixed and presumably large sum, the right to levy taxes, to exploit every conceivable resource of the soil, and to operate state enterprises for their own account. Unfortunately, we have not too much information about the amounts involved in these leases; what we do know derives from the occasional observations of contemporary chroniclers.

Chalcocondylas tells us, for example, that the Danube fords were leased out every year for many thousands of ducats and that the lessee, usually a Greek, was able to make a good profit in spite of the high rent. The Rumelian saltworks on the coast, Anchialus and above all Enez, brought in 90,000 ducats. The lessees of the salt flats of Enez were for the most part Jews. The harbor duties of Istanbul and Gelibolu were evaluated at 42,000 ducats in 1470. The receipts from the piers of Gelibolu and Galata were leased early in January 1476 to several Greeks, among them Andreas Chalcocondylas, Manuel Palaeologus, and another Palaeologus. In the fall of 1468 a number of mines were leased to Yani Palaeologus and Thomas Cantacuzenus. The head and prisoner taxes (*ispence, pençik*) of the mines of Kratovo in Serbia and Siderokapsa in Thessaly were farmed out to two other members of the Cantacuzenus family, Yani, a close relative of Catherine of Cilli, and Yorgi, and their partner, one Nikola "Danjo-vil" (?), but in September or October 1476 all three with their whole families were executed in Istanbul on the sultan's orders and were buried in Galata.[20]

The customs duties of Edirne, Philippopolis, Sofia, Aidos, and Thessaloniki netted the state treasury 90,000 ducats. Anatolian leases mentioned are those of Kastamonu (10,000 ducats), of Bursa and the Hudavendigâr mountain passes (16,000), and others amounting to 29,000 ducats. Chalcocondylas estimates the proceeds of the leases on the Istanbul lighthouse and fords at 200,000 florins. The famous alum mines of Anatolia yielded 50,000 ducats a year, the iron mines of Kastamonu and Sinop the same amount. The total state receipts from the lease of mines have been estimated at 200,000 ducats, half of which must have come from the Rumelian mines, especially Novo Brdo and Srebrnica (Serbia).[21]

The seemingly reliable Jacopo de Promontorio provides additional information for the time around 1475. In that year state receipts from the lease of mines amounted to only 120,000 ducats; the leases ran for three years and the lessees took in 360,000 ducats annually. The same observer eval-

---

[20] For the head tax on non-Moslems see "Ispendje" (H. Inalčik), *EI²* IV, 211.

[21] For these figures see N. Iorga, *Geschichte des Osmanischen Reiches* II (Gotha, 1909), 216–217. Cf. N. Beldiceanu, *Les Actes des premiers sultans* I: *Actes de Mehmed II et de Bayezid II du ms. fonds turc ancien 39* (= *Documents et Recherches* III, ed. P. Lemerle; Paris, 1960), 113.

uates the tithe on the silver mined at 120,000 ducats a year. The monopoly ("comerchio," i.e. Latin *commercium*, modern Greek, *koumerki*, whence Turkish *gümrük*) of the duties and royalties of the Morea over a three-year period brought in 31,500 ducats. The lease of Vlorë, along with the fishing rights, amounted to 445,000 ducats and the Negropont monopoly, including all duties (*gabelle*) and the head tax, to 12,500 ducats a year. For other leases Promontorio gives the following figures (in ducats), each for a three-year period: the leases for Edirne, including transit taxes on slaves and city taxes: 36,500; the imperial bathing establishments in all "Greece" and adjoining territories: 27,000; the rice tax of Philippopolis, Zagora, Serrai, and other localities in "Greece" and adjoining territories: 45,000; the pasturage tax in the entire empire: 30,000; the salt-panning fees in all "Greece" and adjoining territories: 276,000; the mints for silver aspers, for the most part leased to Venetians: 360,000. Gold ducats "with Venetian imprint" yielded 3,000 ducats a year, while the Gypsy monopoly (*comerchio di cingali*) brought its beneficiary 9,000 gold pieces a year.

Weighing fees must have brought in considerable receipts. At the end of 1478 the state treasury demanded 1,926,000 aspers which a certain Muslihuddin had collected in weighing fees in Istanbul, Bursa, Amasya, Tokat, and Kastamonu. The following spring (March 14, 1479) the sultan issued a decree to the effect that Prince Bayezid's income should no longer be derived from weighing fees, but that certain small fiefs (*timar*) should be made over to him instead. The soap monopoly seems also to have been profitable. On July 14, 1479, the right to produce and sell soap was conferred on an Italian named Antonio Uberto (Oberto), but he was enjoined from selling cakes weighing less than 200 *dirhem* (approximately 1 lb. 6 oz.). This shows that foreigners were also permitted to lease business rights.[22]

The farming-out system had disastrous social consequences. The administration and collection of the sums owed the state were in the hands of a commissioner (*emin*). In some cases the commissioner could transfer to his own account the *mukataa* he was administering for the state. In return, of course, he was obligated to make corresponding payments in money or produce. The leasing of the rights inherent in a *mukataa*, or even of a part of them, was called *iltizam*, the lessee *multezim*. As a rule

[22] For the documents referred to here, see Halil Inalcïk, "Bursa şer'iye sicillerinde Fatih Sultan Mehmed'in fermanlari," *Belleten* 11 (1947), 698–700 (documents 4, 5, and 9), together with summary German translation (704–705). Cf. Marie Magdeleine Lefebvre, "Quinze firmans du Sultan Mehmed le Conquérant," *Revue des études islamiques* 39 (1971), 152, 159, and 160–161, for annotated French translations.

a lease ran for three years, but often it was conferred for life in return for a specified payment; then the lease was called *malikane*.

The drawbacks of such an institution are obvious. We need only consider the West: before the outbreak of the French Revolution, for example, a similar system aroused deep-seated dissatisfaction among the people. For the conduct of his incessant wars Mehmed required enormous sums of money, which could be raised only in part by tribute, head taxes, debasement of the coinage, and so on. If they wished to raise the enormous sums required of them and at the same time to make a satisfactory profit, the tax farmers selected by the Porte were obliged to gouge the population mercilessly. Similarly, in order to make the required payments to the state and also to realize a profit, the lessees of state enterprises had to drive those who worked for them beyond endurance. The consequence was that even at the times of the greatest Ottoman power, the Turkish provinces never achieved anything like Western prosperity. No attempt was made to husband human or natural resources. Wasteful farming methods exhausted the soil and consumed what little the tax collectors left.

The Ottoman Empire had seen mutinies and uprisings since its earliest days. The chroniclers merely mention them but say nothing of the causes, which must have been economic. Unfortunately, the meagerness of the sources thus far available makes it impossible to establish definite ties between such rebellions and abuses in the feudal system or the system of leases. But incidents such as those which took place in the capital immediately after the Conqueror's death and culminated in the pillaging of foreign emporia and storehouses were undoubtedly rooted in abuses of this kind. Karamani Mehmed Pasha, the Conqueror's last grand vizier, had infuriated the populace with his fiscal policy toward ground tenants and especially the clergy, who compensated for the reduction in their receipts from pious foundations (*vakif*) and other sources by devising new ways of exploiting the common people. It was no accident that Yakub Pasha (Maestro Iacopo) appears to have fallen victim to the popular fury. The obvious preference which he accorded over a period of years to his coreligionaries in the conferring of lucrative concessions led such independent critics as the dervish Aşikpaşazade to make caustic remarks about his activity and that of the Jews in Turkey. Similarly, all the chroniclers, even those attached to the court, concurred in condemning the executed grand vizier Rum Mehmed Pasha for having favored his Greek compatriots in the same way. What makes this all the more striking is that normally the official historians made no mention of such matters, but merely registered the sultan's acts, the worthy and unworthy deeds of great and small, marriages, fires, earthquakes, and epidemics, all with the

454

same equanimity: without praise or blame, and above all without proffering any opinion of their own. For at the Ottoman court, as earlier in Byzantium and at Oriental courts in general, no one other than the sovereign was entitled to a personal opinion. It was a very different matter, of course, with the handful of unofficial, for the most part anonymous, chroniclers or with Aşìkpaşazade, whose chronicle must have been designed chiefly for reading to members of the order and to the common people. Thus, there is nothing so surprising about the extraordinary frankness with which this writer speaks of certain events that redounded to the harm of the common people and so aroused his anger.

Apart from the head tax, the state treasury derived considerable sums from the tributes paid by Walachia, Moldavia, the Republic of Ragusa, and the island of Chios. A Venetian survey of the receipts of the Ottoman state lists the following sums in the column devoted to the head tax of the vassal countries: Bosnia and Herzegovina, 18,000 ducats; Walachia, 17,000; Moldavia, 6,000; Trebizond, 3,000; Kaffa, 3,000; Amasra and Sinop, 14,000. The tribute paid by the Venetian possessions in the Morea and in Albania is not included.

Chalcocondylas estimates the total state receipts at 4,000,000 ducats, which seems impossible. The figure put forward by the Venetians is only 1,196,000, or less than a third of the Byzantine chronicler's estimate. Cardinal Bessarion held that the sultan collected at most 2,000,000 ducats a year.

The sultan in person received a fifth of all war booty of every kind. In the Moslem view, this portion belonged originally to God (Koran, VIII, 42), but was later accorded to the *imam*, the temporal head of the community, who was to use it "in Allah's name" for state purposes, to the best of his judgment. The higher dignitaries had allegedly to contribute 200,000 ducats whenever Mehmed II undertook a campaign.

State expenditures were modest and do not seem to have amounted to more than 810,000 ducats a year. Of this sum the army alone claimed 300,000. The annual distribution of cloth and of cash for bows and arrows to the Janissaries required 28,000. Not included in this sum is the pay of the Janissaries, which, as in the Byzantine Empire, was usually paid quarterly in advance.

The sultan's treasury also had to meet the needs of the palace and the household, which consisted of 1,500 persons, or 5,000 including slaves. Forty-eight thousand ducats went to the gatekeepers, barbers, physicians, shadow players (*karagöz*), 17,000 to the 200 noble youths raised in the palace and their four educators. Considerable sums were spent on the dress of the household (29,000 ducats), silks and gold brocades (50,000), costly stuffs imported from abroad (Florence, 60,000), and on the garments of honor and ceremonial caftans distributed at receptions and at the great and small *bayram* festivals (25,000). Thus, all the funds that poured in were spent exclusively either on the sultan's household or on warfare.[23]

On an earlier page we have spoken of Mehmed's monetary policy. Here we should add that he issued a decree strictly forbidding the exportation of silver, a prohibition which was later extended to lead. His greatgrandfather, Bayezid I, had probably been the first sultan not only to withdraw the old coinage from circulation and debase the new coinage but also to prohibit the exportation of silver. Unquestionably, this measure was motivated far less by the religious law against providing the enemies of Islam with weapons and war material than by the Ottomans' desire to make use of these resources for their own ends. Under Murad II the Ottomans had already shared in the exploitation of the mines of Trepča, which still belonged to Serbia; despite the bitter protests of the injured parties the Turks had succeeded in stopping the flow of silver from there to Ragusa and directing it to their own mints.

In accordance with old custom, Mehmed continued to mint silver coins (*akçe*, aspers) every ten years, but each time he reduced the silver content. The first of his coinages occurred in 855 H. (1451), on the occasion of his second and definitive accession to the throne; the second and third in 865 (1460/61) and 875 (1470/71). After that, the Conqueror modified the interval, for in 880 (1475/76) aspers were again issued, probably because of the increased need for currency during the campaign against Uzun Hasan. The last silver coins to bear the Conqueror's name were minted in 886 (beginning March 2, 1481), the year of his death. On one occasion in 875 (1470/71) a silver ten-*akçe* piece was minted exclusively in Istanbul; and the first and only gold piece issued by the sultan in his name also made its appearance in Istanbul, in 882 (1477/78) with two later reprints. In addition to Istanbul, there were mints in Edirne, Bursa, Skoplje, Tire, Amasya, Ayasoluk, Serrai, and Novo Brdo. Copper coins (*mangĭr*) were issued in large quantities. Here the usual interval was not observed. Thus, in Istanbul *mangĭr* were minted in 867 (1462/63), 875 (1470/71), 878 (1473/74), and 886 (1481); in Edirne in 861 (1456/57) and 875 (1470/71); in Amasya in 859 (1454/55); and in Bursa in 861 (1456/57), 865 (1460/61), 867 (1462/63), and 868 (1463/64). In ancient Tire (Anatolia) silver and copper coins were once minted simultaneously, that is in 886 (1481); otherwise, only copper coins were produced (865). In Ankara and Bolu copper coins were minted without indication of the year; this would seem

[23] Iorga, 220.

to have been an emergency coinage. In Ayasoluk, where ordinarily only aspers were coined, copper coins also were issued in 865 (1460/61). In Serrai and Novo Brdo, where the famous silver mines were situated, no copper coins were minted.

Since the silver content was reduced in each new coinage, the purchasing power of the asper fell continuously. We have seen that at the beginning of Mehmed's first reign such a deterioration in the currency, in which the weight of the asper fell from six to five *kirat*, led to an uprising of the Janissaries in Edirne, who demanded and obtained an increase in pay. Mehmed several times ordered "recalls" (*revocationes, renovationes*) of the coinage such as had been customary in the West since the days of the Carolingians. The forced exchange, designed to increase the state's profit, seems to have been determined much less by any economic principles than by immediate financial stringencies or the needs of warfare. A document from the year 1478 (April 1) gives us a precise picture of such a recall.[24] The old money (*eski akçe*) was abolished. An official endowed with broad powers was sent out to collect the old silver coinage and all privately owned silver. His methods were Draconian. Under orders to deliver all the money he found to the government mint, he was even authorized to search travelers' baggage, cash boxes, and the rooms of lodging houses. From one *dirhem* (roughly one-ninth of an ounce) of silver two new *akçe* were coined. No goldsmith or silver embroiderer was permitted to keep more than 200 *dirhem* (1 lb. 6 oz.) of silver. At such times the so-called *gümüş sarraflari*, or silver changers, were especially feared. They traveled about the country issuing ten new pieces for twelve old ones. They were under obligation to return the old coins to the mint, and infringement of this regulation brought heavy punishment. The office of silver changer was farmed out by the state, and, according to Theodoros Spandugino, brought in some 800,000 ducats. The whole institution, which was hated throughout the country, was abolished by Bayezid II, who ceased to tamper with the silver content of the coinage.

In consequence of such measures, the ratio of the asper to the Western ducat was always changing. In the late Middle Ages the currencies employed in the commerce of southeastern Europe were the Venetian ducat, a high-grade gold coin, the equivalent Florentine gold florin (*fiorino d'oro*), which took its name from the fleur-de-lis (*flos*)—the

---

[24] The document is given by Inalcĭk, "Bursa şer'iye sicillerinde," 697–698 (document 2) together with German summary translation (704). Cf. M. Lefebvre, 150–151. Haiil Sahillioğlu suggests a connection between Janissary unrest and fiscal imbalance in his "*Sivis* Year Crises in the Ottoman Empire" in M. A. Cook (ed.), *Studies in the Economic History of the Middle East* (London, 1970), 230–252.

emblem of the city—on its reverse, and the Hungarian gold gulden, which enjoyed equal standing. The devaluation of the Ottoman asper is clearly reflected in its relation to the ducat. Originally, the ratio was ten to one. In the days of Mehmed a ducat was equivalent to no less than forty and finally fifty aspers, and in the sixteenth century to fifty-four and ultimately eighty. An asper corresponded to one-quarter of an Arabian silver *dirhem* (from Greek *drachme*); since three *dirhem* were equivalent to one *dinar* (from Latin *denarius*), the Arabian gold coin (roughly one-seventh of an ounce of pure gold), twelve aspers were equal to one *dinar*. At the end of the seventeenth century, when the asper was superseded by the *para,* its silver content was only a little more than 1/350th of an ounce. It seems possible that even in Mehmed's lifetime so small and unstable a coin was no longer adequate to its function as the only denomination intermediate between the gold and copper coins and was complemented by the silver coins of Western countries.

The Ottoman copper coinage stood in even worse disrepute than the asper. At one time eight coppers were equivalent to one asper; later, if Spandugino is to be believed, the figure rose to twelve, sixteen, twenty-four, thirty-two, forty, and forty-eight. It appears that in issuing gold coins in 1477–1478 Mehmed took the Italian gold florin as his model and intended to maintain his *sultani* at par with the Western currency. But in trade with the West the Italian gold florin (*efrenk* or *firenk filori,* i.e. Frankish florin) remained the standard currency and Mehmed's gold piece was assuredly limited to the domestic market.

The Turkish and even the foreign sources thus far available to us say nothing about commerce in the Conqueror's empire. That the sultan took special interest in handicrafts, industry, and foreign trade, particularly in his capital, is demonstrated by the wooden market buildings, the so-called *bezistan* (literally, linen market), which he built in 1461 and which were replaced by new buildings, also of wood, during the reign of Süleyman the Magnificent. In 1651 these in turn gave way to stone bazaars. Thus far, we have no knowledge of the craftsmen's guilds, which appear in sixteenth- and especially seventeenth-century accounts. The superintendence over all merchants and artisans, over textiles and especially the food supply of the capital, was exercised by the *Istanbul kadīsi,* the city judge of Istanbul, assisted by a number of subordinate officials, whose duty it was to supervise the weights, measures, and prices of foodstuffs, and the flour, fat, and oil warehouses. The city judge, who tended to be the colonel of a Janissary "chamber" (*oda*), was also in charge of the administration of justice in the capital. He promptly arrested any seller of foodstuffs caught giving false weight or selling adulterated products, and often had him nailed by his ear to the gate. The markets were carefully regulated, and in general the sultan's purview extended to all spheres of human endeavor.

We have seen in the course of this work that disastrous plagues more than once devastated the entire empire and in particular Istanbul. The sultan always sought safety from the Black Death in flight to the Balkan Mountains. We have the impression that nothing was done to combat the dread epidemics and that the population, resigned to the will of Allah, had no recourse other than to wait for them to subside. At that time the absence of public health measures was not limited to the Ottoman Empire. The sultan compensated for the loss of human life, which was usually large, by removing whole populations from the western parts of his empire and resettling them in Istanbul. Now and then, Western reports speak of famine or abrupt rises in prices, which Mehmed, for fear of popular uprisings, was at pains to remedy in all haste. A steady and ample supply of bread was one of his chief concerns.

The state of medical science was assuredly none too brilliant. The physicians were seldom natives but almost exclusively Jews or Persians. With a single exception, the sultan entrusted the care of his own health to non-Turkish physicians. This exception was Necmeddin, known as Altuncuzade. He seems to have been a skillful practitioner, and was said to have been the first physician to make use of catheters. Others among the sultan's private physicians were Şükrullah of Şirvan (Persia), who, however, was more prominent as a court chronicler; the above-mentioned Hamiduddin al-Lari (from Laristan in southwestern Persia), who employed his arts in vain at the sultan's deathbed and himself came to a bad end; and "Arab" of Jerusalem, who before the Conqueror took him into his service had been in the employ of Ishakoğlu Isa Bey, the march warden in Skoplje. Probably more important than he was Kutbeddin Ahmed of Kirman (Persia), who came of a respected family of viziers and perhaps learned medicine from his father, the *hekim-i Kirmani* (physician from Kirman), who was executed by Uzun Hasan. In 1468 or 1469 (873 H.) Kutbeddin drifted to Istanbul, where he died in 1497 or 1498 and was buried in Eyüp. A student of the physician Necmeddin was a certain Akhi Çelebi Mehmed ibn Kemal of Tabriz, who was later reported to have officiated as head physician of the hospital (*darüşşifa*) endowed by Mehmed in Istanbul. A manuscript in ten chapters on kidney stones (*mesane taşlari*) has come down to us from his hand. But by far the strangest and most important figure among the Conqueror's personal

459

physicians was undoubtedly Maestro Iacopo of Gaeta, later Yakub Pasha, though all we know about his medical abilities is based on anecdote. If these have any foundation in truth, he was the first physician to cure Addison's disease, the disorder of the suprarenal gland first described by Thomas Addison (1793–1860) in 1855. It is from Yakub Pasha, no doubt, that his royal patient acquired his special interest in medicine, concerning which his library contained no less than fourteen celebrated works.[24a]

In the Ottoman state of the Conqueror's day, with its military and theocratic organization, there were no castes but only ranks of office. The servant class formed a kind of extension to the administration; it was often a trial stage preparatory for government office. Superior education or specialized knowledge was not required of those who aspired to state posts. A servant was free to enter public life. No obstacles or limitations were put in his path. Since every Ottoman laying claim to the slightest prestige had to employ servants and to be accompanied by a groom wherever he went, the servant class formed a conspicuously large part of the population. The number of an individual's servants depended on his rank, for high office was tantamount to wealth in a society where power was the sole source of income and property. Distinctions of rank based on property were unknown to the old Islamic society of the Ottoman Empire. In each province the administration, fiscal system, army, and judiciary were in the hands of the governor, who made appointments as he saw fit: power was not conferred by the office, but emanated from the personality. Then and later most dignitaries had no objection to the enrichment and advancement of their subordinates. With the help of good fortune and the sultan's favor, persons of humble origin not infrequently rose to high government office, surpassing their former masters in power and influence. Superiors and underlings alike sprang from the community at large, rather than from different castes; this was the chief difference between the social system of Turkey, as of the entire Moslem Orient, and that of the Christian Occident. The notions of state and civil service were alien to the patriarchal outlook of the old Ottomans. The sultan conferred office and took it away, and government service was looked upon as a privilege to which one acceded through the sultan's favor and from which one could at any time be removed by his disfavor, to make way for others who were more fortunate. Public office was a benefice granted for an indeterminate period.

[24a] Insight into the state of Turkish medical knowledge in the fifteenth century is given by Pierre Huard and Mirko Drazen Grmek's translation of Şerefeddin Sabuncuoğlu's work, *Kitāb al-Cerrāhīye-i Ilhānīye: Le premier manuscrit chirurgical turc* (Paris, 1960).

Since there was no hereditary nobility in the Ottoman Empire, the Ottoman Turks attached no importance to lineage. It was regarded as perfectly natural for one who had sprung from the lowest strata of the people to become a general or a vizier, or through marriage to enter into close ties of kinship with the sultan. And it was considered no more strange for descendants of once leading dignitaries to earn their living as artisans or servants. Although from the accession of Mehmed II until the proclamation of the *Hatt-i şerif* of Gülhane (November 3, 1839) a violent end was virtually the hallmark of a vizier, few men to whom the supreme office was offered hesitated to accept it. Neither fatalism nor the striving for glory and prestige seems to account adequately for this phenomenon, and even the old Ottomans were puzzled by it. Once when a newly appointed grand vizier asked a sheikh of dervishes what man he held to be the biggest fool, the dervish answered frankly: "You, O mighty vizier. For you have done everything in your power to gain your office, although you rode past the bleeding head of your predecessor, which lay in the same spot as that of his predecessor." Like everything else in the old Ottoman Empire, executions were subject to a rigid customary law. Every detail was exactly prescribed according to the victim's rank and person. The head of a vizier with three horsetails, executed in Istanbul, was displayed on a silver plate on a marble pillar at the middle gate of the serai, that of a lesser dignitary on a wooden plate at the first gate, and that of a subordinate on the ground without any special preparation. The heads of civil servants executed in the provinces were preserved in brine and sent to the capital as visible proof that the sultan's order had been carried out.

The requirements for advancement were very different for the learned class, that is, the corporation of the *ülema*, the theologically trained scholars whom Mehmed for the first time organized into a strict hierarchy, defining their duties as judges (*kadı*), interpreters of the law (*mufti*), and prayer leaders (*imam*). The hierarchy of the *ülema* culminated in the supreme juridical offices, namely those of the two army judges and later that of the mufti of Istanbul, from which office that of the sheikh al-Islam was to develop. Thus, the *ülema* comprised not only priests, for in Islam jurisprudence and theology are a single discipline governed by the Koran. Immediately after the conquest of Constantinople, Mehmed laid the groundwork for education in theology and jurisprudence by building *medreses* near Hagia Sophia and seven other churches which had been transformed into mosques. After erecting his own mosque, he radically transformed the entire organization of the *ülema* by building eight theological schools at once, where the teachers (*müderris*) were especially

461

well paid. The grand vizier Mahmud Pasha, who himself endowed a *medrese* near his mosque, took a special interest in the gradations within and also in the well-being of the entire teaching profession. Development, however, was not possible. Every Moslem looked upon the Koran as the seal and culmination of revelation, and this belief that the essential knowledge was already complete continued to exert a stultifying effect on theology and through it on life itself. The Moslem view of the world had undergone no change in centuries, and it was still taught in the same strictly traditional terms. It had long since taken on a character of contemplative old age, which has nothing but death to look forward to.[25]

III. ART, LITERATURE, AND SCIENCE

During the thirty years of Mehmed's reign his energies and those of the Ottomans in general were devoted largely to warfare. Unquestionably, wars played an even larger part in their lives than in the lives of a people as warlike as the early Romans. There was room for inner life only when one of the rare interruptions in warfare, imposed on the sultan in his later years by illness and physical exhaustion, obliged him to turn to peaceable occupations.

His interest in architecture seems very meager beside that of his father or of his successor, Bayezid II, not to mention his great-grandson, Süleyman the Magnificent. His only religious edifice, for example, seems to have been the Conqueror's mosque. Murad II not only adorned Edirne, his capital, with three mosques, among them the majestic one whose minaret with three galleries gives it its name (*Üç şerefeli cami*), but also erected a house of worship in Bursa, his former residence, where he was buried amid the tombs of his ancestors. In Istanbul Bayezid II built a mosque impressive for its solemn simplicity, achieved by use of the basic forms of Hagia Sophia. And in Edirne, whence the court had long since removed, he built (1484–1488) that unique mosque bearing his name which with its magnificent benevolent institutions—a *medrese*, a food kitchen for the poor, a hospital, and an insane asylum—may be numbered among the most splendid buildings of the entire Islamic world. In its prime it made its builder famous in all Moslem countries as one of the greatest benefactors among the Ottoman sultans.

[25] For the complex of schools built by the sultan around his mosque and for the leading members of the *ülema* in his time, see A. Süheyl Ünver, *Fatih külliyesi ve zamani ilim hayati* (Istanbul, 1946). Cf. Richard Repp, "Some Observations on the Development of the Ottoman Learned Hierarchy," in *Scholars, Saints and Sufis*, ed. Nikki R. Keddie (Berkeley, 1972), 17–32.

Mehmed contented himself with the one mosque erected on the site of Justinian's crumbling Church of the Holy Apostles. This building has been termed hardly inferior to Hagia Sophia, whose basic design is not merely taken over but also developed, an achievement that can plausibly be compared with that of the Italian architects of St. Peter's. The other mosques built during Mehmed's reign owe their existence not to him but to his high dignitaries. And even these are small in number: the Eyüp mosque (1458?), the mosque and *türbe* of the grand vizier Mahmud Pasha (1463), the mosque and *türbe* of the grand vizier Rum Mehmed Pasha in Üsküdar, and finally the mosque of Hass Murad Pasha (1466). The small and unimpressive mosque of the sheikh Mustafa Vefa of the Zeyniye order of dervishes on the Golden Horn, which was built in 1476, and not as some have supposed during the reign of Bayezid II, is deserving of mention only for the sake of completeness. In Edirne the only mosque of any importance to have been built during the Conqueror's reign was that endowed by his wife Sitt Hatun. Bursa possesses no important building of the Conqueror's day. Even the mortuary chapel of his own mother is of almost unequaled modesty and drabness. Nowhere else in the Ottoman Empire is there a religious edifice attributable to Mehmed unless we count the insignificant so-called conquest celebration (*Fethiye*) mosques, which are merely remodeled Christian churches.[26]

Only once did the Conqueror seek fame as a builder, when he caused the mosque which was to bear his name to exceed the dimensions of Hagia Sophia. There was nothing in his example to stir the emulation of the grandees of his empire, as was so often the case in the following century throughout the territories of Süleyman the Magnificent. Mehmed nowhere made a name for himself as the creator of richly endowed mosques or charitable institutions, or even as the generous friend and protector of the poor, who were certainly not lacking during his reign. Those of the Conqueror's documents of endowment to have been saved and published, in which the usufruct of various villages and districts is made over to certain Istanbul mosques, scarcely lend themselves to such inferences.[27]

[26] Ayverdi gives a detailed list of all buildings of the reign of Mehmed for which there is any evidence of construction in his *Fatih devri mimarisi*, 11–86. See also the same author's review article, "Prof. F. Babinger'in Fatih devri mimarisi hakkinda mutalaalari," *IED* 1 (1955), 145–151.

[27] Documents of this sort which have been published appear in the following works: Tahsin Öz (ed.), *Zwei Stiftungsurkunden des Sultans Mehmed II. Fatih* (Istanbul, 1935; as *Istanbuler Mitteilungen*, no. 4); *Fatih Mehmet II Vakfiyeleri* (Ankara, 1938; as *Vakiflar Umum Mudurluğu Neşriyati: Türk Vakfiyeleri* no. 1); Osman Ergin (ed.), *Fatih Imareti Vakfiyesi* (Istanbul, 1945).

Similarly, few secular buildings worth the mention have been preserved from the Conqueror's day. It was only natural that inns (*kervansaray*) should be built in numerous towns, especially along the military roads, for travel facilities were of the utmost importance for the cohesion and administration of so large a state. His encouragement of road building, however, was limited to the main arteries and traffic centers. To his mind by far the most important road was the military highway which constituted the only land route between East and West and cut diagonally across the Balkan peninsula from the Bosporus to the southern edge of the Hungarian Danube basin. All the other roads of the peninsula, except perhaps for the coastal highways and the ancient Via Egnatia from Byzantium via Thessaloniki to Durrës, were only branches of this main artery, whose course had been determined by nature in remote antiquity. On this military road the sultan's troops marched westward year after year, led by their sovereign in person as long as his health permitted. Critoboulos, his panegyrist, informs us that immediately after the capture of Constantinople, one of the Conqueror's first thoughts was to repair the military highway near his new capital. He restored the important bridges across the lagoon of Rhegion (Büyük Çekmece) and Athyras (Küçük Çekmece). Here it may be of interest to note that the present bridge across the lagoon of Rhegion was built by Süleyman the Great and his son Selim II, for by then the old Roman-Byzantine bridge repaired by Mehmed was beyond saving. Mehmed also had the parts of the military highway that had become impracticable paved with new stones and had inns built for travelers. But in his reign these repairs were largely limited to the stretch between Istanbul and Edirne, which he himself often traveled. Little attention was paid to the rest of the highway. All roads were maintained by the corvée of the Christians. But the further westward one traveled from Edirne, the less care was taken of them. Even later the construction of often magnificent mosques, baths, schools, bazaars, and aqueducts along the highway was limited to the region between Istanbul and Edirne. Along this link between two imperial residences the dignitaries of the empire could perpetuate their memory by such buildings and above all call themselves to the attention of the sultan.

Murad II and his grandson Bayezid II secured a place of honor in the memory of their people by building bridges which endured for centuries, and some of which are still in use today. During the reign of Mehmed II not a single one, associated with his name, was built at his behest. Some of his viziers—for example, Ishak Pasha, who in 1469–70 built the Kadin Most (Bridge of the Judge, across the Struma at Dupnica), which is still in use, or Saruca Pasha, who built a bridge in Edirne—glorified their names by such works.

There would be little to say of the Conqueror's secular building were it not for his two palaces, the one in Edirne, the other in Istanbul. The serais in the two capitals are not distinguished by magnificent buildings comparable to the numerous palaces built in the same period by princes and nobles in the West, especially in Italy. Both in Edirne and in Istanbul the serai under Mehmed comprised a considerable number of buildings, serving very different purposes; some of them were presumably not of stone but of wood. The so-called Old Serai, destroyed by fire in 1714, had been built of wood, and the fact that in the New Serai virtually nothing has survived from the Conqueror's day can hardly be attributed solely to the architectural enthusiasm of later sultans. It is more likely that these buildings were also of wood and fell a prey to fire or the ravages of time. The old Byzantine palaces—for example, the Imperial Palace (not far from Hagia Sophia), the Blachernae Palace, the palace of Constantine Porphyrogenitus—had been reduced to rubble during the fighting over the city; none was thought to be worth rebuilding. The young sultan was too modest in his tastes to desire such sumptuous buildings, whose destruction merely gave him ground for melancholy reflections. On entering the city, he lived in the monastery of the Latin Franciscans. When the Conqueror later planned his "new palace" (Topkapï) north of Hagia Sophia on the site of the old acropolis, on the tongue of land between the Golden Horn and the Bosporus, he first erected a high, thick crenellated wall pierced by gates, and behind this impregnable bastion proceeded to build his own residence and the seat of his government. Here he lived in the style of an Oriental potentate, far from the eyes of the world.

Nothing is more characteristic of the Conqueror's attitude toward architecture than the fact that, as far as we know, he did not call in a single architect from the West. He invited eminent painters and bronze-casters to his court, but none of the great architects of the day. In a Greek letter of July 30, 1465, to George Amirutzes, the importunate Francesco Filelfo reports that Filarete of Florence (ca. 1400–ca. 1469), was setting out for Istanbul in the summer of that year "just for a visit." But this statement is very much subject to doubt. It is true that the great sculptor and architect had only recently abandoned work on the Ospedale Maggiore, the hospital founded by his patron Francesco Sforza, and may have thought of trying his luck in Istanbul. But there is little reason to suppose that the brilliant eccentric carried out his plan and ended his days on the Golden Horn rather than in Rome. In any case, Mehmed did not send for him and nowhere in the Ottoman Empire is there any trace of his architectural activity.

No observer of the scant remains of the large palace on the Tunca island in Edirne can fail to note Western, probably Italian, influence. The Istanbul serai, however, shows no such influence, and even the Conqueror's mosque clearly discloses the activity of Byzantine architects. None of these is known to us by name. As has been related above, a certain Christodoulos is mentioned as the architect of the "new mosque," while Ottoman sources speak of a freedman named Sinan, who can safely be assumed to have been a convert. Accordingly, the Greek has been identified with Sinan on the assumption that he espoused Islam. We know of this architect's sad fate, and the statements of native chroniclers, confirmed by his tombstone, which has been preserved though in a very damaged state, make it difficult to interpret the story of his execution as merely a traditional *topos*; similar stories are told about architects in the employ of Trajan and Justinian. Still another architect of the Conqueror's day is mentioned by name: Iyas Ağa, son of Abdullah, also a recent convert no doubt, born perhaps in Afyon Karahisar (Anatolia), where in any event he erected a small mosque and made various endowments. Little biographical research has been done on the development of art and architecture in the Ottoman Empire of the fifteenth century, and it is impossible to make any definite statements. In any case, the small number of significant buildings erected by Mehmed makes it clear that he cannot have employed many architects of any importance. As builder of the so-called Çinili Köşk, which in its well-balanced plan and its every detail is Persian or Seljuk, one Kemaleddin is mentioned, undoubtedly from Karaman or Iran.

In the Çinili Köşk we possess an architectural monument which shows, perhaps more than any other of the Conqueror, the startling resemblance between the Turkish and the Central Asian styles in certain fields of applied art. The Far Eastern origin of the ceramic arts is reflected in the name, Çinili, or Chinese wares, as the Ottomans called ceramics (cf. the English "china"). Thus, the sources of these skills are not to be sought in the old Greek cities or in Byzantium itself. After the destruction of the Byzantine Empire, the Greek forms, ordinarily known as "Byzantine," quickly vanished from the capital and from all Asia Minor. The Greek craft, it would seem, was entirely abandoned or withdrew to the remote monasteries on Mount Athos. In the West the art of ceramics had died out at the time of the migrations. But the Islamic peoples had further developed and fortunately preserved the ancient Oriental art of enameling clay plates and vessels, which Egypt and the ancient Mesopotamian empires had developed to an amazing state of perfection in the second millennium B.C. Possibly Islam took the art from India and from there introduced the glazed tiles, used chiefly for covering walls, into its territories, especially Persia and Anatolia. In these regions such tiles had replaced the marble slabs of the late Roman Empire. This art reached its peak with the tin glaze and unparalleled colors of the Persian mosaic tiles and with the Ottoman semiglazed tiles and vases. The mosques of Bursa, Edirne, and Istanbul offer fine examples of such tiles, magnificent for their unchanged colors, rich tracery, floral designs, and arabesques. The ground as a rule is white, while the ornaments are turquoise, cobalt blue, bright metallic brown, green, and, very rarely, cinnabar red.

Under Mehmed the ceramic arts experienced a magnificent revival, although they were already flourishing under his father and grandfather, as their mosques reveal. It would seem, however, that the technique of glazing clay, which provides the chief charm of the Seljuk buildings and of the early Ottoman mosques, especially in Bursa and Edirne, had gradually declined on Turkish soil and in some places even been lost, while it continued to thrive in the lands of the extinct Seljuk empire. Also in Kütahya and especially in Iznik ceramic production had been virtually uninterrupted. The state of this irrevocably lost art under Mehmed is best shown by the sultan's order of 1466 to Mahmud Pasha, then grand vizier, to resettle the artists and artisans of Konya and Laranda in Istanbul. It can hardly be an accident that work was begun on the Çinili Köşk shortly afterward. The whole conception of this unique edifice may well have been the work of the Karamanian masters; they were probably responsible for the disposition of the rooms and their decoration with tiles and with color-glazed bricks.

Persian influence is unmistakable in the art of book production, which received all possible encouragement under the Conqueror. Persian calligraphers and miniaturists would seem to have opened a kind of school, to judge by the magnificent examples of book decoration preserved from that period. These include not only copies of the Koran but manuscripts of a secular character as well. Persian influence is also clearly discernible in the bindings of the time. It is not true that the Ottoman techniques of blind and gold tooling and of leather filigree were first practiced or perfected in the sixteenth century, although, to be sure, they attained unprecedented heights at that time thanks to the immigration of artists from Herat.

The absence of independent sculpture and painting has its root in religious considerations. Whereas the artists of antiquity and of the Christian world devoted their main effort to the portrayal of living things and especially the human form, representational art ceased to exist in Moslem countries. The prohibition is not contained in the Koran itself but only in a *hadith*. Apart from images of the Godhead, the founder of Islam never forbade the representation of living figures; moreover, the prohibition was applied in its full severity only to mosques and other buildings connected with the cult. Since the accent in the prohibition was on three-dimensional naturalistic representation, figures were deprived of their depth. Painters had to content themselves with flat figures without relief or shadow. In mural painting, illumination, and the related arts, this produced remarkable results, especially among the Shiite Persians, who never felt bound by the tradition in question. The Conqueror's pleasure in pictorial representations and especially in richly illustrated manuscripts may well have increased the number of artists in his capital. Here and in Bursa there seems to have developed a school of painting which, forgoing Western influence though allegedly under Western guidance, produced remarkable works, of which only a few, unfortunately, have been preserved.[28]

The craft workshops set up under the Byzantine emperors came to an end with them. Wonderful ceramic wall coverings replaced the Byzantine mosaics of marble and glass. The singularly naturalistic use of certain decorative fruits and flowers, precisely those for which the Occident is indebted to the Turks (pomegranate, carnation, hyacinth), continued under the Conqueror, particularly in the interior decoration of the mosques, where it replaced painting and statuary. Dynamic linear ornament still performed its artistic function. Inscriptions from the Koran and poems describing the building show that the art of calligraphy had preserved its ancient splendor. It would be a mistake to regard these borders and tablets in fine script as a late stage of the capricious monograms of the Byzantines; they were an indigenous, skillfully cultivated form of expression.

We know very little about the weaving of carpets and textiles in the Ottoman Empire of the day, but it seems likely that this art was still carried on, especially in Anatolia. Fine knotted rugs, chiefly for use as wall coverings, were exported in quantity to Flanders and Italy; we see them in the paintings of the period. Konya appears to have been one of the first cities to adopt the use of decorative carpets, but the art of carpet making, which was at first practiced only by nomadic Turkmen, soon lost its original rustic character through contact with the civilization of the cities, and achieved a degree of perfection which even in the Conqueror's day made the products of Uşak, Gördes, Isparta, Demircik, Ladik, and so on, among the most coveted treasures in the West. As for weaving, it must have been favored for home consumption and for

[28] For a survey of the known art work under the Conqueror see Esin Atıl, "Ottoman Miniature Painting under Sultan Mehmed II," *Ars Orientalis* 9 (1973), 103–120.

export to the West, especially in Bursa, whose workshops turned out costly velvets and silk brocades. Italian visitors to Bursa may at that time have conceived the idea of establishing a similar industry at home.

The Conqueror gave no heed to the prohibition of images, as is amply demonstrated by his fondness for the Italian paintings with which he adorned the interior of his palace. As we have seen, none of these works have survived, because Bayezid II on his accession either destroyed them or, as in the case of certain paintings, had them sold in the bazaar. It was thanks to the young Conqueror's intervention that the famous three-headed snake pillar in the hippodrome (*At meydanï*), the votive offering of the thirty-one Greek cities to the temple of Apollo in Delphi (480 B.C.), did not fall a victim to blind religious zeal at the capture of Constantinople. From the pedestal of the bronze pillar grew a mulberry tree, which he caused to be removed with a hot iron. There can be no doubt that superstitious considerations contributed to saving the mysterious monument from destruction. The sultan also gave orders for the equestrian statue of Justinian surmounting a high column in the square known as the Augustaion to be carefully removed, no doubt to save it from the religious frenzy of his troops. These two incidents demonstrate the Conqueror's freedom from religious prejudice, even in his younger years. A further indication is that immediately after the conquest of Constantinople, when the paintings of Hagia Sophia were being whitewashed, he caused the mosaic of Mary in the half-dome of the choir apse to be spared. Toward the end of his life he was totally indifferent to such matters as the prohibition of images. It was not without reason that his pious son branded his liberalism as godlessness.

In the Italy of the quattrocento princes felt their eternal fame to be dependent on the writers of their day and rewarded these bestowers of immortality with hard cash, benefices, or honors for their epics, elegies, odes, panegyrics, letters, and, last but not least, their epitaphs. At Mehmed's court we look in vain for a poet or even a historian who earned his keep by adulation of the sultan. Non-Turks, it is true, tried their luck with panegyrics but without encouragement from the sultan. In Byzantium and above all in Italy, the humanist's supreme goal was the honored and well-paid post of court scholar and court poet; it never occurred to the Ottoman ruler in Istanbul to attach writers and poets to his person as heralds of his fame. As a man of action, as the "king of fortune" (*re della fortuna*), he had no thought of gaining the admiration of posterity in this way, and he was far from regarding the literary talents of his courtiers as his best hope of escaping oblivion.

From this, however, it would be a mistake to infer that Mehmed failed to appreciate poetry or historiography. His father, Murad II, had held gatherings of scholars twice a week to discuss scientific and religious topics; after the manner of his ancestors, he had endowed schools in all the larger cities, especially in Bursa and Edirne. After the conquest of Constantinople, Mehmed carried on this venerable tradition, becoming in his own way a protector and patron of letters and the sciences. When we consider that the thirty years of his reign were taken up almost entirely with wars and the complex tasks arising out of the growth of the empire, we cannot fail to be impressed by his feeling for the world of the Muses, all the more so as he made no attempt to use his patronage of the arts as a means of glorifying his name.

It may well be that an occasional rhymester tried to curry favor with the sultan by glorifying his warlike deeds. A certain Kâşifi, for example, a member of the Bursa circle of the first Ottoman lyric poet, Ahmed Pasha, celebrated the Conqueror's victories in a Persian *Gaza-name-i Rum*. But the works of most of these poets have disappeared; their names do not even figure in the numerous Ottoman anthologies of later days, which often include the most insignificant poetasters. The life and deeds of no sultan could have been more conducive to a heroic epic than those of the Conqueror, but no poet felt equal or inclined to this task. The same is true in the realm of historiography. An indication to the contrary can hardly be found in the work, written in an intricate style quite unintelligible to the simple layman of those days, of Tursun Bey, who toward the turn of the century wrote a history of Mehmed II, in which he included the first six years of Bayezid II's reign. Although as a participant in Mehmed's campaigns and as secretary to the *divan* he was undoubtedly close to the Conqueror, he did not write his work until long after the sultan's death. The same is true of the *Book of the Conquests of Sultan Mehmed*, written in Turkish prose and rhyme and completed only in April 1488 by a certain Kîvami; this was at one time in the library of Bayezid II and ultimately found its way to Germany, where it was discovered only recently.[29]

Quite different from such stylistic exercises, which received little atten-

[29] Kâşifi's work is discussed by Adnan S. Erzi, "Türkiye kütüphanelerinden notlar ve vesikalar ii.," *Belleten* 14 (1950), 596ff. The work of Kîvami was presented in facsimile with an introduction by Babinger as *Fetihname-i Sultan Mehmed* (Istanbul, 1955). Tursun Bey's work was published as *Ta'rih-i Ebu'l-Feth* (Istanbul, 1330 H. [1911/12]) as a supplement to the *Tarih-i osmani encumeni mecmuasi*. A transcribed text has been published by Mertol Tulum: Tursun Bey, *Târih-i Ebü'l-Feth* (Istanbul, 1977). A facsimile edition by Inalcîk is in preparation.

tion and served merely for the entertainment of the upper classes, are the anonymous *Stories of the House of Osman,* which apppeared in numerous versions toward the end of Mehmed's reign and which seem to have been widely distributed among the people. These simply written annals relate in chronological order the most important events of Ottoman history, though carefully passing over anything that might have detracted from the honor of the House of Osman. The narrative is occasionally interrupted by rhymes taken from the *Iskender-name* (Book of Alexander) of Ahmedi (1334–1413). Any tendency to shape events into a unity or to explain their sequence, in other words, to look for the overall significance of the episodes recorded, is absent from such popular chronicles. They were evidently intended to be read to simple people, perhaps including soldiers. Stylistically, the early Ottoman annals of the Conqueror's day whose authors are known to us—for example, Uruc or the dervish Ahmed Aşiki, known as Aşikpaşazade—differ little from their anonymous counterparts. Karamani Mehmed Pasha, the Conqueror's last grand vizier, who was murdered after his master's death, also wrote a history of the Ottoman Empire in Arabic, which neither adds to our knowledge of the subject nor redounds to its author's reputation as a stylist. In none of these histories is the reign of Mehmed II especially emphasized, except occasionally when the authors expatiate on an incident which they themselves witnessed.[30]

It is no exaggeration to say that the profession of literary courtier was not held in high honor during Mehmed's reign. It is all the more surprising to learn that the same sultan sent royal gifts to poets and stylists even in remote Herat. Each year, for example, he dispatched a thousand gold pieces to Abu'l Fadl Mahmud ibn Sheikh Muhammad of Gilan, better known under his surname Khoja-i jihan (i.e. teacher of the world), the celebarted stylist and vizier, author of the admired and much used *Panoramas of the Art of Style,* who in 1481 was executed by order of his sultan, Muhammad Shah Behmen II of the Deccan. He sent the same amount each year to Jami (1414–1492), the last classical author of Persia and the most famous Oriental poet of those days. Whether Mehmed

---

[30] For Ottoman historical writing in general through the 15th century, see Halil Inalcik, "The Rise of Ottoman Historiography," and V. L. Ménage, "The Beginnings of Ottoman Historiography," both in *Historians of the Middle East,* ed. Bernard Lewis and P. M. Holt (London, 1962), 152–167 and 168–179, respectively. For a German translation of Aşikpaşazade's chronicle see above, book 2, n. 55; for Karamani Mehmed and his work, book 6, n. 19. Babinger himself published the chronicle of Uruc: *Die frühosmanischen Jahrbücher des Urudsch* (Hanover, 1925). Cf. the recent modern version: *Oruç Beğ Tarihi,* ed. Atsiz (Istanbul, n.d.).

cherished the hope of attracting them to his court can only be conjectured. Such an assumption is supported, to be sure, by the fact that the sultan sent Mullah Jami 5,000 ducats for his pilgrimage from Khorasan to Mecca, at the same time inviting him to his court through Khoja Ata'ullah al-Kirmani. The message, however, did not reach the poet in Damascus. He had already returned to Khorasan by way of the territories of Uzun Hasan, where he was received with great distinction. The sultan also accorded his special favor to the philosopher Jalal al-Din al-Dawani (1427–1501), perhaps also with the intention of bringing him to Istanbul and removing him from the influence of Uzun Hasan, to whom he had dedicated his most important work, a treatise on ethics. In all these designs, in any case, the Ottoman sultan showed his marked predilection for the Persian language and literature, and in general for the Persian spirit, which was doubtless much closer to him than the sober simplicity of the Arabs. His preference for Persians, whom he distinguished with important government posts and who to the end were his favored associates at court, naturally aroused envy and dissatisfaction among native Turks. We have a number of satirical poems deploring that a man must be a Persian, Jew, or "Frank" to enjoy the sultan's esteem and rise to fortune and standing in his empire. But the lot of these Persian favorites was not always enviable, as is shown by the example of a doubtless mediocre poet surnamed Le'ali, who, though born in Tokat in eastern Anatolia, had learned Persian through association with Jami and other Iranian celebrities. He came to Istanbul as a dervish and was brought before the sultan, who took him for a real Persian, presented him with a ruined Greek church near the Seven Towers (Yedi Kule) as a *tekke* (monastery), and probably settled an income on him. But envious persons discovered that he was not a genuine Persian and denounced him to the sultan, who took away his monastery and benefices. He spent the end of his life in straitened circumstances in Yiannitsa (Yenice-i Vardar) and wrote an embittered satire against his enemies, with an allusion to his own surname (Le'ali = pearl):

Would you be well liked at court, you must be a Persian or a Kurd. A jewel is without value in the mine, or a pearl in the night of the sea. Only too true is the old saying: "It is never light at the foot of the candle." If it is intelligence you want in a man, what difference does his country make? The gem, it is true, comes from stone, but no one cares from what stone. Shouldn't Persians go to Rum, where fame and fortune await them? Those who come from Persia hope to become *sancaks* or even viziers.

The number of literati rhyming in Persian was greater under Mehmed than before or after. Those who did not write in Persian imitated Persian models or tried to render them into Turkish. One of the favorite genres was the so-called *Khamsa* (Five), a collection of five long epic poems by Nizami (1141–1209), which was several times translated or imitated. Also the *Shahname* (Book of Kings) of Firdawsi (ca. 941–1021), which relates the whole legendary history of Persia up to the Arab conquest, was more than once chosen as a model for Turkish imitations or adaptations. We are told, for example, that a certain Şehdi of Kastamonu, a wealthy but unknown poet, who gained access to the Conqueror thanks to rich gifts brought from Persia, planned to celebrate his sultan's deeds in a Persian poem employing the meter of Firdawsi's *Shahname*. Among his assets was a perfect command of the Arabic and Persian languages. He embarked on his task, but abandoned it after completing some four hundred couplets. Unquestionably, neither early Ottoman literature nor the Conqueror's fame was greatly the loser. Perhaps the most admired poet of the day was the Eastern Turk Mir Ali Shir Neva'i (1441–1501), founder of the Chagatai literary language, whose writings vied in popularity with the masterworks of Persian literature.[31]

Many of the Ottoman historians of those days wrote in Persian, and only the scholars, especially the theologians, wrote in Arabic. The eastern countries of Islam, which in former days had boasted numerous centers of Moslem culture and science, had been hardest hit by the Mongol invasions. In these regions Arabic gradually gave way to Persian, which achieved almost exclusive predominance in the fields of poetry and history. Apart from the theologians, only the proponents of the mathematical sciences made use of Arabic. They will be discussed separately.

Surprisingly enough, Mehmed, who under the pseudonym of Avni (i.e. the helper, the helpful one) left a collection (*divan*) of some eighty poems, wrote exclusively in Turkish. A few interspersed Persian poems are nothing more than paraphrases of ghazels of the Persian poet Hafiz. In the Ottoman lives of the poets Avni is numbered among the greatest,

---

[31] For the influence of Persian scholars and writers in the Ottoman Empire, see Hanna Sohrweide, "Dichter und Gelehrte aus dem Osten im osmanischen Reich (1453–1600)—Ein Beitrag zur türkisch-persischen Kulturgeschichte," *Der Islam* 46 (1950), 263–302. The only English survey of Ottoman Turkish poetry—often outdated but not replaced—is Elias J. W. Gibb, *A History of Ottoman Poetry*, 6 vols. (London, 1900–09; reprinted 1958–63). The author died prematurely after the publication of only the first volume; the remainder of the work came out under the editorship of E. G. Browne. The latter half of the 15th century is treated in vol. II.

but even a superficial examination of his ghazels shows that he is hardly deserving of such praise. A sample from the sultan's *divan* will no doubt corroborate this impression and show that the sultan was quite devoid of originality in his choice of images and metaphors, in his ideas and language. Things that have been better said a thousand times over recur in these lines, and no unbiased critic would think of calling them a masterpiece of Turkish poetry.[32]

> *When the rosebush in the garden dons its coat*
> *It fashions the buttons from rosebuds.*
> *When in speech the tongue weaves roses and buds together*
> *Its words are as nothing compared to her sweet lips.*
> *When you stroll through the garden with a hundred coy deceits*
> *The jasmine branches are so amazed at the sight that they sway*
> *   with you.*
> *When the dogwood sees the roses strewn in your path*
> *Then it too strews its petals before you.*
> *Until that rose-cheeked beauty comes to see the garden,*
> *O Avni, may the ground be always damp with the tears of your*
> *   eyes!*

Two of our sources, Latifi and Kīnalizade, assure us that the Conqueror sent gifts of 1,000 aspers monthly to each of thirty Ottoman poets.[33] If true, this may be taken as evidence of his generosity, but hardly of an overly critical attitude toward poetry. In the thirty years of his rule, there was only one Ottoman poet of any stature, and he did not consistently enjoy his sultan's favor. This was Ahmed Pasha. He came of an illustrious family, for his father Veliyüddin, who traced his genealogy to the Prophet through Ali's son Husayn, enjoyed high honors in the reign of Murad II, under whom he had served as army judge. The son Ahmed is mentioned first as a teacher at a *medrese* endowed by the sultan, later

---

[32] The sultan's *divan* was published by Kemal Edip Ünsel as *Fatih'in şiirleri* (Ankara, 1946; *TTK*: XI. seri, no. 1). A more recent critical study is A. Karahan, "Fatih, Şair Avni," *Türk dili ve edebiyati dergisi* 6 (1954), 1–38. See also the brief remarks of E.J.W. Gibb, who did not, however, have access to any manuscripts of the work (II, 22–39). The poem given here was first translated by von Hammer and published in his *Geschichte der Osmanischen Dichtkunst* I (Pesth, 1836), 138. The Turkish text is given in transcription by Ünsal, 65–66, no. 58.

[33] The "poet biographers" Latifi and Kīnalizade are two of two dozen recognized compilers of biographical dictionaries of Ottoman poets. For a German translation (by O. Rescher) of that of the former: *Latifi's tezkere* (Tübingen, 1950). The genre and its representatives are discussed by J. Stewart-Robinson, "The Ottoman Biographies of Poets," *Journal of Near Eastern Studies* 24 (1965), 57–74.

as judge of Edirne. His many-sided talents, his affability, and above all his ready wit soon won him the special favor of Mehmed, whose confidant he became. He quickly rose to the position of army judge, but was then selected as the sultan's private preceptor and so was exposed to his unpredictable moods. He soon experienced the inconstancy of the sultan's favor. Mehmed first gave him the rank of vizier and with it the title of pasha, but soon there was a falling out, allegedly caused by jealousy in connection with a page at the serai: there is ample evidence of Mehmed's leanings toward the male sex. The sultan had Ahmed Pasha imprisoned in the palace. Later he set him free, but removed him from court and transferred him to Tire as head of the district, then to Ankara as administrator of a foundation, and finally to Bursa. There the bachelor led a none too pleasant existence, which was relieved only on the accession of Bayezid II, who made him prefect of that city, which post he held to the time of his death in 1496/97. He was buried in a *türbe* of his own beside the *medrese* which he had had built.

Although Ahmed Pasha was unquestionably the first and most important of Ottoman poets, it has long been evident that his poetry was based on Persian models, especially Hafiz and Jami, and that he later slavishly imitated Mir Ali Shir Neva'i. Sultan Bayezid II was said to have received thirty-three ghazels from this east Turkish poet and thereupon asked Ahmed Pasha to compose pendants to them. The poet filled the order and used the occasion to ask for an improvement of his post and hence of his income. His dexterity and amazing command of the language enabled Ahmed Pasha to improvise his lyrical effusions with ease. He owed a number of personal advantages to this gift. Thus, it is related that one day when Mehmed was playing the game of *fal*, popular in the Orient, with his intimates, Ahmed Pasha participated in this Moslem counterpart of *sortes Virgilianae*. The game consists in opening the Koran—or, among the Persians, usually the poems of Hafiz—with closed eyes, in counting back seven pages, and then reading the first passage that offers itself and interpreting it as an omen. In the *Divan* of Hafiz the sultan hit on the verses:

> *Would that those who by their glances*
> *Transform dust into gold*
> *Would only turn well-wishing*
> *The corner of their eye on me!*

whereupon Ahmed Pasha, quickly improvising, modified the second verse in a way highly flattering to the sultan. The story goes that Mehmed was so enthusiastic at the poet's skill and deft transformation of the rhymes that he filled his mouth with jewels.

Ahmed Pasha's inventiveness and consummate command of his native language gave his poems, despite his obvious borrowings from Persian models and even from older Ottoman poets, the breath of originality and the power to stir the hearts of his contemporaries. His name, however, has long been overshadowed by later poets and even in his lifetime by the younger Necati (d. March 17, 1509), one of his friends in Bursa, who in turn was forgotten in the sixteenth century when such brilliant poets as Baki and Fuzuli made their appearance. Necati's main work was written under Bayezid II, though he knew Mehmed, who also esteemed him as a poet. Toward the end of the Conqueror's life Necati sent him a poem in his praise by secreting it in the turban of one of the sultan's courtiers. Mehmed caught sight of the piece of paper while playing chess, took pleasure in the skillful verses, and appointed their author secretary to the *divan* with a daily wage of seven aspers. Necati was presumably of Christian descent, for he was sold as a slave in his childhood, which precludes Turkish origin.

The ghazels and qasidas (odes) of Ahmed Pasha and even of Necati have long since lost their charm and have not even survived in quotation, and it has fared no better with the other writers of Mehmed's reign, whom Turkish authors of the sixteenth century praised as a kind of golden age. With the possible exception of the grand vizier Mahmud Pasha, who under the pseudonym of Adni wrote Persian and Turkish rhymes, the period offers no further poets of above-average quality.[34]

Among the poets it seems fitting to mention as curiosities two women who improvised rhymes, which also, however, did not surpass the average. Zeynep Hatun of east Anatolian origin, who according to malicious tongues led a licentious life after an unsuccessful marriage and to the end of her days pursued a certain poetaster with her assiduities, composed a *divan* in Persian and Turkish, which she dedicated to Mehmed II. Her contemporary Mihri Hatun, the "Sappho of the Ottomans," was said to have led a far more virtuous life. She associated on the most honorable terms with well-known contemporaries, such as the supreme judge Abdurrahman Müeyyedzade, who, suspect as the bosom friend of Prince Bayezid in Amasya, would no doubt have fallen victim to the sultan's assassins if he had not, with the prince's help, escaped to Syria (1476).

[34] For the works of the two prominent poets during the time of Mehmed, see Ali Nihat Tarlan, *Ahmed Paşa Divani* (Istanbul, 1966) and idem, *Necati Beg Divani* (Istanbul, 1963). Gibb gives samples of the poetry of both, together with an evaluation (II, 40–69 and 93–122).

Her love for him and for the young Iskender Çelebi, a son of Sinan Pasha, was purely platonic, and "not the slightest cloud darkened her reputation for virtue." "Despite this poetic love," wrote the biographer of poets, Aşik Çelebi of Skoplje, "this 'woman of the world' ceded to the desires of no one, no lover's hand touched the treasure of her maidenly charms, and no arm excepting her amber-scented necklace embraced her pure neck, so that she lived and died a virgin." Only scant samples of her poetry have been preserved; despite their natural simplicity, they suggest that she was more remarkable for her virtuous life than for her poetry.

Zeynep Hatun died in 1474/75 (879 H.) while Mihri Hatun lived until 1506/07 (912 H.). They both died in Amasya. What perhaps distinguishes them to their advantage from the male rhymesters of their day is their language, which is not derived from Persian models but flows naturally from the heart. As long as their *divans* are not available in scholarly editions or even published, it is impossible to arrive at a conclusive judgment.[35]

If we include the authors of official letters, which were assembled in special collections (*inşa*), writers in prose were assuredly no less numerous. Mahmud Pasha was reputed to be a great stylist. All his writings were said to have been distinguished by great polish of language and profundity of thought. Thus far, no authenticated examples have come to light, and moreover, Mahmud Pasha's literary mastery was overshadowed by that of his successor in office, Karamani Mehmed Pasha. But what with the rapid change in taste and style, the latter's prose writings also failed to stand up under the critical appraisal of subsequent generations. It was the supreme judge (*kadiasker*) Cafer Çelebi, executed by Selim I in 1515, who with his collection of official papers in Turkish and Persian first won a lasting name in the history of Ottoman letters.[36]

We cannot speak much more favorably of the scientific writing of the time. True, there is an adequate explanation for the conspicuous lack of fundamental works. The Mongol invasions had ruined all sources of culture in the East and in particular destroyed the spiritual unity of Islam. The eastern Islamic countries, which had formerly boasted several important centers of Moslem learning, had been hardest hit. Since then, Bukhara, Samarkand, and Herat had preserved only feeble traces of their former importance. In those regions Arabic gave way more and more

[35] For the two women poets, see Gibb, II, 123–137.

[36] The collection of documents has been published by Necati Lugal and Adnan Erzi as *Taci-zade Sa'di Çelebi: Münşeati* (Istanbul, 1956). For more details on the life of the scholar and poet, see "Dja'far Čelebi" (V. L. Ménage), *EI²* II, 374.

to Persian, which now held almost undisputed sway in the fields of poetry and historiography. Only theologians and scientists continued to use the language of the Koran. It was from Persia that the scholars of the Ottoman Empire drew their chief intellectual nourishment and inspiration, especially as not a few theologians from the Iranian east emigrated to Anatolia and even to Rumelia, where they soon acquired a following. The Ottoman princes were never indifferent to intellectual activity; the schools they founded and endowed attracted recognized scholars and provided them with sufficient leisure for writing. True, their activities were strictly limited. The salient characteristic of that period, in which Moslem science succumbed almost entirely to the sclerosis of scholastic hairsplitting and sophistry, is to be sought in the restriction of learned studies to practical daily needs and in the incorporation of scientists into a rigidly hierarchical state officialdom. Since the gates of free inquiry based on personal conviction (so-called *içtihad* [*ijtihad*]) had been regarded as closed since the days of al-Ghazzali, the celebrated philosopher (1058–1111), by far the greater number of those devoted to science, especially the theologians, philologists, and jurists, contented themselves with acquiring the knowledge necessary for the exercise of their profession as teachers, judges, or muftis, which they gleaned chiefly from a limited number of current texts and manuals and the appended commentaries and marginal notes. Occasionally, a scholar would as a sideline try his hand in some other field that particularly appealed to him, such as historiography, stylistics, or poetry. These literary endeavors, of course, remained outside the sphere of officially sanctioned studies.

By and large, dogma and practical life had soon imposed narrow limits on the subject matter of science and its treatment. Nevertheless, the steadily increasing number of commentaries and glosses had produced an enormous body of literature, although each work had to make the rounds in manuscript and its acquisition involved considerable expense. The study of the material thus accumulated was extremely time consuming; this made it difficult for a scholar to strike out for himself and develop ideas of his own. Time and occasion were lacking for independent creative projects. The circumstances and especially the monotonous daily routine impeded the development of striking personalities or of outstanding scholars. Nowhere does this fact become more glaringly evident than when we consider the scientists who flourished under the Conqueror, although in his time the opposition of the Sufis (mystics)—hostile in varying degrees to the empirical sciences—was not yet very pronounced and the tendency to combat and finally to eliminate the sciences of the *medrese* was still held in check. The most important reason for this unusual situation is probably to be sought in the Conqueror's dislike of the Sufi brotherhoods, which he may well have suspected of being opposed to his freethinking views. It is certain in any case that the sultan expressed his liberal opinions only among his intimates and that as a sovereign he imposed, both in theology and in jurisprudence, the dogmas of the Orthodox Sunnite Abu Hanifa, founder of the doctrine prevailing in the Ottoman Empire, and tolerated no deviation from it in public life. In the field of dogmatics, he revived the long-buried controversy between theology and philosophy by organizing a kind of contest devoted to a critical comparison between al-Ghazzali's celebrated treatise *Tahâfut al-falâsifah* (The Inconsistency of the Philosophers) and philosophy itself. Mustafa, known as Hocazade, one of the few independent thinkers in the Ottoman Empire of the time, won the prize with a work bearing the same name as al-Ghazzali's.

Hocazade was one of those scholars who served as preceptor to the sultan and kept him acquainted with intellectual developments. Under Mehmed this preceptorship became a permanent institution, belonging to the juridical hierarchy. In rank, the sultan's teacher followed immediately after the mufti, the chief of the *ülema*. One of his chief tasks, at least under the Conqueror, was to select appropriate theological texts, to read them aloud, and to comment on them. Most of Mehmed's private teachers became the butt of their sultan's unpredictable moods and only very few held this dangerous position for any considerable period.

The most important of them was Mullah Ahmed ibn Ismail, known as Gürani, mentioned earlier. Once on his return from the Arabian pilgrimage to Cairo, where he taught in the *medrese*, he made the acquaintance of Mullah Mehmed ibn Armağan, known as Yegân, who persuaded him to move to Anatolia. There he soon attracted the attention of Murad II, who appointed him to several successive teaching positions in Bursa. The sultan entrusted him with the instruction of his son, who was then living in Manisa and had already driven several tutors to despair. The fearless and energetic Mullah Gürani took the position and Mehmed Çelebi seems to have been indebted to him for the groundwork of his education, especially his knowledge of Arabic literature. When Mehmed mounted the throne for the second time, he wished to give Gürani the rank of vizier. But the mullah declined with the shrewd words that the sultan's court officials served him only in the hope of achieving high positions later on, and that if an outsider were chosen for the vizierate, the administration would suffer. Pleased at this remark, the young sultan appointed him army judge. Mullah Gürani made use of this position to select candidates agreeable to himself for educational and juridical positions. The sultan did not dare to oppose him, but after conferring with his viziers, transferred him as a judge to Bursa, where, so he claimed, the institutions founded by his grandfather were in urgent need of attention. Despite the distance, a quarrel developed with the sultan when Gürani, allegedly on receiving an order from Mehmed contrary to the religious law, thrashed the messenger without further ado. Thereupon the mullah turned his back on the Ottoman Empire and returned to Egypt, where he was well received by Sultan Ashraf. Mehmed II later regretted his break with Gürani and asked him to return to Istanbul. With the remark that the relation between him and the sultan was that of father to son, the mullah accepted the invitation. The Mamluk sultan was reluctant to let him go, but finally dismissed him with rich gifts for himself and the Ottoman sovereign (1458). For a time Gürani served again as judge in Bursa and then took the post of mufti in Istanbul, where he enjoyed the special favor of his former pupil. He kept large numbers of slaves of both sexes, led a pleasant, carefree life, and wrote several books on the Koran. In addition, he gave lectures, attended by numerous students, on the Koran and the "tradition" (*hadith*) of the prophet Mohammed. A man of imposing stature with a long dyed beard, Gürani all his life displayed manly pride in the presence of kings and always spoke the unvarnished truth. He addressed not only the viziers but the sultan himself simply by name. When he met the sultan in the street, he greeted him without obsequiousness. He simply held out his hand, but did not kiss the sultan's hand as custom prescribed. On feast days he went to the palace only if expressly invited. He was never jealous of any of his colleagues. Mullah Gürani died in 1488, under Bayezid II, in Istanbul, where he was buried. As he lay on his deathbed, he said to the vizier Davud Pasha, "Take my greetings to Bayezid. My last request to him is that he should attend my funeral and pay my debts out of the state treasury." Sultan Bayezid II did indeed take part in the prayer for the dead and paid the sums, amounting to 180,000 silver pieces, out of his treasury, without even asking for receipts. On the day of the burial the city was filled with wailing and lamentation, especially on the part of women and children.

There can be little doubt that the occasion for all this mourning was the death not so much of a great scholar as of a striking personality. It was his vigorous activity and strength of character that called forth the grief of the common people. Beside him the young prince's older tutors pale into insignificance. Of Mustafa ibn Ibrahim at-Temşid, commonly known merely as Ibn Temşid, we know little more than his name and his ability to rhyme in the three chief Islamic languages. Since he died in 1451, he must have been among Mehmed's earliest instructors. Not much more is related of Hoca Hayreddin, who also taught the sultan and earned favor by his witty conversation and congenial company. As a scholar, he was unimportant and esteemed only as an industrious copyist. A more significant scholar was another sometime teacher of the sultan, Mullah Mehmed, known as Hatipzade, reputed for his pride in the presence of princes. In the end his frankness aroused his pupil's anger. Once he was dismissed but was reinstated thanks to the intervention of Mullah Gürani. One day, however, Mehmed asked him if he felt equal to a debate with the celebrated mullah Hocazade, and he replied in the affirmative, saying that he was, after all, the sultan's teacher. With this he fell into disgrace for good and was obliged once again to earn his living in a *medrese*. His pride and utter freedom from servility led him to quarrel several times even with the far more genial Bayezid II. His works, for example, the "Glosses on the Supercommentary of the Commentary" of the well-known Arabic philosopher and theologian Seyyid Jurjani, are without independent thought but do show a critical mind.

All these teachers to the sultan, who at most were significant for their personalities, are overshadowed by Mullah Mustafa, known as Hocazade (i.e. the merchant's son). Concerning him numerous anecdotes have come down to us representing him as a world-removed eccentric indifferent to honors and earthly happiness, whose rich intellectual gifts were in consequence never adequately appreciated. His father was a well-to-do merchant in Bursa, who was none too pleased at the scientific leanings of his shabbily dressed son. His lamentable attire, resulting from his nature but perhaps also from his scant pocket money, finally attracted the attention of patrons. He earned his keep and money to defray his studies by copying books. Toward the end of his reign Murad II appointed him to a judicial post and finally to the directorship of a *medrese* in Bursa. Later Mehmed II took notice of the quick and knowledgeable mullah and made him his private preceptor. The grand vizier Mahmud Pasha, it is related, became envious of him and attempted by all manner of means to deprive him of the sultan's favor. One day he convinced the sultan that Hocazade desired the post of an army judge. When asked why he wished to leave his present service, Mahmud Pasha reportedly could think of no other answer than that this was the mullah's wish. He informed the mullah that Mehmed had chosen him for the post of army judge. Though not at all pleased, Hocazade finally accepted the position. He kept it only a short time, however, for shortly thereafter he went as a teacher to the Sultaniye *medrese* in his native Bursa, where he liked best to live. But then the sultan, who may have missed his company, called him back to Istanbul, where the position of judge was finally given him. When Karamani Mehmed Pasha became grand vizier, however, he succeeded in persuading the sultan that the climate of Istanbul did not agree with Hocazade and that he would like best to remove to Iznik. The sultan believed his grand vizier and in addition to his judgeship appointed the mullah to a teaching position at the *medrese* of Iznik. The death of Mehmed II and of Karamani rescued him from his banishment to this remote spot. Bayezid gave him a new teaching position and later the respected post of a mufti in his native Bursa, where he died in 1488.

He often complained that the position of judge left him no time for scientific endeavor. Nevertheless, he produced a number of works, mostly commentaries and glosses on older theological writings. He seems to have left behind him numerous rough drafts, but they were dispersed far and wide. "The west wind carried off one part and the east wind another," says one of his biographers.

The list of positions which an original and independent thinker like Mustafa Hocazade was forced to occupy in the course of his career, because the sultan's whim or the intrigues of a grand vizier left him no peace, shows the hazards of a scholar's existence in the Conqueror's day. Caught in the trammels of an official career, Hocazade, who more than any of his contemporaries, with the possible exception of Mullah Husrev, might have been able to go his own way and become a creative writer, completed no work worthy to preserve his memory. Whatever originality he may have possessed was squandered in debates with the sultan and in ruses to check his master's dangerous fits of temper.

Those who taught and studied far from the atmosphere of the court fared rather better. But even among them there hardly is an outstanding figure. A case in point is that of Mullah Abdurrahman, surnamed Çelebizade, who had won the Conqueror's affection by his wealth of knowledge and brilliant conversation. After long sunning himself in the sultan's favor and so arousing the envy and hostility of many of his colleagues, he was one day banished from court for "unseemly conduct." If he did not make short shrift of him, so the angry sultan informed Çelebizade, it was only because his father, Mullah Mehmed, had once been Mehmed's teacher. Abdurrahman was sent as judge to Kütahya, where he outlived his former patron by twenty years. In his Anatolian refuge he found leisure for literary activity.

The intrigues of suspicious viziers, especially of Mahmud Pasha and later of Karamani Mehmed Pasha, were often responsible for the withdrawal of the sultan's favor. To the examples already recorded, we may add that of Mullah Abdulkadir of Isparta (Anatolia), who was Mehmed's private teacher for a time, and on the friendliest terms with him. Regarding him as a rival, Mahmud Pasha managed by guile to undermine his position with the sultan. The mullah returned to his home, where he ended his days in contemplation. In the time of his favor, the sultan had greatly appreciated his wit. One day as he was riding through Konya by his master's side, the *ülema* of the city rode out in a body to greet the sultan. The sultan declared: "Look at those staunch scholars! You yourself have been rather fatigued by the journey!" Mullah Abdulkadir retorted with a verse from the Persian poet Sa'di: "Even emaciated, an Arabian horse is better than a whole drove of donkeys." Mehmed laughed at his companion's apt reply.

A number of mullahs who knew how to profit by Mehmed's intervals of good humor and appeal to him with a joke achieved offices for which they seem to have had no particular aptitude. The more pious than learned mullah Hüseyin of Tabriz, surnamed Umm Walad, who was married to a slave woman belonging to the mufti Fahreddin, won the sultan's respect by his rectitude and strength of character and obtained a teaching position at one of the eight *medreses* attached to the Conqueror's mosque. Sometimes when Mehmed rode out to the *türbe* of Abu Ayyub, he passed by the Persian mullah's home, conversed with him, and perhaps accepted a drink from his hand. One day when the sultan gave him his hand to kiss, the mullah turned it over and asked, "To what am I pointing?" When the sultan had no answer, Umm Walad proceeded to answer his own question: "To the [*medrese* of] Aya Sofya." For in Turkish the word *aya* means the palm of the hand. The sultan understood the allusion and gave him a professorship at the institution in question.

As far as possible, the sultan reserved for himself the right to confer teaching positions even in the provinces. A certain Mullah Mustafa, with the strange surname Kïzïl Katïr (Red Mule), had just been transferred from Bursa to the New Medrese in Edirne. The sultan decided to appoint him to a position that had just become free in one of the eight *medreses*. The grand vizier, who was present, called attention to the fact that he had just tranferred the mullah to Edirne. "That is of no importance," the sultan cut him short. "He is worthy of the post." Still another story illustrates the sultan's spur-of-the-moment decisions in such matters. Mullah Hamiduddin, known as Efdalzade, Mehmed's former teacher, then teaching at the *medrese* in Bursa, lost his post on the accession of Mehmed II. Subsequently, he went to Istanbul. As he was riding through the streets, he met the sultan, who in accordance with his custom was strolling about surrounded by a number of slaves. Recognizing him at once, the mullah dismounted and stood in an attitude of reverence. The sultan greeted him and asked him if he were not Efdalzade. When he replied in the affirmative, he was asked to come to the *divan* the following day. No sooner had the sultan appeared in the council chamber than he inquired after the mullah, called him to his presence, and forthwith gave him a well-paid appointment at the *medrese* of his father Murad. Touched by such kindness, the mullah kissed the hand of his benefactor, who told him to devote himself to science and promised not to lose sight of him. And indeed he was subsequently called to Istanbul as a professor at one of the eight *medreses*, where he conscientiously met his obligations. During an outbreak of the plague he moved to the country with his wife and children but came to the city to teach every day. The sultan was campaigning at the time; on his return to the capital, Mullah Efdalzade was among those who came out to welcome him. When the Conqueror, who had heard of the mullah's conduct during his absence, caught sight of him, he called him, praised him highly, and gave him two prisoners of war, whereas the rest of the *ülema* received only one. In addition, he appointed him judge of Istanbul. Bayezid II raised him to the rank of mufti. He died in the capital about 1502, on terms of friendship with all, for he never lost his composure and judged all human affairs with patience and indulgence. As a scholar, he did no significant work, although his commentaries on certain fundamental books of Islam enjoyed great popularity in his lifetime.

A further example of the interest which Mehmed, to the very end of his reign, took in the affairs of his *ülema*, is provided by the life of Mullah Muhyiddin, surnamed Manisazade, who in his youth was Mullah Husrev's favorite student at the *medrese* of Aya Sofya. The story goes that the light burned all night in Muhyiddin's study, which was situated on the top floor of the *medrese*. One night the sultan in his neighboring serai saw the lamplight. The next day he asked Mullah Husrev who his best student was. "Manisazade" was the answer. And who came after him, the sultan asked. "Manisazade," Mullah Husrev replied again. "Are these two different students?" the Conqueror asked. "No," said the mullah, "but he alone is equal to a thousand." "Does he by chance live in the room where the light shines at night?" the sultan finally inquired, and received an affirmative answer. From that moment on the young scholar enjoyed Mehmed's sympathy and was all but assured of a brilliant career. He taught for a time at one of the eight *medreses*, then was promoted to the position of judge and finally of army judge. But he too soon fell afoul of his patron's moods. One day as they were returning from Rumelia to the capital, the sultan asked the mullah about a certain Arabic rhyme. Manisazade was at a loss for an answer and replied that he would like to ponder the matter at home. "Must you rack your brains so long over a single line?" the Conqueror asked with displeasure. When the perplexed man was silent, the sultan sent for Mullah Siracuddin, secretary of the *divan*, who had formerly taught at one of the eight *medreses* and owed his present appointment to his excellent memory and gift for statistics, but who was to die in the prime of life. Asked about the verse, Siracuddin replied without a moment's reflection that it was by such and such a poet, and identified the poem and its meter. Not content with this, he quoted the preceding and following rhymes, whereupon the sultan represented him to the stricken Manisazade as a model of scholarship. Immediately after arriving in Istanbul, the unfortunate lost his position as army judge and was sent back to one of the eight *medreses* with instructions to study some more. Later he returned to favor and obtained the rank of vizier, only to lose his position once again. But Bayezid II, who particularly liked to reinstate dignitaries who had fallen into disgrace under his father, reappointed him army judge of Rumelia, in which post he died unexpectedly in October 1483. Largely preoccupied with obtaining high state offices, he neglected scholarship and left no work of any importance.[37]

The Conqueror liked to spend his leisure hours in the company of poets and scholars, whom he encouraged to engage in debates. These often went on for whole days and the sultan never wearied of listening. On one such occasion the learned and Orthodox mullah Mehmed, surnamed Zeyrek (Keen Mind), was obliged to debate with Mullah Hocazade, because he had claimed in the sultan's presence to possess far more knowledge than Seyyid ash-Sherif Jurjani. The disputation went on for six whole days. Mullah Husrev was the arbiter. Finally, the Conqueror ordered that each of the two contestants should look at the other's notes, whereupon Mullah Zeyrek declared that he possessed no copy. Not so Hocazade, who immediately declared his willingness to give his opponent a copy of his notes. But the exchange never took place because of Zeyrek's obstinacy and especially because of his religious fanaticism. Mullah Zeyrek was extremely displeased at the outcome of the debate and retired to Bursa, where he found a patron in the person of a wealthy merchant, who guaranteed him the income he had previously been receiving. A short time later Mehmed regretted his brusque conduct at the debate and offered him another lucrative position. But the mullah declined with the remark that his sultan was now Hoca (merchant) Hasan. Zeyrek died in Bursa about 1502, but his name has survived only in Istanbul—not because of his

[37] For all of these scholars, see the work of Taşköprüzade cited above, book 1, n. 23. A. Adnan Adıvar also treats the scholars of Mehmed's time and their works in *La Science chez les turcs ottomans* (Paris, 1939). The Turkish edition is *Osmanli türklerinde ilim* (Istanbul, 1943; reprinted, 1970).

importance as a scholar but because of the mosque and *medrese* endowed by him and built from the materials of the Byzantine Church of the Pantocrator. While the mosque still bears his name, in other respects he has been quite forgotten.

All these figures, even the most original, are quite overshadowed by the celebrated mullah Husrev, who by his extensive teaching activity and the almost uninterrupted favor he enjoyed with Mehmed remained the uncontested master. Most of the others were his students. His real name was Mehmed, and his native place was Karkin in eastern Asia Minor. His father, Feramurz, was said to have belonged to the Turkmen tribe of the Varsak. There is little to support the theory that he was the son of a "Greek emir," who was converted to Islam. Actually, his family came from "Rum," that is, eastern Anatolia, which a misunderstanding seems to have transformed into "Rhomaean," or Greek. One legend even makes him of French origin. Mullah Husrev had attracted the attention of Murad II, who attached him to his son. During Mehmed's first brief reign he appointed Husrev army judge, a post he was soon compelled to abandon when Murad resumed the reins of command. When young Mehmed Çelebi was banished to Manisa, all his former dignitaries turned their backs on him, with the exception of Mullah Husrev, who declared that it was the duty, the *mürüvvet*, of an honest man to remain faithful to his friends in ill fortune as in good. Mehmed never forgot these words and in 1451 when he mounted the throne for good, he showered him with honors and financial blessings. When Hizir Bey, the first judge of Istanbul, died, Husrev received the post, and in addition the suburbs of Galata and Üsküdar were included in his jurisdiction. At the same time, he obtained a professorship at the *medrese* of Aya Sofya. The Conqueror knew and esteemed the mullah's vast knowledge and wished as many disciples as possible to benefit by it. His courses were abundantly attended. His students came to his home in the morning, shared his meal, and then accompanied their master, they on foot, he riding on a mule, to the school. Mullah Husrev is described as a man of medium stature with a long flowing beard. He liked to dress shabbily, but when on Friday he went to the mosque of Aya Sofya to hold services, all those present arose and lowered their eyes until he had reached the prayer niche (*mihrab*). As he was saying his prayer, the sultan looked down from his screened gallery (*mahfil*) and said to those who were with him, "Take a good look at him. He is the Abu Hanifa of our time."

Mullah Husrev was modest but dignified and was everywhere held in high esteem. Although his income permitted him to keep numerous servants, he himself kept his study in order, swept it, and lighted the fire and the candles. A quarrel which arose in connection with a banquet planned by the Conqueror had bitter consequences. Asked which place he wished to occupy, Mullah Gürani replied that he regarded himself as a member of the household and consequently wished to help receive the others rather than be treated as a guest. Pleased at these words, the Conqueror assigned the place at his right side to Gürani and reserved that at his left for Mullah Husrev. The latter did not accept this solution, but wrote a letter to the sultan's chancellery. In it he declared that his zeal for the faith and for science forbade him to attend the banquet if he were to be given a place inferior to that of Mullah Gürani. He immediately left the capital for Bursa, where with the ample means at his disposal he founded a school of his own and set to work teaching. As happened not infrequently, Mehmed regretted what he had done, called him back to Istanbul, made him mufti, and treated him with every honor. Mullah Husrev died shortly before the sultan (1480); he had stipulated in his will that he was to be buried in Bursa, not in Istanbul.

Mullah Husrev was perhaps the only Turkish scholar of the time to leave works in Arabic of lasting importance. He wrote famous commentaries on the works of the great exegetes Taftazani and Baydawi. Best known of his books is that on Islamic law, on which he further wrote a comprehensive commentary. This work on the principles of jurisprudence, intended for practical use, was repeatedly reprinted in Cairo and, along with an often published dogmatic work, has retained its standing and popularity to this day. In his lifetime Mullah Husrev was a celebrated jurist, and most of the theologians of his day were his students. Only Hïzïr Bey can be compared with him as a teacher and that with reservations.

Mullah Hïzïr Bey deserves mention, however, for another reason. He was the founder of a family of scholars who were much talked of even in the Conqueror's lifetime and enjoyed particular esteem at court. Hïzïr Bey also came from eastern Anatolia (Sivri Hisar). A descendant of Nasreddin Hoca, the Turkish Till Eulenspiegel, he studied under Mullah Yegân, whose daughter he finally married. Mehmed's attention was drawn to him on the occasion of a controversy between Hïzïr Bey and a North African occult scientist, in which the Anatolian was victorious. The sultan, who had attended the debate, was delighted that a scholar from among his subjects, and a young man at that, should have reduced the foreigner to silence, and immediately appointed him director of the *medrese* of his grandfather Mehmed in Bursa. There many theologians who later achieved fame attended his lectures. One of these was Mullah Muslihuddin Mustafa, surnamed Kesteli or more pompously

Kastallani, after the great scholar of the Tradition, who was roughly his contemporary. Mullah Kesteli later taught at several *medreses*, became army judge of Rumelia in 1480, and wrote a number of highly regarded books in Arabic as well as marginal glosses to various fundamental works.

In Bursa, Hïzïr Bey had two assistant teachers, the previously mentioned Hocazade and Mullah Şemseddin, surnamed Hayali, whose learning won him the sultan's recognition but who died young. Later Hïzïr Bey was active in nearby Inegöl, in Edirne, and finally in Yambol (Bulgaria) as a teacher or judge; his lectures always attracted large numbers of students. His wide knowledge of his field and his almost unerring memory caused the little man to be known as a "walking library." After the conquest of Constantinople, he became the city's first judge. Apart from a few poems in the three Islamic languages, Hïzïr Bey is not known for any literary achievement. His main distinction lay in his talent as a teacher, and his fame has been preserved largely through his gifted sons, Ahmed, Sinan, and Yakub, all three of whom eventually received the title of pasha; it has also survived in the name of a town situated across the straits from Istanbul, namely, Kadïköy (Village of the Judge; the ancient Chalcedon), so-called because Hïzïr Bey possessed large estates there.

Sinan Pasha was for a time close to Mehmed, whom he served as private teacher. Soon he obtained the rank of vizier and became the sultan's adviser and confidant. It was Sinan Pasha who recommended to the sultan his former student, the celebrated Mullah Lutfi of Tokat, as librarian of the serai. One day a quarrel broke out between the sultan and Sinan Pasha, and the pasha was thrown into prison. Then an unexpected thing happened. The *ülema* of the capital appeared at the *divan* and declared that they would all burn their books and leave the country if Sinan Pasha were not set free at once. Their threat produced its effect. The sultan freed Sinan Pasha and handed him over to the *ülema*. Then, to get rid of him, the Conqueror sent him as judge and teacher to the remote Sivri Hisar, the city of his ancestors, and ordered him to leave Istanbul the same day. When he reached Iznik in the course of his journey, a physician, sent by Mehmed to diagnose his mental condition and treat him, was waiting for him. The course of treatment was one often employed in the Orient for mental disorders: the physician prescribed large quantities of numerous medicines and fifty strokes of the rod every day. Mullah Mustafa, surnamed Husam (ed-Din), who was then in Bursa as a teacher or perhaps already as mufti, heard of the shameful incident and wrote the sultan a letter demanding that the mistreatment

488

of Sinan Pasha cease at once, or else he would leave the country. As a result the unfortunate was able to resume his journey to Sivri Hisar, but suffered attacks of melancholia, which may have been relieved later on by his friendly treatment at the hands of Bayezid II, who gave him a professorship in Edirne. He ended his days in Istanbul and was buried in Eyüp.

His two brothers fared better. Yakub Pasha died in 1486 as judge of Bursa, while Ahmed Pasha, who made a name for himself as a friend of the poor and unfortunate, occupied the same position at the end of his life. He lived to be over ninety and also died in Bursa (1521). Both had sons, and the line continued for some time to come.

Another highly respected family of scholars, the Fenarizade, achieved new fame in the Conqueror's day with Ali el-Fenari, a grandson of Mullah Şemseddin, who had enjoyed high esteem under Bayezid I. After Fenari had completed his studies in Herat, Samarkand, and Persia, Mullah Gürani persuaded Mehmed II to call him to Bursa. There he occupied first a teaching position and then the judgeship, and was finally elevated to the rank of army judge. For ten years he held this important position, taking advantage of it to help many scholars and to obtain teaching posts for those whom he held to be worthy. It became customary to regard his term in office as a historical period in which the sciences attained the peak of their splendor.

Later he too fell into disfavor with his sovereign, but was retired with an adequate salary; his children were also well provided for. Mullah Fenari also gathered around him a group of enthusiastic students, whom he instructed every day except Tuesday and Friday. In Bursa he moved to the slope of the Bithynian Olympus, where he lived and studied, undismayed by the snow. He was said to have had strange ways: he did not sleep in a bed, but leaned against a wall when overcome by fatigue. The books he had been engaged in reading lay before him, and when he woke up he returned to them at once. Although he had an excellent understanding of various sciences, including mathematics, he produced no written work of his own; toward the end of his life, he virtually abandoned his scientific pursuits and turned to Sufism. He was influenced by the well-known ecstatic sheikh Haci Halife (d. end of May, 1489, in Bursa). All his life he took special pride in his early association with the sultan. When someone asked him what had given him the greatest pleasure in his life, he said it was a journey he had taken one winter's day with the sultan. On the way they had stopped to rest; as usual, a carpet was spread out before the sultan on which he sat before his tent was set up. Before sitting down on the carpet, he was in the habit of leaning on a page who removed his shoes. On this occasion, the page was not present, and the Conqueror had leaned on Mullah Fenari. This confidence on the part of his sovereign, so he assured the questioner, had been the source of his greatest pleasure in his dealings with the sultan. Bayezid II also seems to have called the scholar, who died only in 1495/96, to his presence. The story goes that one very hot day they climbed a mountain near Istanbul together. When the sun began to decline, but too slowly for Fenari's liking, he cried out, "On such a day even the sun can make no progress!" This and other sallies have come down to us from the mullah, but no book is associated with his name.[37a]

Another such eccentric was his cousin Hasan Çelebi el-Fenari, who even as a teacher at the Halabiya *medrese* in Edirne went about in hair garments and out of humility refused to ride like everyone else with any claim to position. He, too, was attracted to Sufism and gave his money to the poor. When his cousin was army judge, he asked him to intercede with the sultan and obtain permission for him to take a trip to Cairo, where Hasan Çelebi wished to visit a scholar from North Africa (Maghreb), the foremost authority on a certain work. Mehmed granted the leave requested but told Mullah Ali that his cousin was insane, apparently because Mullah Hasan Çelebi had dedicated a book to Prince Bayezid rather than to Mehmed himself. When he returned home from Egypt and a pilgrimage to Mecca, he hastened to dedicate a book to the sultan as well, whereupon the sultan's feeling toward him underwent a change for the better.

One day he attended a gathering at the house of the grand vizier Mahmud Pasha. Also present was the well-known author and sheikh Ali al-Bistami, who proudly traced his descent back to the caliph Umar and had written numerous books. In the course of the conversation Hasan Çelebi criticized one of these books, declaring that he could refute any number of passages in it. Had he never met the sheikh? Mahmud Pasha asked him. He replied in the negative, whereupon the grand vizier pointed al-Bistami out to him. Mullah Hasan Çelebi was highly embarrassed, but the master of the house comforted him by telling him that the sheikh was deaf and had not heard a word of the conversation. Mullah Hasan, the author himself of a number of commentaries and supercommentaries long since forgotten on works of Jurjani and Taftazani, died in Bursa, withdrawn from the world, in 1486.

Mehmed made frequent attempts to attract important representatives of intellectual life to his court from the Iranian East, holding out the

[37a] Further information on Mullah Fenari and his family appears in J. R. Walsh's article "Fenari-zāde" *EI²*, II, 879.

prospect of rich rewards and royal treatment. He succeeded only in one notable instance. In his father's reign not a few theologians, especially Sufi sheikhs from Persia and elsewhere in Central Asia, had turned up in Edirne, where they had continued their activities, often in high positions. Most of these, for example, the mufti Fahreddin, or Mullah Alaeddin et-Tusi (from Tus in Khorasan), remained in the Ottoman Empire under Mehmed, although after a disagreement et-Tusi returned to Persia and finally to Samarkand, where he fell completely under the influence of Sufism. He died there in 1482.

It was from Samarkand that a fecund and many-sided scientist, perhaps the last heir to the ancient learning of Central Asia, found his way to the Ottoman Empire: this was Mullah Alaeddin Ali, surnamed Kuşçi (Falconer) because his father served as a falconer to Ulugh Beg (1394–1449), son of Shahrukh and grandson of Tamerlane. Inspired by Prince Ulugh Beg, who was a master of astronomy and geometry and later built an observatory in Samarkand which passed at one time as one of the wonders of the world, Ali Kuşçi had early devoted himself to the natural sciences. Mullah Mahmud ibn Musa, surnamed Kadizade-i Rumi, a celebrated astronomer who had emigrated from Bursa to Samarkand, was his teacher. But the chief influence on his scientific development was probably that of the emir Ulugh Beg. One day Ali slipped away secretly to Persia, where he spent several years in study. On his return to Samarkand he brought the emir a dissertation on the phases of the moon, written in the course of his travels, which the emir read with enthusiasm. When about 1420 Ulugh Beg built his observatory, Ali directed the construction, for the two scholars who had previously been entrusted with the task had died. The astronomical observations which the two of them gleaned were recorded and compiled by the emir in his famous work *Zij-i jedid-i sultâni* (The Star Tables of Ulugh Beg). In 1449 Ulugh Beg was murdered, and Ali could not make up his mind to serve the emir's successors. He undertook a pilgrimage to Mecca as a pretext for leaving Samarkand and in Tabriz he called on Uzun Hasan, who welcomed him and kept him at court. Here he was employed as an ambassador to Mehmed II, who was so pleased with the ambassador's person and learning that he not only gave him a brilliant reception but offered him a well-paid post in Istanbul. Mullah Ali accepted the proposal and promised to return after completing his mission in Tabriz. He kept his promise; the sultan dispatched courtiers as a guard of honor to meet him and sent him abundant funds for his journey. With an impressive retinue—his escort is said to have numbered 200—Ali Kuşçi arrived in the Ottoman capital. As a gift he brought the sultan a book of 194 pages, written on the journey, the *Muhammadiya*, in which he discussed knotty mathematical problems. Its concluding words tell us that it was completed in the middle of February 1472, thus suggesting that the author arrived in Istanbul early in the spring of 1472. When in the following year Mehmed campaigned against Uzun Hasan, he took Ali with him to eastern Anatolia. Here Ali wrote another treatise of 140 pages, this one on astronomy. As noted at the end of the book, it was completed in the first half of August 1473, immediately after the decisive battle. Therefore he gave it the title *Risâla al-Fathiya* (Book of Conquest). The originals of both manuscripts, bound together, are preserved in the library of Aya Sofya (no. 2733). On his return to the capital, the sultan conferred a professorship at the Aya Sofya *medrese* upon the mullah. An ample salary permitted him a carefree life, which he enjoyed with his children and his large household, but he died in the following year, on December 17, 1474. His family, which had intermarried with the Hocazade and Kadïzade families, flourished for many years, producing such esteemed scientists as Mullah Mahmud, surnamed Mirem Çelebi, the distinguished astronomer.

Ali Kuşci is one of the very few scholars of the Conqueror's day to have made a lasting name for himself as an independent thinker. Apart from his treatises on astronomy and mathematics, he left works on theology, grammar, and jurisprudence, which were prized by connoisseurs and used long after his death. His premature death reduced his activity in the Ottoman Empire to a period of less than two years and deprived his patron of the glory of encouraging one of the most celebrated scholars in Islam to compose works of still greater scope. With him died the last light of classical Oriental astronomy.[38]

Mehmed took an interest not only in astronomy but also, as he openly avowed, in astrology. He need not have studied Ptolemy's *Tetrabiblos*, as he probably did, to be a convinced follower of the ancient magical traditions of the East. Before making any important decision, especially before embarking on a military campaign, he sought the advice of his court astrologers, based on the positions of the planets in relation to each other and to the signs of the zodiac. The astrologers fixed the day and the hour for all his undertakings, which need not surprise us when we consider that even in the more enlightened West the popes as late as the sixteenth century made no secret of their faith in the planets. Pius II was one of the few exceptions. There is also reason to suppose that Mehmed

[38] A. Adnan Adïvar gives references to the sources concerning the astronomer from Samarkand in the article "Ali b. Muhammad al-Kushdji," *EI²* I, 393. Cf. A. S. Ünver, *Ali Kuşci. Hayati ve eserleri* (Istanbul, 1948).

believed in omens and was guided by premonitions in public as well as private affairs. In all these pseudosciences Persians seem to have exerted a dominant influence. The astrological opinion which a certain Khatâ'i of Gilan (northern Persia) gave his master in a horoscope drawn up on May 24, 1480—during a decisive phase in Mehmed's life—demonstrates the deplorable state of the soothsayer's art at the sultan's court. In defense of the Persian stargazer, it must be admitted, however, that fear of the sultan's wrath led him to take his cue not so much from the course of the planets as from political insight and calculation. His own life may well have meant more to him than the language of the stars.

It would be interesting to obtain some precise information about Mehmed's attitude toward music. All we know is that a certain Mullah Şemseddin from Aydïn-eli, thought to have studied in Persia and Arabia, impressed the sultan with his knowledge of music and was his close companion for quite some time. One day, after he had done something "tactless," he was banished from the sultan's presence. The rather odd man went to Bursa, shut himself up in his house, and did not emerge until his provisions were exhausted. Then he appeared again in public and lovers of music sought his company. He made his living teaching music, but then went into seclusion again and carried on the life of an eccentric to the very end. Only his daughter Yetima was permitted to share his solitude. Shortly before his death he lost his mind; his madness was attributed to the loss of his sovereign's favor. He obviously suffered from persecution mania, for he refused gifts of food, believing them to be poisoned. He sent poems of praise to the grandees of the land, but if certain changes were made in the first and last lines, the poems proved to be insults. Mullah Şemseddin wrote several treatises on the musical sciences, which circulated among theoreticians and seem to have been highly regarded.

Finally, a few words about Mehmed's librarian. If dignitaries who did not enjoy Mehmed's full favor had every prospect of being distinguished by his son, Bayezid in turn tended to look askance at his father's favorites, who were not always sure of their lives. The most shocking example of this is the case of the clever but heretical mullah Lutfullah ibn Hasan of Tokat, usually called Mullah Lutfi or Deli Lutfi (crazy Lutfi). He was a student of Hoca Sinan Pasha and of Ali Kuşci. Sinan Pasha, whom he had followed into banishment to Sivri Hisar, recommended him for his learning and knowledge of books to the sultan, who put him in charge of the imperial library. The mullah's sharp tongue made him quite a few enemies, and when Bayezid II mounted the throne their number increased. Accused of heresy, he was finally condemned to death by the

493

mullah Muhyiddin Mehmed, surnamed Hatibzade, and beheaded on the Hippodrome Square in Istanbul (December 28, 1494). This unjust sentence was an act of vengeance on the part of the vain old Hatibzade, who felt that Mullah Lutfi failed to appreciate his scholarship at its true worth. His cruel decision put an end to the career of one of the wittiest and most original thinkers of the Ottoman Empire. It is safe to say that Mullah Lutfi exerted an important influence on the Conqueror's literary taste. Various commissions with which the sultan entrusted certain scholars, such as the preparation of a compilation of the six best-known dictionaries, or the recension of *The Book* of Sibawaihi (ca. 753–793), the great work on the Arabic language, had probably been suggested by his librarian.[39]

IV. MEHMED THE CONQUEROR AND THE WEST

There can be no doubt concerning Mehmed's intentions toward the Western world. By his grandiose campaigns Alexander the Great had, in the brief period of eleven years, changed the face of the whole Oriental world as far as the Punjab and Ferghana. He had striven with at least partial success to achieve a synthesis of the Oriental and the Greco-Macedonian systems and ushered in an order that was to endure for centuries. Mehmed regarded himself as a new Alexander, with the difference that his plans were for Western rather than Eastern conquest. He dreamed of carrying his arms at least to Rome and of raising the victorious crescent banner over the churches of Christendom. Long before Ottoman troops set foot on Italian soil, the battle cry of the sultan's armies, if Ladislas Vetesius, the ambassador of King Matthias Corvinus to Pope Sixtus IV, is to be believed, was "Roma! Roma!" The seat of the papacy had long been represented to them as the supreme goal and the crowning of the sultan's lifework. To the Conqueror's contemporaries the "red apple" (*ḳızıl elma*) of Turkish popular legend, which recurs in countless tales and has been interpreted in many different ways, came to mean the Eternal City. Its conquest by a "padishah of the Turks," who would seize the land of the heathen, win and hold the "red apple," is alluded to in an old prophecy.

The Italians were well aware of the Conqueror's designs on their country. As early as January 31, 1454, Niccolò Sagundino, who had recently returned to Naples from Istanbul and knew the Orient well, informed King Alfonso I of Aragon that on the basis of old prophecies and

---

[39] For a modern edition of one of Lutfi's works, see Abdulhak Adnan (Adïvar), Henry Corbin, and Ş. Yaltkaya, *Mollâ Lutfî'l Maqtûl: La duplication de l'autel (Platon et la problème de Delos)* (Paris, 1940).

omens, the conqueror of Constantinople had resolved to make himself the master of Rome and all Italy; just as he had taken possession of the daughter, Byzantium, so he would also conquer Rome, the mother. The sultan, Sagundino went on, had learned all about the strife among the Italian states from his spies; the crossing from Durrës to Brindisi presented no difficulty and Mehmed angrily rejected the counsels of his statesmen who were trying to dissuade him from such undertakings.

But the heir to the Eastern Empire dreamed of more than Italy. He made frequent attempts to conquer Hungary, and no one in southeastern Europe had the slightest doubt about his plans. Stjepan Tomašević, the last king of Bosnia as well as the last despot of Smederevo, wrote a desperate letter to Pope Pius II, which his ambassadors read before the solemn conclave, calling the pope's attention to the dangers threatening Christendom at the hands of Mehmed. In this almost uncannily prophetic document, which has been quoted verbatim in a previous chapter (p. 216), the king of Bosnia clearly predicted his fate and foresaw the critical position in which his downfall would place his neighbors.

Ten years later, in 1473, if we can believe Matthias Corvinus, Mehmed offered once again to conclude an armistice or peace with Hungary and even to spare Bosnia if he were granted free passage through Hungary to Germany. In the same year the emperor Frederick III showed himself to be quite incapable of stemming the devastating flood of Ottoman raiders who had invaded Carniola, Carinthia, and Styria and were wreaking havoc on the defenseless populations. There is every reason to suppose that if Mehmed had not been busy fighting Uzun Hasan, he could at that time have penetrated to the heart of Europe by way of Austria. In any case, it is hard to doubt that he nourished such purposes as long as he lived.

At least for a time his network of spies extended to Germany. They were active in the towns where the diets convened to deliberate on the measures to be taken against the Turks. In the German provinces, the Bavarian duchies, for example, he had enlisted the services of native agents. Some of these were clergymen. "And the Turkish emperor," writes Jakob Unrest, the Carinthian ecclesiastic, in the autumn of 1472 in his *Chronicon Austriacum*, "has had all the cities in these countries indicated on his map, and has received information from an exiled priest and two prelates."

In Austria and southern Germany, these activities were probably sporadic. In Italy, on the other hand, the Ottomans seemed to have maintained a permanent information service, covering the whole peninsula. There the sultan's agents were almost exclusively Italians. They were motivated partly by gain and partly by hatred and rivalries between the various Italian states. Some openly avowed the services they performed for the Turks. Perhaps the most striking example of an agent who made no bones about his efforts in behalf of the Porte is Benedetto Dei of Florence, the mortal enemy of Venice, whose activities have been recorded above. His career clearly indicates the extremes to which an Italian of the quattrocento could be led by hatred of a neighboring state. Benedetto Dei had no scruples about taking employment with a Venetian merchant of Pera, from whose far-flung influence he expected to benefit, or about serving the declared enemy of Christendom who, he must have known, was not in his heart of hearts any more benevolently disposed toward his native Florence than toward the detested Venetian Republic. Of course, a considerable part of what he says can be attributed to his tendency to exaggeration and self-aggrandizement. But making all due allowances, we cannot help regarding the often confused notes of this vainglorious braggart as an important source of information about events in the Ottoman Empire at the time. We know for sure that Benedetto Dei was employed by Mehmed on espionage missions. There is little doubt that he received money for his services. But what impelled certain others among his compatriots to enter into personal relations with the Conqueror is by no means clear. It is certain, however, that the sultan made use of them all for his purposes, even those who, it was formerly thought, were solely engaged in fostering his supposed love of classical antiquity.

In this connection, we must think first and foremost of Ciriaco de' Pizzicolli. He had been personally acquainted with Murad II, who had so much confidence in the Anconitan that he gave him a safe-conduct enabling him to travel freely throughout the empire and to enter all the cities, towns, and villages without payment of duties. He too, even in his lifetime, earned the reputation of an unreliable story teller, braggart, and mountebank. Impelled by the ingenuous self-adulation characteristic of his century, he collected high-flown testimonials from respected contemporaries in rhyme and prose. He was widely esteemed; princes received him with honor. Men of importance, among them Niccolò Niccoli, Leonardo Bruni, Ambrogio Traversari, and even Francesco Filelfo, who ordinarily respected no one but himself, frequented him and corresponded with him assiduously. Indefatigably, he traveled about, collecting and interpreting the inscriptions and relics of the ancient world. He was animated by a boundless desire to visit the ends of the earth. Since in those days only commercial activity could make such travel possible, he became a merchant, though from his earliest youth his one real enthusiasm had been for the monuments of antiquity. His commercial training often came in handy when he had to raise funds for new discoveries. To accept no help or guidance, to do everything for himself: this principle determined his whole development, the key to which is to be sought in the outward circumstances of his life. He had no teacher in the classical languages in which he was so expert, and he often declared that he had learned nothing from any master. Without regular education but versatile, bold, and eager to learn, he went his own intricate ways. Ciriaco explored all Hellas, the Aegean islands, Egypt, and Asia Minor, searching for the sites of ancient civilization. More than once he informed his friends that he had undertaken to investigate the remaining accessible regions as far as the most distant promontories and the isle of Thule. Beginning in the fall of 1443, he traveled untiringly through Achaea and Euboea, Delos, and the Cyclades, visited Constantinople (which was then Byzantine), the coasts of Asia Minor, Thrace, northern Greece, Thessaly, Macedonia, the Aegean islands, and Crete. Everywhere he made contact with the native dynasts and undoubtedly involved himself in diplomatic affairs and intrigues. As an expert on the Orient, he felt called upon to participate in councils devoted to the great Oriental question, to promote the common war against the Turks with the Palaeologus emperor, the pope, and his legates, and to provide his intimates with political news.

Unfortunately, we possess little reliable information about his wanderings in Greece and the Near East during the twelve years preceding his death, which seems to have occurred about 1455 in Cremona. He apparently returned home toward the end of 1448 from his first great journey in quest of the traces of antiquity, begun at the end of October 1443. In the summer of 1449, he went abroad again. For this journey Genoa provided him with a safe-conduct, the draft of which has been preserved. But up until 1452 we find no trace of his travels, though there is reason to believe that he made use of his safe-conduct to visit the Genoese settlements in the Levant. Presumably, he was active as a merchant, perhaps in the alum trade, and entered into close contact with Mehmed Çelebi, the future sultan, in Manisa. For it is virtually certain that after Mehmed's second accession to the throne in February 1451, Ciriaco was a member of the sultan's retinue, that he was with him at the siege of Constantinople and entered the conquered city with him in May 1453. The reliable Giàcomo de' Languschi states expressly that Ciriaco was a member of the sultan's immediate entourage. As related above, the Grand Turk listened while he read historical works and stories dealing with antiquity, which stood in such high favor that even the meal hours were employed in reading. Ciriaco's position at the court of Edirne and later Istanbul was known in Italy, as can be seen from the above-cited letter of Francesco

Filelfo to Mehmed, in which he mentions the sultan's "secretary," that is, Ciriaco.

The particulars of the role which Ciriaco de' Pizzicolli played, perhaps involuntarily, up to 1454 as the sultan's adviser and teacher in matters of ancient history and geography are still in need of clarification. It is a demonstrable fact that the Anconitan and another Italian were engaged in teaching Mehmed the elements of ancient history. But we are without information about what decided the unstable adventurer to leave Istanbul and spend the rest of his days in Cremona. The remainder of his restless life is shrouded in mystery. It seems possible that, ill or frightened at the Conqueror's plans for the future, he could no longer bear living abroad and resolved to end his earthly pilgrimage at home.

If it is true that Maestro Iacopo of Gaeta was already physician to Murad II, he must have been one of the earliest Italian advisers at the Ottoman court. His influence, however, extended over at least three decades and bore on some of the Conqueror's most important decisions. He was probably one of the two doctors who, according to Niccolò Sagundino, enjoyed the favor of Mehmed II, one of whom was said to know Greek, the other Latin. Jewish physicians had long played an important part at the sultan's court. They combined the wisdom and experience of ancient nations with a hereditary talent for medicine. What caused Iacopo to leave home can only be conjectured. After the death of Murad II, he became Mehmed's chief physician, and it was he who attended the young prince at the siege of Constantinople. By then he enjoyed the full confidence of his master, who in the spring of 1452 was said to have issued him a patent exempting him and his descendants of both sexes from all taxes. From then on Maestro Iacopo never left his master's side and was soon appointed treasurer (*defterdar*). The nature of his duties is not known to us, but he must have become a kind of financial adviser; in any case, his position carried sufficient power to arouse the envy of Moslem circles. He accompanied the Conqueror on his campaigns. A few successful cures enhanced his prestige with the sultan, who, increasingly tormented by gout, pathological obesity, and other ailments, became more and more dependent on him over the years. In Istanbul, Maestro Iacopo soon made contact with his fellow Italians, especially the Venetians, who prized his counsels and were not chary of their rewards. He often met with the *bailo*, whom he entertained with court gossip, and no doubt gathered various information that the *bailo* considered it politic to pass on to him. Occasionally, he did not take too strict a view of the truth—for example, when he confided in the Venetian ambassador that Mehmed had turned Christian in secret. He also managed to take a hand in peace conversations when the situation of the republic, exhausted by the war, began to grow desperate.

We have seen above that mysterious threads were gradually spun between Maestro Iacopo and the Signoria, which tried to make use of him in a plot to murder the sultan. The plan was worked out in every detail and a second Jewish court physician was drawn in. It went up in smoke for reasons which it has not yet been possible to elucidate. The hypothesis that the sultan discovered his physician's dealings with Venice does not hold water, for if he had, even Iacopo could hardly have escaped with his life. It seems reasonable to infer either that Maestro Iacopo was playing a double game and never seriously intended to murder his master, or that he changed his mind at a certain point and dropped the project. In any case, he must have been a man of remarkable tact, who knew how to remain in the background and avoid his master's rages. He attained the rank of vizier, which distinction aroused indignation among the people. Certain sources maintain that he was converted to Islam. There are various indications to the contrary, not least the fact that some of his children and grandchildren seem to have remained true to the faith of their fathers and to have enjoyed certain tax exemptions in the sixteenth century. Another branch of the family must have been converted, for a document of 1489 mentions the grandchildren of the "old physician Yakub," namely, Ahmed, Mahmud, Ishak, Bayezid, the sons of Ali, son of the physician Yakub.

The destinies of those Westerners who had any connection with Mehmed would be a worthy object of scholarship. If we disregard the Serbs, Bulgarians, and Albanians who espoused Islam, they consisted almost entirely of Italians and Greeks. Such a study would have to include all the humanists and specialists who entered, for the most part briefly, into the service of the Porte and served as advisers to the sultan. Thus far, only a few names are known to us, but they are enough to give an idea of the nature and extent of the Western influence to which the Conqueror was exposed.

All our informants are agreed that the young sultan took an interest in the heroes of classical antiquity. Alexander the Great, whose life and exploits were probably familiar to him from the Islamic legends, struck him as a shining example, which he was determined to emulate. Alexander, Iskender, the "two-horned," was for Orientals not only the conqueror of the world and the founder of cities but also the hero who traveled to the ends of the earth. His deeds were motivated not by desire

499

for conquest but by thirst for knowledge. He was accompanied everywhere by philosophers and the wonders and riddles of nature aroused
his special curiosity.

The oldest treatments of the Alexander legend in the Persian language
were those of Firdawsi and Nizami. From the Persian the material passed
into east Turkish and Ottoman Turkish. The *Iskendername* (Book of
Alexander) of Ahmedi, who lived at the court of Emir Süleyman in
Edirne, is the first west Turkish attempt to deal in epic form with the
deeds of Alexander the Great. It can hardly be doubted that Mehmed
knew of these works in his earliest youth. And we know for certain that
he was familiar with the classical accounts of Alexander's heroic deeds,
for the best early history of Alexander the Great to have come down to us,
the one written in Greek by Flavius Arrianus, was among the Conqueror's
books in the Istanbul serai.[40]

Scholars of future years will no doubt derive pleasure and profit from
examining those Greek and Latin manuscripts which have definitely
been identified as belonging to Mehmed II for possible marginal notes
and entries by his Italian teachers. A dense fabric of legends has formed
around the so-called serai library, which is believed to have been founded
by Mehmed the Conqueror. An accumulation of romantic notions has
contributed to the picture of Mehmed as a kind of Renaissance prince
and intermediary between the cultures of the East and West. Imaginative
viewers of the books in the Topkapï palace have regarded them as the
"heritage and image of a secular man" (Adolf Deissmann). None of all
this has any foundation in truth. The supposition that the sultan's palace
houses the remains of the old library of the Palaeologi, which Mehmed
in clear cognizance of their significance and value caused to be rescued
and gathered together, made its appearance not, as might be supposed,
soon after the conquest of Constantinople but only centuries later. In the
fifteenth and sixteenth centuries no one, to judge by the information at
our disposal, suspected the presence of these treasures. Chance remnants
of King Matthias Corvinus's famous collection of books, pillaged when
the Ottomans captured Buda in 1526, were carried off to Istanbul and
apparently incorporated in the serai library. Only much later did Westerners conceive the desire to share in and consult these treasures. It goes
without saying that they were thought to include the lost books of Livy.
Even the original of the Gospel according to St. Matthew was supposed
to be in Istanbul and eagerly hunted. Neither one nor the other was ever

[40] For Mehmed's interest in Alexander, as reflected in the accounts of Westerners,
see Babinger, "Mehmed II., der Eroberer, und Italien," *Byzantion* 21 (1951), 136ff.
and especially 142, n. 1.

found, and to this day it is not known with certainty when and how the manuscripts of the Corvinus library made their way to the serai, much less whether the parts thus far unearthed constitute the totality of what was moved. The legend of the remnants of the Palaeologus library rescued by Mehmed and of the Corvinus library developed only in the eighteenth and particularly the nineteenth century, when the curiosity of Western scholars was really aroused. What finally came to light through the common efforts of Turkish and foreign scholars after the First World War, when the sultan's palace was taken over by the new Turkish republic, by no means justifies the exaggerated hopes of former years.[41]

In their enthusiasm scholars then took a highly exaggerated view of the "authentic remains" of the Conqueror's library. The manuscripts in the Islamic languages had not been kept in the palace for many years. Many had been transferred to the Aya Sofya library, which was, to be sure, also founded by the Conqueror but later declined; it was reestablished only in 1743 by Mahmud I. Certain treasures, such as the books sent to Mehmed by the Persian poet Jami, found their way to Ankara.

As for works in the Western languages, the vast majority are Greek. Thus far, only isolated volumes of Latin works, such as Seneca's *Epistolae* (Letters) and a translation of the *Cosmographia* of Ptolemy have been found. A number of our sources tell us that the sultan commissioned Turkish translations of ancient works which especially appealed to him: Leonardo Bruni speaks expressly of the three *Commentaria de Bello Punico*, an adaptation of the first books of Polybius. But none of these translations has ever been located. Hopes that the complete original work of Polybius (only five books of whose history are extant) would be discovered in the serai have not been fulfilled.

These non-Islamic works in the Conqueror's library, which can definitely be traced back to his original collection of manuscripts, clearly reflect his tastes and inclinations. We find books on history, geography, and military science, as well as religious works, chiefly translations of the Bible.

It takes a good measure of romantic enthusiasm and hero worship to characterize the Conqueror, on the basis of these findings, as a Renaissance prince animated by a Western humanistic spirit. It may well be that his Italian teachers helped to kindle his passion for fame. They may well have acquainted him with shining models from the classical world, in whose peoples the yearning for glory may have been the noblest and

---

[41] The principal investigations of the Topkapï palace library are Emil Jacobs, *Untersuchungen zur Geschichte der Bibliothek im Serai zu Konstantinopel* (Heidelberg, 1919) and Adolf Deissmann, *Forschungen und Finde im Serai* (Berlin, 1933).

profoundest motive of action, the innermost heartbeat of their history. But if we look into the matter more closely, there is in Mehmed no trace of that kind of ambition which Petrarch, for example, awakened from the dead to make it a new force in the modern world. The Conqueror was interested in learning how men like Alexander the Great and Xerxes, Caesar and Ptolemy had achieved their world-shattering triumphs. But his Western mentors never taught him that from time immemorial wars and political achievements, victories and defeats have been quickly engulfed in the waves of time, whereas the acts and creations of the spirit are borne onward through the ages. For Alexander the Great himself had soon become aware that his military victories could draw justification only from the second and perhaps even more arduous part of the task he had set himself, the labors of peace.

What Mehmed was interested in obtaining from his Italian teachers was concrete knowledge of the Western countries, especially Italy, and their military skills. He particularly desired information about their political conflicts, their mutual hatreds and rivalries. If his manner of thinking can be summed up in any motto, it is "Divide and conquer," words which are attributed, mistakenly perhaps, to Louis XI of France, but which were definitely in the spirit of the times. Niccolò Machiavelli later used them in his portrait of a prince who is entitled to be as cruel and disloyal as he pleases provided he has the *virtù,* the power, to overcome political disunity. How closely the Conqueror corresponded to Machiavelli's ideal of a potentate and despot is shown by every page of his biography. All his actions, all his thoughts and passions were inspired by a burning desire for something great and memorable, by insatiable ambition and yearning for glory.

The chief Western powers to seek the sultan's favor were Venice and Florence; Milan and Naples played a less conspicuous role, though, as we shall see, Ferrante of Aragon entered into relations with the Conqueror toward the end of his life. Genoa, whose Levantine trade was already on the wane, enjoyed the sultan's favor at first but later became the constant butt of his rancor and hostility, until the seizure of Amasra and later of Kaffa destroyed the last hopes of an understanding. Among the smaller Italian states, Rimini and Ancona tried to secure the sultan's friendship and benevolence, but their overtures brought no political results. All these states were in competition; each slandered the others and did everything to undermine their position at the court in Istanbul.

The involvement of court poets, scholars, painters, and sculptors in such efforts has puzzled students of the arts and sciences in the fifteenth century and fired their imaginations more than a closer and more dispassionate view of the situation would seem to justify. Unquestionably, more Italian humanists and artists paid brief visits to the sultan's court than our records show. Most of these visits were probably arranged by members of the Italian colonies in Galata or Pera or on the west coast of Anatolia who had personal or business connections with Mehmed.

Before the outbreak of the long war between Venice and the Ottoman Empire certain Venetians were assuredly well regarded by the sultan. It is related that Niccolò Sagundino accompanied the Conqueror on his march to Trebizond and was an eyewitness of the downfall of the Comneni (August 1461). Soon thereafter, it became known in Venice that Mehmed was holding secret meetings with Florentines, Genoese, and Ragusans, probably deliberating on measures to be taken against Venice (autumn, 1465).

All direct political as well as unofficial ties between Venice with Mehmed II seem to have been suspended during the sixteen years of war between the two states. These ties were replaced by underground contacts, partly through Ragusa, partly through the sultan's stepmother Mara, and above all by assassination attempts for which a variety of figures, from a Carthusian monk and an Albanian barber to the sultan's own physician, offered their services.

During the war only one important Venetian seems to have been active at the sultan's court. This was Gian-Maria Angiolello of Vicenza, who was delivered into Turkish captivity at the fall of Negropont (summer, 1470) and remained in the service of the sultans even after the death of Mehmed II. For three years he was the companion of Mustafa Çelebi, the favorite prince, after whose death he was drawn into the father's entourage. His notes, of which there is still no satisfactory edition, provide excellent insight into the history of the period and particularly into the character and personality of the sultan himself. They are by far the most fruitful Western source that has thus far come to light concerning the circumstances and events of the last decade of the Conqueror's life. Angiolello, who had never been obliged to abjure his faith, returned to Vicenza in 1490 and was still living in 1525 as president of the college of notaries (*Collegio dei Notai*).

Far more is known to us of the influence which the Signoria of Florence was able to exert at the sultan's court through adroit diplomatic maneuvers and the individual efforts of various Florentines. "From 1460 to 1472," writes Benedetto Dei, the Florentine agent posing as a merchant, in his *Cronaca*, "Florence has constantly maintained friendly relations with the Grand Turk and with the grand vizier Mahmud Pasha; Florentines have always been with them in their army encampments, and 5,000 ducats each year are not being spent in vain." It will be well to attribute a portion of his remarks to his vanity and boastfulness, which make the exploitation of his notes—especially of the thus far little-used *Chronicle* of his experiences and observations in Turkey from 1453 to 1479—a hazardous undertaking. Nevertheless, there is little reason to doubt his privileged position with the Conqueror, though here too he is no doubt prone to exaggeration. "If this is true," he threatened one day, "I will appeal to the Osman-oghlu [i.e. Mehmed II] for revenge." The Venetians had intercepted some of his letters to Lorenzo de' Medici and sent them to their Signoria.

The Venetian Republic had indeed every reason to keep an eye on Dei and to seize his correspondence with Florence. He reports at length his alleged first conversation with the Conqueror on his arrival in Istanbul; it is quoted above (p. 182). We have also spoken elsewhere of the favor which the Florentine colony in Pera enjoyed with the sultan and of which they took every advantage in their struggle with their Venetian rivals.

As far as we know, there were no leading figures among the Italian humanists who visited the sultan in the last years of his life. One such visitor in earlier times had been Angelo Vadio of Cesena, who at the end of 1461 wrote a letter home from Istanbul to his fellow townsman Roberto Valturio. If we did not know that Valturio, as author of the book *De re militari*, played a certain role in the life of the Conqueror, we should attach no particular importance to the sudden appearance of Angelo Vadio at the sultan's court almost simultaneously with a curious incident.

This brings us to the most complex and delicate aspect of Mehmed's relations with the West: art. The long-known fact that Italian artists, especially painters and bronze-casters, were active at times at the Conqueror's court has also led to romantic notions about the sultan as a patron of Italian art. If we take a closer look and consider the nature of the commissions he gave these Western masters, we shall come to very different conclusions.

The earliest example of such contact with the world of Italian art is probably provided by the strange incident of late 1461, with which there is every reason to associate Angelo Vadio. For it can hardly have been an accident that Sigismondo Pandolfo Malatesta, the lord of Rimini, should have entered into shady relations with Mehmed during the humanist's stay in Istanbul. Malatesta expected more glory from his poets than from his deeds, and since he looked upon the honor he showed his court scholars and poets as his own, humanists, artists, and poets thronged to Rimini, where they were showered with gifts and distinctions. His first literary favorite was Roberto Valturio, who recommended to him talented men from Rimini and elsewhere. Angelo Vadio from nearby Cesena was almost certainly one of these.

How Mehmed allegedly appealed to Sigismondo Malatesta to send a suitable artist to paint his portrait, how Malatesta recommended his intimate Matteo de' Pasti, how Roberto Valturio took advantage of the occasion to offer the sultan, in his Latin letter, a magnificent manuscript of his work on the art of war as a present from his patron, how Matteo de' Pasti started out for Istanbul with this royal gift but was captured by Venetian vessels en route and brought before the Council of Ten in Venice, which at the beginning of December 1461 finally sent him back to Rimini—all this has been related above.

There can be no doubt whatever about the Conqueror's calculations in seeking contact with Malatesta. For whether his court painter carried with him only a map of the Adriatic or one of all Italy, it is certain that the sultan wished in this way to obtain information about the geography of the peninsula. Soon after the capture of Constantinople, the Florentine Iacopo Tedaldo spoke of a war plan conceived by Mehmed, for the execution of which he would have to build a bridge from the present-day Forte Marghera ("Malghera") to Venice.[42] The clear-sighted strategist in the East had recognized at an early date the importance of the "key to the Adriatic," as Fort Marghera was rightly called, and of the bridge across the lagoon connecting Venice with the mainland. Such knowledge can only have been gained through association with Italian advisers.

The number of Italian painters whose destinies took them to Istanbul is probably greater than can at present be demonstrated. Even Benedetto de Maiano (1442–1497) has been mentioned in connection with Mehmed; others of lesser importance are "Maestro Paolo" (of Ragusa) and an Italian renegade who bore the name usual for new converts, Sinan. Little is known about the occupations of Costanzo da Ferrara at the Istanbul court.[43] It is certain that his stay, which is presumed to have covered several years, took place late in the life of the Conqueror. To all appearances, it was connected with the delegation from King Ferrante of Naples which went to Istanbul in the spring of 1478 in response to an Ottoman embassy and undoubtedly hastened the conclusion of peace between Venice and the Porte. The medal bearing the effigy of the sultan must have originated at this time; it is our only evidence of Costanzo's activity during his residence in Istanbul. It may be regarded as by far the most faithful and

[42] Tedaldo fled the city of Constantinople immediately after it fell. For his account see the translation of J. R. Melville Jones, *The Siege of Constantinople*, 3–10.
[43] For Costanzo da Ferrara and (a different?) Sinan, see above, p. 380, n. 8b.

successful of all the medal portraits of Mehmed II and probably served as a model for the Mehmed medal of Bertoldo di Giovanni. Laden with distinctions of all sorts, Costanzo returned from Istanbul to Naples about 1480.

Thus far, the only Italian painter of whose work in the Ottoman capital we have definite evidence is Gentile Bellini. In addition to the particulars set forth above (pp. 378ff.), it seems worth mentioning in this connection that according to Angiolello, he was asked to prepare a plan of Venice (*Venezia in disegno*). This commission and the lascivious murals in the palace of Topkapï probably provided the Venetian painter's chief occupation during his stay of some sixteen months at the Ottoman court. Apart from a few sketches the only surviving products of his work during this period are the two or three portraits of the Conqueror mentioned above. Still according to Gian-Maria Angiolello, the sultan had Bellini do portraits of several persons reputed for their special beauty; when a portrait was completed, he would compare it with the model for likeness. But all these paintings have disappeared.

In the early 1480s the famous Florentine Francesco Berlinghieri sent a magnificent manuscript of his *Geographia* to the sultan's court with typical Renaissance-style dedications; this work turned up in the library of the serai only a short time ago. Although it was not sent to Mehmed, who had meanwhile died, but to his successor Bayezid II, it must originally have been intended for the father. What purposes Berlinghieri was pursuing with this gift—whether he expected something from the sultan in return, whether the gift had been commissioned by Lorenzo de' Medici, or whether Berlinghieri merely wished to enhance his reputation as a humanist—is not known.[44]

The situation is much clearer with Francesco Filelfo's son, Giovanni-Maria. During his stay in Ancona he had made the acquaintance of Othman di Lillo Freducci (Ferducci), who had commissioned and no doubt paid him to write his *Amyris*, a Latin poem of four cantos and 4,706 lines, in praise of Mehmed. The Anconitan family of the Freducci, a branch of which had been living since about 1430 on the island of Tinos in the Aegean, later moving to Gelibolu, boasted close connections with Murad II. Filelfo's friend and patron had been named after the founder of the house of Osman. His sister was married to Angelo Boldoni, who fell into Turkish hands at the conquest of Constantinople, but was set free by Mehmed as soon as he mentioned his kinship with the Freducci.

[44] For Berlinghieri see Babinger's *Spätmittelalterliche fränkische Briefschaften aus dem grossherrlichen Seraj zu Stambul* (= *Südosteuropäische Arbeiten* 61; Munich, 1963), 19ff.

Later he represented his native city as consul in Pera, but became involved in a plot against the sultan and had to flee. In the fourth canto of the *Amyris* (from *amir*, prince) the shrewd poet, the true son of his father, suddenly addresses Galeazzo-Maria Sforza, duke of Milan, exhorting him to join the rulers of the Christian West in attacking and defeating the common Turkish enemy. From this turnabout it may be inferred that Gian-Maria Filelfo had decided for one reason or another to offer the work, originally intended for the sultan, to the duke of Milan, in the hope of drawing profit from the house of Sforza, which his father before him had exploited with dexterity and perseverance. He was no doubt less dismayed by his loss of the opportunity to enhance his own fame by celebrating that of the sultan than by the reduced financial prospects. The *Amyris* has long been forgotten and has been preserved only in a single manuscript, but what a sorry spectacle is presented by this laborious singer of heroic deeds![45]

Thus far, we have no knowledge whatever of the names and works of the architects and builders of fortifications, chiefly Italian, it may be presumed, whom Mehmed employed. Equally unknown are the bridge builders, whose works often suggest Italian influence although they are usually attributed to Greeks or Bulgarians. Their resemblance to Italian bridges of the same period leaves no doubt that Italian architects were employed. We know nothing at all of the business relations between the sultan's court and Italian merchants and commercial firms, if we disregard the names of the Florentine merchants and bankers in Pera known to us through the boastful garrulousness of Benedetto Dei. Until the discovery of the rich alum deposits of Tolfa in 1462 provided an unexpected source of that mineral, the profitable Levantine alum trade remained in the hands of Venetian merchants, in particular the Michiel family; they drew profit from import duties, controlled the soap trade, exploited the copper monopoly, and even enjoyed the privilege of striking coins in all the Ottoman mints.

Apart from the Italian city-states of Genoa, Venice, Florence, and perhaps Ancona, no other country in Europe maintained diplomatic or other relations with Mehmed the Conqueror. No German, no Frenchman, and scarcely any Spaniard can be mentioned in this connection. The Nordic states and England are entirely excluded. Nor did any son of these lands seek refuge in the sultan's service as a renegade. A number of Italians, however, abjured their faith and achieved wealth and honor in the Ottoman Empire. Here again we lack important names except for that of

[45] For further remarks on the *Amyris* and its author, with references to the sources, see Schwoebel, *The Shadow of the Crescent*, 148–149.

Iskender Pasha, whose father was from Genoa and whose Greek mother was from Trebizond. Iskender Pasha was three times *sancak beyi* of Bosnia and for a time governor of Rumelia; he died under Bayezid II. His descendants intermarried with the ruling family, and long played a role as large landowners in Rumelia. Beside the considerable number of renegades who a few generations later left their homes in the West to try their luck, often enough successfully, in the service of the Porte—Germans, Frenchmen, Hungarians, South Slavs, and more Italians—the few turncoats of Mehmed's day pale to insignificance.

It need not surprise us that Mehmed's Moslem subjects were displeased at the increasing influence of Westerners in many fields of public and artistic life and reproached him for favoring not only Persians and Jews but also Christian "Franks." Their complaint is stated in a poem by an unknown author which must have originated in the Conqueror's lifetime:

> *If you wish to stand in high honor*
> *on the sultan's threshold,*
> *You must be a Jew or a Persian or a Frank,*
> *You must choose the name Hâbil, Kâbil,*
> *Hâmidî,*
> *And behave like Zorzi: show no knowledge.*[46]

[46] For the verse see Babinger, "Mehmed II., der Eroberer, und Italien," 167, n. 4.

APPENDIXES

1

LISTS OF RULERS AND POPES

A. Ottoman Sultans[1]

1299–1326 Osman
1326–1360 Orhan
1360–1389 Murad I
1389–1402 Bayezid I
1402–1413 Interregnum

1413–1421 Mehmed I
1421–1451 Murad II[2]
1451–1481 Mehmed II
1481–1512 Bayezid II
1512–1520 Selim I

1520–1566 Süleyman I

B. Byzantine Emperors (Palaeologus Dynasty)

1391–1425 Manuel II
1425–1448 John VIII
1448–1453 Constantine XI } (sons of Manuel)

C. Popes

1417–1431 Martin V
1431–1447 Eugenius IV
1447–1455 Nicholas V

1455–1458 Calixtus III
1458–1464 Pius II
1464–1471 Paul II

1471–1484 Sixtus IV

D. Doges of Venice

1414–1423 Tommaso Mocenigo
1423–1457 Francesco Foscari
1457–1462 Pasquale Malipiero
1462–1471 Cristoforo Moro

1471–1473 Nicolo Tron
1473–1474 Nicolo Marcello
1474–1476 Pietro Mocenigo
1476–1478 Andrea Vendramin

1478–1485 Giovanni Mocenigo

[1] Down to the early seventeenth century the line of succession remained unbroken from father to son, except that Mehmed I succeeded his father only after a decade of civil war when each of four surviving sons of Bayezid, dethroned and captive until his death, struggled to assert his rule and gain legitimacy.

[2] Murad voluntarily retired from his throne in 1444, yielding the reins of government to his twelve-year-old son Mehmed who, under the tutelage of his father's viziers, "ruled" for a year and a half until Murad returned to his throne.

E. Holy Roman Emperors

1410–1437 Sigismund[3]
1438–1439 Albert II (son-in-law of Sigismund)[3]
1440–1493 Frederick III

F. Hungarian Kings

1387–1437 Sigismund
1437–1439 Albert II
1440–1444 Vladislav VI[4]
1444–1457 Ladislas V Posthumus (son of Albert)[5]
1458–1490 Matthias Corvinus (son of John Hunyadi)

G. Serbian Despots

1402–1427 Stephen Lazarević
1429–1456 George Branković (nephew of Stephen)
1456–1458 Lazar Branković (son of George)

H. Medici Rulers of Florence

1434–1464 Cosimo
1464–1469 Piero (son of Cosimo)
1469–1492 Lorenzo (son of Piero)[6]

I. Dukes of Milan

1402–1447 Filippo Maria (Visconti)
1450–1466 Francesco Sforza (son-in-law of Filippo)
1466–1476 Galeazzo Maria Sforza (son of Francesco)
1476–1494 Gian Galeazzo Sforza (son of Galeazzo Maria)

J. Kings of Naples and Sicily

1435–1458 Alfonso V of Aragon
1458–1494 Ferrante (also called Ferdinand), illegitimate son of Alfonso

[3] Simultaneously king of Bohemia and Hungary.
[4] Simultaneously king of Poland.
[5] Only four years old in 1444, Ladislas did not actually rule Hungary until 1452. John Hunyadi, voivode of Transylvania, was regent for the young king until that date.
[6] With his brother, Giuliano, from 1469 until 1478.

2

GLOSSARY

akçe	Ottoman silver coin.
azap	irregular foot soldier.
bab	gate.
bailo	head of the Venetian community in Constantinople, appointed from Venice, holding consular responsibilities.
bey	Turkish title, signifying a rank lower than that of pasha.
beylerbeyi	governor general (*"bey* of *beys"*).
beylık	principality; particularly a political entity ruled by one of the *beys* of Anatolia.
cami	mosque.
çavuş	state messenger.
cıhad	Moslem holy war against unbelievers.
defterdar	treasurer, chief treasury officer.
devşirme	Ottoman system of forced recruitment of non-Moslem children for military and palace service.
divan	(1) Ottoman imperial council; (2) collection of poems.
eyalet	province; military-administrative subdivision.
fetva	legal opinion issued by a mufti.
ghazi	warrior for the faith; a title used by Ottoman sultans.
gümrük	customs duties.
haraç	head or poll tax paid by non-Moslems in Moslem-ruled lands.
hatıp	mosque preacher, with the special responsibility of invoking God's blessings on the ruling sovereign at the Friday prayer.
imam	prayer leader.
kapu	door, gate.
kapucı	gatekeeper.
kapudan pasha	chief admiral of the Ottoman fleet.
kazasker	army judge.
köşk	"kiosk"; a small palace or pavilion.
lâlâ	tutor, particularly of a prince in the Ottoman family.
mahalle	neighborhood, quarter.
mangır	copper coin.
medrese	Moslem college.
mıhrap	prayer niche of a mosque indicating the direction of Mecca.
müftı	"mufti"; expounder of Moslem law.
mukataa	tax-farm.

nişancı	official responsible for inscribing the Ottoman imperial monogram.
pasha	Ottoman title; applied primarily to viziers and *beylerbeyis* in the fifteenth century.
podestà	head of the Genoese community in Constantinople.
pregadi	the Venetian senate.
protostrator	marshal or commander (Byzantine title).
provveditore	commissioner; Venetian official elected to serve in an advisory capacity to a military commander.
reaya	"flock"; applied to the mass of Ottoman civilian subjects.
rettore	Venetian governor of a city recognizing the authority of Venice.
sancaḳ beyi	"lord of the standard"; military commander, with the rank of one horsetail, who also acted as governor of a *sancaḳ*.
savi	body of six men which prepared the agenda for the Venetian senate and framed and defended resolutions.
seğmen başı	head of the corps of dog keepers.
Signoria	Venetian ruling council of ten, including the doge.
sipahi	cavalry troop.
subaşı	prefect.
tekke	dervish lodge.
timar	fief; particularly one whose annual yield was less than 20,000 *akçe*.
türbe	mausoleum.
uç beyi	frontier lord.
ülema	body of Moslem learned men.
vaḳıf	pious foundation.
voivode	prince; particularly used here of the Transylvanian ruler John Hunyadi.

INDEX

INDEX

Cantacuzenus family, 452
Caoursin, Guillaume, 382, 396, 398, 409
Capello, Francesco, 289, 290
Capello, Giovanni, 257
Capello, Vettore, 212, 213, 226, 237, 258
Capistrano, see Giovanni da Capistrano
Cappadocia, 190
Capponi, Francesco, 276
Capranica, Angelo, 303
Capsali, Elijah, 106
Capsali, Moshe, 106
Caraffa, Oliviero, 303, 307–08
Carducci, Lorenzo, 277, 385, 386
Carinthia, 323, 338; Turkish raids on, 347, 349–50, 366, 400, 495
Carniola, 274; Turkish raids on, 323–24, 347, 349, 366, 373, 400, 495
carpets, 468
Carroll, M., 77n
Çarşamba River, 270
Carso (Kras) plateau, 400
Carter, Francis W., 11n, 155n, 401n
Carvajal, Juan de, 140, 156, 198, 238, 267–68
Casimir IV of Poland, 67, 306, 321, 338, 340
Castel Tornese (Chlomoutsi), 125, 176
Castello Belgrado, 388–89
Castiglione, Raffaele, 29–30
Castriota, Andronike, 54
Castriota, George, see Skanderbeg
Castriota, John, son of Skanderbeg, 264
Castro, Giovanni de, 240
Catalans, 210, 211; pirates, 209
Catavolenus, Thomas, see Yunus Bey
Caterina Cornaro, Queen of Cyprus, 320, 334
Catherine, Countess, see Cantacuzena, Countess Catherine
Cattaneo, Maurizio, 87
Cedhin, 252
Çelebi, title, 12n
Cem (Sultan Cem), son of Mehmed II, 74, 316, 411; birth, 173; circumcision, 299; represents his father in Istanbul, 312, 318; attempted usurpation, 313, 317; governor of Karaman, 332; emissary from, to Knights of St. John,

381; suggested as sultan, 404, 405, 406
Cephalonia (Kefalina), 265, 372, 383, 384
ceramics, 466–67; wall decoration, 467, 468
Cerknica, 400
Cervantes Saavedra, Miguel de, 200
Cesarini, Giuliano, Cardinal, 18, 22, 25, 33, 39
Chalcis (Khalkis), 281–83
Chalcondylas, Andreas, 452
Chalcondylas, Laonicus, 5n, 6, 37, 39, 48–51, 56, 64, 77n, 83, 84, 103, 129, 152, 160, 191, 205, 206, 207, 213, 217, 452; on character of Murad II, 61–62; on sack of Constantinople, 96, 97; on incident of ox and executed man, 228–29
Chambers, D. S., 4n, 111n
Charles V, Emperor, 23
Charles VII of France, 123, 147, 188; Filelfo's letter to, 67–68, 120; in conflict over throne of Naples, 169, 183; death, 188
Charles VIII of France, 411
Charles XII of Sweden, 285
Charles the Bold, Duke of Burgundy, 324, 326
Chios, 66, 103, 130, 134, 145, 236, 278, 345, 354, 455; Draperio's claim against, 130–32; Mehmed II tries to take, 278
Chlomoutsi, 125, 176
Choniates, Michael, 160
Christian I of Denmark and Norway, 120
Christianity: schism between Western and Eastern churches, 21–22; Mehmed II's interest in, 118, 199, 248, 410–11; relics collected by Mehmed II, 411–12; see also Greek (Eastern) Orthodox Church; Roman Catholic (Western) Church
Christians: boys conscripted for Janissaries, 6, 160, 195, 438–39; former, as government officials, 7–8, 15; taxes and tribute paid by, 26–27, 103, 451; attitude toward Mehmed II, 67, 69–70, 160; in Ottoman Empire, 434–37;

—Index by Delight Ansley

Library of Congress Cataloging in Publication Data

Babinger, Franz Carl Heinrich, 1891–1967.
Mehmed the Conqueror and his time.

(Bollingen series, 96)
Translation of Mehmed der Eroberer und seine Zeit.
Includes bibliographical references and index.
    1. Turkey—History—Mehmet II, 1451–1481.
2. Mehmet II, the Great, Sultan of the Turks, 1430
(ca.)–1481.   I. Title.   II. Series.
DR501.B313   956.1′01′0924 [B]   77–71972
ISBN 0–691–09900–6   .